Perspectives on International Relations

World Regions

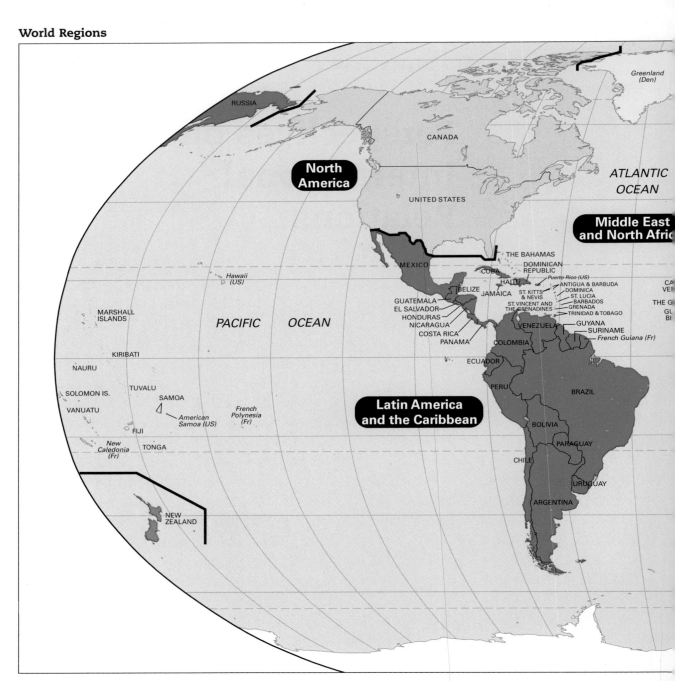

Note: Bold lines and shading demarcate world regions.

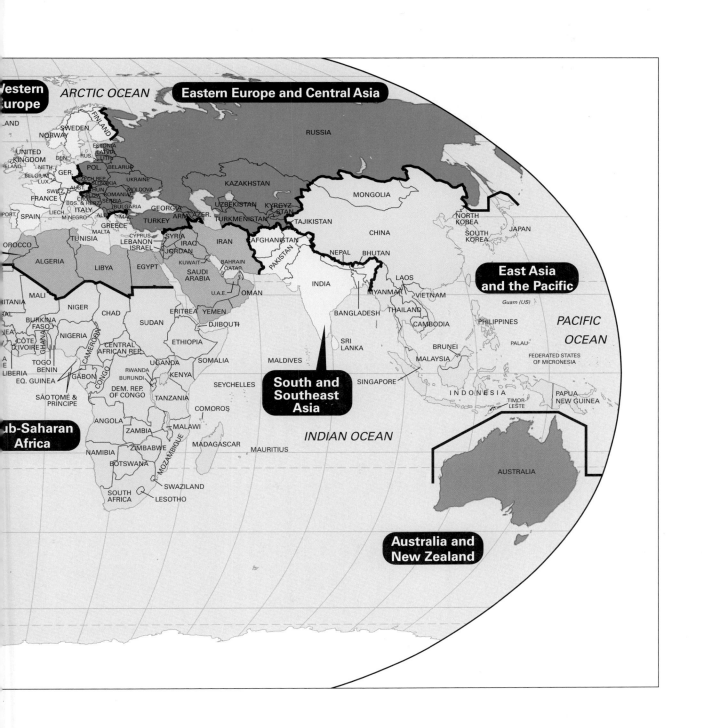

Perspectives on International Relations

SECOND EDITION

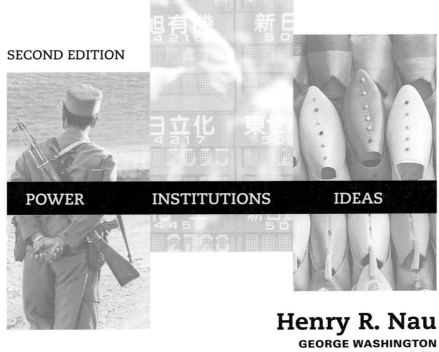

POWER   INSTITUTIONS   IDEAS

Henry R. Nau
**GEORGE WASHINGTON
UNIVERSITY**

CQ PRESS

A DIVISION OF SAGE
WASHINGTON, D.C.

CQ Press
2300 N Street, NW, Suite 800
Washington, DC 20037

Phone: 202-729-1900; toll-free, 1-866-4CQ-PRESS (1-866-427-7737)

Web: www.cqpress.com

CQ Press is a division of SAGE and a registered trademark of Congressional Quarterly Inc.

Cover design, interior design, and typesetting by Naylor Design Inc.
All maps by International Mapping Associates

♾ The paper used in this publication exceeds the requirements of the American National Standard for Information Sciences—Permanence of Paper for Printed Library Materials, ANSI Z39.48-1992.

Printed and bound in the United States of America

12   11   10   4   5

Library of Congress Cataloging-in-Publication Data

Nau, Henry R.
  Perspectives on international relations : power, institutions, and ideas / Henry R. Nau. — 2nd ed.
     p. cm.
  Includes bibliographical references and index.
  ISBN 978-0-87289-924-7 (pbk. : alk. paper) 1. International relations. 2. World politics. I. Title.

  JZ1305.N34 2009
  327.101—dc22   2008025357

To all my former students,
especially Ann, Gabriel, Jim, and Roy

About the Author

Henry R. Nau has taught political science and served in government for more than thirty-five years. He is currently professor of political science and international affairs at the Elliott School of International Affairs, George Washington University. He taught previously at Williams College and has held visiting appointments at Johns Hopkins School of Advanced International Studies, Stanford University, and Columbia University. Since 1989, he has directed the U.S.-Japan and U.S.-Japan-South Korea Legislative Exchange Programs, semiannual meetings among members of the U.S. Congress, Japanese Diet, and Korean National Assembly.

Nau has served in government in several capacities, including from 1975 to 1977 as special assistant to the undersecretary for economic affairs in the Department of State and from 1981 to 1983 as senior staff member responsible for international economic affairs on President Reagan's National Security Council. He was the White House sherpa for the annual G-7 economic summits in Ottawa (1981), Versailles (1982), and Williamsburg (1983), and for the special summit with developing countries in Cancun (1982). He is a former member of the UN Committee for Development Planning and the U.S. Department of State's Advisory Committee on International Investment. Nau has served on the Board of Editors of the journal *International Organization* and has consulted with numerous organizations, including the National Academy of Sciences, National Science Foundation, and the World Bank. In 1977 he received the State Department's Superior Honor Award. From 1963 to 1965 he served as a lieutenant in the 82nd Airborne Division at Fort Bragg, North Carolina.

Nau's published books include *At Home Abroad: Identity and Power in American Foreign Policy* (2002), *Trade and Security: U.S. Policies at Cross-Purposes* (1995), and *The Myth of America's Decline: Leading the World Economy into the 1990s* (1990). His most recent articles and chapters in edited books include "Scholarship and Policy-Making: Who Speaks Truth to Whom?" in *The Oxford Handbook of International Relations,* eds. Christian Reus-Smit and Duncan Snidal (2008); "Conservative Internationalism: An Overlooked Historical Tradition of American Foreign Policy," *Policy Review* no. 150 (August–September 2008); "A Caucus Race and a Long Tale" (a forum on Great Powers in Wonderland), *The National Interest,* no. 94 (May–April 2008); and "Iraq and Previous Transatlantic Crises: Divided by Threat, Not Institutions or Values," in *The End of the West? Crisis and Change in the Atlantic Order,* eds. Jeffrey J. Anderson, G. John Ikenberry, and Thomas Risse (2008).

Brief Contents

Contents

Boxes, Tables, Figures, Timelines, and Maps

Boxes

Tables

Figures

Parallel Timelines

Maps

Preface

Confucius, the Chinese philosopher, once said, "To learn without thinking is in vain; to think without learning is dangerous." Learning or knowing anything requires both thought and investigation, theory and facts.

I confirmed Confucius's insight when I took a break from teaching to serve in government. Having spent a decade in the classroom, I thought I would at last learn how policy was really made. I would have access to all the facts, even the secret ones kept by intelligence agencies, and I would understand the logic behind how facts related to policy choices. My first awakening came when an officer from one of the intelligence agencies paid me a visit, not to give me the facts I so wanted, but to ask me which facts I might be interested in. Oh, I realized, "the facts" depend on which theory or set of ideas I might wish to test. Now I had to do some thinking. What did I really want to know? Did it have to do with what motivated other countries to shape their policies and behavior or what motivated my own government to shape its policies? What were the president's priorities, and how might I help him design international economic policies to achieve his objectives? I learned subsequently that intelligence officers seldom agree on the facts, let alone the interpretation of the facts. There is no one theory about what motivates policy, no one set of facts that defines the situation objectively. There are many theories and many facts—far too many for me to take them all into account.

When I left the government, I understood better than ever that the policy world is not all that different from the classroom. Both require commitment. You have to decide what you want to learn, what interests you. And that's a function of your thinking—or perspective—and your values. And both require real effort. You assemble and investigate as many facts as you can; then you test your ideas against the facts. But, in the end, you make judgments about which questions and which answers are more important. The one big difference is that you have more time to deliberate and choose in the classroom. In government, you have to act quickly because events move quickly and you lose the opportunity to influence outcomes if you wait too long. As one colleague said to me, you consume thought in government; you accumulate it in the classroom.

The idea for this textbook began to emerge the day I left government service. I wanted to demonstrate for students the relationship of perspectives and facts to understanding international relations. It was a long way from there to here, but ultimately the textbook emerged through happenstance and history.

The happenstance part is that I started teaching a large introductory course in international relations a few years after leaving the government. I was eager to do this, but it also coincided with efforts at George Washington University's Elliott School of International Affairs to design a more coherent interdisciplinary foundation for undergraduate majors in international affairs. My task was to come up with a course that not only shepherded students through the nuts and bolts of world politics but also taught them how to look at world problems through different disciplinary lenses. I knew a lot about economics and loved history, and I had always considered my strengths to lie more on the conceptual than methodological side of political science, but was I ready for such a demanding task?

The history part had to do with waiting until I was fully prepared to write this book. My academic research interests progressed over the years from a narrow focus on the technological aspects of U.S. foreign policy and international affairs to broader economic aspects and finally, in the 1990s, to strategic and military aspects. As I broadened my focus, I taught the introductory course in increasingly bolder strokes, exposing students to alternative theoretical perspectives—the realist, liberal, and constructivist approaches in particular—as well as hefty doses of historical narrative and how economic policy mechanisms work. I worried initially that the design expected too much of students. But I worked hard to simplify and illustrate complex issues, especially the role of perspectives. To my joy, the students really cottoned to this approach. They grasped the big ideas and applied them, often bringing me newspaper articles to illustrate the different perspectives and levels of analysis. After fifteen years of teaching and thirty years of research, I put pen to paper, and happenstance and history came together. Happily for me, and hopefully for students too, the book you now hold in your hands is the fruit of that labor.

Approach of the Book

There are several important ways in which this book differs from others currently available to students of international relations.

First, the book uses the concepts of perspectives and levels of analysis to highlight the practical role of theory in understanding international relations. Perspective is more commonplace than theory in everyday discussions and, in that sense, more student-friendly. It represents a scaled-down version or ideal type of a particular theory. Theories tend to be complex and, for that reason, also less accessible to students who are just beginning to get their bearings in world affairs. While most textbooks introduce theories in an opening chapter, many do not follow up in subsequent chapters because the theories are too unwieldy and difficult to integrate into the discussions of subsequent topics and world events. By contrast, I illustrate perspectives initially through the simple device of the prisoner's dilemma. Introduced in this way, perspectives highlight power, institutions, and ideas as the primary, mainstream causes of international events and facilitate comparisons among these causes. Similarly, I simplify the levels of analysis. While perspectives highlight the causes of events, the levels of analysis highlight the levels or sources from which these causes come: individuals, domestic characteristics of countries, and the systemic position or interactions among countries. I then use these two analytical devices of perspectives and levels of analysis to discuss historical events and contemporary issues throughout the rest of the book. Students learn how different perspectives and levels of analysis illuminate many of the historical and contemporary debates about world events and issues.

In this second edition, I have added significant new material on the critical theory perspective. The critical theory perspective offers an important critique of the mainstream perspectives on international relations. It suggests that individual causes and sources of events cannot be isolated or separated from deeply embedded historical processes of social and economic change. Students learn that from this perspective all knowledge conceals the power of certain actors and cannot be objectively dissected to provide universal answers for the future. Examples of critical theory perspectives appear in most chapters, and there is an extended discussion of critical theory assessments of globalization in Chapter 13, "Global Inequality, Imperialism, and Injustice."

I have also included for the first time substantial discussions of the foreign policy level of analysis. This level of analysis links the domestic and systemic process levels of analysis and plays a particularly important role in understanding policy making in international affairs.

Second, the book treats the mainstream realist, liberal, and constructivist or identity perspectives evenhandedly. I avoid presenting our knowledge of international affairs from the standpoint of only one perspective, such as the realist rational choice or liberal institutionalist perspectives. Scholars often have a preference for one perspective over another and separate themselves into schools of thought that duke it out in the academic literature. Students, however, should be given the right to learn about all perspectives. They will encounter opinions throughout their lives from all points of view and need to be equipped to understand and critique those points of view from alternative perspectives. One frightful piece of information from the American Institutes for Research tells us that only 38 percent of college graduates can successfully perform tasks such as comparing viewpoints in two newspaper editorials (see Thomas Toch and Kevin Carey, "Where Colleges Don't Excel," *Washington Post,* April 6, 2007, A21). Somewhere, we instructors are dropping the ball.

Thus, this book does not start with the presumption that I, the instructor, know *a priori* which perspective is best. Rather, I lead the student into different worlds, looking at the same evidence from different angles. This approach, I believe, is the essence of a liberal arts education, equipping students to think critically—that is, by alternatives—and to make their own intellectual choices. I strive to present the alternative perspectives not only accurately but also sympathetically, convinced as I am that they are all well-intended and logically coherent ways of dealing with the factual world. Even though we have to choose among them and know that some perspectives do better in certain situations than others, we short-circuit a student's education when we bias our discussion primarily toward one perspective.

Third, by taking into account more recent constructivist perspectives on international relations, the book updates the field. It develops what I call an ideational or identity perspective. This perspective emphasizes the causal role of ideas, belief systems, norms, values, speech acts, and social discourse in international affairs, particularly as these factors affect the identities of actors and thus define their material interests as well as their behavior in interactions and institutions. The identity perspective highlights new constructivist research, including different varieties of constructivism, while also identifying some of its ideational antecedents, such as idealism and neofunctionalism. The book then contrasts this identity perspective with the more familiar realist and liberal perspectives.

Fourth, the book is genuinely interdisciplinary. It includes a good deal of history and economics. Too often in international affairs we do not sufficiently understand other disciplines, or we simply append them to our instruction in a multi- rather than interdisciplinary fashion. In this book, the student learns relevant political science concepts through the day-to-day unfolding of historical and economic events. For example, the security dilemma is illustrated by the difficulties European states encountered in the late nineteenth century when coming to terms with a unified Germany as a new, strong power in the middle of the European continent. The concept of collective security is presented through the design and experience of the League of Nations in the interwar period, when the concept did not work, and subsequently through the example of the United Nations in the 1991 Persian Gulf War, when the concept did work. The book devotes at least a third of the discussion to political economy. This economics is not topical or graphical, let alone mathematical; it is practical and historical. The student learns how globalization actually works in practice—for example, when an American consumer uses domestic tax cuts to purchase imports or borrows money to refinance a mortgage from capital made available by foreign purchases of U.S. Treasury securities. Policies—including fiscal and monetary—and concepts—such as comparative advantage and strategic trade—are explained through historical examples and disputes rather than by abstract formulas. None of this interdisciplinary instruction lessens the need for students to take subsequent courses in history and economics, but it provides them with an invaluable framework for understanding why historical events are relevant and how economic concepts drive policies and fuel disputes among countries.

Fifth, this book reinforces an emerging trend toward less encyclopedic, more focused texts, but goes beyond that trend by tying the textbook together through a coherent and central theme about how the world works from the vantage points of different perspectives. The book, in short, has a pedagogical "plot," not just a series of "one-act" topics. It is my hope that students will experience this book as an adventure, different to be sure from a fictional novel or historical biography, but inviting, evolving, and delivering insights that give the sense of moving toward a dénouement. If that happens, the book succeeds in not only instructing but also educating and becomes a reference work that students will revisit as they pursue the adventure of international studies through more advanced courses and indeed throughout their lives.

Sixth, and to this end, I write the book in a direct and engaging style that avoids professional jargon and textbook ennui. Students are easily bored by concepts and topics presented in an obligatory fashion, much like an endless list of addresses in a telephone book. They sense the difference between professional and pedantic instruction. The prose in this book is professional, yet light and, I hope, occasionally humorous. It seeks to educate a generation raised on the Internet through enticement and perhaps even a little bit of entertainment as well as earnestness.

Organization of the Book

Perspectives on International Relations is laced together by the theme of perspectives and levels of analysis. In every chapter—including the sections on the world economy and global forces—I discuss how the realist, liberal, identity, and, from time to time, critical theory perspectives view the subject at hand. I do the same with the individual, domestic, foreign policy, and systemic levels of analysis, so that the perspectives and levels of analysis are not forgotten but, instead, are developed and enriched throughout the later chapters. There is some variety, too, in how the chapters are organized internally, with some beginning with realist approaches, others with identity views, and others with the liberal perspective. I have tried quite hard not to prejudice the presentations in favor of any single perspective.

The Introduction is, in effect, an argument for the book's approach, why we have to select and make judgments to understand international affairs. It walks the students through the basic contours of the different perspectives, the concept of levels of analysis, the purpose of methods, the function of judgment, the role of history, and the place for ethics and morality in decision making. Chapter 1 then further develops and contrasts the perspectives and levels of analysis, introducing students to the basic emphasis of each of the perspectives through the story of the prisoner's dilemma and various modifications of that story.

Part I of the text covers military and cultural affairs. Chapters 2–5 review world history from early civilizations through the end of the Cold War. Chapters 6 and 7 address in turn the post–Cold War era—the hopeful years of the 1990s—and then the new millennium in which terrorist attacks and ethnic and religious conflicts intensified. These chapters not only give students a basic understanding of the formative events in world history, they put historical flesh on core political science concepts in contemporary affairs, such as partition (the balance of power), humanitarian intervention (state sovereignty), nation-building (state institutions), and conflict resolution (collective security), to name a few.

Part II addresses economic issues, including the historical precedents as well as contemporary debates associated with globalization. Chapter 8 recounts the history of the world economy under British and, later, U.S. leadership. Most important, Chapter 9 acquaints the student with basic economic policy mechanisms and institutions, such as currencies, balance of payments, and macroeconomic policies, that show how globalization actually works in practice. Chapter 10 then looks at the intricacies of international trade, investment, and finance. Chapters 11 and 12 treat development issues at great length and do so at both the global and more comprehensible regional and local levels. These chapters contrast the experiences of Asian, African, Latin American, and Middle Eastern countries and pay particular attention to domestic policies and the rights of women. In all these chapters, the student learns how the liberal, realist, and identity perspectives differ in their evaluation of the sources and consequences of globalization and development. Chapter 13 then gives special weight to critical theory perspectives on globalization. The student learns that from this perspective world economics may be less about common interests and comparative advantage than about core-country coercion and imperialist exploitation.

Part III looks at global forces for change in the contemporary international system. Chapter 14 surveys the broad range of environmental issues in international affairs, from population and energy to pollution and pandemics. It contrasts national (realist), international (liberal), and ideological (identity) approaches to dealing with refugee flows, global warming, and energy shortages. Chapter 15, new to the second edition, devotes special attention to global civil society—the numerous nongovernmental organizations that proliferate beneath the nation-state and shape broad transnational events today, including, potentially, an emerging consensus on human rights. Chapter 16 looks at the international governmental organizations of international affairs and the long-standing effort to build common institutions of global governance, including supranational institutions. Is it possible that such institutions will one day manage world affairs in a more cooperative and peaceful way that respects basic human rights and international law? This chapter gives students insights into the unprecedented success of the European Union as well as the continuing travails of the United Nations and shows again how alternative perspectives and levels of analysis assess these institutions differently.

Finally, the Conclusion wraps up the concepts of perspectives and levels of analysis developed throughout the book by applying them to the various explanations of the democratic peace. Students finish the book with newfound knowledge of the complexity and limits of good social science research, in part, because they have mastered by this point some simplified tools and can use them to dissect complicated controversies. Above all, the Conclusion warns students to be modest about what they can know with certainty and to prepare to spend the rest of their lives with open minds, learning even as they act without complete knowledge to fulfill their obligations as good citizens of their countries and their world.

Key Features

Each of the book's pedagogical features contributes directly to the balance and coherence of the book by helping students keep track of the different perspectives and levels of analysis and allowing students to see how they are applied in contemporary debates.

This edition has three new features:

Spotlight on
. . .

- To help students easily recall the core international relations concepts discussed in early chapters when they come up in later historical and contemporary coverage—such as alliances, balance of power, collective security, and anarchy—I've placed **Spotlight** icons, such as the one you see here in the margin, next to the relevant text. This means that the field's "terms of art" never get lost in substantive discussions of practical world affairs.

causal
arrow

- **Causal arrow** icons point to passages in the book where there is explicit discussion of the interaction of perspectives and levels of analysis. One perspective or level of analysis is being explicitly emphasized over another. Here, students hone their ability to see which perspective or level of analysis a scholar or world leader is emphasizing as the cause of a particular problem or world event. Students see, for instance, whether power imbalances (realist), weak institutions (liberal), or cultural differences (identity) weigh more importantly in a particular explanation.
- A **marginal glossary** has been added to the book. Succinct definitions of the key concepts now appear in the margin the first time each term (in boldface) is discussed at length.

I've also included updated features from the previous edition:

- **Feature boxes,** "Using the Perspectives to Read Between the Lines," showcase the statements of contemporary politicians, pundits, and academics and use commentary to unpack those statements and identify the perspectives from which these individuals are writing or speaking. These boxes illustrate for students the relevance of perspectives in everyday discussions of international affairs and help them discern the different viewpoints in situ. This edition includes new entries on the EU, American foreign policy toward Iraq, and globalization.
- Graphic **"Parallel Timelines"** appear in the historical and economic chapters, offering simultaneous chronologies of major historical events or movements and plac-

ing the different events under the particular perspective that would most likely emphasize that event.
- Many more "Perspective and Levels of Analysis" **tables** appear throughout the book to help students summarize and keep track of the various explanations of events covered from the different perspectives and levels of analysis.
- Twenty-three unique **maps** help students absorb important geopolitical, demographic, and thematic information.
- More than seventy **photos** greatly enhance the book's art program and help students visualize important events and issues.
- **Key concepts** appear in boldface when first discussed in the book and are listed at chapter end with their page reference for ease of review.
- Thought-provoking **study questions** at the end of each chapter provide a basis for in-class discussions and help gauge student comprehension.
- A complete **glossary** at the end of the book fully defines each of the key terms and helps students prepare for exams.

Ancillaries

The book comes with a full range of high-quality, class-tested instructor and student ancillaries prepared by Sally Anderson (Florida State University). Each ancillary is specifically tailored to *Perspectives on International Relations,* and all are available online.

Adopters can register to access the Instructor's Resources at www.cqpress.com/ college. Click on "Ancillaries for Download" and you can find:

- A comprehensive test bank with over eight hundred factual, conceptual, and vocabulary multiple-choice and long- and short-essay questions. The test bank is available in Word and WordPerfect formats, as well as fully loaded in Respondus—a flexible and easy-to-use test-generation software that allows instructors to build, customize, and even integrate exams into course management systems.
- Two sets of more than 180 class-tested PowerPoint lecture slides each, the first set designed and organized to parallel the book itself and the second designed to emphasize core concepts in international relations.
- An Instructor's Manual with chapter summaries, talking points for discussion, sample syllabi, and several simulations to run in class.
- A set of graphics from the text, including all the maps, tables, and figures, in PowerPoint and .pdf formats for classroom presentations.

Students also have access to a customized companion Web site at http://nau .cqpress.com that offers them opportunities to self-test, study, and explore additional resources: clear and concise chapter summaries with review questions; multiple-choice quizzes; interactive flashcards; annotated Web links with exercises devised to help students evaluate online information; and "Using the Perspectives" exercises that get students analyzing and critiquing a variety of statements, speeches, and writings. Students can even e-mail quiz results or answers to their instructors for credit or a grade.

Acknowledgments

I wrote the first edition of this book faster, and more intensively, than I have any previous book. And I spent more time on this second edition than I expected. I hope the effort is evident in the final product. I know that I could not have done either edition without the help of colleagues and students over many prior years as well as of the professional staff at CQ Press. I dedicate the book to all of my former students, both graduate and undergraduate, who inspired me to teach better. I mention four in particular: Ann Becker, who runs her own consulting firm in Chicago; Gabriel Szekely, who taught at El Colegio de Mexico and served in past years as chief of staff to the Mexican minister of tourism; Jim (or James P.) Lester, who taught at Colorado State University until his untimely death; and Roy H. Ginsberg, who teaches at Skidmore College. Their friendship and success are the true rewards of teaching.

Colleagues who have helped are far too numerous to all be mentioned. Several, however, were particularly encouraging and read the whole or portions of the manuscript and contributed comments. One even volunteered to use an early draft of the manuscript in his undergraduate class; that was especially helpful. I am deeply grateful to all of them: Colin Dueck, George Mason University; Marty Finnemore, George Washington University; David Forsythe, University of Nebraska–Lincoln; Roy Ginsberg, Skidmore College; Jolyon Howarth, Yale University; Aida Hozic, University of Florida; Bruce Jentleson, Duke University; Peter Katzenstein, Cornell University; Stuart Kaufman, University of Delaware; Bob Keohane, Princeton University; Charles Lipson, University of Chicago; John Mearsheimer, University of Chicago; Rob Paarlberg, Wellesley College; Thomas Risse, Free University of Berlin; Randy Schweller, Ohio State University; David Shambaugh, George Washington University; and Janice Stein, University of Toronto.

Other colleagues who offered helpful advice at various stages include Christine Barbour, Indiana University; Larry Berman, University of California–Davis; Bruce Bueno de Mesquita, New York University and the Hoover Institution; Dan Caldwell, Pepperdine University; Gary Jacobson, University of California–San Diego; Sam Kernell, University of California–San Diego; Robert Lieber, Georgetown University; Mike Sodaro, George Washington University; and Steve Wayne, Georgetown University. I had a string of research assistants to help me on this project. I thank, in particular, Bethany Remely, Jordyn Cosmé, and Serena Golden. I owe a special debt to Sandy Snider-Pugh, David Tarre, Jamie Kebely, and Ikuko Turner, who helped me balance this project with other obligations and thus preserve my sanity through very intense months of work.

I have never worked with a more professional and pleasant staff than the one at CQ Press. Charisse Kiino has been there from the beginning. I never thought negotiating a contract could be done without stress, but it was with Charisse. Elise Frasier made so many contributions to the original book and to this second edition that it would not be what it is without her. She and Charisse not only solicited numerous detailed and thoughtful critiques of the manuscript from outside reviewers, but they dived into the details of the project, drafted summaries and tables of issues raised, and discussed these issues with me during numerous extended brainstorming sessions. I was astonished at their professionalism—they must have had good instructors in international relations—and deeply grateful, even when they pinned my ears back on many needed adjustments. Brenda Carter was enormously supportive throughout, and Julie F.

Nemer had the thankless task of editing my prose, which she has done with the same incredible skill and patience she applied on previous books of mine. Gwenda Larsen moved mountains to see the book through production in a timely way, somehow never losing sight of the most important and intricate details. I was warned that a textbook writer's nightmare is to have editors interfere either too much or not enough. I lived a dream because the CQ Press touch was absolutely perfect.

I can't thank my past and current reviewers enough. They were the most thorough and tough I have encountered in any peer review process. Some have consented to be mentioned here. They include:

Richard Anderson, University of California–Los Angeles
Marc Genest, University of Rhode Island
Amy Gurowitz, University of California–Berkeley
Kathleen Hancock, University of Texas–San Antonio
Matthew Hoffmann, University of Toronto
Ian Hurd, Northwestern University
Nathan Jensen, Washington University–Saint Louis
Peter Katzenstein, Cornell University
Stuart Kaufman, University of Delaware
Alan Kessler, University of Texas at Austin
John Masker, Temple University
Waltraud Morales, University of Central Florida
Richard Nolan, University of Florida
Timothy Nordstrom, University of Mississippi
John Owen, University of Virginia
Robert Poirier, Northern Arizona University
Richard Price, University of British Columbia
Randall Schweller, Ohio State University
James Scott, Indiana State University
Nicole Simonelli, Purdue University
Ronald Vardy, University of Houston
Patricia Weitsman, Ohio University

I also thank three other reviewers who chose to remain anonymous. The advice of all these colleagues was so pertinent and penetrating that it was taken into account in almost every single case.

No one gave more to this project, just by letting me do what I do, than my wife and best friend for now more than forty-three years. Marion, or as I call her, Micki, has always been there for me, even when I was so often absent from her, physically present perhaps but lost in my thoughts about this or some other book. Kimberly, my daughter, is another source of inestimable joy and pride, which sustains me in everything I do. They give me my life in the small, which is the nurturing bedrock of my life in the world at large.

Perspectives on International Relations

Introduction
Why We Disagree About International Relations

Let's say you are interested in the ethnic warfare going on today in Darfur, a western province of Sudan, an African country just south of Egypt (see map at the front of this book). You go to the Library of Congress's online catalogue and find more than two hundred book titles on Sudan. You Google "Darfur, Sudan" and get over 8 million Web sites on the subject. Do you start by reading every single one of these materials? Maybe, if you have ten years to do the research. Otherwise you select certain readings. On what basis do you make this selection? Even if you read them all, what would you know? You would know a bunch of facts, but you would not know all the facts and some facts might be disputed. Would you know what caused the ethnic conflict? Not unless you formulated and chose a particular perspective. A **perspective** is a hypothesis that suggests which facts or events cause other facts or events. For example, have economic or other material disparities between Arab and African tribes in Darfur caused the ethnic violence? Or did the colonization of Sudan by Egypt and Britain in the nineteenth century create a deep-seated discrimination that persists today? Maybe the cause of the conflict is religion—Christian blacks fighting against

Darfuri refugees in a camp near the Sudanese border in March 2008. What causes such human sadness (a matter of perspective), and who is responsible (a matter of level of analysis)?

perspectives
hypotheses or explanations that emphasize one of three causes (power, institutions, or ideas) of world events over the others.

Muslim Arabs. You might test all of these explanations to see if the facts support them, but you can't test every possible explanation in every situation. So which perspectives do you select to test when an unlimited number of explanations are possible?

There is a further problem. From what level of analysis do you test your perspectives? A **level of analysis** is the location from which causes of events originate. If economic disparities are the cause of ethnic tensions in Darfur, from what primary location or level of analysis do these causes come? Do they derive from elite leaders who manipulate inequalities to maintain their authority? Do they derive from a domestic system of law and property rights that discriminates consistently among various ethnic groups regardless of who their leaders are? Do they derive from the abject poverty of the country (compared to other countries in the international system) that makes a country such as Sudan prey to foreign intervention and exploitation? Causes may come from all these levels, but which is more important? In the real world, we have to decide what to do about the situation in Darfur. If we decide to replace the leadership but domestic property rights turn out to be the more important cause of the violence, we have not done much to solve the ethnic crisis.

Our objective in this book is to develop the tools of analysis—perspectives and levels of analysis—you need to understand international situations like the one in Darfur. Along the way, you will learn many facts about world history and contemporary events. But this is not a traditional textbook that presents events and topics one after the other and calls them international relations. We will encounter and memorize many facts, to be sure, and it is important that we know the major events of European, Asian, African, Middle Eastern, and Latin American history and contemporary life if we are going to be serious students of international affairs. But that is not the ultimate payoff of this exercise. The payoff is strengthening your intellectual tool kit and ability to think about and understand world affairs. We will be working mostly on your central processor—not your memory storage—although we hope to fill up the latter as well.

The Role of Perspectives and Levels of Analysis

We see and understand international relations through different perspectives and levels of analysis. Both perspectives and levels of analysis are what we call **ideal types.** They help boil down a complex reality, allowing us to see which causes and levels of analysis we are primarily emphasizing when we try to explain and sometimes predict world affairs. Serious students of international affairs try to consider all causes and levels of analysis. They test their perspectives and levels of analysis against as many facts as possible. But time is not unlimited, and no human mind or even a computer can take into account every fact of history or contemporary affairs. Nor can a mind or machine consider every possible explanation of those facts. Think about the newspapers and Web sites you read. Do front pages give you all the news that is fit to print? No, they don't and they can't. Someone decides what news is fit to print and that decision involves selecting and emphasizing certain facts

level of analysis
the direction, or "level," from which different causes of international change emerge. Four types are identified here: the systemic, foreign policy, domestic, and individual.

ideal types
perspectives or simplified characterizations of theories that identify the most important aspects, not all of the intricacies and variations.

Standing in front of the damaged Askariya shrine in Baghdad, an Iraqi policeman views the world from this Muslim country. How others see the world and we see others are a matter of perspectives.

Why did Al Qaeda attack America on September 11, 2001: the weak balancing the strong, a reaction to U.S. diplomacy in the Middle East, or a rejection of western values?

over others. It is crucial to ask on what basis, from what primary perspective and level of analysis, publishers and Web site masters make that selection. Similarly, from what principal perspective and level of analysis do diplomats and politicians act? And from what primary perspective and level of analysis do you evaluate their actions? This textbook will help you develop the skills to understand alternative perspectives and levels of analysis in international relations and use them to draw your own conclusions.

There is a crucial point to understand from the outset. Ideal types single out primary perspectives and levels of analysis. The various perspectives and levels of analysis we discuss in this book are not exclusive of one another. In the real, not ideal, world, they overlap and every situation contains facts important from all perspectives and levels of analysis. But, as we have suggested already, people cannot consider all the perspectives and levels of analysis in any specific situation. Even if they could, they would have to emphasize some causes and levels over others to decide what to do. If we don't know why something happens, we can't fix it. If everything is a cause of an event, nothing is the cause. Based on the best evidence we can gather, we have to decide at some point which perspective and level of analysis are more important. Ideal types help us to detect this relative emphasis in the points of view expressed by others and in our own conclusions.

Perspectives help us decide what the primary cause of an event is. We consider three principal perspectives in this book. The first claims (hypothesizes) that a struggle for power is the primary cause of what happens in international affairs; this we call the realist perspective. The second, the liberal perspective, argues that interdependence and institutions exert the primary influence on world events. The third, the identity perspective, asserts that ideas are more important than power or institutions in shaping international outcomes. From time to time, we'll take note of a fourth perspective, the critical theory perspective, which questions whether events can be explained apart from historical circumstances and focuses instead on social and political change that unfolds within history. This perspective tends to project novel, sometimes utopian and radical solutions, such as revolution, to achieve a world of greater justice and equality. Critical theory reminds us that any understanding of a complex world is fragile and always subject to critique.

Levels of analysis tell us the direction from which different causes come. We consider three principal levels of analysis. The individual level, sometimes called the decision-making level, emphasizes the leaders and decision-making institutions within a country. The domestic level focuses on the internal characteristics of countries as a

Figure Intro-1

Perspectives and Levels of Analysis: A Synopsis

				Perspective "Ideal types" reflect primary but not exclusive emphasis on the following elements:			
				Realist	Liberal	Identity	Critical theory
				Struggle for power	Interdependence and institutions	Ideas	Social change
Level of analysis These are the directions or "levels" from which causes emerge	Systemic	Structure	Relative position of one country vs. another				
		Process	Interactions between countries				
	Foreign policy		Links domestic and systemic-process concerns				
	Domestic		Internal cultural, political, and economic characteristics				
	Individual		Leaders and decision-making groups				

In describing and explaining world events, as the arrows indicate, the perspectives and levels of analysis can be combined in virtually any pairing. In subsequent chapters, we show how different explanations of world events can be arrayed on this matrix.

whole such as their cultural, political, and economic systems. And the systemic level highlights the way countries are positioned (structure) and interact (process) with respect to one another. At times we will consider a fourth level, the foreign policy level of analysis; this level links domestic politics and international relations and falls between the study of comparative politics (comparing countries domestically) and the study of international relations (looking at how countries interrelate internationally). (See Figure Intro-1.)

Because we have to emphasize different perspectives and levels of analysis to make sense of international relations, we often disagree about international relations (just as we do about domestic politics). When disagreements arise from ignorance and prejudice, we try to resolve them by testing alternative perspectives and levels of analysis against the facts. We use various methods to see how well the facts fit our perspectives and level of analysis. In this book, we consider two principal types of methods: rationalist and constructivist. But disagreements often persist even after we've tested perspectives. In that case, disagreements result because different people legitimately hold different perspectives and emphasize different causes. Often, the available facts support competing explanations.[1] Thus, when we have to decide and act, we often exercise judgment, or informed opinion, based on experience, character, and other factors that go beyond theoretical and empirical knowledge. Socially derived standards of good conduct for human behavior—ethics and morality—come into play, and for many people in today's world, religion plays a key role. Figure Intro-2 shows how these elements—different perspectives, levels of analysis, methods, judgments, and ethical and moral convictions— interact to explain events and account for disagreements. The rest of this introduction looks at each element more closely as we think about the 9/11 attacks.

Figure Intro-2

How One Thinks About International Relations

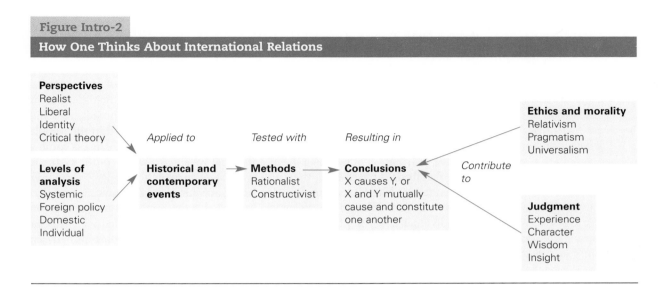

Understanding the 9/11 Attacks

How do perspectives and levels of analysis help us understand contemporary debates? Take the terrorist attacks of September 11, 2001, against the World Trade Center in New York and Pentagon in Washington, D.C. Let's look at four different interpretations of those attacks.

Weak vs. Strong

Three days after 9/11, Ronald Steel, a professor at the University of Southern California, characterized the attacks in the *New York Times* as "a war in which the weak turned the guns of the strong against them . . . showing . . . that in the end there may be no such thing as a universal civilization of which we all too easily assume we are the rightful leaders."[2] Steel interpreted the attacks of Al Qaeda as weak actors rebelling against strong actors, with the weak actors rejecting the notion that the strong ones can dictate what is right and therefore universally valid in international affairs. Steel is applying a perspective emphasizing the struggle for power. This perspective we call the **realist perspective.** It sees the world largely in terms of a struggle for power in which strong actors seek to dominate weak ones and weak actors resist strong ones to preserve their interests and independence. The most important fact driving international behavior from this perspective is that there is no overarching or universal center of power in the world that is recognized by all actors as legitimate. The decentralized distribution of power requires states and other actors to defend themselves because they cannot rely on anyone else to defend them. In so doing, they often come into conflict with one another. They try to manage this conflict through the reciprocal acquisition and use of military arms, or what is called the balance of power.

 The struggle for power goes on at all levels of analysis: between state and nonstate actors at the systemic level, among groups within states at the domestic level, and among leaders making decisions for states and nonstate actors at the individual or decision-making level. Traditionally, realists have focused on the actors with the great-

realist perspective

a perspective that sees the world largely in terms of a struggle for power in which strong actors, especially states, seek to dominate weak ones and weak actors resist strong ones to preserve their interests and independence.

est capability to exercise power. Today, these actors are states. But the realist perspective can apply at any level of analysis.

The weak in the case of the 9/11 attacks are individuals or nonstate actors coming from the **individual level of analysis.** However, if we emphasize the Taliban government in Afghanistan where Al Qaeda trained, we might be thinking of weak or failed states that have been taken over internally by terrorists and conclude that the cause is coming from the **domestic level of analysis.** Or, if we think more broadly still and argue that "the weak" refers to the poor Muslim countries dominated in the Middle East and elsewhere by the strong western powers, we might decide the cause is coming from the distribution of power in the international system as a whole, or the **systemic level of analysis.** At each level, the cause is the same, namely the struggle for power between the weak and the strong. But, depending on which level of analysis we emphasize, we respond differently to the attack. In the first case, we focus our attention on the individual terrorists. In the second, we react to domestic problems in weak or failed states. And in the third, we address problems in broader relationships between Muslim and western countries (Table Intro-1).

Perspectives emphasize causes—in the realist case, the struggle for power. Levels of analysis emphasize where the cause is coming from—in the 9/11 event, from weak nonstate actors such as Al Qaeda. We need both perspectives and levels of analysis to draw a complete picture. Think of it like hitting a baseball. Perspectives tell us what kind of pitch is coming: fastball, curveball, or changeup. Levels of analysis tell us from which direction the pitch is coming, whether it is thrown overhand, sidearm, or underhand. Unless you know both, you'll miss the pitch or, in international affairs, you'll fail to explain the event you are interested in.

As we mentioned, perspectives do not exclude other factors. They just emphasize them differently. Notice how Steel tells us what is not important as well as what is. He discounts the possibility that ideas help bridge the gap between the weak and strong. Ideas, he says, are relative, not universal. There "may be no such thing as a universal civilization." In this brief passage, he also does not mention international institutions as a way to resolve differences between the weak and the strong without resorting to force. He is making the realist point that the struggle for power has a greater impact on outcomes than ideas or institutions do.

Failed Negotiations

Writing two days after Steel in the *Washington Post,* Caryle Murphy, a journalist, saw the attacks quite differently. September 11, 2001, was not a result of the weak striking back against the strong but of unresolved diplomatic disputes, such as the Israeli-Palestinian conflict, that created unfairness and grievances between the feuding par-

---

individual level of analysis

a level at which individuals or small groups of individuals make decisions and cause events using power, institutions, or ideas.

domestic level of analysis

a level that focuses on domestic features of a country as a whole, such as capitalist economic system or nationalist ideology, from which the causes of a realist, liberal, or identity perspective come.

systemic level of analysis

a level that identifies causes that come from the positioning and interaction of states in the international system.

Table Intro-1	
The Causes of the 9/11 Attacks: From the Realist Perspective	
Level	**Perspective** Realist: Struggle for power between the "weak" and the "strong"
Systemic	Muslim countries reject U.S. oppression in the region/world
Domestic	Taliban takeover of the weak Afghan state
Individual	Individual terrorists plotting against the United States

ties. She argued that "if we want to avoid creating more terrorists, we must end the Israeli-Palestinian conflict in a way both sides see as fair."[3] Murphy is using the **liberal perspective.** It emphasizes relationships and interdependence among actors in international affairs, how groups interact, communicate, negotiate, and transact exchanges such as trade with one another. She is saying that the cause of the 9/11 attacks is the failure to include all parties—terrorists and nonterrorists, Palestinians and Israelis—in a negotiated agreement that is fair and legitimate. An outcome decided by a power struggle or imposing one side's ideas on the other would not be fair or legitimate and would probably just create more terrorists. On the other hand, negotiating an agreement might actually reduce the threat of terrorism. Note how diplomacy trumps power. The liberal perspective holds out the prospect that solutions to international conflicts do not require a balance of power but derive from common rules and institutions that include all actors regardless of their relative power or ideas.

Palestinian (Yasser Arafat, left) and Israeli (Shimon Peres, right) leaders meet in late September 2001 to discuss an end to the conflict between Israel and Palestine. Why do some negotiated agreements fail: strong militants, a flawed agreement, or irreconcilable ideologies?

Murphy is emphasizing the systemic level of analysis because international negotiations are a more important cause of and, therefore, solution to the problem of terrorism than institutional aspects of domestic governments or the specific behavior of individual leaders. From the liberal perspective, actors at any level—systemic, domestic, or individual—behave not so much on the basis of their relative power, whether they are weak or strong, but on the way the other party behaves, how the parties interact and negotiate, the patterns of behavior they create, and the roles and rules they establish in institutions that regularize their relationships (Table Intro-2).

liberal perspective
a perspective that emphasizes relationships and negotiations among actors in international affairs, as well as how groups interact, communicate, and transact exchanges with one another, such as trade; liberal perspectives tend to focus on the role of institutions in solving international conflicts.

Democratic Reform of Governments

Writing a year after the September 11, 2001, attacks, as prospects of war against Iraq loomed, Jim Hoagland, a columnist for the *Washington Post*, suggested still a third way to think about the attacks of 9/11. He was skeptical of finding a solution to terrorism through a better balance of power between the weak and strong or through negotiations of the Arab-Israeli dispute. He felt that the problem was one of nondemocratic governments in the Middle East. "The removal of Saddam Hussein [then Iraq's leader] and Yasser Arafat [then leader of the Palestinian Authority] are necessary but not sufficient conditions for stabilizing the Middle East. . . . The administration cannot rely

Table Intro-2	
The Causes of the 9/11 Attacks: From the Liberal Perspective	
Level	**Perspective** Liberal: Failed negotiations, problematic relationships
Systemic	Failure to include all parties in a balanced and fair agreement
Domestic	Institutional aspects of domestic governments
Individual	Behavior of specific leaders

Iran's president, Mahmoud Ahmadinejad, speaks at a ceremony in Tehran marking the Iranian New Year holiday, March 17, 2008.

identity perspective

a perspective that emphasizes the importance of ideas that define the identities of actors and that motivate the use of power and negotiations by these actors.

critical theory perspective

a perspective that questions whether events can be explained apart from historical circumstances and focuses instead on social and political change that unfolds within history; it offers broad critiques of international relations and generally advocates radical solutions such as revolution.

. . . on a now discredited peace process. . . . Only a level and clarity of American commitment to democratic change . . . will calm an ever more deadly conflict." [4] Note how Hoagland deemphasizes the negotiation process, which a liberal perspective would emphasize, by describing it as a "discredited peace process" and says that the mere removal of Saddam Hussein and Yasser Arafat from power, which the realist perspective would emphasize, is not enough. Instead what is needed, he maintains, is a change in the nature of Arab governments and their political identities in the Middle East. They need to reform and, with U.S. help, become more democratic.

Hoagland is employing the **identity perspective.** This perspective emphasizes the importance of ideas that define the identities of actors and motivate their use of power and negotiations in international affairs. He is projecting that democratic reforms at the domestic level of analysis are more important than removing individual leaders—the individual level—and may subsequently change the way Middle East states behave toward one another at the systemic level. If actors identify themselves in adversarial or diverging terms, negotiations are more difficult to achieve and power balancing is more likely to occur. If, on the other hand, actors have similar or converging identities, cooperation is more likely. Hoagland argues that, until Arab identities become more democratic and their identities converge with that of Israel, negotiations (the liberal solution) will remain discredited and shifts in power such as removing Hussein and Arafat (the realist solution) will not change much (Table Intro-3).

Pervasive Violence

From a **critical theory perspective,** the cause of 9/11 is the pervasive violence in the present international system caused primarily by the United States, which as the preeminent power fights terrorism lawlessly while never acknowledging the terror it deploys against the rest of the world, including its own citizens, through imperialism and the curtailment of civil and human rights. As one radical critic puts it, "the probability of 'apocalypse soon' . . . is surely too high . . . because of Washington's primary role in accelerating the race to destruction by extending its historically unique military dominance" [5] (Table Intro-4).

Table Intro-3		
The Causes of the 9/11 Attacks: From the Identity Perspective		
Level	**Perspective** Identity: Understanding of and changes in how actors and entities define and identify themselves	
Systemic	Divergent identities generate conflict, converging identities cooperation	
Domestic	Democratic reforms in Arab governments would make them less adversarial toward Israel and others in the region	
Individual	Removing individual leaders not as important as more democratic institutions	

Table Intro-4		
The Causes of the 9/11 Attacks: From the Critical Theory Perspective		
Level	**Perspective** Critical theory: View of events in historical/political context with emphasis on social justice and change	
Systemic	Pervasive violence in international system, primarily on the part of the United States	
Domestic		
Individual		

More Perspectives and Levels of Analysis

The three primary perspectives we've discussed—realist, liberal, and identity—and three primary levels of analysis—individual, domestic, and systemic—help us better understand the protean world of international affairs. Each perspective emphasizes a different primary cause of world events that can come from a variety of levels of analysis. The realist perspective emphasizes power—human nature at the individual level, aggressive states at the domestic level, and the balance of power at the systemic level. The liberal perspective emphasizes institutions—a leader's role at the individual level, government institutions at the domestic level, and international institutions at the systemic level. And the identity perspective emphasizes ideas—shared or conflicting ideas at the systemic level, a country's culture or political ideology at the domestic level, and leaders' ideas at the decision-making level.

These are not the only perspectives and levels of analysis we could study. There are more complex variations of each perspective as well as additional levels of analysis. For example, the realist perspective includes classical realist and neorealist, offensive and defensive versions of the power struggle. The liberal perspective covers classical liberal

President George W. Bush meets with the National Security Council at Camp David, September 15, 2001. Does the United States run and terrorize the world?

and liberal institutionalist or neoliberal theories of trade and international institutions. The identity perspective treats idealist, normative, social constructivist (constructing identities through discourse), psychological, and methodological variants of international affairs. And critical theories include Marxist, feminist, and other historically embedded approaches. We refer to these more complex variations in our discussions as theories, not perspectives. Perspectives deal with what theories emphasize, not with all the variations of each theory. All realist theories, for example, emphasize the struggle for power, although some, such as classical realism, give a larger role to ideas than do others, such as neorealism.

Similarly, there are many more levels of analysis between the individual and systemic levels, such as the **foreign policy level of analysis.** In addition, there are a public- vs. private-sector level of analysis domestically and a regional level of analysis internationally, useful in analyzing the European Union. We distinguish between two types of systemic levels of analysis, process and structure, later.

But we don't need to understand all these more complex variations at this point. Reality is always more complex than the analytical tools we use to understand it. That's why we use ideal types to help us judge which real-world theories and arguments are, *relatively,* being emphasized. Without ideal types we would not know in the 9/11 example that Steel is emphasizing the power struggle and deemphasizing shared values among international actors. Because we cannot include and emphasize everything, we need analytical devices such as ideal types to help distinguish what is primary and secondary in scholarly theories as well as in day-to-day political arguments.

foreign policy level of analysis

a level of analysis between the systemic process and domestic levels where foreign policy officials actually make decisions.

The Role of Methods

All knowledge starts with theories. Even natural sciences use theories to select and order facts. Before Galileo, scientists thought about motion only in linear terms, in straight lines from one point to another. Galileo was the first to think about motion in periodic terms, that is, as the back-and-forth motion of a pendulum or the movement of the Earth around the sun. As a result, he discovered and emphasized new facts such as inertia, a precursor to Isaac Newton's discovery of the force of gravity. The difference between the natural (physics) and social (political science) sciences is not that social sciences depend on perspective and natural sciences do not. The difference lies in the kinds of facts they deal with. The natural sciences deal with facts that do not have minds of their own. A social science, such as international relations, deals with human beings, who do have minds of their own and often change them. That people can and do think for themselves makes social science facts somewhat more elusive, but they are still real. And it means that we need to be more conscious of our perspective when we deal with social science subjects. We are dealing with people whose perspective may differ from our own and may change in response to the information we provide. If we ask them questions, they may not understand or answer our questions in the same way we would. And they could always change their answer the minute after we ask the question.

Scholarly theories seek to *describe, explain,* and *predict* events. **Methods** provide rules to test theories against facts. They allow us to conclude whether our theories or perspectives are consistent with the world out there. But methods are not miracles. They cannot tell us the way the world out there actually is, just that the way we are thinking about that world is not falsified by what is out there. We can never know what

methods

the formal rules of reason (rationalist) or appropriateness (constructivist) for testing perspectives against facts.

is true or actually out there. That's the case in the natural sciences too. Newtonian physics, which helped us reach the moon, assumes the universe is made up of fixed bodies, time, and space. Quantum physics, which helps us explode the atom, tells us it is made up of probabilities and relative time and space. Which world is the real world? We won't know until we find a unified theory that subsumes both theories, and even then a rival theory may always be possible.

Rationalist vs. Constructivist

In the social sciences, we speak of two general types of methods: **rationalist** and **constructivist.**[6] Realist and liberal perspectives of international affairs generally employ rationalist methods. Identity perspectives use both rationalist and constructivist methods, and some identity perspectives are actually called constructivist because they are considered to be methodologies only, not full-blown theories comparable to realism or liberalism. We use constructiv*ism* to refer to full-blown theories, such as social constructivism, and constructiv*ist* to refer to methodologies only.

Both methods start by naming or labeling facts. Before we can test whether sunlight causes plant growth or power balancing causes war, we need definitions of sun, sunlight, plants, growth, power, and war. Rationalist methods assume that such labeling can be done in a reasonably objective way; constructivist methods pay more attention to the discourse or subjective language game that produces labels. For example, why did U.S. policymakers name the first atomic weapon "Little Boy"? Did that reflect a subjective discourse that discriminated against women and fostered male predilections for war?

More important, the two methods differ over whether facts or events *cause* or *constitute* one another. Rationalist methods see **causation** as sequential. One fact or event exists independently of the other and precedes or comes before it. The first event links up with and causes a second event that comes after it. The preceding event is cause; the subsequent event is consequence. For example, the sun exists before a plant and drives plant life. Sunlight initiates photosynthesis, producing carbohydrates, the fuel of plant growth. Plants grow and reproduce as a result of the sun's light. Rationalist methods apply this kind of sequential causation to international affairs. For example, various types of power balances, whether two great powers or several great powers exist, precede and cause different types of interactions between states, ranging from cooperation to war. Realist perspectives argue that polarity, the number of great powers in the system, causes or determines the prospects of war.

Unlike rationalist methods, constructivist methods see events as bound together in context, not as separate and sequential occurrences. They fit together, not because one causes the other but because they *mutually* cause one another. Social relationships have this constitutive characteristic. Take, for example, the relationship between a master and a slave. One does not precede and cause the other. The master, unlike the sun, does not exist before the slave; instead, the master is defined by acquiring a slave, and the slave is defined by succumbing to a master. The two entities appear together chronologically, and one has no meaning without the other. They mutually cause or constitute one another and in that sense explain one another. Two things fit together in a given context or situation because they are appropriate to that context. This logic of appropriateness replaces the logic of consequence by which one event precedes and causes the other.

rationalist methods

methods that assume that causal factors can be disaggregated and described objectively, explaining one event by a second event occurring in sequence.

constructivist methods

methods that pay more attention to the way that meaning is formed discursively, through language, and that see events as mutually causing or constituting one another rather than causing one another sequentially.

causation

one fact or event causing another.

Sovereignty as Consequence or Construction

For example, we might ask which facts caused the rise of sovereignty or legal equality among states in international relations. Social scientists using rationalist methodologies might hypothesize that it was caused by an independent and preceding event such as the Treaty of Westphalia in 1648. Monarchs who existed in Europe prior to Westphalia gathered together and established (caused) the practice of sovereignty to assert their independence of the pope in Rome and holy Roman emperor in Vienna. Social scientists using constructivist methodologies might hypothesize that sovereignty derived from broader historical developments, "a change . . . in the basic *structure* of property rights that characterizes an entire social formation" (meaning an entire historical period rather than a particular event) and came about through the "growth in the volume and dynamic density" (meaning interdependence) of international society.[7] Before the concept of sovereignty emerged, property or territory among rulers was not considered separable or exclusive. Rulers viewed themselves as local members of a single universal community of Catholic Europe. The new definition of property or territorial rights involved separateness or exclusiveness. Territory now belonged to one and only one monarch or state. How did this change in the concept of property rights come about? Not by one prior thing causing another subsequent one but by a combination of factors—population pressures, diminishing returns to land, a widening of trade, and institutional innovations—that accelerated the "growth in the volume and dynamic density" of international social relationships. Notice how constructivist methods explain things in terms of broad context and appropriateness (at some point, sovereignty and states seemed appropriate to the situation) and how, in this example, ideas—a new conception of property rights—altered institutions and power, rather than the reverse. This is characteristic of identity perspectives; our example reflects one such perspective, known as social constructivism.

Correlation, Causation, and Process Tracing

correlation
one fact or event occurring with another fact or event.

process tracing
a method of examining events in detail to identify cause and effect.

Rationalist methods separate events from context and examine many cases to find patterns of correlation among them. Some rationalist methods become formalistic and mathematical. Because statistical studies show that wars seldom, if ever, occur among democracies, rationalist methodologies conclude that democracies do not go to war with one another. **Correlation** is not the same as causation, however. Correlation does not tell us whether democracy causes no war or no war causes democracy. Nor does it tell us that the two variables appearing together, such as democracy and no war, may not be caused by a host of other factors or omitted variables that we have not considered. These factors may all be interrelated with one another, creating what methodologists call multicolinearity. To move from correlation to causation requires a method known as **process tracing,** which examines events historically and in context to trace how different variables interact with one another. Does one variable appear in time before the other and thus can be said to cause it? Constructivist methods assume that we cannot separate variables in sequence or time. We have to substantiate them through a thick description, or narrative of the repetitive practices and interactions by which they emerge. Constructivist methods offer plausible, rather than predictive, explanations. They call attention to how situations might be interpreted rather than replicated and sensitize us to future possibilities rather than making precise predictions. Thus, constructivist studies might conclude that the peace among democracies is hard to abstract from the deeply embedded structure of American and British culture in the contemporary world and may be a consequence of unique rather than replicable factors that apply to future situations.

Counterfactual Reasoning

Both rationalist and constructivist methods use what we call **counterfactual reasoning.** History, because we look back on events that have already occurred, appears to have a single outcome. It appears to be factual. But we know that along the way many choices were made. With each choice, history took one path and abandoned others. Maybe an event such as World War I was going to happen. But it did not have to begin in July 1914, and it did not have to cost 20 million lives. How do we determine what choices or paths were *not* taken and use that knowledge to judge present circumstances? We ask *counter*factual questions. What if Archduke Franz Ferdinand of Austria-Hungary had not been assassinated in Sarajevo in June 1914, the triggering event for the start of World War I? What if Germany had not had a military plan to fight a war at the same time against both Russia and France? What if the United States had given United Nations (UN) inspectors more time in 2003 to do their work in Iraq? We make educated guesses about alternative paths that history might have taken, and that helps us to look for missing facts and test alternative explanations.

counterfactual reasoning
a method of testing claims for causality by inverting the causal claim. The counterfactual of the claim "event A caused event B" is to ask, "if event A had not happened, would event B have happened?"

Is One Perspective or Method Best?

Is one perspective or method better than another? Perhaps, but there is no general consensus among specialists and, like all other analysts and even professors, you will eventually have to make a judgment for yourself. This book familiarizes you with the arguments of each perspective and method and thus helps you decide which one works better for a given set of facts and circumstances.

The realist perspective may have certain advantages in situations of greater threat. When someone draws a gun on you, you tend not to ask what that person believes or whether you can refer the dispute to a court or institution. You duck or fight back to even the balance of power if you can. But how do you determine situations of greater threat? Often a threat is not obvious. It depends on what you are looking for. So, the realist perspective may exaggerate threat.

The liberal perspective may be better at finding ways to cooperate. Long before someone draws a gun on you, you try to find out what is aggravating that person and negotiate a compromise or alleviate the circumstances, such as poverty or lack of education, that may be driving him or her to violence. But what if the individual intends all along to harm you, not because of anything you do or he or she doesn't have but just because he or she doesn't like you? You may be compromising with someone who will take advantage of you later. How do you protect yourself? So, the liberal perspective may underestimate the risks of cooperation.

The identity perspective may be best at distinguishing between potential allies and enemies. It looks for similarities or differences in collective and individual self-images and asks how these self-images get constructed. If identities can be brought closer together, you might be more willing to risk cooperation (for example, if it's your brother who pulls the gun on you). If identities diverge, you might prefer to protect yourself. But how do you manage relations with an enemy country to avoid war and maybe mutual destruction? Don't you have to risk cooperation, especially with enemies? And what about friends? Don't they sometimes change and become enemies? Maybe the identity perspective is too rigid—some would say ideological—and leads to more fear or more complacency than power disparities or opportunities for compromise might otherwise prescribe.

This book presents and discusses the different perspectives (and methods) evenhandedly. By doing so, each perspective, in effect, critiques the others. What the realist perspective relatively deemphasizes—for example, the role of institutions or ideas—the liberal and identity perspectives emphasize. What the liberal perspective deemphasizes—for example, the role of power and ideas—the realist and identity perspectives emphasize. And so on. Thus, when we discuss the Cuban Missile Crisis or terrorist attacks from the three different perspectives, we will see the strengths and weaknesses of each perspective. We can keep an open mind toward each perspective rather than being told at the outset that this or that perspective is best.

F. Scott Fitzgerald, the novelist, once said that a well-educated person can hold two contradictory ideas in mind at the same time.[8] We will try to hold three (and, at times, four) different ideas—the perspectives and levels of analysis—in mind at the same time. We do this for two reasons. First, each of us already has a preferred way of thinking about the world, although we may not be conscious of it. That is how we conclude whether we are for or against a particular policy, such as the current war in Iraq. By being open to alternative perspectives, we discover which perspective we prefer and decide whether we want to continue to hold that perspective. Second, by considering all perspectives evenhandedly, we remain open to the opinions of others, even after we have decided our own point of view. This is healthy. Too much contemporary debate about international affairs is personalized and vitriolic. People label one another wicked or stupid instead of listening carefully to one another. Once we are used to thinking in terms of alternative perspectives, we may become more patient and generous in our debates with fellow citizens. We may concede that they are just as well-meaning and smart as we are but may be viewing the world from a different perspective.

The Role of Judgment

weapons of mass destruction (WMDs)
weapons that can kill large numbers of humans and/or cause great damage to fabricated and natural structures and to the biosphere in general; they include nuclear, biological, chemical, and, increasingly, radiological weapons.

judgment
the broader assessment of what makes sense after accumulating as many facts and testing as many perspectives as possible.

What is certain is that there will always be differences and controversies in international affairs. World War I occurred almost one hundred years ago. Yet we still don't agree on what caused it. Why? Don't we know all the facts by now? Probably, although a historian may still discover a lost diary or set of letters left by some participant. But will these last few facts resolve the controversy? Probably not. The reason is that people bring different perspectives to bear on the facts. Chapter 3 demonstrates this conclusion in the case of World War I.

Contemporary controversies are no different. Take the recent war in Iraq in 2003. Did Saddam Hussein have **weapons of mass destruction (WMDs)**? At the time the United States invaded Iraq in March 2003, the major intelligence services around the world in the United States, France, Russia, China, Great Britain, and Australia thought he did, particularly biological and chemical weapons. UN inspectors thought so as well. After the invasion, however, no weapons were found. Was that simply a case of bad intelligence? To some extent, no doubt it was. On the other hand, decision makers never act on the basis of perfect information. They have to rely on conjecture and **judgment.** As the *Washington Post* columnist Jim Hoagland writes: "Most of the time you are not going to have perfect knowledge for making decisions. If you look at the way Saddam Hussein acted, any reasonable person would have concluded that he was hiding those weapons, just from what he said and did. The key point is always going to be the judgment you then make from what is almost always imperfect intelligence."[9]

After we have assembled all the facts and done all the testing of perspectives we have time for, judgment comes into play. This is especially true in policy making, where time is always a pressing factor. We make decisions on the basis of some broader judgment about what we think makes sense. What is judgment? Is it instinct? Is it experience? Is it character? It is probably all of these. Whatever it is, it is different from facts and tested knowledge, yet it does not substitute for them. The best judgment, we say, is informed judgment—judgment enriched by facts and accumulated knowledge.

Thus, judgment is indispensable for good statesmanship as well as good scholarship. Oliver Wendell Holmes, the Supreme Court justice, once described President Franklin D. Roosevelt as a man with "a second-class intellect but a first-class temperament."[10] Many said the same thing about President Ronald Reagan. Neither man had a brilliant mind, yet, arguably, these two men were the greatest American presidents of the twentieth century. They had first-class personalities and instincts; they were excellent judges of people and events. As the *Economist* observed on Reagan's death in June 2004, Reagan knew "that mere reason, essential though it is, is only half of the business of reaching momentous decisions. You also need solid-based instincts, feelings, whatever the word is for the other part of the mind. 'I have a gut feeling,' Reagan said over and over again, when he was working out what to say or do."[11] A gut feeling without facts is ignorance, but incomplete knowledge without a gut feeling is often useless, especially under time constraints.

The Role of Ethics and Morality

Judgment is part of character, and character in turn is guided by **ethics** and **morality.** Because judgment plays a role in decision making, personal honesty is very important in intellectual and human affairs more generally—which is why we emphasize it in academic and other activities. What are our obligations to one another as human beings and to the world we inhabit? Ethics and morality deal with standards of right conduct and behavior—what we ought to do, not what we need, can, or prefer to do. Thus, ethics and morality go beyond mere facts and perspectives. They involve what we believe, not what we want, have, or know. Belief often delves into intangible, maybe religious, worlds that we cannot access or test through logical or scientific means. But that does not mean that ethics and morality are incompatible with the material world. Indeed, ethical and moral beliefs are an essential guide for directing contemporary scientific and technological debates. The question of what we do with nuclear technology or the technology used to clone human beings involves moral and ethical dilemmas.

In international affairs, we can distinguish three broad views about ethics and morality: relativism, universalism, and pragmatism.[12]

ethics and **morality**
standards of good conduct for human behavior.

Relativist Values

Relativism holds that all truth is relative. There are no universal moral principles that apply to all people under all circumstances. Each culture or religion is entitled to its

relativism
a position that holds that truth and morality are relative to each individual or culture and that one should "live and let live."

own view of truth. Because relativists do not believe in an ultimate truth, they are willing to tolerate multiple truths. Their attitude is live and let live—respect all views of ethics, morality, and religion. This became the moral view, at least within Christendom, in the seventeenth century. Protestants and Catholics who had been fighting one another for over a hundred years decided to tolerate one another and agreed in the Treaty of Westphalia in 1648 to respect the right of each sovereign to choose the religion for his or her own country. Sovereignty meant that each sovereign, and subsequently each state, agreed not to interfere in the domestic life—meaning, at that time, religion—of other sovereigns. This principle of nonintervention in the domestic affairs of other states remains enshrined today in the Charter of the United Nations. It now accommodates a world of diverse religions, going beyond Christianity. But such moral relativism, taken to an extreme, could also accommodate genocide, the purposeful slaughter of human beings because of their race, religion, or ethnicity, because there are no moral absolutes or prohibitions to condemn it. Shouldn't it be possible to proscribe morally the slaughter of Jews in Germany, Muslims in Bosnia, and Tutsis in Rwanda under all circumstances at all times?

Universal Values

universalism

a position that holds that truth and morality are universal; one cannot adjust moral behavior to circumstances without sliding down the slippery slope to relativism.

Universalism rejects relativism and argues that some absolute moral principles apply to all people in all countries at all times. After World War II and the murder of 6 million Jews in Europe, many decided that genocide should never happen again, that the world community has a moral obligation to prevent or stop it. Thus, the United Nations has evolved a standard of humanitarian intervention that directly contradicts its charter. Kofi Annan, then secretary-general of the United Nations, framed the contradiction this way. Even though the UN Charter rules out intervention in the domestic affairs of states, "is it permissible to let gross and systematic violations of human rights, with grave humanitarian consequences, continue unchecked?"[13] The international community may be moving beyond Westphalia's relativist morality and insisting that there are universal standards of basic human rights that all states, whatever their cultural or moral beliefs, must follow. But where do we draw the line? Saddam Hussein grossly violated the human rights of the citizens of Iraq. Yet neither the UN nor the North Atlantic Treaty Organization (NATO) authorized America's invasion of Iraq in March 2003. Was America nevertheless right to intervene based on universal standards of human rights? If so, how do we know whose standards are the universal ones?

Pragmatic Values

pragmatism

the idea that morality is proportionate to what is possible and that one should do what one can to uphold proper standards under present and potential future circumstances but that one should not be dogmatic.

Pragmatism offers a third point of view. Pragmatists answer the question of whether to intervene based on certain practical requirements, for example, stability and not setting a precedent. That is, they ask, will an intervention create disproportionate consequences that actually reduce world solidarity, and will an intervention set a standard that encourages repeated future interventions? U.S. intervention in Iraq, pragmatists might argue, increased rather than reduced the scale of violence. Moreover, it sanctioned the doctrine of preemption, attacking another state *after* you see it preparing to attack you, or, worse, the doctrine of prevention, attacking another state *before* you see any preparations because you fear it may attack you at some point in the future. Whether Iraq was an imminent threat or not is much disputed. But some pragmatists might conclude that the threat was not imminent and that America's intervention encouraged unlimited repeated interventions in the future. Pragmatists look to the immediate circumstances surrounding the action and ask whether intervention minimizes instability in that situation while at the same time securing whatever just outcome is possible. Pragmatism does not abandon a notion of universal morality but opposes its application at all times in all places. It is willing to compromise, even though compromise risks slipping into relativism. Indeed for pragmatists, the greatest moral good is compromise.

Moral Choice

A simple story illustrates the differences among these moral views.[14] An officer and a small group of soldiers involved in war enter a village, which enemy forces recently occupied. Overnight, one soldier is killed by a single shot. The next morning, the officer assembles the village residents and asks who did it. The villagers remain silent. So the officer announces that he will randomly select and kill three villagers in retaliation for this atrocity. You are a member of the officer's group. What should you do?

If you are a relativist, you will not object. Each side has its own standards of morality. If the other side can justify killing you, certainly you can justify killing them. Killing three people instead of one sets an example in a situation where force is the only arbiter of order because there is no common morality.

If you are a universalist, you will object. No one can kill innocent villagers under any circumstances at any time. To do so may be committing a war crime. So you say to the officer, "This is wrong; you can't do it." At this point, the officer turns to you and says, "OK, you shoot one, and I'll let the other two go." As a universalist, you still have to say no because it is wrong to kill innocent people, whether the number is one or three. You may go on to report the incident as a war crime.

If you are a pragmatist, however, you might accept the officer's offer and shoot one villager, thereby saving the lives of two others. For the pragmatist, killing three villagers would be disproportionate because only one person on your side was killed and the disproportionate retaliation might encourage further arbitrary killing. By killing one villager, the pragmatist minimizes the violence and sets a standard—tit for tat, not triple tit for tat—that potentially limits a chain of future retaliations.

The Role of History

History is the laboratory of international relations. We use historical examples to gather the facts and test the perspectives that enable us to explain and anticipate how the world works. Students often ask why we have to study history. That was then, they say; this is now. Things change, so why is the past relevant? Everything is totally new under the sun, right? Well, if that's the case, how do we recognize when something is totally new under the sun? Don't we need to know, at least, how the new differs from the old? Take globalization, for example. Is it new? Many commentators say it is. But globalization existed before World War I at levels that were not surpassed again until after the mid-1970s. We need patterns from the past to identify the trends of the future. Of course, history never repeats itself exactly. But if we don't examine it, we learn nothing from it and may inadvertently repeat it.

History is also fun. Perhaps you like to read novels? They contain all the elements of human tragedy, triumph, mystery, adventure, and romance. Well, so does history.

After all, it is the *real* story of human triumph and tragedy. History is also personal. Think of where you come from. Where was your family during the Vietnam War or your grandparents in World War II? Do you know from what part of the world your family comes? Unless you are Native American, your family came from someplace else. All these personal stories are part of the historical narrative. As we go through the book, I'll share some snippets of my family's history. I do this not to focus on my life but to help you discover how your life, too, is linked with history.

This book therefore covers lots of history, but at a high level of generalization. We use this history to gain insight into contemporary and future international affairs. We start in Part I with *military* history and contemporary conflicts such as the recent terrorist attacks. In Part II, we take up *economic* history and current controversies about globalization and the world economy. In Part III, we explore *transnational and global* issues that may be creating a new world community or dividing it in different and more dangerous ways. In each part, we seek to understand what has existed in the past to see more clearly what may be coming in the future. Knowing that perspectives matter, we already know that international relations are not just about world events. Somebody has to decide what events matter, and somebody can decide that only through an examination of the past.

Summary

Refer back to Figure Intro-2 for a minute. It suggests how the various elements of understanding international affairs fit together. We start with perspectives because we could not start at all if we tried to consider all the facts that make up world affairs. We theorize about what causes events and select or consider as many facts as we can from the different levels of analysis. Then we test our perspective against other perspectives using rationalist or constructivist methods or some combination of the two. Finally, we draw conclusions relying on judgment, ethics, and morality to fill in the gaps that analysis inevitably leaves.

Every student or participant in international affairs has to approach the subject in this manner. Take a 900-page book entitled *Diplomacy* that former secretary of state Henry Kissinger wrote in 1994. In it, he argued that the United States was entering a world after the end of the Cold War for which it was poorly prepared. He used a realist perspective to survey centuries of world history and show that balancing power is the best approach to preserving peace in a world of relatively equal powers. Today, Kissinger observed, America is entering a world of relatively equal powers—comprising China, Russia, India, Europe, and the United States—but America's self-image, which is exceptionalist and considers democracy appropriate for all countries, is an obstacle to dealing with other countries that share equal power but have different political identities. From a realist perspective, Kissinger wants the balance of power to prevail over any specific country's identity. Do you agree with Kissinger? How can you know unless you have some idea what history he selected and what history he left out? Now you see why, if you want to participate in this debate, you need to understand perspectives and history. In the next chapter, we distinguish more carefully among the three perspectives and levels of analysis to better prepare ourselves, if we are so inclined, to argue with Kissinger's perspective.

Key Concepts

causation 11
constructivist methods 11
correlation 12
counterfactual reasoning 13
critical theory perspective 8
domestic level of analysis 6
ethics 15
foreign policy level of
    analysis 10
ideal types 2

identity perspective 8
individual level of analysis 6
judgment 14
levels of analysis 2
liberal perspective 7
methods 10
morality 15
perspectives 1
pragmatism 16
process tracing 12

rationalist methods 11
realist perspective 5
relativism 15
systemic level of
    analysis 6
universalism 16
weapons of
    mass destruction
    (WMDs) 14

Study Questions

1. Why is ethnic conflict that occurs in one part of the world front-page news but not ethnic conflict that occurs in another?

2. Do you think terrorism is caused by American imperialism or American diplomacy? Which answer reflects the realist perspective? Which reflects the liberal perspective?

3. How would you test your perspective that American imperialism is the cause of terrorism—by measuring relative power over different periods of time or by examining the social purposes of American foreign policy embedded in specific historical circumstances? Which method is rationalist and which is constructivist?

4. Do you believe the U.S. invasion of Iraq was wrong because it violated Iraq's independence or right because it ended genocide in Iraq? Which argument is relativist and which is universalist?

5. Why is history relevant to what is new even though it deals with what is old?

1

How to Think About International Relations

Perspectives and Levels of Analysis

We study the world together from many different analytical perspectives and social settings.

What are the differences among the following statements?

1. The rise of German power caused World War I.
2. Kaiser Wilhelm II's clumsy diplomacy caused World War I.
3. Germany's militarist ideology, which glorified aggressive war, caused World War I.

The statements offer different explanations of the causes of World War I, which we explore more fully in Chapter 3. The purpose here is to help you see that these explanations come from different perspectives and levels of analysis. As already noted, we cannot describe everything in international affairs. Perspectives on international relations help us make selections. They point us in certain directions to find facts, and they order these facts differently to explain events. One fact becomes the cause or independent variable; a second fact becomes the effect or dependent variable. Or, in the case of constructivist methods, two facts mutually cause or constitute one another. What is the problem you are interested in, and what do you think causes or constitutes that problem? As political scientists would say, we have to start with a problem, something that puzzles us, and formulate hypotheses to explain that puzzle. We draw these hypotheses from the major perspectives outlined in this book. Then we look at the facts to test our hypotheses. Often we go back and forth between the hypotheses and the evidence many times refining our analysis. Then we make judgments. As Professor Thomas Risse says, we see "how far one can push one logic of action [perspective] to account for observable practices and which logic [perspective] dominates a given situation." [1]

The realist perspective focuses on separate actors and military conflict and argues that the relative distribution of power among actors in international affairs is the most important cause of war. When one actor becomes too powerful, the other actors feel threatened. They form alliances to counterbalance the first actor and that can lead to war. Did this happen before World War I? The realist perspective finds it did. The rise of German power (see statement 1) upset the relative distribution of power among states in Europe and set in motion a security competition that eventually caused World War I. The liberal perspective focuses on global society and international institutions and argues that the reciprocal process and quality of interactions and negotiations among actors have more to do with peace and war than the relative power of separate actors. If actors lack sufficient social and economic connections to build trust or institutions do not provide clear rules and information for communicating effectively, war may result. This perspective looks at the facts before World War I and finds that the German monarch, Kaiser Wilhelm II, was not an effective diplomat and caused the war by provoking unnecessary rivalries, especially with Great Britain (see statement 2). The identity perspective focuses on ideas and norms and argues that the way actors think about themselves and others—their identities—influences international behavior more than specific institutions or power disparities. This perspective holds that countries with aggressive self-images are more inclined to go to war and finds that prior to World War I Germany had just such a domestic ideology of military aggressiveness, which caused conflict with its neighbors (see statement 3).

Explanations also differ in terms of the level of analysis at which they operate. Perspectives tell us what the substance of the cause is—power, institutions, or ideas; levels of analysis tell us where the cause is coming from. Notice that statement 1 sees the cause of war as coming from the level of the state system as a whole. The rapid rise of German power relative to that of all other states in Europe caused instability and war. The specific characteristics of Germany and its leaders did not matter; any country rising in power relative to other countries would have caused the same instability. This type of explanation we call a systemic level of analysis. Statement 2 sees the cause of war as coming from a specific leader; Kaiser Wilhelm II's bad diplomacy caused the war. If someone else had been in charge of Germany under the same historical circumstances, war might not have occurred. The cause did not come from the nature of the domestic or international system; it came from an individual policymaker or the small group of decision makers around him. This is a very specific level of analysis, which we call the individual or, sometimes, decision-making level of analysis. Finally, statement 3 argues that Germany's militarist ideology, which caused war, came from the nature of Germany's domestic system, not the relative rise of German power or Kaiser Wilhelm II's inept diplomacy. In such a domestic system any leader would have behaved in the same way, regardless of individual and decision-making factors or international conditions. We say that this type of explanation comes from the domestic level of analysis.

In the rest of this chapter, we spell out the details of the three principal perspectives and levels of analysis. From time to time, we also discuss a fourth perspective and level of analysis—critical theory offers a broad critique of mainstream international relations perspectives, and the foreign policy level of analysis suggests how levels of analysis interact. We use the story of the prisoner's dilemma and various modifications of this story to highlight the assumptions of the three core perspectives. Then we investigate the principal concepts that distinguish each perspective and review the characteristics of the multiple levels of analysis from which each perspective may be applied.

Prisoner's Dilemma

prisoner's dilemma
a game illustrating the realist perspective in which two prisoners rationally choose not to cooperate in order to avoid even worse outcomes.

The basic **prisoner's dilemma** story is simple. Two individuals are caught with illegal drugs in their possession. Police authorities suspect that one or both of them may be drug dealers but do not have enough evidence to prove it. So the warden in the prison where the individuals are being held creates a situation to try to get them to squeal on one another. The warden tells each prisoner separately that if he squeals on the other prisoner he can go free; the accused prisoner will then be put away as a drug dealer for twenty-five years. If the other prisoner also squeals, each prisoner gets ten years in prison. On the other hand, if both prisoners remain silent, each will get only one year in prison because there is no further evidence to convict them. The prisoners do not know one another and are not allowed to communicate. Table 1-1 illustrates the choices and outcomes.

How the Realist Perspective Sees the Situation of the Prisoner's Dilemma

The individual prisoner's dilemma is the following. If actor A remains silent, in effect cooperating with his fellow prisoner, he gets either one year in prison if the other prisoner also remains silent (see upper left box) or twenty-five years if the other prisoner squeals (lower left box). On the other hand, if actor A squeals, he may either go free if the other prisoner remains silent (see upper right box) or get a sentence of ten years in prison if the other prisoner also squeals (lower right box). From each prisoner's standpoint, it is logical to squeal (hoping for the best outcome—freedom) even though this

Table 1-1

Prisoner's Dilemma: A Realist Game				
			Actor A	
			Cooperate (C) (silent)	Defect (D) (squeal)
Actor B	Cooperate (C) (silent)		Both get 1 year	**A** goes free **B** gets 25 years
	Defect (D) (squeal)		**A** gets 25 years **B** goes free	Both get 10 years (outcome of game)

- A and B can get their best outcome (go free) only if they squeal and the other prisoner remains silent (DC).
- They can get their second-best outcome (one year) only if they both remain silent (CC), but by remaining silent each gets the worst outcome (twenty-five years) if the other squeals (CD).
- They settle for their third-best outcome (ten years) in order to avoid their worst outcome (twenty-five years [DD]).
- Notice how the outcomes are ordered for each actor: DC > CC > DD > CD. If this order changes, the game changes. See subsequent tables.

choice cannot achieve the second-best outcome that might occur if each prisoner remains silent—getting only one year in prison. But by remaining silent, each prisoner also risks the worst outcome if the other prisoner squeals, namely twenty-five years in prison. The point of the story is that each prisoner cannot achieve the second-best goal of one year in prison or the ideal goal of going free because circumstances outside the control of the prisoner—the various consequences or payoffs of the different choices set by the warden—make squealing the less risky alternative. Each settles for a less desired outcome (ten years) but avoids the worst one.

The realist perspective argues that this sort of dilemma defines the logic of many situations in international affairs. Countries desire peace (analogous to cooperating) and do not want to arm or threaten other countries (analogous to squealing). They prefer less risky or more peaceful strategies such as mutual disarmament (analogous to cooperating and staying only one year in prison). But one country cannot disarm without risking the possibility that the other country may arm and perhaps seize territory or take away the first country's sovereignty, eliminating its independence and, if it is a democratic state, taking away its freedom (analogous to the maximum penalty of twenty-five years). The country that arms is not aggressive. It is just looking for the best outcome, and if it arms and the other country does not, it is safer than it would be otherwise. The situation is set up such that each party cannot have peace (going free or spending one year in prison) without risking loss of territory or sovereignty (twenty-five years in prison). If both countries arm, on the other hand, they can protect their territory and sovereignty but now risk the possibility of mutual harm and war. Because the possibility of war is less risky (equivalent to ten years in prison) than the actual loss of territory, let alone sovereignty (or democracy), they squeal or defect. Thus, from the realist perspective much of international relations is about mutual armaments and conflict. Notice too that when one country gains the most (analogous to one prisoner squealing and going free), the other country loses the most (analogous to one remaining silent and getting twenty-five years). In this specific case, the game approaches what political scientists call **zero sum.** What one actor gains, the other loses, and the sum of gains and losses is zero, as in a conflict over territory. While that's not completely true here because the gains and losses do not add up to zero and the prisoner's dilemma game also includes situations of mutual gain (one year or ten years in prison), both countries cannot achieve their best outcome (going free) simultaneously, and in that sense, the game reflects conflicting goals among international actors which realists stress.

zero sum

situations in international affairs in which what one actor gains, the other loses.

How the Liberal Perspective Sees the Situation of the Prisoner's Dilemma

The liberal perspective argues that situations described by the prisoner's dilemma do exist in international affairs but they are not the only or even most prevalent situations and can be overcome. Three factors help surmount these situations and change the prisoner's dilemma to a more cooperative game: repeated reciprocal interactions or communications, common goals, and technological change. In the original game, the prisoners are not allowed to communicate and build trust, and they play the game only once. What if they were allowed to play the game over and over again, the equivalent of meeting regularly in the prison yard to exchange moves and perhaps make small talk? It's not so much the content of what they say that produces more trust (from a realist perspective, familiarity breeds contempt as easily as cooperation) but, rather, the mere fact that they play the game over and over again. In game theory, this is called creating the shadow of the future, that is, the expectation that the prisoners will have to deal with one another again and again—tomorrow, the day after, and every day in the future. As long as the prisoners can avoid the expectation that they will not meet again—what game theory calls the last move, equivalent to playing the game only once—they might gain enough trust in one another to discount significantly the possibility that the other prisoner will defect if the first prisoner remains silent. Now, as Table 1-2 shows, they end up in the upper left box—the second-best outcome of a one-year sentence—rather than the lower right one. The liberal perspective argues that if countries develop habits of regular interaction and communication through diplomacy, membership in common institutions, trade, tourism, and other exchanges, they can overcome the security dilemma that drives mutual armaments and conflict.

What is more, according to the liberal perspective, many goals in international relations are common and mutually beneficial, not self-interested and conflicting as depicted in the prisoner's dilemma. Countries seek to grow rich together or protect the environment together. These goals are **non-zero sum.** Both sides gain, albeit perhaps not equally.

So, what if we change the goals of the prisoners in the original version of the prisoner's dilemma from going free to frustrating the warden by reducing the total number of years the warden is able to hold the prisoners in jail? Now the prisoners have a common goal, not a self-interested one. Nothing else in the situation changes, but notice how the outcome of the game changes. As Table 1-3 shows, the logical choice that now meets the goal of both prisoners is to remain silent (upper left box). That gives the warden only two prisoner-years (one year for each prisoner), while squealing by one or both prisoners gives the warden twenty-five or twenty (ten years each) prisoner-years, respectively. The prisoners still can't influence the warden. He is outside their control. But now both prisoners can get their second-best outcome simultaneously by cooperating.[2]

Further, what if the warden changes the payoffs, or consequences, of the original game? For example, if both prisoners squeal, that should give the warden enough evidence to convict them both as drug dealers and now, let's say, put them to death.

non-zero sum

situations and goals in which all parties can gain.

Table 1-2				
Situation of Prisoner's Dilemma from Liberal Perspective: Allow Communications				
			Actor A	
			Cooperate (C) *(silent)*	*Defect (D)* *(squeal)*
Actor B	*Cooperate (C)* *(silent)*		Both get 1 year (outcome of game)	**A** goes free **B** gets 25 years
	Defect (D) *(squeal)*		**A** gets 25 years **B** goes free	Both get 10 years

- Same payoffs and goals as original game.
- Assume A and B can communicate repeatedly:
  —meet for one hour in prison yard each day.
  —becomes part of regular schedule or "shadow of the future" (relationships become patterned or institutionalized).
- A and B gain one another's trust.
- A and B choose to cooperate.

Table 1-3

Situation of Prisoner's Dilemma from Liberal Perspective: Change Goals (Frustrate the Warden)

		Actor A	
		Cooperate (C) (silent)	Defect (D) (squeal)
Actor B	Cooperate (C) (silent)	Both get 1 year (outcome of game)	**A** goes free **B** gets 25 years
	Defect (D) (squeal)	**A** gets 25 years **B** goes free	Both get 10 years

- Same payoffs as original game, but the goals have changed. Notice that the new goal of frustrating the warden rather than going free is non-zero sum, because both prisoners can now get their best outcome simultaneously. An example may be two countries trading to increase wealth for both (non-zero sum), rather than fighting over territory that only one can gain (zero-sum). Look at how the countries of the European Union have overcome historical disputes over territory by building a common trade and economic union.
- By cooperating, A and B can limit gains to the warden to two prisoner years, one year for each prisoner (upper left).
- If either or both defect (i.e., choose upper right or lower right or lower left boxes), the warden gets more prisoner years (twenty-five or twenty).
- Hence, A and B can achieve best outcome in terms of new goal by cooperating.

Table 1-4 shows the new game. All we have done is increase the worst possible cost of defecting (death) over that of cooperating (twenty-five years). That might be the equivalent in international affairs of a technological change such as developing nuclear weapons that raises the penalty of arms races and war. Nuclear weapons increase the dangers of mutual armaments by states, just as the death penalty increases the cost of mutual defection by the prisoners. Now the actors no longer have a dominant strategy to defect, as in the original game. Each knows that defecting carries the risk of death, the worst outcome; they would like to cooperate. But each still wants most to go free, and that can be achieved only by defecting. So the actors are torn now between the two strategies depicted by the upper right and lower left boxes: defecting if the other actor cooperates (and going free) or cooperating if the other actor defects (and getting 25 years). While the prospects of both cooperating and ending up in the upper left hand box are not assured, they have improved significantly over the original game. The scale tips toward cooperation. The cost of twenty-five years in prison if the other prisoner does not cooperate is still less than that of death.[3]

Technological change may work the other way of course. It may reduce the costs or increase the benefits of cooperating rather than increasing the costs of defecting. Let's go back to the original game and reduce the cost of remaining silent if the other prisoner squeals from twenty-five to five years. Now, as Table 1-5 illustrates, the prisoners risk less if they cooperate (five years) than if they squeal (ten years). Their preferred strategies again are the upper right and lower left boxes. But now, because they risk only five years in prison if they guess wrong about what the other party will do, the prospects of cooperating are better than in the original game. A real-world example of reducing the costs or increasing the benefits of cooperation might be technological advances that make the prospects of ballistic missile defense more feasible. Reassured by such defenses, countries may be more willing to cooperate in a nuclear crisis. If the

Table 1-4

Situation of Prisoner's Dilemma from Liberal Perspective: Change Payoffs (Increase Costs of Defection/Conflict)

		Actor A	
		Cooperate (C) (silent)	Defect (D) (squeal)
Actor B	Cooperate (C) (silent)	Both get 1 year	**A** goes free **B** gets 25 years (outcome of game)
	Defect (D) (squeal)	**A** gets 25 years **B** goes free (outcome of game)	Both get death

- The warden increases the cost of defection and hence changes the order of preferences for each of the prisoners: DC > CC > CD > DD (different from the original order: DC > CC > DD > CD). An example of increased costs in international relations might be the threat of nuclear versus conventional weapons, which increases dramatically the costs of defection or conflict.
- A or B gets the best outcome only if one defects (squeals and goes free) and the other actor cooperates (remains silent).
- But if they both defect, they risk getting their worst outcome (death).
- So they have a greater tendency to cooperate but still prefer to defect, because that is the only way they can go free, assuming the other cooperates.

Table 1-5

Situation of Prisoner's Dilemma from Liberal Perspective: Change Payoffs (Reduce Costs of Cooperation)

		Actor A	
		Cooperate (C) (silent)	Defect (D) (squeal)
Actor B	Cooperate (C) (silent)	Both get 1 year	**A** goes free **B** gets 5 years (outcome of game)
	Defect (D) (squeal)	**A** gets 5 years **B** goes free (outcome of game)	Both get 10 years

- The warden reduces the costs of cooperation and hence the order of preferences for each actor: DC > CC > CD > DD (different from the original order: DC > CC > DD > CD). A real-life example may be a country that has missile defense and does not risk as much damage if it cooperates (remains silent) and the other country attacks (defects).
- A or B gets the best outcome (freedom) if one defects and the other cooperates.
- But if both A and B defect, they risk getting their worst outcome (ten years).
- Hence, they have a greater tendency to cooperate but still prefer to defect, because that is the only way they can go free, assuming the other cooperates.

other country defects and attacks, the first country can defend itself and not lose as much (the equivalent of getting five years) as it might if it also attacked (the equivalent of getting ten years).

In all of these ways—promoting communication and diplomacy, focusing on common rather than conflicting goals, and exploiting technological changes that alter payoffs in favor of cooperation—the liberal perspective argues realist logic can be overcome.

How the Identity Perspective Sees the Situation of the Prisoner's Dilemma

The **identity** perspective takes still another tack on the situation described by the original prisoner's dilemma game. It challenges the implicit assumption that the prisoners have independent identities and receive payoffs that are exclusive of one another. If the payoffs were interdependent, the two prisoners would seek to maximize their joint score, implying that they have common, not self-interested, motives and identities. What if, for example, the two prisoners knew that they were both members of the Mafia? Members of the Mafia, an underground criminal organization, take a blood oath that they will never squeal on other members of the organization or reveal anything about its criminal activities. This oath becomes part of their identity. They remain silent because of who they are. They may also remain silent, of course, because they fear that someone in the Mafia will kill them if they squeal. But, in that case, the scenario mimics a realist situation because their behavior is determined by external circumstances. In the case as seen from the identity perspective, they do not squeal because their obedience to the Mafia code has been internalized and is now part of their identity. If each prisoner knows that the other prisoner is also a member of the Mafia, they are unlikely to squeal on one another. No feature of the game has changed except that the prisoners now know they have similar or shared identities. Yet, as Table 1-6 shows, the outcome of the game changes substantially. It is now logical for the two prisoners to remain silent and get off with only one year each in prison.

In the same way, the identity perspective argues that two countries may behave differently depending on their identities. They may see one another as enemies, rivals, or

identity

the ideas that shape an entity's sense of self either through a shared or collective relationship with others or through relative similarities and differences with other groups.

Table 1-6				
Situation of Prisoner's Dilemma from Identity Perspective: Change Identity				
			Actor A	
			Cooperate (C) (silent)	*Defect (D) (squeal)*
Actor B	*Cooperate (C) (silent)*		Both get 1 year (outcome of game)	**A** goes free **B** gets 25 years
	Defect (D) (squeal)		**A** gets 25 years **B** goes free	Both get 10 years

- Original payoffs, goals, and no communications (except knowledge of the other's identity).
- Assume that A and B are not self-interested actors but members of a common organization—say the Mafia—and know that about one another.
- Because of their shared identities, they know that the other will not squeal.
- Hence, they can choose to cooperate without fear that the other will defect.

friends, depending on the way their identities are socially constructed. Or their identities may converge or diverge with one another depending on their relative similarities or differences. Thus, democracies behave more peacefully with one another than they do with autocracies, and countries that identify with common international norms and ideas behave differently than those that see themselves struggling over the balance of power.

Let's leave the game metaphor and develop these three perspectives in the real world.

The Realist Perspective

The realist perspective focuses on conflict and war, not because people adopting this perspective favor war or believe war is necessary, but because they hope by studying war to avoid it in the future. War, according to the realist perspective, is a consequence of *anarchy,* the decentralized distribution of power in the international system. In anarchic situations, actors have to rely on *self-help* to defend themselves; there is no central power they can appeal to. So, throughout history wherever anarchy existed, individuals, tribes, clans, villages, towns, and provinces provided for their own security. Today the *state* is the principal actor charged to assemble military and other forms of *power* to protect security. In pursuing power, however, states inevitably threaten one another. Is one state arming to defend itself or to attack another state? States cannot be sure about one another's intentions. They face a *security dilemma,* like the prisoner's dilemma. If one state arms and the other doesn't, the first one may lose its security. To cope with that dilemma, they both defect or pursue a *balance of power.* They form *alliances* against any country that becomes so strong it might threaten the survival of the others. The number of great power states or alliances involved in the balance of power constitutes the *polarity* of the system. Two great powers or alliances form a bipolar system, three form a tripolar system, and four or more form a multipolar system. Different system polarities produce different propensities toward *war.*

Let's look a little closer at these key (italicized) concepts of a realist perspective on world affairs. (The concepts appear in bold where they are most succinctly defined.)

Anarchy and Self-Help

For realist perspectives, the distribution of power is always decentralized. They refer to this fact of international life as an*archy.* The word means no leader or center, as opposed to mon*archy* (or empire), which means one leader or center, and poly*archy,* which means several overlapping leaders or centers, such as the shared authority of the pope and holy Roman emperor in medieval Europe. In the world today, **anarchy** means there is no leader or center of authority that monopolizes coercive power and has the legitimacy to use it. The United States may be the only world superpower, but, as the Iraq War suggests, the rest of the world does not recognize its legitimacy to use that power as a world government, not in the same sense that citizens of a particular country recognize the legitimacy of the domestic government to monopolize coercive power. There is no world government with the authority of a domestic government and no world police force with the authority of a national police or military force. In short, there is no *world 911.* If you get in trouble abroad, there is no one to call for help,

anarchy
the decentralized distribution of power in the international system; no leader or center of authority exists that monopolizes power and has the legitimacy to use it.

no one except your own clan, tribe, or state. If a student from the United States is arrested in Singapore, for example, the student calls the U.S. embassy in Singapore, not the UN in New York. Similarly, if a country is attacked, it provides its own defense or calls on allies. It is not likely to depend on international organizations.

Anarchy places a premium on **self-help,** which means that whatever the size or nature of the actor in any historical period—whether it is a tribe, city-state, or nation-state—it has to provide for its own protection or it risks succumbing to another actor. The size or nature of the actor may change over time. Some states

The realist perspective emphasizes military and economic power, on display here in 2007 by Chinese soldiers during military exercises.

unite like the European Union, while others collapse like the Soviet Union. But the condition of anarchy and need for self-help do not change. Unless the world eventually unites under a single government that all the peoples of the world recognize as the sole legitimate center of military power, decentralized actors will be responsible for their own security.

self-help
the principle of self-defense that arises from the situation of anarchy in which states have no one else to rely on to defend their security except themselves.

State Actors

The realist perspective tends to focus on the largest decentralized actors that exercise self-help because they command the greatest power. Today, the largest actors are **states.** But the realist perspective also focuses on nonstate actors. Earlier, provinces, villages, and city-states provided security. Today, nonstate actors such as Al Qaeda use force, and international drug cartels commit murders. In the future, perhaps regional actors, such as the European Union (EU), or nonstate actors, such as domestic minority groups (for example, the Kurds in Iraq), will provide their own security. The EU has yet to develop an integrated security policy; but if it does, it will function like any other state, according to the realist perspective. Similarly, if current states dissolve and domestic minorities form separate states, as happened in the previously united Yugoslav republic, the new states—Croatia, Slovenia, and so on—face the same imperatives of anarchy and self-help.

How does a territorial unit become a state? From the realist perspective, the most important requirement is that a state commands the resources and power to defend itself. When states emerged in Europe during the period from 1000 to 1500 CE,[4] they had to demonstrate that they could establish and defend their borders. Once a state monopolized force within its borders and mobilized that force to defend its borders, it was recognized by other states. Because the realist perspective is especially interested in conflict and war, realist scholars find it more important to study states than nonstate actors. States command and use military and police forces. Corporations, labor unions, and human rights groups do not; and if they do—for example, private security forces defending corporate properties overseas—these groups are not recognized by

states
the largest actors in the contemporary international system that can legitimately use military force.

domestic authorities or international institutions as having the right to use force. Only states have that right, and therefore, state behavior is the most important reality affecting the prospects of war and peace.

Power

power

material capabilities of a country such as size of population and territory, resource endowment, economic capability, and military strength.

States monopolize power, but what is power? For the most part, **power** from the realist perspective is concerned with material capabilities, not influence or outcomes. Normally, we define power and influence as getting others to do what they would not otherwise do. Power does that by coercion, influence by persuasion. But how do we know what others might have intended or done had we not sought to influence them? Their intentions may be manifold and very hard to discern. And outcomes that might have occurred if we had not sought to influence them are part of that counterfactual history we can only speculate about. As the realist perspective sees it, it is too difficult to measure power and influence in terms of intentions or outcomes. It is better to measure power in terms of inputs, or material capabilities. It is then assumed that these capabilities translate roughly into commensurate influence and outcomes.

How does the realist perspective measure capabilities? Kenneth Waltz, the father of what is known in international political theory as neorealism or structural realism—a realist perspective based primarily on the systemic structure or distribution of power—identifies the following measures: "size of population and territory, resource endowment, economic capability, military strength, political stability and competence."[5] Population, economics, and military might are obvious elements of state power. Territory and resource endowment are too. They involve geography and contribute to what realist perspectives call more broadly **geopolitics.** Some countries have more land than others, some have more natural resources, and some have more easily defended geographical borders. For example, Switzerland is protected on all sides by mountains, while Poland sits in the middle of the great plains of northern Europe and, as a result, has been more frequently invaded, conquered, and even partitioned. Island nations have certain power advantages by virtue of being less vulnerable to invasion. England was never defeated by Napoleon or Hitler, while states on the European continent succumbed to both invaders.

geopolitics

a focus on a country's location and geography as the basis of its national interests.

Other nations, such as the United States and Russia, occupy the heartland of vast continents. They have geographic depth that aids their defense. When Napoleon invaded Russia, the tsar's forces did not directly engage Napoleon's forces but conducted a scorched-earth retreat and drew Napoleon's army deeper and deeper into Russia, farther and farther away from its supply lines and communications. Eventually Napoleon's army ran out of supplies, and the Russian winter destroyed it. The United States has similar geographic depth. It felt safe enough in its continental sanctuary surrounded by two oceans to stay out of World War I until nearly the end and might have stayed out of World War II, even after Britain was almost defeated, if the Japanese had not attacked Pearl Harbor.

Notice, however, that Waltz also mentions capabilities such as political stability and competence that are not, strictly speaking, material capabilities. These political capabilities involve institutional and ideological factors that are more important in liberal and identity perspectives, what some analysts call "soft power." The neorealist perspective does not emphasize such political capabilities. It focuses more on the material power than on the domestic political institutions and ideologies that mobilize the power. Another version of the realist perspective, known as classical realism, pays more attention to domestic values and institutions. But as Professor Hans Morgenthau, the father of classical realism, also concludes, "the main signpost . . . through the landscape of international politics is the concept of interests defined in terms of power." [6]

The realist perspective differentiates states in terms of great powers, middle powers, and small powers. States acquire different interests or goals depending on the size of their capabilities, not on the characteristics of the institutions they belong to or the political ideas they espouse. Great powers have the broadest interests. They have a concern for the well-being of the international system as a whole because they make up a good part of that system. When states fade from great power to middle power status, as Austria did after the seventeenth century, their interests shrink. By the time of World War I, Austria was interested only in its immediate surroundings in the Balkans. Small powers often remain on the sideline in realist analysis or succumb to the power of larger states, as happened to Poland through repeated invasion and conquest.

Security Dilemma

When states pursue power to defend themselves, they create a security dilemma from which the possibility, although not the inevitability, of war can never be completely excluded. The **security dilemma** results from the fact that, as each group or state amasses power to protect itself, it inevitably threatens the other group or state. Other states wonder how the first state will use the power it is amassing: Will it use its power just to defend its present territory, or will it use that power to expand its territory? (This is analogous to the possibility that the other prisoner will squeal in the prisoner's dilemma.) How can the other states be sure what the first state intends? If it is only seeking to defend itself, other states have nothing to worry about. But if it has more ambitious aims, then the other states too must arm. Exactly how much power is consistent with defense, and at what point does the accumulation of power signal aggressive intent? Because no state can be sure, the other states arm too; and in this process of mutual armament, states face all the uncertainties of what exactly constitutes enough power to be safe. As Ronald Reagan once said, we seek a "margin of safety" vis-à-vis the Soviet Union, which to the Soviet Union probably meant that the United States sought "superiority." Scholars who emphasize the realist perspective have never agreed on whether states seek just "security," or enough power to balance and defend themselves, or whether they seek "maximum power" on the assumption that more power always makes the state more secure. Theories of defensive realism say states seek security; theories of offensive realism say they seek maximum power.

security dilemma
the situation that states face when they arm to defend themselves and in the process threaten other states.

Balance of Power

The best states can do then, according to the realist perspective, is to pursue and balance power. The **balance of power** is both a process by which states seek to ensure that no other state dominates the system and an outcome that establishes a rough equilibrium among states. In balancing power, it does not matter what the rising state's intentions are. Does the United States today seek to dominate the world? Many would say no. But the European states, Russia, or China may have reasons for concern. From the realist perspective, they cannot worry about America's intentions; they have to worry about America's power.

As a process, the balance of power focuses on the formation of alliances and requires that states *align against the greatest power* regardless of who that power is. The

balance of power
the process by which states counterbalance to ensure that no single state dominates the system, or an outcome that establishes a rough equilibrium among states.

greatest power is the state that can threaten another state's survival. So it does not matter if that greater power belongs to the same institutions or believes in the same values, the smaller state must align against that power. After all, a growing power may change its institutional affiliations or values. Hence, the state does not align against the greatest threat, which may be a function of the state's institutions and values, but against the greatest power, whatever its institutions and values. Aligning *with*, rather than against, the greatest power, is known as **bandwagoning.** A smaller power joins the dominant power because it expects to share the spoils of conquest with the dominant power. From a realist perspective, however, this strategy is very dangerous because a state can never be sure the greater power won't change its intentions and attack the smaller state when it gets the chance. Think how Hitler turned around and attacked Stalin in 1941 after Stalin had aligned, or bandwagoned, with Hitler and signed a non-aggression pact in 1939 (see Chapter 4).

As an outcome, the balance of power prescribes equilibrium, or a situation of **power balancing.** Presumably states that are relatively equal in power do not threaten one another. They offset one another's power and thus lessen the risk of attack and conflict. What causes instability is the movement away from equilibrium toward one power dominating others. But not all realist scholars agree. Some argue that **hegemony,** a situation in which one country is more powerful than all the others, is more stable than equilibrium. The dominant power, or **hegemon,** deters other powers from attacking because the other powers have no chance of defeating the dominant power; the dominant power creates what is called **hegemonic stability.** Hegemony stabilizes—not destabilizes—the situation, and what causes instability is the movement away from hegemony toward equilibrium. Rising states gain relative power and challenge the dominant state. The moment they pass the dominant state—the moment of **power transition**—is when war is most likely to occur. Rising powers may seek to impose different objectives on the international system and go to war to achieve those objectives. Or declining powers may fear that their decline will only get worse and they have to go to war now before the rising state becomes too powerful, even if the rising state shows no current inclination to attack.

In subsequent chapters, we refer to the power balancing and power transition schools to capture this difference among realist perspectives on which configuration of power—equilibrium or hegemony—is most conducive to stability.

Polarity and Alliances

How do states balance power? It depends on how many states there are. We call the number of states holding power in a system the **polarity** of the system. If there are many states or centers of power, the system is **multipolar.** In a multipolar system states balance by forming **alliances** with other states to counter the state that is becoming the greatest power. These alliances have to be temporary and flexible. Why? Because the balance of power is always uncertain and shifts, sometimes quickly. States must therefore be ready to shift alliances. Remember the purpose of alliances is to balance power, not to make permanent friends or permanent enemies. Winston Churchill, Britain's prime minister during World War II, once said that "if Hitler invaded Hell, I would at least make a favorable reference to the Devil in the House of Commons."[7] Alliances in a multipolar system are expedient, not emotional attachments.

What if there are only two great powers? In a **bipolar** system, the two most powerful states can't align with other states because there are none, except small and inconsequen-

bandwagoning
the aligning of states with a greater power to share the spoils of dominance.

power balancing
a school of realism that sees hegemony as destabilizing and war as most likely when a dominant power emerges to threaten the equilibrium of power among other states.

hegemony
a situation in which one country is more powerful than all the others.

hegemon
the dominant power in the international system.

hegemonic stability
stability provided by a hegemon rather than through equilibrium or a balance of power.

power transition
a school of realism that sees hegemony as stabilizing and war as most likely when a rising power challenges a declining one and the balance of power approaches equilibrium.

polarity
the number of states holding significant power in the international system.

tial ones that can't contribute much to the balance of power. The great powers have to balance internally. That means they compete by mobilizing internal resources to establish a balance between them. The United States and the Soviet Union balanced power during the Cold War by domestic economic and technological competition. Of course, they formed alliances first to create bipolarity. The United States aligned with western Europe and Japan, the Soviet Union with eastern Europe and, until the 1960s, China. These alliances formed, according to some realist accounts, because the post–World War II system was initially **tripolar,** not bipolar. Europe and Japan, although destroyed in World War II, were the potential and decisive third power that could tip the postwar balance of power between the Soviet Union and the United States. Whichever superpower dominated them would have the advantage. Because of this competition for the third power, tripolarity is believed by some to be uniquely unstable.[8]

Polarity determines the propensity of different international systems for war. Here again, realist scholars don't agree on what distributions of power or numbers of powerful states—polarities—contribute to greater stability. Kenneth Waltz and John Mearsheimer argue that bipolar worlds are the most stable because two bigger powers, such as the United States and the Soviet Union, have only one another to worry about and will not make many mistakes.[9] But Dale Copeland, a professor at the University of Virginia, contends that multipolar systems are more stable because a declining power, which is the one most likely to initiate war, has more partners to ally with and is therefore more inclined to deter than fight the rising power.[10] So far, the statistical evidence from large-scale studies of war yields no definitive answer to this disagreement.[11]

War

No state seeks war, but the possibility of war is always inherent in the situation of anarchy. Diplomacy and other relationships may help clarify *intentions* but never enough to preclude the possibility of military conflict. Ultimately, states have to base their calculations on *capabilities* not intentions. That is why the realist perspective notes that even democracies, which presumably are most transparent and accessible to one another and best able to know one another's intentions, still cannot fully trust one another. From the realist perspective, the democratic EU is highly suspicious of American motivations in Iraq and the war on terror, and some European leaders call for a united Europe to become a counterweight or military counterbalance to the United States, despite the fact that Europe and the United States share the same democratic institutions and values.

There are many types of war that realists study: central wars involving all great powers, great power vs. great power wars, great power vs. minor power wars, and so on. The dynamics of power balancing and power transition often lead to two types of war: preemptive and preventive. **Preemptive war** is an attack against a country that is preparing to attack you. You see its armies gathering on your border, and you preempt the expected attack by attacking first. Israel initiated a preemptive war in 1967 when Egypt assembled forces in the Sinai Peninsula and Israel attacked before Egypt might have. **Preventive war** is an attack against a country that is not preparing to attack you but is growing in power and may attack you at some point in the future. War is considered to be inevitable. And, so, a declining power, in particular, may decide that war is preferable sooner rather than later because later it will have declined even further and be less powerful. It attacks at the point when its power peaks or has not yet declined very much.

---

multipolar

when three or more states are involved in a balance of power.

alliances

a formal defense arrangement wherein states align against a greater power to prevent dominance.

bipolar

when two states dominate a distribution of power.

tripolar

when three states dominate a distribution of power.

preemptive war

an attack against a country that is preparing to attack you.

preventive war

a war against a country that is not preparing to attack you but is growing in power and may attack you in the future.

It is often difficult to distinguish between preemptive and preventive wars. The U.S. invasion of Iraq in 2003 was labeled by many observers a preemptive war. If you believed the intelligence information that Saddam Hussein had WMDs and might use them or pass them on to terrorists at any time, the war was preemptive even though Iraq's mobilization was covert and not as clearly visible as massing armies on the border would have been. If you believed Saddam Hussein did not have WMDs but would surely get them in the future, the war was preventive because the United States decided to attack before Iraq actually had the weapons. If the United States had waited, it would have been relatively less powerful because Iraq, once it had the weapons, might use them to deter a U.S. attack by threatening to retaliate with such weapons.

One thing is certain. The balance of power does not prevent war. Over the past five centuries, there have been 119 major wars in Europe alone, where most of the great powers have been located. (A major war is defined as one in which at least one great power was involved.) Many of these wars were horrendously destructive. How do we defend a way of thinking about international relations that accepts such destructive wars? Well, remember that realist scholars are trying to see the world as it has been and remains. They don't favor or want to encourage war any more than anyone else. In fact, they study war to prevent it. Indeed, from the realist perspective, the quickest way to have war is to assume that it cannot occur. Anti-war advocates made such arguments both before and after World War I. Political leaders assumed war was unlikely before World War I, and they assumed it could be prevented without balancing power after World War I.

Until the world unites under a single system, wars cannot be excluded because of the condition of anarchy. Even if a single global system existed, civil wars might still occur. And because the system was now global, civil wars might be, in effect, great power wars and equally destructive. As we learn in Chapter 7, wars within states, or *intrastate* wars, are more common today than wars between states, or *interstate* wars. So far, intrastate wars have not ignited global interstate wars. But there is no guarantee they might not do so in the future, and intrastate wars have caused devastation and suffering on a scale comparable to interstate wars, although not as concentrated. Thus, the realist perspective advocates constant vigilance to power and power balancing as the only path to peace. As Morgenthau explains, the transformation of the world system into something else "can be achieved only through the workmanlike manipulation of the perennial forces that have shaped the past as they will the future." [12]

The Liberal Perspective

The liberal perspective is interested in the problem of cooperation, not because it is naïve and does not recognize the prevalence of violence and conflict. Rather, it is more impressed by the extent to which villages, towns, provinces, and communities over time have been able to overcome violence and conflict by centralizing and legitimating power in institutions, always at higher levels of aggregation. The state is just the most recent level at which groups of people have been able to overcome the balance of power and centralize authority. Why could this kind of consolidation not happen eventually at the international level?

The liberal perspective, therefore, focuses on the causes of cooperation and finds them in the way in which states interact with and relate to one another through repet-

The liberal perspective emphasizes diplomacy and getting together repeatedly to solve problems, such as nuclear proliferation by North Korea. Shown here are diplomats from six countries (left to right: Mitoji Yabunaka from Japan, James Kelly from the United States, Kim Yong II from North Korea, Wang Yi from China, Alexander Losiukov from Russia, and LeeSoo-Hyuck from South Korea) who gathered in Beijing, China, in August 2003 to discuss North Korea's nuclear weapons program.

itive processes and practices. It assumes that individuals and groups behave more on the basis of how other groups behave toward them than on the basis of how much relative power they possess or what their initial cultural or ideological beliefs are. Just as anarchy is a central concept in the realist perspective, *reciprocity,* or how states respond to one another, is a central concept in the liberal perspective.

States have a better chance to reciprocate if they interact more frequently. Thus, in contrast to the realist perspective, the liberal perspective pays more attention to interdependence than independence or self-help. *Interdependence* links groups and countries together through trade, transportation, tourism, and other types of exchanges and makes countries mutually or equally (hence, inter-) dependent on one another. As this happens, they get used to one another and develop habits of cooperation that facilitate the formation of international regimes and institutions.

International regimes coordinate the expectations and behavior of countries without necessarily incorporating them into a single institution, while *international institutions* facilitate specialization which enables certain groups or countries to take on specific bureaucratic roles (for example, the presidency of the European Union) and coordinate their activities through centralized and integrated organizations. Regimes and institutions lower transaction costs of international activities by handling large volumes of exchanges (for example, multilateral trade transactions) and increasing the amount of information available to actors. Greater information reduces secrecy, uncertainty, and the chances of miscommunications and misperceptions.

Once created, institutions tend to evolve through feedback and reinforcement, a process called *path dependence,* whereby cooperation to solve initial problems creates further problems that require expanded cooperation. One of the best examples of path dependence is the spillover in the European Union from intensifying interdependence in trade, which magnified the costs of multiple exchange rates, to a monetary union, which unified currencies.

Global institutions also enhance the *legitimacy* of international action. Because all countries representing multiple cultures participate, international institutions act with greater authority than regional or national institutions. Their decisions create *international law,* which provides common guidelines for all nations.

Finally, global institutions allow for the pursuit of *collective goods,* or goals that actors can only achieve together or not at all. Collective goods include *collective security* and *human security,* which provide protection from violence for all countries and human beings by centralizing institutions at the global level just as citizens have done at the national level; clean air and protection against global warming, which can be achieved for all peoples or for none; and greater wealth from trade and economic growth, which enables all peoples to gain, albeit perhaps not equally.

The liberal perspective emphasizes developments that accelerate interdependence. Hence, this perspective views favorably the historical processes of *technological change* and *modernization.* The agricultural, industrial, and information revolutions steadily expanded the scope and intensity of human contacts and created new opportunities for the formation of interdependent organizations at both the domestic and international levels. Markets spawned the proliferation of *nongovernmental organizations (NGOs)* or nonstate actors, such as the multinational corporation and International Red Cross; new technologies such as the telephone and telegraph prompted governments to establish *intergovernmental organizations (IGOs),* such as the International Telecommunications Union, to regulate ballooning telephony traffic. Compared to the realist perspective, the liberal perspective places more emphasis on NGOs or *global civil society* and on IGOs or *global governance* than it does on state sovereignty or national interests.

Let's look more closely at the key (italicized) concepts that provide the logic of the liberal perspective. (Again the concepts appear in bold where they are most succinctly defined.)

Reciprocity and Interdependence

reciprocity
states behaving toward one another based largely on mutual exchanges that entail interdependent benefits or disadvantages.

From the liberal perspective, reciprocity and interdependence among states matter more than independence and self-help. **Reciprocity** means that states behave toward one another based largely on mutual exchanges that entail interdependent benefits or disadvantages. The focus on reciprocal behavior places great emphasis on how countries communicate, negotiate, trade, and do business with one another. It also places great emphasis on compromise, swapping or logrolling objectives (for example, trading territory for peace in the Arab-Israeli dispute) or splitting the difference between objectives (drawing territorial borders halfway between what disputants claim).

interdependence
the mutual dependence of states and nonstate actors in the international system through conferences, trade, tourism, and the like.

Interdependence refers to the frequency and intensity with which states interact. How often states interact with and interdepend (that is, mutually depend) on one another increases the opportunities for reciprocity and, hence, cooperation. Cooperation is not automatic. It requires repetition and time to emerge. But, in the end, it is not a product of relative power or shared ideas; it's a product of the cumulative interrelationships through which power and ideas are exercised. How countries relate to one another changes the way they perceive one another and use their relative power. Interactions are doing the heavy lifting of changing ideas and power relationships.

One widely acclaimed study of international relations demonstrates the power of reciprocity and interdependence in changing how states behave. Professor Robert Axelrod did a massive computer study of different strategies for playing the prisoner's dilemma game if one allowed the game to be played over and over again.[13] By playing the game repeatedly, the study tested the impact of interactions on behavior over that of exogenous factors, such as the material power of participants or what their particular culture or ideology was. He found that of all the strategies tested, the one that produced the most cooperation over the long run was the simple strategy of "tit for tat," or one actor treating the other actor not on the basis of its power (aligning against the greater power) or its ideas (cooperating with like-minded countries) but on the basis of how the other actor treated it. Cooperative behavior, in short, was a function of reciprocity, which in turn was a function of repeated interactions or interdependence.

Technological Change and Modernization: Civil Society and Human Security

The imperative from the liberal perspective, then, is not to balance power but to increase interdependence. Two forces, in particular, make possible the widening of human relationships and institutions. The first is **technological change,** the application of science and engineering to increase wealth and alter human society; think of the consequences of the technological change in communications and transportation alone. The second force is **modernization,** the transformation of human society from self-contained autarchic centers of agrarian society to highly specialized and interdependent units of modern society that could not survive without the coordinated exchanges at the national and now international levels.

NONGOVERNMENTAL ORGANIZATIONS AND CIVIL SOCIETY. As the liberal perspective sees it, technological change and modernization bring more and more actors into the arena of international affairs. This pluralization of global politics broadens and deepens the context of international relations. **Nongovernmental organizations (NGOs)** are nonstate actors such as student, tourist, and professional associations that are not subject to direct government control. They include economic actors such as multinational corporations, international labor unions, private regulatory bodies, and global financial markets. They involve international humanitarian, foreign assistance, and environmental activities. In all these areas, nonstate actors expand the nongovernmental sector or **civil society** of international relations and engage in what are called **transnational relations,** namely relations outside the direct influence of national governments and international institutions set up by governments.

HUMAN SECURITY. According to the liberal perspective, the broadening and deepening of international relations through nonstate actors expand and change the concept of security. International relations are no longer just about the security of states; they are also about the security of people within states. **Human security** focuses on weak actors, not just the strongest or most capable ones emphasized by the realist perspective, and is concerned with violence caused by wars and oppression within states, not just among them: family violence, especially against women and children; genocide; diseases; pollution; natural disasters; and large displacements of populations. Since the end of the Cold War, liberal perspectives point out, human security issues have become more prevalent than great power or national security issues. Nonstate actors or NGOs play a bigger and more effective role in human security issues.

Thus, the liberal perspective pays more attention to nonstate actors than the realist perspective does. While the realist perspective anticipates conflict and focuses on actors such as states that have the greatest capabilities for conflict, the liberal perspec-

technological change
the application of science and engineering to increase wealth and alter human society.

modernization
the transformation of human society from self-contained autarchic centers of agrarian society to highly specialized and interdependent units of modern society.

nongovernmental organizations (NGOs)
nonstate actors such as student, tourist, and professional associations that are not subject to direct government control.

civil society
the nongovernmental sector.

transnational relations
relations among nongovernmental as opposed to governmental authorities.

human security
a focus on violence and security within states and at the village and local levels, particularly against women and minorities.

tive anticipates cooperation and focuses on nonstate actors that trade and pursue common goals that can potentially benefit everyone.

How the Liberal and Realist Perspectives View Change: Nuclear Weapons

Let's take a short digression and see how differently the liberal and realist perspectives evaluate one of the most important technological changes in international affairs, the advent of nuclear weapons.

As in the prisoner's dilemma, the liberal perspective sees technology altering payoffs and strengthening incentives for cooperation. Thus, it is more inclined to see nuclear weapons as making traditional balance of power politics obsolete. **Deterrence,** which uses the threat of force to deter aggression, replaces defense, which involves the actual use of force. The defending state threatens to retaliate against the attacker with enough force that the attacker is likely to lose more than it might gain. The potential attacker is thus deterred from attacking in the first place. All a state needs now to defend itself are a few nuclear weapons that can survive an initial attack and be launched against an attacker's civilian population and industry. With the destructive power of nuclear weapons, this strategy of **minimum deterrence** makes any war too costly, and states will be very reluctant to build up and use arms at any level of violence. Technology reduces the need for arms to a minimum, encourages **disarmament,** or the mutual reduction of arms, and thereby ameliorates the security dilemma. States can go on to cooperate and develop common institutions to promote the peaceful settlement of disputes. From a liberal perspective, therefore, nuclear weapons work toward arms control and the peaceful settlement of disputes just as collective security does.

The realist perspective, by contrast, sees technology reinforcing existing payoffs and serving the purpose of traditional institutions, such as the state. Thus, it sees nuclear weapons working in the opposite direction, not ameliorating the security dilemma but sublimating it to another, equally dangerous level of psychological warfare. Deterrence does not replace defense but requires "thinking the unthinkable" about how nuclear weapons might be used at every level of potential conflict. The effectiveness of deterrence depends on the credibility of threats. For nuclear threats to be credible, the realist perspective argues, states must possess a great number and variety of nuclear weapons, not just a minimal few. It is not enough to have only a few missiles to use against an adversary's civilian population. One may also need counterforce weapons designed to destroy the other country's nuclear weapons as well as its industry and population.

An example is given by the strategy of **extended deterrence,** which means extending deterrence to defend other countries, not just your own. The United States used this strategy to defend distant allies in Europe during the Cold War. If the Soviet Union threatened to attack Europe with intermediate-range nuclear missiles stationed in eastern Europe and capable of hitting western Europe but not the United States, how could the United States deter such a threat? The United States could threaten to retaliate against the Soviet Union with intercontinental missiles launched from the United States. But that would automatically involve the United States in a global war with the Soviet Union and might not be considered credible. The Soviet Union and even America's European allies might wonder if the United States would really risk New York to retaliate for an attack on Paris. To ensure credibility, Europe or NATO would

deterrence

preventing an attack by threatening retaliation against the potential attacker.

minimum deterrence

a strategy of deterrence that calls for a relatively few nuclear weapons that can survive an enemy strike and threaten unacceptable damage in retaliation on civilian and industrial centers.

disarmament

the process of mutual reduction of military arms by international agreements or convention.

extended deterrence

a strategy of deterrence in which a country agrees to strike back at missile attacks against its allies from its own territory.

have to have its own intermediate-range missiles stationed on western European territory. Now a threat from Soviet intermediate-range missiles could be counterbalanced by a threat from intermediate-range missiles in western Europe. An attack from the Soviet Union on Paris would be met by an attack from France on the Soviet Union. The conflict would not immediately escalate to the global level, and the threat from Europe would be considered more credible.

But would any of this make any difference if nuclear weapons were actually used? Could the Soviet Union and Europe exchange nuclear missiles without the United States also being attacked? Does it make sense even to think this way if the consequences of nuclear war are so unimaginable? The liberal perspective argues that technology transcends the old reasoning and makes possible a different kind of cooperative politics that replaces the traditional balance of power.

International Institutions, Law, and Path Dependence

The liberal perspective emphasizes the role of international institutions. **International institutions** are **intergovernmental organizations (IGOs),** both global and regional, that are set up by national governments (hence, intergovernmental) in part to retain or assert control over transnational activities and other interdependencies spawned by the forces of change. Governments charge these institutions to serve their common interests, defined as areas where their national interests overlap. But once these institutions exist, they take on a life of their own and constitute a system of **global governance,** or network of intergovernmental organizations that make up a kind of primitive world system. In some cases, these institutions make decisions and undertake activities that compromise national interests or supersede them by defining and implementing broader global interests. To the extent that they are not completely under the control of national governments, they become quasi-independent actors in the international system.

Institutions form by an iterative process; relationships cluster in regularized patterns of interactions. Trade relationships, for example, crystallize into markets or cartels. Diplomatic relationships cluster into international conferences and treaties. These regularized patterns of interactions become regimes and institutions that implement certain rules and channel behavior along certain paths.

Institutions may not always coincide with physical organizations. For example, global financial relationships are regularized but not incorporated in any overarching organization. The International Monetary Fund (IMF) affects only a small part of global finance; yet global finance depends on common rules. The annual economic summits among the major industrialized countries and the Bank of International Settlements, an international organization that brings together the heads of national central banks, also play key roles. A network of institutions come together to form an **international regime** that coordinates expectations and rules in a particular issue area, such as finance. The UN, for example, might be considered an international institution for the purpose of dispatching peacekeeping forces to manage ethnic conflicts, but the International Atomic Energy Agency, a UN body, might be part of an international regime to stop the spread of nuclear weapons, along with U.S.-Russian bilateral agreements and the Proliferation Security Initiative, an independent multinational effort to interdict nuclear materials and equipment on the high seas.

international institutions
formal international organizations and informal regimes that establish common rules to regularize contacts and communications.

intergovernmental organizations (IGOs)
formal international organizations established by governments.

global governance
the various international institutions and great powers groups that help govern the global economy.

international regimes
a network of international institutions.

international law

the customary rules and codified treaties under which international organizations operate; it covers political, economic, and social rights.

human rights

the most basic protections against human physical abuse and suffering.

path dependence

a process emphasized by liberal perspectives that results in outcomes from a long sequential historical chain of cause and effect; for example, the kind of institutions a state develops depends on earlier developments because, once a country starts on a certain path, it accumulates advantages or disadvantages along that path.

INTERNATIONAL LAW. International regimes and institutions create international law. **International law** constitutes the customary rules and codified treaties under which international organizations operate. International law covers political, economic, and social rights. **Human rights** provide the most basic protections against physical abuse and suffering. International law and human rights are more disputed than national law. Democratic countries emphasize how the law is made by free institutions and champion political and human rights. Nondemocratic countries emphasize how the law is enforced and, in the case of socialist countries, champion economic and social rights. But the liberal perspective argues that the more treaties and international law there are the better because states are acquiring the habit of obeying central norms and guidelines and will eventually move toward greater consensus on the making and enforcement of law.

PATH DEPENDENCE. In many situations, according to the liberal perspective, international organizations, both nongovernmental and intergovernmental, and international law become the most important facts determining outcomes. They are the independent variables that cause other events, the dependent variables, to occur. International institutions may gradually become more important than states. They evolve through feedback and path dependence. **Path dependence** means that later outcomes depend on previous outcomes and that institutions grow by learning and reinforcement. In the liberal perspective, learning means choosing policies based on more scientific experimentation and information. International institutions provide the relatively impartial platform, at least compared to individual states, from which policy proposals can be developed, tested, and improved.[14] An early example is provided by the role of the European Commission in the European Communities and now in the European Union. When European integration was launched, the founders insisted on creating one organization that would focus not on national but on community-wide interests; that was the European Commission. As we learn in Chapter 16, it is the only institution in the EU that has the right to initiate legislation independently. The idea was that individual states would be forced to react to community needs and, in the process, would get used to taking into account community as well as national needs. In time, they might begin to think differently about their own needs and identify more with the European Union.

International institutions alter the relationships through which people interact and pursue common interests. Through repeated interactions, participants acquire different habits and change their perceptions through better information and greater trust. Over the longer run, they may even change their material interests and identities. Notice how, in the example of the European Commission, process influences thinking and eventually loyalty. Habitual and routine contacts do the heavy lifting in the liberal perspective and cause material power and self-images to adapt. The liberal perspective does not ignore power or identity; it just concludes that these variables are shaped more by institutions than institutions are shaped by them. That's how the liberal perspective differs from the realist and identity perspectives.

Collective Goods: Collective Security, Trade, and Environment

Common institutions facilitate the provision of collective goods. As in the prisoner's dilemma story, if countries focus on common rather than conflicting goals (the prisoners frustrating the warden rather than going free), they can achieve non-zero sum outcomes in which all gain. One country does not have to win and the other lose. The overall pie grows, and everyone's slice grows in absolute terms.

Collective goods have two properties. They are indivisible—they exist for everyone or for no one—and they cannot be appropriated—they do not diminish as one party consumes them. The classic example of a collective good is clean air. It either exists for everyone or for no one. And breathing by one person does not diminish the air available for another person. Global warming is another example. If it is to be prevented, it will be prevented for all countries or for none. And if the benefits of preventing global warming are enjoyed by one country, that does not subtract from the benefits available to other countries.

The liberal perspective sees peace and security as collective goods, especially in today's nuclear and globalized world. If they exist for one member of a society, they exist for all members because using nuclear weapons would destroy peace for everyone; and the benefits to one member do not diminish the amounts of peace and security available to other members. **Collective security** does just what it says—it collects military power in a single global institution, such as the United Nations, that provides peace and security for all countries, just as national governments do for all citizens at the domestic level. This global institution sets up rules that states must follow to resolve disagreements and then creates a **preponderance of power,** a pooling of the military power of all nations, not a balance of power among separate nations, to punish aggressors who violate the rules. Collective security thus serves as an alternative way to organize military power compared to the balance of power.

Because the global institution monopolizes military power, it can reduce military weaponry to a minimum. Arms control and disarmament play a big role in the liberal perspective, just as the opposite dynamics of mutual armaments and competitive arms races play a key role in the realist perspective. Thus, liberal perspectives emphasize the possibility of converting security from a national or competitive process to a collective or public good.

Absolute vs. Relative Gains

Another collective good is wealth. It is not quite as pure a collective good as clean air because it may be appropriated and consumption by one party may reduce, at least relatively, the amounts available to other parties. Wealth, unlike air, does not exist in infinite supply. But the liberal concept of comparative advantage and trade, which we examine in detail in Chapter 10, makes it possible to increase wealth overall and therefore, at least theoretically, increase it for each individual or country, although some individuals and countries may gain more than others. Trade is a classic non-zero sum relationship in which two parties can produce more goods from the same resources if they specialize and exchange products than if they produce them separately. The liberal perspective emphasizes such non-zero sum relationships because they shift the focus away from conflicting goals and demonstrate that, even under conditions of anarchy, cooperation is not only possible but profitable.

The realist perspective, of course, is not convinced. It focuses more on relative gains or zero-sum outcomes and wonders, even if the overall pie grows, whether the relative size of one slice might not go down. For example, one country may get 10 percent of a 15-unit pie before cooperation (or 1.5 units) but only 5 percent of a 40-unit pie after

collective goods
goals, such as clean air, which are indivisible, meaning they exist for everyone or not for any one particular person or group, and which cannot be appropriated, meaning that they do not diminish as one party consumes them.

collective security
the establishment of common institutions and rules among states to settle disputes peacefully and to enforce agreements by a preponderance, not a balance, of power.

preponderance of power
an aggregation of the power of all states (rather than a balance of power) to deter or punish aggressors in a collective security arrangement.

cooperation (or 2.0 units). Even though the *absolute size* of the slice has gone up (from 1.5 to 2.0 units), the *relative size* has gone down (from 10 to 5 percent). Before cooperation, the first country had 1.5 units and the second country 13.5 units. The difference was 12 units. After cooperation, the first country has 2 units and the second country 38 units. The difference is now 36 units or three times the difference before cooperation. The second country has increased its relative power and capability to do the first country harm. Hence, the realist perspective favors trade only with allies that, at least as long as they are allies, are not likely to use their relative gains from trade to harm one another.

The liberal perspective emphasizes **mutual** or **absolute gains,** the increase each side gains over what it had before; the realist perspective emphasizes **relative gains,** the increase one side gains over the other. Thus, scholars emphasizing the liberal perspective are more inclined than those emphasizing the realist perspective to argue that no one won the Cold War or that all countries won the Cold War.[15] And from their perspective they are right. Everyone gained from the end of nuclear terror. Scholars using a realist perspective, who see goals being in conflict with one another, are more likely to say the United States won and the Soviet Union lost. And from their perspective, they too are right. The Soviet Union does not exist anymore. The same facts are evaluated differently from different perspectives.

Diplomacy, Compromise, and Legitimacy

Diplomacy is the business of communications, negotiations, and compromise and thus weighs big in the liberal perspective. From this perspective, talking is always better than not talking, especially with adversaries. Whatever the differences among countries, whatever their relative power or beliefs, they can profit from discussions. Discussions clarify and narrow differences by encouraging bargaining, which produces trade-offs and compromises. **Compromise** swaps the achievement of an interest in one issue area for the achievement of another interest in a second issue area. An example might be the Cold War linkage or trade-off between arms control and human rights in the 1970s. To achieve its interest in reducing arms stockpiles, the United States backed off its interest in promoting human rights in the Soviet Union. Realists, of course, who emphasize interests rather than institutions or ideas, worry that the process of compromise may sacrifice vital interests. They do not spurn diplomacy, but advocate it only from a position of military strength and often with the objective of achieving rather than compromising a country's objectives.

From the liberal perspective, the objective of diplomacy is to include all actors, often nonstate participants as well, and to encourage compromise regardless of the ideologies or beliefs participants hold. All countries and points of view are respected. Tolerance and coexistence are the most important virtues. As Michael Steiner, a UN representative in Kosovo, notes, "the United Nations wields unique moral authority *because* its members represent a wide spectrum of values and political systems. Most of the world trusts the United Nations more than it trusts any single member or alliance, . . . not because of the inherent virtue of any individual member but because the United Nations's temporizing influence imposes a healthy discipline on its members."[16] Notice how **legitimacy,** or the right to use power in international affairs, derives from participation by actors of widely differing values and political systems, not from any specific actor's values such as democracy. There is an implicit faith that participants will learn from one another and that, whatever results emerge, all partic-

mutual or **absolute gains**
the increase each side gains over what it had before.

relative gains
the increase one side gains over the other.

diplomacy
discussions and negotiations among states as emphasized by the liberal perspective.

compromise
swapping the achievement of an interest in one issue area for the achievement of another interest in a second issue area.

legitimacy
the right to use power in international affairs.

ipants will be better off. Diplomacy ultimately produces the same outcome as trade, in that everyone gains.

Thus, as a contemporary example, analysts looking at the world from a liberal perspective are more inclined than those using a realist perspective to favor negotiations with North Korea to stop its nuclear weapons programs. Nothing can be achieved without such negotiations to reduce distrust, according to the liberal perspective, whereas little is likely to be achieved by negotiations because of distrust, according to the realist perspective. The liberal perspective sees negotiations as helping or at least not harming relations. The realist perspective sees them as potentially lowering one's guard and creating even bigger problems down the road should North Korea use talks to buy time and develop nuclear weapons. The differences are matters of perspective and judgment, not ignorance or evil intentions, as the media or partisan debate sometimes suggests.

Separating Democracy from the Liberal Perspective

The liberal perspective focuses more on the process of diplomacy or dialogue, while the identity perspective (which we examine next) focuses more on the ideas, values, and substance of diplomacy. In many books, however, the liberal perspective is identified with the value or political ideology of democracy. From this liberal point of view, the net effect of interdependence and diplomacy is to nurture tolerance, pluralism, and, ultimately, democracy. One scholar, for example, identifies four strands of what he calls liberalism. Three of these strands—economic, ecological, and institutional—involve relationships and interactions characteristic of the liberal perspective as defined in this book. A fourth, however, involves democratic values that may be shared by nations but are not, strictly speaking, a set of interactive interrelationships among nations like trade or institutional links.[17] Classical liberalism, an early version of the liberal perspective, does include individual freedom and democracy. But classical realism, an early version of the realist perspective, does as well. Neoliberalism, a later version of the liberal perspective, puts more emphasis on interactions and institutions than on democracy, just as neorealism, a later version of the realist perspective, puts more emphasis on the distribution of power than on democracy.

A focus on democracy is not unique to liberalism or realism. To identify the liberal perspective with democracy, therefore, seems to prejudice our study of perspectives. It muddles relational and ideational aspects of reality and biases the treatment of perspectives toward the liberal perspective. Who wants to be a realist if only the liberal perspective cares about democracy? In fact, the realist perspective too cares about democracy. It developed during and after World War II precisely to urge liberal democratic countries to pay more attention to power so they could defend themselves more effectively against fascist and communist enemies of freedom.

Including democracy as part of the liberal perspective also biases the treatment of values other than democracy by putting them in a separate category called radical or revolutionary perspectives. Indeed, that is how many books treat ideas such as Marxism, socialism, feminism, and constructivism. They label these approaches alternative or radical perspectives, even though we might just as easily consider democracy an alternative or radical idea, as many analysts do when they point out, for example, how democracy opens up opportunities for nondemocratic forces, such as Hamas in the West Bank and Gaza or the Mahdi Shiite militia in Iraq. Yet so-called radical theories are no different analytically than theories of liberalism or realism. All involve ideas, relationships, and power, and all differ primarily in terms of the relative emphasis they place on these variables.

Marxism, for example, places emphasis on the dialectical interaction between capitalist (manager) and proletariat (worker) social classes. In that sense, it seems to adopt a liberal perspective. But it sees this interaction originating in material forces of capitalist production. So, at root it may be a realist perspective. Finally, it sees these forces of production driving the dialectic not toward equilibrium, as realist perspectives expect, or to democracy, as classical liberal perspectives expect, but to the eventual triumph of the proletariat over the capitalists and, thus, of communism over democracy. In this book, we treat Marxism as a critical theory perspective because it emphasizes social change deeply embedded in historical processes from which it is difficult to isolate the primary role of material, institutional, and ideological factors.

Even though most of us might consider communist and other nondemocratic outcomes as radical, we should not bias our labels in this way. For analytical purposes, we should recognize that other ideas or conceptions of how relationships and institutions work might not lead to democracy. As Robert Keohane, a neoliberal scholar, suggests, we should separate our preferences for specific ideas from our analytical perspective:

> [L]iberalism associates itself with a belief in the value of individual freedom. Although I subscribe to such a belief, this commitment of mine is not particularly relevant to my analysis of international relations. One could believe in the value of individual liberty and remain either a realist or neorealist in one's analysis of world politics.[18]

There are advantages, therefore, in separating the role of ideas and the role of relationships. Relationships or interactions can be driven by many different ideas or ideologies—liberalism, fascism, socialism, Marxism, and the like. The identity perspective, as defined in this book, draws attention to the causal or constitutive role of ideas, including but not limited to democracy, and sees ideas driving relationships more than interactions driving ideas, as in the liberal perspective. From the identity perspective, it is not just the process of communications that matters (which the liberal perspective also emphasizes); it is the content of what is being communicated—the definitions of words, concepts, and the meaning of language itself—that matters much more.

The Identity Perspective

The identity perspective is more interested in the ideas that guide cooperation and the use of power than in cooperation or the pursuit of power per se. *Ideas* define the *values, norms,* and *beliefs* that governments and international institutions hold and for which they pursue and apply power. Taken together, these ideas define or construct the *identity* of actors, and these identities in turn interpret or give meaning to the material capabilities and institutional behavior of actors. Interests now are not defined just by anarchy or geopolitical circumstances, as the realist perspective highlights, or by institutional relationships and rules, as the liberal perspective argues. They are also defined by independent and collective identities.

How are identities constructed? Just as anarchy is a key concept in the realist perspective and reciprocity is a key concept in the liberal perspective, construction is a key concept in identity perspectives. *Construction of identities* means that identities are not given or exogenous (as in realist or liberal perspectives) but are themselves aspects of reality that have to be accounted for. Realist and liberal perspectives spend little time worrying about how the identity of states come about or whether states develop friendly or adversarial self-images of one another. Whatever the identities are, actors behave mostly in response to fixed conditions of anarchy and institutions. Identity perspectives, by contrast, focus on how identities develop and how they change.

For some identity perspectives, identities are collective or shared, not autonomous, and can be constructed only through repetitive social interactions. Known as *social constructivism,* this school sees identities emerging from communicative action, social discourse, and the shared knowledge that participants develop. Actors engage in speech acts, essentially substantive communications about truth claims, to influence, persuade, and learn from one another. In this process, they shape *shared identities* that define them and their counterparts. Thus, social constructivists argue that anarchy in international affairs is not fixed. Rather anarchy is what states make of it, meaning state behavior is not defined by the position states hold in the distribution of power or by the role

The identity perspective emphasizes shared ideas and truthful opinions, such as those exchanged between Ronald Reagan and Mikhail Gorbachev while they were in office in the 1980s. They are shown here later, in 1992, upon the arrival of Gorbachev and his wife, Raisa, for a two-week tour of the United States.

they play in international institutions but, instead, by the shared or external identities they construct. And these identities may be adversarial and distrustful, or they may be friendly and cooperative. In contrast to realist perspectives, states shape anarchy; they don't just respond to it. And, in contrast to the liberal perspective, states focus on the content, not just the process, of communications. Words and identities matter and are not to be traded off just for the sake of compromise.

Other constructivist perspectives place emphasis on autonomous as well as social identities. Autonomous or *internal identities* derive from the capabilities of individual human beings or agents to think creatively and shape or critique the social discourse in which they are involved. Or, in the case of countries, autonomous identities involve the internal political, cultural, or economic ideas that organize the domestic life and history of specific countries and influence their behavior in external relationships. These internal identities are distinct from the shared or *external identities* emphasized by social constructivists. This more agent-oriented (involving autonomous agents, not just shared structures) school of constructivism has no single label. Its advocates talk about *relative identities* as well as shared or collectivist identities. Thus, individuals or countries may have similar or dissimilar as well as shared identities. The *distribution of identities,* not the distribution of power or institutional roles, then determines whether countries behave as friends, rivals, or enemies toward one another. Seen from the identity perspective, relative and shared identities create an international culture that shapes behavior, more than the balance of power and international institutions. Different cultures create different types of balances of power.

Identity perspectives may include other approaches that emphasize ideas but are less concerned with the construction of identities. Later in the chapter, we consider studies that focus on *soft power, belief systems,* and *psychological* aspects of international relations. Thus, identity perspectives come in multiple variations just like realist and liberal perspectives.

Still other approaches might be considered identity perspectives because some of them are constructivist. But they pose a broader critique of contemporary international affairs and question whether we can understand international relations from the standpoint of single or multiple perspectives that operate as ideal types, abstracting situations from their historical structures. We call them *critical theories*. *Feminism* draws on both social and physical (biological) sources of identity and critiques contemporary international studies as thoroughly male-centered and -dominated. *Marxism* emphasizes material forces of production but also social classes and identities to highlight deep and persisting divisions in world politics between rich and poor countries. *Postmodernist* and *deconstructivist* studies deny that there is any abstract or objective pivot from which we can study international relations and look to expose hidden meanings, discrimination, and oppressive power in every situation in international life.

Once again, we explore the italicized concepts in the subsections that follow. (The terms are boldface where they are most clearly defined.)

Ideas and the Construction of Identities

values
ideas that express deep moral convictions.

norms
ideas that govern the procedural or substantive terms of state behavior, such as reciprocity or human rights.

beliefs
ideas about how the world works as emphasized by identity perspectives.

constructivism
a perspective that emphasizes ideas, such as word content and social discourse, over institutions or power.

construction of identities
a process of discourse by which actors define who they are and how they behave toward one another.

Ideas come in many forms. **Values** reflect deep moral convictions, such as freedom. **Norms** guide how groups and states interact and what they jointly prefer; there are procedural or regulatory norms such as sovereignty and substantive norms such as human rights. And **beliefs** constitute comprehensive views about how the world works, such as communist or capitalist ideologies. Ideas, norms, values, and beliefs are not physical entities, as capabilities and some institutions are, but they are no less real. We cannot touch sovereignty the way we can a tank or building. But sovereignty still exists and exerts a powerful influence on international behavior and outcomes. Other ideas do so as well. Democracy, capitalism, fascism, and human rights—all play powerful roles in shaping history and international affairs.

Idealists—those who emphasize ideas over material realities—have always argued that ideas matter. When I was a student of international affairs in the 1960s, idealism and realism were the two main schools of thought. Idealism posited the notion that reasoning or ideas preceded and could be made to shape specific realities. After the horrendous destruction of World War I, "the passionate desire to prevent war" contributed to the idea that a League of Nations, as President Woodrow Wilson said, "must be made to work."[19] For Wilson, the idea would be the cause of the formation of an institution that would then change the way states used power. The disastrous results of World War II discredited idealism and installed realism as the preeminent theory of international relations. Realism argued that reality must be accepted as it is, namely anarchy and power politics, not as we might wish it to be, or ideas and utopian institutions. By the early 1970s, however, some scholars "became increasingly concerned that the postwar aversion to idealism . . . had gone too far [and] . . . was responsible for the discipline's poor grasp of the role of ideational factors of all kinds in international life—be they collective identities, norms, aspirations, ideologies, or ideas about cause-effect relations."[20]

Two decades later, **constructivism** emerged as an approach to international relations that revived the primary causal or constitutive role of ideas. It argues that actors behave on the basis of how they construct their identities. The **construction of identities** involves a process of discourse by which actors define who they are and how they behave toward one another. This approach to understanding international behavior follows in the idealist tradition because it is ideational, seeing ideas as more influential causes than institutions or power. But it also emphasizes cumulative practices such as repetitive communications. These practices are not institutions that influence material interests, as the liberal perspective emphasizes. Rather, they are verbal practices or substantive narratives that cumulate to substantiate and construct identities, which then influence interests and institutions. Such verbal practices constitute who the actors actually are, which in turn defines what their interests are and how those interests might be played out through institutional processes.

Some political scientists do not consider constructivism to be a perspective on the same level as the realist or liberal perspectives. They see it as a method, not a perspective. As we discuss in the Introduction, the realist and liberal perspectives rely primarily on causal reasoning: X causes Y. Many constructivist approaches rely on constitutive reasoning; X and Y constitute or mutually cause one another rather than one factor causing the other sequentially. In constitutive reasoning, causes emerge from cumulative practices and narratives, not from independent and sequential events.

But other constructivists consider their approach to be more than a method. They seek to explain and interpret events. They don't try to predict specific outcomes by a logic of consequences: Y is a consequence of X. They seek, instead, to elucidate structures of discourse that make certain events possible by a logic of appropriateness. An event occurs because it fits a particular narrative, not because it is caused by a specific preceding event. Today, for example, it is considered increasingly appropriate that when countries intervene to protect human rights, they do so multilaterally. No specific event caused this fact, but one hundred years ago unilateral intervention was much more common. Similarly, constructivists do not try to predict the future in terms of one event causing another. Instead, they project future scenarios that make certain outcomes possible and plausible.

In this book, we treat constructivism as a perspective equivalent to the realist and liberal perspectives. Constructivism comes in different varieties, as we explore next: social constructivism and a more individualistic or agent-oriented constructivism. And we include constructivism under the still broader identity perspective because it is only one of several approaches, along with studies of ideology and psychology, that give priority to what people and countries believe and, hence, the ideas by which they act or define themselves.

Social Constructivism

One type of identity perspective, called **social constructivism,** stresses social or collective identity formation. According to Professor Alexander Wendt, whom many consider the father of social constructivism in international affairs, "structures of human association are determined primarily by shared ideas rather than material forces," and these ideas are social, that is, not reducible to individuals.[21] Thus, as we note in the Introduction, the master and slave are defined by their relationship; one cannot be recognized without the other. Similarly, according to social constructivism, states recognize one another only by association with one another. A state does not exist separately in an objective condition of anarchy, as realist perspectives argue, but defines its condition by subjective or intersubjective dialogue with other states. This dialogue between states creates structural social categories, such as friends or enemies, that can-

social constructivism
an identity perspective in which states and other actors acquire their identities from collective discourses in which they know who they are only by reference to others.

not be reduced to the existence of two or more separate states. States, in short, construct anarchy.

A second type of constructivism is less social or structural and more individualistic or agent-oriented. **Agent-oriented constructivism** allows for greater influence on the part of independent actors. As Professor Thomas Risse tells us, actors "are not simply puppets of social structure" but "can actively challenge the validity claims inherent in any communicative action."[22] That means they can come up with new ideas and change prevailing social structures. Outcomes are explained by a logic of argumentation, not a logic of appropriateness, as social constructivists argue, or a logic of consequences, as realist and liberal perspectives argue. As we discuss later, some constructivist accounts see this happening at the end of the Cold War when Gorbachev changed his mind about German membership in NATO in the middle of a meeting, after being persuaded by the arguments of other participants. In both types of constructivism, ideas play the dominant role. In fact, ideas create the material and institutional worlds because without ideas those worlds would have no meaning. The difference lies in level of analysis. Social constructivism operates at a high level of the system's structure, what Wendt called "structural idealism." More agent-oriented constructivism operates also at the domestic and individual levels of analysis, where an individual or group can come up with ideas based on internal reflection and imagination and change the external social discourse.

Anarchy Is What States Make of It

Identity perspectives focus on social discourse and communicative action, meaning not just the physical interaction between actors in institutions or regimes but the speech acts that establish the content, veracity, trustworthiness, and, indeed, identity of the actors. Actors use ideas to construct relationships and material reality. So ideas precede negotiations and interpret history to make relationships either conflictual or cooperative. For example, the Cold War ended, according to constructivists, when "new thinking" emerged in the Soviet Union and Mikhail Gorbachev, the Soviet leader, changed his mind about western countries being enemies and accepted the reunification of Germany within NATO rather than as a neutral country. Negotiations between the Soviet Union and western countries were not just instrumental in the sense that they facilitated a compromise of interests. Splitting the difference would have probably meant reunifying Germany, the western preference, but keeping it neutral, the Soviet preference. Instead, Germany was reunited and stayed in NATO. A logic of argumentation and persuasion prevailed over a negotiating logic emphasized by liberal perspectives. Gorbachev changed his mind on the spot and accepted a united Germany in NATO because he no longer saw NATO as an enemy and believed that Germany had the right of self-determination to make alliance decisions for itself.[23]

Social constructivists emphasize the shared or social elements of communications and identity. For some, such as Professor Wendt, almost all identity is collective or shared, not autonomous or individual. Indeed individualism itself, they argue, is a social construct. States, like individuals, have to be recognized socially before they can act independently. After all, sovereignty was the social construct that originally gave states their independence. Thus, states and other actors constitute one another. Yet it is not the relationships that are most important, as the liberal perspective emphasizes, but, rather, the images such as sovereignty that are embedded in social discourse and history. These are the crucial building blocks of our identity and behavior. If we learn

agent-oriented constructivism

an identity perspective that allows for greater influence on the part of independent actors in shaping identities.

to see one another as friends, we act one way; if we see one anther as enemies, we act another way. Hence, in challenging the realist and liberal perspectives, social constructivists argue, "anarchy is what states make of it."[24] International relations can be either competitive and full of conflict, as the realist perspective contends, or cooperative and institutionalized, as the liberal perspective argues. It depends, says the social constructivist, on how we imagine or construct these relations. In short, it depends on shared and collective identities.

Relative Identities

Other constructivists, namely the more agent-oriented ones, emphasize the separate or individualistic, not just social, aspects of identity. They insist that "actors' domestic identities are crucial for their perceptions of one another in the international arena."[25] They see domestic or internal identities influencing how countries perceive international threats. The internal ideas or identities of states differ, and the ideological distance between them creates threat, either because one state fears that the other's ideology may spread or because their ideologies impose impediments to communicating with one another.[26] Thus after World War II, France and Britain did not see the United States as threatening because they shared a democratic ideology with it, even though the United States was very powerful and American troops were stationed on their soil. On the other hand, they did see the Soviet Union as threatening because its domestic identity was different, even though Soviet forces were not physically located on their territory. Actors therefore have both an internal and external identity, one shaped by discourses at home and another by discourses in the international arena.

Knowing who we are, therefore, may always require being different from others, according to more individualistic constructivism. A "we" group requires a "they" group, and psychological studies suggest that people discriminate between the group they identify with and other groups.[27] That means that identities are not only social and collective but also competitive and separate. To be constructed at all, more individualistic constructivists argue, identities have to have some independent component.[28] Individuals can think critically and come up with new ideas that society has never known before. That's how the slave stops being a slave; the slave, the master, or someone else in society has to come up with an alternative idea about the relationship. Even if the alternative ideas are ultimately also social, they have to originate somewhere. For example, Gorbachev allegedly got his idea that NATO was no longer an enemy from peace research institutes in western Europe.[29] Social constructivists would say such ideas originate in repetitive social practices; more individualistic constructivists insist on tracing them back to agents, norm entrepreneurs or self-reflective individuals, and their capacity for critical thinking and independence.

Distribution of Identities

Thus, as Professor Peter Katzenstein tells us, "the identities of states emerge from their interactions with different social environments, both domestic and international."[30] The **distribution of identities** includes both a domestic, or internal, and an international, or external, dimension. The domestic dimension of identity, or **internal identity,** derives from individual self-reflection and national memory. This dimension animates the domestic life of separate societies. Over the years, individuals have identified with different clans, tribes, ethnic groups, religions, cultures, political systems, and ide-

distribution of identities
the relative relationship of identities among actors in the international system in terms of their similarities and differences.

internal identity
the domestic dimension of identity of a country; it derives from individual self-reflection and national memory.

ological beliefs, reflecting how these groups imagine themselves internally. As we will see, the way these factors are prioritized at different times becomes critical in history and politics. In seventeenth-century Europe, religion was a crucial element of the internal identity of states. By the twentieth century, political or ideological ideas such as fascism and liberalism had become more important, at least in the industrialized world. Today, religious identities may be reasserting themselves again.

The international dimension of identity, or **external identity,** concerns associations with other individuals or countries that shape the social role and conscience of international actors. This external dimension is a function of historical experiences, trade relationships, and membership in alliances and other international organizations. For many years, France and Germany shared a history of enmity and war. Over the past sixty years, however, they developed another history of friendship and peaceful integration. Perhaps crucial to their being able to do so was the convergence of the internal or domestic dimensions of their identities, in which common democratic features came to weigh more importantly in domestic life than past cultural differences. But equally important may have been the convergence of their external associations with one another and the United States as they aligned to confront the Soviet Union.

External and internal dimensions of identities distribute themselves across the international system to establish relative and shared identities among actors. At one level, **relative identities** position actors' self-images with respect to one another as similar or dissimilar, just as relative power positions actors' capabilities with respect to one another as bigger or smaller. We can speak of relative identities in the identity perspective just as we speak of relative capabilities in the realist perspective. But at a higher level, identities overlap and fuse to constitute **shared identities,** or norms and images that cannot be traced back to specific identities or their interrelationships. This is the level at which, according to social constructivists, a common international culture emerges and gives meaning to the physical world of institutions and power; states, in effect, create various versions of anarchy, some more cooperative than others.

Table 1-7 illustrates how we might map the convergence or divergence of relative and shared national identities. In this example, the internal dimension of identity is measured in terms of domestic political ideologies, whether countries are democratic or not. In other examples, it might be measured in terms of similarities and differences among domestic cultures or religions. The external dimension of identity is measured in terms of how cooperative or conflictual historical relations have been among the countries. Again, in other cases, it might be measured in terms of trade or common membership in international organizations. Identity is multifaceted, so measuring it, at least in rationalist studies, presents difficulties. Now, in Table 1-7, countries such as the United States, France, the United Kingdom, and Canada that have strong democracies and historically close relations cluster in the upper left-hand box. In this box, identities converge so strongly they take on a collective character and common culture that we call the democratic peace. As we discuss in the next section, strong democracies seem to escape anarchy altogether and do not go to war with one another. In the lower left-hand and upper right-hand boxes, countries converge on one dimension of identity but diverge on the other. For example, in the lower left-hand box, Germany and Japan are now strong democracies like the United States, but they have been enemies of the United States more recently than the United Kingdom, France, or Canada. Their relationships with the United States are strong but perhaps not as intimate as those of countries in the upper left-hand box. Similarly, in the upper right-hand box, China during the Cold War was not a democracy like the United States, but China did

---

external identity

the international dimension of identity of a country; it is determined by its historical and external relationships with other states.

relative identities

identities that position actors' self-images with respect to one another as similar or dissimilar.

shared identities

identities that overlap and fuse based on norms and images that cannot be traced back to specific identities or their interrelationships.

have friendly historical ties with the United States before it became communist, and after it became communist it worked closely with the United States against the Soviet Union in the later stages of the Cold War. In the lower right-hand box, countries diverge on both dimensions of identity, and the common culture is weakest. This box constitutes the situation of anarchy, such as that characterizing U.S.-Soviet relations during the Cold War and, as some might argue, U.S.-Chinese relations today.

Identities thus change and converge and diverge. This is the dynamics that drives international affairs from an identity perspective. Countries that identify with one another get along with one another and may eventually merge, as seems to be happening among the countries of the European Union. Countries that no longer identify with one another go separate ways and compete to preserve their independence. That was the case with the countries of the former Soviet bloc (Poland, Hungary, Czech Republic, Slovakia, and so on) and also with the republics of the former Soviet Union (Lithuania, Estonia, Turkmenistan, Georgia, and so on). This dynamics explains where states and international actors come from, which realist perspectives often take as given. And it explains where institutions may arise and why they may arise and work in certain situations and not in others, which liberal perspectives often take as given. Democracies, for example, may be better able to establish binding international institutions than societies with other identities.

Democratic Peace

A powerful example of how identities influence international relations is provided by the democratic peace. Studies show that, as countries become stronger and stronger democracies, they appear to escape the security dilemma. They do not go to war with one another or engage in militarized threats. If this behavior is a result of converging or shared democratic identities, it suggests the importance of looking at identities as well as power and institutions. It may be that other shared identities—for example, between Muslim states or fascist states—also produce different behavior than would be predicted from liberal or realist perspectives. As Professor Michael Barnett observes, "a community of Saddam Husseins is unlikely to father a secure environment, while a community of Mohatma Gandhis will encourage all to leave their homes unlocked."[31]

We refer to the democratic peace several times in the following chapters. It was a key factor that played into "the end of history" debate and President Bill Clinton's policies of democratic enlargement as the Cold War ended, and it showed up again in

Table 1-7

Relative and Shared National Identities			
	Internal dimension of identity (measured in terms of political ideologies)		
		Democracy	*Nondemocracy*
External dimension of identity (measured in terms of historical memories)	*Cooperative*	Strongest convergence: U.S.–UK U.S.–Canada U.S.–France	Weak convergence: U.S.–China (Cold War) U.S.–Russia (today?)
	Conflictual	Strong convergence: U.S.–Germany U.S.–Japan	Weakest convergence: U.S.–China (today?) U.S.–Russia (Cold War)

President George W. Bush's thinking about his Greater Middle East Democratic Initiative. The democratic peace studies are complex and ongoing, but they offer us a great way to see how different perspectives and levels of analysis influence our thinking about international relations. So we use it in the conclusions as an example to summarize and pull together the various concepts developed throughout this book. We'll see that it's not completely clear that democracy or ideas cause the phenomenon of peace. It could be economic relationships, contract or bargaining factors, or alliance legacies. And if it is democracy, it's not clear exactly what it is about democracy that is most important: institutions, civil liberties, elections, or something else. Social science research is always burdened by questions of how the causal arrows run between perspectives and levels of analysis and whether we can even establish causality at all or have to settle for constitutive narratives or critical theories that consider all understanding as historically bound.

Other Identity Approaches

Other identity approaches emphasize the causal role of ideas but are less concerned with how ideas construct identities. Some scholars might not include them under identity perspectives. But remember that identity perspectives share one big thing in common—they focus on the causal or constitutive role of ideas. In this sense, the following approaches are identity perspectives.

soft power
the attractiveness of the values or ideas of a country as distinct from its military and economic power or its negotiating behavior.

Professor Joseph Nye has popularized the concept of **soft power.**[32] By soft power, he means the attractiveness of the values or ideas of a country as distinct from its military and economic power or its negotiating behavior. Countries influence one another not so much by force (the realist perspective) and compromise (the liberal perspective) but, often, by just being who they are and attracting other countries to accept their policies by the magnetism of their values and moral standards. A good example may be the way the prospect of membership in the democratic communities of the European Union and NATO encouraged the countries of eastern Europe and the former Soviet bloc to reform their domestic systems—military, economic, and political institutions—to meet the ideological requirements of joining the EU and NATO (such as civilian control of the military). While this process involved lots of negotiations to modify regulations and institutions, it may have been motivated in the first instance by the attractiveness of the values and institutions of the western democratic countries. The negotiations did not split the difference between eastern European and western regulations; rather, they moved the former communist countries decisively toward the standards of the western democracies. Relative identities converged and shared identities deepened, all toward democratic ideals, not communist or socialist ones. All the prospective members, for example, had to privatize industries and create a mixed market where previously state firms dominated.

belief systems
ideas about how the world works that influence the behavior of policymakers.

Still other identity studies focus on countries' **belief systems** and worldviews as ideas that influence their behavior as much as power and institutions.[33] In this case, ideas do not cause or constitute identities, which then cause behavior, but, instead, suggest to leaders how the world works and point them in various policy directions. Leaders embrace certain ideas as "road maps" telling them, for example, what causes prosperity, such as free-market economic policies. Or they conclude agreements that elevate certain ideas as focal points to help interpret issues when multiple outcomes are possible, such as principles of mutual recognition of regulations or arbitration panels to resolve issues that cannot be foreseen. Or institutions themselves embody ideas that regulate state behavior, such as the laws of the European Union, which all states must adopt before they can become members. Ideas, in short, are pervasive throughout the international system, and they are not just reflections of material and institutional power. Rather, they guide or, in some cases, alter the use of power and institutions.

Finally, **psychological studies** of international affairs emphasize ideas that define actor personalities, although the ideas in this case may not be conscious but subconscious and sometimes irrational. Many psychological studies focus on cognitive or rational factors that emphasize the many ways in which our perceptions may mislead us.[34] Two leaders in the same situation may act differently, not because they have different information but because they process it differently. One may associate a piece of information about the behavior of another state with a generally favorable view of that state and discount any hostile intent of the behavior. The second leader, with a different view of the other state, may not discount the hostile information. Psychologically, we like our views of others to be consistent, and we tend to avoid what psychologists call cognitive dissonance. Thus, in 1941, Stalin refused to believe British warnings that Hitler was preparing to attack Russia because Russia had just signed a non-aggression pact with Germany and the idea that Germany would attack Russia was inconsistent with Stalin's broader view of Germany. Psychological factors may also explain why some actors behave like defensive realists while others behave like offensive realists. Defensive realists, for psychological reasons, fear losses more than they value gains; hence, they settle for security rather than conquest. Offensive realists do the reverse. Other psychological studies focus on personality development and subconscious factors. Leaders have different formative experiences as children or young adults. Hitler and Stalin had abusive parents, and even Woodrow Wilson, some argue, was constantly trying to counter feelings of inadequacy branded into him as a child. There is also group think, a psychological phenomenon in which a group of decision makers reinforce a single way of thinking about a problem and rule out alternatives because they want to remain part of the group.[35]

> **psychological studies**
> studies that emphasize ideas that define actor personalities, although the ideas may not be conscious but subconscious and sometimes irrational.

Critical Theory Perspectives

Critical theory perspectives offer broad critiques of international relations and generally advocate radical solutions such as revolution. They deny that we can study international relations by abstracting from historical circumstances and separating the observer from the particular time and period of which the observer is part. To critical theorists, all ideas, institutions, and power are historically bound and contingent. The individual, including the observer or social scientist, is never truly free, and thought as well as behavior is a consequence of specific historical structures. Notice how critical theories refuse to separate ideas, power, and institutions; for them reality is a seamless web. This is also true for many constructivists who capture reality as narratives not causal sequences, which is why some critical theories such as feminism are considered constructivist. But critical theories do more than reconstruct the past; they also focus on the future. They look for the forces of change and evolution in history that define a future, usually more desirable, outcome. As Robert Cox, a well-known critical theorist tells us, "critical theory . . . contains an element of utopianism" but "its utopianism is constrained by its comprehension of historical processes."[36] Critical theory often has a teleological aspect to it; it tells us the direction in which history is moving and therefore what likely, although not certain, futures we may contemplate.

Let's look briefly at three critical theories: Marxism, feminism, and postmodernism or deconstructivism. We'll consider these theories from time to time throughout the rest of this book, especially when we are examining deep material and social divisions in the contemporary international system.

Marxism

Karl Marx was a refugee from revolution in Germany when he met and collaborated in London with Friedrich Engels, another radical son of a German merchant. In 1845, Engels published a scathing critique of British industrial society, *The Condition of the Working Class in England in 1844*. In 1848, Marx and Engels together wrote the *Communist Manifesto,* and in 1867 Marx produced the first volume of his monumental work, *Das Kapital.*

Marxism
a theory that emphasizes the dialectical or conflictual relationship between capitalist and communist states in the international system leading to the triumph of communism, not democracy.

Marx, whose work became known as **Marxism,** foresaw permanent revolution on behalf of the oppressed working class until the last remnants of bourgeois industrial society were destroyed and bourgeois politics and the state faded away. He based his understanding of this historical outcome on three factors: the underlying material forces shaping industrialization; the dialectic that these forces ignited between social classes, specifically between the working classes or proletariat manning the factories of industrialization and the managerial classes or bourgeoisie directing and financing industrialization; and the superstructure of states and interstate imperialism that the struggle between social classes generated. The forces of production ensured that capitalism would expand. Industrialization exploited workers by limiting their wages, in the process ensuring that new markets would have to be found because workers could not consume all of the products produced. Capitalism thus built up pressures to export surplus products and colonize other parts of the world. Here the superstructure of states and interstate competition played a role, inviting aggression and wars of imperial expansion. Wherever capitalism expanded, however, it built up its antithesis of working classes resisting and rebelling against exploitation. Through this dialectic, the workers of the world would unite and eventually break the chains of capitalism. Capitalism would gradually give way to communism, a future state of relations in which workers would control their own lives and destinies, and the state and traditional interstate relations would wither away.

Marxism evolved subsequently under Vladimir Ilyich Lenin in Russia and Mao Tse-tung in China. Lenin emphasized the vanguard of the proletariat, or leading states such as the Soviet Union that would hasten the demise of capitalism. Mao saw peasants, not workers, as the vanguard of the revolution. Today, after the collapse of the Soviet Union and the embrace of capitalism by China, the future envisioned by Marx and his followers seems unlikely. Still Marx's diagnosis of global economic processes retains its relevance for many analysts, even if his solutions have been overtaken by events. Globalization, while it has created an ever-larger middle class and spread economic gains to millions over the past century, has also carved deep divisions in the world between the upper and middle classes and the poorest classes, even within developing countries such as China and India. World systems approaches that borrow heavily from Marxism seek to explain this inequality—how core countries, such as those in the advanced world, continue to exploit semi-peripheral (for example, the Middle East) and peripheral (for example, Africa) parts of the world. Other Marxist-related accounts, such as the one developed by Antonio Gramsci, an Italian Marxist, focus on the dialectic from the other end and point out how hidden social purposes as well as material forces of production exercise a hegemonic grip on social consciousness and identity in any given historical period. Critical theorists argue that the historical dialectic that Marx discovered is still at work, spawning inequalities and tensions that increase the need to restructure radically the future global system.

Feminism

Feminism critiques international relations as a male-centered and -dominated discipline. As Professor Ann Tickner writes, "the discipline of international relations, as it is presently constructed, is defined in terms of everything that is not female." [37] By that she means that all perspectives, but the realist perspective in particular, place too much emphasis on military struggle and war instead of peace, sovereignty and self-help instead of community, and environmental exploitation instead of environmental preservation. Conventional studies value differences and disaggregation. They exalt individualism and aggression. They encourage the exploitation and abuse of natural resources. And they privilege system and statist solutions while downplaying the local and private spheres of activity, especially those where more women than men are involved, such as home making, child raising, care giving, and community service.

Feminist perspectives, and there are many, call for more attention to comprehensive rather than national security, to protecting homes where women and children are often exposed to domestic violence and not just safeguarding states. They emphasize the practices of mediation and reconciliation, peace-making, community-building, and nurturing trust and goodwill in the private as well as public sectors. Instead of large-scale corporate and state-run institutions, they prefer small-scale and often self-reliant and self-sufficient economic solutions that care as much about reproduction and preservation as they do about growth and disruptive innovation. Like all critical theories, feminist theories contain an element of utopianism. The past tragedies of war and violence may be overcome by recognizing that they took place in a particular time and place when women were not free or equal and can be overcome once women are given full equality and social justice.

Some feminist outlooks see this male domination as deeply rooted in the language and culture of international affairs. They note how diplomacy exalts masculine and denigrates feminine attributes. Alexander Hamilton accused Thomas Jefferson of a "womanish attachment to France"; Walt Whitman talked about the "manly heart" of democracy; bombs were given male names, such as "Little Boy" for the first atomic bomb, exploded in 1945; and success in testing the first hydrogen bomb was reported as "it's a boy" rather than "it's a girl," as if the birth of a girl implied failure. These feminist outlooks see men and women as fundamentally different, in some sense biologically hard-wired, and they seek a qualitative change in international life. It's not just a matter of adding a few more women to the military or diplomatic establishments; it's a matter of revolutionary change that converts a male-centered world of international affairs to the virtues of female culture.

Other feminist theories seek simply equal rights and participation for women across the broad spectrum of domestic and international life. They note that women have played roles in history since the beginning of time, and prominent women such as Cleopatra, Joan of Arc, Elizabeth I, and Catherine the Great have not so much changed the fundamental character of international relations as added to its diversity and richness. They acknowledge that men may act the way they do because of circumstances, not gender, and that once females are allowed to act in similar circumstances,

feminism
a theory that critiques international relations as a male-centered and -dominated discipline.

they may act similarly. If women had been the hunters and men the homemakers, would there have been no conflicts over scarce food and territory? Women add talent, not magic, to human affairs. A world that subjects half its population to inferior status is a world that moves at half speed or achieves only half a loaf. Women need to be given a fair chance, and then the world will see not that women are inherently more virtuous or peace-loving but that they are different and add immeasurably to the talents and treasure of the world community.

Postmodernism and Deconstructivism

Some critical theories argue that all attempts at knowledge involve the exercise of power, particularly of words, language, texts, and discourses. They argue that commonplace dichotomies in the study of international relations—sovereignty and anarchy, war and peace, citizen and human—mask a power structure that marginalizes many peoples. Sovereignty, for example, legitimates state power and serves the agenda of state elites while delegitimating domestic opposition by minorities, the poor, or indigenous peoples. Anarchy justifies war and imperialism, marginalizing the weak and nonwestern cultures, all in the name of establishing world order and civilizing the backward. The citizen is privileged over the human being because citizens gain authority to murder human beings, or go to war, in the name of the state. Economic modernity is portrayed as politically neutral when, in fact, it legitimates western economic hegemony.

Much of this language originates with modernization and the ascendance of western elites to the apex of global power. Hence, critical theories that seek to unmask the rhetorical dominance of western thought are often called postmodern. **Postmodernists** seek to expose the hidden or masked meanings of language and discourse in international relations to gain space to imagine alternatives. They hope to find a more socially just form of discourse, and many of them hold to a belief in causality, albeit a causality that is constructed rather than objective. However, other postmodernists want to go no further than to demonstrate that all social reality is constructed by language and discourse. They seek to deconstruct that reality wherever they find it and show that all politics conceals the power of words and discourse. They are called **deconstructivists,** and their approach is sometimes called radical constructivism. They are a bit like radicals or revolutionaries in the realist world who believe that all politics conceals coercive power and seek to expose and destroy that power wherever they find it. Neither radical constructivists nor revolutionaries feel any obligation to offer alternative ideas for order or justice. They are interested simply in deconstructing. In this sense, we may agree they do represent extreme or radical viewpoints.

Levels of Analysis

Perspectives deal with the substantive content of the cause making something happen in international relations—power, institutions, or ideas. Levels of analysis deal with the origin of that cause—an individual, a country, or the international system as a whole. And just as we cannot describe everything of substance in the world, we also cannot describe everything from all levels of analysis. And even if we might, we'd still have to decide which level to emphasize or we would not know where to act to change the outcome. Levels of analysis interact, just as perspectives do. But the decisive question is which way the causal arrows run. Until we can say that the domestic level forces are

postmodernists
theorists who seek to expose the hidden or masked meanings of language and discourse in international relations in order to gain space to imagine alternatives.

deconstructivists
theorists who seek to deconstruct social reality wherever they find it and show that all politics conceals the exercise of power through words and discourse.

driving the systemic forces, we do not know that the systemic factors may not be driving domestic ones. And if we say everything is equally important, again we have an overdetermined outcome, which means we don't know what really caused it.

The struggle for power may be the cause of war (a realist perspective). But the struggle for power may originate in the individual human being's lust for power, the aggressive characteristics of a particular state, or the uncertainties of a decentralized system of power.[38] The individual's lust for power represents an *individual* level of analysis, an aggressive or warlike state represents a *domestic* level of analysis, and the uncertainties of the balance of power represent a *systemic* level of analysis. The systemic level of analysis is often broken down further into a *process* level, involving interactions among states, and a *structural* level, involving the relative positions of states. So, in our example, war may originate from the failure of alliances (a process level) or the relative rise of a new power (a structural level of analysis).

There are, of course, an unlimited number of levels between the three primary ones. A regional level falls between the systemic and domestic levels. For example, a cause may originate in the way power is exercised within the European Union rather than within the global system as a whole. Another intermediate level is the *foreign policy* level of analysis. This level captures the interplay of domestic politics and international politics. It links foreign policy actors both with constituents in their own states at the domestic level, such as cabinet ministries and interest groups, and with counterpart actors in other countries at the systemic process level of analysis. Thus, at the foreign policy level of analysis, we might argue that war is a consequence of a leader being constrained by domestic politics and failing to react in a timely fashion to a threat from the systemic process level. An example might be President Franklin Roosevelt's being constrained by isolationist forces in American politics and being late to respond to fascist aggression in Europe and Asia in the 1930s. We will pay attention to this foreign policy level of analysis from time to time because it is quite important in democratic countries and provides a critical focal point where individual, state, and systemic forces come to bear on a particular country's actions in the international system.

In all these examples, the substance of the cause is the same—namely power—but in each case the cause comes from a different level of analysis. Can we conclude that causes from all these levels matter? Sure, but which level matters most? If the individual level is more important than the domestic level, we might change the leader; but if the domestic or systemic level is more important, changing the leader won't have much effect.

Systemic Level of Analysis

The systemic level of analysis explains outcomes from a systemwide level that includes all states. It takes into account both the position of states (actors) in the international system and their interrelationships. The position of states constitutes the systemic structural level of analysis. This involves the relative distribution of power, such as which state is a great, middle, or small power, and geopolitics, such as which state is a sea or land power. The interaction of states constitutes the systemic process level of analysis. At this level, we are concerned with which state aligns with which other states and which state negotiates with which other states. Thus, we can explain World War I in terms of the absence of systemwide institutions, such as the League of Nations, which was not created until after World War I to prevent such wars in the future. That would be a liberal explanation from a systemic *structural* level of analysis. Or we could explain World War I in terms of a loss of moderation in the practices of international diplomacy. That would also be a liberal explanation but from a systemic *process* level of analysis. Another way to think about the difference between the structural and process levels of analysis is to use the analogy of a card game. The cards you hold constitute the structural level; the cards themselves represent the relative power states hold. Playing the cards takes place at the process level. When a state forms an alliance with another state, it commits some of its power, or plays one of its cards.

The systemic level of analysis is the most comprehensive. If we emphasize this level of analysis, we are unlikely to leave out a significant part of the international situation we are looking at and therefore omit a particular cause. On the other hand, this level is also the most general; we will come up with explanations that lack specificity. For example, we may conclude that the relative rise of German power caused World War I, and it may well have. But now we wonder, why did the relative rise of American power not cause World War I? America had surpassed Britain at the end of the nineteenth century and was more powerful than Germany. Maybe we have to look just at Europe, the regional level of analysis, because America did not see itself as part of Europe. But why, then, did America not feel part of Europe? Perhaps because the United States had fewer interactions with Europe than Britain did—less trade and tourism. Now we are at the system process level of analysis. But it might have also been America's ideology of isolationism. Now we are at the domestic level of analysis. And so on. It is hard to be very specific at the systemic level.

But because causes are remote does not mean they do not affect outcomes. More generally, structural level studies predict outcomes, not behaviors. Neorealists, for example, say that bipolarity decreases the likelihood of war; but they cannot say that bipolarity causes a specific country not to go to war. On the other hand, a structural distribution of power can widen or narrow the options a country faces. In a bipolar world, for instance, neither major actor can find additional allies that will be of much help. Hence, in a bipolar world, states compete through internal competition, not external balancing. In a unipolar world, the hegemonic country may not be able to withdraw, regardless of its domestic preferences. Structural studies help us see the things we take for granted. That's why, as we already discussed, critical theories are often deeply structural—they are trying to show us alternatives that no one has considered because of the hegemonic structure dominating discourse.

Certain perspectives emphasize the systemic level of analysis. Social constructivism, for example, sees identity shaped more by international relationships (system process level) and shared knowledge or culture (system structure level) than by separate country histories (domestic level) or specific leaders (individual level). Neorealism emphasizes the systemic level of relative power almost to the exclusion of domestic and individual factors. Often perspectives differ primarily in terms of level of analysis. Neoliberal institutional perspectives, for example, differ from classical liberal perspectives by emphasizing the systemic more than the domestic level of analysis. Agent-oriented or argumentative constructivism, as we have discussed, is similar in all respects to social constructivism, but gives more emphasis to agency, that is, the domestic and individual levels of analysis; social constructivism gives more emphasis to systemic structure.

Domestic Level of Analysis

The domestic level of analysis locates causes in the character of the domestic system of specific states. Thus, war is caused by aggressive or warlike states, not by evil, inept, or misguided people (individual level of analysis) or the structure of power in the international system (systemic level of analysis); this is a realist perspective from a domestic level of analysis. The failure of domestic institutions may also cause war. In World War I, the internal collapse of the Austro-Hungarian Empire, or the brittle coalition inside Germany of agricultural (rye) and industrial (iron) interests are often cited as important causes. These are also explanations from a domestic level of analysis but now from a liberal perspective; the breakdown of institutional relationships at the domestic level led to war.

Domestic level causes are more specific than systemic level causes but not as specific as individual level factors. We can point to a specific domestic political coalition, such as the iron and rye coalition in Germany, which led to the expansion of German power and caused World War I, rather than the relative rise of German power, which occurred over a longer period of time and does not tell us exactly when that power became sufficient to precipitate war. On the other hand, at the domestic level we now downplay causes that might come from other countries or the structure of international power. What if the buildup of military power in another country, such as Russia, was the principal cause of German armament, and the need to arm Germany brought together the iron and rye coalition? Now the iron and rye coalition is not a cause of World War I but a consequence of systemic factors and an intervening, not independent, variable causing war. Similarly, the iron-rye coalition had existed for some time, and war did not occur. Was there an even more specific cause that came from the individual level of analysis, such as the brinksmanship of the German Chancellor Theobald von Bethmann-Hollweg during the critical month of July 1914?

Domestic level causes may come from various characteristics of the domestic system. Capitalist and socialist economies generate different attitudes and behavior. The Muslim and Christian religions or democratic and nondemocratic political ideologies do as well. Stable and failed institutions are domestic level factors affecting state behavior. A great worry today is the existence of **failed states,** meaning states whose domestic institutions have broken down, such as Somalia. Another worry is the existence of a **rogue state,** such as North Korea, which may pass nuclear weapons on to terrorists. Both types of state come from the domestic level of analysis, but a failed state usually means an institutional breakdown, a liberal cause, whereas a rogue state often implies evil intentions, an identity cause.

Individual Level of Analysis

The individual level of analysis locates the cause of events in individual leaders or the immediate circle of decision makers within a particular country. Now the cause of World War I comes not from some general characteristic of the German domestic system as a whole—the iron and rye coalition—but from the particular leaders in power at the time. Kaiser Wilhelm II is considered to be the level from which the cause originated. It may have been his need for power to hide a sense of inferiority; this is a realist explanation. Or it may have been his inability to understand the intricacies of statecraft, the way Otto von Bismarck, the German chancellor until 1890, did; this is a liberal explanation. Or it may have been his ideas about the monarchy and German destiny; this is an identity explanation. But all three of these explanations are drawn from an individual level of analysis.

The individual level of analysis is the most specific level. Now we can see the proximate or most immediate cause of some action. President George W. Bush and a small

failed states

states whose domestic institutions have collapsed.

rogue states

states that seek systematically to acquire nuclear weapons with the possible intent of passing them on to nonstate terrorists.

group of neoconservative advisers made the decision to invade Iraq and cause war in 2003. This level of analysis has great appeal, especially among historians and the media. Much of history is written as the work of great men (and a few great women). The stories of Napoleon, Frederick the Great, Samurai families in Japan, and the strong men of Africa who led their countries to independence after World War II resonate with human interest and human tragedy. Newspapers sell when they report personal peccadilloes or more serious evils that leaders are alleged to have caused. And the individual level of analysis is important, especially in democratic countries, where accountability is at the heart of domestic politics.

Nevertheless, this level of analysis is the least general level of analysis. It soft-pedals all the domestic and international level factors that may have set up the situation in which the American president or other leaders acted. Working at this level of analysis is akin to watching a baseball game and concluding that a home run in the bottom of the ninth inning caused the final outcome without considering how the rest of the game set up the situation in the bottom of the ninth that made the home run decisive. Was the neoconservative role in the decision to invade Iraq all that significant? Had those six or eight people not been there, would the decision have been a different one? Conceivably, but it's hardly a sure thing. To reach that conclusion we would need to investigate comprehensively all the other domestic groups and factors that weighed in for and against the Iraq invasion, not to mention the international factors at play. It may be politically useful to exaggerate the role of an individual or small group, but that's not the same as proving it is so.

Foreign Policy Level of Analysis

Another important level of analysis, as we noted, is the foreign policy level of analysis. The foreign policy level of analysis is where foreign policy officials actually make decisions. It operates between the systemic process and domestic levels of analysis. In this sense, as Robert Putnam tells us, the foreign policy level of analysis is a "two-level game."[39] Beneath the foreign policy officials are domestic groups that have their own interests, associations, and ideas about what the foreign policy of the country should be. Above the policymakers are foreign groups that also seek to influence the first country's foreign policy. The foreign policy officials thus are sandwiched in between the systemic process and domestic levels. What is more, the foreign policy officials themselves are not necessarily neutral. They may have independent preferences that come from the individual level of analysis. They aspire to be power brokers and put their own personal stamp on foreign policy. Thus, the individual, domestic, and systemic process levels of analysis are all involved in the game of foreign policy making. This is the complex setting in which foreign policy is made.

Let's take a snapshot of one case of foreign policy making to see the different levels at work. I was personally involved as the White House aide, or sherpa, in the negotiations leading up to the Group of Seven (G-7) economic summit in Williamsburg, Virginia, in May 1983. The G-7 countries are Canada, France, Germany, Great Britain, Italy, Japan, and the United States. Three sherpas from each country—one from the prime minister's or president's office, one from the finance ministry, and one from the foreign ministry—met for a full year to develop the agenda and action plan for the summit. This level constituted the official intergovernmental negotiations, or the *systemic process level of analysis*. These negotiations were difficult enough, but also intense were the domestic, transnational, and even transgovernmental (coalitions between

U.S. and foreign bureaucrats) interactions that swirled around the sherpas. President Reagan's policies sparked sharp opposition in the United States and abroad. His economic policies were seen as unconventional and had not yet generated the strong economic recovery that followed later in 1983 and lasted the rest of the decade. Thus, domestic interest groups opposed to these policies sought to reverse them. Like-minded economists from the private sector in both the United States and Europe met in December 1982 as a *transnational level group (international NGO)* to mobilize support against U.S. policies. France under President François Mitterrand also strongly opposed U.S. policies and used other IGOs in addition to the official summit process, such as the Organization for Economic Co-operation and Development (OECD), to persuade other countries to oppose the United States. Even some U.S. government officials did not agree with Reagan's policies and dropped hints to their counterparts in foreign governments that foreign leaders should press the U.S. president hard at the summit to change course, an example of a *transgovernmental level coalition* from different countries. Sometimes, in international diplomacy, the toughest negotiations are with domestic not foreign opponents; it is indeed a two-level game. The U.S. sherpas faced repeated attempts by domestic groups not only to change foreign policy but to change domestic policy through the foreign policy process.[40]

Thus, when we study international relations from the foreign policy as opposed to systemic level of analysis, we look more fully at domestic politics and institutions and at how different domestic groups perceive the international system and exercise their domestic capabilities (power), connections (institutions), and ideas to shape that country's foreign policy. In the United States, for example, we pay attention to an array of nongovernmental or private interest groups that lobby for various American foreign policies. These include business and labor groups; the military-industrial complex; think tanks and universities; and numerous trade, environmental, foreign aid, and human rights NGOs. At the foreign policy level, we also worry about the constitutional structure of the country and the division of powers among the various government institutions that have responsibilities for foreign policy. Again, in the United States, we're looking at the House of Representatives, which controls the purse strings of foreign policy; the Senate, which confirms cabinet appointments and ratifies international treaties; the president, who serves as commander-in-chief of the armed forces; and the Supreme Court, which rules on the constitutionality of legislation. The story of America foreign policy is in many ways the story of a struggle for power among these various institutions to make foreign policy decisions. A good example is the face-off in 2007 between President Bush and the new Democratic Congress to set the course of U.S. policy in Iraq. Finally, we are concerned at the foreign policy level with the media and civil society institutions of a particular country. These might include the national and local press and broadcast media, educational and religious institutions, and the other sources of public opinion in the society.

A well-known foreign policy level perspective in international relations is the rational choice approach. From this approach, as Professor Bruce Bueno de Mesquita tells us, "international relations is the process by which foreign policy leaders balance their ambition to pursue particular policy objectives [such as security, economic prosperity, and so on] against their need to avoid internal and external threats to their political survival."[41] Foreign policy leaders have certain preferences or objectives that motivate their behavior; they pursue these preferences through the pursuit of power; they calculate the costs and benefits of various policy options based on their perceptions of available power and political risk; and they decide which option maximizes the achievement of their goals. Notice how the focal point is the foreign policy level of individual leaders who have mostly fixed identities and institutional roles and who pursue power at both the domestic and international level to maximize their self-interest in political survival. We might conclude that rational choice is primarily a realist perspective at the foreign policy level of analysis.

Interaction of Perspectives and Levels of Analysis: Causal Arrows

Thus far in this chapter, we have accomplished two tasks: (1) examining the underlying logic of the three main perspectives on international relations—realist, liberal, and identity—using the story of the prisoner's dilemma; and (2) defining the principal concepts of each perspective and the chief characteristics of each level of analysis. Now, we are ready to undertake a third most important task, understanding the way in which perspectives and levels of analysis interact. As we have already suggested several times, careful studies of international relations focus on factors important to all perspectives—power, institutions, and ideas—and coming from all levels of analysis—systemic, domestic, and individual. The perspectives and levels of analysis do not differ because they focus on only one factor or level of analysis and exclude the others. Liberal perspectives do not exclude power or identity factors, and a systemic level of analysis does not exclude domestic or individual level factors. The difference lies in which factors and levels of analysis each perspective judges to be most important in causing outcomes. In other words, in which direction do the causal arrows run among power, institutions, and ideas and among the various levels of analysis?

The box on page 63 illustrates this crucial point about causality among the factors important to each perspective. In realist perspectives, power factors ultimately cause institutional and ideological outcomes. In liberal perspectives, institutional factors ultimately cause power and identity outcomes. And in identity perspectives, ideas ultimately cause power and institutional outcomes. Notice in the box that realist explanations of World War I do not ignore the identity factors associated with Social Darwinism but, rather, conclude that Social Darwinism was a consequence of the fear generated by the decentralized distribution of power and the security dilemma. The identity perspective, by contrast, sees Social Darwinism not as a consequence but as a cause of the security dilemma, generating a sense of difference and fear that caused countries to arm and struggle for power.

Similarly, the levels of analysis interact. For example, domestic level factors may be judged to be more important than systemic, foreign policy, or individual level factors. The domestic level of analysis does not exclude the other levels. Rather, the causal arrows run from the domestic level to the systemic and other levels of analysis. Or, alternatively, when we judge systemic factors to be most important, we have not excluded domestic or other level factors. We have simply concluded that systemic factors are more important than the others in causing the outcomes.

Remember we have to make these judgments about which way the causal arrows run because we cannot conclude that everything causes something to happen. Such a conclusion would not only tell us nothing that we did not know at the beginning of our study. It would offer no guidance about how to change the outcomes; we would not know which factor was causing the others and hence what to change. And we cannot change everything. So, all mainstream students of international affairs examine

Which Way Does the Causal Arrow Go?

Determining the Primary Cause of an Outcome

How can we tell whether a scholar, pundit, or leader is emphasizing the realist, liberal, or identity perspective when the analyst draws a conclusion? Don't just listen for synonyms for power, institutions, or ideas. Good analysts will consider all three factors. Focus instead primarily on what the analyst says is *causing* something else to happen. Is power causing the ideas and institutional behavior? Or are institutions causing power and ideological factors? Below, we give three examples illustrating the debate about World War I.

To realists, an increase in German power was responsible for intensifying the security dilemma, which in turn gave rise to a mentality of Social Darwinism and led to the interruption of interdependence. Notice in this example that power, ideas, and interdependence (institutions) are all present in the explanation but that power developments are causing the ideas and institutional outcomes.

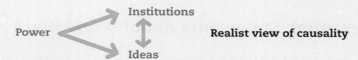

From the liberal perspective, the causal arrows shift. Now the absence of universal institutions before World War I, such as the League of Nations (set up after World War I), did not allow for sufficient trust to develop between nations to overcome the security dilemma and avoid the competitive mentality of Social Darwinism. Had those institutions existed, they would have overcome the power and ideological competition.

From the identity perspective, the causal arrows shift yet again. Now the mind-set of Social Darwinism caused countries to engage in a competitive arms race, which made it difficult for them to trust one another and resolve disputes peacefully. In short, conflicting identities drove the power struggle and made institutional cooperation difficult if not impossible.

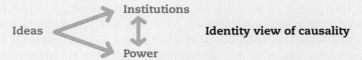

Understanding which way causality flows is a crucial part of the process of analyzing what scholars, pundits, and politicians have to say about world events. To alert readers to places where causality is our focus, we place an arrow icon in the margin to indicate that causal logic is at work:

causal →
arrow

facts from all perspectives and levels of analysis, but then judge, based on the evidence they have collected, that one perspective and one level of analysis are more important than the others. Is the judgment of any one study or scholar then definitive? If it were, there would be no controversies among scholars or other students of international affairs about either historical or contemporary events. Yet controversies abound because no scholar or student can consider all the facts, and each scholar or student judges when he or she has enough facts and which facts seem most important on the basis of his or her own preferences with respect to perspectives and levels of analysis.

The three mainstream perspectives return again and again to the facts because they believe that an objective reality exists independently of the observer even if the observer has to make certain assumptions—employ certain biases—in order to test the facts. Critical theory perspectives differ in that they do not believe that such an objective pursuit of knowledge is possible. They believe that the observer is inextricably part of the situation being studied and cannot escape the biases of the social and historical circumstances in which the observer operates.

Revisiting Statements About World War I

Now, we can revisit the three statements made at the beginning of this chapter about the causes of World War I and add to them the other causes we have mentioned. In Table 1-8, we organize the different explanations by perspectives and levels of analysis.

Statement 1 at the beginning of the chapter is a realist explanation from a systemic level of analysis (see upper left box). It attributes the cause of war to a shift in the distribution of power away from equilibrium within the system as a whole. It appeals to the dynamics in power-balancing realist thinking that inequality or rapid shifts in the distribution of power are destabilizing and bring into play competitive forces that eventually rebalance power, sometimes by war. It cannot explain exactly when war occurs; the systemic level of analysis is too general. But as we will see in the next chapter, it does draw on a centuries-old historical pattern that suggests when one country becomes too powerful other countries align to counterbalance it. And that process of counterbalancing often leads to war.

Statement 2 is a liberal explanation from an individual level of analysis (see lower center box). The cause comes from the Kaiser himself, from his lack of bureaucratic skills. If someone else had been in power, that person might have acted differently, for example, not given the Austrians a blank check to mobilize armies, which then triggered war on two fronts and ensured a world war. The cause of the war, then, was misguided diplomacy. There was no inherent reason why the shift in the balance of power had to cause war. If we shift the emphasis to the Kaiser's need for power to conceal his inferiority complex, the argument is still at an individual level but now becomes a realist explanation (see lower left box).

Statement 3 is an identity-based account from a domestic level of analysis (right middle box). It is identity-based because it sees the cause of the war in the German militarist ideology or self-image, how the German people thought about themselves, particularly in relation to the aggressive use of force and heroism of war. The explanation comes from the domestic level of analysis because the cause derives from a characteristic of the domestic political system as a whole, not the foibles of a particular leader or unbalanced relationships with external powers.

A foreign policy level explanation from a realist perspective might point to the

Table 1-8

The Causes of World War I: By Perspective and Levels of Analysis

Level of analysis	Perspective		
	Realist	Liberal	Identity
Systemic	The rise of a powerful German state, causing changes in the distribution of power away from equilibrium	The absence of systemwide institutions to prevent war (structural level), or the loss of moderation in the practices of international diplomacy (process level)	
Foreign policy	Kaiser's diplomatic flexibility constrained by domestic interest groups	Kaiser's diplomacy facilitated by weak parliamentary institutions	
Domestic		The internal collapse of the Austro-Hungarian Empire, or the brittle coalition inside Germany of agricultural (rye) and industrial (iron) interests	Germany's militaristic ideology, which celebrated war
Individual	Kaiser Wilhelm II's need for power to hide a sense of inferiority	Kaiser Wilhelm II's inability to master the intricacies of statecraft	

domestic interest group divisions in Germany (especially between the iron-rye coalition and the socialists) that restricted the Kaiser's flexibility to respond to peace overtures. A foreign policy level explanation from a liberal perspective might highlight the German parliament's lack of institutional control of military spending. Other explanations mentioned in this chapter fall into the center column, upper and middle boxes. They are liberal explanations based on institutional considerations but from the systemic and domestic levels of analysis. We'll consider all these explanations in more detail in Chapter 3. By then, this approach of distinguishing arguments in terms of perspectives and levels of analysis will be more familiar.

Summary: Relevance in the Real World

The realist perspective hypothesizes that actors in international affairs behave primarily on the basis of what they *have*, how much relative power they control and how their use of power inevitably threatens others. The liberal perspective hypothesizes that actors behave primarily on the basis of what they and other actors *do*, how actors interact and the processes of reciprocity and interdependence that create institutions and facilitate the pursuit of collective goods. The identity perspective hypothesizes that actors behave primarily on the basis of who they *are*, the ideas that construct their identities or serve as causal guidelines for choosing policies in the real world. Most social science scholars believe that testing perspectives can yield knowledge that is universal and can be applied to a better future. But the critical theory perspectives deny that we can break up reality into testable hypotheses, seek to expose the power and politics of all social science research, and look for forces of change and prospects of better worlds that act inside history.

Each perspective can be tested at multiple levels of analysis. The systemic level involves process and structural features of the global system that influence the behavior of state and individual actors. The domestic level focuses on causes that come from broad features inside countries, such as their political ideologies, economic systems, institutional structure, or public opinion. The individual or decision-making level highlights causes that lie inside individuals or within their immediate decision-making environment. It is the most specific level, but it may exaggerate the independence of decision makers. Finally, the foreign policy level isolates the specific leaders making foreign policy and filters forces from both the domestic and systemic levels of analysis through the preferences and perceptions of these leaders.

We have introduced a lot of concepts in this chapter. The rest of the book illustrates how these concepts work in the real world, and we will remind you of them as we see them at work in explaining historical and contemporary events. Perspectives and levels of analysis are grippingly relevant. To drive this point home, we provide three pedagogical features in the margins of subsequent chapters. First, when practical events are being covered that illustrate a particular concept, a "Spotlight on . . ." feature appears in the margin referring you back to that concept in this chapter. Second, in the discussion of historical or contemporary events in which one perspective or level of analysis is being identified as more important than others in explaining the outcome of some event or argument, a causal arrow feature appears in the margin, referring you back to the discussion in this chapter about how the perspectives and levels of analysis interact. Third, when a major concept appears for the first time in subsequent chapters, it appears in bold, and we continue to provide in the margin an accompanying glossary definition of the concept, as we have done in this chapter.

Let's end this chapter with two examples of how perspectives matter in day-to-day international affairs.

The box on page 67 uses the three perspectives—realist, liberal, and identity—to dissect the worldview of Secretary of State Condoleezza Rice. Her views are taken from an article she wrote in 2000 before she became President George W. Bush's national security adviser and from an interview she conducted in November 2004 after she was nominated to become secretary of state. Read the box carefully. Notice several things. First, she considers facts emphasized by all three perspectives. Second, she evaluates each perspective. Is the balance of power enough? Should the United States always adhere to international agreements and institutions? Is acting on the basis of values arrogant? Third, she judges which perspective should have priority in achieving U.S. foreign policy goals. She concludes that we should act on the basis of our values, not the dictates of the balance of power or international institutions. The solution to world conflict is to spread democratic values and use the balance of power and institutions toward that end. See how values are *relatively* more important than power and institutions.

The box on page 68 offers a second example. This time a columnist, Sebastian Mallaby, analyzes Rice's worldview. Unfortunately, he has not taken a course on the role of perspectives in international relations, but he uses them, nevertheless, as everyone must. Notice how he begins by saying Rice looks at the world from a realist perspective but then suggests in the middle of the article that she switched at some point to an identity perspective; now, she considers the character of regimes or

Understanding Secretary of State Condoleezza Rice's View of the World

The ideal types we discuss in this chapter help differentiate the realist, liberal, and identity elements of any foreign policy argument we encounter. The three quotations below address Secretary Rice's view of the roles of the balance of power, international institutions, and values in U.S. foreign policy. Let's see how she emphasizes and judges each element:

1. **Balance of Power:** *"The reality is that 'multi-polarity' was never a unifying idea, or a vision. It was a necessary evil that sustained the absence of war but it did not promote the triumph of peace. Multi-polarity is a theory of rivalry, of competing interests—and at its worse—competing values."* [1]

   Notice that Rice rejects a pure realist perspective. Multi-polarity, which relates to balancing power, is "a necessary evil" that has kept war at bay, but it is not enough to "promote the triumph of peace." Moreover, multi-polarity is not just about power; it is "at its worse" also about "competing values." Rice hints that "competing values," not the security dilemma, may be driving the balance of power and making it worse. So, how does one cope with competing values driving competing power? Through international institutions?

2. **International Institutions:** *"Multilateral agreements and institutions should not be ends in themselves . . . the United States has a special role in the world and should not adhere to every international convention and agreement that someone thinks to propose."* [2]

   Clearly international institutions are not the primary solution for Rice. She is not adopting the liberal perspective here. She takes liberal factors into account, but she does not emphasize them. So what is the solution?

3. **Values:** *"America can exercise power without arrogance and pursue its interests without hectoring or bluster. When it does so in concert with those who share its core values, the world becomes more prosperous, democratic and peaceful."* [3]

   The solution is to use power (a realist solution) but to aim for more than the "absence of war," to work "in concert with those who share [America's] core values." Ideas, in this case democratic values, define America's partners and its policies, not relative power or institutions per se. And the objective is not just stability but the spread of democratic values.

Do you see why we might conclude that the identity perspective is most important in how she views the world?

1. Quoted in Glenn Kessler, "The Power-Values Approach to Policy," *Washington Post*, November 21, 2004, A9.
2. Condoleezza Rice, "Campaign 2000: Promoting the National Interest," *Foreign Affairs* 79, no. 1 (January–February 2000): 47, 48–49.
3. Ibid., 62.

Columnist Sebastian Mallaby's Understanding of Secretary of State Condoleezza Rice's View of the World

In a *Washington Post* column on January 23, 2006, Sebastian Mallaby identifies "Rice's Blind Spot." What do you think this blind spot might be? Is she overlooking power (realist perspective), values (identity perspective), institutions (liberal perspective) or the inevitability of history (critical theory perspective) and, if so, from what level of analysis?

Mallaby begins by showing that Condoleezza Rice in 2000, before she became national security adviser, adopted a realist perspective on world affairs, focusing on great powers at the systemic structural level of analysis, not on the internal values or institutions of states operating at the domestic or decision-making levels of analysis:

> In January 2000, as the Bush campaign got underway, Rice published a manifesto in Foreign Affairs that laid out the classic "realist" position: American diplomacy should "focus on power relationships and great-power politics" rather than on other countries' internal affairs. "Some worry that this view of the world ignores the role of values, particularly human rights and the promotion of democracy," she acknowledged. But the priority for U.S. foreign policy was to deal with powerful governments, whose "fits of anger or acts of beneficence affect hundreds of millions of people."

Later in the article, Mallaby notes a shift in Rice's emphasis from relative power to the internal characteristics (values and institutions) of regimes (states). She adopts an identity perspective still from a systemic structural level of analysis (different positions of democratic and nondemocratic states) but with more attention now to what is going on within (domestic level of analysis) as well as between (systemic process level) states:

> Fast-forward to 2006. Rice gave two speeches last week calling for "transformational diplomacy," meaning diplomacy that will transform undemocratic societies: The internal affairs of other countries turn out to be important after all. "The greatest threats now emerge more within states than between them," she said Wednesday. "The fundamental character of regimes now matters more than the international distribution of power. In this world it is impossible to draw neat, clear lines between our security interests, our development efforts and our democratic ideals."

Up to this point, Mallaby has characterized Rice as operating from a realist and subsequently an identity perspective, mostly from the systemic structural level of analysis. What has he left out? You guessed it—the liberal perspective and the domestic level of analysis. Notice in the next part of the article how he chastises her for not paying enough attention to failed states and institution-building at the domestic level of analysis. In the end, he doubts that such nation-building is possible through the efforts of outside countries, suggesting that local or internal norms (values/identity) may be more powerful after all than external values, power or institution-building:

> Rice has caught up with the 1990s consensus that powerful states may pose less of a problem than disintegrating weak ones and that the best hope for peace in the long term is a world of stable democracies. But she's only half-acknowledging the next question: Yes,

Secretary of State Condoleezza Rice speaks on "transformational diplomacy" in this January 18, 2006, photo.

weak and autocratic states are a problem, but can we do anything about them?

The best formulation of this new debate comes from Francis Fukuyama, who famously proclaimed the universality of the democratic urge in his 1989 essay on history's end. Fukuyama certainly believes in spreading U.S. values, but he has emerged as a critic of the Iraq war because he believes its ambitions were unrealizable. The United States lacks the instruments to transform other societies, Fukuyama argues; to build nations you must first build institutions, and nobody knows how to do that. Conservatives, who have long preached the limits to what government can achieve with domestic social policies, should wake up to government's limits in foreign policy as well.

Rice shows some signs of seeing this. She is not content with the instruments of foreign policy as they exist, and her speeches last week were about fostering new ones—a strengthened office for post-conflict stabilization and a reconfigured foreign aid program. But this only begins to confront Fukuyama's worry, which is that no amount of tinkering with the apparatus of government will make nation-building possible. Creating a functional Iraq or Afghanistan requires creating norms of work and trust and honesty, and such norms can't be conjured by outsiders, no matter how well organized they are.

Finally, Mallaby questions whether a problem like Iraq is manageable at all, at least by intellectual means of identifying specific causes and effects. Is he sliding toward a critical theory perspective, in which history unfolds based on a dynamic of its own?

The big question today in foreign policy is not whether you are a realist or an idealist. It's whether you are an optimist or a pessimist: whether you think that Iraq has gone badly merely because the Bush administration mishandled it, or whether you believe that no amount of skillful management could have achieved stability after three years. I've watched Rice handle squadrons of aggressive journalists, and there's no doubting her intellect. But her forays into grand theory are disappointing. Last week's call for "transformational diplomacy" merely slides past today's big question. It doesn't offer an answer.

identity to be more important than the distribution of power. Before reading the rest of the article, ask yourself which perspective he has left out so far and from which perspective he is most likely to criticize Rice. Yes, you guessed it—the liberal perspective. He says she pays too little attention to nation-building and institutional development. He's working from the domestic level of analysis, but he might have also made this criticism from the systemic level of analysis. Many critics have accused Secretary Rice (and President Bush) of not paying sufficient attention to multilateral diplomacy and international institutions. See how perspectives and levels of analysis help us not just to read between the lines of what contemporary commentators are saying but even to anticipate what they are going to say? Now you are beginning to think critically about the subject of international relations.

Key Concepts

absolute gains 42
agent-oriented constructivism 48
alliances 33
anarchy 28
balance of power 31
bandwagoning 32
beliefs 46
belief systems 52
bipolar 33
civil society 37
collective goods 41
collective security 41
compromise 42
construction of identities 46
constructivism 46
deconstructivists 56
deterrence 38
diplomacy 42
disarmament 38
distribution of identities 49
extended deterrence 38
external identity 50
failed states 59
feminism 55
geopolitics 30

global governance 39
hegemon 32
hegemonic stability 32
hegemony 32
human rights 40
human security 37
identity 27
interdependence 36
intergovernmental organizations (IGOs) 39
internal identity 49
international institutions 39
international law 40
international regimes 39
legitimacy 42
Marxism 54
minimum deterrence 38
modernization 37
multipolar 33
mutual gains 42
nongovernmental organizations (NGOs) 37
non-zero sum 24
norms 46
path dependence 40

polarity 32
postmodernists 56
power 30
power balancing 32
power transition 32
preemptive wars 33
preponderance of power 41
preventive wars 33
prisoner's dilemma 22
psychological studies 53
reciprocity 36
relative gains 42
relative identities 50
rogue states 59
security dilemma 31
self-help 29
shared identities 50
social constructivism 47
soft power 52
states 29
technological change 37
transnational relations 37
tripolar 33
values 46
zero sum 23

Study Questions

1. How do ideal types, perspectives, and theories differ?

2. What do the realist, liberal, and identity perspectives each relatively emphasize?

3. Can any perspective apply at any level of analysis?

4. Is constructivism both a theory and a method?

5. Why is former Secretary of State Henry Kissinger identified more with the realist perspective, while Secretary of State Condoleezza Rice might be identified more with the identity perspective?

Part I

International Conflict and War

Violence comes in many forms and exists all around us, affecting us individually, as citizens of states, and as members of the international system. It comes in the form of hunger, disease, and natural disasters, and it comes in the form of human conflict. These conflicts take place at all levels of analysis: major interstate and world wars, regional and global terrorism, ethnic and civil wars, village and neighborhood rioting, gang and racial pogroms, international drug and sex trafficking, and child and spousal abuse. In this part of the book, we focus on understanding these international conflicts, especially major wars, and consider what we should do about them.

As we will see, the three perspectives approach the study of conflict differently and prescribe different solutions. The realist perspective tries to find the solution in the correct configuration of power, the liberal perspective in the proper design of communities and institutions, and the identity perspective in humane dialogue and empathetic images of self and others. Critical theory perspectives view conflict as a consequence of deeply embedded historical structures and expose repression, empower particular groups, and even advocate revolution as solutions to conflict.

The perspectives offer these solutions at all levels of analysis: systemic, foreign policy, domestic, and individual. The realist solution to family, ethnic, or interstate violence is to create either a dominant center that monopolizes the use of force (according to the power transition school of realism) or a system of checks and balances that preserves independence and equilibrium (according to the power balancing school of realism). The liberal solution to conflict is human or collective security, which stresses equal participation in family, state, and international institutions and addresses problems of both military security and individual safety. The identity perspective strives for more open, accountable, and truthful dialogues that create healthy self-images and nonadversarial images of others through both humanistic and, in some cases, democratic principles. Critical theory perspectives focus on the holistic interaction of individual, domestic, foreign policy, and systemic forces that mutually cause or constitute oppression and see the emancipation of marginalized groups by giving them a voice in the process as the best remedy to inequality and conflict.

Why focus on conflict? One reason is to better understand and control it. Interestingly, while conflict seems ubiquitous in international affairs, it may be decreasing. From 1816 to 1980, for example, interstate wars, despite our memories of World Wars I and II, did not increase in number, severity, or magnitude if we adjust for the growing number of states that emerged during this period.[1] Neither did civil wars. Absolute magnitudes of violence, of course, did increase because there are a larger number of states involved in the international system. Our awareness of these conflicts has also increased; globalized media report more conflicts and often do so dramatically. But a recent study suggests that the global media may be giving us a false impression. From the end of the Cold War through 2005, the number of armed conflicts around the world declined by more than 40 percent; the number of genocides plummeted by 90 percent.[2] As of 2004, forty-three armed struggles for self-determination were contained or ended, while another twenty-five continued, the lowest number since 1976; international crises, which often precede conflicts, declined by 70 percent; the dollar value of arms transfers declined by 33 percent; the number of refugees dropped by 45 percent; and five of six developing regions saw a net decrease in core human rights abuses.[3] The only form of political violence that is getting worse is international terrorism.

These are encouraging, albeit limited and always debatable, statistics. There have been other periods of relative calm in international affairs, for example most of the nineteenth century, which was then followed by the devastating wars of the twentieth century. So we should not read too much into these numbers and become complacent. Nevertheless, they suggest that we don't have to approach our study of international affairs with alarmist or gloomy expectations. Maybe the international community has learned something from the past about managing international conflicts.

What have we learned? Well, we can't know until we examine the past, right? In Part I, we review the major events of world history. Chapter 2 explores conflicts from the earliest days of recorded history. Chapter 3 looks at World War I, and Chapter 4 discusses World War II. Chapter 5 examines the origins and end of the Cold War. Then Chapter 6 addresses the period between the end of the Cold War and September 11, 2001—the world of the 1990s. Chapter 7 offers a sustained look at the growth of international terrorism post-9/11, as well as other recent ethnic, religious, and national conflicts. The perspectives do not agree on this history; hence, we explore the history from each of the perspectives. Seeing how and why they disagree may help us to draw better conclusions of our own and apply the lessons of the past more effectively to our world of the twenty-first century.

1. Melvin Small and J. David Singer, *Resort to Arms: International and Civil Wars, 1816–1980* (Beverly Hills, Calif.: Sage, 1982).
2. Human Security Brief 2006, available at: www.hsrgroup.org/images/stories/HSBrief2006/contents/finalversion.pdf.
3. Human Security Report 2005, *War and Peace in the Twenty-first Century* (New York: Oxford University Press, 2005), 1–2.

Perspectives on World History
Change and Continuity

Our identity comes in part from history, sometimes buried right beneath our feet, as in the case of the ancient Muslim city of Medina Azahara in southern Spain. Ninety percent of this Islamic metropolis remains unexcavated.

Three miles west of the modern city of Córdoba, Spain, lies the buried city of Medina Azahara. Constructed in the tenth century, Medina Azahara was the political and cultural hub of the Islamic kingdom of al-Andalus, the Arabic name for the Iberian Peninsula (current-day Spain and Portugal). There was nothing in Europe to compare to it. It was, in the words of a current scholar of that period, "like New York versus, well, a rural village in Mexico."[1] The Islamic world, not Christian Europe, was the center of the universe. Today, even though excavations began in 1910, only about 10 percent of the buried city has been uncovered and restored. Now, the site is threatened by urban sprawl and the vagaries of government funding to preserve the ruins. Too few people know about it and care to preserve it. Yet this history, however ancient, constitutes the basis of our global political heritage. It is worth studying to gain insights about our contemporary world. How we view this history, of course, depends on our perspective.

The realist perspective looks at world history through the lens of power distribution. It sees a dynamic of two major configurations of power over the past 5,000 years: empire and equilibrium. These two configurations cycled back and forth, as empires consolidated dominant power and smaller powers resisted to reestablish equilibrium.

From the beginning of recorded history (around 3000 BCE until about 1500 CE), empires dotted the historical landscape and, in some cases, lasted for hundreds of years. But after 1500 CE, Europe, and then the world as a whole, moved toward equilibrium and the decentralized system we have today of separate and more or less equal nation-states.

The liberal perspective views this same history focusing on expanding societies and governing institutions. In the first period, from 3000 BCE to 1500 CE, human society grew from agricultural villages and sea-based trading towns to large, contiguous territorial states. After 1500 CE, the territorial states in Europe spawned an industrial revolution that subsequently drew the world closer together through exploration, commerce, and, most recently, the information revolution. Today we speak about the *global* village.

The identity perspective sees this history in terms of the evolution of ideas, how people over the years imagined themselves and others. Ethnicity, mythology, and religion defined the self-images of people in the earliest societies. Then, starting around the fifteenth century, the Renaissance, Reformation, and Enlightenment in Europe invented the modern age of national, ideological, and secular identities. Today, secular states coexist warily with religious, ethnic, and traditional cultures from other parts of the world.

Let's look briefly at this history up through the third quarter of the nineteenth century. We pick up the threads leading to World War I in the next chapter. The Parallel Timeline on page 77 offers a chronology of this history and helps you see which events the different perspectives might emphasize. Try to grasp the big picture and not simply memorize every detail.

Some of this ancient history, I realize, may seem distant and hard to absorb. But remember your family is part of this history. And history illuminates many activities we engage in today. For example, when you visit the Great Wall in China, do you know when and why it was built? History also provides context. Do you know, for example, that the Buddha and Confucius lived about the same time or that Mayan and Islamic civilizations flourished in the same era?

My daughter once asked a pretty significant question. She was ten years old and traveling in Europe for the first time. "Dad," she said, "where did Europe come from?" An innocent yet profound question! We can't study international affairs and not know the answer to that question. We need to know where Islam, the Great Wall, Hinduism, and Mayan temples came from. And don't think the answers to those questions are not relevant today. In January 2005, an American Iraqi was asked why he voted (by absentee ballot) in the elections held in Iraq that month. "I'm an Assyrian," he said. "That's now a small province in northwest Iraq." Think of it—he's from one of the oldest recorded civilizations in the world. And his part of the world, known then as Mesopotamia, is still in the center of the news. Everything changes and nothing changes, right?

The Realist View of World History

empire
a configuration of government where a hegemon consolidates power primarily through conquest.

From a realist perspective, two logics drive the course of world history: a logic of empires or domination, emphasized by the power transition school, and a logic of equilibrium or counterbalancing, emphasized by the power balancing school. Ancient history from 3000 BCE to 1500 CE is mostly about **empires** in different parts of the

Events of World History from Different Perspectives

Realist		Liberal		Identity	
Egypt and Mesopotamia	3000 BCE	Agricultural settlements	3000 BCE		
Hindu (India) and Shang (China) dynasties	1500 BCE			Hindu traditions	1500 BCE
Kingdom of Kush (Africa)	1000 BCE	Mediterranean trade	1000 BCE		
Olmec culture (Latin America)	1000 BCE				
				Buddha (Buddhism)	600 BCE
Period of warring states (China)	400 BCE			Confucius (Confucianism)	600 BCE
Peloponnesian Wars (Greece)	400 BCE			Classical Greek culture	400s–300s BCE
Alexander the Great	350 BCE				
Ch'in dynasty (China)	200 BCE			Hellenistic Greek culture	200s BCE
Roman Empire	200 BCE–500 CE				
				Jesus Christ (Christianity)	25 CE
Gupta dynasty (India)	400 CE				
Golden Age of Islam	600–1200 CE			Muhammad (Islam)	600 CE
Sui, T'ang, and Sung dynasties (China)	600–1200 CE				
		Spread of monastic orders	900–1200 CE	Holy Roman Empire (Europe)	900–1700 CE
Various African civilizations	1000 CE				
Mayan civilization (Americas)	1000 CE				
		Consolidation of territorial states in Europe	1100–1500 CE		
Yuan (Kahn) dynasty (China)	1300 CE	Asian-European trade—Silk Road	1300s CE	Magna Carta	1215 CE
Aztec and Inca empires (Americas)	1400s–1500s CE	Black Plague	1400s CE	Renaissance	1400s CE
				Reformation	1517 CE
Manchu dynasty (China)	1600s CE	Agricultural revolution	1600s–1700s CE	Cromwell and Glorious Revolution (Liberalism)	1600s CE
Japanese isolation—Tokugawa era	1600s–1800s CE	Treaty of Westphalia	1648 CE		
Thirty Years War	1618–1648 CE				
Louis XIV bid for empire	1670–1715 CE				
Colonial empires	1700–1900 CE	Treaty of Utrecht	1713 CE	Enlightenment	1700s CE
				American Revolution	1770s CE
Napoleonic Wars and empire	1792–1815 CE	Industrial revolution	1780s CE	French Revolution	1789 CE
		Congress of Vienna	1815 CE	Nationalism	1800s CE
German unification	1871 CE	Laissez-faire trade	1846 CE	Marxism	1870s CE

equilibrium

a distribution of political or economic power in which the different parts of the world interact on a more or less decentralized basis.

Spotlight on security dilemma

world that sometimes competed within a specific region, such as the Middle East, but did not interact much with one another across different regions of the world. Modern history from 1500 CE to the present is mostly about **equilibrium** or the growing interaction of separate and more or less equal states, first within Europe, and then throughout the rest of the world.

In the sections that follow, we observe the repetitive impact of the security dilemma in international affairs that realist perspectives emphasize. One city-state arms either to protect itself or to attack another city-state. Other city-states cannot be sure which motivation is paramount, and they arm too to balance power and avoid losing their independence. At times, when the other party is overwhelmingly powerful, groups bandwagon. Empires highlight the advantages of economies of scale (sharing the spoils of conquest) and consolidation or integration (exercising influence from inside rather than outside an empire) rather than balancing. Empires in Asia developed stronger centralizing features than those in Europe. Many centuries before European states did so, for example, an earlier Ch'in dynasty in the fourth century BCE conscripted soldiers, taxed rather than borrowed money to finance state affairs, monopolized property, developed extensive secret police and informant systems, and allocated administrative offices more on merit than due to bribes.[2] But notice that both of these logics of consolidation and balancing focus on material forces. Liberal and identity perspectives, which we take up subsequently, emphasize more interactive or institutional and ideological forces.

Age of Empires

History begins not with the first societies to exist but with the first societies to record their existence (which tells us something about the importance of public relations in human affairs—when you do something, record it and be sure others know about it). So we start with ancient empires in Mesopotamia, which were the first to record their existence, but we move on quickly to Asia, the Americas, and Africa, where other empires also existed but records started only later.

MESOPOTAMIA. Around 3000 BCE, a dozen or so separate cities in Mesopotamia began to record their exploits. At times, over the next 1,500 years, the most powerful ones dominated their neighbors. Around 2450 BCE Sargon established the first known empire of Akkad. The Akkadian empire linked Babylonian cities located near modern-day Baghdad and in southern Iraq with Assyrian cities located in northern Iraq and parts of contemporary Turkey and Syria. Also about the third millennium BCE, another empire, Egypt, sprouted in the Nile Valley. Pharaohs built the pyramids to grasp eternity. Later, the Ur and Babylonian empires flourished. Hammurabi of Babylon produced his famous code of laws that laid out practical guidelines such as an eye for an eye and a tooth for a tooth. But after Hammurabi, a period of equilibrium or balancing began. In this period, known as the Amarna period, the Egyptian empire came into contact and competed with empires in both Mesopotamia and Anatolia (the Hittites, in present-day Turkey). Subsequently, the Assyrian (800–700 BCE) and Persian (600–400 BCE) empires reestablished hegemony (see Map 2-1), until Rome conquered the Mediterranean region, a time marked in our memory by the marriage of Mark Anthony, the Roman general, and Cleopatra, the queen of Egypt, in the present-day Gaza Strip.

INDIA AND CHINA. By the second millennium BCE, Indian and Chinese civilizations also began to record their existence. The Aryans, an Indo-European people, invaded and settled India around 1500 BCE, bringing with them Brahmanic or Hindu religious traditions and a social structure that influenced the Indian caste system. In the sixth century BCE, Siddhartha Gautama, who came from a non-Aryan tribal clan and became known as the Buddha, founded the religion that bears his name. Buddhism challenged the Hindu caste system and flourished in the third century BCE under the Mauryan king Asoka (see Map 2-2). In 2005, Amartya Sen, the Nobel Prize–winning economist, pointed out that Buddhist councils under Asoka predated the Roman Senate in offering some of the earliest forums for democracy, in which adherents of different viewpoints argued issues.[3] But then Buddhism declined in India. Today, Hindu traditions prevail in India, although India also hosts the second largest Muslim population in the world (after Indonesia).

The Shang dynasty in China, governing a much smaller area than present-day China, emerged around 1500 BCE. It was later overthrown by the Chou dynasty, which ruled with declining effectiveness first from the western capital of Hao and then the eastern capital of Lo-yi. Confucius, who came from the lower nobility in China, propagated his teachings in the sixth and fifth centuries BCE, about the same time as the Buddha in India. Confucianism, which emphasized hierarchical relations within family and society, did much to strengthen Chinese unity but not before the Chou dynasty dissolved and, in the fourth and third centuries BCE, China went through a period of anarchy and equilibrium known as the Period of Warring States. Sun Tzu described this period in his classic study, *The Art of War*, and left rules for war and peace comparable to those of the Greek historian Thucydides, who wrote about the Peloponnesian wars in Greece.[4] Notice in the box on page 80 how this Chinese history is still relevant to contemporary policy debates. In 221 BCE, the Ch'in dynasty reunited China and built the Great Wall to defend it—which you can visit today outside Beijing—as well as a vast army of terra-cotta soldiers to honor the Emperor, which was unearthed in 1974 in the old capital in Xian. The Han dynasty followed and ruled with one interruption until 220 CE. China was divided again in the third century CE, and although it is identified with empire and the concept of the Middle Kingdom (with China as the center of civilization) throughout the rest of its history, it continued to experience periodic divisions and anarchy, most recently under western colonialism in the nineteenth century.

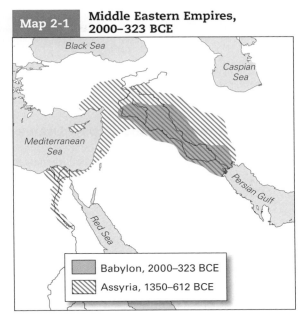

Map 2-1 Middle Eastern Empires, 2000–323 BCE

Babylon, 2000–323 BCE

Assyria, 1350–612 BCE

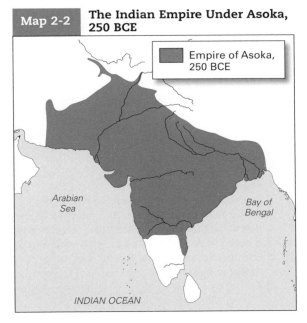

Map 2-2 The Indian Empire Under Asoka, 250 BCE

Empire of Asoka, 250 BCE

Contemporary China Expert Draws from Ancient Chinese History

On September 8, 2005, the *Wall Street Journal* ran a front-page story about a Pentagon China expert, Michael Pillsbury. If you think that some of the history covered in this chapter is irrelevant to contemporary policy debates, listen to what Mr. Pillsbury has to say about China's foreign policy. See also if you can identify the perspective behind his use of history, in this case from the Period of Warring States in China around the fourth century BCE.

> After decades spent nurturing contacts within China's military, Mr. Pillsbury has amassed mounds of Chinese-language military texts and interviewed their authors to get a grip on China's long-term military aims. His conclusion has rattled many in Washington. . . .
>
> "Beijing sees the U.S. as an inevitable foe, and is planning accordingly," warns the 60-year-old China expert. . . .
>
> Chinese writings, Mr. Pillsbury says, show a military establishment obsessed with the inevitable decline of the U.S. and China's commensurate rise. On the economic front, he cautions that Americans shouldn't be taken in by the profusion of fast-food restaurants in China or other signs that make China look like the West. Beneath the growing trade ties with the U.S., he says, runs a nationalistic fervor that could take American investors by surprise. . . .

[Mr. Pillsbury] is increasingly convinced that China's military thinkers and strategists derive much of their guidance and inspiration from China's Warring States period, an era of pre-unification strife about 2,300 years ago. This is the thesis of his latest book, *The Future of China's Ancient Strategy*, which [argues] . . . that China's history and culture posit the existence of a "hegemon"—these days, the United States—that must be defeated over time.

First, notice Pillsbury's conviction that history influences present-day military thinking in China—if you do not know that history, you cannot understand China today. Second, China's military thinking, according to Pillsbury, is fixated on the conflict between declining and rising states, the realist cycle of empire and equilibrium that China experienced during the Warring States period before the Ch'in dynasty reunited China and built the Great Wall to defend it. Third, notice how Pillsbury discounts the liberal expectation that China will be converted by wealth to become more like the West. Nationalistic fervor will prove stronger than trade ties, he warns. Finally, Pillsbury never suggests that the United States might actually be a hegemon and hence a threat to China, or that American military planning may also be based on the balance of power. According to Pillsbury, China's conviction that America is a foe derives from its historical memory or mentality, not the contemporary structure of power in Asia. Can you see why, in the end, Pillsbury analyzes China from an identity perspective?

GREEK CIVILIZATION. Around 1000 BCE, activity in the Mediterranean shifted westward. Seafaring people, such as the Phoenicians based in Carthage on the North African coast and the Philistines (from which Palestine gets its name), descended on the Levant (today's Syria, Lebanon, and Israel). Overland invasions brought Greeks from the northwest and Aramaic-speaking people from the southeast, including the Israelites, into the Mediterranean basin and the Middle East. Israelite kings, David and Solomon, worshipping the deity they knew as Yahweh, briefly established a kingdom centered in Jerusalem. By the eighth and seventh centuries BCE, some city-states in Greece, as earlier in Mesopotamia, began to dominate their neighbors. Sparta established an empire, then Athens. The two city-states united briefly to confront Persia, a new empire in the eastern Mediterranean that united the old Assyrian and Egyptian kingdoms. Classical Greek civilization flourished, but Sparta and Athens soon fell into hegemonic wars against one another. Sparta defeated Athens, and Thucydides left a realist account of these Peloponnesian Wars (431–421 BCE and 414–404 BCE) that influences our understanding of international relations to the present day.[5]

In the mid-fourth century BCE, a new Greek empire took over under the reign of Philip II of Macedon and his son, Alexander the Great. Alexander briefly united the Greek and Persian kingdoms into an empire greater than any seen before, stretching from Greece and Egypt in the west (and founding today's city of Alexandria) across present-day Iran and Afghanistan into the Indus River valley of India. Hellenistic Greek culture, named after the straits of Hellespont, the ancient dividing line between east and west now known as the Dardanelles, added elements of cosmopolitan life and art to the small city-state traditions of classical Greek culture.

ROMAN EMPIRE. On the Italian peninsula, still another empire was being born. Rome had existed as a city since the seventh century BCE. But in the third century BCE, it expanded, first conquering southern Italy and then spreading beyond the Italian peninsula. It fought two major wars, known as the Punic Wars (264–241 BCE and 218–202 BCE), against Carthage, the Phoenician city-state. The Punic Wars live on in our imagination because Hannibal, the Carthaginian general, crossed the Alps with elephants to fight the Romans. In the early second century, Rome defeated the last remnants of Alexander's empire, and the Roman Empire consolidated control and lasted for the next 800 years. As Map 2-3 shows, it extended its rule to the Rhine-Danube Rivers in Europe and across the English Channel to England, Wales, and southern Scotland. Hadrian's Wall, the northernmost outpost of Roman civilization, still stretches across the landscape of northern England. Roman rule evoked early ethnic resentments in both the Middle East (the roots of Judean nationalism) and Europe (the roots of German nationalism). And Roman colonial administrators in Judea executed the Jewish prophet Jesus of Nazareth, known to his followers as Christ, the anointed one and the son of God. Christ's life and crucifixion inspired the religion of Christianity. After persecuting Christians for several centuries, the Roman Empire in the fourth century CE under Constantine adopted Christianity as the state religion. Christianity supplanted Roman authority when the empire

Map 2-3 | **The Roman Empire, 218 BCE–116 CE**

Mediterranean Sea

☐ Roman Empire, outbreak of Second Punic War, 218 BCE

■ Roman Empire under Trajan, 116 CE

| Map 2-4 | The Islamic Empire, 632–750 CE |

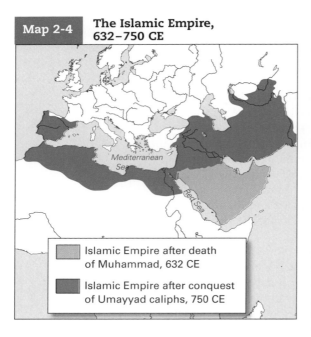

Islamic Empire after death of Muhammad, 632 CE

Islamic Empire after conquest of Umayyad caliphs, 750 CE

collapsed in the fifth century CE, and the Christian church played a major role in European politics for the next millennium through the pope in Rome, the seat of the Roman Catholic Church, and the patriarchs in Constantinople (today's Istanbul), Kiev, and then Moscow, the various centers of the Eastern Orthodox Church.

GOLDEN AGE OF ISLAM. Rome and Greece, Christianity and Judaism, became the crucibles of western civilization. But other civilizations flourished nearby, as well as far away. Arab civilization existed long before the seventh century CE but left no recorded history. The Queen of Sheba, known from biblical stories, came from the kingdom of the Sabaens in what is now Yemen. Romans and Persians attacked the kingdoms of southern Arabia but never subdued them. The Arabian peninsula escaped conquest, as did Saudi Arabia many centuries later, the only Middle Eastern country not colonized by European powers. Nomadic Arabs ruled in northern Arabia. From one such nomadic tribe, the Quraysh, came Muhammad, the founder of Islam. A pious youth turned off by materialism, he received the call in 610 in Mecca to become God's prophet. Persecuted by worldly merchants, he fled in 622 to Medina and organized there a godly society that ignited the expansion of the Islamic Empire—an empire that in conquest and culture rivaled that of Rome (see Map 2-4).

By mid-century, Islamic conquests extended across North Africa to Europe and across Mesopotamia to the Indus River valley of India. Islamic forces were finally stopped at Tours, France, in 732 and occupied Spain, or al-Andalus, for the next four hundred years. Arabs besieged Constantinople several times during this period but never conquered it. The Umayyad dynasties in Syria and later the Abbasid dynasties in Baghdad maintained Arab rule until the twelfth century, fighting back both Christian crusades from the west (1097–1100 and 1147–1149) and Mongol assaults from central Asia. In the eleventh century, the Seljuk Turks converted to Islam, and a succession of Turkish dynasties established the Ottoman Empire. Centered in Constantinople, Ottoman rulers conquered territories as far north as the outskirts of Vienna and as far east as India. This Golden Age of Islam made numerous contributions to culture and science, including algebra, advanced irrigation techniques, and the art of papermaking (possibly obtained from China) that facilitated the translation and preservation of Greek and Roman classics. Without the efforts of Islamic scholars, many of the writings of Plato, Aristotle, and others would have been lost to us forever.

ASIAN DYNASTIES. About the same time as the rise of Islam, China experienced a renaissance. Yang Chien, a leading statesman in the northern kingdom, seized the throne and reunited the country under the Sui dynasty. Known as Emperor Wen, he invaded Korea and battled Turkish invaders from central Asia. In 615, a noble family in northwest China, known as Li, temporarily allied with the Turks and overthrew the Sui dynasty. Li-Yuan became emperor and founded the T'ang dynasty (see Map 2-5). China now expanded its rule to include inner and outer Mongolia, parts of central Asia, and, briefly, Korea. The T'ang dynasty crumbled in the tenth century and was followed by the northern (960–1126) and southern (1126–1279) Sung dynasties. During the southern Sung period, China shrank under the onslaught of another empire, that of the Mongolian chief, Genghis Khan. Khan conquered territories from the Pacific to the Adriatic (Italy's eastern coast) and organized the Great Khanate to rule China under the Yuan dynasty (1280–1367). The Venetian explorer Marco Polo visited China during this period and reported on the beauty and achievements of Chinese civilization, stimulating Europe's appetite for trade with the east.

Further east, still other civilizations flourished. Japan's early recorded history describes an emperor system in the eighth century CE, centered near present-day Kyoto, heavily influenced by Chinese culture and Buddhism. When the emperor, and to a lesser extent Buddhism, declined in influence thereafter, great aristocratic families such as the Fujiwara and warriors such as Minamoto ruled the country. A *shogun* system maintained nominal unity through the puppet emperor, while *daimyos,* the lords, and *samurai* warriors divided authority and exercised real power.

In the fourth century CE, India consolidated Hindu orthodoxy under the Gupta dynasty but then divided after the sixth century into some seventy kingdoms, which competed with one another until the Turks invaded and established Muslim rule from the twelfth to seventeenth centuries.

EMPIRES IN THE AMERICAS. Mayan civilization in southern Mexico, Guatemala, and northern Honduras reached its zenith in the first millennium CE (see Map 2-6). The Maya raised stone temples, pyramids, and tombs comparable to those of ancient Egypt and developed calendars based on astronomical observations that involved sophisticated mathematics. As the Mayan civilization went into decline, the Aztecs built another empire in central Mexico, known for its magnificent capital, Tenochtitlán, and its horrific rituals of human sacrifice. Farther south, the Incas established an Andean empire that stretched from Ecuador to central Chile. They organized complex governmental structures and built roads and cities, such as Machu Picchu, in the most remote and difficult mountain retreats. Extensive mining for silver and copper resulted in the exquisite adornment of cities like Cuzco, which fascinated the Spaniards when they arrived.

Recent discoveries have illuminated even older civilizations in what is now Latin America. The Olmec culture, which flourished along the Gulf of Mexico in Veracruz and Tabasco, dates back to around 1000 BCE. A stone slab found recently in southern Veracruz bears what experts believe to be a true writing system.[6] If this discovery holds up and leads to further evidence, empires in the Western Hemisphere as old as those in the Middle East may be confirmed.

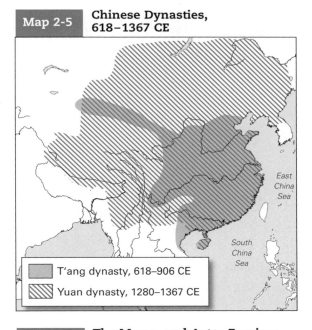

Map 2-5

Chinese Dynasties, 618–1367 CE

T'ang dynasty, 618–906 CE

Yuan dynasty, 1280–1367 CE

East China Sea

South China Sea

Map 2-6

The Mayan and Aztec Empires, 250–1521 CE

Mayan empire, 250–900 CE

Aztec empire, 1300–1521 CE

Caribbean Sea

PACIFIC OCEAN

| Map 2-7 | African Empires, 300–1400 CE |

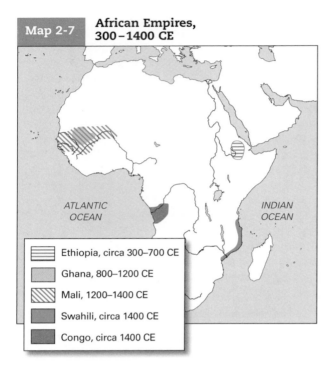

ATLANTIC OCEAN

INDIAN OCEAN

Ethiopia, circa 300–700 CE

Ghana, 800–1200 CE

Mali, 1200–1400 CE

Swahili, circa 1400 CE

Congo, circa 1400 CE

AFRICAN CIVILIZATIONS. African civilizations existed in Ghana, Mali, Congo, Ethiopia, and southeastern Africa. In the eighth century CE, the empire of Ghana spanned an area from the Saharan desert to present-day Niger and Senegal. Arabs spoke of it as the "land of gold," and Ghana traded gold with the Arabs, as well as salt and slaves. The empire of Mali succeeded Ghana in the thirteenth century and was twice as large (see Map 2-7). Its ruler is said to have had ten thousand horses in his stable. Bantu-speaking people in Nigeria spread south into the Congo and eventually across most of southern Africa. The kingdom of Congo flourished on the lower Congo river. Swahili-speaking tribes settled on the east coast of Africa and traded with seafaring peoples as far away as Indonesia. Interior kingdoms in central Africa flourished. Traces of magnificent stone buildings from the fifteenth century can be found today throughout Zimbabwe (which means "stone houses"). Ethiopia is perhaps the oldest African civilization, dating back to the kingdom of Kush, which had connections with ancient Egypt.

EUROPE IN THE EARLY MIDDLE, OR DARK, AGES.
While the Arab, Chinese, African, and American civilizations flourished after 600 CE, Rome collapsed and Europe descended into what early historians called the Dark Ages. Later historians documented a period of comparative decline and stagnation in which much of the learning and technological achievements of the ancient Greeks and Romans were lost for the time being. Germanic and other tribes, the most warlike of which were the Huns led by Attila, raided the Italian peninsula and the rest of Europe. In the sixth century, the Christian church in Rome declared its independence from Constantinople and turned to the Germanic tribes to help defend the western empire. In 800, the pope crowned the Frankish king Charlemagne, from a German tribe in today's northern France, as holy Roman emperor. Charlemagne's empire encompassed much of modern-day France and Germany and seemed for a while to be a worthy successor to Rome. But continuing raids across Europe, this time by the Vikings in the ninth and tenth centuries, and the fact that Charlemagne's empire had to be continuously divided among his heirs fragmented Europe once again. The papacy lost influence and became corrupt. Local princes and dukes seized control, claimed divinity, and invested or appointed local bishops. In 1054, the Christian world formally split into two. Orthodox Byzantium, with the patriarch in Constantinople, became the inspiration for the later Slavic and Russian civilizations; the papacy in Rome competed with emerging territorial-based kings to reconstitute a weak version of the Roman Empire in Europe, which now, because of the church's influence, became known as the Holy Roman Empire.

Around the turn of the millennium, the Roman church made a comeback. In 962, the papacy anointed another German king—Otto of Saxony, today a region in eastern Germany—as holy Roman emperor. Major reforms of the church followed, including the founding of monastic orders, the most influential of which was the Benedictine order in Cluny outside Paris. These orders fanned out across Europe, renewing faith, inspiring the Crusades, and providing essential services in the feudal society (such as loans to purchase land). In the late eleventh century, during the so-called Investiture Conflict, Pope Gregory VII took back the right of the church to select or invest local bishops and authorities. The conflict sparked a series of wars between Rome and Otto's successors, the Hohenstaufen kings—Frederick I, or Frederick Barbarossa, and his son Frederick II. The two Fredericks tried to expand the empire to incorporate the rich trading cities and provinces of Italy. The pope fought back, encouraging Italian provinces to align against the emperor under alliances such as the Lombard League of northern Italian cities. This balancing of power weakened the holy Roman emperor and devolved power to the individual German and Italian provinces and cities, which remained divided until the late nineteenth century. The Hapsburg kings, initially from Switzerland, seized the emperor's crown in the thirteenth century. They relocated to Vienna and led the Austrian dynasty that campaigned against the Protestant Reformation in the sixteenth and seventeenth centuries.

MEDIEVAL EUROPE. While small, fragmented **city leagues,** such as the Hanseatic League of German cities on the Baltic Sea, and **city-states,** such as Venice, Florence, Genoa, and Milan on the Mediterranean Sea, dominated the area of present-day Germany and Italy during the early Middle Ages, a new form of authority, the **territorial state,** emerged in France, England, the Netherlands, Spain, and Portugal.[7] Starting in 987, the Capetian kings expanded Frankish, or French, authority outward from Paris. They weakened the pope, even moving the papacy in 1309 from Rome to Avignon. The Valois kings from Burgundy succeeded the Capetians and waged a long conflict, known as the Hundred Years War (1337–1453), to expel England from the continent, where English monarchs had expanded through intermarriage and conquest. Eventually victorious, France developed a highly centralized administration that consolidated feudal authorities and asserted independence from the holy Roman emperor. England, in defeat, consolidated its domain across the English Channel. Unlike France, however, it developed a more decentralized system. In the thirteenth century, the nobility and local leaders extracted from King John the first bill of rights, the Magna Carta, and established the practice of more and more frequent assemblies of nobles and notables known as *parlers*—the precursors of the present-day Parliament—to decide affairs of state. Meanwhile, Spain and Portugal, after expelling the Muslims, opened up long-distance sea trade and began an age of exploration that led to the discovery and colonization of the New World, as well as Africa and Asia. The Dutch entered the sea trade and became the ship-building and financial center of early modern Europe. We mention more about Europe's economic expansion in Chapter 8.

The period from 1300 to 1600 witnessed both a decline and renaissance in Europe. The Black Plague in the fourteenth century wiped out a third of Europe's population. But the period of cultural innovation known as the Renaissance, which began in Italy and spread through Europe, ushered in the modern age of science, art, and political thought. Michelangelo painted the ceiling of the Sistine Chapel, and Machiavelli wrote *The Prince,* giving his name thereafter to a type of politics, Machiavellian, that epitomized realist maneuvering to benefit the interests of the sovereign.

EUROPE ASCENDS AND OTHER EMPIRES RECEDE. By 1500, Europe had begun to reemerge from its thousand-year decline following the fall of Rome. Curiously, just as it did so, several other great civilizations fell into decline. The Islamic world slipped back, although the Ottoman Empire besieged Vienna in 1529 and 1683 and played a role in Europe until the early twentieth century. China, which had built impressive

city leagues
collections of city-states united for protection or trade.

city-states
cities that are controlled by sovereign governments.

territorial states
highly centralized administrations emerging in the late tenth century CE that consolidated feudal authorities and asserted independence from the holy Roman emperor.

fleets in the fifteenth century, abandoned long-distance sea trade and succumbed in the seventeenth century for the second time to foreign rule under the Manchu Qing dynasty. Japan forbade all contact with foreign intruders (except a few Jesuit traders around Nagasaki) and isolated itself from western influence for three centuries. The Mayan, Aztec, and Inca civilizations in the Americas offered little resistance when the Spanish conquistadors arrived in the early 1500s. The African empires also disintegrated under the assault of western explorers and slave traders.

Age of Equilibrium

Thus, we turn to Europe to investigate the age of equilibrium and the rise of the contemporary system of independent states. Europe became the center of technological innovation and change after 1500, and its modern history epitomized the cycling back and forth between empire and equilibrium that the realist perspective sees as the principal dynamic of world politics. But we should not forget other great civilizations that continued to evolve—Islam, China, Japan, and those in Africa and Latin America. Today they play equally important roles in world affairs and bring experiences that differ from those of modern Europe.

REFORMATION. Beginning in the mid-fifteenth century, the Hapsburg kings Frederick III and Maximilian expanded the Holy Roman Empire to include much of Europe, other than France. In the 1500s, their successors, Charles V and later his son, Philip II, incorporated Spain and the Spanish Netherlands into the empire. Now, France was surrounded on all sides by Hapsburg rulers. Empire once again threatened to unite all of Europe.

At this very moment, however, the Catholic Church, which gave the holy Roman emperor its imprimatur, imploded. In 1517, Martin Luther, a devout monk, nailed his ninety-five theses to the church door in Wittenberg, Germany, which criticized corrupt church practices. His protest launched the religious upheaval known as the Reformation or "Protest-antism." A religious dispute to reform the church soon became a political dispute to redistribute power in Europe. Numerous princes throughout the empire as well as the French kings exploited the Lutheran or Protestant split with Rome to fight back against the Hapsburgs. Francis I of France attacked Hapsburg territories in Italy, and Protestant kings in the Netherlands, Denmark, Sweden, and northern Germany challenged Hapsburg rule across northern Europe. By the end of the sixteenth century, England under Henry VIII had withdrawn from the Catholic Church and established the Protestant Anglican Church, with the monarch as its supreme head. When the papacy rallied forces to punish England, now ruled by Henry's daughter Elizabeth I, the English fleet defeated the Spanish Armada in 1588. Where Catholic rulers had once dominated, Protestant states now consolidated their authority.

COUNTER-REFORMATION AND THE THIRTY YEARS WAR. The holy Roman emperor did not give up easily. In the first half of the seventeenth century, the Hapsburg emperor, Ferdinand II, led a counter-reformation campaign against France and the Protestant states. Religious wars, known as the Thirty Years War (1618–1648), ensued and decimated the villages and peoples of Europe. To this day, Europeans remember which towns are Catholic and which are Protestant.[8] Gustavus Adolphus of Sweden led the Protestant states, and France, although Catholic, exploited the conflict against the Hapsburgs to expand its territory and power under the French king, Louis XIII.

Cardinal de Richelieu, first minister under Louis XIII, was a leading figure in the Thirty Years War and became one of the fathers of the modern state system. Ferdinand and Protestant rulers fought about religion and the true faith, but Richelieu, although a Catholic prelate, fought only to expand the power of his sovereign and the aristocratic class to which he belonged. He appealed to what he called ***raison d'état*** (reason of state) or what later became known as the national interest. **Sovereignty** became the new watchword of the territorial state; the sovereign yielded to no other authority in matters of religion or power. The state pursued independent interests and rejected universal values, such as Catholicism or Protestantism, as a basis for managing interstate relations. Reason was beginning to supplant religion as the rationale for state power, although, as identity perspectives stress (see later discussion), Europe remained Christian, a fact that stirs debate today as the European Union considers membership for the Muslim state of Turkey.

raison d'état
the principle of national interest or what the state requires.

sovereignty
a condition under which a state yields to no other authority in matters of religion or power.

TREATY OF WESTPHALIA. The religious wars ended in 1648. The **Treaty of Westphalia** established a new order of sovereign monarchs. From this point on, individual states—not the Holy Roman Empire—ruled Europe. Negotiated over four years, the treaty came out of the first multilateral, interstate diplomatic conference of its kind, involving 145 delegates representing 55 jurisdictions. So bitter were the divisions that the Catholic delegates gathered in Münster and Protestant delegates in Osnabrück. Couriers carried proposals back and forth over the fifty kilometers separating the two towns in northwest Germany.

Treaty of Westphalia
a multiparty European treaty signed in 1648 establishing the modern international system of state sovereignty.

Two critical issues had to be resolved: religion and power. On religion, the delegates agreed to a formula already established at the Peace of Augsburg in 1555. Individual sovereigns had the right to decide the religion of their own people. Monarchs were independent in all matters of domestic jurisdiction and, in turn, recognized the equality or mutual sovereignty of other monarchs. The Protestant Netherlands, or Holland, became independent of Catholic Hapsburg rule and established the principle of statehood through recognition by other states. On power, Westphalia extracted a renunciation of imperial ambitions from the holy Roman emperor and gave individual sovereigns the right to participate in and consent to all dealings of the empire. Thereafter, some three hundred separate political entities made up the Holy Roman Empire and decided policies through electors meeting in the Imperial Diet. France and Sweden were granted the right to intervene to enforce these provisions. Both inside and outside the empire, Westphalia established the expectation that equilibrium, not empire, would govern European affairs.

LOUIS XIV. Like many peace settlements, Westphalia focused on the last war, not the next one. Everyone worried that the holy Roman emperor in Vienna might seek empire again. No one anticipated that France, a guarantor of Westphalia, would make the next bid. Building on Richelieu's legacy, Louis XIV, the Sun King, envisioned himself as a universal monarch and built a glorious palace at Versailles to symbolize the new center of Europe. In the late seventeenth century, he attacked the Low Countries, which included Hapsburg lands located in present-day Belgium but which were then part of Holland. This threat eventually forced an alliance between Holland and Great Britain, which had been naval rivals in the 1650s. (Remember, in one of these naval wars, New Amsterdam, located on present-day lower Manhattan, passed from Dutch to English hands and was renamed New York?) In 1688, under the threat from Louis XIV, England invited William of Orange, the Dutch Protestant ruler, to become, along with his wife Mary (daughter of James II, the Catholic King being deposed), king and queen of England. From the realist perspective, power dictated this alliance, although, as we note later, identity perspectives stress the convergence of English and Dutch religious identities. Britain and Holland joined Austria to save the new state system from French imperial ambitions. In 1700, the last Spanish Hapsburg king died without a direct heir. Louis XIV named his grandson Philip V to take over the Spanish throne. Philip V was also in line to become the next king of France. Uniting the dynasties, Louis saw the opportunity to dominate the entire Atlantic coastline, thus jeopardizing British and Dutch commercial interests. The War of the Spanish Succession followed and extended the conflict for another decade. It ended eventually in 1713 in another multistate European treaty, the **Treaty of Utrecht.** France was stopped, and Spain began its retreat from the stage of great powers. England, which had been absent at Westphalia because of a domestic revolution in the 1640s and 1650s under Oliver Cromwell, stepped forward to guarantee the settlement. Great Britain, formed in 1707 with the merger of England, Wales, and Scotland, went on to play a prominent role in Europe until the present day.

CLASSIC BALANCE OF POWER. The eighteenth century was one of relative equilibrium. Great Britain and France fought one another, off and on, throughout the century. Many of these wars had ramifications outside Europe. The Seven Years War (1756–1763) cost France its North American empire; known as the French and Indian War in North America, the Seven Years War also led Britain to tax the American colonies and triggered the battle cry of the American Revolution—"no taxation without representation." France later became a crucial American ally to help win American independence, among other things controlling the Chesapeake Bay as George Washington defeated Charles Cornwallis at Yorktown in 1781. Austria remained a significant power in Europe, but two other powers—Prussia and Russia—also ascended. Prussia under Frederick the Great seized Silesia, a resource-rich province in present-day Poland, and ignited a long struggle with the Hapsburg rulers in Austria for dominance of the German provinces. Russia expanded even more dramatically. In the late seventeenth and early eighteenth centuries, Peter the Great injected western technology and customs into Russia society; and the German princess, Catherine the Great, who became tsarina by marriage to Peter's grandson, later expanded the Russian empire. Russia surged toward central Asia, seizing the Crimea on the Black Sea, and moved toward the Balkans where it rolled back a declining Ottoman Empire and threatened Austrian provinces. At the end of the century, as a portent of things to come, the three eastern powers Russia, Prussia, and Austria absorbed and divided the independent kingdom of Poland, which disappeared from the map of Europe until the end of World War I.

The balance of power in the eighteenth century worked in classic fashion, with flexible alliances, periodic but limited wars, and territorial compensation. As realists see it, there was no conscious direction of the system; the system was laissez-faire, like an economic marketplace, with the outcomes unintended but determined by an "invisible hand." A balance or equilibrium resulted even though no one state deliberately sought it. Britain, it is true, acted as a kind of off-shore balancer of power. It did not seek to dominate on the continent but to prevent any other power from dominating. When Prussia and France threatened Austria in the 1740s, Britain aligned with Austria. But when Austria and France threatened the status quo in the 1750s, Britain sided with Prussia. Alliances formed and dissolved on the basis of shifts in power, not ideological

Treaty of Utrecht
a multistate European treaty established in 1713 that helped end the War of Spanish Succession and eventually signaled the rise of Great Britain.

Spotlight on
balance of power and alliances

affinities or permanent alliances. Equilibrium in Europe was accompanied by colonial competition abroad. French, British, Dutch, Spanish, and Portuguese fleets colonized much of North and South America and the coastal areas of Africa, South and Southeast Asia, and China. The industrial revolution began in England and spread to Europe. The development of military technology accelerated and began to shift material power decisively.

FRENCH REVOLUTION AND NAPOLEON. Domestic political revolutions soon refashioned the European landscape. The American Revolution of 1776 had a long-term impact, but the French Revolution in 1789 changed Europe immediately. The identity perspective sees these revolutions originating from new ideas of liberty and constitutionalism at the domestic and foreign policy levels of analysis. The liberal perspective highlights the advent of specialization and markets at the systemic process level. But the realist perspective sees these events as part of the ongoing struggle for power at both the domestic and international levels of analysis. A new kind of military dictatorship, uniting the state with the people, emerged to replace the monarchy. By 1799, Napoleon Bonaparte, a commoner and army officer, had seized absolute power in France. He crowned himself the successor to Charlemagne as holy Roman emperor, showing that temporal authority no longer needed the pope, and waged a series of wars to subjugate the rest of Europe. Empire was back. But as the realist perspective predicts, the other nations resisted. The Napoleonic Wars from 1792 to 1815 checked French expansion, and the Congress of Vienna in 1814–1815, which ended the Napoleonic Wars, restored equilibrium.

CONCERT OF EUROPE. The grandest of all international conferences up to that point, the **Congress of Vienna** shaped Europe for the next century. While Westphalia and Utrecht made only modest provisions to monitor the peace, the Vienna settlement set up the **Concert of Europe,** an elaborate system of conferences and consultations among the great powers to manage the balance of power. The four victorious powers—Britain, Russia, Prussia, and Austria—restored the French monarchy and established the **Quadruple Alliance** to prevent another revolution in France. In 1818, France joined the other four in the **Quintuple Alliance,** which assumed special rights and responsibilities to settle international disputes and, if necessary, enforce them.

According to the liberal perspective (see later discussion), the Concert of Europe was a giant step forward from the classical or laissez-faire balance of power instituted by Westphalia and Utrecht, and it played an important role in preserving the general peace in Europe over the next century. But as the realist perspective sees it, the Concert did not last very long as a working system. Active conferences dropped off after 1830, and the system failed almost from the beginning to deal with the new forces of nationalism stirring in Europe.

NATIONALISM. In the early nineteenth century, nationalism ignited independence movements both inside and outside Europe. National revolutions occurred in Spain (1821), Greece (1829), Belgium (1830), France again (1830), and other European countries. Colonial rebellions in South America (1820s) freed the Spanish colonies. **Nationalism,** while manipulated by elites, appealed to ordinary people to become part of the life of the state and to identify with a common language, culture, and history. From the nineteenth century on, we speak of the **nation-state,** a fusion of the masses and state, not just the territorial or aristocratic state.

Congress of Vienna
a major international conference (1814–1815) that shaped Europe by setting up the Concert of Europe.

Concert of Europe
a system of conferences and consultations, in the early nineteenth century, among the great powers to manage the balance of power.

Quadruple Alliance
an alliance established in 1814 by Britain, Russia, Prussia, and Austria to prevent another revolution in France.

Quintuple Alliance
an alliance established in 1818 when France joined the four nations of the Quadruple Alliance in which members assumed special rights and responsibilities to settle international disputes peacefully and, if necessary, enforce them.

nationalism
a sentiment, emerging in the 1800s, that sees nations as the core unit of identity.

nation-states
states defined by a fusion of the masses and the state, which occurred in the aftermath of the French Revolution.

causal arrow →

The realist perspective sees nationalism as an instrumental not independent force. Aristocratic elites operating from a foreign policy level of analysis used advancing technology to draft the masses into state service and created myths of nationhood to yoke them firmly to the foreign policy objectives of the state. Napoleon pioneered conscription and replaced the mercenary army with a citizen army. Military service, as historian John Keegan writes, became a *rite de passage* from boyhood to manhood and "an important cultural form in European life."[9] But notice that the state created the military culture, not the other way around. The nineteenth century, while relatively peaceful after 1815, witnessed an increasingly virulent tension between a new order of nation-states, which harnessed the power of the people to the state, and the old order of territorial or aristocratic states, which pursued the interests of aristocratic elites.

GERMAN UNIFICATION. The most decisive nationalist movements came in the second half of the nineteenth century with the unification of Germany and Italy (and, we might argue, the reunification of a divided United States through the Civil War)—all occurring in the 1860s. As realists see it, Germany and Italy, divided into autonomous provinces, city leagues, and city-states since the early days of the Holy Roman Empire, served as buffers to cushion the contest for power on the European continent. They separated the relatively new powers of eastern Europe—Russia, Prussia, and Austria—from the earlier powers of the west—Britain and France. Once this buffer was gone, there were fewer margins for error in managing the balance of power. Disputes became more intense, and competition that normally played out among the divided German and Italian provinces now spread to the Balkans where the empires of Austria and the Ottomans were crumbling. The Crimean War (1854–1856) gave an early indication of trouble ahead. Britain, France, and Austria allied to stop Russia's advance to the Black Sea. But Germany's unification seriously weakened Austria and created a big new power in central Europe that could now threaten France, Russia, and ultimately Britain.

Prussia unified Germany in the 1860s through three unilateral wars against European sovereigns. The effect was to overturn the cooperative system of the Concert of Europe. First, in 1864, Prussian forces seized Schleswig-Holstein, a province in today's northwest Germany, from Denmark. Second, in 1866, Prussia defeated Austria, its longtime rival for mastery of the German provinces, and united the German provinces without Austria, which became in 1867 the dual monarchy of Austria-Hungary. Third, the united German provinces attacked and defeated France in 1870–1871. Germany annexed Alsace-Lorraine, a chunk of French territory in the southwest, which France had taken two centuries before, and proclaimed the new German Empire from the Hall of Mirrors in Versailles. The Prussian king William I retrieved the old title of caesar—kaiser in German—used by earlier holy Roman emperors and became Kaiser Wilhelm I. France was humiliated, and the stage was set for the great European conflagrations of the twentieth century—the First and Second World Wars.

Otto von Bismarck, chancellor of Prussia, and then of the united Germany under Kaiser Wilhelm I, was the architect of German unification. In realist annals, he ranks as the master statesman and preeminent practitioner of the balance of power. He not only unified Germany through separate wars that avoided counterbalancing from the countries surrounding Germany, but he managed to reassure neighboring states for the next twenty years, until he left the chancellorship in 1890, that the new, increasingly powerful, united Germany was not a threat to their safety or interests. Had he continued in office, some believe, arguing now from an individual level of analysis—

because the cause comes from Bismarck—that Germany would have evolved very differently and Europe might have avoided the devastating world wars of the twentieth century.

Emphasizing Power over Institutions and Ideas

Realist perspectives do not ignore institutions and ideas. They simply emphasize power relative to them. Why do they believe power is so important? Writing from a realist perspective, Thomas Hobbes, the seventeenth-century English philosopher, believed that people need power for innate or psychological reasons. Hans Morgenthau, whom we met in the last chapter, also believed that people need power, not, however, for its own sake but largely to pursue other objectives. They seek more worthy goals, often different ones such as religion, glory, and freedom, but they all need power to achieve their goals. This common need for power, Morgenthau argues, makes it possible to develop a systematic study of international relations. The values (goals and identities) of states vary too dramatically to study international relations from this point of view. But since all states need power, students could study the pursuit of power and achieve a more scientific understanding of international politics.

Thus, for logically consistent reasons, realist perspectives do not make too much of the varying values, motivations, and aims of historical actors. They note that each empire or warring state has always had its own purposes for pursuing power but that what matters most in terms of outcomes is which states acquired and used power most successfully to achieve their purposes.

Listen to Paul Kennedy, a realist who wrote a best-selling book in 1987, *The Rise and Fall of the Great Powers.* Surveying the age of equilibrium in Europe after 1500, he tells us explicitly that he is not going to focus on the motives, goals, or values of countries; he's going to focus on their ships and firepower:

> There are elements in this story of "the expansion of Europe" which have been ignored . . . . The personal aspect has not been examined and yet—as in all great endeavors—it was there in abundance. . . . For a complex mixture of motives—personal gain, national glory, religious zeal, perhaps a sense of adventure—men were willing to risk everything, as indeed they did in many cases. Nor has there been [in this account] much dwelling upon the awful cruelties inflicted by these European conquerors upon their many victims in Africa, Asia, and America. If these features are hardly mentioned here, it is because many societies in their time have thrown up individuals and groups willing to dare all and do anything in order to make the world their oyster. What distinguished the captains, crews, and explorers of Europe was that they possessed the ships and the firepower with which to achieve their ambitions, and that they came from a political environment in which competition, risk, and entrepreneurship were prevalent.[10]

Remember from Chapter 1 that we cannot focus on everything. Kennedy's book is over 650 pages long. Covers everything, right? Not quite. Kennedy, like others, cannot cover everything. He has to select, emphasize, and make judgments. Notice from the quotation that for him material factors ("the ships and the firepower") do the heavy lifting of history, while ideas ("national glory, religious zeal") and values ("awful cruelties") are relatively ignored. This is a quintessential realist approach, not because realist scholars don't care about values but because values are so varied ("complex mixture of motives") and dispersed ("many societies in their time") that they matter less in determining what happens than the relative material factors and anarchic conditions ("political environment [of] competition, risk, and entrepreneurship") that all individuals and groups have to consider.

Nor do realist perspectives ignore diplomacy and institutions. Remember Kissinger, the realist scholar, named his long book (mentioned in the Introduction) *Diplomacy*. Diplomacy is bargaining and negotiating, often within common institutions, to settle disputes peacefully. The problem for Kissinger and other realists is not that negotiations and institutions are unimportant but that the problems to be negotiated are very tough. They involve conflicting goals or what, as we learned in Chapter 1, are often zero-sum situations. What one country gains, the other loses. Recall the wars in the sixteenth century between Francis I of France and Charles V of Austria. When asked once what differences existed between him and Charles to cause such wars, Francis responded, "None whatsoever. We agree perfectly. We both want control of Italy!"[11] Issues of territory and control are pretty tough problems! Kissinger quotes Bismarck's 1853 lament about the long-standing rivalry between Prussia and Austria over control of the German provinces: " 'We deprive each other of the air we need to breathe.' "[12] Realist problems don't yield easily to compromise. Territorial issues, which dominated world and European politics for so long, are classic zero-sum situations, and they continue to exist today, as Muslims' and Serbs' battling over the territory of Kosovo remind us.

Spotlight on

diplomacy and use of force

Because stakes are so antithetical, realist perspectives believe that negotiations and institutions can never succeed unless they are backed by force. The balance (or correlation as communist leaders phrased it) of forces on the ground circumscribes the effectiveness of diplomacy and the achievement of ideas such as peace; hence follows the realist refrain that countries should always seek "peace through strength." Realist accounts often criticize liberal assessments because they put too much emphasis on arms control and pursue negotiations as a substitute for rather than complement of military power. Liberal perspectives, realists argue, see force as a last resort after diplomacy fails or in some cases as a "past" resort outmoded by modern times. By contrast, realists see force as a pervasive resort. Without the will to back up one's claims with cannons, diplomacy is ineffective and negotiations become appeasement. Frederick the Great, the eighteenth-century Prussian king who seized Silesia from Austria, once phrased this axiom in memorable terms: "negotiations without arms are like music without instruments."[13] You can't get the results of agreement—the music—without the use of arms—the instruments.

Liberal Accounts of World History

Liberal perspectives interpret the realist history of empire and equilibrium very differently. They are less impressed by the cycling between empire and equilibrium than with the gradual but inexorable expansion of international interdependence among the people and societies of the world. Because liberal perspectives focus on relationships rather than power, they see more clearly the increasing volume and complexity of global interactions. These interactions have grown geometrically over time and crystallized in regularities and patterns that constitute widening domestic societies and international institutions. This broader social context constrains the balancing and use of military power. International politics may be an anarchical system, but it is also an anarchical *society,* that involves specialized and cooperative, as well as conflictual, interactions.[14]

From Villages to States

Cooperative interactions include economic exchanges, which have been going on at least since the beginning of recorded history. Sargon's Akkadian empire consolidated trade in wood from present-day Lebanon and precious metals from the mountain ranges between present-day Syria and Turkey. In the second millennia BCE, during the Amarna period, trade became an alternative to imperial expansion to broker relations among relatively equal powers.[15] Phoenicia and Rome spread shipping throughout the Mediterranean. Commerce accelerated enormously in the second millennium CE. Marco Polo later spurred trade between east and west. Social interactions between different societies also increased. The Aryans brought the caste system with them to India; the Confucian social order stabilized China after the Period of Warring States; and monastic or religious orders spread across Europe in the eleventh and twelfth centuries. Other interactions grew with commerce, such as pandemics. Ships brought the Black Plague to Europe in the fourteenth century, and western explorers brought smallpox to the New World.

Most important, liberal perspectives emphasize political interactions and the role of expanding domestic (NGOs) and international institutions (IGOs). From earliest times, societies slowly widened, albeit often through struggle. Rome coalesced in a war against Hellenistic Greece, and modern France formed out of the struggle against the papacy and Holy Roman Empire. By 1500, contiguous territorial states populated much of Europe. Consider this: at the end of the first millennium over 3,000 political entities existed just within the confines of the Holy Roman Empire (today roughly Germany and parts of Italy). By the time of the Treaty of Westphalia in 1648, that number was down to about 300. In 1815, it dropped to fewer than 40; and today, of course, Germany and Italy are not only united but gradually becoming part of a still further united entity known as the European Union. In 2008, there are fewer than 200 political units or states in the entire world. Political society and legitimacy are clearly coagulating, liberal perspectives observe. Historical processes appear to reinforce and widen economic and institutional jurisdictions, moving societies by path dependence and unintended consequences toward higher aggregations of authority. How does this happen, and why can't it happen in the future at the level of regional and international organizations, such as the EU and the UN? If the cycling between empire and equilibrium is a broad pattern, so is the steady broadening of political governance.

Spotlight on
expanding governance of society

From Anarchy to Legitimacy

Liberal perspectives point out that relationships come in greater variety than empire and equilibrium. Political units may be independent and exist in a situation of anarchy. Yet their actions need not threaten one another and may actually produce a larger harmony. The distribution of power is not the decisive factor; the distribution of legitimacy is. Legitimacy is the right or authority to use force, not just the capability of using force. It can be centralized, while capabilities remain decentralized. Some political scientists call this arrangement "negarchy," a hierarchy of legitimacy but an anarchy of capabilities.[16] This was the seminal insight of the Buddhist courts under Asoka and the Roman Senate under Julius Caesar. Oligarchic families and elites competed to make decisions, but they all accepted the central authority of republican councils in India and Rome. Merchants discovered this principle in trade. They competed with one another to acquire and sell goods, but they all respected the law of a central

Spotlight on
legitimacy

authority or treaty that did not allow them to trade at gunpoint and thus nullify the mutual gains of voluntary exchanges.

Similarly, liberal perspectives argue, political units may be interdependent or even subordinate to one another, that is, exist in a situation of hierarchy or empire, but the outcome may be not be security but insecurity. As political scientist Michael Doyle explains, the outcome under imperial rule depends on four factors: the dispositions or identities of the imperial and peripheral powers make up two factors (the identity perspective), the differences in international power between them make up a third factor (the realist perspective), and the interactions or connections among them make up a fourth (the liberal perspective). After considering all four factors, Doyle concludes that connections or interdependence, not identities or power, might play the decisive role: "transnational agents—metropolitan merchants, for example, or missionaries—often take on a role significant in shaping the particular content of each imperial rule." [17]

causal **arrow**

Thus, empire depends on the nature of authority between social units, not just the hierarchy of power. This fact accounts for why some empires in history have been aggressive and others have not. Empires should be stable, right? No one is able to challenge the central power. Yet empires never seem to be stable; hegemons do not know when to stop expanding. Louis XIV could not stop before he was defeated. Nor could Napoleon or Hitler. This momentum for expansion must have had something to do with the internal institutions of empires, not just their external monopoly of capabilities. Also, some empires survive; others do not. Why? To be sure, empires are always challenged from outside by the forces of anarchy, but the ones that succumb are usually softened up from inside by the forces of decay. Their institutions fail and, as a result, their power fails. That was the case, for example, with the Indian and Roman empires of the fifth and sixth centuries CE, both of which fell eventually to the Huns. Notice, in these cases, how institutional factors drive power factors and a domestic or individual level of analysis dominates over the systemic level of analysis.

causal **arrow**

From Modernization to Institutions

The liberal perspective emphasizes the steady march of modernization, technology, and material progress. Technical progress is largely the result of process, participation, and compromise, not the ascendance of a specific political ideology. The liberal perspective upholds the political neutrality of science, technology, commerce, expertise, and learning. Modern institutions promote such developments. They help countries overcome obstacles to cooperation by increasing information, lowering transaction costs, spurring efficiency, facilitating specialization and expertise, testing alternative policy choices, solving common problems, and enforcing agreements. [18] They encourage reciprocity and enable cooperation over time even among antagonists. [19]

Thus, as we defined the liberal perspective in Chapter 1 and as it is generally understood outside the United States and Europe, the liberal perspective refers to modernization, not westernization or democratization, and implies interactions based on procedures and rules that can be embraced by all political ideologies. Neoliberal institutional perspectives, unlike classical liberal perspectives, emphasize pragmatism over principle and institutions over ideology in thinking about how to promote cooperation and overcome conflict. The political scientist John Ikenberry, for example, writes, using a neoliberal perspective: "The possibility of an institutional settlement stems from the ability to achieve agreement on institutional arrangements even if the underlying substantive interests remain widely divergent and antagonistic." [20] Institutional agreements

Spotlight on
institutions
shaping identities

causal **arrow**

do not require converging or similar ideologies, as identity perspectives might. Instead, institutional processes accommodate diverging ideologies. From the liberal perspective, legitimacy to use power derives from procedural rules such as inclusiveness and tolerance, not from substantive ideologies such as democracy.

THE CONCERT OF EUROPE. The historian Paul Schroeder writes a liberal account of European history in the age of equilibrium—the period after 1500—that is very different from Henry Kissinger's account in *Diplomacy.* Schroeder treats the same facts as Kissinger, but chooses to emphasize different ones. Kissinger writes, "nations have pursued self-interest more frequently than high-minded principle, and have competed more than they have cooperated." [21] Notice how for Kissinger self-interest and competition (the realist emphasis) trump high-minded principle (the identity emphasis) and cooperation (the liberal emphasis). By contrast, Schroeder writes, "the history of international politics is not one of an essentially unchanging, cyclical struggle for power or one of the shifting play of the balance of power, but a history of systematic institutional change—change essentially linear, moving overall in the direction of complexity, subtlety, and capacity for order and problem-solving." [22] Note the emphasis on systematic institutional change and linear progress toward order and problem solving (the liberal emphasis), not the cyclical struggle for power (the realist emphasis) or convergence around similar aims or ideas such as democracy (the identity emphasis).

The industrial revolution, depicted here in this nineteenth-century engraving of steel works in Sheffield, England, changed many things but not the struggle for power as realist perspectives see it.

Schroeder goes on to examine European politics in terms "of the constituent rules of a practice or a civic association: the understandings, assumptions, learned skills and responses, rules, norms, procedures, etc. which agents [actors] acquire and use in pursuing their individual divergent aims within the framework of a shared practice." [23] OK, sounds like a bit of mumbo jumbo. But mark the number of words Schroeder uses that emphasize relationships or interactions. Practice, rules, and procedures suggest repetition and reciprocity. Civic association emphasizes the NGOs that figure prominently in liberal accounts. Learning denotes the feedback and path dependence of the liberal perspective. He considers other factors such as understandings, assumptions, and norms, but these cognitive factors or ideas relate primarily to procedures, not principles or ideologies. Indeed, despite "individual divergent aims" or principles, he expects countries to work together "within the framework of a shared practice." Common practice, in short, dominates divergent ideologies. And he does not mention power at all; there is no emphasis on ships and firepower, as in the case of Paul Kennedy.

How does Schroeder's institutional approach affect his interpretation of specific events? Considerably. A good example is how he treats the Vienna settlement in 1815. Realist perspectives interpret that settlement as restoring the balance-of-power system following the upheavals of the French Revolution. Schroeder is more impressed by the

Spotlight on
interactions

causal
arrow

institutional innovations adopted at Vienna, which altered the nature and outcomes of the balance of power. The eighteenth-century balance-of-power system involved long and frequent wars; the nineteenth-century system was relatively more peaceful; that was because, as Schroeder explains, "The 1815 settlement did not restore an 18th-century-type balance of power or revive 18th-century political practices; the European equilibrium established in 1815 and lasting well into the 19th century differed sharply from so-called balances of power in the 18th."[24]

Spotlight on institutions

Notice the emphasis on international institutional factors. For Schroeder, three "major institutionalized arrangements and practices" are of particular note. First, the Vienna or Concert of Europe system created more credible security guarantees than the Utrecht Treaty did. Critical to these guarantees was the practice of periodic multi-lateral conferences. Regular conferences occurred between 1815 and 1830; and, although less frequent thereafter, twenty-five more took place between 1830 and 1884. Second, the congresses of Paris in 1856 and Berlin in 1878 involved heads of state, not just foreign ministers, a very rare occurrence at that time.[25] Third, the system fenced off colonial issues from European politics. In the eighteenth century, British and French rivalries outside Europe reinforced rivalries inside Europe. Recall how the Seven Years War (1756–1763) in Europe between France and Britain (among others) was replicated in the United States by the French and Indian War and subsequently led France, which lost the Seven Years War, to revenge its defeat by supporting the American colonists against Great Britain in the colonists' war of independence. This sort of interaction between colonial and continental wars occurred less frequently in the nineteenth century. Finally, the Vienna system gave smaller or secondary powers a larger role in buffering great power conflicts. The Netherlands, Scandinavian countries, Switzerland, and the German Confederation, which reduced the number of German provinces, all served this purpose. Poland, of course, remained partitioned. But Schroeder believes the evidence is enough to show that institutional changes helped countries overcome the worst aspects of the security dilemma and expand the number of participants to include middle and small powers. This is a classic liberal interpretation of the nineteenth-century European international system.

causal *arrow*

MISPERCEPTIONS, THREAT, AND BANDWAGONING. Liberal critiques spotlight the ambiguities and flaws in the diplomacy associated with the balance of power. These flaws result from insufficient emphasis on communications, types of goals, and the existence of alternative behaviors to balancing.

Spotlight on flawed diplomacy

First, countries miscalculate or misperceive the balance of power.[26] They have insufficient or erroneous information. France in 1865 thought Austria was the dominant power in the German Confederation, not Prussia. That's why France didn't align with Austria when Prussia attacked Austria in 1866. Then, after Prussia beat Austria, France saw itself as the strongest power and pressed Prussia in 1870 to apologize for the Spanish succession affair in which Bismarck had backed a German prince to take over the Spanish throne. Even though that prince subsequently withdrew, France, feeling its superiority, demanded an apology from Bismarck. The kaiser, relaxing at a spa in Bad Ems, responded conciliatorily, but Bismarck (operating at the foreign policy level of analysis, linking and manipulating domestic and systemic process factors) doctored the telegram to make it shorter and less conciliatory. France was offended and declared war against Prussia—a war that France ultimately lost. The balance of power failed because of bad information. More open diplomacy and effective institutions might have prevented war.[27]

Second, countries react to threats, not capabilities. Threats are a function of geographic proximity, technological balances between types of weapons, and intentions.[28] While realists also emphasize geography, liberal accounts pay more attention to the strategies and intentions that influence how capabilities are deployed, not just how big they are. They argue that states align against the greater threat, not the greater power. England, for example, fought Holland in the early 1660s, even though France had attacked Holland and was clearly becoming the greater power in Europe. But Holland and Britain were both sea powers and threatened one another's trade. France was a land power, and its armies seemed less threatening. Alignment thus involves an assessment of the other country's type of power and intentions, which liberal perspectives emphasize, not just its total capabilities, which realist perspectives stress.

Third, countries have options other than balancing. They can bandwagon with the greater power, that is, cut a deal with the stronger party or pursue appeasement. Spain's 1796 alliance with France, even though France was winning on the battlefield, is an example of bandwagoning. Or they can hide, as Prussia did in 1795 when it withdrew from the coalition against France. Or they can wait and watch, engage in what is called **buckpassing,** and let other countries do the fighting. Britain followed this strategy partially throughout the Napoleonic Wars until it weighed in decisively at the final battle at Waterloo.

Some of the disagreement here between realist and liberal perspectives has to do with whether we are trying to predict behavior or outcomes. Realist perspectives point out that countries may not always behave by balancing but that balances eventually form anyway, as they did in the end against Napoleon. Liberal perspectives point out, however, that behaving differently affects the types of balances that result. The new balance of power that formed in 1815 after Napoleon was defeated was different from the previous one, and the differences contributed to the relative peace of Europe in the nineteenth century.

INDUSTRIAL REVOLUTION, TRADE, AND NONSTATE ACTORS. The liberal perspective not only emphasizes the role of international institutions in helping states overcome conflicting goals. It also emphasizes the role of nonstate institutions and how common goals, such as peace and wealth, inspire both intergovernmental and nongovernmental organizations to achieve benefits for all.

The liberal focus on wealth as a common goal spotlights trade. Trade is not a pure collective good like clean air. One party may gain more than the other and, in relative terms, lose. But the liberal emphasis on trade makes it possible to increase wealth overall and therefore, at least theoretically, increase it for each party. Trade and economics are the focus of our discussion in Part II of this book. Trade creates a multitude of nonstate actors that participate increasingly in domestic and international politics. In ancient and medieval society, landowners were stationary, and religious leaders ventured abroad mostly as emissaries of governments, as was the case for the Crusaders and the monastic orders of the eleventh and twelfth centuries. From the time of the Amarna great powers and Phoenician seafarers, however, traders moved across political boundaries without representing governments, creating what political scientists call transnational relations, or relations among nongovernmental, as opposed to governmental, authorities. Traders founded the early city-states and leagues in Europe, and river commerce helped consolidate feudal estates to form modern European states. Western exploration and colonialism extended the process to the global level.

Spotlight on intentions not capabilities

buckpassing
a free-riding strategy wherein one country allows others to fight conflicts, while it stays on the sidelines.

← **causal** *arrow*

Spotlight on common goals such as trade

Spotlight on transnational relations

British and Dutch trading companies were among the first transnational corporations in world markets.

But the big breakthrough came with the industrial revolution in the eighteenth century. Governments established functional IGOs to manage the growing interdependence in commerce, shipping, and communications. The earliest of these included various interstate river commissions in Europe, which regulated the collection of tolls, and the International Telegraphic (1865) and Universal Postal (1874) unions, which regulated early forms of global communications. Purely NGOs also proliferated, reflecting not only commercialization, but political and human rights movements in the nineteenth century. Transnational banks such as the Rothschild Bank of France conducted business abroad, and organizations to abolish the slave trade and help in natural disasters, such as the International Red Cross, operated across national borders.

Even more important, industrial and political change created more and more domestic actors with an interest in international affairs. Domestic coalitions and institutions, such as transnational bankers and corporations, became prominent in foreign affairs. The role of these domestic actors, however, varied depending on the ideology of the countries in question. The variety of ideas and ideologies that inspired individuals and societies over the millennia is emphasized by the next perspective on world history—the identity perspective.

Identity Views of World History

Identity perspectives root the explanation of historical events in the ideas and dialogues by which international actors acquire or choose their identities. Realist and liberal perspectives tend to take for granted who the actors are and focus primarily on their interests and relationships. Recall how, from realist perspectives, it is not possible to study systematically the enormous variety of values and motives by which states identify themselves and for which they pursue power. Realist perspectives prefer to focus instead on how states pursue power, which they all have to do. And recall how liberal perspectives prefer to focus on practice or procedural norms, not substantive principles and ideologies. For both realist and liberal perspectives, the identities of actors are what we call **exogenous variables,** falling outside their specific focus. By contrast, identity perspectives focus directly on who the actors are and see the use of power and institutions as a consequence of the actors' identities, not as something that is given or unchanging.

Identity views emphasize the influence of ethnicity, religion, culture, domestic ideologies, international norms, and social discourse on historical events. Let's look at these factors in selected historical outcomes.

Religion and Pope Innocent III

Family, ethnic, clan, and tribal identities dominated early societies. Mythology reinforced and, in some cases, superseded blood ties. Ancient peoples defined themselves and others through their gods. As Professor Stuart Kaufman notes, in Sumer, one of the early Mesopotamian dynasties, "the theology held that each city existed primarily to serve a particular god, with each city-state's ruler considered the delegate of his city's god." [29] Although Greek philosophy introduced a more rational basis for identity,

Spotlight on IGOs and NGOs

Spotlight on the construction of identities

exogenous variables

autonomous factors that come from outside a particular model or system and that are not explained by the system.

which influenced, among other things, public debate in the Roman Senate, religious sources of identity remained strong. Christianity dominated the late Roman Empire and medieval life in both western and eastern Europe, while religious commitments drove the rise of the Islamic Empire. Institutional rationality may have played a more important role in China, as Confucianism, a set of practical rather than spiritual rules, eventually became more important than Buddhism.

As identity perspectives see it, religious power often made the difference in European medieval conflicts between the pope and temporal or worldly authorities. Pope Innocent III, who ruled the church in the early thirteenth century, was particularly effective at using religious or ideational power. His legions could not always match the armies of the Hohenstaufen and other kings that sought to dominate the Holy Roman Empire. But he understood how to use the enormous spiritual power that the church exercised over ordinary citizens, especially through excommunication. As Rodney Hall tells us, when two princes, Philip and Otto, battled for preeminence, Innocent sided with Otto and forced the bishops attached to Philip to abandon him by threatening to depose them from their sees and excommunicate them. Then, when Philip was assassinated in 1208 and Otto ungratefully used the occasion to defy papal power, Innocent excommunicated Otto and released Otto's subjects from their oaths of allegiance to their king. Otto lost his legions not by force but by fiat. In the end, Otto could not find a single priest to marry him, let alone support him, and, as Professor Hall writes, "Otto was utterly and unequivocally deposed by 1214." His successor, Frederick II, learned a lesson and made more concessions to the pope than Philip or Otto ever did.[30]

Spotlight on religious identity

French Culture and Richelieu

When temporal authority challenged the pope again, it did so with ideas not armies. Recall from the history recounted earlier how Cardinal de Richelieu counseled King Louis XIII to ignore his religious ties to the pope and use force to expand French territory at the expense of the holy Roman emperor in Vienna. His critics saw this counsel as blasphemy. Kissinger recounts how one critic at the time asked Richelieu incredulously, "Do you believe that a secular, perishable state should outweigh religion and the Church?" Richelieu's answer was a resounding yes. "In matters of state," he observed, "he who has the power often has the right, and he who is weak can only with difficulty keep from being wrong in the opinion of the majority of the world."[31] Richelieu was saying that ideas and identities in Europe were changing. The state identified in terms of religion was giving way to the state defined in terms of power. This is the identity of states, which realist perspectives take for granted. But identity perspectives are concerned with how identities emerge in the first place and how they might change again in the future.

Spotlight on secular identity

England and Domestic Ideologies

From an identity perspective, not all states are alike. Their identities change, and domestic factors play a role. The example of England in the seventeenth century is instructive. Just at the moment that Richelieu exalted the power of his king, English noblemen and commoners cut off the head of their king. Under Oliver Cromwell, English rebels beheaded Charles I, but Stuart kings, Charles II and James II, restored royal rule in the 1660s. Nevertheless, English Protestants and the Anglican Church of

England, which had broken with the pope already under Henry VIII in the sixteenth century, continued to oppose the Catholic Stuart kings. In 1688, they finally prevailed in Parliament and brought the Protestant leader from Holland, William of Orange, to the English throne as William III.

Now, according to the logic of the identity perspective, this change of English domestic identity from Catholic to Protestant had the decisive impact on English foreign policy behavior during this period. Remember that at the same time Louis XIV, the French Catholic king, was making a bid for European empire. According to realist logic, England and other states should have balanced against France. Instead, England fought Holland in the early stages of French aggression (1660s and 1670s) because, liberal accounts say, they saw one another as the greater threat even though France was the greater power. But identity perspectives point to still other factors that eventually caused England to balance against France—a change in domestic religious identity that occurred in 1688 when the Protestant king William of Orange took the English throne. As Paul Schroeder points out,

> had not William III become king of England . . . England would have never balanced against France. The legitimate Stuart King James II whom William overthrew depended on Louis to support and subsidize him in his religious-political struggle with Parliament and the Church of England.[32]

So a change in England's ruling coalition from Catholic to Protestant was necessary before England could oppose France, a Catholic country, and make the balance of power work. Relative power was not the decisive factor; relative religious identity was. If we emphasize the parliamentary or institutional struggle going on inside England, as Schroeder does, the explanation is a liberal one from the domestic level of analysis. If we emphasize the ideological struggle between Protestants and Catholics, the explanation is an identity one, also from the domestic level of analysis. The difference depends on whether we judge institutional processes or ideological convictions to be more important.

Identity and Westphalia

When the state emerged in Europe at Westphalia in 1648, monarchs identified with one another as Christians, even as they separated into distinctly Protestant and Catholic states. They defended one another against both higher authorities—Rome—and lower authorities—the feudal aristocracy—through the doctrine of mutual sovereignty. Neorealist perspectives, as we noted earlier, say that the monarchs pursued independent interests and the balance of power resulted from unintended consequences. But classical realists and identity perspectives emphasize that the monarchs also shared a convergent or collective identity. They operated under a set of common Christian beliefs, which they took for granted.

Thus, as Morgenthau, a classical realist, observes, from 1648 to the French Revolution of 1789, "the princes and their advisors . . . referred as a matter of course to the 'republic of Europe,' 'the community of Christian princes,' or 'the political system of Europe.' "[33] This sense of community did not prevent war. Smaller, localized wars were more frequent in the eighteenth than the nineteenth century. But the perception of community constrained widespread war and avoided another bloody marathon like the Thirty Years War. As social constructivists argue, there are different types of anarchy, some more violent than others. "Anarchy is what states make of it."

causal *arrow*

Spotlight on relative identities

Spotlight on shared identities

At the Congress of Vienna in 1815, Tsar Alexander of Russia sought to reconstruct the Christian community of Westphalia. He proposed the Holy Alliance to go along with the realist Quadruple and Quintuple Alliances (see earlier discussion). The **Holy Alliance** proclaimed the adherence of all rulers to the principles of Christianity, with God as the actual sovereign of the world. The tsar wanted Christian ideals to inform all institutional activity and use of power by the Concert of Europe. In the end, only the most conservative monarchs of Prussia, Russia, and Austria signed on to the Holy Alliance.

Holy Alliance
an alliance established in 1815 that proclaimed the adherence of all rulers to the principles of Christianity, with God as the actual sovereign of the world.

Norms and the Concert of Europe

The French Revolution injected a large transfusion of ideas into European politics. It forced European statesmen to make their compact more explicit. They did so through the conference system established at the Congress of Vienna, and that system helped avoid general war for the rest of the century. Liberal scholars such as Schroeder emphasize this institutionalization of the system and give it high marks, at least compared to the eighteenth century. But identity perspectives see ideas as being more important. Some emphasize the social construction of shared identities and norms that governed diplomacy and the use of force after Vienna, not just the common institutions. Others emphasize the role of relative or diverging national ideologies unleashed by the French Revolution. Underneath the structure of common norms and institutions, according to more agent-oriented constructivists, competitive nationalisms weakened the sense of European community and in the twentieth century blew it wide open.

According to political scientist Martha Finnemore, the Concert system involved five relative changes in the norms affecting the balance-of-power system. First, it established the normative expectation that states would resolve problems through consultation and negotiation, not the use of force. Second, it placed new emphasis on expectations of association and international society that created a balance of duties and

Spotlight on
common norms

The statesmen of Europe meeting in Vienna in 1815 established an international conference system, the kind of repeated meetings that liberal perspectives hope may someday replace the balance of power.

rights to go along with the balance of power. Third, it institutionalized face-to-face personal meetings, which enabled for the first time in international diplomacy an ongoing social discourse. Fourth, it "normatively devalued war as a tool of foreign policy." And fifth, it identified domestic revolution as the principal threat to international solidarity. The Concert aimed to prevent at all costs another revolution like that in France that elevated ideological disputes over common purposes.[34] Most of the new norms were procedural, although the last one involved an ideological preference for conservative regimes. According to Finnemore, these norms account for outcomes better than institutional roles or the balance of power.

Political scientists John Owen and Mark Haas emphasize the ideological or identity struggle that emerged in Europe in the nineteenth century.[35] This struggle between absolute and constitutional monarchies went on inside countries at the domestic and foreign policy levels (for example, the liberal Whigs and conservative Tories in England) as well as between countries at the systemic process and structural levels (for example, constitutional Britain and France versus the autocratic Holy Alliance powers). Absolute monarchies exercised unrestrained power, while constitutional monarchies respected an increasing measure of domestic law and custom. Britain, which was the most advanced constitutional monarchy at the time, found itself increasingly opposed to Concert interventions. When liberal revolutions broke out after 1820 in Spain, Portugal, Naples (Italy), Piedmont (Italy), and Greece, Britain could not cooperate with absolute monarchies to suppress these revolutions. It ceased to participate in the Concert system and became an observer only. In 1826, Britain actually acted to oppose the norms of the Concert. It intervened unilaterally in Portugal not to suppress but to defend a constitutional monarchy. And by 1830 France joined Britain in supporting Belgium's liberal revolution from the Dutch crown. Outcomes are explained more in terms of converging and diverging identities than norms held in common by all.

Spotlight on diverging identities

International Law and Liberal Constitutionalism

As the nineteenth century wore on, Christian beliefs faded but international law and liberal constitutional ideas flourished. States increasingly accepted more legal obligations toward one another. A rudimentary body of international law took shape, codified earlier by, among others, Hugo Grotius, the Dutch seventeenth-century jurist, in his classic work *On the Law of War and Peace* and Eméric Vattel, the Swiss eighteenth-century legal scholar, in *The Law of Nations*. Between 1581 and 1864, as Morgenthau reports, states concluded some 291 international agreements to protect the wounded and innocent in war. The Geneva Convention of 1864 became the basis of Hague Conventions in 1906 and an expanded Geneva Convention of 1949, which regulate conduct in war to the present day and are points of issue in the contemporary debate on the handling of prisoners in the conflict with terrorism.

Did liberal constitutional ideas in democratizing states drive this development of international law, or did international law gradually shape a consensus on basic human rights and democracy? You say both, and certainly you are right. But which was more important overall or in any given situation in time? Identity perspectives see ideas or shared beliefs (such as Christianity in the classic balance of power) creating the basis of procedures and law, whereas liberal perspectives see procedures and law (such as the conventions to protect the wounded) gradually altering ideas and identities. Again, it is not a question of one perspective ignoring the other but of which key variable emphasized by each perspective causes the other.

causal arrow

Sometimes scholars point to a different understanding of law in Europe and the United States. According to Professor Jed Rubenstein,

> Europeans have embraced international constitutionalism, according to which the whole point of constitutional law is to check democracy. For Americans, constitutional law cannot merely check democracy. It must answer to democracy—have its source and basis in a democratic constitutional politics and always, somehow, be part of politics, even though it [politics] can invalidate the outcomes of the democratic process at any given moment.[36]

Can you see that the difference between these two understandings of international law depends on the direction the causal arrow runs from law to democracy or from process to ideas? For the European view, law must be inclusive of all cultures and check democratic as well as nondemocratic states. The causal arrow runs from law to democracy. Thus, when the United States acts outside the law of the United Nations, which is the most inclusive and therefore legitimate institution in contemporary world affairs, it breaks the law. For the American view, democratic politics legitimates law. Nondemocratic states cannot make legitimate law. The causal arrow runs from democratic ideas to law. The danger is that democratic politics may always bring nondemocratic groups to power that then break the law, as the elections of Hamas did recently in the Palestinian community. Or, just as bad, one democratic country, such as the United States, may decide that it alone makes the law, as some believe it did by invading Iraq. Many disagreements in international affairs lie behind these subtle distinctions in the causal relationship of variables, which is why we work so hard on understanding and using alternative perspectives in this book.

causal arrow

Bismarck and German Identity

By the last half of the nineteenth century, domestic ideologies or identities were increasingly at war with the Concert's procedural norms. Europe fragmented into more liberal states—Britain and France—and more conservative states—Austria, Prussia, and Russia. Each type of state feared a revolution that might put the other ideology in power. They feared that, if other states adopted the opposing ideology, the position of their ideology in the world would be weakened and the ideology of the other states would be strengthened. The opposing ideology might come to be seen as "the wave of the future." Thus, a kind of ideological war increasingly accompanied European balance-of-power politics. Would common norms of the Concert of Europe or competing liberal and conservative political ideologies win out?

The test came, some believe, with the unification of Germany. Did Bismarck act within the institutional constraints of the Concert system, or did he shatter that system for good? From the first point of view, Bismarck united Germany without a continental war, something that would not have been possible in the eighteenth century. So the Concert's institutions must have constrained Bismarck's behavior. This is a liberal argument. From the second point of view, Bismarck attacked and defeated fellow monarchies: Denmark in 1864, Austria in 1866, and France in 1870–1871. He went on to establish the principle not of sovereign solidarity but of "my sovereign over all others." For the sake of nationalism, he destroyed the Concert system. This is an identity conclusion.

causal arrow

Let's end this discussion of identity perspectives with a conversation Bismarck had in the 1850s with one of his Prussian mentors. The conversation is a classic example of how identities change in the process of social discourse and reveals the tension in nineteenth-century Europe between nationalist identities and the collective sentiments of the Concert of Europe.[37]

Recall that Bismarck was ready to use any means to unite the German Confederation under Prussian rule. Austria was a fellow German and conservative monarchy under the Concert of Europe, but Austria was also Prussia's principal rival in the German Confederation. Bismarck wrote to his mentor Leopold von Gerlach that "present-day Austria cannot be our friend" and suggested an alliance with France in order to gain leverage over Austria. France was led by Napoleon III, a nephew of the great Bonaparte. Napoleon III had assisted revolution in Italy and was considered by many to be a romantic and hardly a dependable ally to preserve a conservative Europe. So Bismarck's desire to align with France did not please von Gerlach. What did Prussia have in common with France? Nothing, von Gerlach told Bismarck, "How can a man of your intelligence sacrifice his principles to such an individual as Napoleon?" Bismarck countered with the mantra of the new nationalism:

Spotlight on discourse

> France interests me only insofar as it affects the situation of my country. . . . as things stand, France, irrespective of the accident who leads it, is for me an unavoidable pawn on the chessboard of diplomacy, where I have no other duty than to serve *my* king and *my* country [Bismarck's emphasis]. I cannot reconcile personal sympathies and antipathies toward foreign powers with my sense of duty in foreign affairs; indeed I see in them the embryo of disloyalty toward the Sovereign and the country I serve.

Von Gerlach wanted to preserve the Christian, anti-revolutionary Europe of the Concert system. Bismarck wanted to unify Germany, and as he put it, *my* king and *my* country come before Europe. He would serve that king and country, even if it meant attacking another conservative state and colluding with an otherwise archrival revolutionary one. Bismarck was putting sovereignty above German culture, just as de Richelieu had put culture above religion. Bismarck ends the conversation by telling his old mentor that he is prepared to discuss practical issues but not ones of right or wrong.

> I know that you will reply that fact and right cannot be separated, that a properly conceived Prussian policy requires chastity in foreign affairs [no alignment with revolutionary France] even from the point of view of utility [calculation of my sovereign's interest]. I am prepared to discuss the point of utility; but if you pose antimonies between right and revolution; Christianity and infidelity; God and the Devil; I can argue no longer and can merely say, "I am not of your opinion and you judge in me what is not yours to judge."

Bismarck had had enough of European sentimentalities. He would focus on what was useful, not what was right. The day of "my country right or wrong" had arrived.

Today we would disapprove of both Bismarck's nationalism and von Gerlach's conservatism. But that is not the point. The story illustrates how identities change through discourse and then, in turn, affect behavior. From this perspective, identities account for the subsequent fragmentation of Europe. Germany, and other countries, went on to embrace an extreme nationalism that plunged Europe into wars in the twentieth century that were far worse than the Thirty Years War.

Critical Theory Views of World History

Critical theory perspectives view world history from a contrarian point of view. For them, all history is an exercise of power, whether material (power), institutional (dependence), or rhetorical (ideas). The perspectives that scholars and policymakers throw up obscure rather than illuminate this power; they hide the marginalization of women in history, the oppression of the working class, and the structural imperialism that divides the world into core (rich) and peripheral (poor) parts. Let's take a look at some reflections on this history from feminist, Marxist, and world system perspectives.

Feminist Views of State Construction

Professor Ann Tickner is a leading feminist scholar who has worked to open up the international affairs discourse to critical perspectives. Listen to her critique of the evolution of the European state system:

> Since the beginning of the state system, the national security functions of states have been deeded to us through gendered images that privilege masculinity.
>
> The Western state system began in seventeenth-century Europe. As described by Charles Tilly [see endnote 7 for this chapter], the modern state was born through war; leaders of nation states consolidated their power through the coercive extraction of resources and the conquest of ever-larger territories. Success in war continued to be the imperative for state survival and the building of state apparatus. Throughout the period of state building in the west, nationalist movements have used gendered imagery that exhorts masculine heroes to fight for the establishment and defense of the mother country. The collective identity of citizens in most states depends heavily on telling stories about, and celebration of, wars of independence or national liberation and other great victories in battle. National anthems are frequently war songs, just as holidays are celebrated with military parades and uniforms that recall great feats in past conflicts. These collective historical memories are very important for the way in which individuals define themselves as citizens as well as for the way in which states command support for their policies, particularly foreign policies. Rarely, however, do they include experiences of women or female heroes.[38]

Spotlight on
feminism

Tickner is taking aim not just at power struggles but at the deep-seated imagery and institutions, especially cultural institutions, that structure and dominate our understanding of power and the role of the masculine figure in this understanding. The privileged masculine view subjugates not only women but also nonwestern cultures. Tickner, not being a deconstructivist, offers numerous suggestions to overcome this situation. She believes women bring very different qualities to the foreign policy enterprise and that once "women occupy half, or nearly half, the positions at all levels of foreign and military policy-making," their contributions as "mediators and care givers" will become as valued as the citizen-warrior images espoused by men.[39]

Marxist Critique of Industrialization

Karl Marx focuses his radical critique of international relations on the plight of the industrial masses uprooted by the industrial revolution. Industrialization or **capitalism,** he argues, distributed wealth unevenly, concentrating economic and social power in the hands of bankers and corporations (bourgeoisie) and exploiting the labor of workers and farmers (proletariat). Marx believes the forces driving this exploitation are buried deep in the structure of history. No single point of emancipation is possible. The salvation of workers, however, lies in the fact that history is on their side. The same powerful material forces driving capitalism will one day drive the emancipation of workers. Exploitation will gradually raise the consciousness of workers and cause them to unite to match big corporations and the state apparatus they control. The struggle will begin in industrialized countries and spread across the international sys-

capitalism
a system that concentrates economic and social power in the hands of bankers and corporations (bourgeoisie), exploiting the labor of workers and farmers (proletariat).

tem. The capitalist need for markets will bring industrial countries into conflict with one another and, through colonialism and imperialism, carry their struggle to the developing world. In response, working classes will unite across the international system, and eventually external resistance along with internal contradictions will do capitalism in. The world capitalist system will implode, leaving in its wake the united masses of working people who will do away with the superstructure of state and interstate institutions constructed by capitalism and refashion the world on communist principles of global justice and equality.

The struggle in actuality proved to be long and extremely difficult. Marxists reasoned that either history was acting too slowly or that some other powerful forces were abetting capitalism. Lenin developed the idea of the vanguard of the proletariat to expedite history. Antonio Gramsci, an Italian Marxist imprisoned by the fascists in the 1920s, developed the idea of the hegemonic social order to show that the bourgeois grip on the working classes was not only material but ideological. According to Gramsci, the state included not only the bureaucracy but "the church, the educational system, the press, all the institutions which helped create in people certain modes of behavior and expectations consistent with the hegemonic social order" or capitalism.[40] This hegemonic social order reinforced the capitalist industrial order and made revolution very difficult without seismic upheavals. Lenin's and Gramsci's ideas fed into the titanic struggle that ensued in the twentieth century among liberalism (bourgeoisie-ism), communism, and fascism.

World Systems Theories

No one could see at the end of the nineteenth century that Marx would prove to be wrong. But the critique of exploitation he advanced acquired an enduring appeal, especially among the poorest peoples of the developing world. Colonization in the nineteenth century and then the long road to independence in the twentieth century left an agonizing trail of tears and trauma, which is still ongoing. **World systems** theories, an updating of Marxism, stepped in to explain how colonialism reinforced capitalism and enabled capitalism to survive by exploiting the peripheral countries of the world.

Professor Immanuel Wallerstein tells the story of how exploitation evolved from feudal times to modern times:

> [I]n the late Middle Ages, [m]ost of Europe was feudal, that is, consisted of relatively small, relatively self-sufficient economic nodules based on a form of exploitation which involved the relatively direct appropriation of the small agricultural surplus produced within a manorial economy by a small class of nobility. . . . what Europe was to develop and sustain now was a new form of surplus appropriation, a capitalist world economy. It was to be based not on direct appropriation of agricultural surplus in the form either of tribute (as had been the case of world-empires) or of feudal rents (as had been the case of European feudalism). Instead what would develop now is the appropriation of a surplus which was based on more efficient and expanded productivity (first in agriculture and later in industry) by means of a world market mechanism with the "artificial" (that is, nonmarket) assist of state machineries, none of which controlled the world market in its entirety. . . . The territorial expansion of Europe hence was theoretically a key prerequisite to a solution for the "crisis of feudalism."[41]

For Wallerstein, growth generates surpluses that one class or group of countries then appropriates unequally from the other. Feudal lords extracted pre-industrial sur-

world systems
theories (updating Marxism) that explain how colonialism reinforced capitalism and enabled capitalism to survive by exploiting the peripheral countries of the world.

pluses from peasants. Capitalist or core states now extract this surplus from poor or peripheral countries. State institutions and particularly the decentralized state system or anarchy serve this process of exploitation. They provide the deep structural forces keeping the system at work because no one state controls the process and world socialist government is impossible. In short, international politics, as the three perspectives outlined in this book see it, is not at all an objective world that we can know by hypothesizing and testing but a subjective instrument of deep-seated social forces that exploit one another. According to Wallerstein, "exploitation and the refusal to accept exploitation as either inevitable or just constitute the continuing antimony of the modern era, joined together in a dialectic which has far from reached its climax. . . ."[42]

Summary

History, we could say, contains too many facts. We can't know all or even most of them. We have to select, and that selection depends on our perspectives. Realist perspectives track the ebb and flow of power and conclude that history is mostly a cycle of empires and warring states. From ancient Mesopotamian empires to the Greek, Roman, Islamic, and now western empires, other states fight back and eventually restore equilibrium. Liberal perspectives see a progressive, not a cyclical, trend in history. This trend moves in the direction of expanding societies and governance. From subsistence villages in ancient empires to the Concert of Europe to the European Union and now a globalized world, technology promotes growing interdependence and the capacity to solve problems that benefit the needs of all. Identity perspectives survey the march of ideas through history and see either a growing consensus on international law, human rights, and progressive governance or a continuing competition of alternative ideological solutions for the needs of human society. From mythology to religion to nationalism and political ideologies, the world constructs and contests alternative social images and political futures. Critical theories deny that we can abstract any of these forces from history. History is a gigantic fly trap in which we are all stuck. The three perspectives are inextricably a part of their specific times and places. If anything, they disguise the larger social system in which they are embedded. Anarchy is a product of capitalism.

Key Concepts

buckpassing 97	equilibrium 78	*raison d'état* 87
capitalism 105	exogenous variables 98	sovereignty 87
city leagues 85	Holy Alliance 101	territorial states 85
city-states 85	nationalism 89	Treaty of Utrecht 88
Concert of Europe 89	nation-states 89	Treaty of Westphalia 87
Congress of Vienna 89	Quadruple Alliance 89	world systems 106
empires 76	Quintuple Alliance 89	

Study Questions

1. Did history begin in Mesopotamia or just recorded history?

2. What are the parallels between the Peloponnesian Wars in Greece and the Period of Warring States in China?

3. What are the parallels between the Greek, Roman, and Islamic Empires?

4. Would the liberal or realist perspective emphasize the crucial role of the Reformation in European development?

5. What aspects of the Concert of Europe would the realist, liberal, and identity perspectives emphasize?

3

World War I
World on Fire

W orld War I was a catastrophe. Over 15 million people died. The world had not experienced this level of butchery at least since the Thirty Years War. How did such a disaster occur? We still do not know; historians and scholars disagree. Undoubtedly there were many causes. Perhaps it was a "perfect storm," with multiple causes coming together at the same time. But which causes were more important? That, we will see, is a matter of perspective.

Europe in 1914

On June 28, 1914, the heir to the Austrian throne, Archduke Franz Ferdinand, was assassinated on a visit to Sarajevo in Bosnia-Herzegovina, then provinces of Austria. This incident touched off World War I. But if you think history has only one outcome, consider the tragic comedy of the assassination itself. A bomb-wielding Serbian nationalist agent had attempted earlier that morning to kill the archduke. The attempt failed, but several people were wounded, including an army officer in the car trailing the archduke. The archduke went on to City Hall where he was welcomed and then later to visit the wounded officer in the hospital. His driver made a wrong turn and stopped the vehicle in front of a shopping area. There, by coincidence,

Kaiser Wilhelm II (left) is accompanied by Winston Churchill on a review of German troops in this photograph from 1909. Why did Great Britain and Germany fail to align and perhaps avoid World War I—because of naval and colonial competition (the realist perspective), inept diplomacy (the liberal perspective), or diverging liberal and autocratic political systems (the identity perspective)?

another of seven agents involved in the plot was standing. This agent stepped forward and this time succeeded in killing the archduke.

Austria considered Serbia responsible for the attack and had to retaliate. The next month brought the world, step by step, closer to war. Now imagine this scene. On the morning of July 28, 1914, Austria-Hungary declared war on Serbia. But before war actually began and before Russia, Germany, Britain, and France joined the hostilities, the monarchs of Germany and Russia exchanged frantic telegrams. The two monarchs were cousins. Kaiser Wilhelm II of Germany was the son of Victoria Adelaide Mary Louise, the first child and daughter of Queen Victoria of Great Britain. Victoria Adelaide had married Prince Frederick, the son of Kaiser Wilhelm I. The second daughter of Queen Victoria, Alice, had married the German duke of Hesse-Darmstadt. Their daughter, Alix, went on to marry Nicholas II, the tsar of Russia in 1914. (She became the famous tsarina who had a hemophiliac son, befriended the mad monk Rasputin, and was subsequently killed with Nicholas and her five children by Bolshevik executioners in 1918.) So by marriage, Tsar Nicholas and Kaiser Wilhelm, known to each other as Nicky and Willy, were cousins. Their frantic exchanges became known as the "Willy-Nicky telegrams." George V, the king of England in 1914 and another grandson of Queen Victoria, was also a cousin. Now all these family members were about to march off to war with one another.

Russia had vital interests at stake in Serbia and had pledged to come to its aid in the event of war, so Nicholas II was under great pressure to mobilize Russian forces to support Serbia. His last chance was to get Germany, an ally of Austria, to pull Austria back from its declaration of war against Serbia. On July 29, he telegraphed Willy, "An ignoble war has been declared on a weak country. . . . I beg you in the name of our old friendship to do what you can to stop your allies from going too far." In reply, Willy warned his cousin that "military measures on the part of Russia, which would be looked upon by Austria as threatening, would precipitate a calamity. . . ." For three days, Willy and Nicky talked past one another—in English, which was their common language—and on August 1 the world plunged into the abyss of total war.[1]

Could the cousins have changed the course of history even if they had wanted to? Many students of history would say no. Applying levels of analysis tools, they would argue that systemic and domestic forces overrode individual influences. Germany felt encircled and devised a war strategy in 1913 to break out before Russia became too powerful. In addition, monarchs no longer had the absolutist power of Louis XIV or Frederick the Great. Kaiser Wilhelm was not really in full control of his military. But when, then, did events veer out of control? Here the three principal perspectives on international affairs offer different answers. Let's summarize the answers and then explore them in more detail.

Realist perspectives argue that the crucial event was the unification of Germany in 1871. German unification created a new power in the heart of Europe that had a larger population and, in short order, a more powerful economy than any other European power. Such a central power inevitably threatened its neighbors. So, these neighbors in response allied against Germany. Now surrounded by enemies, Germany felt even more threatened.

Spotlight on security dilemma

Notice here the security dilemma at work. How could Germany be sure that its neighbors intended only to defend themselves, and how could its neighbors be sure that Germany would not use its dominance to attack them? No country was being particularly aggressive. The problem, as realist perspectives see it, "was Germany's growing economic and military power, not its aggressive behavior."[2]

Ultimately, the problem could be resolved only by reducing German power, which the victors attempted to do after World War I, or integrating German power into western Europe and then into the whole of Europe, which was done after World War II and the Cold War. History, realist perspectives argue, bears out the fact that a free-standing Germany in the center of the European balance of power is destabilizing. Europe is stable today only because a united and once again powerful Germany is now part of a new supranational actor known as the European Union.

Liberal perspectives see it differently. It was not a shift of power due to German unification that made countries insecure; rather, it was the lack of adequate institutions and diplomacy to make commitments openly and to develop information about who was complying with those commitments and who was not. It was, in short, the secrecy and manipulation of European diplomacy from the late nineteenth century on that created the uncertainty, not the situation of unbalanced power driven by the security dilemma. Notice here the problems of lack of information, miscommunications, and lack of institutions to enforce compliance that liberal perspectives emphasize. Interestingly, European diplomacy and institutions failed just as powerful new forces of economic and political interdependence emerged that could have overcome distrust. Industrialization was creating new linkages among banks and corporations that opposed war. International institutions were being set up to regulate trade, settle political disputes, and reduce armaments. The Hague Conferences, started in 1899, might have headed off World War I if their potential had been properly recognized. When the war ended, liberal perspectives proposed an entirely new system of collective security to manage international military relations. The League of Nations was their hope to replace the balance of power.

Identity perspectives focus on yet another primary force leading to World War I—that of shared and competitive identities. Nationalism, ignited by the French Revolution, grew out of different cultures and, in its most virulent form, was associated with different races. Different cultures and races struggled to survive in world politics, much as different species struggled to survive in the natural world. Social Darwinism, drawn from Charles Darwin's new theory of natural evolution, became the shared mind-set among European nations and drove them apart. It constructed a particularly virulent form of anarchy, which eventually proved a stronger force than peace movements, the Hague Conferences, and international trade and investment that drove nations together. European countries raced off into the inferno of World War I eager to prove that their culture was the superior one. Notice here how ideas, which identity perspectives emphasize, shaped conflicting identities that, in turn, generated military competition and overrode the cooperative opportunities offered by common institutions and trade.

Let's take a further look at these three explanations of World War I and then assess their relative validity. As we go along, we will also take note in matrix tables of explanations from each perspective at different levels of analysis. The Parallel Timeline on page 112 provides a chronology of the historical events. Not only can it help you remember the main events, but it can also help you sort them out in terms of which perspective might emphasize them. Remember that historical events always involve all three principal causes of international behavior—ideas, institutions, and power. But realist perspectives highlight events that suggest power struggles, liberal perspectives highlight developments that increase interdependence, and identity perspectives highlight events associated with new ideas.

If you still doubt that this history has much relevance for today, take a look at the

Spotlight on secret diplomacy

Spotlight on distribution of identities

causal arrow

Parallel Timeline

Events Leading to World War I from Different Perspectives

Realist		Liberal		Identity	
				Nationalism	1800s
		Prussian Zollverein (economic customs union)	1830s	Liberal nationalism in Britain, France, and United States	1800s
German unification by war	1864–1871	Demise of Concert of Europe	1860s–1870s	Militant nationalism in Germany	1860s
		Three Emperors' League	1873	Marxist socialism	1870s
Germany-Austria/Hungary secret alliance	1879	Berlin Conference	1878		
German-Italian alliance, creating Triple Alliance	1882	German-Russian Reassurance Treaty	1887		
Franco-Russian alliance	1894	Krüger telegram	1895	Social Darwinism	1890s
German-British naval rivalry	1900s	Hague Conferences	1899 and 1907	Cult of the offensive	1900
French-British Entente Cordiale	1904				
Russo-Japanese War	1905				
Triple Entente	1907	Moroccan Crises	1905 and 1911		
		Balkan crises	1908–1909 and 1912–1913		
Schlieffen Plan	1913				
German naval program completed	1914	"Blank check" of July 5	1914		

"Using the Perspectives" box on page 113. Notice the many similarities between the world before 1914 and the world today. There are, of course, many differences as well; the existence of nuclear weapons is but one of them. So, we know that history never repeats itself exactly. But we also know that we cannot know what is the same or what is different unless we know the past.

Realist Explanations

From a systemic structural level of analysis, Germany's unification in 1871 significantly altered the balance of power in Europe. Recall that Germany, as well as Italy, had been divided for over a thousand years. From comprising more than 3,000 units at the time of Charlemagne to 300 at the Treaty of Westphalia to a little more than 30 at the Congress of Vienna, the Holy Roman Empire had always been divided. As Map 3-1 on page 114 shows, this fragmentation provided a kind of buffer as other great

History Redux?

Have you concluded that the events leading up to World War I are ancient history and not terribly relevant to the world today? Think again. Here is just one example of how the period before World War I may be relevant to understanding contemporary international affairs.

According to a *Wall Street Journal* article on August 4, 2005, Professor Niall Ferguson of Harvard University told a group of Merrill Lynch clients in New York that:

> [W]e need to go further back than living memory to understand the predicament in which we currently find ourselves. . . . There is a striking resemblance between what is happening now and what was happening 100 years ago.[1]

According to Professor Ferguson and other experts quoted in the article, uncanny similarities exist between these two periods, the current era of globalization and the original one, from roughly 1880 to 1914, that first harnessed global communications (telegraph and telephone) and swift transportation (steamships) to tie the world together economically:

- a dominant but financially overstretched global power—then the United Kingdom, today the United States.
- rival powers that define themselves largely in opposition to the dominant power, especially regional powers with global aspirations like Germany then and China today.
- the existence of failed states—then the collapsing empires of Turkey and Austria-Hungary, today the disintegrating societies of Somalia, Sudan, Afghanistan, and other Muslim countries in central and southeast Asia.

- competition over access to resources—then the rivalry among Britain, France, and Russia over colonial territories and access to India, now the competition over oil and access to the Middle East and central Asia.
- the presence of anti-western doctrines and armed militants—then the teachings of Karl Marx and radical revolutionaries and anarchists, one of whom killed the Archduke of Austria and ignited World War I; today the pronouncements of Osama bin Laden and the proliferation of Muslim fundamentalists determined to wage "a holy war."

So what do we do in the face of these parallels? In his other writings, such as *Colossus: The Price of America's Empire,* Ferguson takes a realist perspective and calls on the United States, the "Colossus," to maintain order. In his view, the United States is far more powerful than Britain was in 1900 and should start acting like it. But, he warns, too many people have adopted a complacent attitude, a "sense of exaggerated security," just as they did before World War I. They take a liberal perspective and conclude that the new globalization is much deeper than the earlier globalization and will serve to keep potential rivals such as China on board to gain economic benefits. Finally, still others take an identity perspective and doubt that the ideas of Osama bin Laden have the appeal of those of Karl Marx. Bin Laden harks back to the past and ancient caliphates; Marx appealed to the future and a utopia of the classless society.

Where do you stand? And do you still think there is no need to study history?

1. Michael R. Sesit, "Geopolitical Risk: History's Constant," *Wall Street Journal,* August 4, 2005, C12.

powers emerged and contended for power in Europe. At times, the European balance of power functioned in two parts, a major rivalry between France and Great Britain in the west and another among Prussia, Austria, and Russia in the east. And even though western and eastern powers participated in wars across the continent—for example, Russia's role in the Napoleonic Wars or Britain's role in the Crimean War—their priority interests remained somewhat separate. Britain was primarily concerned with the low countries of Belgium and the Netherlands; Russia was primarily concerned with Poland. Once Germany was united, the European balance of power became a single whole, and it was more likely now that a disruption in one part would trigger a wider war among all great powers. This was especially true because Germany occupied the northern plains of Europe, which offered few geographical obstacles to invasion. A united country in this part of Europe would feel vulnerable, just as Poland, which also occupies the northern plains, was historically vulnerable and indeed subject to repeated partition. Geography matters, a realist perspective would point out; a united Germany would have to be either very strong and threaten its neighbors or very weak and become the potential prey of its neighbors.

The Rise of German Power

Zollverein

a customs union created by Prussia involving other German states that lowered barriers to trade and ignited rapid industrial development beginning in the 1830s.

As it turned out, a united Germany was going to be very strong. Already in the 1830s, Prussia had created the **Zollverein,** a customs union with other German states that lowered barriers to trade and ignited rapid industrial development. Through this trade community, which a liberal perspective might emphasize, Prussia between 1850 and 1870 increased sixfold the number of steam engines driving its industry and tripled its railway capacity. Germany was changing so fast that Karl Marx, visiting Berlin in 1859, said, "whoever last saw Berlin ten years ago would not recognize it again."[3] (A possible parallel with the contemporary world is that many visitors say

Map 3-1 **Europe Prior to German Unification in 1871**

the same thing today about cities in China.) By 1870, Prussia/Germany had pulled ahead of France in both population and gross national product (GNP, or the total income of the residents of a country) and had eight times the relative wealth of Russia. And, by 1900, Germany had pulled even with Great Britain, the preeminent power in Europe, and was three times wealthier than France or Russia. In 1913, one year before the war broke out, German wealth exceeded that of Great Britain by 40 percent.[4]

Germany was also able to convert its wealth into military power. Countries do this with differing degrees of efficiency, and **power conversion** becomes one of the factors complicating the assessment of power in balance-of-power politics. Remember from Chapter 1 how realist perspectives include political competence and stability as measures of power capabilities—not something we can touch but clearly something vital for mobilizing and converting resources into military arms. Russia, for example, had substantial wealth, particularly natural resources. But it did not have an efficient bureaucracy and could not support its military the way Germany did. By 1900, Germany, with less than half the population of Russia, had an army (including reserves) bigger than Russia and was building a navy to challenge British dominance on the seas.[5] During World War I itself, Germany massively outproduced Russia across the whole range of military equipment: planes, machine guns, artillery pieces, and rifles.[6] This administrative capacity to convert wealth into military power was also one of America's great strengths as it rose to great power status around the time of World War I.[7]

Power conversion reflects one of the ways in which the levels of analysis interact in the realist perspective and in international affairs more generally. Different domestic capacities to convert resources into power affect the relative systemic structural balance of power. Germany and Poland were both affected by vulnerable strategic positions. The one survived, while the other succumbed, in part because of domestic factors. But both too were driven by structural vulnerabilities, Germany to aggression and Poland to submission.

power conversion
the administrative capacity of a country to convert wealth to military power.

← **causal**
arrow

Power Balancing—Triple Entente and Triple Alliance

What was Europe going to do with this efficient colossus sitting across the strategic northern plains? Balance it, the realist perspective says. And that's exactly what Germany's neighbors proceeded to do. For a while, through the masterful but secretive diplomacy of Bismarck, Germany was able to reassure its weaker neighbors and keep them from aligning against Germany's greater power. But, in 1894, four years after Bismarck left the scene, the two countries most directly affected by Germany's power, France and Russia, formed an alliance. Now, with the Franco-Russian Alliance, Germany had potential adversaries on both borders. As Map 3-2 shows, Poland did not exist at the time, so Germany and Russia shared a border. A lot now depended on what Great Britain did.

For two decades prior to World War I, Britain and Germany had flirted with the idea of alliance. Remember that Kaiser Wilhelm's uncle, Edward VII, and cousin, George V, were the English monarchs during this period. In the 1890s, Willy spent his summer vacations in England participating in yacht races with his relatives and admiring the British naval fleet. A British-German alliance might have avoided the encirclement that Germany feared. From a realist perspective and systemic level of analysis, alliances tend to develop in a checkerboard rather than a domino pattern.

Spotlight on
alliances

| Map 3-2 | **Europe and Germany in 1914** |

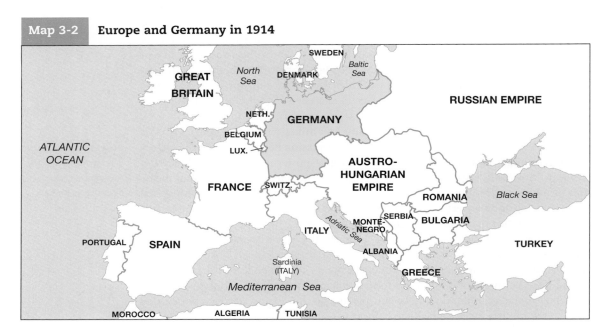

Rather than aligning with threatening neighbors, countries leapfrog over neighbors to find the counterbalances that help offset border rivalries. An alliance with Germany might have also made sense for Britain. By 1900, the United States had surpassed Great Britain in terms of total wealth and power. Britain and the United States did not share a border but they competed increasingly on the high seas. The American navy was expanding rapidly under the influence of Admiral Alfred Mahan and the inspiration of President Theodore Roosevelt. Thus, Germany and Britain might have acted to check the growing specter of American power. But geography matters as well as total power, realist perspectives argue, and Germany was closer to Great Britain and hence a more proximate threat than the United States. Great Britain had long defended the neutrality of the low countries of Belgium and the Netherlands, and Germany's new power potentially threatened these countries, just as French power had in the eighteenth and nineteenth centuries.

Observe that, from the realist perspective, it does not matter that the United States and Britain shared similar cultural and political systems. This factor is important from an identity perspective and a domestic level of analysis. Some analysts attribute the eventual alliance between the United States and Great Britain primarily to the shared Anglo-Saxon culture of the two countries.[8] They believe domestic and dyadic level (systemic process between two countries) forces of culture and democracy overrode the systemic structural level forces of power competition.

Thus, in 1904, Britain and France signed an agreement, the **Entente Cordiale,** that settled colonial disputes between them (they had almost come to blows at Fashoda in the Egyptian Sudan in 1898) and, although not explicitly directed against Germany, ended a century of "splendid isolation" for British policy, during which it had avoided specific commitments on the continent. That the Entente Cordiale had broader purposes became evident within a year. In 1905, Russia suffered a major naval defeat in the Russo-Japanese War. Japan was another rising power in Russia's neighborhood, this time in Asia. Worried that Russia was now seriously weakened vis-à-vis Germany,

Spotlight on geopolitics

causal arrow

Entente Cordiale
an agreement signed in 1904 between Britain and France that settled colonial disputes between them and ended a century of British isolation from conflicts on the continent.

Great Britain and France expanded their alliance in 1907 to include Russia. The Entente Cordiale became the **Triple Entente.**

Sir Eyre Crowe, permanent secretary of the British foreign office, wrote a famous memorandum in 1907 that summed up the realist logic driving British policy. He noted that Germany might have two intentions, "aiming at a general political hegemony and maritime ascendance" or "thinking for the present merely of using her legitimate position and influence as one of the leading Powers in the council of nations." However, "there is no actual necessity for a British government to determine definitely which of the two theories of German policy it will accept." Either way, Crowe concluded, "the position thereby accruing to Germany would obviously constitute . . . a menace to the rest of the world. . . ."[9] Regardless of German intentions, the Crowe memorandum argued, German power had to be balanced.

And the balance of power seemed to be working. Many scholars estimate that German power reached its peak around 1905. Just as it did so, its major neighbors came together in the Entente Cordiale and Triple Entente to check that power. In 1913, the Triple Entente had about 50 percent of European wealth. The other 50 percent was accounted for by the **Triple Alliance,** an alliance first between Germany and Austria-Hungary in 1879, which then added Italy in 1882. In 1914, the two alliances offered a near-perfect offset.[10] According to the power balancing school of realism, equilibrium existed and should have prevented war. What went wrong?

Here realist perspectives split in explaining the breakdown of the balance of power. Some argue that the offsetting alliances became too rigid and converted a flexible multipolar balance of power into a rigid bipolar balance. The tense standoff eventually precipitated a preemptive war, an attack by one country on another country because the second country is getting ready to attack the first. Others argue that a bipolar distribution is the most stable but that the problem was not the current balance of power but the potential future balance of power. By this account, Germany saw Russia as a rising power in the future and therefore launched a preventive war to avoid Germany's decline at a later date. Recall that a preventive war is an attack by one country on another country not because the second country is getting ready to attack the first but because it may do so in the future. Still others argue that hegemony or unipolarity is the most stable configuration of power and that Britain, whose hegemony ensured the long peace of nineteenth-century Europe, was now a declining power, leading to a multipolar scramble to decide which country would be the next hegemon. Let's look further at each of these realist arguments.

Rigid Alliances and Preemptive War

How could countries balance against German power and still preserve flexibility? As we have noted, if Germany had aligned with Britain to avoid encirclement, it would have created an even more powerful grouping, accounting for about two-thirds of Europe's wealth in 1913. And France and Russia would have felt even more threatened. So, the balance of power required Britain to align against Germany. In that sense, encirclement and confrontation of the two alliance arrangements may have been unavoidable. It was a consequence of Germany's superior power *and* its position at the center of the European continent. It was, in short, an outgrowth of the security dilemma. Any effort to counterbalance Germany within Europe would necessarily involve encirclement; and encirclement meant that Germany had to plan to fight a war on two fronts.

Triple Entente
an agreement signed in 1907 in which Great Britain and France expanded the Entente Cordiale to include Russia, accounting for 50 percent of European wealth at the time.

Spotlight on
capabilities not intentions

Triple Alliance
an alliance first between Germany and Austria-Hungary in 1879, which then added Italy in 1882, that accounted for 50 percent of all European wealth in the early twentieth century.

Spotlight on
preemptive and preventive wars

Spotlight on
hegemonic stability

Spotlight on
security dilemma

Schlieffen Plan

Germany's plan (named after General Alfred von Schlieffen, who first developed the plan in 1892; it did not become official strategy until 1913) that called for an attack on France first, by way of Belgium, followed by an attack on Russia.

causal
    arrow

Spotlight on

offensive/defensive technologies

causal
    arrow

This logic led Germany as early as the 1890s to consider a preemptive war, a lightning strike or *blitzkrieg*, against one neighbor, say in the west, so that German forces could then turn and concentrate against the other neighbor, say in the east. The **Schlieffen Plan** (named after General Alfred von Schlieffen, who first developed the plan in 1892; it did not become official strategy until 1913) called for an attack on France first, by way of Belgium—undoubtedly bringing Britain into the war—followed by an attack on Russia.

Notice that, in the realist argument, the strategic situation dictated the military strategy and was the primary cause of war. Sometimes scholars say that geopolitics is a necessary but not sufficient explanation for war. They want to emphasize more specific factors at the foreign policy, domestic, and individual levels of analysis. Later we consider liberal arguments, for example, that bureaucratic factors, such as military and mobilization plans, not strategic imperatives, were the primary cause of war.

But why must bipolarity of alliances be unstable? The common argument is that each side is supersensitive to any gains by the other side because there are no other allies to turn to for balancing. But a counterargument to this is that the two powers have only one another to consider and will therefore focus on one another "like a laser beam" and not allow either side to gain advantage. Perhaps the balance was unstable in 1914 because both sides believed that military technology favored offensive strategies—machine guns, motorized vehicles, and other attack weapons. In a balanced bipolar situation, offensive technology would give the advantage to the attacker and therefore place a premium on preemption. As it turned out, however, technology actually favored defensive strategies; World War I was a stalemate for most of its duration, involving stagnant trench warfare.

An explanation that hinges on whether weapons are offensive or defensive slides into liberal and identity explanations of the outbreak of World War I (see subsequent discussion). Such an explanation depends on bureaucratic and cognitive factors that influence perceptions and cause misperceptions. In this case, military leaders had incorrect information about weapons (an argument from the liberal perspective and foreign policy level of analysis) or saw only the facts they wanted to see based on their ideas or beliefs (an argument from the identity perspective and individual level of analysis). From a strictly realist perspective, perceptions are not a primary variable. Facts speak for themselves, especially the power realities.

Future Balances and Preventive War

A more consistent realist argument is that the balance ultimately broke down not because of current imbalances but because of fears of future imbalances. This argument hinges on Germany's fear of Russian power and whether that fear was reasonable. If the fear is not reasonable, liberal or identity factors are at work distorting the perception of material balances. According to this argument, Germany feared that Russia would surpass Germany in military and industrial power by 1916–1917. Theobald von Bethmann-Hollweg, the German Chancellor, visited Russia in 1912

In this 1916 photograph from the Battle of the Somme in northern France, British troops ascend from trenches to no-man's land, the devastated landscape between battle lines that changed little during World War I.

and observed "Russia's rising industrial power, which will grow to overwhelming pro-portions."[11] Russia was rapidly developing a railroad network that would permit it to move forces more quickly to the front. This would give Germany less time to deal with France before it would have to turn and confront Russian forces as well.

But why then didn't Germany attack before 1914? Its power peaked in 1905, when Russia was weak after the disastrous naval defeat by Japan and when Britain and France had just concluded the Entent Cordiale, which was not strictly an alliance against Germany. From 1905 on, there were plenty of occasions for war. Germany and other European powers were involved in a series of diplomatic crises in Morocco (1905 and 1911) and the Balkans (1908–1909 and 1912–1913) that were at least as serious as the assassination of the Austrian archduke in June 1914.[12] One answer to why Germany waited is that Germany's naval program was not completed until July 1914 and Germany relied on this naval program to either deter or hold Great Britain at bay while it attacked France. Thus, all the pieces for a preventive war were in place by the July crisis. Germany knew that Russia was not getting ready to attack it. Hence, the war was not preemptive, that is, in anticipation of an imminent Russian attack. In fact, Germany had to goad Russia into war. Now foreign policy level factors become important. According to this account, Bethmann-Hollweg and military leaders such as Helmuth von Moltke, the German army chief of staff, used diplomacy "with Machiavellian dexterity" to provoke Russian mobilization, even delaying for twelve hours the transmission of the kaiser's instructions to settle the dispute peacefully so that Austria had time to declare war (see more discussion later).[13]

In this realist account, notice how diplomacy plays a role but as an intervening, not independent, variable. The projection of future relative Russian predominance drives the diplomacy, not the other way around. And this projection of future balances is systemic as long as it is reasonable. If it is unreasonable, then other factors at the diplomatic, domestic, and individual levels of analysis must be distorting leaders' perceptions. Were those projections reasonable? At the time, some believed they were.[14] But in retrospect historians know that Russia was not much of a match for German military forces. Russia eventually capitulated in 1917 to a German force that repre-sented only half of Germany's capabilities (the other half of the German force was fighting against France). And Russia disintegrated into civil war in 1917 and did not emerge to play a role in European politics for the next fifteen years.

← **causal** *arrow*

Power Transition and Hegemonic Decline

A final realist perspective is that World War I was caused not by the rising power of Germany or the projected future dominance of Russia but by the declining hegemo-ny of Great Britain. According to this realist version, it is not present or future bal-ances that produce stability but imbalance or hegemony. The dominant power has interests that span the system as a whole and, therefore, more than any other coun-try, looks after the maintenance of the balance of power. Britain played this role dur-ing the Pax Britannica, the long century of peace in the nineteenth century. It exer-cised naval superiority around the globe and watched on the European continent so that no power gained ascendance. By the end of the nineteenth century, however, Britain no longer had that kind of power. The United States had surpassed Britain, but the United States was not yet powerful enough to play a global role. It was only beginning to assert its foreign policy and did not see its interests affected yet by the larger system or balance of power in Europe.

Thus, in the early twentieth century, the world experienced a dangerous interregnum in which Germany faced no leading power to temper rivalries. British diplomacy was not specifically at fault because its diplomacy was a product of British power, and British power was simply declining. The opposite was true for the United States. Its diplomacy was not at fault either because it was not yet powerful enough to direct events in Europe. Notice that, in this explanation from the systemic structural level of analysis, diplomacy is an intervening, not primary, variable. Structural power shifts explain diplomacy, not the other way around.

This explanation draws from the power transition school of realism, which alerts us to dangerous periods of transition when a declining power falls and a challenging power closes in. Moving toward balance from this school's perspective is viewed as destabilizing, whereas moving toward balance from the power balancing perspective is viewed as stabilizing. This difference in how balance is viewed stems in part from a focus on different actors and different assumptions about goals. Power transition perspectives focus on the declining power and assume that it seeks to preserve the status quo. Thus, the loss of hegemony threatens stability. Power balancing perspectives focus on the rising power and assume that it would like to change the status quo. Hence, the emergence of hegemony threatens stability.

Cartelized Domestic Politics and German Aggression

Realist explanations of World War I also operate at the domestic level of analysis. One domestic level explanation argues that World War I was caused by German aggression and that German aggression, in turn, was caused by German domestic politics. According to this explanation, Germany's domestic politics was cartelized or united among various elite groups, all of which had independent interests in one or another aspect of German expansion. The agricultural landowners of large estates in East Prussia, or Junkers, were primarily interested in high tariffs to protect grain prices; military elites were primarily interested in offensive war plans and weaponry; and industrial leaders advocated high tariffs to develop industry and military arms, including a naval fleet. As political scientist Jack Snyder explains, "these groups logrolled their interests, producing a policy outcome that was more expansionist and overcommitted than any group desired individually." [15] Thus, grain tariffs antagonized Russia, a large grain exporter; heavy industry and naval plans antagonized Great Britain; and military leaders and their offensive war plans alienated France and Russia. These cartelized domestic interests "embroiled Germany simultaneously with all of Europe's major powers." [16]

Snyder does not ignore international factors: "International circumstances did affect German expansionist policy, but only by influencing the domestic political strength of imperialist groups. . . ." [17] He simply judges domestic expansionist forces to be more important than systemic ones. (See Table 3-1 for a summary of realist explanations.)

Liberal Explanations

Liberal accounts of World War I focus on diplomatic miscalculations and institutional deficiencies, both in the international system and in the domestic politics of key players such as Germany, Austria-Hungary, Russia, and the Ottoman Empire.

---

causal arrow

Spotlight on power transitions

Spotlight on security dilemma

Table 3-1

The Causes of World War I: The Realist Perspective and Levels of Analysis

Level of analysis		Realist perspective
Systemic	*Structure*	• Rise of German power engenders threat of empire (power balancing school)
		• Decline of British power signals end of Pax Britannica (power transition school)
		• Loss of flexibility, rise of rigid alliances—Triple Entente verus Triple Alliance—that intensifies bipolarity which is unstable and increases incentives for preemptive war
		• Future rise of Russian power—bipolarity is stable in present but not in future (power transition school), leads to preventive war
		• Power vacuum—disintegration of Austro-Hungarian and Ottoman Empires, which sucked in Great Powers
	Process	• Alliances: Interactive formation of Triple Entente and Triple Alliance
Foreign policy		• German leaders use Machiavellian diplomacy to provoke war and unite domestic interests
Domestic		• German bureaucratic efficiency; Russia not so efficient (contributed to shift in power)
		• Cartelized German domestic interests combine expansionist aims and provoke other major powers
Individual		• Weak leaders: Emperor Franz Joseph (tired, old man), Tsar Nicholas II (isolated autocrat), Kaiser Wilhelm II (weak ruler)

International diplomacy had been building under the Congress of Vienna toward a more multilateral and open system for settling disputes. But Bismarck's diplomacy used to unite Germany dealt this emerging system structure a damaging blow. Although Bismarck tried to replace the Concert of Europe with an intricate series of offsetting alliances, his secretive style of diplomacy bred suspicion. Once Bismarck was gone, Kaiser Wilhelm II proved less capable at navigating the system. Notice here the individual level of analysis—Bismarck was able to offset domestic and systemic factors to make diplomacy work to preserve peace; the kaiser was not.

← causal
arrow

As the liberal perspective sees it, the Kaiser blundered his way into a naval competition with Great Britain and military strategies toward France and Russia that ultimately produced rigid alliances and self-initiating mobilization plans. The explanation thus far emphasizes diplomatic mistakes at the individual level of analysis. Wilhelm was not being pressured to do what he did by domestic or systemic forces. In the crisis of July 1914, German and European diplomacy then got caught up in a spiral of action and reaction, compounding the march to war. Each decision narrowed the options of the next decision in what liberal perspectives call path dependence. Eventually, the process led to the last move of the prisoner's dilemma, in which war seemed to be inevitable. Now the explanation draws on the interactive or systemic process level of analysis. Meanwhile, promising international economic and legal ties did not develop in time to constrain military action. Expanding trade at the systemic process level and a new Hague Conference process that included small as well as great powers at the systemic structural level proved too weak to head off war.

Spotlight on
path dependence

Diplomatic miscalculations were abetted by domestic institutional weaknesses in most of the major continental powers. At the domestic level of analysis, Germany's political system was sharply divided between royalist and socialist forces, and its parliament, the Reichstag, had minimal controls over military plans and spending. The tsar in Russia was a weak leader with a crumbling imperial administration, and nationalism was eating away at the vital organs of the once mighty Austrian (after 1867, Austro-Hungarian) and Ottoman empires. A closer look at these diplomatic and institutional developments illustrates how liberal perspectives emphasize interactions and institutions, rather than power balancing or ideologies, as the primary causes of war and peace.

Secret Diplomacy—Bismarck

After weakening, if not effectively destroying, the Concert of Europe system through wars with Austria and France, Bismarck reconstituted in 1873 the Three Emperors' League, a faint reproduction of the old Holy Alliance. (Identity-based explanations might give more weight to the "Holy" aspect, whereas Bismarck was more interested in the "Alliance" aspect.) Germany, Austria-Hungary, and Russia, still led by traditional monarchs, as opposed to the emerging constitutional monarchs in Britain and France, pledged to suppress subversion and manage their affairs cooperatively. The Three Emperors' League was immediately tested in the Balkans, a region that produced most of the crises after 1870 and eventually war in 1914. In 1876, Bulgarians, who had lived for centuries under Turkish rule, revolted. Russia proclaimed support for its orthodox religious brethren in Bulgaria. The tsar was either genuinely motivated to protect Christians in the Balkans or using this identity factor for realist expansionist aims. Austria-Hungary and Great Britain suspected the latter—concerns that had led them earlier to block Russia's advance in the Crimean War in the 1850s. Britain feared Russian dominance of the Dardanelles, as well as its relentless push through central Asia toward India, then Britain's prize colonial territory. Thus, when Russian and Bulgarian forces reached the gates of Constantinople in 1878 and announced the Treaty of San Stefano, creating a Bulgarian state and drastically weakening Turkey, Bismarck with British support called a conference, the last major conference of the Concert of Europe era. Britain and Russia solved the most contentious issues before the conference, leading to significant Russian concessions. Hence the Berlin Conference in 1878 left a bad taste in the mouth of the Russians, and Russia thereafter blamed Germany.

Over the next fifteen years, Germany and Russia grew apart, creating one of the fault lines that contributed to World War I. In 1879, Bismarck concluded a secret alliance with Austria-Hungary against Russia. Austria, in turn, gave Germany veto power over its policies in the Balkans. This was the basis for the crucial role that Germany played in Austrian diplomacy in 1914. Bismarck renewed the Three Emperors' League in 1881, but its purpose was now purely defensive. Each country pledged to remain neutral if one of them went to war against a fourth country. Russia would stay out of a war between Germany and France, and Austria-Hungary would stay out of a war between Russia and Great Britain. In 1882, Bismarck concluded still another alliance with Italy. This one pledged Italian assistance to Germany against a French attack and to Austria-Hungary against a Russian attack. One of the rigid alliances, the Triple Alliance—Germany, Austria-Hungary, and Italy—was now in place. Another Bulgarian crisis in 1885 shattered the Three Emperors' League for good. Bismarck made one final effort to maintain ties with Russia, the Reassurance Treaty of 1887. But when Bismarck left office—essentially fired—in 1890, Kaiser Wilhelm II did not renew the treaty.

Although Germany rose rapidly in power from 1870 to 1890, Bismarck's diplomacy preserved the peace. Could others have replicated his virtuoso performance? Some prominent realists think so.[18] They judge that systemic factors were driving Bismarck's policy, not individual level factors. Hence, someone else as adept as Bismarck might have been able to continue his success. But, the liberal and identity perspectives might argue that that is expecting too much from any individual. Indeed, even by realist logic, Bismarck's performance was lacking. For example, he did relatively little to reassure France, except to avoid rivalry in colonial disputes. Instead, he was the principal architect of annexing Alsace-Lorraine after the Franco-Prussian War of 1871, even though he knew this policy would poison French-German relations thereafter. He did it to weaken France, expecting France to be an enemy for good: "An enemy, whose honest friendship can never be won, must at least be rendered somewhat less harmful."[19] Bismarck apparently considered France a permanent enemy and contaminated the realist requirements of a flexible balance of power with identity factors. Realism says to never regard a country as either a permanent enemy or a permanent friend and to be ready to align with any country, regardless of friendship or animosity, to counter greater power. Even if Bismarck had followed that rule, could he have reassured France any more than he was able to reassure Russia? After all, Russia made the first alliance with France relatively soon (four years) after Bismarck left office. Would that not have happened eventually, whoever succeeded Bismarck? From realist perspectives, diplomacy can only do what the balance of power allows. And, from the liberal and identity perspectives, the balance of power in Europe before World War I was flawed either because it relied too much on secrecy and manipulation or because it demanded perfect—we might say angelic—statesmanship, which even Bismarck was unable to deliver.

Thus, realist perspectives enthrone Bismarck as the master statesman, while liberal and identity perspectives point out that only a God could have pulled it off.

Clumsy Diplomacy—Wilhelm II

From a liberal perspective, Kaiser Wilhelm II was clearly a less capable diplomat than Bismarck and quickly stoked further antagonism between Germany and Russia, contributing to the Franco-Russian Alliance of 1894. He also initiated a colonial and naval rivalry with Great Britain, something that Bismarck had astutely avoided. In 1895, he sent a famous telegram to President Paul Krüger of the independent Boer states, settled by Germans in the South Africa Transvaal. Krüger's army had just defeated a raid into the Transvaal supported by British colonialists. The so-called Krüger telegram congratulated the Boer leader for the victory. It was a gratuitous slap at the British. The Kaiser carried the insult further and launched a major shipbuilding program to challenge British naval supremacy. Envious of the British ships he saw on his summer vacations in England, he launched an arms race that witnessed the production of more and bigger battleships, culminating in the famous Dreadnought competition.[20] The secret and rapid buildup of the German navy under the determined leadership of Admiral Alfred von Tirpitz was a key factor contributing to growing rivalries before World War I.

Other colonial conflicts followed. German and French interests clashed in the Moroccan Crises in 1905 and 1911. Russia and Austria-Hungary almost went to war in a Balkan crisis in 1908–1909 after Austria-Hungary annexed Bosnia-Herzegovina (where Sarajevo is located, the site of the assassination of Archduke Ferdinand, which

Spotlight on flexible versus rigid alliances

triggered World War I, and, by the way, the central city in the Bosnian crisis of 1992–1995). Balkan wars broke out again in 1912–1913. In October 1912, Montenegro, another small Balkan state, declared war on Turkey and was quickly supported by Bulgaria, Serbia, and Greece. After this crisis was settled, Bulgaria attacked Serbia and Greece in June 1913. In both crises, Austria and Russia stood eye-ball to eyeball, fearing that the other might gain an advantage. Germany supported Austria but had significant influence over Austrian policy, as called for by the Treaty of 1879. Great Britain, which sent its war minister, Richard Haldane, to Berlin in 1912, sought to ensure that Germany would not threaten Belgium. Suspicions were mounting for the final drama of war.

Misperceptions and Mobilization Plans

Why did war break out in 1914 and not in 1912 or 1913? From a liberal perspective, diplomacy had prevented war in earlier crises. Why didn't diplomacy do so again in 1914? For three reasons, liberal accounts suggest. First, Germany expected Britain to remain neutral in 1914, thus permitting a local settlement of the crisis, as in previous incidents. Second, mobilization plans—such as the Schlieffen Plan—were finalized in 1913 that called for an automatic escalation to war. Now the slightest spark could ignite a firestorm. And third, civilian institutions in various countries broke down, contributing to a last move situation familiar in game theory when the only choice remaining is to go to war. Notice that all these factors are contingent on the process of interaction, a typically liberal focus in explaining international events.

On July 5, a week after the assassination of the archduke, the Kaiser met the Austrian ambassador in Germany and told him that Germany would back Austria against Serbia "whatever Austria's decision." German Chancellor Bethmann-Hollweg confirmed this commitment the next day in what became known as a "blank check," giving Austria a free hand to start a war.[21] The Kaiser did not expect Russia, Serbia's ally, to go to war and did not even discuss the possibility that Britain might inter-vene. The Kaiser left town for his regular summer North Sea cruise. Austria sent an ultimatum to Serbia on July 23. The Serbs replied on July 27 and appeared to con-cede to Austria's demands. The Kaiser, who had just returned from his cruise, ordered negotiations, proposing that Austria "[h]alt in Belgrade," meaning occupy Belgrade temporarily until Serbia met other demands. But the Kaiser's instructions did not arrive in Vienna until July 28, after Austria had declared war against Serbia—perhaps deliberately delayed, according to some realist accounts that we have dis-cussed, to start a preventive war.

Now the issue hinged on whether the war could be localized between Austria and Serbia without involving their allies, Germany and Russia. British neutrality was key. If Britain did not support Russia, an ally under the Triple Entente, a wider war might be avoided. As already noted, some German officials did not expect Britain to inter-vene. But on the evening of July 29, a telegram from London warned firmly that Britain would support Russia if war occurred. Germany now tried to rein in its Austrian ally. Early in the morning of July 30, Bethmann-Hollweg fired off his famous "world on fire" telegrams urging Vienna to implement the Kaiser's instructions to negotiate—just a smoke screen, as some realist accounts see it, to shift blame for war on Russia.

Military plans and mobilization, however, now made diplomacy difficult. War plans were based on quick strikes, and Germany's Schlieffen Plan, as we have noted,

Spotlight on interactions

called for an attack first on France and then on Russia. Military plans relied on precise timetables and the complex movements of troops. In response to Austria's declaration of war against Serbia, Russia had already partially mobilized on July 29, and the tsar actually ordered full mobilization that same evening but cancelled the order two hours later when he received another telegram from his cousin Willy. Under intense pressure from his generals, however, Nicholas went ahead the next day with full mobilization. In response, Germany sent an ultimatum to Russia on July 31 and declared war on August 1. When the Kaiser met with his generals to order them to limit the war to Russia and not attack France, von Moltke, the German army chief of staff, protested:

> Your Majesty, it cannot be done. The deployment of millions cannot be improvised. If Your Majesty insists on leading the whole army to the East, it will not be an army ready for battle but a disorganized mob. . . . These arrangements took a whole year of intricate labor to complete and once settled they cannot be altered.[22]

The Last Move

The Kaiser won the argument, and German troops in the west were pulled back. Although a German infantry unit had already crossed into Luxembourg, another unit went in and, following the Kaiser's instruction, ordered the first unit out.[23] France mobilized the same day, even though it positioned its troops ten kilometers from the border to avoid accidents. Nevertheless, German military and political leaders doubted that France would stay out of the war, and on August 3 Germany declared war on France. The next day, German troops invaded Belgium, and Britain entered the war. A general European war was underway.[24]

From the liberal perspective, no one sought a general war but rational behavior ultimately led to it. Why? The process of interaction broke down. In iterative game theory—which is the liberal perspective, illustrated by the example of the prisoners interacting regularly in the prison yard in Chapter 1—actors count on being able to play the game again tomorrow. This expectation, or shadow of the future, helps cooperation. But if they come to believe that they are playing the game for the last time, the so-called last move, they face the static prisoner's dilemma or realist situation and defect. In a sense, liberal accounts argue, this is what happened to ignite World War I. Listen to the conclusions of political scientist Marc Trachtenberg: "[Bethmann-Hollweg] had not set out to provoke a great war. . . . He had made a certain effort to get the Austrians to pull back. But war was almost bound to come eventually, so he would just stand aside and let it come now."[25] No one wanted war, but by a process of action-reaction the great powers became dependent on a path that eventually resulted in war.

Notice the language of the pending last move ("almost bound to come eventually"). Under these circumstances, it was rational for Bethmann-Hollweg to behave the way he did. Now, compare this argument to the previous, realist one that Germany sought a general war to avoid the future dominance of Russia. In the realist argument, Germany always intended war because future relative power projections required it. In the liberal argument, Germany did not reach that conclusion until late in the process of diplomatic action and reaction. In the realist case, relative power projections at the systemic structural level caused the war; in the liberal case, negotiating dynamics at the systemic process level brought it about. Observe that in neither argument do Germany's intentions cause the war. Intentions are a function of what actors

Spotlight on path dependence

causal *arrow*

want, not how much relative power they have or how they interact. These cognitive or identity factors were certainly present before and during the July crisis, but according to these accounts, they did not influence outcomes as much as power projections or interactive factors.

But the debate goes on because, as one scholar notes, World War I "appears to offer at least some empirical support for practically any theory or explanation." Other scholars see a larger role for intentions and identity factors. On the basis of new materials obtained from former East German archives after the Cold War, Professor Kier Lieber concludes that the war was neither unintended, as power balancing (defensive) realists might argue, nor a consequence of diplomatic blunders, as liberal accounts might suggest, but "that German leaders went to war in 1914 with their eyes wide open."[26] The war, in short, was intended. For Lieber, the intentions were caused primarily by hegemonic aspirations. He is a proponent of the offensive realist school that assumes that countries always seek more power, not just enough to balance. But, for others, the intention may derive from ideational or identity factors such as Germany's heroic self-image and militant ideology, as we examine under identity perspectives later.

causal **arrow** →

Weak Domestic Institutions

The last move argument assumes that diplomats were in control of institutions, especially the military, and acted rationally. But other liberal explanations suggest that diplomats may not have been in control and that institutions malfunctioned. Institutional weaknesses contributed to fragmentation and faulty coordination of policy. German diplomacy, for example, was weakened by "an astonishing lack of coordination between the political and the military authorities."[27] Political interests that sought to avoid war, or at least shift the blame for war, worked at cross-purposes with military strategies that counted on the precise timetables and a two-front war set out in the mobilization plans.

German domestic institutions were also divided. The conservative—iron-rye—coalition that ran the German government consisted of landed agricultural interests (rye) and industrial leaders (iron). It excluded for the most part the growing working class and its socialist leaders who held the majority in the Reichstag. The only way this growing division could be overcome was by war. A policy of war diverted resources to the military, which the Reichstag did not fully control, and coopted socialist opponents by appeals to nationalism. As one historian concludes, Germany "sought to consolidate the position of the ruling classes with a successful imperialist foreign policy."[28]

Domestic cleavages in the other monarchies were even stronger. Austria-Hungary was disintegrating from within, the Russian tsar was in a precarious position, and the Ottoman Empire was barely surviving. Within four years of the outbreak of war, all three of these institutions would cease to exist.

Elsewhere domestic institutions were becoming more popularly based and representative. Representative government made it more difficult to conduct foreign policy in a timely and coherent way. In the United States, President Woodrow Wilson campaigned for reelection in 1916 on a promise to keep the United States out of war, even though by January 1917 Germany's policy of unlimited submarine warfare and the sinking of the *Lusitania* forced the United States into war. American involvement may have been decisive and suggests a blunder of German diplomacy in alienating the United States. Germany defeated Russia in early 1918 just as American doughboys arrived to counter additional German forces moved from the Russian to the western front. Germany may well have worn down the western allies if American troops had not entered the battle.

Insufficient Interdependence: Trade and the Hague Conferences

International commerce and banking had expanded dramatically in the last quarter of the nineteenth century. Not only colonial trade but also trade among the industrial powers reached levels before World War I that would not be reached again until the 1970s. Britain had led an effort to liberalize trade unilaterally, and some countries followed, such as France. But there were no effective multilateral institutions to coordinate and expand this effort; and other countries, such as Germany and the United States, did not liberalize their trade policies. Still the growing number of bankers and merchants benefiting from commercial interdependence denounced the costs of military conflicts and trade barriers and called for the peaceful resolution of political disputes. A best-selling book published just two years before the outbreak of World War I proclaimed that war was a "great illusion" because its costs from the breakup of lucrative trade and investment now far exceeded its benefits. War had become obsolete, its author Norman Angell declared.[29] Multilateral diplomacy was a better way to resolve disputes. The Hague Conferences, convened in 1899 and 1907 by initiative of the Russian tsar, brought small as well as large states into the diplomatic process (twenty-six states in 1899, forty-four in 1907). Although these conferences solved no major issues, they reformed the rules and methods of diplomacy and started discussions to control arms races.

From the liberal perspective, trade and law were becoming more important aspects of international affairs than power and secret diplomacy. William Gladstone, who became British prime minister in 1880, foresaw this development and observed that:

> a new law of nations is gradually taking hold of the mind, and coming to sway the practice, of the world; a law which recognizes independence, which frowns upon aggression, which favours the pacific, not the bloody settlement of disputes, which aims at permanent not temporary adjustments: above all, which recognizes, as a tribunal of paramount authority, the general judgement of civilized mankind.[30]

Notice Gladstone's emphasis on classic liberal themes—law, practice, pacific settlement of disputes, permanent solutions, and universal participation—which he terms the "general judgement of civilized mankind." Gladstone's insights became the banner of another great statesman in the next century. The American president Woodrow Wilson championed worldviews that emphasized open markets, the rule of law, and collective, rather than national, security. From the liberal point of view, these factors were too weak to head off World War I. But after the war, they formed the edifice of a whole new approach to managing military relations in international politics, which we discuss more fully in the next chapter. (See Table 3-2 for a summary of the liberal explanations.)

Spotlight on collective security

Identity Explanations

Identity perspectives on World War I emphasize the ideas and norms that motivated prewar diplomacy and military rivalries. These ideas were both shared and autonomous, rational and psychological. The dominant ideology in prewar Europe was nationalism. Three broad varieties emerged in the nineteenth century. **Militant nationalism** focused on cultural and ultimately racial differences and advocated a kind of aggressive, heroic

militant nationalism
a form of nationalism emerging in the nineteenth century focusing on cultural and racial differences and advocating an aggressive, heroic approach to international relations.

Table 3-2

The Causes of World War I: The Liberal Perspective and Levels of Analysis		
Level of analysis		**Liberal perspective**
Systemic	*Structure*	• Weakness of common institutions initiated by Hague Conferences
		• Collapse of Concert of Europe conference system
	Process	• Interactions and path dependence: —Clumsiness of Kaiser's policy—dropped treaty with Russia, antagonized Britain —Secretive diplomacy: German misperception that Britain would not intervene —Automatic mobilization plans—"last move" —Growing but insufficient trade, social, and legal interdependence
Foreign policy		• Lack of coordination between diplomatic and military policies in Germany pushing Germany toward war
		• Differences between Congress and the presidency in the United States keeping United States out of war until 1917
Domestic		• Domestic politics of Germany—iron-rye coalition used imperial expansion to unify society
		• Domestic disintegration of Ottoman and Austro-Hungarian Empires/ institutions
Individual		• Bureaucratic pressures overwhelm policy

liberal nationalism

a form of nationalism emerging in the nineteenth century focusing on political ideologies and calling for wider participation and the rule of law in both domestic and international politics.

socialist nationalism

a form of nationalism emerging in the nineteenth century that sought greater economic equality and social justice, especially in class and colonial relationships.

approach to international relations. **Liberal nationalism** focused on political ideologies and called for wider participation and the rule of law in both domestic and international politics. **Socialist nationalism** sought greater economic equality and social justice, especially in class and colonial relationships. Each variety of nationalism also had an international or collectivist dimension. Militant nationalism, for example, embraced Social Darwinism, a collectivist norm of political and military struggle. Liberal nationalism supported the Hague legal process and later collective security under the League of Nations, while socialist nationalism embraced a series of international meetings known as the Second International, which advocated the solidarity of the working classes. Let's look more closely at these different types of nationalism.

Militant and Racist Nationalism

We observed in this last chapter that rising nationalism weakened the solidarity or collective identity of the European conference system, the Concert of Europe. Bismarck personified the kind of nationalism that recognized no higher principle or purpose than service to one's country. This kind of nationalism exalted the culture and language of each nation, which did not change much and could not be shared easily with other nations.

It was a short step from this type of cultural nationalism to the virulent militarist and racist doctrines that spread in Europe in the late nineteenth century. Militarism reflected the imperative to organize and train a citizen army, often including extensive reserves. Prior to the eighteenth century, armies consisted mostly of nobles, peasants recruited for each campaign, and mercenaries. Wars were fought among the tens

Across Europe, World War I was greeted with nationalistic enthusiasm. Here German citizens rally in late July 1914 in front of the kaiser's palace (right) in Berlin.

of thousands, not millions, and direct casualties were relatively low (most soldiers died of diseases). In the eighteenth century, Prussia began to change this model for the army by introducing "limited military conscription, intensive tactical training, efficient artillery barrages, and skillful generalship." Napoleon accelerated these developments. As Robert Osgood and Robert Tucker write, he "created a 'nation in arms' . . . [and] transformed warfare into a national crusade, involving not just tactical maneuver and attrition of the enemy's supply lines but annihilation of the enemy's forces, occupation of his territory, and even political conversion of his people."[31] War now had the objective of regime change. The industrial revolution completed this transformation. It created not only new technologies of military power but a whole new arms industry that promoted and thrived on accelerating arms races, such as the Dreadnought battleship competition mentioned earlier.

Military technological changes contributed to a widespread belief in European military establishments that offensive strategies would hold the advantage in the next war. This belief led to the need for rapid mobilization plans and secret military planning. In this way, ideas created the mobilization spiral that caused World War I, not the mobilization process itself, which liberal perspectives emphasize. A militarist mentality created the **"cult of the offensive"**.[32] This belief in offensive military power was the reason rapid mobilization plans were developed in the first place; the mobilization plans and their interaction at the end of July 1914 were simply a consequence. Notice again how arguments are differentiated in terms of the way the causal arrow runs among ideas (cult of the offensive), interactions (mobilization plans), and power (relative military capabilities).

cult of the offensive
a belief in offensive military power.

⟵ **causal arrow**

Liberal Nationalism

The second type of nationalism that emerged in the nineteenth century was more ideological and political than racial. It too emphasized culture and military struggle.

But it offered political rather than racial visions of the way the world was unfolding. Liberal nationalism saw a trend toward increased individual freedom, fundamental human rights, and the rule of law. It emphasized equality of opportunity, especially the possibility of education and participation of all members of society in the political life and institutions of the country.

The United States and Great Britain led the development of liberal nationalism. By 1830, the United States had enfranchised all white male citizens. Through two major reform laws in 1832 and 1867, Great Britain also extended the franchise. Britain first and then the United States, after a bloody civil war, eliminated slavery, although political and economic, as opposed to legal, emancipation of black citizens took another century or more to achieve. Women too waited another century. Still, these countries planted the seed of expanding individual freedom and developed some of the early international movements for human rights and law—for example, the British campaign against the international slave trade in the early nineteenth century and the Hague Conferences.

More utopian versions of liberal ideology proclaimed universal peace. Immanuel Kant, the eighteenth-century German philosopher, wrote an *Idea for a Universal History and Perpetual Peace* predicting that democracy would spread and lead to a federation of peaceful states.[33] This type of thinking may have contributed to a complacency before World War I that war was increasingly obsolete and that international organizations, law, and trade could resolve disputes, as Gladstone and Angell had envisioned.

Spotlight on democratic peace

Socialist Nationalism

Socialist nationalism focused more on the social and economic equality of individuals and advocated that state institutions restrict economic freedoms and redistribute economic wealth from the capitalist to the working classes. While communism, a more radical version of socialism, did not yield political fruit until Vladimir Ilyich Lenin installed it in Russia in 1917, many European and global societies—for example, India—adopted moderate versions of this class-oriented outlook.

Socialist parties emerged and sharpened conflicts with liberal and conservative parties. Socialist parties met in international conferences in 1907, 1910, and 1912, known as the Second International, and denounced militarism and war. In the end, however, nationalism proved stronger than internationalism. Although Social Democrats, representing the interests of the working class, actually held the majority in the German parliament in 1914, they voted on August 4, 1914, unanimously for war. In the 1860s, Bismarck had used war to co-opt the liberal nationalists and unify Germany. Now in 1914 conservatives in Germany, Russia, and other countries used war to co-opt the social nationalists and forge ideological unity through conservative and militant nationalism.

Social Darwinism

Militant, liberal, and socialist spirits came together at the end of the nineteenth century in the worldview of **Social Darwinism.** Charles Darwin, an English scientist, published in 1859 his theory of evolution in *The Origin of Species.* Darwin identified a process of competition and natural selection that accounted for the evolution and survival of biological species. In *The Descent of Man,* published in 1871, Darwin applied

Social Darwinism
a worldview that emerged in the nineteenth century that claimed that, as in the natural world described by the scientific writings of Charles Darwin, there exists a struggle among nations for a survival of the fittest.

his theory to the origins of human beings. Many nineteenth-century political leaders concluded that it must also apply to the survival and evolution of human societies and, indeed, nation-states. Bismarck, for example, said that "without struggle there can be no life and, if we wish to continue living, we must also be reconciled to further struggle."[34] President Teddy Roosevelt once famously mused, "Unless we keep the barbarian virtues, the civilized ones will be of little avail."[35] Thus was born the idea of a struggle among nations for the survival of the fittest. Only strong nations survived, and the strength of a nation involved its military power and its cultural cohesion.

Race inevitably became a measure of cultural cohesion for the Social Darwinists. It linked culture to biology and seemed to follow from Darwinist logic. It affected all countries during this period. America openly discriminated against Chinese immigrants and continued to disenfranchise Black Americans. But German leaders were particularly blunt about race. Kaiser Wilhelm II suggested on more than one occasion that the issue for him was race: "[N]ow comes . . . the Germanic peoples' fight for their existence against Russo-Gallia [Russia and France]. No further conference can smooth this over, for it is not a question of high politics but of race . . . for what is at stake is whether the Germanic race is to be or not to be in Europe."[36] His army chief of staff, von Moltke, agreed: "a European war is bound to come sooner or later, and then it will be, in the last resort, a struggle between Teuton and Slav." And so did his foreign minister Gottlieb von Jagow: "the struggle between Teuton and Slav was bound to come."[37]

These comments reflect an identity perspective. The Kaiser explicitly rules out the possibility that liberal factors might resolve the problem ("no further conference can smooth this over") and says the question is not one of "high politics," a frequent reference to great power relations or realist factors. Moltke's and Jagow's comments suggest that identity differences are bound to override diplomatic efforts for peace and lead to the last move ("war is bound to come sooner or later"). In each case, ideas are driving diplomacy and conflict, not the other way around.

causal arrow

Here was a witch's brew of culture and race stirred together in a kind of **hypernationalism** that would afflict world politics for the next century. Some historians see German war aims as the direct cause of World War I. Others agree that hypernationalism was present but came to the fore much more virulently in World War II. (See Table 3-3 for a summary of identity explanations.)

hypernationalism
a form of nationalism in the early twentieth century, most prominent in Germany, that stirred together race and culture to heighten national cohesion.

Critical Theory Explanations

Lenin saw World War I as a product of capitalist dynamics. The capitalist countries would fight one another for markets, and communist countries would be left to pick up the pieces. As soon as Lenin seized control in Russia in 1917, he pulled the Russian forces out of the capitalists' war. He concentrated on building communism in a single country, knowing that the historical dialectic of class conflict was on his side. Critical theories, such as Marxism, emphasize the deeper material forces propelling history toward its predetermined end. In the case of Marxism, the predetermined end is communism; in other cases of critical theory, it might be emancipation of marginalized voices or simply deconstruction of all power relationships. Critical theories remind us that attempts to understand history through perspectives is always selective and therefore biased. Social forces are holistic. They drive social science research no less than the political, economic, and military events that that research tries selectively to understand.

Table 3-3

The Causes of World War I: The Identity Perspective and Levels of Analysis

Level of analysis		Identity perspective
Systemic	*Structure*	• Social Darwinism—common mentality of international struggle
	Process	• Spread or alignment of ideas and ideologies: —Loss of moderation—spread of militarism, "cult of the offensive" drove mobilization plans —Britain and United States align as democracies even though they are the two largest powers
Foreign policy		• Racist clique hijacked German foreign policy
Domestic		• Hypernationalism (mixture of race and militarism in Germany as a whole) drove Germany to war
		• Liberal nationalism in the United States and Great Britain—precipitated alliance of democracies that isolated Germany
Individual		• Evil or emotionally unstable leaders: —Bethmann-Hollweg? —Kaiser Wilhelm II?

For example, one way realist perspectives distort history is by diminishing the role of identity in shaping events. Most historians do not see World War I primarily as a war caused by racism or political ideologies. Germany and Japan would give World War II a greater racist character, and the Cold War would emphasize ideological fault lines between capitalism and communism. But even in these later conflicts realist perspectives downplay the role of national identities. They fear the loss of restraint in foreign policy if domestic political passions drive policy.

Yet much of the history of Europe has been written from realist perspectives. That history, therefore, may relatively neglect identity factors. Realists always point to a famous statement by Lord Palmerston, a British prime minister in the nineteenth century. Speaking for Britain, Palmerston said, "we have no eternal allies and no permanent enemies." As we have noted, this statement became realism's mantra—countries should not align with one another based on domestic ideological sentiments, whether or not they feel friendly toward one another; alliance decisions should be made solely on the basis of relative power considerations to confront and balance the greater power. But, as we have seen in the case of Bismarck, few realists actually followed this prescription consistently. Bismarck succumbed to German **irredentism,** domestic passions and pressures to regain from France the territory of Alsace-Lorraine where German-speaking peoples resided. Here identity factors apparently overrode realist ones, even in the diplomacy of one of the most revered realist statesmen. Lord Palmerston, too, did not always follow the realist rule of no permanent friends or enemies. He once observed that "the independence of constitutional states . . . never can be a matter of indifference to the British parliament, or, I should hope, to the British public. Constitutional states I would consider to be the natural allies of this country." [38]

In other words, contrary to his realist outlook, Palmerston was now saying that the domestic political identities of countries matter more than their relative power in making foreign policy. He is hinting at the tendency of democracies (he calls them

irredentism

the annexation of or claim to territory in one state by another on historical or purported grounds of common race, ethnicity, or culture.

constitutional states) to align and not go to war with one another, thereby creating the "democratic peace" (we consider this in Chapter 6 and the conclusion of this book).

Why isn't this idea of democracies aligning with one another the proper prescription for foreign policy rather than having no permanent allies or enemies? Maybe countries align with other countries of similar cultural or political identity rather than against the country that has greater power (the realist solution) or the one that poses the greater threat (the liberal solution). There are examples of such alignments in history. The Holy Alliance was an alignment among conservative monarchies that shared similar religious identities. The Anglo-American special relationship that emerged in the late nineteenth century was an alignment between countries that shared common democratic ideologies. Maybe, as we note earlier in this chapter, Britain did not align with Germany and against the United States before World War I, not because Germany was a more proximate threat but because the United States was a more "natural" ally. Britain and the United States shared a similar heritage and democratic political system.

Critical theories make us skeptical of all these efforts to select and emphasize specific factors to understand international relations. Realist scholars writing about the past do not tell the whole story, not because they are devious but because they can't. Neither, of course, can scholars writing from liberal or identity perspectives. Nor can scholars from any single perspective isolate factors at one level of analysis and say that one level overrides or causes another. Reality is holistic not fragmented or capable of being decomposed piece by piece.

Critical theories, on the other hand, face a comparable limitation. Even though they insist on studying history as a whole, not by selecting and focusing on specific hypotheses, they have to concede that they can never tell us the whole story of history. History is too gargantuan, which is why mainstream scholars turn to selective perspectives in the first place. Critical theory can tell us the story of history only from the particular social vantage point of a particular critical theory scholar. As we see in this book, the social vantage point that critical theorists often select is the interests of the poor, oppressed, and disenfranchised peoples of the world, which in their view are systematically deemphasized in mainstream perspectives. (See Table 3-4 for a summary of critical theory perspectives; bear in mind that critical theories do not consider the factors at the various levels of analysis to be separable but, rather, interrelated as an inseparable whole.)

Table 3-4

The Causes of World War I: The Critical Theory Perspective and Levels of Analysis[a]

Level of analysis		Critical theory perspective
Systemic	Structure	• Historical materialism drives clash between capitalist and communist states; Russia pulls out of World War I to let capitalist states fight it out
	Process	• Dialectic drives history through class conflict
Foreign policy		—
Domestic		• Russia becomes vanguard of the proletariat
Individual		• Lenin builds communism in one country

a. Critical theories do not consider the factors at the various levels of analysis to be separable, as the mainstream perspectives do.

Summary

Our discussion of World War I shows how the concepts emphasized by each perspective play out in the actual course of historical events. Realist perspectives emphasize material factors such as anarchy and the security dilemma (self-help), rising (Germany) and declining (Great Britain) states, power conversion through more and less efficient bureaucracies, imperialistic domestic interest groups (cartelized politics in Germany), and weak leaders (Russia and Austria-Hungary). Liberal perspectives emphasize the absence or demise of common international institutions (Concert of Europe), the depth or shallowness of interdependence (the Hague Conferences), the misperceptions and accidents of diplomacy (secret diplomacy and path dependence leading to the last move), and the breakdown of domestic policy coordination and institutions. Identity perspectives emphasize the variety of nationalist ideologies and their accompanying international discourses. Social Darwinism, the spread of hypernationalist ideologies glorifying the "cult of the offensive," won out over Kantian liberal and Marxist socialist discourses. Evil or emotionally unstable leaders may have also contributed.

The mainstream perspectives emphasize these concepts from different levels of analysis. The kaiser may have been a uniquely weak leader (individual level), Germany an aggressive militarist state (domestic level), the leadership manipulative in using war to overcome domestic fissures (foreign policy level), or Germany just too powerful to contain (systemic level).

Critical theories weave all these causal factors from different perspectives and levels of analysis into a single historical drama, such as dialectical materialism in the case of Marxist theories. This drama is driven by factors beyond the control of theorists and thus not subject to rational manipulation. The future cannot be understood or made by applying tested propositions from the past to policy prescriptions for the future.

The variety of explanations is bewildering. But our analytical tools help us distinguish and organize them. Then, as scholars and students, we have an obligation to keep testing and evaluating the explanations. We may never obtain definitive answers, but we can know better how and why we disagree.

Key Concepts

cult of the offensive 129	militant nationalism 127	Triple Alliance 117
Entente Cordiale 116	power conversion 115	Triple Entente 117
hypernationalism 131	Schlieffen Plan 118	Zollverein 114
irredentism 132	Social Darwinism 130	
liberal nationalism 128	socialist nationalism 128	

Study Questions

1. Do you believe that the two cousins, Willy and Nicky, could have prevented World War I? What level of analysis does your answer reflect?

2. Why is Bismarck's diplomacy, which included the Berlin Conference in 1878, considered to be realist rather than liberal?

3. What are the differences among the following domestic level explanations of World War I: imperialistic cartels, poorly coordinated military and political institutions, and nationalist political ideologies?

4. Can you give three explanations, one from each perspective, why World War I started in 1914 and not earlier?

5. Which perspective is reflected and which rejected in the following argument about World War I from John Mearsheimer's *The Tragedy of Great Power Politics*? Explain your conclusion.

   Even if Bismarck had remained in power past 1890, it is unlikely that he could have forestalled the Franco-Russian alliance with clever diplomacy. . . . France and Russia came together because they were scared of Germany's growing power, not because Germany behaved aggressively or foolishly.[39]

6. What level of analysis is Professor Jack Levy emphasizing when he writes: "it is certainly plausible that the July crisis might have ended differently if other individuals had been in positions of power at the beginning of July 1914"?[40]

7. What level of analysis is Professor Jack Snyder using when he concludes, that "Germany's expansionism was compelled by its position in the international system . . . is fundamentally unconvincing [because] [e]ven a cursory look at Germany's international position will show that the nation's vulnerability and insecurity were caused by its own aggressive policies"?[41]

4

World War II
Why Did War Happen Again?

The German nation salutes its Führer, Adolf Hitler, in 1938 after the annexation of Austria. At the time, was Hitler trying to reunite German-speaking people (the identity perspective), negotiate a better peace than Versailles (the liberal perspective), or prepare for a war to acquire *Lebensraum* (the realist perspective)?

Lebensraum
the Hitlerian expansionist ideology that proposed a larger living space for the German racial community.

On November 5, 1937, Adolf Hitler summoned his generals to a meeting in Berlin. The meeting was expected to be routine. But once it began Hitler swore the participants to secrecy and proceeded to outline his plans for war. According to minutes drafted from memory a few days later by an army adjutant, Colonel Friedrich Hossbach, Hitler said that the aim of German policy was to secure a larger living space—*Lebensraum*—for the German racial community. This expansion could only be done by war, which had to occur before 1943–1945, when German power would peak. The first steps would be to seize Czechoslovakia and Austria. Hitler believed that France, England, and Poland had already written off the Czechs and had too many problems of their own to resist. But if they did, Germany must counter with lightning strikes. The deck would then be cleared for the final strike against the primary enemy, Russia.[1]

Is this the explanation for World War II? A premeditated plan by a single man (notice, the identity perspective and individual level of analysis) who had written two books ten years earlier—the two-volume *Mein Kampf* in 1925–1926 and a secret, unpublished book in 1928—that not only laid out a strategy for conquering territory in the east but also hatched his horrific plans for the extermination of the Jews. The war followed this plan pretty closely. So, the explanation seems convincing, right? Case closed. We can go straight to the next chapter.

Causes of Madness

Not so fast. How did a man like Hitler ever come to power in the first place? What domestic level factors facilitated his rise, and what systemic factors permitted another colossal catastrophe so soon after the death trenches of World War I? Weren't 15 million dead enough? What about causal forces from the liberal perspective? Hadn't European diplomats abandoned the balance of power and built a bold new international institution called the **League of Nations** to settle disputes peacefully? Massive mistakes that set the conditions for war must have been made long before Hitler came to power in January 1933. Did Hitler just exploit these mistakes? Could someone else have started World War II even if he had not? Or would Germany have gone to war eventually because realist factors, such as Germany's unity and exposed central location, continued to fuel the security dilemma, even if Germany and other countries had done almost everything right? We have to try to answer these questions, whether we succeed or not, because three times as many people (approximately 35–50 million) died in World War II as in World War I, six million of them Jews in the Holocaust. What could have caused such madness?

Once again, there is disagreement. Realists ask if World War II wasn't really just a continuation of World War I. The basic problem was the same: anarchy, the security dilemma, and an unstable balance of power. After World War I, Germany was not occupied or destroyed. It remained intact and potentially a looming menace again in the exposed (remember the open plains) center of the European system. True, Germany was much weaker. It had lost about 13 percent of its prewar territory, the monarchy had ended, and runaway inflation and economic depression had followed. The Versailles Treaty limited its arms and stripped it of its colonies. But Germany continued to have the largest population in Europe and one of the most resilient, talented, and efficient societies in the world. The major powers in Europe did not see this problem in the 1920s, distracted, as realists see it, by utopian liberal schemes of collective security such as the League of Nations. When they did see it in the late 1930s, it was too late. Germany had gathered momentum, as it had before World War I, and the security dilemma intensified with renewed force. Germany was too big to contain without encirclement and too little to feel safe with encirclement.

From the liberal perspective, the balance of power itself was the problem. As the dilemmas with German encirclement suggested, such a balance could never be stable. It had to be replaced by new institutional arrangements. Liberal advocates led by President Wilson proposed a whole new scheme for managing military relations in international politics. The concept of collective security organized force on a different principle, one based on common institutions and the preponderance of power rather than separate national interests and the balance of power. The League of Nations was an imaginative new approach, but it didn't work at the time. Why? Liberal accounts lay the blame largely at the door of the United States. It refused to play its role as a new, leading great power. After helping win World War I, the United States did an about-face, refused to join the League, and retreated into isolationism during the 1920s and 1930s. Without the leading power, the League could not muster a preponderance of power, and the world marched off into another nationalist struggle for power.

League of Nations
an institution founded after the Paris Peace Conference in 1919; it was the first international institution to embody the collective security approach to the use of military power.

Spotlight on
security dilemma

Spotlight on
collective security

But why does nationalism have to lead to war? How do identities get constructed so as to lead to war? If all nations were satisfied with the status quo, no state would seek to upset it. What kind of nationalism leads to aggression? Identity perspectives have an answer—the kind that derives from revanchism (the desire for revenge), irredentism (the desire to regain territories), racism, and xenophobia. German nationalism after World War I had all these characteristics. Many Germans felt that they had been unjustly blamed for World War I and humiliated by the Versailles Treaty that ended the war. They considered it only reasonable to regain territories where Germans lived, such as Alsace-Lorraine, which France had seized in World War I. Many Germans also indulged in a racism of Aryan superiority and murderous antisemitism, and they dehumanized foreigners not of their superior race. This was the extreme nihilistic nationalism that Bismarck unleashed in the 1860s and talked about in his conversations with von Gerlach: "I can even think out the idea that some day 'unbelieving Jesuits' will rule over the Mark Brandenburg [core of Prussia] together with a Bonaparte absolutism. . . ."[2] Aggressive missionaries (Jesuits) without any beliefs (unbelieving) ruling over Berlin with a Napoleon-like absolutism—not a bad description of the Nazis who controlled Germany from 1933–1945.

This time let's start with liberal explanations of the war. President Wilson and the League of Nations may have failed to prevent a second world war, but they left a powerful example of collective security through universal international institutions that later bore practical fruit in the UN intervention in 1990–1991 in the first Persian Gulf War (see Chapter 6). Liberal perspectives argue that if there is hope that the world community might someday go beyond the balance of power and domesticate military force—that is, convert it to police power, as in domestic society—it will have to grow out of the seed of institutional arrangements in which all nations and people participate. As we will see, other perspectives disagree. Realist perspectives say it still matters more who holds power within those institutions, while identity perspectives argue that the values these institutions promote matter more than the rules or power they employ. The Parallel Timeline on page 158 helps organize events by perspectives.

Liberal Solutions to War

In asking Congress to declare war on Germany, Woodrow Wilson emphasized that "the world must be made safe for democracy."[3] Subsequently, in January 1918, he laid out to Congress his famous Fourteen Points plan to restructure the world order after the war. Listen to the emphasis in these points on liberal themes of relationships, negotiations, interdependence, and peaceful pursuits (non-zero-sum goals): open diplomacy, freedom of the seas, general disarmament, removal of trade barriers, impartial settlement of colonial claims, internationalization of the Dardanelles, and establishment of the League of Nations. The program also had realist elements involving territorial and military adjustments: restoration of Belgium, return of Alsace-Lorraine to France, evacuation of Russian territory, readjustment of Italy's frontiers, evacuation of the Balkans, and creation (actually recreation—remember that it had been partitioned among Prussia, Russia, and Austria at the end of the eighteenth century) of Poland with access to the sea. And there was an important identity element as well, the granting of autonomy or **self-determination** to the national minorities of the Austro-Hungarian and Ottoman Empires. Wilson expected that self-determination would lead to democracy, hence his theme "to make the world safe for democracy." But the plan relied over-

self-determination
the right of autonomy for nations; that is, nations may adopt whatever substantive identities they wish, democratic or nondemocratic.

whelmingly on the expectation that repetitive practices of trade and diplomacy would condition state behavior to preserve the peace and prepare the way for democracy to spread and the balance of power to recede. Liberal procedures would steadily trump identity and power disparities.

As we know now, it was not to be. The League failed for various reasons (discussed later): American isolationism, utopian disarmament schemes, unanimity, and Japanese and Italian aggression. Nevertheless, Wilson believed the League of Nations would eventually overcome the divisions of nationalism and in the long run lead to more open, democratic, peaceful societies. From his liberal perspective, he expected procedural institutional factors to reduce the significance of power disparities and of nationalist or identity differences. Institutions would shape identities toward common ends, supplanting relative power that drove nations toward separate national interests.

causal arrow

Collective Security, Not Balance of Power

What was this new approach? Collective security started with a fundamentally different configuration of power. From the liberal perspective, the decentralization or balance of power had failed disastrously. Wilson was an unrelenting critic of the secret treaties, arms races, colonial rivalries, and great power maneuvering that drove the balance of power into perpetual flux and uncertainty. Restoring that system after World War I, as the Congress of Vienna did after the Napoleonic Wars, was out of the question. Wilson wanted "no odor of the Vienna settlement" at Versailles.[4] The new approach of collective security would centralize, not decentralize, military power. It would require all nations to join together in a single universal institution and pool their military power to create an overwhelming central military force. This central force would be so powerful it could reduce the overall level of force through disarmament and operate largely on the basis of economic, not military, sanctions. Now if a particular country threatened another country, the common institution would order the offending power to desist and, if necessary, threaten it with economic sanctions. Overpowered, the offending country would be deterred or, if it persisted, defeated. No country could withstand the centralized power of the entire global community. Protection for all countries would be achieved not through the balance but the preponderance of power.

How would the central institution decide which country was threatening the system? This was crucial because the system depended on organizing against the country that was the greatest threat, not the country that was the greatest power. This was a key difference from the balance-of-power and realist solutions to war. From a liberal perspective, countries align against the country threatening the system regardless of its size, not against the greater power based on its size or capabilities. So how would the liberal perspective measure threat, as the realist perspective had to measure power? It would do so through a set of institutional procedures that spelled out the obligations states must follow in resolving international disputes. If a state failed to meet these obligations, it was the threat. Common institutions and rules defined threat, not relative power.

League of Nations

The League of Nations was the first international institution to embody the collective security approach to the use of military power. The Covenant of the League spelled out the various provisions of collective security.

Article 5 established the principle of **unanimity.** All nations, great and small, par-

unanimity
a principle in Article 5 in the Covenant of the League of Nations that established that all nations, no matter what size, must agree on what constitutes a threat to international peace and security.

The League of Nations meets in Geneva, Switzerland, in 1921 to resolve disputes peacefully under the auspices of collective security.

ticipated in the League and decided collectively what constituted a threat to international peace and security. Remember Gladstone's appeal in the nineteenth century to the "general judgement of civilized mankind"? The League was, as Woodrow Wilson said, the "general judgment of the world as to what is right." [5] Consequently, all countries, regardless of size or domestic ideologies, made decisions on an equal basis. The League of Nations buried the old Congress of Vienna system in which great powers had special responsibilities.

Article 2 created the two main common institutions of the League: the Council, composed initially of nine members, and the Assembly, composed of all members. Article 4 made the five great powers that had just won the war (the United States, which of course never joined; Great Britain; France; Italy; and Japan) permanent members of the Council. But these members did not have any special privileges. All Council members, great and small, had a veto, the practical consequence of unanimity. Moreover, the Council had no special responsibilities. The Assembly, on which all members sat and also decided by unanimity, had exactly the same responsibilities. Indeed, Articles 3 and 4 establishing the responsibilities of the Assembly and Council, respectively, used the same language: either body "may deal at its meetings with any matter within the sphere of action of the League or affecting the peace of the world." There was no hierarchy between the Council and Assembly.

Articles 10 and 11 of the League Covenant established the collective commitment to deter or defeat aggression. Article 10 committed members to "respect and preserve as against external aggression the territorial integrity and political independence of all Members of the League." Article 11 committed members to consider "any war or threat of war, whether immediately affecting any of the Members of the League or not, . . . a matter of concern to the whole League."

Notice that all members had to see a threat anywhere as a common concern even if the particular threat did not immediately affect them. Conflict anywhere affected everyone. Peace was indivisible; it was a collective good, hence, collective security. It existed for all or none, and its enjoyment by one did not diminish its enjoyment by others.

How was this possible? As realists argue, don't countries have separate geopolitical interests and see threats differently? Think of the differences between the United States and some of its allies in the 2003 war on Iraq. True, but the hope in the League was to channel these differences through a process, a discussion of disputes, a set of rules and procedures that would lead to compromise and define the aggressor as any country that stood in the way of compromise.

Articles 12–15 set out the League's rules. They created a path of procedures that would identify the aggressor. Notice how this liberal approach defines threat by iterative interactions and path dependence, not by power disparities or ideological dif-

Spotlight on collective goods

Spotlight on interactions

ferences. Article 12 said members must submit disputes to peaceful arbitration, judicial settlement, or the Council—which in turn could submit disputes to the Assembly. Countries must then refrain from war until after the League made a decision. If the issue was suitable for arbitration or judicial settlement, Articles 13 and 14 set up the Permanent Court of International Justice to render judicial decisions. If the dispute went to the Council, Article 15 required the Council to settle the dispute or issue a report with its recommendations. If the Council issued a unanimous report except for the parties to the dispute, the members agreed that they would not go to war with any party to the dispute that abided by the Council's recommendations. This provision was intended to isolate the aggressor party and make it feel the full condemnation and power of the common community of nations.

Article 16 then said that if any member went to war in disregard of Council or judicial recommendations as prescribed in Articles 12–15:

> [I]t shall, *ipso facto,* be deemed to have committed an act of war against all other Members of the League, which hereby undertake immediately to subject it to the severance of all trade or financial relations, the prohibition of all intercourse between their nationals and the nationals of the Covenant-breaking state, and the prevention of all financial, commercial or personal intercourse between the nationals of the Covenant-breaking state and the nationals of any other State, whether a member of the League or not.

The word "immediately" implied that these sanctions would be automatic.

Presto, the world had a new system to define threat and deal with it. But didn't such a system risk turning every dispute, however minor, into a global war? After all, everyone had to confront the aggressor. That made a local dispute a global one, just the way the balance of power turned a local clash between Austria and Serbia into World War I. The League had an answer. As Article 16 said, League members would use economic sanctions, not military force. Because everyone would be participating, economic sanctions would suffice to deter the aggressor. The aggressor would be isolated and relent or starve to death if it did not relent. Military force would not be necessary, except as a backup or last resort should sanctions fail—for example, if the aggressor attacked out of desperation. Military power, in fact, could be reduced. Article 8 called for "the reduction of national armaments to the lowest point consistent with national safety and the enforcement by common action of international obligations."

Spotlight on disarmament

Here is the classic liberal solution to conflicts. Get everyone to participate, negotiate peacefully, use economic sanctions if necessary, and maintain military power only to the extent necessary to implement economic sanctions. Don't think this approach is irrelevant today? As we have already noted (and examine further in Chapter 6), it worked like a textbook case in the first Persian Gulf war in 1990–1991. And critics of America's policy in the second Persian Gulf war in 2003 argued straight from the collective security rule book: the United Nations was the only legitimate institution to make the decision to go to war because it included everyone (the general judgment of the world); negotiations were the only way to facilitate inspections and resolve the issue of WMD; economic sanctions were sufficient to convince Iraq to come clean; and military force was necessary only to support economic sanctions—that is, to get the UN weapons inspectors back into Iraq by positioning an invasion force in the Persian Gulf but by not invading the country. The idea of collective security survives today in the operations of the UN, even if it failed under the League of Nations.

Why the League of Nations Failed

What went wrong with the liberal solution of the League of Nations? Several things. First, the United States, the leading world power, did not join. Nor did the Soviet Union until 1933, by which time two other major powers, Germany and Japan, had withdrawn. The League of Nations never achieved the preponderance of power it required to work effectively. Second, the League never organized effective security guarantees. It failed to provide credible military commitments to defend countries, and eventually countries scrambled outside the League to protect their security. Third, although it made some progress in reducing arms, disarmament without credible security commitments only led to more, not fewer, security fears. Fourth, unanimity proved to be the League's Achilles' heel. The aggressor country also had a veto. The League could issue a report without concurrence of the parties to the dispute, but the report was toothless unless the League either followed it up with specific actions, which the aggressor could veto, or implemented Article 16 sanctions automatically, which might mean war. When the League condemned Japan's invasion of Manchuria, Japan vetoed the report and withdrew from the League. When the League imposed economic sanctions on Italy, the League eventually backed off because France and Britain feared it might mean war with Italy and they were more concerned at the time about Germany than Italy. Peace in this case proved not to be indivisible. One threat (Germany) was not considered to be the same as another threat (Italy). And given different perceptions of threat, the veto for everyone became a loophole for inaction.

Let's see how American isolationism, utopian disarmament agreements, unanimity, and Japanese and Italian aggression undermined the League.

AMERICAN ISOLATIONISM. Woodrow Wilson literally died trying to persuade the Congress and American people to join the League. He returned in July 1919 from the peace negotiations in Paris to campaign nonstop across the country for Congress to approve the Treaty of Versailles and the League of Nations. But in early October he collapsed and suffered a massive paralytic stroke. When the treaty came up for votes in November and again in March 1920, the League's greatest champion was still seriously ill.

A favorite counterfactual question from the liberal perspective is whether different leadership (for example, someone like Franklin Roosevelt, who deftly guided an isolationist country into World War II) or a healthier President Wilson might have persuaded Congress to approve the League. The country was not of one mind on the League issue. One group opposed the League and any American military entanglement abroad. It was led by William Jennings Bryan, a frequent Democratic presidential candidate and Wilson's first secretary of state, and by Senator William E. Borah of Idaho. This group harked back to George Washington's warning in his farewell address to stay out of foreign alliances. A second group, led by former president Teddy Roosevelt and Senator Henry Cabot Lodge, did not oppose military commitments per se, but preferred specific ones and recoiled at the automatic sanctions under Article 16 to act without congressional deliberations. Finally, a third group led by former president William Howard Taft supported the League.

In order to win the confirmation battle in the Senate, Wilson had to win over the second group, the one that demanded reservations on Article 16 preserving the constitutional power of Congress to declare war. He failed, and analysts still argue about the causes. Was it because the constitutional structure of the American government prevented Congress from giving up its power to declare war—a liberal argument from the domestic level of analysis? Or was it Wilson's high-mindedness and ideological inflexibility? Did, in effect, identity factors from an individual level of analysis outweigh institutional ones from the domestic level? Or maybe it was simply a political struggle for domestic power between Wilson and his foes—a realist explanation from the domestic level of analysis. Notice again how our analytical tools of perspectives and levels of analysis help sort out a sometimes bewildering array of conflicting arguments explaining a historical event.

← *causal arrow*

The result, in any case, was a League of Nations that was supposed to mobilize preponderant power but lacked from the outset the world's then most important power, the United States. Another soon-to-be great power, the Soviet Union, also went into isolationism. The October 1917 Russian Revolution toppled the tsar from power, and Vladimir Ilyich Lenin, whom the Germans had transported into Russia in 1916 in a secret railroad car, seized power with his Bolshevik faction and not only pulled Russia out of the war—which is why the Germans helped him—but also out of world diplomacy. Russia slipped into civil war and then, under Stalin after 1925, concentrated on the transformation of its domestic society to communism. Marxist-Leninist ideology—an identity factor—convinced some communist leaders that the state would wither away and that diplomacy, at least as conventionally understood, would not require much of their time.

Disarmament Agreements: The Washington Naval Conference and Kellogg-Briand Pact. Liberal perspectives tend to downplay military power compared to realist perspectives. As we have noted, Article 8 of the League Covenant called for disarmament. Other international agreements at the time similarly restricted military capacity. The Treaty of Versailles imposed stringent arms control measures on Germany. The Washington Naval Conference of 1921–1922 set ceilings on sea power, placing the United States on a par with Great Britain and holding Japan to three-fifths of the U.S. level. Disarmament talks continued episodically throughout the 1920s and 1930s. Even after Germany left the League in 1933, Hitler concluded a naval pact with Great Britain in 1935 that limited the German surface fleet to 35 percent of Britain's.

Spotlight on disarmament

The idea of getting rid of arms and war itself was behind the Kellogg-Briand Pact signed in 1928. Originally proposed as a U.S.-French agreement, the pact called on all signatories "to condemn recourse to war for the solution of international controversies, and renounce it as an instrument of national policy."[6] Practically all the nations of the world signed it, including Germany, Japan, and Italy. As a statement of moral and legal sentiment, the Kellogg-Briand Pact was unsurpassed. But as a practical matter, it barely survived its signing. Immediately, countries, especially the United States, entered reservations of self-defense, regional security, and sovereignty that gutted the commitment. The pact became meaningless. When asked why the United States should be interested if another nation broke the treaty, U.S. Secretary of State Frank Kellogg replied, "There is not a bit of reason."[7]

Japanese Aggression in Manchuria. The first real test for the League came in 1931. Japan invaded Manchuria, a northern province of China. China appealed to the League, and the League called on Japan to withdraw its troops. But Japan voted against the resolution. Here was the core problem of collective security. Unanimity, and the veto, let the bad guys hold the world community at bay.

When the Qing dynasty fell in 1911, and China lapsed into civil war, Japan increased its military position along the Manchurian railroad where it had already stationed troops under agreements stemming from the Russo-Japanese War in 1905 (brokered, by the way, by U.S. President Theodore Roosevelt, one of America's first forays on to the stage of world diplomacy). In September 1931, the Japanese military, with or without orders from Tokyo (it's still disputed), staged an incident and invaded the rest of Manchuria, creating the puppet state of Manchukuo.

Spotlight on unanimity

After Japan blocked League action, the League established a commission to investigate the incident. The Lytton Commission (named after its chairman, Lord Lytton of Great Britain) issued a report in September 1932 that asked League members not to recognize Manchukuo. But the report did not invoke Article 16. When the League voted in February 1933 to accept the Lytton report, Japan cast the lone dissenting vote and then abruptly withdrew from the League. The League was exposed as a paper tiger. It was not long before the European powers dealt the finishing blow to the League.

ITALIAN AGGRESSION IN ETHIOPIA. In the nineteenth century, Italy acquired colonies in Eritrea, an African territory at the mouth of the Red Sea. It tried at the time to colonize neighboring Ethiopia as well, but it failed. In October 1935, the Italian government, under fascist dictator Benito Mussolini, tried again—Italy invaded Ethiopia. This time, the League got around the unanimity requirement. It convened a special conference. Fifty members attended and defined Italy as the aggressor. They invoked specific but not complete sanctions—an arms embargo, cutoff of loans to Italy and imports from Italy, and embargo on certain exports to Italy such as rubber and tin. But they did not embargo steel, coal, and oil exports to Italy, break off diplomatic relations, or close the Suez Canal, through which Italy supplied its forces in Eritrea. The League seemed to be working, at least partially and certainly better than in the case of Japan and Manchuria.

Spotlight on indivisibility of peace

By December 1935, however, Britain and France were having second thoughts because they needed Italy to make the balance of power work against Germany. Here was the problem with collective security arrangements. These arrangements considered every threat to be of equal concern to all League members, regardless of where the conflict occurred or which countries it involved. Peace was assumed to be indivisible. But in this case, Britain and France did not consider the threat from Italy to be as great as that from Germany. Thus, the British and French foreign ministers met and came up with the Hoare-Laval plan, which divided Ethiopia into two parts, awarding one part to Italy and the other to the League. When word of the plan leaked, the British minister, Samuel Hoare, had to resign. Public opinion was outraged, as were the representatives of small nations, one of whom warned, "Great or small, strong or weak, near or far, white or colored, let us never forget that one day we may be somebody's Ethiopia."[8]

The fate of the weak in this case was nevertheless sealed. When Hitler marched into the Rhineland in March 1936, Britain and France met with Italy in Stresa and gave the green light to Italy's conquest of Ethiopia. The balance of power had prevailed over collective security. Would it now work better than it had in 1914? Don't hold your breath. (See Table 4-1 for a summary of liberal explanations.)

Table 4-1

The Causes of World War II: The Liberal Perspective and Levels of Analysis

Level of analysis		Liberal perspective
Systemic	*Structure*	• Collective security problems and the failure of the League of Nations: 　—Major powers not involved to create preponderance of power 　—Weak centralized security commitments and hence no incentives to disarm 　—Aggressor states not members of League and hence not subject to institutional constraints • Economic depression
	Process	• Misperceptions of threat: 　—UK saw France as stronger than Germany 　—France thought defense dominant and "chain-ganged" with UK and Poland (left initiative to Hitler) 　—UK appeased instead of balanced Hitler at Munich (1938) and failed to align with Soviet Union after Hitler invaded Czechoslovakia in March 1939
		• Spread of immoderate goals: Germany and Japan were revisionist states, sought to overturn Versailles and create Greater East Asia Co-Prosperity Sphere
Foreign policy		• British foreign minister resigns from domestic opposition to plan to divide Ethiopia
Domestic		• Divided domestic interests in United States reject League
		• Economic collapse in Germany
Individual		• Ineffective leadership of Congress by a dying President Wilson

Realist Accounts

From the realist perspective, the problem was always Germany. As Map 4-1 shows, its unity and location in the center of Europe made the balance of power difficult to operate. Germany was either too little and thus vulnerable or too big and thus threatening. This reality triggered a virulent security dilemma of encirclement and fear. So, Germany had to be either weakened or divided again, as it was before 1871. The Versailles Treaty tried the first solution. It weakened Germany. But then Germany scratched its way back. It aligned with Russia, joined the League, and accepted border guarantees with France and Belgium in the west but not with Poland and Czechoslovakia in the east. Hitler systematically reclaimed territories and people in the east that Germany had lost in World War I. By 1939, Germany faced the prospect of another two-front war. This time it initially defeated both France and Russia. Germany now dominated on one side of a weakened Russia (now the Soviet Union, Map 4-2), and Japan threatened on the other side (Map 4-3). The United States became concerned. It tightened the noose on Japan, and Japan attacked Pearl Harbor. The United States joined Great Britain and the Soviet Union and eventually destroyed German and Japanese power. Now, after World War II, the allies tried the second solution—they divided Germany again. But we save that story for the next chapter; here we take up the tragedy of Versailles and the interwar period.

Spotlight on security dilemma

Map 4-1 Germany Before World War II, 1938

Map 4-2 Germany and Occupied Territories, 1942

Greater German Reich
Territories controlled by Germany
German allies

Spotlight on
balance of power

Versailles Treaty

After World War I, the victorious allies met in the Versailles Palace outside Paris to conclude the peace treaty. The Versailles Treaty gutted the former German empire. Germany lost territory and its colonies. Alsace-Lorraine went back to the French. The Rhineland was permanently demilitarized and administered for fifteen years by an international authority. Poland was restored with a corridor to the sea and the port of Danzig, which became a "free city" under League supervision. The Polish corridor split East Prussia from the rest of Germany, in the way Kaliningrad, a Russian province in former East Prussia, is separated today from Russia. Versailles cut Germany's army to 100,000 volunteers and its navy to six cruisers and a few smaller vessels. The British demolished the German navy after the war. Germany was forbidden to have a general staff and any offensive weapons such as submarines, aircraft, tanks, or heavy artillery. Most punitively, Versailles pronounced in Article 231, the famous "war guilt" clause, that Germany was solely responsible for the outbreak of World War I (adopting a domestic level of analysis explanation of World War I), and Germany was required to pay massive reparations (then about $33 billion; in today's dollars, some $300–400 billion) that subsequently burdened the German economy and international trade.

Problem solved, right? Not quite. France knew that Germany would not remain weak permanently. Like the victorious powers at Vienna in 1815, France wanted a military alliance to subdue the defeated power should it rise again. Britain, however, saw France as the more powerful country. In the 1920s, France had a smaller share of European wealth than Britain, but it had an army of around 600,000 men, double or triple the size of Britain's and six times Germany's allotted number.[9] Neither Wilson and the U.S. Congress nor a Bolshevik and isolated Russia were ready to make military commitments to defend France. So France turned to keeping

Germany weak as long as possible and finding smaller allies. It occupied the Ruhr Valley—the heart of Germany's industrial establishment next to the Rhineland—in January 1923 to extract reparations. And it concluded alliances with the small states of eastern Europe—Poland, and the "Little Entente" of Czecho-slovakia, Romania, and Yugoslavia—to serve as a substitute, it hoped, for the Franco-Russian Alliance before World War I.

Rapallo and Locarno

Excluded and humiliated by the Versailles Treaty, Germany responded to encirclement by meeting in April 1922 with the Russians at Rapallo, a seaside resort in Italy. Both countries nurtured grievances against the west (Russia at western involvement in its civil war from 1918 to 1920) and agreed to establish full diplomatic relations. Over the next fifteen years, Russia helped Germany evade some of the Versailles restrictions on its military forces and training. Think of

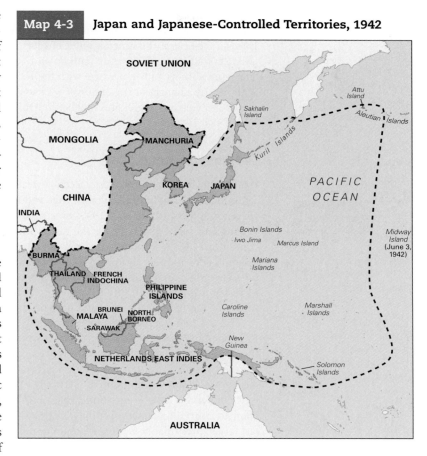

Map 4-3 **Japan and Japanese-Controlled Territories, 1942**

it. Here was a classic realist alignment. Even then ideological foes, the two countries (one recently monarchist going fascist—Hitler's failed barroom *putsch* occurred in 1923—the other already communist) shared a common interest in radically revising the established order coming out of World War I.

Spotlight on

realist alliances between ideological adversaries

Seeing the dangers of alienating Germany, the western powers rushed to reassure Berlin. France ended the Ruhr occupation in fall 1923, and Great Britain proposed the alliance that France had always wanted. But Britain did not want to isolate Germany further, so it proposed an alliance to guarantee French and Belgian borders as part of a broader agreement under the League that would also make Germany a member. The Locarno Pact, signed in 1925 (and for which the French, British, and German foreign ministers won the Nobel Peace Prize), guaranteed Germany's western borders with France and Belgium. But this guarantee was not against German aggression per se. Rather, it was a general commitment in the spirit of collective security against any threat from any direction, making it, of course, less meaningful. At the same time, Germany undertook general obligations as a League member to settle disputes peacefully and concluded arbitration agreements with its eastern neighbors—Poland, Czechoslovakia, and Romania. Significantly, however, it did not recognize its borders with these countries as it did with its western neighbors. Nor did League members guarantee the eastern borders.

So, here was a huge hole in the balance of power. In the west, where France and Great

Britain were relatively strong, the League guaranteed borders. In the east, where small states had replaced Russia and Austria-Hungary and the balance of power was relatively weak, the League did not guarantee borders. All that existed in the east were a few frail alliances that France had set up with Poland, Romania, Yugoslavia, and Czechoslovakia. This vulnerability only got worse with the Kellogg-Briand Pact, which promised peace without any alliances or use of power whatsoever. From the realist perspective, the stage was set for German aggression well before Hitler showed up, especially in the east where World War II started.

Germany Expands

Spotlight on concealing intentions

If Germany had ever intended to accept a weakened role in the postwar Versailles order, Hitler decided emphatically against that option. But he disguised his plans masterfully for several years. In October 1933, nine months after coming to power, Hitler left the League and immediately broke the restrictions on German rearmament. At the same time, however, he concluded a non-aggression pact with Poland, which weakened Poland's commitment to France if Germany attacked France, and signed a naval treaty with Great Britain. He also started a major propaganda campaign that Germany sought to reclaim only what an unjust Versailles Treaty had taken away—once Germany had united all Germans again, it would have no further designs on its neighbors.

Thus, when German troops marched into the "permanently demilitarized" Rhineland in March 1936 to liberate German residents, no western power resisted, even though this step violated German as well as League guarantees. The next target was the German people in Austria. Germany signed an alliance with Italy in 1936 creating the Axis powers and weaning one of Germany's perennial rivals in Austria away from the west (remember how France and Britain had backed off on sanctions in the Ethiopian affair to court an alliance with Italy?). Hitler then annexed Austria in March 1938. His last target, presumably, was the German population in the Sudetenland—Germans, living on the Czechoslovakian side of the border, who had been separated from Germany by Versailles. Hitler demanded the annexation of the Sudetenland. In late September 1938, Neville Chamberlain, the British prime minister, met Hitler in Munich, together with the French and Italian heads of government. The western allies agreed to return the Sudetenland to Germany, and the Munich Conference went down in history as the classic symbol of **appeasement,** a policy of making concessions to a stronger foe because one is unwilling to consider the use of force. Now that Germany was whole, the allies hoped, Hitler would surely cease to upset the status quo.

appeasement

a policy of making concessions to a stronger foe because a nation is less willing to consider the use of force.

Another Two-Front War

Unfortunately, not so! From a realist perspective, whatever Hitler's intentions, Germany still faced a security dilemma. Did that explain why Hitler did not stop after Munich? By 1939–1940, Germany was again superior. It controlled 36 percent of Europe's wealth, compared to 9 percent for France, 24 percent for Great Britain, and 28 percent for the Soviet Union.[10] It was too big for its neighbors to feel comfortable individually, but if those neighbors got together Germany was too small to feel comfortable alone.

Germany faced the same situation of superiority and encirclement as it had before World War I. The security dilemma still dominated. And Germany followed roughly the same strategy to deal with this situation. It strengthened its position in the east, turned west, eliminated one adversary, and wheeled around for the final stroke against Russia.

Spotlight on security dilemma

Some realists find it uncanny that this strategy repeated itself. It's too easy, they argue, to attribute the war simply to Hitler's megalomania. Larger structural forces had to be at work.[11]

Germany invaded the rest of Czechoslovakia in March 1939. Now Germany's neighbors knew it was not just trying to unite Germans, and Britain immediately signed defense guarantees with Poland and Romania. The Triple Entente (remember, Britain, France, and Russia before World War I) struggled to reemerge. Counterbalancing was happening, but it was happening late. Why? Some realists argue, because Germany's power, especially military power, did not peak until 1939–1940, unlike before World War I when it had peaked already in 1905.[12] This time, Germany had disguised its military buildup as well as its intentions. But now the chess pieces were almost in place. Britain and France had defense commitments with Poland and Romania. The missing piece was the Soviet Union.

Joseph Stalin succeeded Lenin in 1925 and brutally yanked his country into the twentieth century. Massive state-driven industrialization raised the Soviet Union to the great power ranks. But Stalin imprisoned and murdered millions of farmers and opponents in the process.[13] The Soviet Union joined the League in 1933 and played a cat-and-mouse game—realists call it buckpassing—with France and Britain, in which each was trying to get the other country to stop Hitler. By summer 1939, however, the cat-and-mouse game was over, and the cat was now, so to speak, in the fire.

> **Spotlight on buckpassing**

Stalin had to decide whether to work with France and Great Britain or to throw in his lot with a fellow dictator. He negotiated with both sides and, to the surprise of the world, announced in August 1939 a non-aggression pact with Hitler, the famous Molotov-Ribbentrop agreement, named after the foreign ministers. (If you want your name to go down in history, become a foreign minister.) Stalin gambled on bandwagoning and joining the stronger rather than the weaker side in the hope that the Soviet Union might benefit from the spoils of war between Germany and the west. Germany and the Soviet Union divided up eastern Europe, including the Baltic states of Lithuania, Estonia, and Latvia. Then in September 1939, Germany invaded Poland and started World War II. The Soviet Union occupied the other half of eastern Europe.

> **Spotlight on bandwagoning not balancing**

Finishing off Poland, Germany turned west. It took Norway in the winter of 1939–1940 and invaded the Low Countries and France in spring 1940. An all-out air war against Great Britain followed, and Britain came perilously close to defeat. But British flyers bested the German Luftwaffe, and Hitler, frustrated, wheeled east in June 1941 and attacked the Soviet Union. Now, as the realist school warns, the dangers of bandwagoning came home to roost. Stalin reportedly couldn't believe the perfidy of his Nazi ally—who was only following, of course, the realist proscription against permanent alliances—and went into a depression for several weeks.[14] The box on page 150 uses the perspectives in this book to answer the question, why were the two dictators, who were alike in so many ways, ultimately unable to cooperate?

Counterbalancing failed again. Why? The reason, say realists, is that Germany was now clearly a revisionist state, unlike Bismarck's Germany or, according to some realist perspectives, even Kaiser Wilhelm's Germany. Revisionist states seek maximum power, not just security or enough power to counterbalance. Following power transition logic, they see equilibrium as unstable and seek more power to dominate. They are unhappy with the status quo and want to change it. Hence, defense alone is not enough. So counterbalancing does not work against revisionist states. Revisionist states may not stop even after they achieve hegemony (see further discussion later in the chapter).

> **Spotlight on revisionist versus status quo states**

Comparing Stalinist and Nazi Regimes

One of the great mysteries of World War II is why Nazi Germany and Stalinist Russia did not sustain the Molotov-Ribbentrop non-aggression pact of 1939 and cooperate to dominate Europe. Had Hitler not attacked Russia, he might have ruled Europe for decades because the West ultimately defeated him only with the substantial help of Russia.

In 2004, Steven Merritt Miner reviewed a book by Richard Overy entitled *The Dictators: Hitler's Germany and Stalin's Russia.*[1] In the book, Overy argues that the two dictators and their respective countries shared more similarities than differences. Presumably, that fact should have enabled them to cooperate to avoid war.

Overy observes that the two dictators had the same adversary in western democracies. As Ribbentrop himself told Stalin, the two countries "were animated in the same degree by the desire for a New Order in the world . . . against the congealed plutocratic democracies."[2] Thus, from a realist perspective, they should have been able to cooperate.

Overy further observes that the two systems were similar economically and ideologically. Stalin had five-year economic plans; Hitler had four-year plans. Stalin had numerous bureaucrats working on the Russian economy; Hitler had seven times as many working on the German economy. Neither country had a free-market capitalist economy. According to Overy, both systems also rested on mass popular support and projected utopian visions of the future, which were similar in form if not in content—one sociological, a world with-out classes; the other biological, a world with a superior race. Thus, also from the institutional (domestic liberal) and ideological (identity) perspectives, the two countries should have cooperated.

But, on identity aspects, Miner dissents. He argues that, compared to Stalin, Hitler had stronger support at home but less diplomatic support abroad. Hitler sent fewer non-Jewish, ethnic Germans to concentration camps, although the number was not insignificant. By contrast, Stalin's camps were full of ethnic Russians, and Stalin killed millions of Soviet peasants when he collectivized farms in the 1930s. So Hitler faced less domestic ideological opposition than Stalin. Conversely, abroad, Hitler's biological vision of the future attracted little support, while Stalin's sociological vision was much more popular in the West.

Miner goes no further with these conclusions. But we might extrapolate from his critique that Stalin faced greater ideological constraints in planning an attack on Germany than Hitler did in planning an attack on Russia. Stalin feared more dissent at home and thought he could count on support abroad to contain Hitler without having to go to war. Hitler, on the other hand, had more support at home and felt isolated and estranged from foreign powers. So Germany was less constrained to attack Russia, and indeed, Germany not Russia was the one that broke the non-aggression pact. Identity (ideological support at home and abroad) factors overrode realist (the United States as a common adversary) and liberal (similar institutions) ones.

1. Steven Merritt Miner, "Engineers of Death," *New York Times Book Review,* December 26, 2004, 15.
2. Ibid.

Japan and the Pacific War

All the while America slept. The United States was long since the wealthiest country in the world. By 1941, its wealth constituted 54 percent of the combined wealth of the United States, Germany, Soviet Union, Great Britain, and Italy.[15] But it was not using this wealth to exert a great power military role. Why? Some realist perspectives explain America's isolationism in geopolitical terms. America enjoys "strategic immunity."[16] As long as it stays out of foreign military commitments, it is relatively invulnerable to attack. Two oceans thwart successful invasion, and America's vast size enables greater economic independence. Thus, it was rational for the United States to stand aside from Europe's wars. Britain eventually repulsed German air power, and the Soviet Union would shortly engulf German land power. All America had to do was wait for other countries to do the balancing.

Other realist perspectives aren't so sure. For them, Hitler's success in Russia would have been intolerable for Americans because German and Japanese power would then dominate the Eurasian landmass. America would face a fascist juggernaut alone. If the European war was not enough to draw America in, certainly a global war was. Russia's fate linked the European and Asian balance of power.

In 1936, Japan signed an anti-Comintern Pact with Germany, a declaration of opposition to communist and hence Soviet principles without being a direct alliance against Russia. From its base in Manchukuo, Japan then invaded China in 1937. It declared its intent to create a Greater East Asia Co-Prosperity Sphere. And in 1940, after Hitler attacked France, Japan seized French colonies in Southeast Asia, Vietnam, and Cambodia. In September 1940, Japan, Germany, and Italy signed the Tripartite Pact committing each to go to war if any other country came to the defense of England. The pact was aimed primarily at the United States, but Stalin might have wondered about this alliance between the two great powers on either side of the Soviet Union. In April 1941, he countered and signed a neutrality pact with Japan. The latter was apparently preparing to strike east against the United States. When Germany attacked the Soviet Union in June 1941, Stalin concentrated his forces against the Nazi onslaught and even then just barely survived.

So, the fact that Japan struck against the United States rather than the Soviet Union was crucial. Some historians attribute this turn of events to the United States. President Franklin Roosevelt moved to save the Soviet Union from the pincer of German and Japanese power (see Maps 4-2 and 4-3). He tightened oil deliveries to Japan, either to deter Japan from striking the Soviet Union or perhaps to distract it toward the United States. As Roosevelt put it, "the United States would slip a noose around Japan's neck and give it a jerk now and then."[17] While Roosevelt did not expect an oil embargo to lead to war, Japan began to see the situation it faced as the last move in a prisoner's dilemma game. If war was coming, Japan had better make a preemptive strike first.

And it did. Japan bombed the American fleet at Pearl Harbor on December 7, 1941, and the United States declared war. Four days later, Germany declared war on the United States. The world was off for its second encounter with Armageddon, this one three times more deadly than the first.

Why Don't Hegemons Stop?

Realist perspectives do not predict that balancing will always prevent war. The power transition school, in fact, predicts that balancing causes war when the challenger creeps

Spotlight on geopolitics

Spotlight on last move and preemptive war

Soldiers at Ford Island Naval Air Station watch in horror—as did all Americans—on December 7, 1941, as Japan bombs Pearl Harbor, Hawaii, drawing America into World War II.

up on the declining power. Nor do realist perspectives predict that states will always balance; states, like the Soviet Union in 1939, often buckpass or try to get others to do the balancing for them. Realist perspectives predict only that balances will result. By war or other means, hegemons do not endure. That prediction seems solid enough. Hitler, like Louis XIV and Napoleon before him, ultimately went too far, and other states counterbalanced and beat him back.

Why don't hegemons stop when they are ahead? As the box on page 150 suggests, Hitler did not have to attack Russia. Look again at Map 4-2. He commanded the continent, in effect, ending Germany's encirclement and security dilemma. Britain, even if it could not be beaten, posed no threat of invasion, and Russia was an ally. But Hitler, like others before him, could not resist the temptation to keep on going.

Realists give multiple explanations: offensive imperatives, domestic cartels, polarity, and preventive war. Let's look briefly at each.

OFFENSIVE IMPERATIVES. Offensive realists, such as John Mearsheimer, argue that states always seek more power because more power brings more security.[18] In Germany's case, Russia was still a looming menace on its border, and Germany was more secure if it controlled Russia than if it didn't. We might respond that it was actually not more secure because conquering and holding territory costs more than it returns, but the offensive realist school argues that conquest pays.[19] Thus, it was rational for Hitler to attack Russia. So far, the argument is pure realist.

But Mearsheimer goes on to argue that states that achieve conquest and hegemony on land cannot achieve hegemony across large bodies of water. The reason is the "stopping power of water." By that, Mearsheimer means that geography (or perhaps more persuasively, as we discuss later, technology) does not permit the projection of land

Spotlight on
offensive realism

power across large bodies of water. And hegemons cannot conquer and hold territory by naval and sea power alone. Thus, Hitler, like Napoleon, did not succeed in conquering Great Britain. And if Hitler could not subdue Great Britain across the English Channel, he certainly could not invade North America across the Atlantic Ocean. The United States was dominant in its region and relatively safe behind two large oceans. True, Japan did attack a territory of the United States, but it did not attack the mainland, and it did so by air, not by land. And although Japan did invade China, it already had established a foothold in China in 1905 on the basis of the treaty ending the Russo-Japanese War and had to traverse only a small body of water to expand its position on the mainland while possessing complete air and sea superiority.

If expanding powers cannot achieve hegemony in other regions, it makes sense for them to buckpass, to let others in that region balance and to intervene only if a hegemon threatens to emerge. Again, by this logic, it was rational for the United States to wait and let Britain and Russia take the power out of the Nazi steamroller. Still, hegemons in one region may find allies and hence footholds in other regions to stage invasions. The United States used England to stage the successful D-Day invasion of Europe in 1944, just as Japan used Manchukuo to stage its invasion of China in 1937. With such a foothold, land invasions across smaller bodies of water may not be impossible, especially if the invader enjoys air and naval superiority, as the United States and Japan did in their respective assaults. Thus, technological constraints, not geography, may explain the stopping power of water. And technology can always change.

> Spotlight on
> **buckpassing**

Notice here that if technological constraints are more important than geography, the argument slips into liberal terrain. As we note in Chapter 1, realist perspectives tend to see technology reinforcing the status quo; liberal perspectives see it as a force for change. Technologies from a liberal perspective are not inherently expanding (offensive) or constraining (defensive). A machine gun, for example, is an excellent defensive as well as offensive weapon. It depends on the strategy by which weapons are deployed. And strategies begin to involve institutional and intentional (ideological) factors, which are emphasized more by liberal and identity perspectives. (See the further discussion under "Role of Misperceptions" on page 155.)

> causal
> *arrow*

DOMESTIC CARTELS. Defensive-oriented realists consider expansion beyond what is needed for security unnecessary from a systemic structural point of view. More power is not always better than less, and balancing suffices to achieve stability. Thus, when states cannot stop expanding, defensive realists look for explanations at other levels of analysis. Some attribute the inability of hegemons to stop their expansion to domestic political factors. As we observe in Chapter 3, Professor Jack Snyder argues that because of its late industrialization Germany had many diverse social groups with narrowly defined interests; remember the iron (industry) and rye (agriculture) coalition before World War I. These groups cannot achieve their objectives independently, but logroll, or combine, to implement them. In the process, their cumulative goals commit the state to overexpansion.

> Spotlight on
> **defensive realism**

Hitler faced similar domestic cartels prior to World War II. He could not stop because he was backed by a wide domestic coalition that supported the need for *Lebensraum* and converted this need into an implacable ideology. According to Snyder, "the Nazis won power . . . by promising incompatible payoffs to every group in Weimar society: labor, industry, farmers, clerks, artisans. . . . Hitler saw conquest as the only alternative to a politically unacceptable decision to cut consumption"[20] But this explanation, Snyder concludes, is not enough because Hitler eventually did cut consumption to finance the war effort. Now, Snyder appeals to ideology. Hitler held the country together with strategic myths such as *Lebensraum.*

Notice how this explanation, while remaining mostly realist (domestic interests compete for power) takes on some liberal (an emphasis on the process by which domestic interests logroll or interact with one another) and ideological (myths) elements. The explanation also drops to the domestic level of analysis. The realist and other additional causes come from the country's political system at home rather than the relative distribution of power abroad.

causal arrow

It is worth quoting Snyder's conclusions in full to show how a sophisticated analysis considers all perspectives but ultimately judges them differently. When you read books or articles, these are the passages you must not miss. They tell you most about the perspective from which the facts are being presented. And if you miss them, you miss the opportunity to critique the facts, which are always partial because the world of facts is so unlimited:

> Domestic explanations of German overexpansion must look not only at the interests of groups, but also at the process by which those interests were reconciled [logrolling] and at the unintended ideological consequences of the strategic myths used to promote those interests.[21]

Interests (power) and hence realist factors are still the primary causal variable. Logrolling and strategic myths tell us more about how these interests produced the eventual outcomes, but these liberal and ideological factors are tied to interests. They do not stand alone. The explanation would make no sense if interests were not the major causal variable.

POLARITY. Still other neorealist perspectives explain Hitler's attack on Russia in purely systemic terms. For political scientist Randall Schweller, the explanation lies in the peculiar distribution of power that preceded World War II.[22] This distribution was tripolar: the United States, Germany, and the Soviet Union. In a tripolar world, no pole can allow the other two to come together, for that would constitute a dominating coalition. Hence, the tripolar distribution of power is uniquely unstable. Either Germany and its allies would dominate Russia or the United States and its allies would. Roosevelt understood that fundamental fact, thus prompting his intervention to weaken Japan.

Spotlight on tripolarity

PREVENTIVE WAR. For Dale Copeland, the factor that drove German policy in World War II was the same as in World War I—not the present balances but Germany's fear of Russian superiority in the future. At the meeting that Hossbach recorded, Hitler said that Russia was the ultimate target and that it had to be attacked before 1943–1945 when Germany's power relative to Russia's would peak. After that, Russia would have the advantage. So Germany undertook a preventive war to prevent Russia from becoming more powerful as Germany became less powerful. As long as this assessment of power shifts was reasonable, and Copeland thinks it was, the realist perspective explains Germany's behavior from a systemic structural level of analysis.[23] For example, Copeland, unlike Snyder (and Mark Haas; see the section on identity explanations), minimizes the role of race and ideology in Nazi decision making. He sees systemic power factors dominating and allows a role for identity only in the distant future (as we note later).

If the assessment of power shifts is not reasonable, meaning warranted by the systemic evidence available to the observer, then the assessment is being influenced by other factors, namely institutional (lack of information) and identity (misperception) factors. For example, German leaders may not have had enough information to make an accurate assessment of Russia's future power. Or they may have been affected by their racist or ideological (for example, anti-communist) prejudices toward Russia. Often, when the perceptions of decision makers matter, the level of analysis drops from the systemic structural level to the foreign policy level. The foreign policy level, as we note in Chapter 1, links systemic process factors such as alliance formation with domestic level factors such as bureaucratic (information) and intentional (ideational) variables. Now decision makers may be limited by domestic forces and unable to respond flexibly to systemic process forces. An example, which we discuss next, is when decision makers, because they lack information or indulge their biases, misperceive the power realities.

Spotlight on
foreign policy level of analysis

Role of Misperceptions in Realist Accounts

Realist perspectives expect assessments of power to be accurate because material forces dominate. When such assessments are inaccurate, as Professor Snyder's analysis shows, realist explanations appeal to liberal and identity factors to supplement material forces. Professor Stephen Walt developed a realist line of reasoning that included judgments about nonmaterial factors such as whether offensive or defensive weapons dominated in a particular historical period and whether leaders' intentions were aggressive or not.[24] As Walt's critics have pointed out, however, the analysis remains realist only if material factors still provide the predominant share of the explanation.[25]

One liberal factor distorting realist behavior is misperception. Stalin, for example, judged French and British power to be much greater in 1939 than it actually was. He thought those two countries would hold out against and drain Germany's resources, allowing Russia to enter the conflict later as the decisive power. Thus, he buckpassed, but in this case he misperceived the realities.

Spotlight on
lack of accurate information

Another realist, the historian A. J. P. Taylor, concludes that the war was the consequence of a long series of such misperceptions and mistakes. Rejecting identity arguments that the war was premeditated, he writes, "The war of 1939, far from being premeditated, was a mistake, the result on both sides of diplomatic blunders." Hitler, he argues, bears unique responsibility for domestic horrors, such as the Holocaust, but he does not bear any more responsibility than other powers for foreign policy mistakes. He sought to restore German power and exploited others' mistakes, especially Britain's failure to negotiate an alliance with Stalin in 1939. "Human blunders," Taylor concludes, "usually do more to shape history than human wickedness." Notice the discounting of values (evil or wicked human beings) and the emphasis on liberal factors (interactions and blunders). Taylor believes the balance of power should work, and when it doesn't, he blames inept diplomacy, which overrides balancing imperatives.[26]

States also misperceive the advantage of offensive versus defensive military power. France thought a defensive strategy dominated and buckpassed in 1938, when it still had an advantage over Germany. It waited for Britain to commit. When Britain finally did commit in 1939, France expected the defense to dominate and chain-ganged with Britain and Poland. **Chain-ganging,** or creating a rigid defensive alliance (the opposite of buckpassing), left the initiative to Hitler. Hitler seized it and neutralized Russia while attacking Poland and France. Offensive power proved dominant. France had misperceived the offensive-defensive balance.[27]

Spotlight on
offensive-defensive balance

chain-ganging
the creation of a rigid defensive alliance.

Identity factors come into play when realists assess risks. Copeland acknowledges, for example, that even if Russia became more powerful than Germany in the future, Germany would still have to assess whether Russia was more or less likely to attack in the future compared to the present. That assessment might depend to some extent on the nature of the political regime in Russia. A declining authoritarian regime, such as Germany, might remain suspicious of a rising authoritarian power, such as Russia, as was the case in the 1930s when Germany feared rising Russian power in the future. But a declining democratic state, say Great Britain, might not worry too much about a rising state that was also democratic, say the United States.[28] As we note in Chapter 3, Britain worried more before World War I about Germany's rise than America's.

In all these cases, realists draw on other factors to supplement relative power explanations. Liberal factors, such as domestic processes and institutions, distort perceptions. And identity factors, such as the ideology of *Lebensraum* and the nature of domestic political regimes, affect risk-taking. When information is missing or misleading, institutions and ideologies fill the gap. (See Table 4-2 for a summary of realist explanations.)

Let's look now at explanations that treat identity factors or ideological factors as the primary causes of World War II, not as supplementary factors to realist explanations.

Table 4-2

The Causes of World War II: The Realist Perspective and Levels of Analysis

Level of analysis		Realist perspective
Systemic	*Structure*	• Distribution/balance of power: —Rise of German and Japanese power —Versailles Treaty alienated rather than reintegrated Germany —Power vacuum caused by many new, weak states in eastern Europe, and a weak China in Asia —Major powers such as the United States and Soviet Union not involved to create balance —Tripolarity sets off scramble between Germany, Russia, and the United States to ally with third country
	Process	• Failure of UK, France, Poland, Russia, and United States to align against the greater power (Germany). Why did they buckpass?: —Kept off-balance by adept (compared to clumsy, before World War I) German diplomacy—Hitler's pact with Poland, naval treaty with Britain, and alliance with Italy —Threats based on different national (geopolitical) not common institutional interests —France formed alliances with Poland, Yugoslavia, Czechoslovakia, and Romania—all weak states—instead of the Soviet Union
Foreign policy		• Germany's assessment of Soviet power (present and future) was accurate and not distorted by domestic bureaucratic or ideological factors
Domestic		• Aggressive interests of various domestic groups in Germany
Individual		• Hitler's war
		• Roosevelt's embargo

Identity Matters

The nineteenth century gradually weakened the old conservative, Christian, monarchic community that had provided a common identity for Europe since the time of Charlemagne; World War I had decisively ended it. The last tsar and his family were still devout Christians, as were Franz Joseph, the Kaiser, and other monarchs. The Versailles Treaty replaced this long-dying Christian community with a more explicit secular one. Whereas the old Europe functioned on the basis of substantive religious beliefs and then the rights of sovereign powers, the new one adopted secular procedural and institutional norms of self-determination and unanimity as the basis of international community. These norms encouraged the proliferation of new nations inside Europe—Poland, Czechoslovakia, Hungary, Yugoslavia, Lithuania, Estonia, and Latvia, among others—but continued to suppress new nations outside Europe. The League of Nations did away with old-style colonialism under national control, but instituted a new form of colonialism under international control. France, Britain, the Netherlands, Belgium, Italy, and Japan received mandates from the League to perpetuate imperial rule in the Middle East, Africa, and Asia. Colonialism, while not being condemned or ended, was at least subjected to some kind of international oversight.

Spotlight on norms of self-determination and unanimity

Recall from Chapter 1 that **procedural norms** govern how states interact and are emphasized by liberal perspectives. Substantive norms involve the values states share or do not share and are emphasized by identity perspectives. As we observed earlier, the League's procedural norms of self-determination and unanimity proved to be rather thin both inside and outside Europe. Self-determination inside Europe meant new nations could adopt whatever substantive identities they wished, democratic or nondemocratic. And unanimity meant every nation, whatever its substantive or ideological commitments, had the same rights to make or veto international decisions. Outside Europe, of course, self-determination did not even apply. So the League tried to hold countries together using rules that were observed differently inside and outside of Europe and did not distinguish among countries in terms of the deeper values or identities they professed. The League tried to hold too many substantive differences together with too little procedural glue.

procedural norms norms that govern how states interact; emphasized by liberal perspectives.

Substantive norms, on the other hand, got stronger and diverged more and more sharply. Cultural nationalism persisted. British and French nationalism were vindicated by World War I, but German nationalism was humiliated and isolated, thus perpetuating and even deepening the Darwinian cultural struggles that preceded World War I. Self-determination added more national cultures to the mix, with many of the new nations being irredentist, or dissatisfied by boundaries drawn after the war that excluded fellow nationals. Political or ideological nationalism compounded cultural suspicions. Liberal nationalism muddled along in Britain and France and thrived in the isolationist mind-set of the United States, which thought of itself as an exceptionalist country. Communist nationalism succeeded socialist nationalism and triumphed in Russia. But fascist nationalism triumphed in Italy and, after a brief democratic interlude, in Germany and Japan as well. The Spanish Civil War in the 1930s became a ferocious battleground between fascism and communism. Antisemitism, periodically erupting in Europe since the time of Christ, reached its zenith with Nazi racism. Jews became the scapegoat for practically every grievance from World War I to the Great Depression.

substantive norms norms that involve the values states share or do not share; emphasized by identity perspectives.

Spotlight on irredentism

Events Leading to World War II from Different Perspectives

Realist		Liberal		Identity	
Versailles Treaty	1919	League of Nations	1919	Nationalism	1900s
Rapallo Pact	1922	Washington Naval Conference	1922	American exceptionalism/ isolationism	1920s
Locarno Pact	1925	Kellogg-Briand Pact	1928	Fascism/communism	1920s
Japan invades Manchuria	1931	Germany and Japan leave League	1933	Hitler's idea of a German Third Reich	1930s
Hitler takes power	1933	Soviet Union joins League	1933	Greater East Asia Co-Prosperity Sphere	1930s
		German-British naval agreement	1934	Spanish Civil War	1934
Italy invades Ethiopia	1935				
Germany occupies Rhineland	1936			Japan and Germany sign anti-Comintern Pact	1936
Japan invades China	1937				
Germany annexes Austria	1938	Appeasement at Munich	1938		
Germany occupies Sudetenland	1938				
Germany invades Czechoslovakia	1939				
Germany attacks Poland	1939				
Molotov-Ribbentrop Pact	1939				
Germany, Japan, and Italy sign Tripartite Pact	1940				

How much did these substantive ideas matter? Identity perspectives say they mattered a lot. They shaped or, as it were, weakened and incapacitated the institutions, such as the League of Nations, that liberal solutions depended on. And they drove the competition for power such that stability was never in the cards, whether by equilibrium or by empire. Consciously or subconsciously, competitive or diverging identities propelled nations toward the abyss. As before World War I, nations constructed identities that exacerbated differences and conflicts, creating an atmosphere of xenophobia and racism. Because realist alliances continued to form among ideological adversaries—the Soviet Union and Germany in 1939 and then the Soviet Union and the western powers after 1941—most historians still hesitate in the case of World War II to attribute primary causal emphasis to ideological factors; that comes in the Cold War after World War II. But identity factors always mattered. Capitalism, fascism, and communism were powerful ideologies as well as useful rationalizations of power.

Cultural Nationalism

Cultural nationalism, the glorification of one national culture over that of others, hit its high-water mark in the period right after World War I. Romania and Bulgaria were already national entities that had been carved out of the collapsing Ottoman Empire in 1861 and 1908, respectively. Now Versailles created new nations out of the collapse of the German, Ottoman, and Austro-Hungarian Empires. Self-determination both justified and contradicted this process. The new countries constituted peoples that shared a common language and culture. But they also included minorities that did not. And these minorities triggered resentment and perpetual grievances throughout the interwar period.

Spotlight on
self-determination

The new democracy of Czechoslovakia had a population of 15 million, which included 3 million Germans, 1 million Hungarians, and one-half million Poles. We saw how that mix played into the hands of Hitler when he claimed that he wanted only to reunite Germans in the new Third Reich. Romania became home to millions of Hungarians, and Poland included millions of Germans. Hungary, created in 1918, was embittered two years later by the Treaty of Trianon that left 5 million, or one-third of, Hungarians outside its national borders. The Baltic states of Lithuania, Latvia, and Estonia gained nationhood. Yugoslavia brought together at least six national groups: Serbs, Croats, Slovenes, Macedonians, Montenegrins, and Bosnians. In addition, it crossed the cultural fault line between Catholic Croatia and Orthodox Serbia and between these two groups and Bosnian Muslims. Turkey emerged as the rump or residual Ottoman state and immediately fought terrible wars of ethnic and national fury with Armenia, resonating to this day with charges of genocide.

Spotlight on
construction of
identities

Not only did new nations contain minorities that did not feel liberated by the process of self-determination, other nations effectively disappeared as the Soviet Union put together its empire and subdued the Caucasus countries of Armenia, Azerbaijan, and Georgia. National peoples in the Middle East, North Africa, and elsewhere also endured four more decades of colonial rule.

What did all this mean? Which peoples should have a nation, and when they have one, how should they govern? In particular, how should they treat minorities? Nationalism based on language and culture inherently discriminates against other cultures. So, by this standard minorities either acquired autonomy, which threatened national unity, or were oppressed, which negated their right of self-determination. President Wilson hoped democratic political ideas would temper and eventually override ethnic and national differences. Democracy protects minorities and celebrates cultural diversity. Unfortunately, Wilson was fifty years or more ahead of his time.

Liberal and Social Democracy

Liberal democracy emerged most prominently in the United States. It built a community ethos around the constitutional rights of individuals instead of the homogeneous culture of the nation (although American folk culture and the English language imposed powerful pressures to assimilate) and promoted a free-market economic system based on private property and competition. Social democracy was more prominent in Europe. It advocated individual political rights, but favored state regulation and ownership of key sectors of the economy to manage class struggle between management and labor. Socialist parties were strong in Europe before World War I, controlling, as we previously noted, the German parliament in 1914.

Spotlight on
political ideologies

Britain and France became exemplars of social democracy. Both suffered traumas in World War I and in the interwar period confronted virulent enemies of freedom in the form of domestic fascist and communist movements. Liberal political forces were weakened, and inflation and later economic depression undermined enthusiasm for free markets. By the mid-1930s France was so divided that conservatives seemed more fascist than nationalist. "Better Hitler than Blum" was the conservative slogan, referring to the French socialist leader, Léon Blum, who came to power in 1936. Ideologies were beginning to transcend national feelings, and this affected foreign policy. As Professor Mark Haas notes, conservative groups in Britain and France preferred to align with fascist countries, such as Italy, to counterbalance Germany, while socialist groups preferred to align with communist countries, such as the Soviet Union, to counterbalance Germany. The unintended consequences of these ideological divisions was indecision and the failure to counterbalance Germany at all.[29]

American Exceptionalism

America suffered economic crisis but, by leadership and national experience, avoided the violent class and cultural cleavages of Europe. The United States began as a conventional nation with a homogeneous culture. Its population was mostly Anglo-Saxon, except for the enslaved black minority. Despite slavery, it was one of the leading democracies of its day, at least in terms of the extent of the white male franchise and protection of that group's individual rights. Other countries such as Britain had a smaller white male franchise during the nineteenth century but abolished slavery before the United States.

Subsequent waves of immigrants slowly transformed America into a multicultural country. The country was tied together less and less by a common culture—although a single language prevailed—and more and more by a common ideological creed of political and economic freedom. Slaves gained legal freedom during the Civil War, a private enterprise system took hold in the late nineteenth century (compared to state-run industries of fascist and socialist governments in Europe), the Progressive Era (1900–1930) broadened suffrage and regulatory reform, and Franklin Roosevelt introduced a national social security system and broader concern for economic equality.

No fascist or socialist party of any consequence ever developed in the United States. While Europe armed, America's military establishment remained miniscule. In June 1940, America had only 267,767 men under arms. Britain had 402,000 and France and Germany over 2.2 and 2.7 million, respectively.[30] And Roosevelt's deft leadership during the economic crisis of the Depression preempted more radical socialist and communist economic alternatives that might have nationalized industries or eroded economic freedoms.

Altogether, America, even with its continuing faults such as political and economic constraints on the freedom of blacks and the poor, was the leading example of liberal democracy in the interwar world. In this sense, it acquired an identity of **exceptionalism,** a country set apart from the rest of the world by its progressive, freedom-loving, and pacifist nature.

But America indulged this sense of exceptionalism too much and shunned Europe. And while the United States remained uninvolved, the lights of liberal democracy went out in Europe as well as the rest of the world. After 1922, as Samuel Huntington observes, liberal democracy disappeared from one country after the other:

exceptionalism

the view that a particular state, and especially the United States, is distinct due to its specific history and unique institutions.

In a little over a decade fledgling democratic institutions in Lithuania, Poland, Latvia, and Estonia were overthrown by military coups. Countries such as Yugoslavia and Bulgaria that had never known real democracy were subjected to new forms of harsher dictatorship. The conquest of power by Hitler in 1933 ended German democracy, ensured the end of Austrian democracy the following year, and eventually of course produced the end of Czech democracy in 1938. Greek democracy . . . was finally buried in 1936. Portugal succumbed to a military coup in 1926. . . . Military takeovers occurred in Brazil and Argentina in 1930. Uruguay reverted to authoritarianism in 1933. A military coup in 1936 led to civil war and the death of the Spanish republic in 1939. The new and limited democracy introduced in Japan . . . was supplanted by military rule in the early 1930s.[31]

Why did America not care? Some identity perspectives might argue that it was America's self-image, not its institutions or geography, that kept the country out of the League of Nations. American democracy was unique or exceptional and did not apply to other countries in the world. And even if the United States had joined the League, it would not have been prepared to use force. The United States needed more justification to participate in world affairs than procedural rules of self-determination or alliance prescriptions of the balance of power. As we'll see in the next chapter, when it finally entered World War II, it came up with another new set of ideas to run the world. The United Nations was somewhat more realistic perhaps, but it was still pretty high-minded in the tradition of American exceptionalism.

← causal *arrow*

Communist Nationalism

The communist movement brought a radical edge to socialism. In Germany right after the war, communists battled conservatives in Berlin.[32] Whites (conservatives) fought Reds (Bolsheviks) in Russia. Eventually, Lenin and then Stalin consolidated communism in Russia. Whereas socialist parties struggled for the rights of workers through the parliamentary system, communism eradicated the party system. It designated the Communist Party as the sole vanguard of the proletariat or workers' movement and used state institutions to uproot reactionary forces—conservative nobility and peasants—and commandeer the nation's property and industry. Stalin forced Russian industrialization through state ministries and planning and uprooted and starved millions of peasants to create collectivized farms. He also purged the military officer corps, a last bastion of nobility and fascist predilections.[33]

Fascist and Racist Nationalism

Radicalization on the left was matched by radicalization on the right. Fascist parties rallied conservative forces to recall old glories of national triumph and marry militaristic virtues with heroic symbols of the ancient Greek and Roman empires. Benito Mussolini's fascist party seized power in Italy in 1922. Fascist and military groups subsequently dominated in Germany and Japan. Both countries had had parliamentary systems in the 1920s. Germany created the Weimar Republic and had, some believe, a moderate foreign policy leadership under Gustav Stresemann that might have brought Germany back peacefully into the European fold.[34] Japan had political parties that struggled to control the military from the late nineteenth century on. By the early 1930s, however, both countries had chosen fascist futures.

Racism became a big part of nationalism in Germany and Japan. While prejudice is hardly unique to these two countries, the maniacal extreme it reached there is still the

genocide

systematic persecution and extermination of a group of people on the basis of their national, ethnic, racial, or religious identity.

ultimate example of human brutality and depravity. The Holocaust, of course, stands out by any standard, with more than 6 million Jews, plus other minorities such as gypsies, systematically exterminated. It epitomizes **genocide,** the extermination of an entire people based on their race or ethnicity. Is there any way to explain it? Probably not to everyone's satisfaction. How much blame do the masses of people share? How much do the leaders deserve? Could it have happened elsewhere? Is this a darkness that lurks in every society? The United States is not blameless. It has its own legacy of slavery and then vigilantism. And the United States did not help the international cause of equal rights when it rejected a Japanese appeal at Versailles for a declaration of racial equality. Japan, of course, indulged its own racism, alienating many of its Chinese and South Korean neighbors and leaving issues, such as its use of "comfort women," or sex slaves, that fester to the present day. Suffice it to note that atrocities happened. They cannot be denied, as a few still do in Germany and perhaps more in Japan. And the explanation may not be as important as the process of forever searching for an explanation. Otherwise, they may happen again.

Ideological Constructions and Chasms

Social constructivists emphasize the collective identities constructed in the interwar period that glorified nationalist traits and military exploits. More agency-oriented constructivists emphasize the chasms that erupted among the self-images of different societies.

The ideological struggles going on in Europe came to the fore vividly during the Spanish Civil War. In 1936, the Spanish people elected a radical socialist government similar to the one in France under Blum. The rightist groups—monarchists, militarists, and fascists—rebelled and started a civil war. Fascism and communism went head to head. The battle fascinated the world, including Ernest Hemingway, who covered the war and wrote his classic novel *A Farewell to Arms* to describe it. Italy and Germany aided the fascist rebels. Russia aided the republican government. For reasons of weakness and ideological divisions of their own (as we have noted), France and Great Britain stayed out of the conflict. After two years, the republican government lost the battle it probably would have won with modest help from the democracies. General Francisco Franco seized power, but then did not join his fascist colleagues in the Second World War.

So how relevant were ideological struggles to the outbreak of World War II? Did identities really have an effect on behavior, or were states responding largely to material and institutional forces? Clearly the Axis powers shared an ideological affinity. Germany, Italy, and Japan were tied together by similar militarist and fascist politics rather than by the monarchist systems that united Germany, Austria, and Italy before World War I. On the other hand, Spain, another fascist system, did not join their cause and for two years Germany allied with its arch-ideological foe, the Soviet Union. That alliance did not last, to be sure, but then the Soviet Union joined up with other arch-ideological foes, the liberal democracies of Britain, France, and the United States. Hence, it cannot be said very easily that the war was about conflicting identities and ideologies.

Did Germany's Nazi identity cause World War II, or did Germany's geopolitical circumstances cause the war? Was identity or power more important overall? As we learned in the Introduction, scholars ask counterfactual questions to tease out the answers to such questions.

Spotlight on
counterfactuals

Professor Copeland writes, "if one imagines a Germany in 1939 with superior but declining military power, but led by military leaders lacking the racist ideology of Nazism, would these leaders have gone to war?" He answers:

> given that to a man senior [German] generals were holdovers from the First World War, and given that the military pushed for war in 1914 because of a rising Russia, . . . racism appears to be neither a sufficient nor even a necessary condition. . . . to explain why Germany initiated world war for a second time in a generation. . . . German geopolitical vulnerability and the desire to eliminate the Russian threat would have existed with or without Nazi ideology.[35]

Now let's listen to Professor Mark Haas. He asks the same question and concludes "that Germany's international decisions in the 1930s would have been very different if the Nazis had not been in power." He emphasizes the fact that a group of German generals led by Ludwig Beck, the army chief of staff, "viewed Britain and France as Germany's ideological allies against the greatest ideological threat in the system: the Soviet Union."[36] Before the German attack on France, this group risked treason by communicating Hitler's battle plans to Britain and France. The dissident generals, Haas contends, would not have put their lives on the line merely to disagree with Hitler about the tactics or timing of Germany's attack, which is Copeland's conclusion. Hitler subsequently purged the Beck group, but Haas concludes that it was not geopolitical factors that predetermined Hitler's policies but an ideological struggle within the German leadership that the Nazis won. Thus, Nazi ideology played a more important role than present or future power balances in explaining the outcome of war. (See Table 4-3 for a summary of identity explanations.)

Massive Nazi rallies, like this one taking place in September 1936 in Nuremberg, Germany, stoked hypernationalism in Germany.

Critical Theory Perspective

We can't do justice in this small space to the rich literature that offers critical perspectives on the origins of World War II. Marxism, as amended by Lenin and Stalin, foresaw, as we note in previous chapters, the advance of capitalism, which in turn would create its antithesis—communism. Lenin introduced the idea that capitalist states would pursue colonialism or imperialism as a means to get rid of surplus production and in the last stages of capitalism fight against one another for world markets. The Great Depression of the 1930s seemed to confirm this dialectic. The capitalist powers suffered economic collapse at home and in turn accelerated the scramble for export markets abroad. Fascist and liberal states were both capitalist and hence in need of foreign markets. They would clash and ultimately hasten the rise of communism. Undoubtedly this expectation influenced Stalin and contributed to his decision to buckpass and ally with Hitler in the hope that Hitler would fight the other capitalist countries to the death and hasten the demise of capitalism altogether. Moscow created

Table 4-3

The Causes of World War II: The Identity Perspective and Levels of Analysis		
Level of analysis		**Identity perspective**
Systemic	*Structure*	• Change in individual and collective identity: —Shared norms of self-determination not uniformly practiced or applied, created many small, weak states (rather than weak states themselves being the cause, as realist perspectives emphasize) —National identities diverged—different nationalisms drove security dilemma (not geopolitics, as realist perspectives emphasize)
	Process	• Spread of fascism, socialism, and racism
		• Decline of democracies
Foreign policy		• Racist views of German decision makers exaggerate Soviet or Bolshevik threat
Domestic		• Bolshevism/communism in Russia
		• Racism/militarism in Germany and Japan
		• Exceptionalism in the United States
Individual		• Stalin's communist beliefs that Germany and other capitalist countries would fight one another and that the Soviet Union could stay out of it

In this Russian poster from 1920, Vladimir Lenin is depicted wielding the broom of history to sweep the world clean of aristocrats and bourgeoisie. The text reads, "Comrade Lenin cleans the world of filth."

the Communist International, or Comintern, to work with communist parties in other countries and foment the revolutionary cause.

The revisionist school of American history, the Wisconsin School (from the location of some of its leading adherents at the University of Wisconsin), developed this thesis as applied to the United States, the leading capitalist country in the twentieth century. Charles A. Beard and William Appleman Williams interpreted America's rising power and influence in the world as a quest for markets on behalf of the capitalist class. In a book Beard published with his wife Mary in 1930, the Beards argued that the Civil War was not an ideological war about human rights but an economic class war between capitalist and agrarian economic systems. The capitalist system won, and American foreign policy after that was one of steady expansion. "As the domestic market was saturated and capital heaped up for investment," the Beards write, "the pressure for expansion of the American commercial empire rose with corresponding speed."[37] The "open door policy" followed, in which the United States pressed for economic access to one part of the world after the other: China, Europe, and the colonial territories. In a later book, Beard placed the blame for World War II squarely on the policies of the United States. These policies were not only imperialist but deceptive and degenerate, a blatant attempt to saddle the American people with the profit plunder of the arms industry.[38]

Table 4-4

The Causes of World War II: The Critical Theory Perspective and Levels of Analysis[a]		
Level of analysis		**Critical theory perspective**
Systemic	*Structure*	• Capitalist states war against one another while communist states pick up the spoils
	Process	—
Foreign policy		—
Domestic		• United States adopts open door policy to dump export surpluses on world markets
Individual		• Lenin modifies Marxism to include imperialist phase of capitalist expansion

a. Remember that critical theories consider levels of analysis to be inseparable.

William Appleman Williams, who spent his academic career at the University of Wisconsin, picked up on this theme about the dark side of U.S. foreign policy and established the Wisconsin School as one of the most influential and controversial interpretations of international relations in general. (See Table 4-4 for a summary of critical theory explanations.) We'll have occasion to visit with Professor Williams again in the next chapter.

Summary

In this chapter, we have revisited numerous concepts laid out initially in Chapter 1. The features in the margins are there to help you see these concepts at work in the history of World War II. The security dilemma figures prominently in realist accounts, collective goods (security) and institutions in liberal accounts, and identity construction and differences in identity perspectives.

Realist arguments often dominate the historical record. Was World War II, then, mostly a struggle for power? Perhaps, but liberal and identity factors were becoming more important. Ironically, one great power—the Soviet Union—joined the League just as the two aggressor powers—Germany and Japan—withdrew. The United States never joined. In that sense the League never got a fair test. Moreover, by the mid-1930s, domestic political systems had diverged to such a large extent that trust was increasingly in short supply. When Britain negotiated with the Soviet Union in summer 1939 to form an alliance against Hitler (an exercise that ultimately failed when the Soviet Union aligned with Hitler), here is what Neville Chamberlain, the British prime minister, wrote:

> I must confess to the very most profound distrust of Russia. I have no belief whatsoever in her ability to maintain an effective offensive, even if it wanted to. And I distrust her motives, which seem to me to have little connection with our ideas of liberty, and to be concerned only with getting everyone else by the ears.[39]

Diplomacy—the liberal perspective—cannot bridge unlimited ideological chasms. Nor can alliances—the realist perspective. The United States and the Soviet Union allied *in extremis* to defeat Nazi Germany. But once that menace was vanquished, the wartime allies had a severe falling out that became the Cold War. Ideology ultimately severed the alliance and the United Nations that the allies intended to lead. That's the topic of our next chapter.

Key Concepts

appeasement 148	League of Nations 137	substantive norms 157
chain-ganging 155	*Lebensraum* 136	unanimity 139
exceptionalism 160	procedural norms 157	
genocide 162	self-determination 138	

Study Questions

1. If Hitler planned and predicted war at the meeting with his generals in 1937 recorded by Hossbach, how can anyone argue that this was not a premeditated war reflecting the identity perspective from the individual level of analysis?

2. Contrast the way balance of power and collective security systems work.

3. Explain why the League of Nations failed from the three different perspectives.

4. What are three realist arguments why hegemons, such as Nazi Germany, France under Louis XIV, and France under Napoleon, cannot stop once they have achieved superiority?

5. Distinguish the following questions in terms of the perspective they reflect. Did the norm of self-determination create weak states in eastern Europe, did weak states emerge from a vacuum of power, or did the Locarno Treaty concluded by the League of Nations fail to protect weak states?

5

The Origins and End of the Cold War

I n mid-February 1946 a young, relatively obscure U.S. Foreign Service officer lay feverish and ill in bed in Moscow. An aide brought him a cable from the State Department in Washington asking why the Soviets seemed unwilling to support the World Bank and International Monetary Fund, two institutions the United States sought to create to manage postwar international economic relations. The query was routine and even trivial. But the sick diplomat, George Kennan, used the occasion to compose his famous **long telegram** outlining the nature of the conflict the United States faced with the Soviet Union and the diplomatic solution to it.[1]

President Kennedy and Soviet Foreign Minister Andrei Gromyko meet in the middle of the Cuban Missile Crisis as the world watches intently. Also shown in this photograph, taken at the White House on October 18, 1962, are Secretary of State Dean Rusk (seated on the couch, left) and Llewellyn Thompson (seated on the couch, right), special adviser on Soviet affairs.

The Long Telegram

Kennan's telegram hit Washington like a thunderbolt and made Kennan an instant diplomatic rock star. In typical telegram shorthand, it made the following six points:

First, the Soviet Union is confrontational. Kennan warned that the leadership of the Soviet Union had adopted an outlook of "antagonistic 'capitalist encirclement,'" expecting a global confrontation between capitalism and socialism. Stalin, Kennan quoted, had stated as early as 1927 that "there will emerge two centers of world signif-

long telegram
George Kennan's diplomatic telegram of 1946 outlining the U.S.-Soviet conflict and arguing for the policy of containment.

167

icance: a socialist center, drawing to itself the countries which tend toward socialism, and a capitalist center, drawing to itself the countries that incline toward capitalism. Battle between these two centers . . . will decide fate of capitalism and of communism in entire world."

Second, Marxism expresses Russian insecurity. This confrontational

Spotlight on
security dilemma

Soviet party line is not based on any objective analysis of the situation beyond Russia's borders. . . . At the bottom of the Kremlin's neurotic view of world affairs is traditional and instinctive Russian sense of insecurity . . . insecurity of a peaceful agricultural people trying to live on vast exposed plain in neighborhood of fierce nomadic peoples. To this was added, as Russia came into contact with economically advanced West, fear of more competent, more powerful, more highly organized societies in that area. . . . Marxist dogma . . . became a perfect vehicle for [this] sense of insecurity. . . .

Third, the Soviet Union will expand its power. Russia will increase

in every way strength and prestige of Soviet state; intensive military-industrialization, maximum development of armed forces, great displays to impress outsiders, continued secretiveness. . . . [And] whenever it is considered timely and promising, efforts will be made to advance official limits of Soviet power . . . for the moment . . . restricted to certain neighboring points . . . such as Iran, Turkey, possibly Bornholm [an island in the Baltic Sea south of Sweden]. However, other points may at times come into question . . . a port on Persian Gulf . . . Soviet base at Gilbraltar [sic] Strait. . . .

Fourth, the Soviet Union leads a worldwide communist effort. Kennan foresaw that the Soviet Union would work "closely together" with leaders of Communist parties in other countries "as an underground operating directorate of world communism, a concealed Comintern [Communist International] tightly coordinated and dominated by Moscow." It would also steer the rank and file of Communist parties "through front organizations" and use national associations such as labor unions, youth leagues, and women's organizations, as well as international organizations, the Russian Orthodox Church, pan-Slav and other movements, and willing foreign governments "to undermine general political and strategic potential of major Western powers . . . to disrupt national self-confidence, to hamstring measures of national defense, to increase social and industrial unrest, to stimulate all forms of disunity."

Fifth, the United States must contain the Soviet Union and let communism fail. Perhaps most famously, Kennan argued for resistance to Soviet power but not overreaction to Soviet ideology:

how to cope with this force is undoubtedly greatest task [U.S.] diplomacy has ever faced. . . . Soviet power does not work by fixed plans. . . . Impervious to the logic of reason, it is highly sensitive to the logic of force. For this reason it can easily withdraw—and usually does—when strong resistance is encountered at any point. . . . [I]f situations are properly handled there need be no prestige-engaging showdowns. . . . Soviet system, as form of internal power, is not yet finally proven . . . never since the termination of the civil war [1921] have [sic] the mass of Russian people been emotionally farther removed from doctrines of the Communist Party than they are today. . . . Thus, internal soundness and permanence of movement need not yet be regarded as assured.

Spotlight on
balancing power

Sixth, the United States will win by improving its own society, not by spreading freedom. Kennan warned that the United States must not

be emotionally provoked or unseated by [the communist movement]. . . . Much depends on health and vigor of our own society. . . . Every courageous and incisive measure to solve internal problems of our own society, to improve self-confidence, discipline, morale, and community spirit of our own people is a diplomatic victory over Moscow worth a thousand diplomatic notes and joint communiqués. . . . We must . . . put forward for all nations a much more positive and constructive picture of the sort of world we would like to see. . . . It is not enough to urge the people to develop political processes similar to our own. Many foreign peoples . . . are less interested in abstract freedom than in security. . . . Finally, we must . . . cling to our own . . . conceptions of human society. . . . the greatest danger that can befall us . . . is that we shall allow ourselves to become like those with whom we are coping.

Long by the standards of a telegram, Kennan's analysis was succinct by the logic of diplomacy. It was also eerily prescient.

Snapshot of the Cold War

Within two years of the end of World War II, the two wartime allies faced off against one another, just as Kennan had highlighted. They used "the logic of force" to checkmate and contain one another. From 1949 to 1955, two massive military alliances, the North Atlantic Treaty Organization (NATO) in the West and the Warsaw Pact in the East, emerged to divide Berlin, Germany, and the rest of Europe not just politically but physically. By 1961, an ugly wall ran down the center of Berlin, and barbed wire, guard towers, and a barren no-man's land scarred the surface of the heartland of Europe.

The two superpowers engaged one another with considerably more ideological fervor and saber rattling than Kennan had advised, and which he later sharply criticized. An intense series of crises followed worldwide. Berlin, Korea, and Cuba brought the superpowers to the brink of war. Nevertheless, in the end the superpowers ended the confrontation without firing a shot directly at one another. They engaged in a **Cold War** of deterrence and diplomatic crises that, although it included plenty of "hot" wars waged through proxy governments as in Vietnam, did not involve the use of force in direct relations between the superpowers. Deterrence sublimated the use of force to a psychological rather than physical level. The superpowers played out the scenarios of war in their imaginations, testing the credibility of threats against capabilities and resolve and ultimately pulling back from the brink and settling disputes before war began. And all the while, as Kennan anticipated, the United States and Soviet Union fought the real battle at home through domestic competition. Forty-five years later, the United States and its allies won that competition decisively. In November 1989, the Berlin Wall came down, and in December 1991, the Soviet Union ceased to exist.

Does Kennan's picture offer the best explanation of the start of the Cold War? Possibly, but first we must ask, what kind of explanation is it—realist, liberal, or identity? What is driving Soviet behavior in Kennan's analysis? At first glance, it might seem to be Marxist ideology. After all, as he points out, the Soviet party line of "capitalist encirclement" was "not based on any objective analysis" but was, instead, a "neurotic view of world affairs." Moreover, in contact with the advanced West, Russia felt less competent, less powerful, making "Marxist dogma" a "perfect vehicle" to express its inferiority. But now geopolitics slips into the picture. This neurotic view was not itself the cause of Soviet behavior but a result of a "traditional and instinctive Russian sense of insecurity." Russia lived on a "vast exposed plain" in a "neighborhood of fierce nomadic peoples" and had suffered three bloody invasions by

Spotlight on stability not freedom

Cold War

the putatively bloodless conflict, starting after World War II and lasting forty-five years, between the United States and the Soviet Union, which nonetheless resulted in massive arms buildups, international conflicts, and proxy wars worldwide.

Napoleon, Kaiser Wilhelm II, and Hitler in just over a hundred years. It was location or geopolitics, not ideology, that explained Russia's paranoia.

The real tip-off comes when Kennan suggests, "Soviet power does not work by fixed plans." Moscow might have an ideology but in the end that ideology bends to "the logic of force." The Soviet Union can "easily withdraw—and usually does—when strong resistance is encountered at any point." How so, if its ideology calls for "drawing to itself the countries which tend toward socialism"? Because in determining Soviet behavior, Kennan judges, strategic and geopolitical realities ultimately trump ideology. They also trump liberal factors. Notice that the Soviet Union uses international organizations and transnational actors—for example, the Russian Orthodox Church—to advance the purposes of Soviet ideology. But institutions are instruments not determinants of Soviet behavior. Thus, when all is said and done, ideology and institutions bend to power factors. Kennan's analysis is realist, and that's why he can be relatively complacent about the ideological component of Soviet policy. Note that he says the "mass of Russian people . . . [is] emotionally . . . removed from doctrines of the Communist Party." This is why he became so critical of others who saw the Cold War more in ideological or identity terms.[2]

This chapter addresses arguments about what caused the Cold War and what caused it to end. As before, there are realist, identity, and liberal explanations of these historical events. And along the way critical theories offer their insights as well.

causal arrow →

Realist Explanations of the Origins and End of the Cold War

Three main realist arguments explain the origins of the Cold War. Each traces events back to power factors, but they come from different levels of analysis. One domestic level explanation suggests that the Soviet Union caused the Cold War because its society was aggressive. A second domestic level argument says the United States caused the Cold War because its capitalist economic system was expansionist. A third explanation, perhaps the most influential, comes from the systemic level. It argues that neither the United States nor the Soviet Union was responsible for the Cold War; rather, the Cold War was a consequence of the security dilemma. The two countries faced one another across a power vacuum in central Europe and had to compete to fill that vacuum whether they were aggressive or not.

Spotlight on power

The principal realist explanation for the end of the Cold War also comes from the systemic level. It holds that the United States eventually won this competition by means of deterrence and an arms race that bankrupted the Soviet Union. Kennan predicted this outcome in a famous article published a year and a half after the long telegram. By confronting "the Russians with unalterable counterforce at every point where they show signs of encroaching upon the interest of a peaceful and stable world," he wrote, the United States would "promote tendencies which must eventually find their outlet in either the break-up or the gradual mellowing of Soviet power."[3]

In the sections that follow, we examine the three realist explanations about how the Cold War started, four realist mechanisms by which the Cold War expanded (atomic bomb, nuclear deterrence, crises such as the Cuban Missile Crisis, and alliances/proxy wars), and finally the realist explanation of how the Cold War ended.

How the Cold War Started

SOVIET AGGRESSION—HISTORICAL EXPANSIONISM. "Russia on the march," Henry Kissinger writes, "rarely exhibited a sense of limits." It "seemed impelled to expand by a rhythm all its own, containable only by the deployment of superior force, and usually by war."[4] This had been the case since the time of Peter the Great, long before the arrival of communism. So, according to this explanation of the Cold War, Soviet aggression was not a consequence of communist ideology or the sense of historical insecurity that Kennan stressed. It was the outgrowth of an aggressive nature of the domestic society that demanded aggrandizement and empire. As Stalin saw it, "Everyone imposes his own system as far as his army can reach."[5] He was, according to this explanation, an offensive realist, seeking to maximize power rather than just provide security. And the cause of aggression came not from Stalin himself or the individual level of analysis because every Russian leader since Peter the Great had been aggressive. Nor did it come from the systemic structural level of analysis or the sense of historical insecurity bred by the security dilemma. Rather, it came from the domestic society as a whole, and it was not the communist ideology or institutions but the aggressive nature of that society that caused the expansionism.

Stalin's army had reached quite far when World War II ended. Soviet divisions occupied Lithuania, Latvia, and Estonia; all of eastern Europe; half of Germany; and northern Iran. Meanwhile, U.S. troops withdrew from Europe, reduced from 12 million down to 1.5 million by mid-1947. Stalin also pressed for a naval advantage, looking for warm-water ports in the Mediterranean and modes of access to the Atlantic Ocean, perhaps as a way to challenge, if not encircle, Britain and the United States on the high seas. Finally, when a million Soviet troops maneuvered in Romania and stayed in Iran beyond the end of 1945, Harry S. Truman saw a threat of aggression and became alarmed: "There isn't a doubt in my mind that Russia intends an invasion of Turkey and the seizure of the Black Sea Straits to the Mediterranean. Unless Russia is faced with an iron fist and strong language another war is in the making."[6]

Although these crises passed, the impression of Soviet aggression lasted, and the "policy of containment, as it came to be called, was adopted at the beginning of 1946."[7] Aggressive Soviet actions convinced Washington policy officials that they had to draw a line of **containment** around the periphery of the territories Soviet armies occupied and defend that line, if necessary by military force. No wonder Kennan's telegram, which arrived about this time, set off such a furor. Policymakers had decided "the Soviet Union was an expansionist power, and . . . only countervailing power could keep her in line."[8]

In the same month, British Prime Minister Winston Churchill declared in Fulton, Missouri, that an **iron curtain** had descended on Europe "from Stettin in the Baltic to Trieste in the Adriatic."[9] Churchill spoke about the impending division of Europe in a political sense. But two years later in 1948, the iron curtain became a physical barrier when the Soviet Union cut off access routes to the western occupied parts of Berlin located inside the Soviet-occupied zone. And two years after that, in 1950, it became a military division when North Korea, a client state of the Soviet Union, invaded South Korea and sparked a global conflict.

As was assumed then and known now, the Soviet Union approved the North Korean invasion beforehand. The attack set off alarm bells in Europe and provoked a military buildup—an **arms race**—to prevent a Soviet-sponsored invasion from happening there. From this realist argument, Soviet aggression was clearly the culprit. And

Spotlight on offensive realism

containment
the policy of the United States during the Cold War that checked aggressive Soviet actions by military alliances.

iron curtain
a metaphor for the political, ideological, and physical (no-man's land) separation of the Soviet Union and western countries during the Cold War.

arms race
the competitive buildup of weapons systems.

now Moscow had allies in Asia as well. In 1949, the communists under Mao Zedong won the civil war in China. The Cold War was in full swing.

U.S. AGGRESSION—CAPITALIST EXPANSIONISM. But wait a minute, you say. What about American or western aggression? Weren't western armies also ensconced in Europe, even if they were being reduced? Didn't American and British fleets dominate the Mediterranean and Baltic Seas, in effect "encircling" the Soviet Union? Hadn't the Soviet Union, not the United States, recently been invaded by Nazi hordes, and didn't the United States and Great Britain delay for almost three years before establishing a second front to help Russia fight off the Nazi invaders? For every one American who died in World War II, fifty-three Russians died.[10] Might Stalin have had reasons to wonder whether the capitalist states were happy watching the fascist and communist states eliminate or at least drastically weaken one another?

When the war ended, Russia was powerful militarily, but the United States possessed the atom bomb. And, while the Soviet economy lay in ruins, the United States was by far the most powerful country economically. It was the only major combatant in World War II to escape entirely any damage to its homeland industrial base. So the Soviet Union had good reason to feel that it was the weaker power and to expect and probably deserve substantial economic help from its western allies, as well as reparations from Germany and conquered eastern European countries. What did it get?

Not much. First, as soon as the war was over in both Europe and Asia, the United States cut off Lend Lease assistance to the Soviet Union, the supply of all kinds of military and economic assistance during the war to countries fighting Germany and its allies. Then, at the **Potsdam Conference** in July 1945, the allies concocted a reparation plan that assumed the unification of Germany. But the Soviet Union preferred a division of Germany and rejected the plan.[11] When the western powers decided in spring 1946 to go ahead rebuilding their own zones, the Soviet Union saw the western powers uniting Germany not only without it but against it. The battle for Germany was joined.

One year later in spring 1947, the United States announced the Marshall Plan. This plan proposed to integrate the western zones of Germany into a larger program of European economic cooperation. The Soviet zone and other eastern European states were invited to join. But let's think about this proposal now from the point of view of the Soviet Union. Economically ravaged and weak, its satellites were being asked to join a western market system that was not only more powerful, given the backing of the United States, but that also operated on the basis of free trade. Quite understandably, Moscow saw this move as western aggression, a plan to penetrate economically, and eventually take over politically, the protective band of countries in eastern Europe that the Soviet Union needed as a security buffer and had just sacrificed so many lives to establish. The U.S. action wasn't military aggression as such, but it could be seen as capitalist imperial aggression. And it threatened the heart of Soviet interests in Europe, whereas alleged Soviet aggression challenged only peripheral western interests in places such as Greece and Turkey.

When the western powers announced in spring 1948 that they would unify the currency of the western zones of Germany, Moscow reacted by shutting down the land routes to Berlin. As Map 5-1 shows, the city of Berlin was located inside the Soviet-occupied part of Germany (East Germany) and was itself divided into western (U.S., British, and French) and Soviet zones. Thus, the Soviet Union controlled land access

Potsdam Conference

the meeting among wartime allies in July 1945 in which they were unable to reach an agreement on the unification of Germany and other issues.

to Berlin. When Stalin blockaded the road and railway routes, the western powers responded with the massive Berlin airlift. Over fourteen months, the allies made 277,804 flights to Berlin, delivering 2.326 million tons of supplies. The **Berlin Blockade** of 1948–1949 was the first physical confrontation of the Cold War. According to the United States-is-the-aggressor argument, however, Russia was not responsible. It was provoked. Moscow could not permit capitalist economic forces to expand and weaken its control of the Soviet zone.

This argument is called the **revisionist interpretation** of the Cold War because it revises the traditional argument that the Soviet Union was the aggressor. To the extent that it emphasizes military causes of U.S. aggressive policy, it is clearly a realist argument. But to the extent that it draws on deeper historical forces of social and economic change, it slides into a critical theory perspective. Critical theorists see a dialectic at work between America's propensity to expand, the so-called open door or open market (for example, the Marshall Plan) policy by which America demanded access to resources and territory in other regions, and the inevitable resistance the United States encountered from the disadvantaged or poorer states that it sought to dominate. Out of this dialectic driven by the forces of capitalist production arose opportunities for change and the liberation of oppressed social classes. Capitalism spread wealth, while class struggle ensured a more just and equitable distribution of wealth. Eventually, a more democratic socialism based on community rather than private property would replace the individualistic, acquisitive character of liberal democracy. The revisionist, or Wisconsin School, argues that Soviet behavior after World War II was defensive in nature and that the dynamic of the American, not the Soviet, empire was the deep-seated cause of the Cold War and subsequent social change.[12]

Berlin Blockade

the first physical confrontation of the Cold War, taking place from 1948–1949, in which Stalin blocked the land routes into Berlin.

revisionist interpretation

an interpretation of the origins of the Cold War that emphasizes American ideological or economic aggression against the Soviet Union and its allies.

| Map 5-1 | The Division of Berlin |

POWER VACUUM AND SPHERES OF INFLUENCE. A third influential realist argument holds that the Cold War was nobody's fault but was a consequence of the situation that the United States and the Soviet Union faced. In April 1945, the two massive allied armies met in the middle of Germany, at Torgau on the Elbe River.[13] Because the allies had agreed in 1943 to pursue the war until the unconditional surrender of the enemy, there was nothing left of Germany when they finished. The entire country lay in ruins.

How was Germany going to be rebuilt? Would it be rebuilt as a western ally, Soviet ally, or neutral country? One thing was sure. As we know, Germany was the centerpiece of the old European state system. It had been divided for centuries; then it was united for nearly seventy-five years. Now it was destroyed. If it were united or divided again, it would matter greatly whether Germany added to western power or Soviet power. The distribution of power at the time, some realists argue, was tripolar.[14] The third country, in this case a reconstructed Germany (or Japan in the case of Asia), could tip the balance. Whoever won this prize would control the center of Europe (or Asia, in the case of Japan). Thus, the stakes were very high. No one had to be an aggressor in this situation. It was a matter of security, not aggression, for each side to seek the best outcome.

So systemic structural forces were driving events. Essentially two great powers (and their smaller allies) sat astride a strategic piece of territory and faced the security dilemma of whether and how much to trust one another. The classic balance-of-power solution was to "split the difference," divide the territory and power evenly. Create two **spheres of influence,** one in which the Soviet Union dominated and the other in which the United States dominated. That way, the relative balance of power would not be affected. Roughly, that is what happened. By 1950, two German governments existed and two alliances divided up the rest of Europe.

The balance of power was apparently working better than it had before World Wars I and II. There was no hot war in Europe, but why did a cold war emerge? Realist perspectives predict no cold war but a spheres of influence solution. That was the solution George Kennan favored. At best, realists might say that the bipolar distribution of power left no room for error and thus provoked a deep security dilemma that made the two superpowers enemies instead of rivals. But identity perspectives (examined later in the chapter) might say that it was the ideological divide that prevented an accommodation, not the security dilemma.

Churchill was an avid proponent of the spheres of influence solution. In October 1944, he met Stalin in Moscow and, on a famous half-sheet of paper, proposed a breakdown of relative influence in the Balkans.[15] The Soviet Union would have predominant influence in Romania and Bulgaria, Great Britain and the United States would have predominant influence in Greece, and both sides would split influence in Yugoslavia and Hungary. Deal done, right? Why not do the same for Germany and eastern Europe? Well, now think how you would administer such spheres of influence arrangements, especially when the two partners already suspect one another. After the war, Soviet troops occupied Poland, Romania, Hungary, Bulgaria, and Czechoslovakia. How could Britain and the United States know, let alone control, what might go on in those countries? At the **Yalta Conference** (held at a Russian resort of that name on the Black Sea) in February 1945, Roosevelt tried to reach an agreement with Stalin about what would happen in Poland. The United States would concede Soviet influence, since Soviet armies already occupied the country, if the Soviet Union would hold free and fair elections. But who then would ensure that the elections were free and fair? Yalta specified few details. In the end, no such elections were held. The Soviet Union

---

spheres of influence
areas of contested territory divided up and dominated by the great powers; the great powers then agree not to interfere in one another's territory in order to preserve the relative balance of power.

Yalta Conference
a wartime conference held in February 1945 where the United States, Soviet Union, and Great Britain agreed on the unconditional surrender of Nazi Germany and postwar occupation of Europe and where the United States conceded Soviet influence over Poland; considered a sellout, especially in eastern Europe, of small powers by the great powers.

installed a **puppet government** in Warsaw that Moscow manipulated. Later in 1948 the Soviet Union stage-managed another coup in Czechoslovakia. To this day, the conference at Yalta stands in the minds of eastern Europeans as a callous sell-out of small powers by the great powers.

How the Cold War Expanded

So the Cold War divided Europe. But why did it divide the globe? The answer, according to realist perspectives, is that a balance of terror replaced the balance of power and made it more difficult to segregate regional conflicts. The atomic bomb and nuclear deterrence provoked a global arms race and put a premium on the credibility of superpower commitments to defend their interests outside as well as inside Europe. Crises became a substitute for conflict, and the superpowers dueled over the Cuban Missile Crisis and **proxy wars** in Vietnam and Afghanistan. The costs were high, and eventually, the Soviet Union went bankrupt and the United States prevailed. From a realist perspective, competition and relative material capabilities decided the outcome. There was no direct conflict, but the persistent terrifying threat of nuclear war produced an equivalent outcome.

THE ATOMIC BOMB AND BALANCE OF TERROR. On July 16, 1945, the first nuclear bomb (called Little Boy) was tested in the deserts of New Mexico, an event Truman reported to Stalin at Potsdam. Stalin was not surprised. Klaus Fuchs, a Soviet spy at Los Alamos, the center of U.S. weapons research in New Mexico, had been supplying Russia with atomic secrets for years. After his conversation with Truman, Stalin instructed V. M. Molotov, his foreign minister, and Lavrenty Beria, the head of the Soviet atomic program, "to hurry up the work" on the Soviet bomb.[16] In 1949, the Soviet Union exploded its own weapon. According to realist logic, the Soviet Union could not depend on the United States or anyone else for security against this type of weapon.

Now a kind of **balance of terror** superseded the balance of power. If either side attacked, the other side might use nuclear weapons. As these weapons became more powerful—hydrogen bombs were developed by 1951 that were many times more powerful than atomic weapons—no country could risk nuclear war and survive. Yet conventional war might still be possible. After all, if no one could risk escalation, then the struggle for power might be decided by regular armies with tanks, artillery, and aircraft. Each country would have to be prepared for the full range of possible conflicts.

Thus, as realists see it, the arms race began even before the Korean War started in June 1950. The United States undertook a massive buildup of conventional forces. NSC-68, a famous U.S. policy document drafted by the National Security Council in early 1950, boosted the U.S. defense budget in one year from $13.5 to $48.2 billion. U.S. troops ballooned again in Europe from 80,000 in 1950 to 427,000 in 1953. NATO, created in 1949 during the Berlin Blockade to demonstrate political solidarity among the western allies, now developed into an integrated military force under a U.S. supreme commander. The military occupation of Germany by the western allies ended, a West German government was established, and West Germany eventually rearmed and joined NATO in 1955.

The **Korean War** globalized Cold War alliances. Korea had been divided at the end of World War II between a Soviet-dependent government in the north and a U.S.-dependent government in the south. In June 1950, North Korea, with permission from Moscow, invaded South Korea. The United States led a United Nations force to drive

puppet governments
governments that are installed, controlled, and/or supported by foreign states or other external parties and that act in the interests of those states or parties.

proxy wars
conflicts sponsored by superpowers elsewhere—in third-party states or through terrorists—as a substitute for direct conflict.

balance of terror
a situation in which two countries fear that, if either side attacks, the other side might use nuclear weapons, resulting in both countries being forced to prepare for the full range of possible conflicts to avoid all-out nuclear war.

Korean War
A war that started in June 1950 by a Soviet-blessed North Korean invasion of South Korea and ended in July 1953 by an armistice agreement (but no peace treaty) that divided the country along the thirty-eighth parallel, roughly where the war had begun.

the North Koreans back. When U.S-led UN forces threatened to cross the Yalu, a river dividing China and North Korea, China entered the war, and the fighting stalemated around the original dividing line until an armistice was signed in 1953. In 1950, the United States had signed a defense pact with Japan, which was upgraded after Korea to a security treaty. In 1954, the United States also created the South East Asian Treaty Organization (SEATO), comprising the United States, Great Britain, France, Australia, New Zealand, Pakistan, the Philippines, and Thailand. SEATO filled the vacuum when France pulled out of its colonial empire in Indochina (Vietnam, Cambodia, and Laos). The United States also concluded bilateral alliances with Australia, New Zealand, South Korea, the Philippines, Thailand, and Taiwan. Although the United Nations, a multilateral institution, authorized the U.S.-led resistance in Korea, bilateral alliances dominated in Asia, unlike the multilateral NATO alliance in Europe.

NUCLEAR DETERRENCE AND ESCALATION. As realists see it, the Cold War now played out through a series of crises—Berlin, Cuba, and so on. In these crises, the superpowers tested one another's resolve to defend specific commitments and maintain the balance of terror. Crisis and the threat of use of force substituted for war and the actual use of force. But each crisis itself could potentially lead to war. In effect, deterrence depended on the credibility of using force that was at some point too horrible to use.

How did nuclear deterrence work? It relied on an interactive process of threat and counterthreat to stop a dispute before the threats were implemented. The idea was to have the capability and to demonstrate the resolve to use that capability at any level of potential conflict. In a crisis, the superpowers tested one another's capabilities and resolve to defend specific interests. For instance, if Soviet armies threatened to invade western Europe, the allies would threaten to use nuclear weapons to deter them. But that threat might not be credible because it would mean an immediate all-out nuclear war. So, initially, the allies might threaten to use only tactical nuclear weapons. In the 1950s, NATO in fact deployed nuclear land mines as well as artillery shells in central Europe. If the Soviet Union threatened to escalate further, say with intermediate-range nuclear missiles capable of hitting U.S. allies in western Europe but not the United States, the United States had to be ready to retaliate against the Soviet Union with nuclear missiles. But would it be credible for the United States to launch intercontinental missiles from the United States and risk retaliation against New York in response to a threat in western Europe? That would only widen the war to a global war. Again, it might be better if the allies had missiles based in Europe that could threaten the Soviet Union. In fact, NATO deployed intermediate-range missiles in western Europe in the early 1980s to match similar Soviet missiles in eastern Europe.

If the Soviet Union was still not deterred, the United States would threaten to launch missiles from the United States, but these missiles would be aimed at Soviet missiles, not Soviet cities, to minimize collateral damage. Such weapons were called **counterforce weapons** and were designed to destroy specific military targets, as opposed to **countervalue weapons,** which were designed to destroy Soviet industries and cities. The threat of counterforce weapons led to hardening of missile sites to ensure that some of these missiles survived a first strike by the other side and would be available to retaliate in a second strike at the next level of escalation.

A **first-strike capability** is the capacity for the preemptive use of nuclear missiles to destroy most or all of the missiles of the other side. A **second-strike capability** involves protecting nuclear missiles so that enough survive a first-strike attack to be used to retaliate and ensure a level of unacceptable damage, thereby deterring the first strike to

counterforce weapons
nuclear missiles aimed at other missiles rather than at population or industrial centers.

countervalue weapons
nuclear missiles aimed at population and industrial centers rather than at other missiles.

first-strike capability
the capacity to use nuclear missiles preemptively to destroy most or all of the missiles of the other side.

second-strike capability
protecting nuclear missiles so that enough will survive a first-strike attack to be used to retaliate and ensure a level of unacceptable damage, thereby deterring the first strike.

begin with. Missiles were hardened in underground silos and dispersed on submarines where they were virtually undetectable and could be launched from underwater. In addition, a strategic bomber force armed with nuclear weapons was kept in the air around the clock to ensure that they would not be destroyed on the ground in a preemptive first strike. The combination of land-, sea-, and air-based retaliatory weapons became known as the **nuclear triad.**

The strategy of nuclear deterrence thus sought to slice the stages of escalation finer and finer so as to avoid the last move to all-out nuclear war. The superpowers would move up the various stages, or rungs of the ladder, of escalation in an incremental and controlled fashion, eventually achieving what was called **escalation dominance,** namely convincing the adversary not to go any farther up the ladder and forcing it to choose between unacceptable escalation and compromise.

Deterrence strategies evolved during the Cold War. For the first decade, when the United States had the capacity to strike the Soviet Union but the Soviet Union could not strike the United States, the United States relied on a strategy of **massive retaliation** or the threat of unleashing a general nuclear war if the Soviet Union attacked western Europe. After the Soviet Union launched the first space satellite, Sputnik, in 1957 and demonstrated its long-range rocket capability to strike the United States, the United States adopted a deterrence strategy of **flexible response,** or retaliating selectively to fight wars at conventional levels without immediately risking nuclear war or, if the nuclear threshold was crossed, engaging in limited nuclear wars.

Eventually, as both sides acquired increasingly equivalent capabilities, the deterrence strategy settled on what became known as **Mutual Assured Destruction** or, appropriately as critics pointed out, **MAD.** If each side could retaliate and assure an unacceptable amount of destruction to the other side, neither side would risk escalation. The strategy involved an emphasis on offensive weapons and a deemphasis on defensive weapons. The **Anti-Ballistic Missile (ABM) Treaty,** signed by the United States and Soviet Union in 1972, limited anti-ballistic missiles except for two installations on each side.

As we note in Chapter 1, however, realist and liberal perspectives part company on how many stages of escalation and offensive nuclear weapons were necessary and whether it was possible to control the process of escalation and manage the use of nuclear weapons in an atmosphere of extreme stress and danger. Realist perspectives feel it was imperative to have capabilities at every level of potential escalation and that it was possible to use diplomacy even in crises to convey the existence of this capability and the will to use it. A robust deterrence capability was especially necessary to provide **extended deterrence** to allies in Europe. Liberal perspectives feel that only a few second-strike nuclear weapons were necessary and that diplomacy should aim to reduce nuclear weapons to this minimum level, known as **minimum deterrence.**

Thus realist perspectives see diplomacy as serving the purpose of projecting credible force; liberal factors (diplomacy) serve realist ones (projecting force). Liberal perspectives see diplomacy as serving the purpose of reducing the level of necessary force; liberal factors (diplomacy) diminish realist ones (reducing arms). The difference between realist and liberal perspectives on deterrence is a matter of how the causal arrows ran between force and diplomacy, not the exclusion of one factor. Realist perspectives worried that if only one person or country in the world decided that something was worth the risk of nuclear war, other countries had better be prepared to deter them. Liberal perspectives worried that deterrence itself increased the risks of nuclear war.

nuclear triad
the combination of nuclear land-, sea-, and air-based retaliatory weapons.

escalation dominance
a strategy of deterrence designed to force another state to choose between compromise and escalation.

massive retaliation
the strategy of threatening to unleash a general nuclear war.

flexible response
the strategy of retaliating selectively to fight wars at conventional levels without immediately risking nuclear war.

Mutual Assured Destruction (MAD)
the deterrence strategy that called for the dominance of offensive over defensive weapons.

Anti-Ballistic Missile (ABM) Treaty
a 1972 treaty between the United States and Soviet Union limiting anti-ballistic missiles.

extended deterrence
a strategy by which a country extends deterrence to its allies by threatening to strike back on their behalf from its own territory.

minimum deterrence
a strategy of deterrence that calls for a relatively few nuclear weapons that can survive an enemy strike and threaten unacceptable damage in retaliation.

← **causal** *arrow*

Deterrence had two broad consequences for conflict. First, it intensified conflicts vertically between the superpowers, seeking to deter war by crisis rather than actual combat. Second, it spread conflicts horizontally as the superpowers worried about their credibility in third-world conflicts. In the two sections that follow, we look at examples of each of these consequences, first the Cuban Missile Crisis and then proxy wars in the third world.

CUBAN MISSILE CRISIS. No crisis illustrates the dynamics of deterrence between the superpowers better than the Cuban Missile Crisis. Soviet leaders risked nuclear war, but in the end superpower diplomacy avoided it. Here we consider realist perspectives, but compare this account carefully with the liberal perspectives presented later in this chapter.

In the summer and fall of 1962, the Soviets moved medium- and intermediate-range nuclear-armed ballistic missiles into Cuba. What induced them to do that? And why did the United States risk nuclear war to get them removed? Here's the calculus according to realist perspectives.

In the 1960s, the United States had a substantial superiority of nuclear weapons and missiles over the Soviets, with roughly 3,000 nuclear warheads, 180 intercontinental ballistic missiles (ICBMs) with a range of 5,000 miles, 630 long-range bombers, and 12 nuclear submarines. The Soviet Union had only 300 warheads, 20 ICBMs, 200 long-range bombers, and 6 nuclear submarines. U.S. bombers were deployed at forward bases in Europe and Asia, and its submarines could patrol waters within range of Soviet targets. In addition, the United States had placed intermediate-range ballistic missiles (IRBMs) with a range of 2,200 miles in Britain and medium-range ballistic missiles (MRBMs) with a range of 1,100 miles in Italy and Turkey. All these missiles could reach the Soviet Union. Soviet bombers had no forward bases or refueling capacity, and Soviet IRBMs and MRBMs could hit Europe but not the United States. Soviet submarines operated from bases 7,000 miles from the U.S. mainland and could not patrol in U.S. waters within the range of Soviet missiles, which was only 600 miles.[17]

Why did the United States have such an advantage? As we have noted, the realist argument is that it needed this advantage to provide extended deterrence to its allies in western Europe. If the Soviet Union launched missiles at Europe, Britain and later France might have had a few missiles to retaliate. But the United States would also have to respond; otherwise, a Soviet attack might not entail sufficient risk of retaliatory damage to deter the Soviet Union in the first place and the Soviet Union might try to divide Europe from the United States. Of course, it made little difference to the Soviet Union why the United States had more missiles. The Soviet Union saw them as an offensive threat, a first-strike capability that could destroy Soviet missiles on the ground before they were launched, thus leaving the Soviet Union defenseless. Might that be why Nikita Khrushchev, the Soviet premier, put missiles in Cuba, to give the Soviet Union an offsetting capability to destroy U.S. missiles before they left the ground?

Perhaps. Missile accuracies were not yet that precise. But once the communist revolutionary Fidel Castro overthrew the U.S.-backed dictatorship in Cuba in 1959, Khrushchev had his own distant ally to defend by extended deterrence. Castro turned to Moscow for help, and the Soviet Union started selling arms to Cuba in fall 1959. In April 1961, the United States backed an invasion of Cuba by anti-Castro exiles. Known as the Bay of Pigs invasion, the attack failed, in part because the United States dropped crucial air support at the last minute. But the United States continued covert activities to support an invasion of Cuba and tried several times to assassinate Castro.[18] Now Khrushchev wondered, as he later wrote in his memoirs, "what will happen if we lose Cuba?"[19] If the United States could defend Turkey by installing missiles, why couldn't the Soviet Union install missiles to defend Cuba?

Soviet and American credibility were at stake. This credibility had just been tested in Berlin. From 1958 to 1961, the Soviet Union tried again to deny western access to West Berlin by threatening to turn over controls to the East German government. East German citizens were fleeing in increasing numbers to the West. Soviet Premier Nikita Khrushchev felt he had to do something to solve the Berlin problem. After renewing his threat to President John F. Kennedy at Vienna in June 1961, Khrushchev built the Berlin Wall in August. Now he saw another opportunity to get the western allies out— trade a Soviet departure from Cuba for a western departure from Berlin.

Berlin was the epicenter of the superpower conflict. If either superpower backed down on this issue, it would undermine their European alliances as well as their own security. That might explain their willingness to march to the brink of nuclear disaster over the Cuban missiles.[20]

In May 1962, the Soviet Union made the decision to deploy to Cuba 48 MRBMs capable of striking Dallas, St. Louis, Cincinnati, and Washington; 32 IRBMs capable of striking all U.S. cities except Seattle; nuclear weapons for coastal defense cruise missiles; surface-to-air missiles (SAMs); 42 light Ilyushin-28 bombers; MIG fighter aircraft; and bases for 7 nuclear submarines. It then proceeded to lie to the United States and other nations as the deployment took place. Moscow, of course, believed the United States was doing the same thing about plans to invade Cuba. Notice here the realist problem of not being able to trust the other party, for good reason realists point out, because the other party lies. Nevertheless, Khrushchev's decision to deploy nuclear missiles in Cuba was bold and breathtaking, not to mention deadly. He had either lost his mind or believed he had taken the measure of Kennedy and could get away with it. Here is a case, realist perspectives remind us, when someone was willing to risk nuclear war. Khrushchev expected to complete the installation by early fall and, as Kennedy himself later noted, "face us [that is, the United States] with a bad situation in November at the time he was going to squeeze us on Berlin."[21] With the missiles installed in Cuba by November, Khrushchev would be in a much stronger position to demand a Berlin withdrawal for a Cuban one.

In October 1962, Kennedy reacted. He ordered a naval quarantine, not a blockade, of Soviet ships going to Cuba. A quarantine was a less belligerent act under international law and, in accordance with deterrence logic, initiated the crisis at a lower rung on the escalation ladder. Kennedy then demanded the removal of the missiles already there. He also prepared to escalate the use of force by mobilizing a major invasion force to storm Cuba if the Soviet Union refused. The superpowers were eyeball to eyeball. On Saturday, October 27, Kennedy, according to his own account, decided to schedule air strikes for the following Tuesday, October 30.[22] We now know that 9 MRBMs had already been assembled in Cuba, and 36 nuclear warheads were also on the island. More important, and unknown to American officials during the crisis, Soviet combat troops in Cuba, altogether some 42,000 (many more than U.S. policymakers thought), were equipped with tactical nuclear missiles with a range of 60 kilometers to resist the invasion. Soviet generals later said they were prepared to use the missiles to hit American ships 10–12 miles offshore when they were grouped together for landing and, hence, most vulnerable to attack. The generals had advance authorization to use the missiles if for some reason they could not reach Moscow for instructions, although

Spotlight on
deceptive diplomacy

that authorization was reportedly rescinded once the crisis began.[23] Nevertheless, earlier on October 27, Soviet generals in Cuba had acted on their own authority, after failing to reach Moscow, to shoot down a U.S. reconnaissance plane over Cuba. Thus, on that Saturday night, the world was very possibly only a couple of days away from Armageddon.

On Sunday, October 28, however, the Soviet Union blinked and the crisis ended. Khrushchev agreed to stop deployments and take out the weapons already there. On the surface, it looked like a complete U.S. victory. But in fact Kennedy had secretly traded in return two substantial concessions: a pledge not to invade Cuba and another to withdraw the Jupiter missiles in Turkey. The secrecy protected alliance relations as well as President Kennedy's own legacy.[24] Moreover, Soviet forces and tactical nuclear weapons stayed in Cuba for several years. Some of the delivery systems, although not the warheads, were never withdrawn.[25]

Why did the Soviet Union back down in the Cuban Missile Crisis? According to realist perspectives, because the American threat to escalate and use force was credible. As Graham Allison and Philip Zelikow conclude, "Khrushchev withdrew the Soviet missiles, not because of the blockade, but because of the threat of further action." Khrushchev believed "he faced a clear, urgent threat that America was about to move up the ladder of escalation." [26] The threat of escalation was decisive, at least according to this account.

ALLIANCES AND PROXY WARS. As realist perspectives see it, alliances and proxy wars were central to the operation of deterrence and the eventual outcome of the Cold War. Deterrence worked in the Cuban Missile Crisis because alliances stood firm. But, in other crises, deterrence placed enormous stress on alliances. To work, alliances had to be tight to preserve credibility. But no country could feel completely comfortable relying on another country to defend it with nuclear weapons. America's European allies, for example, feared the alliance might not be tight enough and that they would be abandoned, as the Berlin crises suggested. Or they worried that the alliance might be too tight and they would be entrapped or drawn into wars that they did not want, as the Vietnam crisis suggested. The United States had concerns as well. In Suez, the United States stopped Britain and France from supporting an Israeli invasion of the Suez Canal because it feared being drawn into a Middle East war with the Soviet Union.

The Soviet Union had even bigger troubles with its allies. It used force in 1956 to crush a revolution and possible "abandonment" by Hungary and again in 1968 to terminate the anti-communist revolt, called Prague Spring, in Czechoslovakia. In 1968–1969, it also fought a border war with China, terminating that alliance and providing the opening that President Richard Nixon exploited in 1972 when he visited China and forged a common alignment against the Soviet Union.

Deterrence was designed to prevent disputes from going up the ladder of escalation to nuclear war. But it also pushed disputes off the ladder into peripheral areas and involved the superpowers in third-world conflicts, or what the Soviets called **national wars of liberation.** The superpowers probed one another's intentions in more distant places and fought proxy wars in Korea, the Middle East, Vietnam, Central America, Africa, and Afghanistan.

Some realists such as Kennan wanted to pursue a strategy of strongpoint, not perimeter deterrence. **Strongpoint deterrence** is a strategy of concentrating on the central states in Europe and on not spreading the Cold War across the entire globe.

Spotlight on compromise

---

national wars of liberation
Soviet term for revolutions in developing countries against western colonialism and for proxy wars during the Cold War.

strongpoint deterrence
Cold War strategy of concentrating on the central points of a conflict and on not spreading the conflict to other, perimeter regions.

Perimeter deterrence is a strategy of confronting disputes early in peripheral and former colonial areas and preventing them from escalating into conflicts that involved central states in Europe.

After World War II, **decolonization** under the United Nations created over fifty new nations in the Middle East, Africa, and Asia. As colonial powers retreated from these areas, the competing superpowers stepped in to fill the vacuum. When Britain left Greece and Turkey in 1947, the United States declared the Truman Doctrine to support free people wherever they may be threatened and implemented a Four-Point Plan to provide economic and technical assistance to Greece and Turkey. In the Middle East, the United States helped create the state of Israel and then supported it in a long series of wars between Arabs and Jews from 1948 to the present, almost coming to blows with the Soviet Union during the October war of 1973. France pulled out of Indochina in 1954, and America began its slow entanglement in Vietnam.

The superpowers exacerbated but also contained many of these conflicts. They competed to establish friendly governments, but cooperated to control the spread of nuclear weapons. From a realist perspective, the problem was less one of spreading democracy or communism than losing bases or allies to the other side. To use a metaphor common at the time, the **domino theory** haunted the superpowers. They feared that if a key country in a particular region went over to the other side, their side would lose momentum and credibility in the larger global struggle. Other countries in that region would fall to the other side like dominoes. This fear, justified from some realist perspectives (not Kennan's) but heavily criticized from other perspectives, led to numerous interventions by both superpowers in third-world conflicts. The United States intervened in Iran (1953), Guatemala (1954), Cuba (1961), Chile (1973), and other places. The Soviet Union intervened in Cuba (1962), Egypt (1973), Angola (1975), Mozambique (1976), and elsewhere. As realists see it, the choice often came down to a communist or an authoritarian regime. An authoritarian regime was to be preferred, particularly if it bolstered U.S. and western credibility to maintain deterrence and protect freedom in western Europe and Japan. President Kennedy captured the dilemma in his comments about U.S. intervention in the Dominican Republic in 1963:

> There are three possibilities in descending order of preference: a decent democratic regime, a continuation of the Trujillo [then the dictator in the Dominican Republic] regime, or a Castro regime. We ought to aim at the first, but we can't really renounce the second until we are sure we can avoid the third.[27]

Many third-world countries took refuge from superpower competition by forming a **nonaligned movement.** Led by India, Yugoslavia, and Egypt, the nonaligned movement stressed nonintervention in the domestic affairs of newly independent nations and international aid for third-world development. The movement tempered the political impact of the Cold War and focused attention on economic development.

perimeter deterrence
Cold War strategy of confronting disputes early in peripheral and former colonial areas and preventing them from escalating to the central states in Europe.

decolonization
the process by which a colony gains its independence from a colonial power.

domino theory
fear of the superpowers that if one country in a developing region went over to the other side, other countries would fall like dominoes.

nonaligned movement
a coalition led by India, Yugoslavia, and Egypt that stressed neutrality in the Cold War, nonintervention in the domestic affairs of newly independent nations, and international aid for third-world development.

Under siege, the United States leaves Vietnam. Here, a U.S. marine helicopter lifts off the rooftop of the U.S. Embassy during the evacuation of Saigon on April 30, 1975.

Map 5-2 Laos, Cambodia, North and South Vietnam

The Vietnam and Afghanistan wars marked the apogee of Cold War rivalry in the third world. Both wars ended in defeat for the superpowers. The Vietnam War was a traumatic experience for the United States. It cost 58,000 American lives and some 3 million Vietnamese lives. France originally had colonized Indochina, which includes Vietnam, Laos, and Cambodia (see Map 5-2). In 1954, Laos and Cambodia became independent, but Vietnam was provisionally divided between a communist north and an authoritarian south. Elections to unite the country were contemplated but never held. The United States backed a fragile military government in the south while the Soviet Union supported the Viet Cong revolutionaries in the north. After fifteen years of fighting with no significant gains to show for it, the United States packed up and left Vietnam in 1973. Two years later, the South Vietnamese government collapsed, and the communists in North Vietnam reunited the country. Then in 1979, the Soviet Union invaded Afghanistan. This conflict proved to be even more fateful for the Soviet Union. Fundamentalist Muslims, called mujahidin, battled Soviet forces in a long war of attrition. The United States armed and supported the mujahidin, creating the radicalized Muslim zealots that later formed the Taliban government in Afghanistan and that threaten today to destabilize Pakistan. In 1989, the Soviet Union finally withdrew from Afghanistan. Shortly thereafter, in part due to the heavy losses it incurred in Afghanistan in both lives and treasury, the Soviet Union collapsed and disappeared.

As realist perspectives see it, such wars were necessary at the time. When America entered Vietnam, the Cold War rivalry in Europe and Asia was intense. The Soviet Union had just put missiles in Cuba, and the eventual collapse of the alliance between the Soviet Union and China was not yet known. Similarly, Soviet interventions in Africa and Afghanistan signaled its recovery from the humiliation of the Cuban Missile Crisis and its ability now to compete with the United States in the projection of power worldwide. Constant vigilance in peripheral areas maintained deterrence in central areas where it may have caused a nuclear holocaust. Other perspectives, of course, disagreed. They saw Vietnam and Afghanistan as symbols of the folly of dominoes and deterrence outside Europe and a dark legacy on the conscience of both superpowers. Defensive realists such as Paul Kennedy predicted the decline of the United States due to **imperial overstretch,** the squandering of resources in conflicts such as Vietnam.[28] In the end, the Soviet Union declined, not the United States, but both superpowers suffered from imperial overstretch in Vietnam and Afghanistan. (See Table 5-1 for a summary of realist explanations for the start of the Cold War.)

imperial overstretch

the squandering of resources by superpowers in proxy conflicts.

How the Cold War Ended

As realists see it, the Cold War ended by the U.S. containing Soviet power until the Soviet Union changed. Realists did not predict, however, that the Soviet Union would

Table 5-1

The Causes of the Origins and Expansion of the Cold War: The Realist Perspective and Levels of Analysis

Level of analysis		Realist perspective
Systemic	*Structure*	• Bipolarity—no flexibility: —Security dilemma: Balance of terror replaces balance of power —Nuclear deterrence discourages attack by threat before it occurs rather than by defense after an attack occurs; credibility as important as capability; leads to repeated crises to test intentions
		• Power vacuum: Germany and Japan surrender unconditionally; reconstructed Germany/Japan could tip balance
	Process	• Dynamics of deterrence spreads conflict to third world
Foreign policy		• U.S. and Soviet leaders resolve Cuban Missile Crisis
Domestic		• Soviet Union aggressive militarily in eastern Europe, Baltic, and Balkan states
		• U.S. expansionist economically in western Europe and Asia
Individual		• Khrushchev takes measure of Kennedy and deploys Cuban missiles

disappear. They expected the two superpowers to remain rivals and compete over spheres of influence, as Churchill had advocated right after World War II. Many realists argue that this is still the case today when the United States and Russia continue to vie for influence in eastern Europe, the Middle East, and central Asia (see Chapter 6). Nevertheless, a vigorous U.S. rebound and a precipitous Soviet collapse in the 1980s decisively shifted the balance of power and ended the Cold War, with the United States as the only remaining military and economic superpower.

U.S. REBOUND. The 1970s was not a good decade for the United States. Its economy fell on hard times, its political system was rocked by the Watergate scandal and racial tensions, it exited Vietnam with a significant loss of face and self-confidence, and it faced a Soviet Union that for the first time projected its forces into areas beyond the European landmass, such as Angola and Mozambique. By 1979, when the Soviet Union invaded Afghanistan and a revolutionary government in Iran seized American hostages, the United States hit bottom.

Then in 1980 Ronald Reagan defeated incumbent president Jimmy Carter and launched a massive military and economic buildup. Defense expenditures rose precipitously. Washington galvanized the NATO alliance to deploy intermediate-range nuclear missile forces (INFs) in Europe. And Reagan announced a major new program of space-based anti-missile systems, known as the **Strategic Defense Initiative (SDI)** or Star Wars by its critics. Under Reagan's policies of deregulating and restructuring, the American economy roared back and grew steadily for the next twenty years. Even taking into account mild recessions in 1990 and 2001, the U.S. economy expanded at unprecedented rates above 3 percent per year.

SDI was more than satellites, rockets, and lasers in space to knock down ballistic missiles. It changed the calculus of deterrence. As already noted, deterrence under MAD depended on offensive missiles threatening mutual assured destruction with no effective anti-ballistic missile (ABM) defenses. Now SDI suggested that defensive systems would be built up and offensive weapons built down. In the short run, this change might increase instability because whoever got the defensive systems first

Strategic Defense Initiative (SDI)

the space-based anti-missile systems that formed the core of Reagan's program to enhance missile defenses.

Mutual Assured Defense
the strategy, proposed by Reagan with his Strategic Defense Initiative, that defensive systems could be built up and offensive weapons built down to ensure deterrence, with the United States sharing defense technology with the Soviet Union to preclude a first strike advantage.

might, in a crisis, launch a first strike against the other side and feel confident that its defensive systems would defeat whatever offensive missiles survived on the other side. To overcome this problem, Reagan offered to share SDI technology with the Soviet Union. Now the superpowers could deter one another by **Mutual Assured Defense,** not mutual destruction. It was certainly more humane than the specter of MAD killing millions of innocent civilians, but at the time it scared a lot of people, including Soviet leaders, and twenty-five years later missile defense has still to be realized operationally.

SOVIET COLLAPSE. While the United States was rebounding under Reagan, the Soviet Union fell on hard times. A series of aging Soviet leaders died in rapid succession—Leonid Brezhnev in 1982, Yuri Andropov in 1984, and Konstantin Chernenko in 1985. Soviet forces bogged down in Afghanistan, and the Soviet economy plummeted. The Soviet economy had never been as strong as U.S. officials thought. It peaked in 1970 at only 57 percent of the U.S. GNP. Reagan's buildup and the advent of the information age hit the Soviet Union at precisely the wrong time. When the younger, more technically sophisticated Mikhail Gorbachev succeeded Chernenko in 1985, his primary goal was to revitalize the Soviet economy and avoid another arms race with the United States, which SDI symbolized. In a Politburo meeting in October 1985, he told his colleagues:

> Our goal is to prevent the next round of the arms race. If we do not accomplish it, the threat to us will only grow. We will be pulled into another round of the arms race that is beyond our capabilities, and we will lose, because we are already at the limits of our capabilities. Moreover, we can expect that Japan and the FRG [West Germany] could very soon join the American potential. . . . If the new round begins, the pressure on our economy will be unbelievable.[29]

Here, from a realist perspective, were the material forces driving the Soviet Union to defeat in the Cold War. The cause was not any new ideas that Gorbachev brought to the table, the "new thinking" that identity accounts emphasize (see later discussion). Nor was it U.S.-Soviet negotiations, which had been in the deep freeze since Reagan took office. It was, pure and simple, an arms race coupled with the information revolution (notice how technology serves zero-sum, not common, goals in a realist perspective) and the coherence of western alliances (notice Gorbachev's reference to America's two principal allies, Japan and West Germany). These material pressures affected old thinkers as well as new thinkers in the Soviet Union, showing that it was not a debate won by new thinkers that decided Soviet policy but material circumstances that neither old nor new thinkers could ignore.[30] A hard-liner and critic of Gorbachev's new thinking, Soviet Chief of the General Staff Sergei Akhromeyev, made the point emphatically: "The Soviet Union could no longer continue a policy of military confrontation with the U.S. and NATO after 1985."[31]

Gorbachev tried in vain to stop SDI. At a summit in Reykjavik, Iceland, in December 1986, he walked away from the possibility of an unprecedented agreement to eliminate all nuclear weapons when Reagan refused to give up SDI. Meanwhile, Soviet defense expenditures as a percentage of GNP climbed from 13.5 percent in 1976 to almost 18 percent in 1988 (before dropping for the first time in 1989), and the Soviet Union increased its nuclear warhead arsenal in the 1980s by over 50 percent (from 7,480 to over 11,320).[32] That the Soviet Union continued the arms race and stuck it out in Afghanistan until 1988 proves to realist analysts that the new thinking had little impact. Although realist forces may not explain every aspect of Soviet behavior (for example, why Gorbachev reformed the political system before opening the

causal arrow →

economy to foreign investment, while China did the reverse), they clearly explain Soviet bankruptcy and the Soviet decision to retreat from eastern Europe and focus on reforming its economy.

So, from realist perspectives, the Cold War ended without a shot but not without a psychological and material struggle, which the United States ultimately won. Nuclear weapons substituted crises, such as those in Berlin and Cuba, for war, and conflicts were fought and won virtually through arms races and economic competition rather than violently through battlefield deaths and destruction. (See Table 5-2 for a summary of realist explanations for the end of the Cold War.) For one attempt to sort out realist from other factors in explaining the end of the Cold War, see the conclusions of historian John Lewis Gaddes in the box on page 186.

Identity Explanations of the Origins and End of the Cold War

Identity perspectives take a very different cut at nuclear deterrence and the Cold War. If war, especially nuclear war, has to be risked, should it be risked for nothing more than a cynical struggle for power for which no one is responsible? Identity perspectives think not. They see the Cold War shaped by values and common humanity. For some identity perspectives, it was a struggle between good and evil, the free world versus totalitarian societies, democracy versus communism. For others, it was a struggle for common human survival, regardless of political philosophy, a quest to save the Earth and human civilization from nuclear winter, the long dark devastation that would follow a general nuclear war.

Three identity arguments explain the origins of the Cold War. Two come from the domestic level of analysis and focus on internal ideological factors: Marxist-Leninism (not Russia's historical insecurity) caused the Cold War, or, conversely, American democracy (not military or economic expansionism) caused the Cold War. The third comes from the systemic level of analysis and focuses on collective identity, on why the United States and Soviet Union saw themselves as enemies rather than just rivals.

Four identity arguments explain the end of the Cold War. The first, from the domestic level of analysis, says the ideology of the Soviet Union mellowed and deadly enemies became less dangerous rivals. The second, from the individual level of analysis, says Gorbachev and advisers around him adopted new thinking and ended the Cold War. The third, from the systemic process level, says that the ideologies of both East and West converged to chart a common course. And the fourth, from the systemic

Table 5-2

The Causes of the End of the Cold War: The Realist Perspective and Levels of Analysis		
Level of analysis		**Realist perspective**
Systemic	*Structure*	• United States outcompetes Soviet Union materially
	Process	• Information revolution bolsters U.S. advantage
Foreign policy		—
Domestic		• United States revives its military and economic power
Individual		• Reagan devises strategy to exploit Soviet weaknesses

Reagan and the End of the Cold War

John Lewis Gaddis wrote a book in 1982 called *Strategies of Containment*. The book evaluated the containment strategies toward the Soviet Union of each American president since Truman and assessed the effectiveness of these strategies. In 2005, Gaddis published a new edition that evaluated what Reagan did differently than other presidents that helped to end the Cold War. Here is what he concluded:

> It seems reasonable . . . to . . . seek no single explanation for what happened in the Soviet Union under Gorbachev; internal developments were surely more important than external pressures and inducements, although in just what proportion may not be clear for decades. What one can say now is that Reagan saw Soviet weaknesses sooner than most of his contemporaries did; that he understood the extent to which détente was perpetuating the Cold War rather than hastening its end; that his hard line strained the Soviet system at the moment of its maximum weakness; that his shift toward conciliation preceded Gorbachev; that he combined reassurance, persuasion, and pressure in dealing with the new Soviet leader; and that he maintained the support of the American people and American allies. Quite apart from whatever results this strategy produced, it was an impressive accomplishment simply to have devised and sustained it. Reagan's role here was critical.[1]

Let's pull his conclusions apart. Fundamentally, Gaddis concludes that internal developments in the Soviet Union had more to do with ending the Cold War than external pressures from the United States. So the domestic level of analysis was more important than the systemic level, and material weakness (the realist perspective), institutional failures (the liberal perspective), and a defunct communist ideology (the identity perspective) were apparently—he doesn't tell us, since he has focused primarily on U.S. policies—the cause in some relative proportion for the change that occurred inside the Soviet Union.

But Gaddis acknowledges that history could change that judgment and that, in any event, Reagan's strategy was impressive. In comparison to previous presidents, Reagan spotted earlier and exploited more effectively Soviet weaknesses, understood that détente delayed rather than hastened the end of the Cold War, did not just respond to change in the Soviet Union but initiated a plan of conciliation even before Gorbachev arrived on the scene, and pulled off this multifaceted strategy with both Gorbachev and the American people largely through reassurance and persuasion or a dialogue of ideas.

Reagan's strategy, in short, had more to do with realist (the focus on weaknesses) than liberal factors (the focus on détente). It also stressed ideas (identity). As Gaddis tells us elsewhere in his analysis, Reagan's strategy challenged rather than accepted the Soviet regime's legitimacy by using "human rights . . . as a weapon more powerful than anything that existed in the military arsenals of either side."[2] Ideas were just as powerful as weapons, and competition was just as powerful as cooperation.

---

1. John Lewis Gaddis, *Strategies of Containment: A Critical Appraisal of American National Security Policy During the Cold War,* 2nd ed. (New York: Oxford University Press, 2005), 375.
2. Ibid., 353.

structural level, says U.S. ideas of freedom and markets outcompeted and ultimately eliminated communist ideas in Europe and the Soviet Union.

In the next four sections we examine the arguments about the construction or origins of the Cold War, and in the fifth section we look at the four augments about how the Cold War ended or was deconstructed.

Soviet Ideology—Marxist-Leninism

The first domestic level identity explanation for the causes of the Cold War is that the Soviet Union genuinely believed its Marxist-Leninist ideology that communism was the wave of the future and would eventually vanquish capitalism. In this case, Marxist-Leninist ideas acted as a belief system that caused Soviet behavior, not as an underlying historical dialectic as in critical theory perspectives (see later discussion). Contrary to Kennan's view, ideology now trumps insecurity or geopolitics in determining Soviet behavior. From this point of view, the Soviet Union was not likely to back down when confronted by superior force. It saw history as on its side and expected the correlation of forces (the Marxist-Leninist term for balance of power) to move steadily in its direction. That's why Moscow took aggressive moves in the 1970s even though its economy was in decline.

The Soviet Union did support, as Kennan projected, a worldwide campaign to promote communism. It established Cominform in 1947 (a replacement for the old Comintern, which was disbanded in 1943) to assist communist parties in France, Italy, and elsewhere. Communists led the resistance in France against the Nazi occupation and Vichy regime (a pro-Hitler puppet government in France that nominally controlled part of the country during the war) and participated after the war in a coalition government. Communists also formed coalition governments in Italy and contested power in eastern Europe, Greece, and Turkey.

When China fell (or, as it was said, "was lost") to the communists in 1949, it set off a virulent fear of communist conspiracies, especially in the United States. Senator Joseph McCarthy of Wisconsin held hearings and developed lists of communist spies and sympathizers throughout the U.S. government who he said threatened American freedom. Richard Nixon, then a young member of Congress, gained notoriety when he accused (correctly, as it turned out) Alger Hiss, a highly respected government official and president of the Carnegie Endowment for International Peace, of lying about his earlier membership in the Communist Party. Ronald Reagan, at that time a young actor and president of the Hollywood Screen Actors Guild, testified before the House Un-American Activities Committee that communists were infiltrating Hollywood, saying "I abhor their philosophy," while adding that he believed they had the right to express it.[33]

Critical Theory Perspective

According to mainstream explanations of the origin and end of the Cold War, individual variables such as communist belief systems inspired Soviet aggression and a worldwide conspiracy to overthrow capitalism. Critical theory perspectives shift the focus from individual causes acting sequentially to deep-seated historical forces acting in an interconnected manner. Critical theory highlights the dialectic process of social change, driven by a combination of material, institutional, and social forces that lead to a more just and peaceful future. In this historical process, the United States was the

Spotlight on
belief systems

leading representative of the capitalist forces and the Soviet Union was the leading representative or vanguard of the communist forces. The two countries were not, primarily, pursuing their own ideologies or interests but were fulfilling a role in a predetermined historical drama of social and political revolution. Individual leaders and countries are secondary. Causality is constitutive and evolutionary, involving a historical consciousness that entraps participants.

However, as the Cold War turned out, Marx's analysis was wrong. It was capitalism not communism that moved history forward. Marx did not see things clearly because he, too, was entrapped in historical consciousness and could not separate himself objectively from the forces that operated around him. But critical theory perspectives would point out that these forces continue to operate whoever the protagonists might be. Inequality persists, and underlying tensions between social classes and the forces of production continue to drive history.[34] (See Tables 5-3 and 5-4 for a summary of critical theory perspective explanations for the causes and end of the Cold War.)

American Ideology—Truman Doctrine

Coming at the issue from the other direction, perhaps anti-communism or America's ideology of democracy caused the Cold War. The United States too made ideas the centerpiece of this struggle. Announcing the eponymous Truman Doctrine on March 12, 1947, the president had this to say:

> At the present moment in world history nearly every nation must choose between alternative ways of life. . . .

Table 5-3

The Causes of the Origins of the Cold War: The Critical Theory Perspective and Levels of Analysis		
Level of analysis		**Critical theory perspective**
Systemic	*Structure*	• Historical dialectic of social change driving a class struggle between capitalist and communist societies leading to a workers state free of oppression and inequality
	Process	—
Foreign policy		—
Domestic		—
Individual		—

Table 5-4

The Causes of the End of the Cold War: The Critical Theory Perspective and Levels of Analysis		
Level of analysis		**Critical theory perspective**
Systemic	*Structure*	• Dialectic process of class struggle that continues even after demise of communism
	Process	—
Foreign policy		—
Domestic		—
Individual		—

One way of life is based upon the will of the majority, and is distinguished by free institutions, representative government, free elections, guarantees of individual liberty, freedom of speech and religion, and freedom from political oppression.

The second way of life is based upon the will of a minority forcibly imposed upon the majority. It relies upon terror and oppression, a controlled press and radio, fixed elections, and the suppression of human freedoms.[35]

NSC-68, the document in 1950 that called for a big boost in defense expenditures, also laid out the case for the spread of democracy. For realists like Henry Kissinger, it went too far. It abandoned a policy based on material interests and "opted for the alternative vision of America as a crusader."[36] In a speech in April 1950, Secretary of State Dean Acheson echoed the Truman Doctrine: "We are the children of freedom. We cannot be safe except in an environment of freedom. . . . We believe that all people in the world are entitled to as much freedom, to develop in their own way, as we want ourselves."[37]

John Foster Dulles, secretary of state under President Eisenhower, was perhaps the most ardent advocate of spreading American freedom. He labeled the eastern European countries "captive nations" and called on the United States to go beyond the defensive policy of containment and make "it publicly known that [the United States] wants and expects liberation to occur."[38] Dulles favored a policy of **rollback,** or recovering the eastern European countries from Moscow's control.

rollback
John Foster Dulles's policy in the 1950s of liberating the eastern European countries from Moscow's control.

Were Truman, Acheson, Dulles, and others just trying to scare the American public into supporting a balance-of-power policy? Was Stalin also manipulating Soviet public opinion for realist ends? Or were public opinion and ideology on both sides driving the Cold War?

Here is where judgment comes in. Take Kennan, for example. On the one hand, he says the contest is an international struggle for power and discounts Soviet ideology; yet, on the other, he expects the contest to be determined mostly by a political struggle of ideas at the domestic level. Kennan is a classical realist. He, like Hans Morgenthau, judges that values matter more at the domestic level while power matters more at the international level. Every country has values, but all countries need power to protect their values. He warned his superiors in Washington, D.C., that other countries worry less about abstract freedom, at least as Americans understand it, than security. Thus, even if Soviet domestic politics mellowed, as he projected, the United States and the Soviet Union would continue to compete for power (a security concern). But, if their values conflicted less sharply, they would compete less intensively as nationalist rivals not ideological enemies. Classical realists move a bit on to the turf of identity perspectives and acknowledge that some balances of power are not as dangerous as others, depending on the degree of conflict among underlying identities.

Spotlight on classical realism

Constructing the Cold War

The third identity explanation of the origins of the Cold War comes from the systemic level and explains why, from a social constructivist perspective, the Cold War superpowers saw one another as deadly enemies rather than less dangerous rivals.

As we have noted, realism expected the great powers to compete across a political vacuum but ultimately to be able to manage their competition through a spheres of influence policy. They would become rivals but not all-out enemies. Unlike enemies, rivals generally exist in comfortable competition with one another, like two football teams playing on a Saturday afternoon. In a rival relationship, neither side interferes in the domestic politics of the other side or tries to change the regime by sabotage or outright elimination. The two sides compete through an external contest without fear that they threaten one another's existence. They also cooperate. As Walter Lippmann, a famous realist author and commentator of the period said, "for a diplomat to think that rival and unfriendly powers cannot be brought to a settlement is to forget what diplomacy is all about."[39]

Enemies, on the other hand, threaten one another because of who they are, not just because they compete or cooperate in some external environment. As identity perspectives see it, opposing ideologies made the United States and Soviet Union enemies and account for the alignments after World War II better than relative power factors. For example, according to realist logic, Europe should have aligned with the Soviet Union against the United States since the United States was supremely dominant after the war over both Europe and the Soviet Union. Why did western Europe fear Russian armies more than American ones? The answer, identity perspectives say, has to do with *whose* the armies were, not how *big* they were. The ideology of the Russian armies led them to impose their will by force. The ideology of American armies called for free elections. Both armies wanted to expand their ideologies, but for western Europeans the content of one ideology based on consent was less frightening than that of the other based on coercion.

How domestic identities related to one another was key. As Professor Thomas Risse argues, "had Stalin 'Finlandized' rather than 'Sovietized' Eastern Europe, the Cold War could have been avoided."[40] Stalin let Finland keep its own domestic system as long as it cooperated with Moscow on foreign policy. In eastern Europe, however, Stalin imposed Moscow's domestic system. And in western Europe, communist parties exploited economic disorder to try to gain power and impose a communist system. Thus, "Soviet power became threatening as a tool to expand the Soviet domestic order."[41]

Realists say Stalin behaved with restraint in eastern Europe. He did not immediately impose communist governments, and he restrained communist parties in western Europe.[42] If the United States had been less ideological, a spheres of influence or **Finlandization** solution may have been possible. Each side would have tolerated the different domestic systems and cooperated on foreign policy. But that's the point, identity perspectives argue. You can't separate domestic and foreign policy that neatly. Stalin could not tolerate noncommunist governments in the heart of eastern Europe without them threatening the communist order back in the Soviet Union. Finland was an exception because it was on the periphery of central Europe. But Poland and Czechoslovakia were a different story; the Soviet Union could not be indifferent about whether democracy or communism prevailed in those countries because they were located in the heart of the continent.

Nor could the United States accept Finlandization in eastern Europe. Political scientist Colin Dueck tells us why. The liberal democratic culture in the United States, he argues, was so strong that practically all American policymakers rejected a spheres of influence policy that involved closed, authoritarian domestic systems in eastern Europe.[43] It was not because the United States insisted that every country be democratic; it was because the United States could not be comfortable in an international system that sanctioned strict controls and barriers between countries. The international system had to be open, at least for trade and travel; otherwise, understanding and diplomacy would not be possible. The United States feared secrecy and authoritarian power in eastern Europe because this type of system might weaken commitments to freedom and markets in western Europe or even weaken democracy back in the United States.

causal arrow

Spotlight on
internal identities

Finlandization

a solution to conflict whereby the Soviet Union agrees to tolerate different domestic systems within its alliance as long as its allies cooperate on foreign policy; contrasts with Stalinization in which the Soviet Union imposes its domestic system on its allies.

Because of who they were, the United States and the Soviet Union pursued conflicting zero-sum goals in the international system. As U.S. Secretary of State James F. Byrnes said in 1945, "There is too much difference in the ideologies of the U.S. and Russia to work out a long term program of cooperation."[44] (See Table 5-5 for a summary of identity explanations for the origins of the Cold War.)

Deconstructing the Cold War

How can a cold war between enemies end peacefully? If ideas can "construct"—cause or constitute—events, they can also "deconstruct" them. From the identity perspective, there are four possibilities.

First, when one side changes its ideas at the domestic level, enemies can become rivals again. That's what Kennan expected when he suggested containing the Soviet Union until it mellowed.

The second possibility is that both systems change and eventually converge at the systemic process level of analysis. The United States becomes more postmodern (community oriented), while the Soviet Union becomes more modern (individually oriented). Writing in the late 1960s, Zbigniew Brzezinski, later President Carter's national security adviser, anticipated such a convergence:

> The 1950s were the era of certainty. The two sides—Communist and Western—faced each other in a setting that pitted conviction against conviction. Stalinist Manicheans [who see the world in terms of good and evil] confronted Dulles's missionaries. That mood quickly gave way to another, with Khrushchev and Kennedy serving as transitions to an era of confusion. Dissension in the communist world prompted an ideological crisis, while the West increasingly began to question its own values and righteousness. Communist cynics confronted liberal skeptics.
>
> There are indications that the 1970s will be dominated by growing awareness that the time has come for a common effort to shape a new framework for international politics . . . an emerging global consciousness is forcing the abandonment of preoccupations with national supremacy and accentuating global interdependence.[45]

Notice that in Brzezinski's prediction ideas ("an emerging global consciousness") are driving out realist factors ("abandonment of preoccupations with national supremacy") and emphasizing liberal ones ("accentuating global interdependence"). Brzezinski does not fail to take realist and liberal factors into account; he simply sees

Spotlight on
relative identities

←—— causal
arrow

Table 5-5

The Causes of the Origins of the Cold War: The Identity Perspective and Levels of Analysis		
Level of analysis		**Identity perspective**
Systemic	*Structure*	• Divergent ideologies: No spheres of influence possible because identities of United States and Soviet Union create relationship of enemy rather than rival
	Process	—
Foreign policy		—
Domestic		• U.S. anti-communism and moralism
		• Soviet Union expansionist ideologically as belief system not as embedded historical dialectic (which is a critical theory perspective)
Individual		—

identity factors as driving or dominating them. The causal arrows run from ideas to power to institutions.

Brzezinski's prediction rested on the expectation that ideas in East and West would converge. He expected them to converge equally toward the center. But the two main identity explanations of the end of the Cold War suggest that Soviet ideas moved more toward the West than vice versa.

GORBACHEV'S NEW THINKING. The third, related, possibility is that old ideas simply fade away and new thinking takes over. In many constructivist accounts, such new thinking, especially in the Soviet Union, gets primary credit for ending the Cold War. Influencing outcomes from an individual level of analysis, Gorbachev and his advisers introduced domestic reforms: *glasnost* to open up political debate and *perestroika* to modernize the Soviet bureaucracy and economy. But, equally important, they also formulated new ideas in foreign policy. Based on **peace research studies** and other contacts initiated with the West at Helsinki in 1975 (a secondary emphasis on the systemic process level of analysis, or on the structural level if you emphasize constitutive reasoning), Soviet officials began to entertain new ideas about security structures in Europe. Gorbachev talked about "a common European home" involving shared identities and less threat or confrontation. He loosened Soviet controls in eastern Europe, and refugees flooded across the iron curtain. The Berlin Wall was breached on November 11, 1989 (which became known as 11/9, to contrast with 9/11, the date of the terrorist attacks on the United States in 2001).

Now the question became, again, what to do about Germany. Not only the Soviet Union but France and Britain harbored doubts about reunification. West Germany, however, under Chancellor Helmut Kohl, acted swiftly to present a plan for reunification. To keep events from spinning out of control, the allies set up the "two plus four" talks, the four World War II allies (United States, Soviet Union, Britain, and France) plus the two German governments. In these talks, according to more agency-oriented constructivist perspectives, the end of the Cold War was decided more by argumentation than by power (as the realist perspectives stress) or bargaining (as the liberal perspectives stress).[46] Through an authentic and serious conversation, the U.S. officials persuaded the Soviet Union to accept a reunited Germany and permit it to join NATO. The key arguments were that Moscow was better off with a reunited Germany inside NATO than an independent one outside NATO and that Germany, once united, should have the right of self-determination to decide whether it wanted to join NATO or not. According to one account, Gorbachev accepted the last of these arguments on the spot, stunning members of his own delegation.[47] As identity perspectives see it, "this incident probably constituted one of the most extraordinary cases of arguing in international affairs" and, as social constructivist perspectives see it, vindicated the focus on discourse and dialogue as the most important influences on state behavior.[48]

REAGAN'S IDEOLOGICAL OFFENSIVE. The fourth explanation from an identity perspective is that the United States and its western allies won the Cold War through a systemic structural competition of ideas. The Soviet Union changed, to be sure, but it changed more radically than realist or convergence explanations expected. It ceased to exist altogether and disbanded in December 1991 into fifteen separate republics. Moreover, Gorbachev's new thinking was not really new but rather a face-saving rationalization to accept western ideas of freedom and self-determination. Instead of the new European home under the Organization for Security and Cooperation in Europe

peace research studies
scholarly inquiry dedicated to the study of the potential for international peace, emphasizing collective and common humanity approaches rather than balance of power.

Spotlight on
communicative discourse

(OSCE) that the Soviet Union had envisioned, NATO went on to expand and include all of eastern Europe. In 2004, it admitted the Baltic states, three of the former republics of the Soviet Union, even though some western officials had promised in the negotiations not to extend NATO jurisdiction to the east.[49] Something more powerful was pushing events than immediate arguments or promises made in negotiations over German reunification.

And that something, according to this identity account of the end of the Cold War, was the power of new ideas—or new thinking—coming from Washington, not from Moscow. When Ronald Reagan took office in January 1981, he rejected containment, which had dominated U.S. thinking since Truman, and called instead for "a crusade for freedom that will engage the faith and fortitude of the next generation." He harked back to the more aggressive American ideology at the beginning of the Cold War and predicted prophetically in 1982 that "the march of freedom and democracy . . . will leave Marxism-Leninism on the ash-heap of history as it has left other tyrannies which stifle the freedom and muzzle the self-expression of the people." [50] His first comprehensive statement on U.S. policy toward the Soviet Union, NSDD-75, issued on January 17, 1983, "went beyond what any previous administration had established as the aims of its Cold War approach" and stated explicitly that U.S. policies toward the USSR are "to contain and over time reverse Soviet expansionism . . . [and] to promote, within the narrow limits available to us, the process of change in the Soviet Union toward a more pluralistic political and economic system. . . ." [51] On the fortieth anniversary of Yalta in 1985, Reagan made it clear that the objective was not containment but rollback: "there is one boundary that can never be made legitimate, and that is the dividing line between freedom and repression. I do not hesitate to say we wish to undo this boundary. . . . Our forty-year pledge is to the goal of a restored community of free European nations." [52]

Reagan's vision included deterrence by mutual assured defense rather than mutual assured destruction, support for freedom fighters in Central America and elsewhere, the eventual elimination of nuclear weapons, and the rending of the iron curtain. In a now-famous speech in Berlin in summer 1987, Reagan stood before the Berlin Wall at the Brandenburg Gate and said:

> There is one sign the Soviets can make that would be unmistakable, that would advance dramatically the cause of freedom and peace.
>
> General Secretary Gorbachev, if you seek peace, if you seek prosperity for the Soviet Union and Eastern Europe, if you seek liberalization: Come here to this gate! Mr. Gorbachev, open this gate! Mr. Gorbachev, tear down this wall.[53]

If ideas have power, Reagan's ideas in hindsight proved to be very powerful indeed. The challenge of freedom was too much, and the military division symbolized by the Berlin Wall as

Spotlight on ideological competition

Speaking to an audience in front of the Brandenburg Gate in West Berlin on June 12, 1987, with the Berlin Wall visible in the background, President Reagan contrasts freedom and communism and calls on Gorbachev to "tear down this wall."

causal →
    arrow

well as the institutions of the Soviet Union bowed to the march of freedom. When the world was finally able to look behind the iron curtain in 1991, it saw the devastation caused by the defeated set of ideas. No one could question any more that ideas shaped institutions and power. Or so it is argued from this particular identity perspective. (See Table 5-6 for a summary of identity explanations for the end of the Cold War.)

Liberal Explanations for the Origins and End of the Cold War

Liberal interpretations of the Cold War emphasize the role of institutions, interdependence, and diplomatic negotiations. From the systemic level of analysis, the United Nations constituted a second attempt—after the League of Nations—to establish collective security institutions. When the United Nations failed, regional NATO and European institutions cultivated security and economic interdependence and, in the case of European integration, transformed political interests and identities. The information revolution further deepened economic ties. Finally, from the systemic process level of analysis, détente and the Helsinki Accords between the superpowers and their respective allies created an alternative mechanism to that of deterrence and crisis escalation. As liberal perspectives see it, the superpowers addressed disputes by communicating and learning from one another rather than by threatening with and manipulating nuclear weapons.

United Nations

The United Nations was established in April 1945 even before the official end of World War II. President Roosevelt was determined to avoid a repeat of the failure of the United States to join the League of Nations. He sought, from a foreign policy level of analysis, to balance the external requirements for collective security with the internal requirements of American constitutionalism. He was determined to succeed where Wilson had failed. He already had sketched out in spring 1942 his idea of the "four policemen," the three main wartime allies—Britain, the United States, and the Soviet Union—plus China, playing a special role to monitor and enforce the postwar peace.

The four policemen, plus France, eventually became the permanent members of the UN Security Council. To ensure their participation and avoid the League experience,

Table 5-6

The Causes of the End of the Cold War: The Identity Perspective and Levels of Analysis		
Level of analysis		**Identity perspective**
Systemic	*Structure*	• U.S. democratic ideas proved superior to Soviet Marxist-Leninist ideas
		• U.S. and Soviet Union constructed new identity as rivals rather than enemies
	Process	• Soviet and U.S. ideologies converged toward the center
Foreign policy		• Gorbachev accepts idea of Germany in NATO to the surprise of his own advisers
Domestic		• Soviet ideology mellowed
Individual		• Gorbachev developed new thinking
		• Reagan revived America's liberal democratic ideas

the permanent members were given a veto (Article 27). The Security Council was also charged with "primary responsibility" (Article 24) for keeping the peace. The General Assembly, in which all members participated, could not consider an issue that was before the Security Council unless asked to do so by the Council (Article 12). In Chapter VI of the Charter (Articles 33–38), the Council had at its disposal all the peaceful means of settling disputes that the League had. But now, in addition and most important, the Council had the military means to back them up. Chapter VII (Articles 39–51) called on all members to "make available to the Security Council . . . armed forces, assistance, and facilities, including rights of passage, necessary for the purpose of maintaining international peace and security" (Article 43) and to "take such action by air, sea, or land forces as may be necessary to maintain or restore international peace and security" (Article 42). A Military Staff Committee made up of the chiefs of staff of the veto powers would command the UN military forces.

At last, here was a collective security institution worth its salt. It combined liberal and realist features for managing world affairs. The great powers had special privileges, a realist feature. But they had to work together through international institutions to accomplish their tasks, a liberal feature. If the veto powers disagreed, members retained "the inherent right of individual or collective self-defense" (Article 51). This provision proved to be a big loophole. But if the great powers were not on board, the institution would not be effective anyway. That was certainly one lesson drawn from the League's experience.

Spotlight on
global collective security among great powers

The whole scheme depended on great power cooperation. Clearly Roosevelt counted on continuing the wartime cooperation with the Soviet Union. "The essential thing," he believed, "was to build a relationship of trust with Stalin." [54] He decided that Russia was neither innately aggressive, as some realists believed, nor ideologically driven, as some identity perspectives suggested. In allied discussions at the Teheran Conference in Iran in late November 1943, Roosevelt called Stalin "Uncle Joe" and commented, "from that time on our relations were personal. . . . The ice was broken and we talked like men and brothers." [55] Later, he told the American people "I believe we are going to get along very well with [Stalin] and the Russian people—very well indeed." [56] Roosevelt's design for the United Nations depended very much on the relationships and interactions within institutions that would breed trust and cooperation. Compared to containment (a realist approach) and anti-communism (an identity approach), this approach was classically liberal.

Truman's Blundering Diplomacy

What went wrong? One liberal explanation is that Roosevelt died and was replaced by Harry Truman. Truman was a much less self-confident and skilled negotiator than Roosevelt. At his very first meeting with Soviet officials in April 1945, Truman berated Foreign Minister V. M. Molotov over the Soviet failure to hold elections in Poland as promised at Yalta. When Molotov left, he said to Truman, "I have never been talked to like that in my life." Truman replied, "Carry out your agreements and you won't get talked to like that." [57]

Hardly a good start, right? Subsequently, at Potsdam in July 1945, Truman used clumsy tactics to impress Stalin with American nuclear weapons. As Churchill noticed, Truman, who was brand new at his job, seemed more self-confident and assertive in his discussions with Stalin once he had received word that Little Boy had been successfully tested in New Mexico. [58] For one week, Truman said nothing to Stalin about the bomb but held intensive discussions with his generals and Churchill to decide whether to use the bomb against Japan. After that decision was made, he "casually mentioned to Stalin that we had a weapon of unusual destructive force."[59] Stalin, well informed by his spy Fuchs, responded offhandedly that he was glad to hear it and hoped the allies would make good use of it against the Japanese.

Whether Truman sought to intimidate Stalin is disputed. But Truman's silence and then assertive diplomacy at Potsdam might have easily seemed to Stalin like American bluster and aggression. And even though the United States subsequently proposed the **Baruch Plan** to establish an international agency under the United Nations to manage nuclear weapons cooperatively, the Soviet Union had every reason to wonder how fair this arrangement would be since America remained the only country outside the agency with the know-how to develop atomic weapons should it choose to do so.

At the UN Foreign Minister conferences held in the fall and winter of 1945, the United States and Soviet Union could not agree on the postwar handling of Germany. The misunderstandings continued over Soviet troops in Iran, reconstruction of Germany, access to Berlin, Soviet policy in Poland, and other issues. Eventually, contacts ended. In 1947, the superpowers discontinued foreign minister meetings, and negotiations went into a deep freeze for the next eight years.

Notice that in this case the causes of the Cold War come mostly from the individual or small group, bureaucratic level of analysis and involve problems of relationships and interactions. The Cold War was not preordained by international circumstances (a realist argument) or domestic ideology (an identity argument). It resulted from a breakdown in negotiations. Opportunities to resolve the Berlin and German problems were lost. Stalin proposed German unity and neutralization in 1952, but the West ignored his proposal. By this time, the western countries had other priorities: supporting the new West German government and building up NATO military forces. President Dwight Eisenhower and Soviet Premier Nikita Khrushchev met at the Geneva Summit in July 1955, but the "spirit of Geneva" did not last very long. Communications deteriorated once again, and the Hungarian, Berlin, and Cuban crises followed.

NATO and the European Community

As an alternative to the United Nations, some liberal accounts look to western institutions as the causal source of international order after World War II.[60] These institutions had their origins before the war in the principles of the Atlantic Charter signed in August 1941 on a ship in the middle of the Atlantic Ocean by Britain and the United States. These principles combined liberal and identity factors. Members would participate equally in Atlantic institutions without veto powers (liberal factor), but they would share closer ideological ties than realist versions assumed (identity factor). The common principles acknowledged, for example, pluralist constitutional procedures based on majority rule and protection of minorities and called for an open international political and economic system. After the war, NATO and the institutions of the European Community embodied these principles.

Liberal accounts of the Cold War emphasize that NATO was proposed initially as a political association, not a military alliance, and that America was drawn into a military alliance only very reluctantly after the Korean War broke out.[61] NATO was not a global institution nor was it an alliance. Rather, it was thought to be a collective secu-

Baruch Plan
a proposal made by the United States in 1946 to create an international agency under the United Nations to control and manage nuclear weapons cooperatively.

causal arrow

Spotlight on
regional collective security

rity arrangement because it was directed against threats in general, not against specific threats from the Soviet Union as in the case of an alliance. In his testimony to Congress, Secretary of State Dean Acheson, a realist who may have been simply acknowledging strong liberal sentiments in Congress, said in reference to the NATO treaty, "It is not aimed at any country; it is aimed solely at armed aggression." [62] NATO's purpose was to strengthen political commitments to open governments and free markets in western Europe, not to arm the West against Soviet military aggression from eastern Europe.

From the liberal perspective, a primary purpose of NATO, therefore, was to back up political and economic integration in western Europe. After a century of war, France and Germany still distrusted one another. Realists had tried various alliance solutions. Now technocrats charged with modernizing the French economy came up with a liberal solution. Jean Monnet, head of the French planning ministry, convinced French Foreign Minister Robert Schuman to create a European Coal and Steel Community (ECSC). This novel economic institution integrated the coal and steel industries of France and Germany, the two industrial sectors most important for war-making, and gradually reoriented these sectors and the two countries toward common non-zero-sum goals of economic growth rather than zero-sum goals of national security. European economic integration was born and became one of the most powerful institutional movements in history.

Integration subsequently transformed the European state system and ended, for all practical purposes, centuries of brutal warfare in Europe. Keep that in mind if you doubt that the liberal perspective has much to offer to the understanding of international affairs. Of course, realists will point out that European unification happened only because after the Korean War NATO became a conventional military alliance and protected Europe from the scourge of Soviet power that ravaged eastern Europe after World War II. Even if NATO were the catalyst, however, integration still happened and realists have no explanation for why it happened, especially when these institutions survive and flourish today even after the Soviet Union has long since disappeared as a galvanizing threat.

The ECSC was established in 1951 among France, Germany, Italy, Belgium, the Netherlands, and Luxembourg. It was followed by a failed and patently premature

Spotlight on interdependence

Foreign ministers of six European nations sign the treaty for a European Coal and Steel Community in Paris, France, on April 18, 1951, and set out on the historic path leading to today's European Union.

attempt to integrate the full defense sectors of France and Germany. The European Defense Community (EDC) was supposed to accommodate German rearmament, all under the protective wing of NATO. But France was not ready to rearm its traditional enemy, and the National Assembly killed the idea in 1954. Germany was rearmed within NATO.

Spotlight on path dependence

In 1968, however, the European states took another big step toward economic integration. The same six ECSC countries created the European Economic Community (EEC) and the European Atomic Energy Community (Euratom). The EEC established a common market in industry—no internal tariffs and common external tariffs—and common policy in agriculture, which managed prices above market levels. Euratom pooled research and development activities to exploit peaceful uses of nuclear power.[63] The Commission of the EEC was a supranational body that had sole authority to initiate legislation. It became the driving force behind European integration, and in 1968 the EEC incorporated the ECSC and Euratom to become the European Communities (EC). Great Britain, Denmark, and Ireland joined the EC in 1973, Greece in 1981, and Austria, Finland, and Sweden in 1986. The European Communities became the European Union in 1993 and extended its activities beyond creating a common market to include monetary and economic union; a common foreign and security policy; and internal police, judicial, and immigration affairs.

The United States encouraged and supported European integration. The Marshall Plan required European countries to cooperate to receive U.S. aid and led to the creation of the Organization for European Economic Cooperation (OEEC). The United States and Canada joined the OEEC in 1961, when it became the Organization for Economic Co-operation and Development (OECD). Although American leaders were always ambivalent about Europe becoming another major power, President Eisenhower actually hoped to make Europe into a "third force" that would relieve the United States of some of the economic and military burdens of protecting Europe.[64] He sought ways to transfer control of nuclear weapons to a European defense force, but these efforts failed and became moribund when France withdrew from NATO's military command structure in 1968.

causal arrow

Despite many crises, NATO and the EC flourished. They enlarged and more members became democratic. From the liberal perspective, these institutions illustrate vividly how regularized patterns of interaction can discipline power (for example, make U.S. power, which was dominant after the war, less threatening to the allies), focus countries on non-zero-sum goals of free trade and currency union (create the unprecedented prosperity of postwar Europe), and narrow different conceptions of national interests such that political union eventually becomes a possibility (the miracle of the EU).

Western institutions alone cannot account for the outcome of the Cold War because they dealt only with western countries. But when the Cold War ended, western institutions were ready to assume larger responsibilities. They were strong and had become more than alliances. They existed as the foundations of a global collective security community that the United Nations, and before it the League of Nations, had never been able to provide.

Cuban Missile Crisis from a Liberal Perspective

The breakdown of U.S.-Soviet negotiations after 1945 was the great failing of western diplomacy, as liberal perspectives see it. It took twenty years to revive that diplomacy and another twenty years for the diplomacy to bear fruit. Until the Cuban Missile Crisis, there were almost no systematic discussions between the United States and the Soviet Union. After the Cuban crisis, President Kennedy remarked about the absence of a process of regular communications and subsequently installed a hot line in the White House to Moscow. In 1963, the United States and the Soviet Union concluded the first arms control agreement, the Test Ban Treaty, which limited the size of nuclear tests in the atmosphere.

Liberal perspectives see the causes and lessons of the Cuban Missile Crisis very differently from realist perspectives. They question whether the U.S. threat of escalation from quarantine to full-scale invasion caused the Soviet Union to back down. They argue that beneath the drama of threat and escalation Kennedy and Khrushchev, operating at the foreign policy level of analysis, actually cooperated to help circumvent domestic pressures from hard-liners. The two leaders engaged in an interdependent process of reassurance and mutual learning that ended in significant compromises on both sides. The United States agreed to remove the Jupiter missiles from Turkey that were creating realist pressures at the structural level of analysis and was ready to undertake a public initiative through the United Nations to exchange Jupiter for Cuban missiles if Moscow rejected the idea of a secret agreement, in effect exploiting a liberal means to resolve a realist confrontation.[65]

← **causal** *arrow*

On Saturday night before he knew that the Soviet Union would accept the secret arrangement the next day, Kennedy instructed his secretary of state, Dean Rusk, to contact a professor at Columbia University, Andrew Cordier, and have him ready to ask the UN Secretary-General, U Thant, to propose the Jupiter missile exchange publicly. While Kennedy could not accept such a demand directly from Khrushchev, he could accept it from the UN, even though it would still seriously damage U.S. credibility with its allies by making it look like the United States was abandoning Turkey's defense to save America's skin. Far from being ready to invade Cuba, according to this account, Kennedy was looking for every possible way to compromise, recognizing that he could not control the process of escalation as realists argued.

Whether Kennedy was more serious about this so-called Cordier initiative or about an invasion, which some advisers deny he ordered, we will thankfully never know.[66] The important point is that the liberal and realist perspectives look at the same facts and make different judgments. Realists emphasize the threat of invasion; liberals emphasize the mutual efforts of leaders to negotiate a compromise. The liberal perspective does not deny the existence and impact of force and deterrence; it just judges that impact to be negative and unhelpful to crisis management. As Richard Lebow and Janice Stein argue, "deterrence can impede early warning, lead to exaggerated threat assessments, contribute to stress, increase the domestic and allied pressures on leaders to stand firm, and exacerbate the problem of loss of control."[67] By contrast, "crisis resolution is most effective when leaders 'learn' about others' interests as well as their own, when they reorder or modify their objectives in light of the risk of war, and then engage in fundamental trade-offs."[68] (See Table 5-7 for a summary of liberal explanations for the causes of the Cold War.)

← **causal** *arrow*

détente
a phase of the Cold War beginning in the 1960s when France and Germany initiated diplomatic overtures to Moscow and western countries subsequently concluded agreements with the Soviet Union.

Détente and Helsinki Accords

The liberal emphasis on diplomacy reached full flower during the **détente** phase of the Cold War. Détente emerged first in Europe in the 1960s. General Charles de Gaulle distanced France from NATO and began diplomatic overtures in Moscow to resolve the

Table 5-7

The Causes of the Origins of the Cold War: The Liberal Perspective and Levels of Analysis		
Level of analysis		**Liberal perspective**
Systemic	*Structure*	• United Nations and Baruch Plan to centralize control of nuclear weapons failed: —Flawed global institutions —Small collective security: Great power veto on Security Council ensured preponderance of power; but United States-Soviets clashed —Big collective security: Unanimity in General Assembly but Assembly was subordinate to Council, used only once in Korea because Soviets were absent in Security Council
		• NATO and EC develop collective security at regional level
	Process	• Soviet Union saw Marshall Plan as threat to communist regimes in eastern Europe
		• United States saw spread of Marxist-Leninism as threat to democratic regimes in western Europe
		• Diplomacy: Differences over Poland, Germany, Greece, etc. could have been negotiated
		• Lack of trade
Foreign policy		• Kennedy and Khrushchev cooperate to circumvent domestic hard-liners and settle the Cuban Missile Crisis
Domestic		—
Individual		• Truman threatened Stalin
		• Roosevelt misinterpreted Stalin

Spotlight on
negotiations

lingering postwar issues of Berlin and the territorial borders of central Europe. West Germany signed a much heralded reconciliation treaty with France in 1963 and also moved toward reconciliation with the East. The Christian Democrats, elected to power in 1948, had put West Germany's integration into NATO and the EEC ahead of negotiations with East Germany and Moscow. In 1966, however, the Social Democrats joined the government and in 1968 took power on their own. The Social Democrats had always favored negotiations with the Soviets. Had they been in power in 1952, they may well have accepted Stalin's offer to unify Germany as a neutral country. Under Foreign Minister and then Chancellor Willy Brandt, the Social Democrats now initiated a series of visits to reconcile Germany with its neighbors in the East and to recognize the East German government.

The United States, alienated from Europe by the Vietnam War, joined the rapprochement process late. President Nixon and his national security adviser Henry Kissinger concentrated on negotiating an end to the Vietnam War and opening up a new alliance with China. Under pressure from the European initiatives, however, the United States and its three wartime allies (Britain, France, and the Soviet Union) signed in 1971 the Berlin Accords, a set of agreements normalizing the situation in Berlin. Although the wall remained in place, East and West Germany recognized one another and Germany accepted the postwar borders in eastern Europe.

In 1972, the United States and the Soviet Union signed the first Strategic Arms Limitation Talks (SALT) agreement setting ceilings on strategic offensive missiles. They also signed the Anti-Ballistic Missile (ABM) agreement, effectively banning significant defensive systems against offensive missiles. The two agreements defined the deterrence strategy of MAD, as previously discussed.

Liberal perspectives advocated significant additional disarmament. They did not accept the realist version of escalation dominance, which required capabilities at all rungs of the ladder of escalation, including limited nuclear exchanges, to compel the adversary to back down in a crisis. They strongly supported the ABM treaty and advocated large further reductions of nuclear arms, including a comprehensive test ban treaty to stop further detonations of nuclear warheads above and below ground.

Détente peaked in 1975 with the **Helsinki Accords.** Thirty-five nations from East and West met in Helsinki, Finland, under the auspices of the UN Conference on Security and Cooperation in Europe (CSCE, a regional UN organization which in 1991 became the OSCE) and concluded three baskets of agreements to encourage diplomatic interactions and economic interdependence between the two blocs—arms control, trade, and human rights. SALT II agreements were signed in 1979, although they were never ratified by the United States. Trade restrictions were relaxed, although the Soviet Union never received most-favored-nation status (meaning entry to markets at the lowest tariff rates accorded to the most favored nation) because it continued to restrict the emigration of Jewish dissidents. And monitoring of human rights (an identity element), especially in eastern Europe, began to open up the closed communist systems, although the Soviet invasion of Afghanistan in 1979 generated new restrictions.

As liberal accounts believe, détente in the 1970s let the genie out of the bottle; and despite the resurgence of the Cold War in the late 1970s and early 1980s, the genie could not be put back in the bottle again. The Helsinki Accords proved especially valuable. Even in the midst of renewed Cold War tensions, conferences followed at Belgrade (1977–1978), Madrid (1980–1983), and Vienna (1986–1989). More important, nongovernmental groups established regularized contacts. Arms control groups in the United States (for example, the Union of Concerned Scientists), peace research institutes in western Europe (for example, the Stockholm International Peace Research Institute), social democratic and labor parties in Europe (for example, the Social Democratic Party in Germany), and policy institutes in the Soviet Union (for example, the Institute of the World Economy and International Relations) intensified contacts and developed concepts of common security, interdependence, and conventional arms reduction that reduced the fear of unilateral offensive operations. Some of these groups penetrated government circles, opening up domestic institutions and creating transnational coalitions. They affected in particular Gorbachev and other Soviet new thinkers. Notice how in the liberal perspective ideas follow from rather than cause institutional interdependence. Without regularized institutional processes at both the international and domestic levels, new thinking might not have emerged. In contrast to identity perspectives, liberal interpretations emphasize the regularity of contacts more than the substance. They emphasize that "ideas do not float freely." [69] They need institutional incubators to sprout and be nurtured.

Helsinki Accords
a series of agreements between East and West concerning arms control, trade, and human rights signed by thirty-five nations in 1975, which encouraged exchanges and interdependence.

← *causal arrow*

The Information Revolution and the End of the Cold War

From the liberal perspective, another factor came into the picture about the same time as détente and decisively contributed to the end of the Cold War. The information revolution ushered in a whole new age of technological innovation comparable to the industrial revolution. Information technologies tied the world together as never

Spotlight on
interactions

before. Computers created the new global highway of the Internet just as earlier steam engines opened up sea travel, electricity powered telegraph and telephone lines, and combustion engines produced the automobile. Countries that wanted to get on board had to participate in international trade. This positive economic incentive, more than any other, liberal accounts suggest, drove the Soviet Union to reconsider its economic and strategic policies. From a liberal perspective, the information revolution emphasized the pursuit of non-zero-sum economic goals more than the zero-sum military goals of SDI emphasized by realists and undermined the last resistance to ending the Cold War ideological division within Europe and throughout the world.

Gorbachev was the product of these new developments. He did not initiate them with new thinking, nor was he just reacting to military threats. He was looking for new opportunities for economic change and growth. Firms were beginning to operate all over the world, form numerous and intricate alliances for the development and production of information age products, and outsource more and more production to foreign shores. The most productive industries were global ones. No country could cut itself off from these developments and keep up with the rest of the world.

In February 1986, Gorbachev noted the importance of these developments. "By the early 1980s," he observed, "the transnational corporations accounted for more than one-third of industrial production, more than one-half of foreign trade, and nearly 80 percent of the patents for new machinery and technology in the capitalist world." [70] The Soviet Union had to become part of this new corporate world, and to do that Gorbachev had to reconsider his foreign policy and persuade western countries to remove Cold War containment restrictions on the exports of high-technology goods and information to the Soviet Union. Unlike China, which had no empire, the Soviet Union had to give up its empire first to gain access to global trade and investment markets.

As liberal accounts see it, Soviet military developments during the 1970s and 1980s were all ephemeral. So was the U.S. military buildup in response to Soviet challenges. Underneath all this misplaced military investment, contacts between East and West demonstrated to the Soviet Union that it was falling steadily behind and would have to make major internal reforms to become a part of the new world information economy. Ideology may have mattered in the sense that Gorbachev still hoped he could reform and save the communist system. But the driving forces for change were not new ideas but new technological forces propelling the world toward unforeseen levels of interconnectedness in the twenty-first century. (See Table 5-8 for a summary of liberal explanations for the end of the Cold War.)

Spotlight on
global NGOs

causal
arrow

Table 5-8

The Causes of the End of the Cold War: The Liberal Perspective and Levels of Analysis		
Level of analysis		**Liberal perspective**
Systemic	*Structure*	• Information revolution elevates non-zero-sum over zero-sum goals
	Process	• Détente and Helsinki deepens interdependence
Foreign policy		• Gorbachev outmaneuvers hardliners to initiate East-West rapprochement
Domestic		• Nongovernmental peace research groups emerge in European countries and Soviet Union
Individual		—

Summary

Realist perspectives emphasize power. At the systemic level, bipolarity and a power vacuum caused the Cold War, and U.S. power outcompeted Soviet power to end the Cold War. At the systemic process level, western alliances proved superior. At the domestic level of analysis, either the Soviet Union caused the Cold War because it was aggressive militarily or the United States did because it was aggressive economically. And the Cold War ended at the domestic level because the United States revived its military and economic power or because the Soviet economy collapsed.

Liberal perspectives emphasize institutions, diplomacy, and interdependence. At the systemic structural level of analysis, the Cold War started because the United Nations failed and collective security could be achieved only within the western region under NATO and the EU. At the systemic process level, it started because the Marshall Plan threatened the Soviet Union, while the spread of Marxist-Leninism in western Europe threatened the United States. And at the individual level, it started because Truman threatened Stalin and Roosevelt misinterpreted Stalin. The Cold War ended, at the systemic structural level, because the information revolution emphasized non-zero-sum goals; at the systemic process level, it ended because détente and Helsinki deepened East-West interdependence; at the foreign policy level, it ended because government bureaucrats formed transgovernmental coalitions; and at the domestic level, it ended because nongovernmental organizations emerged in European countries and the Soviet Union that opened up domestic institutions.

Finally, identity perspectives emphasize the configuration and construction of ideologies. At the systemic structural level, ideological divergence caused the Cold War. And at the domestic level, it was Soviet ideological zealotry or American anti-communism—take your pick—that caused the confrontation. The Cold War ended from this perspective at the systemic structural level because U.S. ideology proved superior, at the systemic process level because Soviet and U.S. ideologies converged, at the foreign policy level because Gorbachev was persuaded by western arguments despite the skepticism of his own advisers, from the domestic level because Soviet ideology mellowed, and at the individual level because Gorbachev developed new thinking or Reagan revived America's classical liberal democratic identity—again, take your pick.

Critical theory perspectives see both the origins and end of the Cold War as the unfolding of deeply embedded historical processes that, although they did not end in the triumph of communism, nevertheless continue to widen economic inequalities and injustices in the global system.

Key Concepts

Anti-Ballistic Missile (ABM)
   Treaty 177
arms race 171
balance of terror 175
Baruch Plan 196
Berlin Blockade 173
Cold War 169
containment 171
counterforce weapons 176
countervalue weapons 176
decolonization 181
détente 199
domino theory 181
escalation dominance 177
extended deterrence 177
Finlandization 190

first-strike capability 176
flexible response 177
Helsinki Accords 201
imperial overstretch 182
iron curtain 171
Korean War 175
long telegram 167
massive retaliation 177
minimum deterrence 177
Mutual Assured Defense 184
Mutual Assured Destruction
   (MAD) 177
national wars of liberation
   180
nonaligned movement 181
nuclear triad 177

peace research studies 192
perimeter deterrence 181
Potsdam Conference 172
proxy wars 175
puppet governments 175
revisionist interpretation
   173
rollback 189
second-strike capability 176
spheres of influence 174
Strategic Defense Initiative
   (SDI) 183
strongpoint deterrence 180
Yalta Conference 174

Study Questions

1. How would you line up the following causes of Soviet behavior in Kennan's analysis in the long telegram: security, ideology, and international institutions?

2. In what way do realist and liberal interpretations of deterrence differ, especially as they relate to the use of force and diplomacy?

3. What led to a resolution of the Cuban Missile Crisis as seen by liberal and realist perspectives?

4. What does "Finlandization" mean, and how did different perspectives interpret it?

5. Do the following arguments about the causes of the end of the Cold War differ in terms of perspectives or levels of analysis: information revolution, emergence and outreach of peace research and other nongovernmental groups in Germany and elsewhere, and détente?

6

From 11/9 to 9/11
The World of the 1990s

U.S. Marine amphibious tracked vehicles deploy in the Arabian desert in February 1991 under UN mandate as part of a massive force to drive Iraq out of Kuwait.

On November 9, 1989, the Berlin Wall came down, and the Cold War effectively ended. On September 11, 2001, the twin World Trade Center towers in New York City came down, and a new kind of global terrorist conflict started.

What happened in the twelve years between 11/9 and 9/11? Did the world blow another golden opportunity to achieve collective security? In 1991, the UN Security Council acted in a classic collective security operation to drive Iraq out of Kuwait. What happened after that? Did American unilateralism cause the disruption of global institutions? The liberal perspective might think so. Or did the world encounter for the first time a truly global hegemon? After the demise of the Soviet Union, the United States emerged as the only unipolar power in history whose power reached across the entire globe. Did the rest of the world inevitably counterbalance against the United States, producing yet another episode in history's cycles from empire to equilibrium? The realist perspective might think so. Or did the idea of democracy triumph and put an end to history, uniting the world around the cause of human rights and constitutional government? If so, why then did a new idea of fundamentalist Islam incubate in this period and begin to strike out against the ideas of western freedom and equality? Was a clash of civilizations emerging? Identity perspectives might have something to tell us.

From 11/9 to 9/11

On August 2, 1990, Iraq invaded Kuwait. In contrast to Japan's invasion of Manchuria in 1931 or Hitler's annexation of the Sudetenland in 1938, international organizations responded this time promptly and decisively—the way they were supposed to. The UN immediately condemned the attack, and the United States, supported by all the great powers, mobilized a UN-blessed military force to eject Iraq from Kuwait. As that unprecedented global action took place, President George H. W. Bush proclaimed to Congress a "new world order . . . in which the rule of law supplants the rule of the jungle" and expressed to the UN General Assembly what appeared to be the fulfillment of liberal hopes to replace the balance of power with collective security:

> This is a new and different world. Not since 1945 have we seen the real possibility of using the United Nations as it was designed: as a center for international collective security.
>
> The changes in the Soviet Union have been critical to the emergence of a stronger United Nations. . . .
>
> Two months ago, . . . once again the sound of distant thunder echoed across . . . the vast, still beauty of the peaceful Kuwaiti desert. . . .
>
> But this time, the world was ready. The United Nations Security Council's resolute response to Iraq's unprovoked aggression has been without precedent.[1]

Shortly after 11/9, the world seemed at last to have a global 911, a world police organization to call in the event of violence.

Almost at the moment Bush spoke of a new world order, however, an Egyptian *jihad*ist, El-Sayyid Nosair, gunned down a right-wing Jewish rabbi, Meir Kahane, in the Marriott East Side Hotel in New York. It was a relatively minor event, but Nosair wrote something in his notebook that portended events to come. **Jihad,** he explained, called for the

> breaking and destruction of the enemies of Allah. And this is by means of destroying, exploding, the structure of their civilized pillars such as the touristic infrastructure which they are proud of and their high world buildings which they are proud of and their statues which they endear and the buildings which gather their head[s], their leaders. . . .[2]

Here was a vision of 9/11 already at the time of 11/9. And Nosair was not acting in isolation. He maintained regular contact with Sheikh Omar Ahmad Abdel Rahman in Egypt. Known as the Blind Sheikh, Rahman had authorized the assassination of Anwar Sadat, Egypt's leader who made peace with Israel in 1979. With Nosair's help, Rahman settled in the United States and then planned the first assault on "their high world buildings"—the truck (actually, van) bombing of the World Trade Center towers in New York City on February 26, 1993.

Let's sort out the differing perspectives on these events. Map 6-1 highlights key features of the world of the 1990s as seen from each perspective. The bar graph on the lower left side of the map displays the realist world of unipolar distribution of military power, in which the United States and western civilization dominate the rest of the world. The starburst symbols show terrorist activity around the world, mostly within states in poor regions of the world, a view of terrorism that emphasizes economics and makes sense from the liberal perspective. Finally, the different shadings and hatch marks outline the nine civilizations that reflect changing identities in the world of the 1990s.

We'll start again, as we did in Chapter 4, with the liberal view of the world of the 1990s, primarily because this view offered so much hope at the beginning of the 1990s and still does today, as its adherents see it.

jihad
for Muslim fundamentalists, a "holy war" or the physical struggle against western civilization in the name of Islam.

Liberal Accounts of the World of the 1990s

Liberal accounts of the interval between the Cold War and the September 11, 2001, attacks focus at the systemic structural level of analysis on the integrating forces of international institutions and economic interdependence. They highlight the promise of a revived United Nations in the first Persian Gulf War and, when that promise dimmed, the enlargement of regional institutions such as NATO and the EU to include former communist countries and the expansion of the global trading system through the World Trade Organization (WTO) and the North American Free Trade Agreement (NAFTA) to include China, Mexico, and other developing countries. Negotiations to resolve the Arab-Israeli dispute flowered and then faltered over the course of the 1990s, as did diplomatic efforts to stanch the proliferation of nuclear, biological, and chemical WMDs. As liberal accounts see it, these failures of diplomacy at the systemic process level, especially in the Middle East, opened the floodgates for the tsunami of terrorism that culminated in violent transnational movements such as Al Qaeda, terrorist-sponsoring states such as the Taliban government in Afghanistan, and the attacks of 9/11.

The United States, after the failed UN intervention in Somalia, retreated from its responsibilities as the preponderant power in collective security institutions. It did nothing in 1994 when genocide occurred in Rwanda and initially let the European Union deal with ethnic conflicts in Croatia, Bosnia, and other former Yugoslavian republics. Eventually, the United States led NATO, not the UN, to deal with conflicts in Bosnia and Kosovo, but the United States failed to ratify significant international agreements, such as the Comprehensive Test Ban Treaty and the Kyoto Protocol, and it did little when Saddam Hussein kicked UN inspectors out of Iraq in 1998 and terrorist threats escalated. Once again, as liberal perspectives see it, collective security failed because of the reluctant participation of dominant powers.

> **Spotlight on**
> **international institutions and interdependence**

Success of Collective Security: The First Persian Gulf War

As President George H. W. Bush noted, the Persian Gulf War of 1990–1991 was a textbook case of collective security. According to liberal accounts, he and Bill Clinton understood the value of strong international institutions. Bush's secretary of state, James Baker, pursued a self-conscious strategy of institution-building. He insisted that Germany be reunified and remain a member of NATO, and he led the first Persian Gulf War effort through the UN. "Men like Truman and Acheson," Baker once said, "were above all, though sometimes we forget it, *institution builders*. . . . I believed we should take a leaf from their book."[3] Clinton's ambassador to the United Nations and later secretary of state, Madeleine Albright, endorsed what she called "assertive multilateralism" or "multilateral engagement and U.S. leadership within collective bodies."[4]

Iraq invaded Kuwait allegedly for many reasons: to control Kuwait's oil, to alter colonially imposed borders, to gain assets to pay off Iraq's huge debt from its eight years of war with Iran (1980–1988), and so on. But whatever the reasons, the entire world wasted no time in condemning Iraq as the aggressor and taking immediate actions to sanction it. One day after the attack, Iraq's fellow states in the Arab League (founded in 1945) denounced the aggression. On the same day, the UN Security Council passed unanimously Resolution 660 to demand Iraq's immediate and unconditional withdrawal from Kuwait. Over the next few months, the Security Council passed no fewer than ten additional resolutions that declared Iraq's annexation of

> **Spotlight on**
> **unanimity**

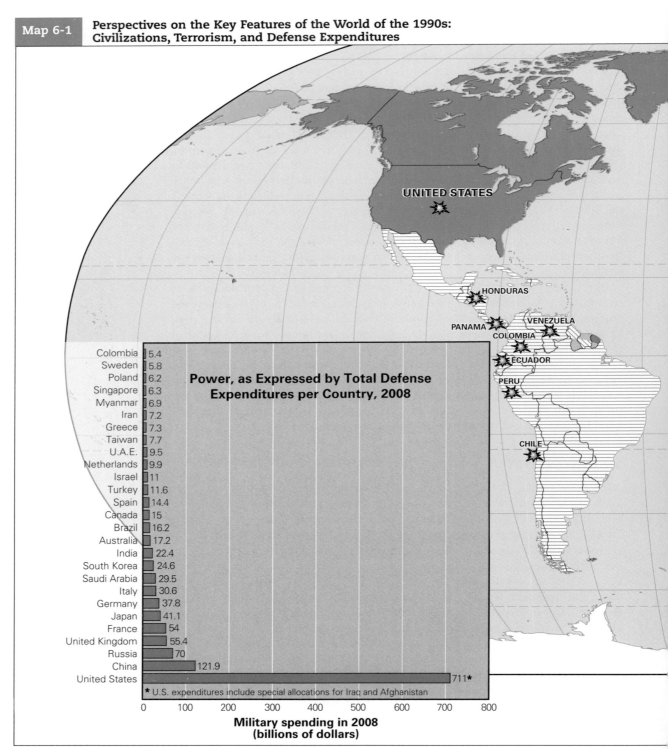

Map 6-1

Perspectives on the Key Features of the World of the 1990s: Civilizations, Terrorism, and Defense Expenditures

UNITED STATES

HONDURAS

PANAMA

VENEZUELA

COLOMBIA

ECUADOR

PERU

CHILE

Power, as Expressed by Total Defense Expenditures per Country, 2008

Country	Military spending in 2008 (billions of dollars)
Colombia	5.4
Sweden	5.8
Poland	6.2
Singapore	6.3
Myanmar	6.9
Iran	7.2
Greece	7.3
Taiwan	7.7
U.A.E.	9.5
Netherlands	9.9
Israel	11
Turkey	11.6
Spain	14.4
Canada	15
Brazil	16.2
Australia	17.2
India	22.4
South Korea	24.6
Saudi Arabia	29.5
Italy	30.6
Germany	37.8
Japan	41.1
France	54
United Kingdom	55.4
Russia	70
China	121.9
United States	711*

* U.S. expenditures include special allocations for Iraq and Afghanistan

Military spending in 2008 (billions of dollars)

Source: Samuel P. Huntington, *The Clash of Civilizations and the Remaking of World Order* (New York: Simon and Schuster, 1996), 26–27. Reproduced with permission. Terrorism data from the U.S. Department of State. Defense expenditures data from The Center for Arms Control and Non-Proliferation, April 2008. www.armscontrolcenter.org/policy/securityspending/articles/fy09_dod_request_global.

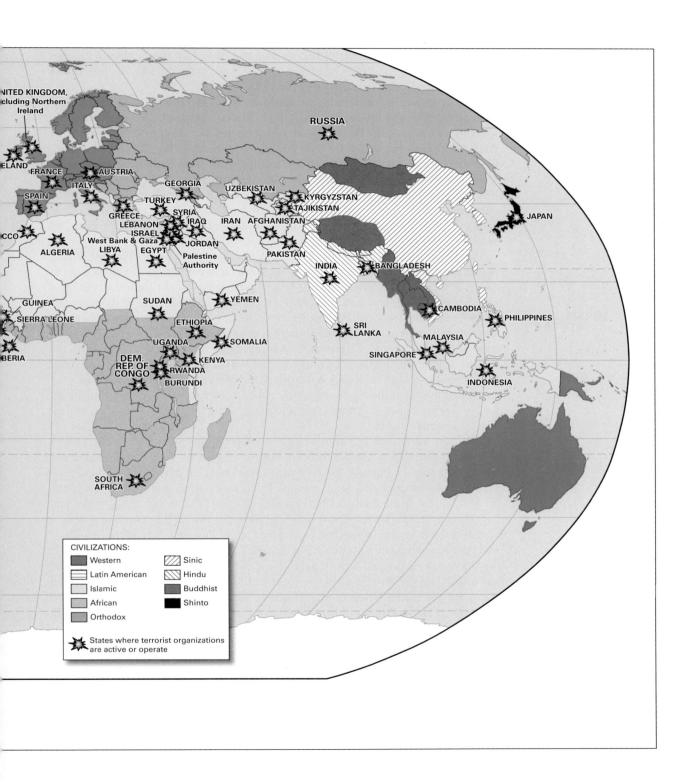

UNITED KINGDOM, including Northern Ireland

RUSSIA

FRANCE
AUSTRIA
ITALY
SPAIN
GEORGIA
UZBEKISTAN
KYRGYZSTAN
TAJIKISTAN
TURKEY
GREECE
SYRIA
LEBANON
IRAQ
IRAN
AFGHANISTAN
ISRAEL
West Bank & Gaza
JORDAN
ALGERIA
LIBYA
EGYPT
PAKISTAN
Palestine Authority
JAPAN

CCO

MOROCCO

GUINEA
SIERRA LEONE
LIBERIA

SUDAN
YEMEN
INDIA
BANGLADESH
CAMBODIA
PHILIPPINES
SRI LANKA
MALAYSIA
ETHIOPIA
UGANDA
SOMALIA
DEM. REP. OF CONGO
RWANDA
KENYA
SINGAPORE
BURUNDI
INDONESIA

SOUTH AFRICA

CIVILIZATIONS:

Western
Latin American
Islamic
African
Orthodox

Sinic
Hindu
Buddhist
Shinto

States where terrorist organizations are active or operate

Kuwait null and void, demanded release of foreign hostages taken by Iraq, held Iraq liable for war and economic damages, imposed trade and financial embargoes, cut off air cargo shipments, and established a naval blockade. Had the League of Nations acted this decisively in 1931 when Japan invaded Manchuria, who knows how differently things might have turned out in the 1930s?

Despite universal condemnation, however, Saddam Hussein, Iraq's tyrannical ruler since 1979, did not budge. The United States and other UN members began to build up forces in the Persian Gulf, initially to defend Saudi Arabia from further Iraqi assaults in what was called Operation Desert Shield. In late October, they doubled these forces and positioned them to expel Iraq from Kuwait by an invasion code-named Operation Desert Storm. On November 29, 1990, the UN Security Council pronounced the diplomatic words of war, authorizing members "to use all necessary means" if Iraq did not withdraw by January 15, 1991. The U.S. Congress debated the issue and, on January 12, also authorized the president to use "all means necessary."

Probably no war in history has been as legitimate as the first Persian Gulf War, if you measure legitimacy by the universal approval of all nations, including all democracies. What produced this consensus? Liberal perspectives might argue the coming of age of international law. Iraq violated the most cherished principle of the interstate system since the Treaty of Westphalia in 1648, namely the sovereignty of another country, and it did so in such a blatant way as to alienate all its supporters. Realist perspectives, of course, might stress oil, which practically all countries needed from the Persian Gulf, or the simple fact that the United States dominated the world and could lead a credible collective security operation, which the League of Nations, without the participation of dominant powers, never could. Identity perspectives might highlight the converging values of east and west and the growing international concern to protect basic human rights.

After last-minute initiatives to negotiate compromises by both the United States and the Soviet Union failed—the two former adversaries cooperating, albeit not always smoothly—Operation Desert Storm commenced on January 17. Massive aerial assaults hammered Iraq for a month. Then, an invasion force swept across the Kuwaiti border. Some 700,000 UN (including 550,000 U.S.) troops, 2,000 tanks, and 1,700 helicopters participated. It was the biggest battle ever in the deserts of Arabia.

By February 28, Iraqi forces had been driven out of Kuwait. UN resolutions authorized expelling Iraq from Kuwait but not changing the regime in Baghdad. Accordingly the U.S.-led army stopped at the Iraq border. It did not pursue Iraqi forces to Baghdad and unseat Hussein. From a liberal perspective, this was the right decision. The United States did not exceed UN authority. However, Saddam Hussein used the reprieve to smash local Shiite and Kurdish rebellions and reestablish his tyrannical control in Baghdad.

One unintended consequence of leaving Hussein in power was the permanent stationing of U.S. and western troops in Saudi Arabia to protect the oil fields. Here is a case, as liberal perspectives see it, of path dependence. The United States did not intend to provoke Islam but to protect an ally. Nevertheless, one step leads to another along a path of events, and the end result is something that no one really anticipated. Radical Islamic fundamentalists, such as Osama bin Laden, saw the presence of infidel troops in the land of the holy places of Mecca and Medina as a declaration of war against Islam.[5]

causal *arrow*

Spotlight on path dependence

Demise of Collective Security: Somalia

The United Nations rode a crest of acclaim after the first Persian Gulf War. Secretary-General Boutros Boutros-Ghali issued a report in 1992 called *An Agenda for Peace.* It set out a plan to use UN forces not only for **peacekeeping activities,** that is, monitoring cease-fires and separating combatants, which the UN had done during the Cold War, but also for **peace-enforcement activities,** compelling countries to follow the terms of UN resolutions as had just been done in the case of Iraq. For a time, both President George H. W. Bush and President Bill Clinton, who took office in January 1993, supported this plan and held talks with the Soviet Union to establish the military staff committee that was intended to assemble and direct UN forces under enforcement actions called for by Chapter VII of the UN Charter. UN responsibilities mounted. By January 1994, the UN was in charge of seventeen military missions around the world, deploying some 70,000 personnel at an annual cost of over $3 billion.

But then almost as quickly as it had risen, the UN fell. The turning point came in Somalia. In December 1992, the United States dispatched forces under UN auspices to provide humanitarian relief to citizens in that country, which was torn by civil war. As in the case of many UN missions, however, it was difficult to feed and clothe people without also protecting them. And protecting them meant inevitably becoming involved in the local conflicts. That happened in October 1993 in Mogadishu, the capital of Somalia. When one of the Somalian warlords, Aideed, attacked UN troops, the UN authorized U.S. forces to capture him. In the fighting that ensued, a U.S. Black Hawk helicopter was shot down (inspiring a subsequent Hollywood movie) and eighteen U.S. soldiers died. One dead American soldier was dragged through the streets of Mogadishu. With Congress in an uproar, President Clinton ordered American troops to pull out by the end of March 1994.

Notice that this explanation comes from the foreign policy level of analysis. Clinton made his decision trying to balance between domestic forces urging withdrawal and systemic process factors urging support for the UN. In this case, realist perspectives would argue, the systemic factors were weaker than domestic institutional divisions because the United States had no material interests in Somalia—no oil or strategic requirement for military bases—and moral or identity factors were not strong enough to sustain U.S. involvement without significant material interests. Once again, as in 1919, the open-ended burdens of collective security proved too much for the United States. The American people were not ready to sacrifice American lives in many places where the United States had no material interests.

While some commentators applauded U.S. intervention in Somalia as an example of a purely moral foreign policy—a universalist position motivated by principles independent of circumstances—others condemned it as immoral, meddling in other peoples' affairs without a sufficient material stake to stick it out when the going got tough—a pragmatist position that asks if the intervention helps more than it hurts. Was peace indivisible and hence a collective good available to all or to none, as liberal perspectives envision? Or was it separable, in the sense that no country, however dominant, could be expected practically or morally to intervene in conflicts where it had no significant private goods (national interests) at stake?

Weakened by Somalia, the United States and the United Nations swung to the other extreme in Rwanda in 1994 and did nothing when Hutus killed over half a million Tutsis in an acknowledged case of **genocide,** the willful and massive slaughtering of one group by another on purely ethnic or racial grounds. Expectations for the UN

peacekeeping activities
the UN monitoring of cease-fires and separating combatants.

peace-enforcement activities
UN actions compelling countries by force or threat of force to follow the terms of UN resolutions.

causal arrow

Spotlight on ethics and morality

genocide
the systematic persecution and extermination of a group of people on the basis of their national, ethnic, racial, or religious identity.

receded steadily after this point and ended up a decade later in the ugly debacle of UN division and corruption during and after the Iraq War of 2003.

Oslo Accords Fail in the Middle East

The first Persian Gulf War sparked the most serious round of Middle East peace negotiations since the creation of Israel. The cause, from the liberal perspective, was path dependence, or the momentum of post–Cold War cooperation between the United States and Russia that spilled over into the revival of UN diplomacy. Building on the UN success in the Gulf War, the United States convened a conference in Madrid, Spain, in October 1991. The conference brought together all the principal parties to the Arab-Israeli dispute, including Palestinian representatives not affiliated with the Palestine Liberation Organization (PLO). At the time, Israel did not recognize the PLO.

Although formal meetings after Madrid stalled, informal back-channel talks started between Israeli and PLO officials outside Oslo, Norway. Back-channel talks allowed the parties to explore options in secret without committing themselves to any option officially and to be able to deny that the talks were taking place, if necessary. The talks eventually led to public agreements, the Declaration of Principles signed at the White House in September 1993, and then a series of agreements known as the **Oslo Accords.** Israel withdrew troops from Gaza and areas of the West Bank and recognized the PLO as the legitimate representative of the Palestinian people. The PLO under Yasser Arafat returned to the West Bank from exile in Tunisia and progressively assumed police and other functions over a wider area of the West Bank and Gaza. Palestinians held their first national elections in 1996, and Arafat became president of a new Palestinian Authority (PA), which replaced the PLO. In October 1994, Jordan signed a peace treaty with Israel. For anyone familiar with the travails of the Arab-

Spotlight on
path dependence

Oslo Accords

a series of agreements reached in 1993 between the Palestine Liberation Organization and Israel calling for Israel to withdraw troops from Gaza and areas of the West Bank and for Israel and the PLO to recognize one another.

As president Bill Clinton looks on during a ceremony on the White House lawn in September 1993, Israel's Prime Minister Yitzhak Rabin (left) and PLO leader Yasser Arafat share a historic handshake on the peace plan known as the Oslo Accords.

Israeli dispute, these were monumental steps forward toward peace. Resolution of one of the most divisive disputes in the Middle East and third world seemed to be at hand.

But it was not to be. And from a liberal perspective, there are a variety of explanations for the failure to reach peace in the Middle East. Perhaps it was because of the diplomatic inflexibility of individuals such as Arafat—the individual level of analysis—who was unable to give up the mace of revolution for the mantle of peacemaker. Or perhaps it was because domestic coalitions—the domestic level of analysis—shifted in Israel, giving more power to parties that opposed negotiations, while the PLO pursued strategies that weakened moderates and empowered radicals among Palestinians. In Israel, orthodox extremists murdered Yitzhak Rabin in December 1995, the Israeli prime minister and Labor Party leader who had led the Oslo initiative. The Likud, Israel's more hard-line conservative party, took power under Benjamin Netanyahu. Smaller Orthodox parties, fueled by Zionist immigrants from Russia and eastern Europe, joined government coalitions and advocated the annexation of occupied territories. Israel stepped up construction of new settlements in the West Bank and Gaza. In the Palestinian Authority, Arafat failed to deliver on policing the West Bank, and extremist elements, such as Hamas and Islamic Jihad, seized control of parts of the Palestinian security forces. Through repetitive interactions and feedback, which liberal perspectives emphasize, extremism in Israel fed on extremism in Palestine, and vice versa. The Oslo process, caught in the middle, was the victim.

Or perhaps the Oslo peace process failed because the great powers had other diplomatic priorities—a systemic level explanation. As we discuss later, once the United States lost its enthusiasm for the UN, Washington's and Europe's attention shifted to NATO and to managing disputes in the Balkans and eastern Europe. The United States reacted slowly to the rise of extremism in both Israel and the PA.

Most important, little came out of Oslo to improve economic prospects in the Middle East. For millions of young people in the Middle East, zero-sum goals of territorial control and religious zealotry remained more important than non-zero-sum goals of professional education and employment. Egypt had been at peace with Israel since 1979. But there was nothing to show for it in terms of trade or higher standards of living benefiting both countries.

Negotiations continued, but the peace process was in deep trouble well before President Clinton made a final futile effort to bring the parties together at Camp David in 2000. That effort failed, and a new ***intifada,*** involving generalized violence and suicide bombings, broke out in the occupied territories in February 2001.

International Regimes: Arms Control, Courts, and Development

The preferred way to deal with global conflict from a liberal perspective is to strengthen international regimes and institutions, including treaties to ban the spread of WMDs, international courts to prosecute both state and nonstate actors that commit genocide or crimes against innocent civilians, and development programs to attack the roots of conflict that lie in poverty and economic despair.

An international regime to ban the spread of nuclear weapons had already been established in 1957. The International Atomic Energy Agency (IAEA), a UN agency in Geneva, was the more modest sequel to the failed Baruch Plan of 1946, which, as noted in Chapter 5, tried to consolidate all nuclear weapons under the authority of a single international institution. The IAEA accepted the possession of nuclear weapons by the great powers but sought to prevent their spread to other states by fostering peaceful

← **causal** *arrow*

Spotlight on
economic development and trade

intifada
Arabic term for uprising; often refers to Palestinian campaigns to end Israeli military occupation and oppose U.S. policies supporting Israel.

Treaty on the Non-Proliferation of Nuclear Weapons (NPT)
a 1968 treaty that seeks to prevent the spread of nuclear weapons and materials while fostering the civilian development of nuclear power.

Spotlight on rogue states

Chemical Weapons Convention
agreement made in 1993 to ban the production and use of chemical weapons.

Biological Weapons Convention (BWC)
agreement made in 1972 to ban the production and use of biological weapons.

Strategic Arms Reduction Talks (START)
meetings that produced agreements (including START I in 1991 and START II in 1993) that lowered by two-thirds the number of offensive ballistic missiles and warheads maintained by Russia and the United States.

development of nuclear power under international inspections and safeguards. Non-nuclear states could exploit peaceful nuclear power to generate electricity while IAEA inspection teams monitored the storage and use of civilian materials that could be diverted to weapons programs. In 1968, the **Treaty on the Non-Proliferation of Nuclear Weapons (NPT)** strengthened the IAEA system. The NPT was extended indefinitely in 1995, and review conferences are held every five years to address problems of implementation.

The NPT, supplemented by cooperation among the major nuclear suppliers, achieved some notable successes. Brazil, Argentina, South Africa, South Korea, and most recently Libya abandoned nuclear weapons programs. Ukraine, Belarus, and Kazakhstan also gave up Soviet nuclear weapons when they became independent. India and Pakistan, however, acquired nuclear weapons in the 1990s. And Pakistan, through an elaborate and illegal global nongovernmental network of individuals and corporations established by A. Q. Khan, a top Pakistani scientist, sold nuclear technology and equipment to other groups and states, including Libya, Iran, and North Korea.[6] Israel is believed to have nuclear weapons. And Israel bombed suspected nuclear weapons sites in Iraq in 1981 and in Syria in 2007. Many nuclear weapons sites in Russia remain inadequately protected. In 1997, Russia acknowledged that 84 of some 132 nuclear bombs of suitcase size had yet to be accounted for.[7]

Iraq, North Korea, and Iran became particularly troublesome cases. Iraq's capabilities, as we now know, were substantially gutted by IAEA inspection teams after the first Persian Gulf War. As liberal perspectives see it, UN arms control regimes functioned in this instance just the way they were designed. However, Iraq kicked the UN inspectors out in 1998, creating the impression that Iraq was proceeding full speed ahead with its nuclear weapons programs. North Korea threatened in 1993 to withdraw from the NPT, but then signed an agreement with the United States that placed its plutonium-producing reactor under IAEA surveillance. However, this agreement did not account for the spent fuel (which contains plutonium) previously extracted from this reactor and did not cover other nuclear programs based on enriched uranium, which later became an issue. Iran initiated a broad-based civilian nuclear program that it claimed was permitted under the NPT even though it did not allow IAEA inspectors to visit all its facilities, as called for by the NPT.

The **Chemical Weapons Convention** (1993) and **Biological Weapons Convention (BWC)** (1972) also exist to ban the production and use of chemical and biological weapons. These weapons are less difficult and expensive to develop than nuclear weapons and are, therefore, easier to hide. When the Cold War ended, it was learned that the former Soviet Union had pursued a vast clandestine biological weapons program in direct violation of the BWC. And Saddam Hussein used poison gas against his own people in the aftermath of the first Persian Gulf War. To be effective, inspection and compliance procedures need to be extremely stringent. But the United States fears that the procedures proposed thus far, including unannounced inspections, will fail to detect weapons violations but succeed in revealing defense secrets. It has refused to accept new inspection protocols. The use of chemical and possibly biological weapons generated widespread alarm when the Aum Shinrikyo group released sarin gas in the Tokyo subway system in 1995 and when still unknown individuals sent anthrax-filled letters to media figures and members of the U.S. Congress in October 2001.

The end of the Cold War offered an unprecedented opportunity to reduce the level of military arms. Besides pooling military power in collective security institutions, liberal perspectives emphasize reducing arms to the minimum level possible. The **Strategic Arms Reduction Talks (START)** produced agreements, including START I in 1991 and START II in 1993, that lowered by two-thirds the number of offensive ballistic missiles and warheads maintained by Russia and the United States. The ABM Treaty signed in 1992 (which we discuss in Chapter 5) banned anti-missile defense systems except at one or two locations. The **Treaty on Conventional Forces in Europe (CFE)** reduced and established a roughly equal balance of major conventional weapons systems (tanks, artillery, aircraft, and so on) and personnel strength among some thirty countries in Europe. The **Comprehensive Test Ban Treaty (CTBT)** concluded in 1996 eliminates all testing of nuclear weapons above and below the ground, and the Anti-Personnel Landmine Treaty, which became effective in 1999, outlaws the use of land mines. From a liberal perspective, the way to end violence is to ban or limit arms. If the instruments of violence are not available or are carefully monitored, the destructive consequences of conflicts in the international system can be sharply reduced. Then international trade and development programs can drain the swamp of poverty and ignorance that foster arms buildups and conflict.

And, indeed, from the liberal perspective, the world made giant gains in the 1990s toward promoting trade and economic development. The Uruguay Round of trade negotiations initiated in 1986 came to fruition in 1994. It not only expanded trade liberalization to agriculture, investment, and services, which had not been covered earlier under the General Agreement on Tariffs and Trade (GATT), but also established the more comprehensive WTO, which acquired limited powers to overrule national law and require offending countries to change their laws or pay penalties and compensate offended countries in other areas. The United States, Canada, and Mexico also signed NAFTA, taking a first step toward the regional integration of markets in North America. China and Mexico became members of the WTO, and the global community accelerated the provision of technical assistance, foreign aid, and investment capital to the developing world.

International courts also play an important role in liberal approaches. They address legal grievances that frustrate alienated groups. The Hague Conferences at the turn of the nineteenth century established the Permanent Court of Arbitration, a standing panel of jurists from which disputants could pick a panel to arbitrate their dispute. The League of Nations created a Permanent Court of International Justice, and the United Nations supplanted the Permanent Court of International Justice with the **International Court of Justice (ICJ).** The ICJ is made up of fifteen judges elected by a majority of the UN Security Council and General Assembly. Most recently, the **International Criminal Court (ICC)** made permanent the practice of trying individuals for wartime criminal acts started by the ad hoc tribunals for war crimes in World War II, Yugoslavia, and Rwanda. The ICC, like domestic courts, decides cases brought by civilians as well as governments, although, unlike domestic courts, it does not have independent police power to enforce its decisions.

The objective from a liberal approach to international affairs is ultimately to domesticate international disputes—to eliminate the role of violence in decision making and subject disputes to the same measures of economic redress and rule of law that apply to domestic disputes. **Constitutional orders** guaranteeing the rule of law replace balance-of-power politics based on violence.[8] Peaceful diplomacy and courts adjudicate where alliances once did. We discuss constitutional orders further in Chapter 15.

Spotlight on disarmament

Treaty on Conventional Forces in Europe (CFE) treaty reducing and establishing a roughly equal balance of major conventional weapons systems (tanks, artillery, aircraft, and so on) and personnel strength among some thirty countries in Europe.

Comprehensive Test Ban Treaty (CTBT) agreement in 1996 to stop the testing of nuclear weapons both above and below ground.

International Court of Justice (ICJ) the UN's main judicial institution, made up of fifteen judges elected by a majority of the UN Security Council and General Assembly and designed to arbitrate disputes among nations.

International Criminal Court (ICC) permanent tribunals started in 2002 to prosecute war crimes.

constitutional orders international orders based on constitutional rules and institutions such as those that exist in the case of constitutional domestic governments.

Spotlight on rule of law

Legitimacy and Intervention: Bosnia and Kosovo

International institutions were still weak, however. The UN was tested in interventions in Bosnia in the early 1990s and Kosovo in the late 1990s, and in both cases, it came up short. In lieu of weak international institutions, therefore, liberal perspectives turned to stronger regional institutions, such as NATO and the EU. These institutions, through spillover and other path-dependent mechanisms, had gathered momentum during the Cold War, and they now stepped into the breach as global institutions faltered in the mid-1990s.

Realist accounts predicted, wrongly thus far, that institutions such as NATO would dissolve once the Soviet threat disappeared.[9] For realists, such institutions were considered to be alliances against specific threats, not collective security arrangements against general threats. To distinguish the difference, realists referred to NATO as a collective *defense* arrangement, not a collective *security* arrangement. When the threats ended, the defense arrangements were expected to end. Liberal perspectives saw it differently. For them, these institutions were regional collective security arrangements that, although not universal, nevertheless consolidated power and authority on a collective rather than selective (alliance) basis. They invested the legitimacy, or authority to use military power, at a regional level higher than the nation-state. Whereas states decided individually when to form alliances and use force, NATO decided these issues collectively. When was it legitimate, however, to act at a regional or NATO level as opposed to a universal or UN level? From the liberal perspective, how broad did the international consensus have to be to act legitimately?

In spring 1991, civil war broke out in the former Yugoslav republic. Ethnic divisions separated western, Slavic, Turkish, and Arab peoples. Religious differences further divided Catholics, Orthodox Christians, and Muslims. Of the six provinces in former Yugoslavia, Slovenia and Croatia were mostly Catholic, with a significant Orthodox Serbian minority in Croatia; Serbia, Montenegro, and Macedonia were mostly Slavic and Orthodox with significant Muslim minorities; and Bosnia-Herzegovina (Bosnia, for short) had roughly equal Orthodox and Muslim populations with a significant Catholic minority. Bosnia, along with Croatia, became the focus of the conflict.

In the first year, the EC (which becomes EU in 1993) took the lead and tried to negotiate a cease-fire and peaceful settlement. By mid-1992, the United Nations had deployed a UN Protection Force (UNPROFOR) in Croatia and Bosnia. UN and EC officials established the International Conference on the Former Yugoslavia (ICFY) to propose cease-fire plans. None worked, and after a mortar round went off in the marketplace of Sarajevo in February 1994 killing 68 people and wounding 197 others, the EU realized it did not have the military power to stop the violence. The United States and NATO were called on to support UNPROFOR with air strikes.

NATO had the power, but did it have the legitimacy to use that power? To be legitimate, as some liberal perspectives see it, NATO needed UN authorization. But working through the UN was ultimately not possible. Russia had veto power on the Security Council and supported Serbia, which the other powers perceived to be the primary aggressor. When violence escalated again in summer 1995, NATO acted without UN authority and launched week-long air strikes against Serb targets in Bosnia. The United States also assumed the diplomatic initiative and called the parties together in Dayton, Ohio, to hammer out the Dayton accords. A NATO-led peace Implementation Force (IFOR) replaced the UN force UNPROFOR.

Eventually, the UN gave its blessing, and NATO, with some 60,000 troops and related equipment, began its first so-called **out-of-area mission,** that is, a mission outside the central European area as defined by the Cold War threat.

In 1999, NATO got a second bite at the apple in Yugoslavia. Fighting broke out again, this time in Kosovo, a province of Serbia, after Serbia tried to crush the Muslim majority in that region. When Russia supported Serbia and again prevented UN action, NATO intervened once more and bombed Belgrade, the capital of Serbia. Serbia relented, and NATO and then EU forces policed a cease-fire in Kosovo.

In Kosovo, however, NATO intervened in a dispute within a sovereign state, not between sovereign states, as in the case of the first Persian Gulf War or within disintegrating entities such as Bosnia. Intervention was directed toward common humanitarian concerns within a unified and functioning country, an area generally reserved by international law and the UN Charter for "domestic jurisdiction." Russia strongly protested this collective security action against a sovereign state and increasingly opposed NATO thereafter.

In summer 1990, U.S. officials had promised the Soviet Union that NATO would not expand its security role eastward. But now in 1999, NATO not only played a key role in securing the Balkans but also expanded to include Poland, Hungary, and the Czech Republic (the western part of Czechoslovakia, which had separated peacefully in January 1993 from the eastern part, known as Slovakia). In 2004, NATO expanded again to admit seven more new members—one republic from the former Yugoslavia, Slovenia; three republics from the former Soviet Union, Lithuania, Latvia, and Estonia; and three more eastern European countries, Slovakia, Romania, and Bulgaria. U.S. officials struggled not to alienate Russia. President Clinton made U.S.-Russian relations a centerpiece of his foreign policy and invited Russia to join a NATO-Russian Permanent Joint Council.[10] The idea was to start with *regional* collective security and eventually expand to include everyone, becoming *universal* collective security. But when the Kosovo crisis occurred, Russia walked out of the Permanent Joint Council (notice, in the case of the word "permanent," how little diplomatic words may mean). President George W. Bush, pursuing a more bilateral rather than collective security approach to Russia, reconstituted the Permanent Council in May 2002 as the NATO-Russia Council.

What makes military intervention legitimate? From a liberal position, many in Europe and the United States still believe it requires prior UN authorization. But can Russia or other nondemocratic countries, such as China, block actions that democratic countries deem necessary to defend freedom or human rights? Others may argue that democratic countries decide legitimacy because they are elected and held accountable by their own people. From an identity perspective, legitimacy derives from democracy, not from universal participation. If the democratic countries in NATO and elsewhere can decide alone, however, won't that eventually cause a new Cold War or worse with Russia or China? And what if even the democratic countries in NATO cannot agree on military intervention? Does France or Germany have the right to veto actions that the U.S. Congress considers in the national interest? From a realist perspective, each nation decides what is legitimate. These issues came to a head in the 2003 Iraq War (see the next chapter) and sharply divided institution-oriented liberal and stability-oriented realist perspectives from more democracy-oriented identity perspectives. (See Table 6-1 for a summary of liberal explanations for world events in the 1990s.)

out-of-area missions
NATO missions outside the central European area as defined by the Cold War threat.

Spotlight on
sovereignty

Spotlight on
legitimacy to
intervene

Table 6-1

The Causes of World Events in the 1990s: The Liberal Perspective and Levels of Analysis

Level of analysis		Liberal perspective
Systemic	*Structure*	• Success of UN collective security in first Persian Gulf War and then failure in Somalia
	Process	• Failure of Oslo Accords to resolve Arab-Israeli dispute
Foreign policy		• George H. W. Bush and Secretary of State James Baker emphasize importance of institution-building despite domestic reluctance to bind American policy
Domestic		• Collapse of moderate governments in Israel and Arab states after 1995
Individual		• Bill Clinton mediates, but fails to implement Arab-Israeli peace settlement in 2000

Realist Interpretations of the World of the 1990s

Realist perspectives see the years after the end of the Cold War very differently. They focus on the distribution of power, not institutional processes. At the systemic structural level of analysis, they see a world that is unipolar under American dominance yet increasingly subject to *asymmetric threats* from smaller powers that use technology to challenge larger foes. The most serious threats are not the occasional terrorist attacks from nonstate actors at the domestic level of analysis but, instead, coordinated efforts by terrorist groups and their state sponsors at the systemic process level to acquire nuclear weapons and undermine stability throughout the world. These antagonists exploit the bewildering blizzard of ethnic and interstate conflicts that resurfaced after the Cold War and use failed and radical states as bases to chip away at western dominance. As realist perspectives see it, domestic level conflicts and poverty are not the source of terrorism, as liberal perspectives argue, but instruments used by process and structural level actors to wage the age-old battle to redistribute power.

Realist perspectives anticipate the historical cycle of empires and equilibrium. Some, following the power transition school, believe that America can preserve its predominance and advocate preemptive measures to forestall challengers. Others, following the power balancing school, anticipate decline and rely on deterrence and containment to contend with rising powers such as China, resurgent powers such as Russia, and wealthy counterweights such as Europe (EU) and Japan. But few realists believe (as liberals do) that international institutions, courts, and economic development can replace the balance of power; the need for flexible alliances, such as coalitions of the willing; or the use of military force to stabilize world politics and underwrite economic interdependence.

Spotlight on power transition and power balancing

Power Transition Realists: Unipolarity and Preemption

Realist perspectives recognized immediately the unique feature of the post–Cold War world. It was not institutional unity or democratic expansion; it was American unipolarity. For the first time in history, a war among great powers, namely the Cold War, had ended without a fight. The country that won not only dominated the postwar landscape; it did so unscathed. The United States had suffered no significant losses in the Cold War, as a victorious England had in World War I or the Soviet Union had in World War II. There was no central Europe to rebuild, although eastern Germany and Europe would require substantial investments for decades to come. And there were no big power threats to parry, as Russia had challenged British power after 1815 and the Soviet Union had challenged U.S. power after 1945. The United States stood at the pinnacle of unchallenged power.

Most realists believed American dominance would not last. After all, historically, empires always succumbed to equilibrium. Therefore, Charles Krauthammer, a well-known realist commentator, called the postwar period "the unipolar moment," or alternatively "a holiday from history," meaning a brief interlude from conflict and the cycle of empire and equilibrium.[11] But how long would "the moment" or "holiday" last? As Krauthammer suggested, it might be decades. Other realists thought it might be much shorter. For Henry Kissinger, the world of equilibrium was already at hand: "Victory in the Cold War has propelled America into a world which bears many similarities to the European state system of the eighteenth and nineteenth centuries. . . ."[12]

Not surprisingly realists broke into two camps: those that focused on how to preserve and extend American hegemony, perhaps for decades, and those who fretted about immediate counterchallenges and sought to accommodate rising powers. The two camps reflected the old realist division discussed in earlier chapters between the power balancing and power transition schools. Power transition realists see wars arising from movement *toward* equilibrium, either by the decline of dominant powers or the rise of challenging powers. They seek, therefore, to preserve hegemony and justify it morally because hegemony fosters peace—a universalist position. Power balancing realists see wars arising from movements *away* from equilibrium. They seek, therefore, to reduce hegemony by accommodating rising power and advocate coexistence—a relativist position. Offensive realists, who emphasize the use of American power to dominate a hegemonic order, take the power transition position, while some neoconservatives, such as Krauthammer, who emphasize the use of power to spread democracy, draw from identity perspectives as well. Traditional defensive realists, who emphasize stability not hegemony or democracy, take the power balancing position.

In 1992, neoconservatives in the Pentagon, led by then secretary of defense Dick Cheney, drafted a controversial strategy document that called on the United States to forestall the emergence of any challenger to American predominance.[13] Although this document was not affirmed as official policy, it later resurfaced in the 2002 national security strategy document and influenced the U.S. decision to take preemptive action in Iraq. The 2002 document laid out the strategic doctrine of **preemption,** a policy to use force to head off potential challengers rather than wait to be attacked. The document stated that "while the United States will constantly strive to enlist the support of the international community, we will not hesitate to act alone, if necessary, to exercise our right of self-defense by acting preemptively against . . . terrorists, to prevent them from doing harm against our people and our country."[14] Preemption implied that the enemy was about to attack. But even if it was not, a more aggressive preventive action might be necessary, power transition realists thought, because the terrorist threat was less visible. The United States could not wait until it saw "armies gathering at the border"; terrorist "armies" did not appear until they actually struck. Thus, the distinction between preemptive and preventive war blurred. The United States might have to attack whether it saw the other side getting ready to attack now (preemption) or just thought it might do so at some

Spotlight on
ethics and morality

Spotlight on
preemptive and preventive wars

preemption
a policy of using force to attack challengers when they prepare to attack you; blurs with preventive war when the preparation of challengers such as terrorists is not readily visible.

unspecified time in the future (prevention). Understandably, other countries viewed this justification of aggressive action with alarm, but for the power transition realists the United States could preempt with impunity since no other nation or even group of nations had the power to oppose it. Compared to previous hegemons, the United States enjoyed in the mid-1990s an extraordinary concentration of power in all categories: national wealth, military expenditures, and composite measures of power. As political scientist William Wohlforth observed, "never in modern international history has the leading state been so dominant economically and militarily."[15]

causal arrow

Thus, preventive war became more likely both because of the nature of the threat and because of unipolarity. Notice that, from the realist perspective, the structure of power drives policy or the prospects of preventive war, not the misguided strategies of Pentagon leaders (liberal individual decision-making level explanation) or the desire of the American people to spread democracy (identity domestic level explanation).

Power Balancing Realists: Stability and Containment

Because realist perspectives expect an unending struggle for power, they pay less attention to the values for which states seek power than to the configuration of power in which they compete. The power balancing school stresses equilibrium. Realists found great comfort, for example, in the stability of the bipolar configuration during the Cold War struggle. Bipolar equilibrium nurtured peace, and for all its problems the bipolar world produced a cold not a hot war. Many realist analysts assumed and perhaps even preferred that the Cold War would go on indefinitely.[16]

Thus, when the Soviet empire and then the Soviet Union itself disintegrated, traditional realists advised caution. They saw the same dilemma that John Kennedy had talked about during the Cold War—before you call for independence to replace one tyrant, be sure you can avoid another tyrant that may be even worse. This was the approach George H. W. Bush and his national security adviser, Brent Scowcroft, took in 1991 to the independence movements in both Yugoslavia and Ukraine. Concerned about the fighting that broke out in Yugoslavia in early 1991, Bush expressed the dilemma openly when he visited Kiev, Ukraine, in August 1991: "Americans will not support those who seek independence in order to replace a far-off tyranny with a local despotism."[17]

Spotlight on stability, not democracy

Dubbed unfairly—because it is a real dilemma from the power balancing realist perspective—the "Chicken Kiev" speech, Bush's remarks highlighted a debate that presaged the later division among realists over Iraq. In 1991, Defense Secretary Cheney opposed the Bush-Scowcroft line, which was also supported by Colin Powell, then chairman of the Joint Chiefs of Staff. Cheney argued for a more aggressive policy to break up the Soviet Union, whatever the consequences for the spread of democracy. Leading the power transition school, Cheney saw an opportunity to extend America's power advantage. Even "if democracy fails" in the fifteen Soviet republics, Cheney argued, "we're better off if they're small."[18] Notice that in Cheney's comment the distribution of power counts more than the spread of democracy. Breaking up the former Soviet Union would increase America's relative power even if democracy, a lesser goal, did not prevail in the now smaller Soviet republics. As we will see in the next chapter, this subtle emphasis also separates offensive-minded or power transition realists such as Cheney from power balancing realists who give the advantage to stability over power and from more identity-oriented neoconservatives who give the edge to democracy over power.

causal arrow

This same argument divided Vice President Cheney and Secretary of State Colin Powell twelve years later over the Iraq War. Cheney wanted to press America's dominance and decisively shift the balance of power in Iraq and the Middle East; Powell worried about destabilizing the region and winding up with even worse fundamentalist governments. He coined the "Pottery Barn" argument, warning Bush, "if you break it [meaning Iraq], you own it [for better or for worse]." Brent Scowcroft, who was now in civilian life, agreed with Powell and became a vocal critic of the American decision to invade Iraq in 2003.

Counterweights—China, Russia, Japan, and the European Union

Realists anticipate counterbalancing. Power transition realists seek to forestall it through preemption or prevention. They are particularly unwilling to rely on international institutions because these institutions become the means by which weaker states often block the use of preemptive or preventive action. The power balancing school, by contrast, expects other countries to become stronger and challenge the United States in the age-old competition for power. The power balancers therefore focus on containing rising powers such as China, Russia, Japan, and the EU.

Spotlight on counterbalancing

China occupies center stage as a preeminent rising power. Since 1979, it has been modernizing. In that year, Deng Xiaoping, the leader who replaced Mao Zedong, reoriented China's economy to world markets. China adopted the strategy of Japan and the smaller Asian "tigers" that used export development to modernize their economies. The results were nothing short of spectacular; China grew by 10 percent per year. Its current potential seems unlimited. Here is how one realist analyst assessed China's prospects in 2001:

> Right now, Japan has a population one-tenth the size of China's and a per capita GNP ($32,350) that is 40 times greater. If China modernizes to the point where it has about the same per capita GNP as South Korea does today ($8,600), it will have an economy 2.5 times the size of Japan's current one and 1.3 times the size of the U.S. economy. And if China achieves a per capita GNP equal to about half of that of Japan, its economy will be 5 times larger than Japan's and 2.5 times larger than that of the United States. For most of the Cold War, it should be remembered, the Soviet economy was only about half the size of the American economy.[19]

China's strength, and its weakness, is its population—1.3 billion people, to be exact. If that population ever achieved middle-class status, and that's a big if, suggesting how difficult it is to develop a country with a large population, China would dwarf the world, except perhaps for India, which also has a population over 1 billion. Although China was nowhere close to that goal in 2007, it is moving rapidly in an upward direction, continuing to grow since 2001 at over 10 percent per year. It is modernizing its military and for more than two decades has increased military spending at double-digit rates. It has used that military power ruthlessly in the past to occupy Tibet in 1950, fight a border war with India in 1971, and briefly invade Vietnam in 1979. It considers Taiwan, an island off the southeast coast of China occupied by nationalist forces in 1949 after the communists defeated the nationalists on the mainland, a renegade part of the fatherland and threatens to invade if Taiwan moves toward independence. In March 1996, China fired missiles into the sea around Taiwan, and the United States sent two aircraft carrier groups into the area to deter Beijing. China competes with Japan and other Asian countries for oil resources in the East and South China Seas. If it develops a blue-water navy, one capable of operating

Spotlight on rising power

over long distances from its coastline, it might ultimately challenge American naval dominance in the Pacific.

Realist perspectives fret about other counterweights to American power. In the years immediately after the Cold War, they saw Germany, the EU, and Japan challenging American power. The saying was, "the Cold War is over, and Japan has won." America had exhausted its treasury in the Cold War, it was widely feared, and was now in economic decline.[20] Meanwhile, Japan had spent very little on defense, was protected by the United States, and was aggressively exploiting export markets to undercut American preeminence. A Cold Peace, it was said, had replaced the Cold War, and America was locked in a struggle for supremacy with its former Cold War allies.[21] The challenge was mostly economic but, as Kissinger warned, "the new international system will move toward equilibrium even in the military field, though it may take decades to reach that point."[22] Better to accept and accommodate than resist this movement toward equilibrium. Even the prospect of nuclear proliferation did not disturb some realists.[23] Thinking in terms of deterrence, they assumed that the spread of nuclear weapons would automatically produce equilibrium and stalemate. Once states and their opponents had nuclear weapons, they would not use them but settle their disputes by other means, such as conventional balances and détente, as the superpowers had done in the Cold War.

Russia was another obvious potential counterweight to the United States. From a realist perspective, NATO was never a collective security organization going beyond the logic of alliances, as the liberal perspectives see it. Rather, it was an insurance policy—or alliance in waiting—to protect against a resurgent nationalist Russia. Just as NATO's creation had reassured western European countries in 1949, NATO's enlargement in the 1990s provided political and economic reassurance for eastern European countries struggling to maintain their independence and reform their societies away from the Soviet model. These regimes did not require immediate military protection because Russia was weak and under Boris Yeltsin, its president in the 1990s, cooperated with the West. But under Vladimir Putin, who succeeded Yeltsin in 1999, Russia became more assertive and less democratic. Putin intervened in Ukraine to oppose a reformist government and pressured it by cutting off gas supplies. He also shut down independent media outlets and shackled foreign organizations assisting democratic groups in Russia. In realist eyes, NATO was still needed to secure new democracies in eastern Europe.

In addition, realist spokesmen, such as Dick Cheney and Donald Rumsfeld, campaigned in the 1990s to terminate the ABM Treaty. They sought to develop more robust missile defense systems, which might be effective against reduced numbers of offensive missile systems that might be negotiated with Russia. Such defensive systems might also counter the threat of proliferation from terrorists and rogue states seeking to acquire WMDs and the missile systems to deliver them. In 1998, Rumsfeld, later defense secretary under George W. Bush, chaired the Commission to Assess the Ballistic Missile Threat to the United States. The commission concluded that

> Concerted efforts by a number of overtly or potentially hostile nations to acquire ballistic missiles with biological or nuclear payloads pose a growing threat to the United States, its deployed forces and its friends and allies. These newer, developing threats in North Korea, Iran, and Iraq are in addition to those still posed by the existing ballistic missile arsenals of Russia and China, nations with which we are not now in conflict but which remain in uncertain transitions.[24]

Spotlight on proliferation

Spotlight on nationalism

Asymmetric Threat and Warfare

From a realist perspective, threat and warfare took on a different character under unipolarity, or American primacy. The unprecedented asymmetry in the distribution of power put a premium on the use of force to disrupt and disconcert an adversary rather than to counterbalance or defeat it. There was no chance to defeat a vastly superior enemy directly, but there was an opportunity to create fear and spread uncertainty throughout the enemy's extended realm. Barbarian invaders had done this on the borders of the Roman Empire for centuries, eventually contributing to the weakening of Roman pride and resolve. And revolutionary groups have done this repeatedly inside countries or empires to spread violence and insurrection. The less powerful therefore have always thought in terms of **asymmetric threat and warfare,** the exploitation of technology and psychology to target the peripheral vulnerabilities of a larger foe and wrestle it to the ground.

> **asymmetric threat and warfare**
> the exploitation of technology and psychology to target the peripheral vulnerabilities of a larger foe.

For this reason, as Professor Richard Betts tells us, "terrorism is the premier form of 'asymmetric warfare.' "[25] **Terrorism** is the use of violence against innocent civilians to advance political aims. It is an old art of statecraft, especially for weaker groups fighting against stronger, more established foes. It had been present for some time in the Middle East and in other parts of the world such as Northern Ireland and the Basque region in Spain. Irgun, for example, was a Jewish terrorist organization that fought the British to secure Israel's statehood. Now Arab terrorist groups fight Israel to achieve Palestinian statehood.

> **terrorism**
> the use of violence against innocent civilians to advance political aims.

The rise of terrorism, therefore, is no surprise from a realist perspective. Several factors, however, sharply escalated the threat of asymmetric warfare in the 1990s.

First, new information technologies empowered individual terrorist groups not only to communicate more effectively but also to develop strategies on a global scale. After Muslim *jihad*ists defeated the Soviet Union in Afghanistan, Osama bin Laden reflected on the threat America now posed: the "collapse [of the Soviet Union] made the U.S. more haughty and arrogant and it has started to look at itself as a Master of this world and established what it calls the new world order."[26] He determined to set up a global network to confront this new "Master of the world." Al Qaeda emerged just as the Cold War ended and became a full-fledged global NGO with corporate and financial operations all over the world. It ran multinational businesses in construction, manufacturing, banking, leasing, commodities, exporting, and importing. Its members included from the earliest days Muslim followers from many nations across the Islamic world—Libyans, Filipinos, Nigerians, Iraqis, Saudis, Yemenis, Jordanians, and Algerians.

Second, modern technology made large powers increasingly vulnerable to the tactics of terrorism. The United States, for example, has almost 600,000 bridges, 170,000 water-treatment systems, more than 2,800 power plants (104 of them nuclear), 190,000 miles of interstate pipelines for natural gas, almost 500 skyscrapers, and hundreds of airports, harbors, sports arenas, and shopping centers, not to mention thousands of miles of open borders. It was relatively easy for violent groups to target strategic links in these systems and send out ripple effects of physical disruption and fear that magnified the impact of relatively specific attacks.

Third, less powerful groups gained a greater advantage in the element of surprise. Offense holds a huge advantage over defense. In guerilla wars, it has been estimated that defensive forces need an advantage of personnel as high as ten to one to defeat insurgency groups. Given all the vulnerable systems where guerillas or terrorists might attack, the cost to defend against terrorism was now much larger. In fact, the need to defend so many vulnerable places at such high costs created an incentive for larger states to preempt or prevent attacks. The money would be better spent trying to locate and kill terrorist cells through advanced espionage techniques and covert operations than to establish passive defenses at all the points of vulnerability. On the other hand, aggressive intelligence measures spread fear and concern, especially among democratic societies, that fundamental civil rights were being violated. Terrorist groups could play on this political vulnerability to weaken the pride and resolve of defending democracies.

Fourth, some states became systematic supporters of nonstate terrorism. Rejectionist states—meaning those rejecting Israel—such as Iran, Iraq, and Syria had long supported terrorist groups such as Hezbollah in Lebanon and Hamas in Palestine. But now other, failed states, internally divided and vulnerable to outside insurgent groups, became potential safe havens and training centers for terrorism. The hijackers who carried out the 9/11 attacks trained in the 1990s in Afghan camps under the Taliban government, a government that had emerged from the tribal warfare and chaos after Soviet troops withdrew in 1989. When bin Laden had his passport taken from him in Saudi Arabia in 1991, he went to Sudan, where an Islamist radical government under Hassan al-Turabi harbored terrorists. From Sudan, Al Qaeda allegedly played a role in attacking American troops in Somalia, at the time another failed and lawless state.[27] Training activities for holy war also took place in Pakistan, the Philippines, Yemen, and other countries.

Fifth, the information age facilitated the spread of WMDs, and some states, called rogue states, sought systematically to acquire such weapons, primarily to threaten retaliation against the unipolar power should it attack but also with the possible intent of passing WMDs on to nonstate terrorists. The discovery after the first Persian Gulf War that Iraq was much closer to having a nuclear weapon than the world community thought and the subsequent unraveling of the A. Q. Khan network selling nuclear technology and equipment to the highest bidder suggested the new dangers. The A. Q. Khan network was an elaborate global nongovernmental network of individuals and corporations that, as it later came out, sold nuclear technology and equipment, including possible weapons designs, to rogue states such as Libya, Iran, and North Korea.[28] Dr. Abdul Qadeer Khan, the group's eponymous leader, was the top scientist in the Pakistani program to develop nuclear weapons. Thus, possible links between rogue states and nonstate terrorists through shadowy global networks exploiting the new information highways of global commerce and communications were becoming a new axis of asymmetric warfare, although little of this was that visible or well understood yet in the early 1990s.

What was visible, as the box on page 226 shows, was a methodical increase in disruptive violence aimed especially at the predominant power, the United States. After the first World Trade Center van bombing in 1993, global

Spotlight on failed states

Spotlight on rogue states

Muslim militants bomb the Khobar Towers marine complex in Saudi Arabia in June 1996, killing nineteen U.S. marines and wounding hundreds more.

Table 6-2

The Causes of World Events in the 1990s: The Realist Perspective and Levels of Analysis		
Level of analysis		**Realist perspective**
Systemic	*Structure*	• U.S. unipolarity prompts preemption and counterbalancing
	Process	• Iraq defies UN resolutions and sanctions to stop weapons programs
Foreign policy		• Power transition realists deflect domestic pressures to spread democracy to extend America's dominance in eastern Europe
Domestic		—
Individual		• Vice President Cheney gives priority to expanding American power over spreading democracy

terrorists bombed Khobar Towers, a U.S. military barracks in Dhahran, Saudi Arabia, in 1996; U.S. embassies in Kenya and Tanzania in 1998; and a U.S. warship, the USS *Cole* in Aden, Yemen, in 2000. Other attacks to blow up a series of U.S. civilian planes in southeast Asia and to disrupt the Los Angeles airport in the United States during the millennium celebrations were thwarted. All these attacks occurred before the sensational events of 9/11. (See Table 6-2 for a summary of realist explanations for the events of the 1990s.)

Identity Perspectives on the World of the 1990s

Identity perspectives see the world through the competition and construction of ideas. One identity explanation of the world that emerged in the 1990s, at the systemic structural level of analysis, argued that the ideas of democracy had won out over the ideas of communism and that democracy was now the solution to the problem of war and peace in eastern Europe, the Balkans, and other parts of the world. In this argument, democracy trumped culture and became a possibility in all countries, western or not. However, another identity argument was made that culture or civilization, the highest form of culture, trumped democracy and that the world was heading into another clash of ideologies not unlike the ideological confrontation of the Cold War. A western world of liberal secular democracy would face off against a series of other cultures that were either illiberal, based on religious fundamentalism, or both. The most significant conflicts would emerge between the western world, on one side, and a possible combination of Confucian China–centered and Muslim Middle East–centered civilizations, on the other side. For realists, this confrontation was simply the age-old struggle for power taking place, this time between civilizations of broadly similar nation-states rather than between nation-states within the same civilization, as in the case of earlier Europe. From an identity perspective, however, it was a struggle for power among very different types of actors—civilizations rather than nation-states—whose interactions might lead to different kinds of international systems, some more anarchic than others, depending on how shared identities were constructed.

Spotlight on internal identities

Democracy: The End of History

In the early 1990s, Francis Fukuyama wrote a book, *The End of History and the Last Man,* that seemed to capture the meaning of the new era ushered in by the events of

Major Terrorist Attacks Against U.S. Targets, 1993–2000

Date	Event
February 26, 1993	Bombing of World Trade Center towers in New York City coordinated by Ramzi Yousef and financed by Kahlid Shaik Mohammed, both Al Qaeda members. Six people killed and over a thousand injured.
January 6, 1995	Philippines terrorist group plot to bomb eleven U.S. airlines foiled. Ramzi Yousef, Kahlid Shaik Mohammed, and the group Jemaah Islamiyah are suspected of involvement.
June 25, 1996	Khobar Towers housing complex in Dhahran, Saudi Arabia, bombed by Hezbollah. U.S. air force personnel and other foreign nationals were housed there; 19 U.S. servicemen and 1 Saudi killed and 372 wounded.
August 7, 1998	Al Qaeda truck bombings target U.S. embassies in Kenya and Tanzania; 224 killed and 4,500 injured.
December 1999	Twenty-eight suspects arrested in Jordan and charged with attempting to bomb U.S. and Israeli tourists as part of the millennium celebration attacks.
December 14, 1999	Ahmed Ressam arrested trying to enter the United States from Canada at the border in Port Angeles, Washington. Ressam later confesses to planning to bomb the Los Angeles International Airport as part of a series of coordinated attacks timed around millennium celebrations.
October 12, 2000	Al Qaeda suicide boat targets the USS Cole in Aden, Yemen; 17 U.S. soldiers killed.

Spotlight on democratic peace

11/9.[29] Communism has just died a peaceful death in the Soviet Union, and democracy, its ideological adversary for a century, stood unchallenged around the world. Fukuyama asked how this had happened. His answer was that democracy supplied something that communism or any other political identity did not, namely a sense of equal recognition among human beings and groups of human beings that ended the historical quest for domination. In international politics, it ended the quest for empire and equilibrium by creating a "democratic peace" in which all countries recognized one another as equal and legitimate, eliminating the struggle for power and status and, hence, the incentive for war.

Fukuyama drew heavily on the work of the German philosopher Georg W. F. Hegel. Hegel developed a nonmaterialist account of history that contrasted with both Marx's materialist and Kant's rationalist accounts. He argued that human beings have three parts to their makeup or soul: a desiring part for objects such as food, drink, and shelter to preserve their bodies; a reasoning part that tells them how best to acquire these material objects; and a "spiritedness" part that seeks recognition from other human beings of the individual's or group's self-worth. The quest for recognition, which Hegel called "thymos," is what drives history. People desire to be recognized by other people, and that spiritedness ignites a struggle for prestige or recognition. Notice that the struggle is for prestige or recognition, not power; hence, Hegel, and his pupil Fukuyama, reflect identity perspectives, not realist perspectives. The struggle for prestige drives the struggle for power between lordship and bondage in domestic affairs and between dominance and revolution—or empire and equilibrium—in international affairs.

Democracy, unlike other sources of identity such as civilization and religion, was supposed to have ended this struggle because it was based on the universal and equal recognition of all human beings and states. Once societies accepted one another as equals, the struggle for recognition was over; thus the **end of history** was at hand. War was unnecessary among democracies, and indeed the statistical evidence of the democratic peace, which we discuss in the Conclusion of this book, shows that democracies do not go to war with one another.

end of history
an idea advanced by Francis Fukuyama that with the spread of democracy and the achievement of universal and equal recognition of all human beings and states the struggle for recognition, and hence violent conflict, will end.

Democracy or Culture?

Fukuyama's updating of Hegel's thesis landed on fertile ground. It offered an ideational explanation for the institutional success of NATO and the EU after the end of the Cold War. The institutional processes themselves were not determinative, as liberal perspectives argued; the political ideas behind democracy were the deciding factor. Even some scholars, who stressed the binding and transformational power of institutions, recognized that democracy might be the causal force behind institutions because democracies were more likely than other states to bind themselves in such institutions.[30] But in liberal perspectives, institutions shape ideas, more than the other way around; in identity perspectives, ideas shape the institutions.

causal arrow

Could democracy transcend western culture? It seemed so. Japan and India were nonwestern democratic countries and, after the Cold War, some eastern European countries, South Korea, Taiwan, Latin America, and even parts of Africa, which were not western, became democratic. Yet the one part of the world where democracy seemed to be excluded was the Middle East. There, Turkey was a struggling democracy, and only Israel, a western-oriented nation, was a strong democracy. Even in Israel's case, radical Orthodox Jewish elements advocated the annexation of Gaza and the West Bank, steps that would almost certainly end the Israeli democracy because Palestinians would then constitute a majority of the Israeli population and would have to become second-class citizens if Israel were to remain a Jewish state. It was not surprising, then, from this perspective that the part of the world where democracy failed to take hold was also the center of regional and global conflict. The absence of democracy, not the failure of Middle East diplomacy or the growing power of extremists, was the cause of such conflict.

Some realist analysts also supported the idea of using American power to spread American ideals. Charles Krauthammer, a neoconservative commentator, called for a realism aimed at democracy, not just stability. He wanted a "democratic realism," a strategic policy that not only went "around the world bashing bad guys over the head" but "at some point . . . implant[ed] something, something organic and self-developing. And that something is democracy. . . ."[31] Secretary of State Condoleezza Rice favored a similar democratic realism when she called for a "balance of power that favors freedom."[32]

Clash of Civilizations

But many scholars of a realist bent remained highly skeptical. Professor Samuel Huntington, for example, wrote a book a few years after Fukuyama's in which he argued that cultures or civilizations "are far more fundamental than differences among political ideologies and political regimes."[33] He detected the contours of a future struggle for power along the borders of different civilizations and foresaw the possibility of

clash of civilizations

a thesis advanced by Samuel Huntington that past and future global conflicts can be traced along the fault lines between nine major world civilizations.

Spotlight on

relative identities

a **clash of civilizations.** Civilizations involved larger groupings of countries than traditional nation-states. Civilizations, according to Huntington, were the highest form of culture. They represented enduring differences among peoples based principally on religion but also on other cultural factors such as language, history, customs, institutions, and the way people subjectively identified themselves.

In a famous article published in 1993, and expanded into a book in 1996, Huntington identified nine major civilizations. Map 6-1 (page 208) displays these civilizations geographically and the borders between them. These nine groupings are Western (North America and Europe), Orthodox (eastern Europe and Russia), Confucian or Sinic (China), Islamic (North Africa; Middle East; and central, south, and southeast Asia), Hindu (India), Buddhist (Tibet and Indochina), Shinto (Japan), Latin American, and African (sub-Saharan Africa). He found that historical conflicts proliferated along the fault lines between these civilizations. For example, the Cold War was waged between the Western and Orthodox civilizations. Repeated crusades and wars took place in the Middle East between the Islamic and Western civilizations. China and Japan were historical rivals, reflecting conflicts between the Confucian (Sinic) and Shinto civilizations, as were India and China, reflecting conflicts between the Hindu and Confucian civilizations, and India and Pakistan, reflecting conflicts between Hindu and Muslim civilizations. And so on. Huntington was particularly intrigued by the conflicts in the Balkans. Here three religious civilizations—Western, Orthodox, and Islamic—came together. In each province of the former Yugoslavia, as we noted earlier, fighting tended to follow the divisions between religions or civilizations. Huntington asked if these fault lines might not become the locus of future international conflicts. He worried, in particular, about conflicts between the Western civilization (North America and Europe) and Islamic countries in the Middle East and the possibility that Islamic countries, such as Iran, might align with Confucian powers, namely China, to counterbalance the United States.[34]

At the time, Huntington's analysis was sharply criticized. Some identity perspectives accused him of creating a self-fulfilling prophecy—thinking about the world in such contentious terms would make it so. Liberal perspectives rejected the implication that diplomacy was not up to the task of integrating Islam as well as China into the existing western world order. Huntington, in his defense, did not see the clash as inevitable; he placed a question mark after the phrase "clash of civilizations." But he did offer lots of evidence to arouse concern.

By suggesting that civilizations were more hardwired in people than the ideological differences that had characterized the Cold War or the cultural and nation-state differences that had divided Europe earlier, Huntington was ven-

The cross of an Orthodox church stands alongside the minaret of an Islamic mosque in this Macedonian town of Tetovo, symbolizing the clash of religious civilizations or cultures that erupted in Bosnia, Kosovo, and other parts of the former Yugoslavia in the 1990s.

turing into the world of changing identities in international affairs. Some analysts therefore interpret his argument as an identity perspective. On the other hand, Huntington's purpose was not to suggest how ideas change and transcend material (realist) or institutional (liberal) circumstances but rather to point out that identities, especially at the level of civilizations, do not change very much. They are historically rooted and serve to divide the world in ways that might be considered permanent. He did not think that democracy, for example, could transcend these civilization differences. He expected that the distribution of power in the world would always remain decentralized, whatever the specific sources of identity in any given era. Since realists have always conceded that states can merge or disappear and identities change but anarchy will still persist, Huntington's argument can also be seen as realist.

causal arrow

Huntington anticipated much of what subsequently happened after the Cold War. He offered, in particular, a framework for understanding the new threat of terrorism and its eventual targeting of the United States. Osama bin Laden and nonstate actors such as Al Qaeda took the lead, but history suggested this effort might find wider global support among states from different civilizations seeking to counterbalance American power. The subsequent discovery of China's assistance to Pakistan in developing nuclear weapons and Pakistan's A. Q. Khan network to supply nuclear technology to Libya, Iran, and North Korea even seemed to outline the dimensions of the Confucian-Islamic alliance that Huntington feared. Altogether, Huntington's thesis generated much debate and raised important questions, even if unintended, about how identities change and shape international events.

Western or Universal?

From Huntington's analysis, democracy as a political ideology is not likely to spread across the fault lines of different civilizations. It is part of Western civilization, not a universal value.[35] Fareed Zakaria, a journalist and realist foreign policy analyst, was similarly skeptical. He argued that many countries in the Middle East and the third world held elections but that they did not have civil societies that protected individual rights and nurtured the basic institutions of a free press and independent courts to ensure real competitive political processes. These countries were illiberal, not liberal, democracies, and democracy there was unstable and easily reversed. (Notice that "liberal" here refers to classical liberal or democratic values, which we disentangled in Chapter 1 from the liberal perspective.) Zakaria pointed out that civil societies in western states developed in parallel with elections over long periods of time and that a similar development would be necessary before other countries could achieve real democracy. Zakaria wanted the United States to go more slowly. "Instead of searching for new lands to democratize and new places to hold elections," he advises the United States and international community "to consolidate democracy where it has taken root and to encourage the gradual development of constitutional liberalism across the globe."[36]

Analysts adopting a liberal perspective concurred with Zakaria and went even further. They pointed out the irony of the United States pulling away from old democracies in Europe and North America to construct new democracies in Iraq and the Middle East. If democracy could not hold the western allies together over Iraq, how could it build bridges between the United States and countries in the Middle East? Perhaps power overrode both democracy and common institutions, as strict realist perspectives argued. The United States had the power to intervene, and therefore it did. Or perhaps the United States would be driven back to common institutions, as liberal

Spotlight on
judgment

Table 6-3

The Causes of World Events in the 1990s: The Identity Perspective and Levels of Analysis

Level of analysis		Identity perspective
Systemic	*Structure*	• Triumph of democracy and end of history
		• Confrontation of radical Islam and secular democracy
	Process	• Al Qaeda emerges as transnational NGO network fomenting terrorism
Foreign policy		—
Domestic		• Radical Islamic forces within individual Muslim nations wage *jihad* against western infidels
Individual		• Osama bin Laden declares holy war against the United States

perspectives believed. Unilateralism and preemption were simply not sustainable. The debate reflected the continuing need to make judgments, after examining as many facts as possible, whether ideational, power, or institutional factors are more important in determining outcomes and prescribing solutions in international affairs. (See Table 6-3 for a summary of identity explanations for the events of the 1990s.)

Critical Theory Perspective: American Empire

From a critical theory perspective, the end of the Cold War did nothing more decisively than reveal the deeply engrained historical dynamic impelling America to create an empire even while professing ever more vigorously that it did not want an empire and was nothing like its historic predecessors Rome and Great Britain. This imperative to create an empire does not stem from specific leaders or ideas—it's not even unique to America—nor is it the product of specific historic periods or configurations of power such as unipolarity. Rather, it stems from social and material forces throughout history that perennially produce a great power that achieves regional or global domination while denying that that is what it is actually doing. It stems, in other words, from deeper forces that drive leaders and societies to power and hypocrisy whether they are aware of what they are doing or not.

Professor Andrew Bacevich gives us an example of a critical theory perspective in the *American Empire*.[37] American policy after the Cold War, he argues, was not a product of George H. W. Bush, Bill Clinton, or George W. Bush. Each of these men followed policies that had characterized American foreign policy from the earliest origins of the republic. America believed that it had founded a new society that ultimately did away with politics, a society based on openness and acquisition that was available to all citizens and all countries of the world if they followed the rules. And those rules were straightforward. First, interdependence was the dominant reality of domestic and international politics. America could no more deny its global role than a citizen could deny the nation. No one could blame America for being an empire; that is what the historical forces of globalization required. Second, the American empire was based on an unassailable commitment to openness,

> the removal of barriers to the movement of goods, capital, people, and ideas, thereby fostering an integrated international order conducive to American interests, governed by American norms, regulated by American power, and, above all, satisfying the expectations of the American people for ever-greater abundance.[38]

Table 6-4

The Causes of World Events in the 1990s: The Critical Theory Perspective and Levels of Analysis		
Level of analysis		**Critical theory perspective**
Systemic	*Structure*	• American empire constitutes another manifestation of social and political change that masks the use of power to dominate others
	Process	—
Foreign policy		—
Domestic		—
Individual		—

In short, the world had to be open and coincidentally accessible for penetration by American power and ideas. Third, in this world of both material and moral interdependence, there was no sanctuary or isolationism for the American people. They must defer to their historical role and follow the nation's leadership, especially in foreign policy.

Bacevich is not clear about whether ideas, institutions, or economics drive this historical drama. But it does not matter. Whether American hegemony is Gramscian, and hence socially based, or Marxian, and materially based, is irrelevant. Individual causes cannot be separated from historical context. America is caught in the powerful undercurrents of historical change and cannot do anything but fulfill its role. What would help most is if it would simply acknowledge its imperial stance. Bacevich writes,

> As the Cold War has receded into the past the conceit that America is by its nature innocent of imperial pretensions has become not only untenable but counterproductive. . . . Holding sway in not one but several regions of pivotal geopolitical importance, disdaining the legitimacy of political economic principles other than its own, declaring the existing order to be sacrosanct, asserting unquestioned military supremacy with a globally deployed force configured not for self-defense but for coercion: these are the actions of a nation engaged in the governance of an empire. [39]

Like many critical theorists, Bacevich develops no alternative plan to guide a different American policy. It is often enough from a critical theory perspective to expose the use of power; to redirect it would assume pretensions that many critical theorists do not wish to adopt. (See Table 6-4 for a summary of critical theory explanations for the events of the 1990s.)

Summary

To explain world events in the 1990s, realist perspectives emphasize the role of other countries counterbalancing America's unipolar power at the systemic structural level, the spread of terrorist threats and WMDs at the systemic process level, and the determination of power transition foreign policy elites to extend American power despite domestic pressures to promote stability or spread democracy. If we take the levels of analysis in the same order, liberal perspectives stress the failure of UN collective security institutions to sustain the success of the first Persian Gulf War, the breakdown of diplomacy under the Oslo Accords, the unsuccessful effort of U.S. foreign policy elites to strengthen international institutions, the collapse of moderate governments in the

Middle East, and President Clinton's well-intended but ill-timed 2000 Arab-Israeli peace agreement. At the structural level, identity perspectives give most attention either to the triumph and spread of democracy or to the emerging clash of civilizations between Islam and the West. At the systemic process, domestic, and individual levels, identity accounts point to the spread of transnational Al Qaeda networks, the rise of fundamentalist groups within individual nations, and the leadership role of Osama bin Laden. Critical theory perspectives attribute developments in the 1990s to the unfolding of an historical drama elevating American power and hypocrisy to the world stage in a manner like that of other overweening historical powers, such as Rome or Great Britain.

Key Concepts

asymmetric threat and
warfare 223
Biological Weapons
Convention (BWC) 214
Chemical Weapons
Convention 214
clash of civilizations 228
Comprehensive Test Ban
Treaty (CTBT) 215
constitutional orders 215
end of history 227
genocide 211

International Court of
Justice (ICJ) 215
International Criminal Court
(ICC) 215
intifada 213
jihad 206
Oslo Accords 212
out-of-area missions 217
peace-enforcement
activities 211
peacekeeping activities
211

preemption 219
Strategic Arms Reduction
Talks (START) 214
terrorism 223
Treaty on Conventional
Forces in Europe
(CFE) 215
Treaty on the Non-
Proliferation of Nuclear
Weapons (NPT) 214

Study Questions

1. How do liberal, realist, and identity perspectives explain the failure of the Oslo Accords?

2. Why did the United Nations succeed in the first Persian Gulf War and fail thereafter? Was it the momentary dominance of the United States after the Cold War ended, the farsighted foreign policy leadership of presidents George H. W. Bush and Bill Clinton, or the religious humiliation of fundamentalist Muslims by the presence of western forces in the Gulf? Which perspective and level of analysis are involved in each argument?

3. From the different perspectives, when is it legitimate to intervene in the domestic affairs of another state?

4. What are different strategies for U.S. and western relations with China from the standpoint of the different perspectives?

5. How might the different perspectives interpret Huntington's thesis about the clash of civilizations?

Terrorism and the World After 9/11

Religious, Ethnic, and National Conflicts

On September 11, 2001, nineteen terrorists, fifteen of them from Saudi Arabia, hijacked four American commercial airliners and used them as missiles to destroy the twin towers in New York, a sizable section of the Pentagon in Washington, and, thanks to some courageous passengers, some open farmland in Pennsylvania instead of the intended target of the Capitol building in Washington, D.C. 9/11, it was often said, changed everything. For someone born or raised in the world after 11/9, that is, after the Cold War ended, perhaps. My daughter, then twenty-six years old and living in New York, was totally horrified. "Dad," she said, "this kind of thing cannot happen in America." The bubble of safety that had secured the states of America since the War of 1812 had burst.

Two of the 9/11 hijackers, Mohamed Atta (right) and Abdulaziz Alomari (center), pass through airport security in Portland, Maine, as they make their way to Boston and American Airlines Flight 11, which they later crash into the World Trade Center in New York.

So 9/11 did change everything, right? Yes, it did in the sense that a major conflict loomed once again above the contours of the international system. But, no, it did not in the sense that reactions to 9/11 should by now be familiar to those of us who understand the role of perspectives and levels of analysis in international affairs. As you read further, recall the reactions to 9/11 from the different perspectives that we outlined initially in the Introduction of this book.

For realists, 9/11 represented an end to the "holiday from history," or reprieve from conflict the world had experienced in the 1990s. After an interlude of converging values between East and West and a burst of interdependence in both diplomacy and trade, the use of force to counterbalance and manage conflict was back on the agenda. This time the use of force took the form of terrorism. But for realists, as we learned in the previous chapter, terrorism is the premier use of force in situations of an asymmetric distribution of power or unipolarity. What was more important from a realist perspective is that this terrorism was not aimed just at local or regional conflicts but at the redistribution of power in the international system as a whole. While this systemic conflict built on local religious, ethnic, and national grievances, foremost in the Middle East, it was not confined nor could it be contained at these levels. It was a global conflict that immediately involved the role of failed states such as Afghanistan that could become training camps for terrorism; rogue states such as Iraq, Iran, and North Korea that could potentially supply weapons of mass destruction to terrorists; and dissatisfied states such as Arab Muslim countries, Russia, China, Venezuela, and others that were not unhappy to see America's hegemonic wings clipped a bit. For power transition realists, 9/11 sparked a new global war on terror and a renewed division of the world into friendly and enemy states. Reflecting this approach shortly after 9/11, President George W. Bush warned the world, "You're either with us or against us in the fight against terror."[1] For other realists, who emphasize power balancing, national conflicts continued to matter as much as ethnic and religious terrorism. They called for regional containment to deter Iraq and Iran and more attention to stability rather than aggressive campaigns to force regime change in places such as Pakistan, which confronts India in a nuclear standoff, and North Korea, which threatens South Korea and Japan with nuclear weapons.

From the liberal perspective, 9/11 was no less horrible, but its dimensions were substantially different. Terrorism was not a new phase in the ongoing struggle for global power but rather the outgrowth of unresolved grievances and lack of economic development primarily at the local and regional levels. Declaring global war against terrorism was the wrong way to go. It only increased terrorism and distracted attention from the ongoing diplomatic and economic grievances that fuel terrorism. The Arab-Israeli dispute festered as President Clinton's Camp David diplomacy failed in 2000; ethnic conflicts raged relentlessly in Somalia, West Africa, Congo, Sri Lanka, and elsewhere; and religious sectarianism divided Muslims and Christians in the Balkans and split Sunni and Shiite Muslims in the Middle East. What was driving these conflicts was not the desire to counterbalance American power but feelings of exclusion, poverty, and marginalization, the same forces that drive crime within individual countries. From the liberal perspective too, terrorism was not new. It was known in advanced countries such as Spain and Northern Ireland. It was violent activity born of unresolved local conflicts and grievances. What was needed was an intensified effort to reconcile conflicts peacefully through international mediation, courts, and control of arms. Liberal responses to 9/11 called for treating global terrorism as international crime, not war, and increasing international police, intelligence, judicial, diplomatic, peacekeeping, and nonproliferation efforts to capture and convict militant terrorists and weapons smugglers while using economic and educational programs to drain the swamp of political alienation, poverty, and misunderstanding. The most unhelpful response from this perspective is to act unilaterally or outside the universal community of the United Nations and fuel the hatred and division that the terrorists and others hope to create. America's unilateralism weakened the international institutions that offered the best hope to deal with terrorism.

Spotlight on counterbalancing and war

Spotlight on diplomacy and poverty

Identity perspectives view the challenge of 9/11 and terrorism still another way. Terrorism is largely a product of ethnic, national, and religious identities, not just a consequence of power struggles or criminal behavior due to poverty, lack of education, and alienation. What matters for identity perspectives such as social constructivism is how these identities get constructed. How do people learn that they belong to different ethnic, national, or religious groups, and how do they come to see one another as mortal enemies, realist rivals, or cooperative friends? Social constructivist perspectives look for ways to integrate the conflicting identities of terrorists, ethnic groups, and other international actors. Some focus on tolerance, norms of common humanity, and developing respect for a multicultural world of diverse religions and cultures. Others look to promote greater secularism and common views of basic human rights, such as women's rights, to moderate religious fundamentalism, whether it be Muslim, Christian, or Jewish. Still others turn to democracy and its ability to offer equality and respect for all minorities and institutional openness to resolve disputes. More agency-oriented constructivists focus on the ideological distance or differences that divide diverse cultures and religions and look for ways to narrow these differences through persuasive discourse or contain them and to allow competition to sort out winners and losers (as happened between capitalism and communism in the Cold War).

Let's start first with how the different perspectives assess the global significance of 9/11 and subsequent events. We begin again with the liberal perspective and its critique of military and ideological approaches that prompted America's break out of the collective security system that seemed so promising before 9/11. Then we look at realist and identity perspectives, which emphasize material and normative rather than institutional solutions. Finally, we look more closely at the local and regional aspects of religious, ethnic, and national conflicts in contemporary international affairs and at the remedies that each perspective recommends to cope with these conflicts.

> **Spotlight on**
> **shared versus dissimilar identities**

American Unilateralism: A Critique from the Liberal Perspective

Why didn't the United States and other great powers respond to the terrorist attacks of 9/11 as they did to Iraqi aggression in the first Persian Gulf War in 1990? Why didn't global threat drive the nations of the world together to implement collective security as Iraq's violation of Kuwait sovereignty had done in 1990? The biggest reason from the liberal perspective is the United States. It overreacted disastrously to the events of 9/11. It took the attacks too personally, unwisely dividing the world into enemies and friends, and rejected the opportunity, as liberal perspectives see it, to define terrorism as a threat to all countries of the world and to deal with that threat through the instrumentalities of common institutions: diplomacy, nonproliferation, intelligence cooperation, criminal apprehension of terrorists, and international judicial proceedings.

From the liberal perspective, there were some signs before September 11, 2001, that the United States might not need international institutions as much as before. Congress never ratified the Comprehensive Test Ban Treaty signed by forty-four states in 1996. Nor did it sign the Anti-Personnel Landmine Treaty concluded in 1998. And it refused to accept a new protocol stiffening inspection procedures to detect biological weapons. Congress also passed resolutions rejecting U.S. participation in the Kyoto Protocol, a landmark agreement signed in 1995 to reduce greenhouse gases in the environment, and U.S. membership in the International Criminal Court, which actually came into

causal
arrow

being without the United States in 2004. Much of this pressure to weaken international commitments came from a more ideological and realist-oriented Congress that took power in 1994 and called for a more assertive American foreign policy. Notice the domestic level of analysis in this liberal explanation of America's growing unilateralism. In this case, liberal accounts see the U.S. response to terrorism provoked more by domestic developments than by actual threat from the systemic level. 9/11 was the occasion for but not the cause of America's unilateralism. The underlying cause was institutional shifts (Republican Congress) at the domestic level of analysis.

Now, as the war on terrorism erupted, NATO and UN institutions came under severe challenge from the United States. After the brazen attacks of 9/11, American officials were scared. As realist perspectives see it, they had good reason to be. No one knew the full dimensions of the threat the country faced. The material threat loomed larger than concerns for international institutions or domestic political advantage.

Spotlight on
international
institutions reducing
uncertainty

From a liberal perspective, however, this uncertainty should have encouraged the United States to look for allies. International cooperation increases information and reduces uncertainty. But America had just fought an air war in Kosovo in 1999 through an institutional committee of allies within NATO. American commanders had been frustrated by the delays caused by international bureaucracy. Each bombing target had to be decided by consensus among sixteen countries.[2]

Thus, when the European allies invoked Article 5 of the NATO Treaty, declaring the 9/11 attacks against the United States to be an attack against all members of NATO, the United States declined the offer to conduct the war through NATO. This was a fatal blow to collective security. If the United States was unwilling to accept multilateral help from its closest allies, it was unlikely to turn to the United Nations for help. Instead, blessed by UN resolutions expressing the world's support, the Pentagon put together an ad hoc alliance or "coalition of the willing" to overthrow the Taliban government in Afghanistan, where most of the 9/11 hijackers had been trained. NATO was sidelined, although it subsequently assumed responsibility for security and reconstruction in Kabul and, after 2006, in Afghanistan as a whole.

The world stood behind the United States in Afghanistan. But thereafter, according to liberal accounts, it began to perceive an America dead set on acting alone. George W. Bush's "in-your-face" diplomatic style did not help. While Clinton had softly rejected Kyoto and the ICC (in the last days of his presidency, asking Congress to ratify the ICC even though he knew Congress would not do so), Bush seemed to relish denouncing these agreements. He also terminated the ABM Treaty with Russia (while further reducing offensive weapon systems in line with the new deterrence strategy of mutual assured defense; see Chapter 6) and suspended negotiations to contain nuclear programs in North Korea, both liberal cornerstones for controlling nuclear weapons. Simultaneously, he pulled back from negotiations to settle long-standing political grievances in the Middle East, which from a liberal perspective fuel terrorism.

The most troubling steps, as liberal perspectives see it, came in the next phase of the terrorist conflict. In his State of the Union message in January 2002, President Bush extended the conflict to include rogue states supporting terrorism, not just Al Qaeda, the nonstate actor that trained the hijackers and was most directly responsible for 9/11. He called Iraq, Iran, and North Korea the "axis of evil" and initiated a hard-line

Spotlight on
rogue states

diplomacy to test Iraq's intentions in the decade-long drama of UN resolutions and sanctions to dismantle Baghdad's WMD programs. A national security strategy document issued in September 2002 made clear that the United States might act alone and defined terrorists to include not only "terrorist organizations of global reach" but "any terrorist or state sponsor of terrorism which attempts to gain or use weapons of mass destruction (WMD[s]) or their precursors. . . ."[3] From a liberal perspective, it was a fundamental mistake to link nonstate and state actors and to convert a criminal issue of apprehending individual terrorists into a global interstate war against terrorism.

causal arrow

In October 2002, Bush secured congressional authority to use force against Iraq. Then, as liberal perspectives see it, he reluctantly or deceptively—assuming he never really expected to gain agreement—took his case to the UN. In November, the Security Council agreed unanimously in Resolution 1441 to afford Iraq "one final opportunity" to come clean on its WMD programs or "face serious consequences." Confronting a gathering invasion force in the Persian Gulf, Saddam Hussein let UN inspectors back into the country for the first time since 1998, when he had kicked them out. Realist perspectives emphasized the role that force played in getting the inspectors back in and creating a diplomatic option that did not exist after 1998. But liberal perspectives emphasized the pressure that the invasion force now created to eventually use force and not give diplomacy adequate time to work. In bitter discussions that followed in winter 2002–2003, the United States and the other great powers could not agree on whether Iraq was complying with UN requirements and, more important, on whether force should be used—in short, what "serious consequences" meant. Many UN members, taking a liberal perspective, argued that widening the war to Iraq would only increase terrorism and divert attention from Afghanistan, the source of the 9/11 attacks. They did not believe that Saddam Hussein would align with Al Qaeda and preferred to stick with international instruments of UN inspections, police and intelligence cooperation, and strengthening international courts to monitor WMDs and apprehend and punish terrorists. The model for them was collective security, in which force is a last resort and does not have to be used in massive assaults, such as the planned invasion, if the world sticks together and reduces arms. When France, Russia, and Germany indicated they would not accept the use of force under any conditions, the United States, with Great Britain, Poland, Italy, Spain, and an assortment of smaller allies, acted without UN or NATO authorization. Coalition forces invaded Iraq in March and secured Baghdad by mid-April. Twelve years after its great success in the Persian Gulf War, the UN was sidelined once again by great power conflicts.

causal arrow

From a liberal perspective, American unilateralism was the clear cause for the breakout from international institutions that had been the bedrock of U.S. policy since World War II. What is worse, the breakout was totally unnecessary—Iraq had no WMDs. The Iraq Survey Group, a team of 1,400 weapons specialists sent in by the U.S. government after the successful invasion of Iraq to find nuclear and other WMDs, found that Saddam Hussein had no chemical or biological weapons and only aspirations for a nuclear program. Subsequently, other commissions— the 9/11 Commission, which published its report in 2004 on who and what were

Secretary of State Colin Powell makes the case to the United Nations in February 2003 that Iraq possesses weapons of mass destruction. Seated directly behind Powell are CIA Director George Tenet (left) and U.S. Ambassador to the UN John Negroponte.

Table 7-1

The Causes of Global Terrorism: The Liberal Perspective and Levels of Analysis		
Level of analysis		**Liberal perspective**
Systemic	*Structure*	• Failure of UN diplomacy to manage Iraq War, largely due to American unilateralism
	Process	• Coalitions of the willing lead instead of alliances or international institutions
Foreign policy		• U.S. leaders, responding to domestic fears, reject Article 5 offer from NATO allies
Domestic		• Republican Congress in 1994 rejects international agreements
Individual		• Bush demonizes rogue states

responsible for 9/11, and the Iraq Study Group, which issued a report in 2006 on future steps in Iraq and the war on terror—confirmed the view that unilateralism was unnecessary and called for more emphasis on multilateralism and the need to strengthen national and international institutions.

From which level of analysis did the cause of this breakout come? Was American unilateralism caused by George W. Bush's belligerent diplomacy (the individual level of analysis), a shift in Congress and American politics toward more conservative or nationalist policies (the domestic level of analysis), or weaknesses in UN and International Atomic Energy Agency (IAEA) institutions that had no answer for the delays caused by Saddam Hussein's deceptive diplomacy or the requirement for great power consensus in the UN (the systemic level of analysis)? The answer matters because when you fix something you can't change everything, even if you'd like to. In fall 2006, the opposition Democratic Party took control of both houses of Congress. Did this shift at the domestic level of analysis suffice to change American foreign policy in Iraq? It initiated a major struggle for control of Iraq policy between the legislative and executive branches. But a decisive shift in policy may require further changes at the individual level of analysis, namely a change in the American president. Even then, what if European or other great powers continue to veto measures to assist Iraq or disarm Iran? Will a new American president have to follow policies similar to those of the previous president because the primary causes of the policy stem from lack of consensus in the international system, not differences in the Congress or the presidency inside the United States at the domestic and individual levels of analysis? You can see how helpful levels of analysis can be for understanding and interpreting everyday policy controversies. (See Table 7-1 for a summary of liberal explanations for global terrorism.)

causal →
arrow

Global War on Terror: A Realist Outlook

Realists expect counterbalancing. Thus, they were focused on systemic events when the 9/11 attacks occurred. From this vantage point, the attacks were not isolated criminal acts or the consequences of some failure of diplomacy or international institutions and aid programs. They were the first attacks in almost two centuries on the American mainland, and the death toll was higher than it had been at Pearl Harbor, Hawaii (which in 1941 was still a U.S. territory). True, this time the aggressor was not a state and the victims were almost exclusively civilian, but from a realist perspective that only compounded, not lessened, the dangers. Nonstate actors might collude with rogue states to magnify the threat and its potential consequences.

Thus, while liberal perspectives emphasized the nonstate aspects of the new terrorist threat and sought to narrow, not widen, the conflict to apprehend specific nonstate terrorist groups, such as Al Qaeda, realist perspectives immediately labeled it a war. This **global war on terror** involved both rogue state and nonstate actors and could not be treated simply as a criminal act adjudicated by international courts and development institutions. Realist accounts suspected a wider conspiracy and reached for familiar instruments of flexible coalitions, sanctions, and war to terminate financial support for and to defeat the global enemy.

This is how power transition realists and the neoconservative school (which goes beyond realism by advocating identity elements of regime change and the spread of democracy) justified the U.S. breakout from standing alliances and international institutions. It was necessary because the threat was different, and NATO was not equipped to respond to terrorism and conflicts outside Europe. Moreover, NATO after the Cold War was largely an American enterprise. The allies brought few military assets to the table to fight conflicts outside Europe, unlike during the Cold War when allies fielded large armies to defend Europe's borders against Soviet forces. In Bosnia, as we observed, the EU had insufficient military capabilities to suppress violence and had to turn to the UN and then to NATO forces to end the crisis. The same thing happened in Kosovo. Thus, from realist perspectives most conscious of America's advantage in preponderant power, standing international institutions offered considerably less value to fight the 9/11 attackers. Greater advantage was achieved through independent action with ad hoc groups of nations that wished to contribute and undertake specific tasks associated with the immediate threat.

Was it a mistake to refuse NATO help in Afghanistan? It probably was, as liberal perspectives argue, because NATO was needed and called on later to help anyway. It might have made a big difference in the run-up to the Iraq conflict if the United States had asked NATO from the beginning to help in Afghanistan. NATO had no forces ready to go into Afghanistan in winter 2001–2002. Thus, U.S. forces could have conducted the initial assaults without NATO interference. Then NATO forces might have arrived in fall 2002 and created a very different diplomatic atmosphere for the debate about Iraq as well as subsequent developments in Afghanistan.

True, realist perspectives concede, but in September 2001 the United States did not know how long it would take to subdue Taliban forces in Afghanistan. The fighting might have stalemated by the time NATO forces arrived, and now the United States would have had to fight the war again by consensus, as it had in Kosovo. Moreover, NATO helped in Afghanistan for the first few years only in policing and reconstruction activities. The initial combat forces were supplied mostly by U.S. and British troops under a separate non-NATO command. Even after NATO assumed overall command in 2006, some NATO allies, such as Germany, refused to accept combat roles or argued conveniently that there was less need to use military force and advocated civilian construction approaches instead. Even in noncombat areas, allies failed to meet their commitments to supply helicopters, transport planes, and other equipment. From a realist perspective, this experience suggests that the decision not to rely on NATO was the right one—how much help would the allies have been in the early, more demanding combat stages of the Afghanistan campaign given that they evaded commitments in the later stages?

global war on terror a military campaign to defeat nonstate terrorist groups such as Al Qaeda and rogue state actors that assist terrorists by supplying training facilities, as the Taliban government did, or potentially WMDs, as it was thought that Iraq or a radical government in Pakistan might do.

Spotlight on threat and distribution of power

Spotlight on alliances

Nevertheless, if NATO had played a more central role from the start, NATO might have been more effective sooner in Afghanistan and, potentially at least, less divided on the Iraq intervention. After all, by 2006, even after bitter allied disputes, NATO was playing not only a central role in Afghanistan but even a modest role in Iraq, training local army and police forces.

Spotlight on international institutions

Traditional or power balancing realists accept the need to work through standing alliances such as NATO. But neoconservative or power transition realists consider such international institutions more as a trap than a support. Weaker countries use them to tie down stronger countries. As they see it, European members in NATO cannot compete with the United States in material capabilities, so, as other weak states have done historically, they use international institutions to restrain larger powers.[4] The European members insist that the United States make decisions only through NATO, while they spend far less on defense capabilities and do not risk the lives of their own troops in combat missions. Allies and other powers use the United Nations for the same purposes.

Spotlight on power transition

Let's think about the Iraq War from this neoconservative or power transition perspective. The United States and Britain positioned 200,000 forces in the Gulf to force inspectors back into Iraq. As we have noted, without those forces, there would have been no UN inspectors in Iraq and hence no diplomatic option to contain Iraq's nuclear program. France, Germany, and Russia did not contribute to these forces, yet now they hoped to use the UN Security Council to block the use of those forces and give the inspectors unlimited time to do their job. If the allies had contributed to the invasion forces to begin with, they may have had more influence over when to use them. And they would have certainly had to answer to their own people about how long they could keep such forces in harm's way without eventually using or withdrawing them. Power transition logic says that sharing influence always requires sharing power and danger.

Spotlight on relative power

The problem in a unipolar world, as power transition analysts see it, is the divorce between capability and responsibility. Smaller powers want responsibility but contribute few capabilities. They always advocate more diplomacy because international institutions give them some influence over diplomacy. They resist using force because once force is used they lose influence because they have no capabilities to contribute. If you have a hammer, you want to use it. If you don't, you don't want others to use it. The dilemma is a consequence of the distribution of power. Until NATO becomes a more balanced institution in which Europeans contribute significantly to combat capabilities, as they did on the central front in Europe during the Cold War, realist arguments suspect that institutions such as NATO and the UN are more committees to delay action than real capabilities to fight nasty wars. In the end, the European allies have to decide to strengthen their defense capabilities independently, convincing their

A statue of Saddam Hussein is brought down in Baghdad on April 9, 2003, symbolizing the toppling of Hussein's regime by coalition military might.

people not only to pay more for military forces but to risk the lives of their own sons and daughters in combat, not just in peacekeeping missions.

As power transition advocates see it, the problem extends to the broader Middle East conflict and policies toward other rogue states such as Syria, Iran, and North Korea. Diplomacy can accomplish only what the balance of power permits. George W. Bush pulled back from diplomatic efforts in the Arab-Israeli dispute and negotiations with North Korea even before September 11. Diplomacy was not working because, from a realist perspective, the balance of forces on the ground was moving against the moderate groups that support diplomatic solutions. After the failure of the Camp David talks in 2000, extremists gained ground throughout the Middle East. In Iran, Mahmoud Ahmadinejad won a rigged presidential election in 2005 and, in a replay of Saddam Hussein's policies, defied repeated UN resolutions and sanctions to stop Iran's nuclear program that included activities, such as enriching uranium, integral to a weapons capability. In the Palestinian Authority, Hamas, the militant Muslim faction, won the parliamentary elections in 2006, took control of Gaza when Israeli forces withdrew, and launched relentless missile attacks against Israel. And in Lebanon, the assassination of the moderate former prime minister, Rafik Al-Hariri, sparked renewed conflict in 2005 between supporters of Syria (which occupied Lebanon in the 1990s and withdrew its forces only under pressure in 2005) and proponents of Lebanese independence. As part of the Lebanese turmoil, Israel invaded southern Lebanon in 2006 and then withdrew without much gain. And, in a continuing effort to stabilize Iraq, the United States surged military forces into the country in 2007 to stem the growing insurgency against the new U.S.-supported Iraqi government. Meanwhile, in North Korea, the regime also became more extreme, increasing repression and not only concealing a secret enriched-uranium nuclear program (which it subsequently denied) but also exploding a primitive nuclear bomb in October 2006.

Thus, across a broad front, as realists see it, moderate forces were in retreat. Until the balance of forces was altered on the ground, diplomacy could not achieve very much. As Secretary of State Condoleezza Rice once said, "you are not going to succeed as a diplomat if you don't understand the strategic context in which you are actually negotiating."[5] To delay diplomacy while improving the balance of forces on the ground, Bush shunned Arafat in the early part of the decade (Arafat died in 2004) and devised the "road map," a framework for peace backed by the United States, Russia, the EU, and UN (the so-called Quartet), to strengthen moderate forces within the PA and Israel. Eventually, in November 2007, Bush launched a new round of Arab-Israeli peace talks. In Korea, the United States established the Six-Party Talks, a coalition of Japan, South Korea, China, and Russia to pressure Pyongyang multilaterally rather than the U.S. negotiating bilaterally with North Korea, as it had done in the 1990s. North Korea eventually concluded an agreement in February 2007 that allowed inspectors to return and dismantle its plutonium program, but Pyongyang still refused to document its enriched-uranium program or its assistance to Syria on the nuclear installation that Israel bombed in 2007. In all these cases, realist objectives sought to strengthen military or diplomatic positions before negotiating seriously, while liberal critics blasted the realist strategy for delaying diplomatic solutions while exacerbating military tensions.

Notice again the different emphasis of the realist and liberal perspectives on the use of diplomacy versus force. From the liberal perspective, the Iraq War constituted an unnecessary diversion from diplomacy in the Middle East and exacerbated terrorism in the region and the world. As liberal perspectives see it, American unilater-

Spotlight on balance of power

causal arrow

alism was the primary cause of increased extremism in Iran, Syria, and the Palestinian Authority. Diplomacy exacerbated war. From the realist perspective, the Iraq War reduced extremism, eliminating one state that rejected Israel, namely Hussein's Iraq, and reinforcing moderate leaders in countries such as Egypt, Jordan, and Saudi Arabia. The use of force strengthened diplomacy. The difference lies in judgments about whether the use of force makes diplomacy less effective (liberal factors being more important) or more effective (realist factors being more important).

causal arrow →

The Iraq debate was bitter and often personal. But, when seen from the vantage point of perspectives, there is no need to assume, as each side did—and immediate participants always do—that the other side was acting in bad faith. EU allies and perhaps also Russia looked to international institutions to solve the crisis (the liberal perspective) because they genuinely felt that the moral weight of the international community backed up by sanctions would suffice to contain and deter Iraq. They were a little disingenuous, we might argue, because they did not admit that force was the only way the inspectors got back into Iraq and they did not willingly accept their share of the burden in providing that force. On the other hand, the United States and Britain looked to the balance of power (the realist perspective) because they genuinely felt that institutional pressures and economic sanctions alone, which had been applied for more than a decade, would not suffice to disarm Iraq. They, too, were a bit disingenuous in the sense they were unlikely to trust any response Saddam Hussein might make to reveal and give up his WMDs. But, altogether, the disagreement between the allies was substantive and real, not contrived and mean-spirited.

Differing Judgments About Al Qaeda and Weapons of Mass Destruction

Perspectives also help illuminate two of the most troubling aspects of the Iraq crisis: the links between Iraq and Al Qaeda and the alleged existence of WMDs. The key information or facts about these two aspects were more or less known at the time by all the participants. But intelligence information does not exist in a vacuum; it has to be discovered, meaning someone has to decide to collect this or that type of information. Human intelligence was particularly limited and often wrong in the case of Iraq. There was the now-famous case of an Iraqi defector known as "Curveball" who supplied erroneous information about mobile chemical weapons factories before the invasion.[6] For years, intelligence agencies had underinvested in credible human agents compared, for example, to satellite information. Then, of course, intelligence information has to be interpreted. Intelligence analysts always disagree about facts. Indeed, good policy making depends on such disagreements, even though policy making is not made any easier as a result. If you have the idea that you would make the right decision if you just knew the classified intelligence that policymakers knew, think again. Intelligence information is never that decisive.

Spotlight on information

The issue of contacts between Iraq and Al Qaeda sharply divided supporters and opponents of the decision to invade Iraq. Here is what the bipartisan 9/11 Commission, which issued its report in summer 2004, found out about such contacts:

> [A]round this time [1997] bin Laden sent out a number of feelers to the Iraqi regime, offering some cooperation. None are reported to have received a significant response. . . .
> In mid-1998, the situation reversed: it was Iraq that reportedly took the initiative. In March 1998, after bin Laden's public fatwa [the declaration of a holy war] against the

United States, two al Qaeda members reportedly went to Iraq to meet with Iraqi intelligence. In July, an Iraqi delegation traveled to Afghanistan to meet first with the Taliban and then with bin Laden. Sources reported that one, or perhaps both, of these meetings were apparently arranged through bin Laden's Egyptian deputy, [al]Zawahiri, who had ties of his own to the Iraqis. . . .

Similar meetings between Iraqi officials and bin Laden may have occurred in 1999 during a period of some reported strains with the Taliban. According to the reporting, Iraqi officials offered bin Laden safe haven in Iraq. Bin Laden declined, apparently judging that his circumstances in Afghanistan remained more favorable than the Iraqi circumstances. The reports describe friendly contacts and indicate some common themes in both sides' hatred of the United States. But to date we have seen no evidence that these or the earlier contacts ever developed into a collaborative operational relationship. Nor have we seen evidence indicating that Iraq cooperated with al Qaeda in developing or carrying out any attacks against the United States.[7]

Opponents of the war did not hesitate to emphasize the conclusion that "no collaborative operational relationship" existed between Iraq and Al Qaeda. But supporters of the war wondered about the "friendly contacts" that did exist, especially the offer by Iraq to give bin Laden safe haven in Iraq, even if he had declined that offer at the time. The offer suggested a very substantial motivation to collaborate. After all, Iraq was offering to become another Taliban government to harbor and support bin Laden and Al Qaeda. And if Iraq offered safe haven once, might it not do so again? Moreover, what constitutes a "collaborative operational relationship" in the shadowy world of nonstate actors?

Our purpose here is not to adjudicate the different judgments that were made. Each citizen must do that on his or her own. We are just suggesting that perspective probably influenced these judgments as much as facts did. Someone looking at this intelligence from a liberal perspective emphasized the specific contacts and the absence of proven collaboration. Someone looking at it from a realist perspective emphasized the broader power context and potential alliance between common enemies of the United States. The first would be reluctant to connect the dots; the second would be more willing. Neither judgment ignored the facts. (See Table 7-2 for a summary of realist explanations for global terrorism.)

Spotlight on judgment

Table 7-2

The Causes of Global Terrorism: The Realist Perspective and Levels of Analysis		
Level of analysis		**Realist perspective**
Systemic	*Structure*	• Islamic and other states (Russia, France, Germany, China) counterbalance the unipolar power of United States
	Process	• Potential links between rogue states with WMDs and transnational non-state actors such as Al Qaeda; for example, nuclear assistance by the Pakistani-led A. Q. Khan network to Libya, North Korea, Syria, and Iran
Foreign policy		• Saudi foreign policy elites forge alliances with the West over opposition of radical Wahhabists at home, such as bin Laden, who reject the West
		• President George W. Bush surges military forces into Iraq over objections of the Democrat-controlled Congress
Domestic		• Rise to power of conservative parties in United States in 2000 and 2004 elections
Individual		• George W. Bush asserts American dominance

The box on page 245 explores similar differences in judgments about whether Saddam Hussein possessed WMDs. It asks the most interesting question of all: Why did Saddam Hussein risk an invasion and lose power if he knew he had no WMDs?

Democracy, Religion, or What? An Identity Perspective

In Chapter 6, we discuss how Professors Fukuyama and Huntington framed the issue of global identities after the Cold War in terms of the ultimate triumph of democracy versus the clash of civilizations. The terrorist attacks of 9/11 now focused this issue anew, especially in the context of the Middle East. Was the root cause of terrorism the tyranny of corrupt governments in the Middle East and, hence, the solution the long-term reform and transformation of these governments toward greater accountability and democracy? Or was the cause a religious fanaticism on the part of fundamentalist Islam that portended a wider, perhaps existential conflict between Islamic and western values and the solution ideological and terrorist warfare until one side mellowed or changed, as in the case of the Cold War? Or were both democracy and fundamentalism the wrong construction of identities for the West and Islam, so that the world would have to discover a new discourse as the solution to terrorism that offers justice and equality to all identities, whatever their roots in differing civilizations or political ideologies?

Greater Middle East Initiative

President George W. Bush apparently agreed with the view that democratic reform in the Middle East was crucial. Either out of conviction or because he found no WMDs in Iraq, he made the promotion of democracy the solution to terrorism in Iraq and the rest of the Middle East. To get at the roots of terrorism, the United States and international community had to transform the political regimes in the Arab and Muslim world into democracies. Notice that, from this perspective, unlike the liberal perspective, the primary sources of terrorism are not economic—poverty, disease, and unemployment. They are political—oppressive regimes that deny their people basic freedoms, such as a practical education, economic ownership, and political opportunity. Instead of allowing basic freedoms, these regimes siphon off millions of dollars in aid and oil revenues to finance corrupt and bloated bureaucracies and to foment foreign conflicts to unite and divert the people from domestic oppression. Unless these conditions of governance are addressed, this approach contends, liberal proposals to open markets and promote trade will be like "spitting into the wind." Political reform is a prerequisite for economic growth, reversing the liberal hope that economic growth brings political liberalization.

George W. Bush pressed for regime reforms in the Palestinian Authority before supporting further negotiations between the PA and Israel. Notice that regime or identity change precedes negotiations or liberal approaches. Bush insisted that regime change in Iraq was the only way that the world could ever be sure that Saddam Hussein would give up his WMDs or verify that these weapons did not exist. He proposed a broad program known as the Greater Middle East Initiative to bring democratic reforms to all the countries of the Middle East. In his inaugural address in January 2005, he declared it U.S. policy "to seek and support the growth of democratic move-

Spotlight on regime change

causal arrow

causal arrow

Using the Perspectives to Read

 Between

the Lines

Intelligence About Iraq's Weapons of Mass Destruction

The intelligence on WMDs provides a good example of differing judgments of the same facts. We can't take up the whole issue here. But consider the following. Not only American, but all the major powers' intelligence services (British, French, German, Russian, Chinese, Australian, and so on) concluded in early 2003 that Saddam Hussein possessed WMDs. As Hans Blix, the head of the UN inspection effort, reported to the Security Council two weeks before the invasion began, "intelligence agencies have expressed the view the proscribed programs [in Iraq] have continued or restarted in this period" since 1998. "It is further contended," he noted, "that proscribed programs and items are located in underground facilities . . . and that proscribed items are being moved around Iraq. . . ." Blix reported that the destruction of arms by Iraq to date "constitutes a substantial measure of disarmament," but he also reported that Iraq's initiatives to resolve questions about its capabilities, "three to four months into the new resolution [referring to UN Resolution 1441 passed in November 2002], cannot be said to constitute immediate cooperation, nor do they necessarily cover all areas of relevance. . . ."[1]

There are always dissenting views within intelligence agencies. So it is possible that the leadership in the United States and Britain manipulated the facts. Many critics emphasizing liberal factors such as the fail-ure of diplomacy and domestic institutions thought so. But German, French, and Russian intelligence agencies also agreed that Iraq had WMDs, and their governments opposed the war. So maybe other factors, such as counterbalancing U.S. power, played a role. Analysts reasoning from a realist perspective might think so.

Let's assume you are the decision maker. Do you act on the consensus intelligence (gathered from 1991 to 1998 and from December 2002 to March 2003) that Iraq still had weapons, or do you give international inspectors more time to gather more intelligence? There is room here for differing judgments without calling those who disagree with you stupid or wicked.

Finally, the greatest mystery of all is why Saddam Hussein risked everything, including ultimately his life, for something he did not have, namely WMDs. If he had WMDs, power balancing realists that opposed the war expected him to act rationally and not give them to terrorists. Liberal observers expected him to compromise at some point and not provoke the entire international community. But if he did not have WMDs, no one expected him to provoke an invasion. Yet he did just that rather than reveal the information that he had no WMDs. Was he motivated more by fanatical ideas than power? Neoconservatives emphasizing the importance of ideas might think so.

1. "In a Chief Inspector's Words: 'A Substantial Measure of Disarmament'," excerpts from reports by Hans Blix and Mohammed El Baradei to the UN Security Council, *New York Times,* March 8, 2003, A8.

ments and institutions in every nation and culture, with the ultimate goal of ending tyranny in our world."[8] And at the National Defense University in March 2005, he repeated the point: "It should be clear the best antidote to radicalism and terror is the tolerance kindled in free societies."[9]

Does the promotion of democracy, especially in the Middle East, bridge or widen the gap between the West and Islam? Or would it be better, as social constructivists might argue, to emphasize common human rights, not regime change, and to focus on economic, social, and cultural, not political, rights? Or is it possible that oil wealth and broader economic growth might simply be invested in WMDs and create more powerful and dangerous enemies, particularly if radical groups seize control of governments, as they did in Iran in 1979? And might not promoting democracy create the very opportunity for radicals to seize power in Saudi Arabia, Egypt, Pakistan, and elsewhere, which the West fears? Then what should the West do? Stand by and let extremists take power, as happened in Germany in 1933? Or intervene and keep a nondemocratic but friendly government in power, as France did in Algeria in 1992, when it installed a military government and ousted the Islamic radicals who had just won the elections? This issue became real in spring 2006 when Hamas, the Palestinian group that rejects Israel, won the PA elections and now sat in the Palestinian government.

causal arrow

There is plenty of room for differences in judgment about these weighty matters. We need to study hard, learn more, and always remember that in the end we have to decide. The facts don't decide for us; perspectives, instincts, and moral convictions have a role to play as well.

Fundamentalist Islam: A New Fanaticism

Another identity argument about the causes of global terrorism emphasizes the political ideas of fundamentalist Islam at the domestic and systemic process level of analysis. According to this argument, fundamentalist Islam operating within and between numerous Muslim states poses an existential threat to western values, much as communism did during the Cold War.[10] It advocates a theocratic world order or caliphate (the governmental form of earlier Islamic empires) that revives the purist values of ancient Islam and rules by religious law, which systematically discriminates against women and excludes most of the secular and market mechanisms of modern societies.

Spotlight on relative identities

Although most Muslims are not fundamentalists and most fundamentalists are not terrorists, there is, as Daniel Benjamin and Steven Simon point out, a "strong connection between the subculture of terrorism and a broader culture in which the basis of terrorist values is well established and legally unassailable."[11] Islam does not openly condone terrorism, but neither does it openly condemn it. In that sense, Islam is on the sidelines in the global war on terror. Which way Islam swings between the reformers and the fundamentalists—toward increasing modernization and secularism, on the one hand, or toward religious fervor and martyrdom, on the other—will determine how Islam relates to the West and whether that relationship becomes one of enemy, the earlier case with communism; rival, the case today between the West and China; or friend, the case among western countries.

Divisions Within Islam: Sunnis and Shiites

Where does fundamentalist Islam come from and how strong is it now and likely to become?

Muslims total about 1.5 billion people, roughly 25 percent of the world's population. They constitute the majority of the populations of a string of countries extending from Morocco across North Africa through the Middle East, to south and southeast Asia. Indonesia is the largest Muslim country, with over 200 million people. The center of Islam lies in the Middle East. Saudi Arabia safeguards the holy places of Mecca and Medina, the birthplace of Muhammad, the prophet who founded Islam, and the city of his famous *Hijra,* or migration, in 622 CE (the beginning, by the way, of the Muslim calendar).

Most Muslims are **Sunnis,** members of the branch of Islam that identifies with the caliphs, the elected successors of Muhammad dating back to the seventh century. A minority are Shia or **Shiites.** They identify with a renegade group that advocated divine rather than elective succession. Their leader was Ali, a paternal cousin of Muhammad and the husband of his only surviving daughter. When the third caliph, Uthman, was assassinated in 656, Ali became caliph. But in 661, he too was assassinated. His son, Husayn, tried to retrieve the caliphate in 680 but was massacred at Karbala and his head sent to Damascus. Later, this tragic slaying of the Prophet's grandson became the inspiration of the Shia movement, which divided Islam between orthodox (Sunnis) and radical (Shiites) camps.

Today the center of Shia Islam is located in the town of Qum in Iran, a Persian country, although many holy sites, such as Najaf and Karbala, are also located in Iraq, an Arab country. Sunni Islam was centered initially in Syria (Ummayad dynasty) and then in Iraq (Abbasid dynasty), and by the thirteenth century it had splintered into various dynasties in Egypt and elsewhere. Today, Egypt and Turkey represent more moderate Sunni branches of Islam, as does Indonesia.

Other radical branches of Islam developed over the centuries. When the Mongols stormed the Middle East in the thirteenth century, Taqi al-Din Taymiyya, a revered Sunni Muslim scholar, elevated *jihad,* or holy war, to the same level of doctrine as the five pillars of Islam—prayer, pilgrimage, alms, declaration of faith, and Ramadan (the Muslim holy days). He authorized holy war not only against infidels, or the "far enemy" (at that time the Mongols and Turks), but also against apostate rulers within Islam, or the "near enemy." Islam had to purify itself internally as well as defeat the infidels externally.

Holy war was not unique to Islam, of course. For two centuries before Taymiyya, Christian warriors had crusaded against Muslims to conquer their holy land of Jerusalem and surrounding territories. The Knights Templar and Hospitallers were Christian orders whose members were both priests and warriors called to wage their own version of holy war against Muslim infidels.[12] Schismatic wars within Christianity were also hardly unknown. Popes and emperors excommunicated and, indeed, executed or poisoned one another during the Middle Ages, and Protestants and Catholics fought the cataclysmic Thirty Years War in the seventeenth century.

As we ask in Chapter 2, why did the Islamic world fade in the fifteenth century and Christian Europe rise? "What went wrong?" as the Princeton scholar of Islam, Bernard Lewis, puts it.[13] For one thing, the Reformation and Enlightenment in Europe passed Islam by. The reasons are many and disputed: no separation of church and state in Islam, no concept of competitive politics or markets, the second-class status of Muslim women, and so on. But one consequence (and perhaps after 1500, also a cause) was western imperialism, the breakout of European energies and avarice that sent sailing ships around the world, western armies into Egypt under Napoleon in 1798, and then western colonialists into the Middle East in the nineteenth century. The experience of western imperialism and then, on top of that, Israel's creation and the imperialist ambitions of some Israelis to annex the West Bank and Gaza seared the Muslim mind and seeded the ground for a broad-based suspicion, if not hatred, of western life and values.

Saudi Arabia, the land of Islam's holy places, escaped imperialism, which made the presence of U.S. troops there in the 1990s all the more intolerable. Intolerance

Sunnis

members of the majority branch of Islam that identifies with the caliphs, the elected successors of Muhammad dating back to the seventh century.

Shiites

members of the minority sect of Islam that identifies with a renegade group in the seventh century that advocated divine rather than elective succession.

Spotlight on religious wars

Wahhabism
a rigid and puritanical form of Islam originating in the eighteenth century with the Arabian spiritual leader, Muhammad ibn Abd al-Wahhab.

causal ⟶
arrow

was based on a virulent version of Islam. In the eighteenth century, Muhammad ibn Abd al-Wahhab, a spiritual descendant of Taymiyya, teamed up with Muhammad Ibn Saud, then ruler of parts of Arabia, to unite the whole of Arabia. Al-Wahhab preached a rigid and puritanical form of Islam known as **Wahhabism,** which harkened back to the radical ancient men, or Salafis, of the early caliphates. Today, the alliance between Wahhabism and the royal family of Saud creates a situation in Saudi Arabia that exists in many other Muslim countries, such as Pakistan. Governments control the wealth and, in Saudi Arabia's case, oil and promote trade and other links with western societies, while religious leaders, the clerical establishments, control the society and educate the young people and wider citizenry to reject modern values and take up *jihad* against the western infidels. Elites balance domestic and systemic requirements at the foreign policy level of analysis, suggesting that, should the elites be toppled, major changes may follow, driven by domestic level (Whahhabist radicals in Saudi Arabia) or systemic level (Iranian intervention in Saudi Arabia) forces.

Today's Radical Islam

Sayyid Qutb, an Egyptian writer and former government official, brought many of the radical strands of Islam together in the mid-twentieth century and focused them on the United States. He came to the United States in 1948 and studied at Northern Colorado Teachers College, where he developed a strong distaste for American cultures and values. His puritanical view rejected not only western consumerism and usury (the charging of interest for the use of money, which earlier Christianity also condemned) but also the liberation of women, sexual license, and the breakdown of the family associated with western culture. Qutb saw the West as the enemy and urged Islam to go back to its seventh-century roots.

Qutb is the prophet of contemporary Islamic fundamentalism. Omar Rahman, the Blind Sheikh who was behind the first World Trade Center attack, and Osama bin Laden, who was behind the second, were both disciples of Qutb. Can these radical proponents of contemporary Islamic fundamentalism lead the rest of Islam to a worldwide confrontation with democracy and the West, much as Lenin and Stalin led radical Marxist forces to a global confrontation between the Soviet Union and the United States? Judgments differ. (See Table 7-3 for a summary of identity explanations for global terrorism.)

Table 7-3

The Causes of Global Terrorism: The Identity Perspective and Levels of Analysis		
Level of analysis		**Identity perspective**
Systemic	*Structure*	• Islamic fundamentalism seeks to reestablish seventh-century global caliphate
	Process	• Sunni and Shia states and groups align and interact transnationally, as in the case of Iranian Shia influence in southern Iraq
Foreign policy		• Saudi elites control foreign policy, while Wahhabists control domestic policy
Domestic		• Taliban fundamentalist forces take over Afghanistan to train 9/11 hijackers
Individual		• Osama bin Laden leads holy war

Whither the West and Radical Islam?

For some identity perspectives, which emphasize the relative distribution rather than the social construction of identities, radical Islam produced militant crusades against Europe in the past and, given the deep-seated resentments and absence of secular modernization, might do so again in the future. Much depends on how the rest of Islam swings. Some believe that there is enough resentment in Islamic countries to swell the ranks of holy warriors for a long time to come. Abdurrahman Wahid, former president of Indonesia, the world's largest Muslim country and a generally moderate one, says, "Wahhabi/Salafi ideology has made substantial inroads throughout the Muslim world. . . . [It is] a well-financed multifaceted global movement that operates like a juggernaut in much of the developing world, and even among immigrant Muslim communities in the West."[14] Estimates are that some 60,000 warriors trained in Afghanistan alone when it was under Taliban control. If we count the thousands trained elsewhere and the additional thousands who sympathize with and finance *jihad*ism, sleeping cells may well proliferate everywhere in the industrialized world.[15] That these time bombs provide the potential for a long-term global war that eventually undermines western stability and confidence is certainly not out of the question. Especially troubling is the possibility that terrorists may join up with state power. What if Saudi Arabia with its oil wealth and Pakistan with its nuclear capability should fall into the hands of the Islamic radicals? Both countries, but especially Pakistan, suffer from political instability. From this perspective, it would not be wise to underestimate the internal values and convictions that drive radical Islam. Without full modernization, the values of radical Islam may not be enough to succeed. But, don't forget, the Soviet Union never fully modernized, yet it produced an enormous challenge for the West and caused untold suffering and death.

causal arrow

Others, taking a more liberal perspective that emphasizes feedback and modernization, disagree. They see radical Islam as being no worse than Christian fundamentalism and worry that Jewish fundamentalism (for example, orthodox demands for annexation of West Bank and Gaza) provokes much Arab resentment. From this perspective, it is better to downplay the ideological causes of the conflict and pursue trade and development to get at the roots of poverty and despair that breed terrorism. The ranks of radical Islam may not be so great. The 9/11 hijackers were educated Arabs who were uprooted from their own societies and disaffected with their experiences in western societies where, like their mentor Qutb, they studied. According to some reviews of the biographies of known terrorists, three-quarters of them come from the upper or middle classes.[16] Only a small percentage came out of **madrassas,** or Muslim religious schools, some of which teach hatred and holy war toward the West. So perhaps, as Oliver Roy, a British author, argues, the number of terrorists is much smaller than the totals we have cited.[17] This smaller number may be better educated, but they are apparently educated for no purpose in that there are few jobs at home to absorb their energies except in corrupt bureaucracies or oil-sodden royal families. Thus, if education alone is not the answer to terrorism, modernization may still be. Diversifying Persian Gulf countries away from oil and opening up manufacturing, investments, and exports might not only create more jobs but also reorient incentives in religious schools to teach more practical subjects.

causal arrow

madrassas
Muslim religious schools, some of which teach hatred and holy war toward the West.

Analysts taking a realist perspective see a more systemic phenomenon of power balancing at work. Although China and Russia cooperated with the United States in Afghanistan, their interest was self-motivated; they wanted to restrain terrorist radicals

causal arrow

Afghan children in Kabul study in a madrassa, or religious school. Under the Taliban, madrassas fostered hatred of the West.

Spotlight on
counterbalancing

in their own countries. From a realist perspective, they have larger systemic interests in opposing U.S. hegemony. Even before 9/11, Russia and China had created the Shanghai Five, which included Kazakhstan, Kyrgyzstan, and Tajikistan, renaming it in 2001 the Shanghai Cooperation Organization (SCO) and adding Uzbekistan as a member and other countries as observers—Mongolia, Iran, Pakistan, and India. The SCO promotes cooperation, including joint military exercises, to defend common interests and counter U.S. dominance. Russia and China also resisted hard-line U.S. policies toward Iran and North Korea. And in 2007 Russia suspended its participation in the Treaty on Conventional Armed Forces in Europe (CFE) and vigorously opposed U.S. plans to deploy missile defenses in the Czech Republic and Poland to defend against Iranian missiles. China cultivated governments in the Middle East and Africa (for example, Iran and Sudan) as well as in Latin America (for example, Cuba and Venezuela), both to gain access to oil and to counterbalance American influence. Radical Islam was becoming a pretext for a wider campaign to reduce American hegemony and influence. Although Huntington's anticipation of a Confucian-Islamic alliance to counterbalance Western power may not yet be fully visible, realist perspectives saw disturbing developments in that direction.

Local and Regional Roots of Conflict

ethnic groups
social organizations in which the group is primarily defined by families and blood relatives or by the idea of some kind of kinship.

The terrorist attacks of 9/11 sparked global responses, but the roots of religious, ethnic, and national conflicts are local and ancient. Ethnic and religious differences have fragmented humankind from earliest times. **Ethnic groups** originate with families and blood relatives and extend outward to include distant ancestors and artificial kinship. The early rulers in Mesopotamia and China were family dynasties, which grew to encompass broader communities, such as clans and tribes. Ancient communities identified with cities, such as Babylon or the Greek city-states, and regions, such as Assyria. Rulers often served as spiritual leaders, interceding between the people and fearsome gods and differentiating communities by religion and mythology. Ethnic differences produced conflict and violence. Germanic tribes, for example, plundered the northern borders of the Roman Empire; and Mongolian clans, such as Attila's Huns, sacked and raided Chinese provinces as well as European villages.

Religious sects divided Christendom and Islam and shaped enduring differences between Catholics and Orthodox Christians and between Shiite Muslims and Sunni Muslims. Catholic bishops and royal dynasties ruled feudal Europe, while Muslim imams and caliphs governed the Golden Age of Islam.

religious sects
social organizations in which the group is defined by participation in a particular religion or subgroup (or denomination) of a religion.

Over the centuries, ethnic groups collected into larger entities that emphasized territorial independence and became known as states and national groups. The Germanic tribes coalesced initially under the Holy Roman Empire and then the German Confederation. The Frankish and Anglo-Saxon tribes established the distinct and contiguous territorial states of France and England. During the Thirty Years War, religious differences demarcated separate Protestant and Catholic states. The French Revolution inspired a more abstract or ideological notion of nationality that went beyond territory. Ethnic peoples, who had once ruled themselves or only imagined that they had or should, clamored for independence. The unification of Germany and Italy symbolized the new nation-state defined by culture and language as well as territory. By the twentieth century, national groups became the basis of statehood throughout the world. Some national movements differentiated themselves on the basis of virulent racist ideologies, such as fascism; others differentiated themselves on the basis of economic forces that determined class, such as Marxist-Leninism; and still others differentiated themselves on the basis of political ideologies, such as liberalism and socialism. But all such movements were identified by distinct territories and borders.

In much of the world, these ancient and local sources of ethnic, religious, and national fragmentation remain strong today. Saddam Hussein, for example, came from a Sunni tribe that identifies with the city and region of Tikrit, located north of Baghdad. His autocratic rule was based mainly on support from his local tribe, and Tikrit became one of the richest cities in Iraq. The Basque people in Spain have their own region, language, and ethnic characteristics and seek independence from Madrid. Quebec province in Canada has a separatist movement that advocates withdrawal from Ottawa and English-speaking Canada. Clan violence divides Somalia. Ethnic and religious divisions fracture unity in numerous other countries. National conflicts, often over territory, divide still other groups—Pakistan and India, Palestine and Israel, China and Tibet, and Japan and China, among others.

There are 2,000–5,000 distinct linguistic groups in the world. The major religious groups number 2.1 billion Christians, 1.5 billion Muslims, 900 million Hindus, 394 million Chinese folk religions, 376 million Buddhists, 300 million tribal and animist religions, 100 million new or syncretistic religious groups formed since 1800, 14 million Jews, 6.2 million Confucianists, and about 900 million atheists.[18] The major religious groups are divided further into numerous sects; Christianity alone boasts more than 2,000 denominations. And there are, as of 2008, 192 nation-states. So, it is obvious that we can't cover all of the conflicts generated by ethnic, religious, and national differences.

In the rest of this chapter, we discuss what causes these conflicts and how they might be resolved. Not surprisingly, realist, liberal, identity, and critical theory perspectives propose different causes and solutions for local and regional conflicts, just as they do for global ones. Then we examine selected conflicts in greater detail: Iraq as a prototype of ethnic and religious differences, China-Taiwan as an example of a dispute within a nationality, and the Arab-Israeli conflict as a national conflict between two civilizations.

Ethnic Conflicts

Realist perspectives see ethnic conflicts as a consequence of two factors: the cognitive needs of individuals to feel positive about their group and the physical needs to cope with the enduring circumstances of anarchy (namely competition and scarce resources). Liberal perspectives see ethnic conflicts as largely the result of learned behavior instilled by political elites or of the failure of domestic and international institutions. Identity perspectives see ethnic divisions as constructed either by conscious choice or, more commonly, social discourses that justify discrimination by race, class, or other means.

Because ethnic conflicts are rooted in enduring cognitive and situational needs, realist perspectives conclude that they are relatively hardwired or primordial. They are based on ancient hatreds or enduring cultural differences and cannot be easily changed. The best way to deal with them is by partition or secession secured by a balance of power among equal and independent states. Liberal perspectives conclude that ethnic conflicts are caused by elite manipulation and can be ameliorated by the enlightened intervention of domestic leaders or international institutions. **Federalism,** for example, offers a way to decentralize power to accommodate tribal and regional differences, and economic development creates more resources to redistribute and ameliorate ethnic conflicts. Growth changes the game from a zero-sum struggle over limited resources to a non-zero-sum increase in mutual gains. Identity perspectives view conflict as ideationally constructed and thus seek to develop new, overarching ideas, such as tolerance and democracy, to integrate multiethnic differences. **Constitutional solutions,** such as divided powers and pluralism, inculcate new norms of equality and human rights, which respect ethnic, religious, and national differences and resolve them by common procedures under the rule of law that protects minorities. The box on page 253 lists selected ethnic conflicts.

federalism
a method of decentralizing power to accommodate tribal and regional differences.

constitutional solutions
resolutions to ethnic and religious conflicts that implement a constitution and promulgate norms of equality and human rights.

Realist Solutions—Partition

As realists see it, ethnic identities serve a necessary purpose. They offer people meaningful associations that make them feel good about their group and provide for their safety and welfare.[19] After all, family is the basic building block of society. It nurtures and protects individual identities. It is not surprising that, since the first recorded political societies in Mesopotamia, ethnic groups have existed and persisted.

From a realist perspective, politics should accommodate this reality rather than trying to reengineer the human family. Historically, accommodation has been achieved by recognizing multiple actors. To be sure, actors have grown in size as technology made it possible to expand the scope of governance. But larger groups have their limits. From the realist perspective, they cannot provide cognitive satisfaction for everyone. The family of common humanity may exist, but, if it is mostly rhetoric, it is too amorphous to galvanize loyalties and, if it is real, it may smother diversity and freedom. Thus, multiple, separate groups, however large, drive the process of international

Selected Ethnic Conflicts Around the World

Democratic Republic of Congo	Fighting in the remote eastern area of the country along the Rwandan border from 1994 on led to the toppling of Mobutu Sese Seko, Congo's postindependence dictator. Laurent Kabila succeeded him, but Rwanda and Uganda intervened to oppose the Kabila government. Other countries—Zimbabwe, Angola, Namibia, Chad, and Sudan—entered the civil war on Kabila's side. Access to diamonds and other resources fueled the fighting.
Rwanda and Burundi	Minority Tutsi elites, originally favored by colonialists, battle majority Hutu tribes. When the first democratically elected Hutu president of Burundi was assassinated in 1993, Hutus went on a rampage in Rwanda, killing almost a million Tutsis and driving another 2 million into exile. Fighting between Hutu rebels and the Rwandan Tutsi government continues along the border with Congo.
Sudan	An Arab Islamic (Sunni) government in the north battles an animist and Christian black population in the south; the two sides are temporarily held together by a fragile agreement signed in 2005, while local Arab militia, known as Janjaweed, raids and pillages African villages in the western province of Darfur. In both conflicts, some 3 million people have been killed and another 6 million driven into exile.
Somalia	Eighty-five percent of the people belong to the same ethnic group, and all of them are Sunni Muslims. But since 1991 clans in the northwest fight to form an independent Somaliland, while other clans in the northeast run a semi-autonomous state known as Puntland. In June 2006, Islamic fundamentalists seized the capital Mogadishu, driving out a group of feuding warlords. Ethiopia intervened to fight the fundamentalists.
Bosnia and Kosovo	When the former Yugoslavia collapsed in 1991, fighting broke out between Orthodox Serbs and Catholic Croats in Croatia, followed by conflicts in Bosnia-Herzegovina among Croats, Serbs, and Bosnian Muslims and in Macedonia between Orthodox Macedonians and Albanian Muslims. In 1999, Muslims and Serbs battled in Kosovo, a province of Serbia, leading to interim autonomy under international auspices. In February 2008, Kosovo, backed by western states, declared independence from Serbia over the objections of Serbia and Russia.
Lebanon	Druze family elites, Maronite Christians, Greek Orthodox Christians, Sunni Muslims, Shiite Muslims, and a series of intervening countries, most recently Syria, vie for power in the country, most violently in 1958, during the long civil war from 1975–1990, and after the assassination of Rafiq Hariri in 2005. Hezbollah controls southern Lebanon monitored by a weak UN force.
Russia	Conflict persists in Chechnya on Russia's southern border, where the people speak a different language and are mostly Muslim, and spills over into the eastern region known as Dagestan, where people speak at least thirty different mutually unintelligible languages.
Afghanistan	Mostly Sunni, principal tribes—Pashtuns (42 percent) in the south and Tajiks (27 percent), Uzbeks (9 percent), and Hazaras (9 percent) in the north and west—fought Soviets in the 1980s and then one another in the 1990s, leading to the fundamentalist Taliban government, Osama bin Laden's terrorist camps, and the 9/11 attacks. Today, U.S.-backed government fights Taliban insurgents who have sanctuaries in Pakistan.
Southeast Asia	Chinese immigrants—who constitute 77 percent of the population in Singapore, 24 percent in Malaysia, 14 percent in Thailand, 3 percent in Indonesia, 2 percent in the Philippines, and 1 percent in Laos, Cambodia, and Vietnam and who control 80 percent of listed companies in Singapore and Thailand, 62 percent in Malaysia, 50 percent in the Philippines, and as high as 70 percent in Indonesia—are often targets of ethnic violence, especially in economic crises.
Latin America	Amerindians constitute a majority or near majority in Bolivia, Peru, Guatemala, and Ecuador, and they fight exclusion and discrimination in Latin American society, which is largely dominated, as Amy Chua writes, by "taller, lighter-skinned, European-blooded elites."[1]
North America	Quebec, French-speaking province in Canada, votes periodically on whether to secede from English-speaking Canada.
Europe	Basque and Catalonian regions in Spain seek autonomy, and Northern Ireland is divided between Unionists (Protestants), who want to remain part of Great Britain, and Republicans (Catholics), who want to become part of Ireland.

1. Amy Chua, *World on Fire* (New York: Anchor, 2004), 57.

politics and indeed prevent the consolidation of dominance by single or hegemonic groups.

From this perspective, it makes sense to separate hostile ethnic groups. While realist observers initially feared instability from the dissolution of the former Yugoslavia and Soviet Union, they subsequently embraced the idea of separate states for individual provinces. Separation worked in the case of the fifteen Soviet republics and the former Yugoslav republics of Slovenia, Croatia, Macedonia, and Montenegro, all of which became independent after 1991. And, for realist observers, **partition** may still be the best solution today in Bosnia and Kosovo, where Serb and Muslim groups resist integration; indeed, in 2008 the world community moved toward the recognition of Kosovo independence. Forcing hostile people to live together is possible only if one group coerces or dominates the others, as Serbia did in the cases of Yugoslavia and Kosovo and as Russia did in the case of the former Soviet Union. It is better for each group to manage its own affairs.

A case in point is Africa. From a realist perspective, colonialism forced diverse ethnic groups to live together in new African nations, and this legacy contributes, at least in some part, to the many ethnic conflicts in Africa today. State boundaries in Africa followed arbitrary colonial boundaries drawn in Europe. Ethnic groups were forced together and postindependence unity was possible only through the dominance of one ethnic group or coalition by another. German colonialists in Burundi and Rwanda, for example, relied on Tutsis, an ethnic group that made up only 14 percent of the population, to control the Hutus, which made up 85 percent (the vast majority) of the population. They instilled in Tutsi elites theories of racial superiority, which Belgium perpetuated when it took over the German colonies after World War I. As realist perspectives see it, the requirements of governing in such multiethnic situations caused the construction of racial theories to justify the rule of one ethnic group by another.

Notice how in this realist case power does not ignore ideas but shapes them to suit the needs of power! Elite leadership and manipulation may be involved, to be sure, but they are now intervening factors between power and ideas, not independent causes, as liberal perspectives might argue. The cause is the requirement of power to govern an unsustainable mix of ethnic groups, and too much is expected of leadership to manage such situations without oppression. Resentment and rebellion by marginalized ethnic groups become endemic.

African ethnicity, of course, may have been so diverse that it was not possible to accommodate all ethnic differences by partition. And referenda or other means to ascertain local preferences for national boundaries may have unleashed a wave of violence of their own. Still, it is worth pondering, from a realist perspective, how different Africa's experience over the past fifty years might have been if national boundaries had been drawn with greater attention to ethnic compatibilities. Nigeria, for example, has over 300 ethnic groups, including four major ones: Hausa (21 percent), Yoruba (21 percent), Ibo (18 percent), and Fulani (11 percent). In 1965, when oil was discovered in the Ibo region, the Ibos declared independence, calling their region Biafra. A civil war followed. Biafra lost, and more than a million people died. Today, fighting in Nigeria persists between the Muslim-dominated Hausa and Fulani tribes in the north and the Christian-dominated Ibo and Yoruba tribes in the south.

But partition also has its downside. It rewards separatists and creates incentives for ethnic groups to expel one another in what is called **ethnic cleansing.** This is what happened in Bosnia. When Yugoslavia dissolved in 1991, ethnic groups proceeded to seize territory held by minority groups and drive them out. Serbians slaughtered 7,000

partition

the separation of hostile ethnic or religious groups into different territories or states.

causal ⟶
arrow

ethnic cleansing

the systematic persecution, torture, and killing or removal of a religious or ethnic group with the intent to take over the territory of that group.

Muslim men and boys in Srebrenica, expecting later to annex Bosnian territory to Serbia. Any resolution of borders in Bosnia, thus, either sanctioned the ethnic cleansing that took place during the war or brought refugees back to re-create the same mix of ethnic groups that existed before violence erupted. Partition, therefore, may not resolve but simply displace conflict. When Slovenia and Croatia separated from Yugoslavia, their separation did not end the conflict. It simply led to more fighting, this time between Serbia and Croatia over the Serbian-inhabited province of Krajina inside Croatia. There, Croatian military leaders committed atrocities for which they now stand trial before a special tribunal in The Hague, Netherlands. Unless a balance of power exists and works well, which is the realist way to accommodate separation, separation merely stimulates competitive armaments and is itself prone to instability. At one point in the Bosnian conflict, for example, some realist solutions advocated arming the Muslims so they could better defend themselves against Serbs and Croats. If some kind of intervention is necessary to ensure the balance of power, however, maybe that intervention could also incorporate institutional and leadership innovations that might mitigate ethnic antagonisms, as liberal perspectives advocate.

Liberal Solutions—Peacekeeping and Reconciliation

Liberal perspectives dispute the claim that ethnic identities are hardwired and require separation. People, they argue, tend to exaggerate the influence of ancient hatreds on behavior and overlook the influence of elite leadership and institutional factors. Weak or failed states are the principal reason ethnic conflicts get out of control. When domestic institutions fail, ethnic groups face more intense security dilemmas. One side resists disarming because it cannot be sure that the other side will disarm. Thus, anything that reduces distrust lessens incentives toward violence.[20] Domestic institutions offer greater transparency and reduce the level of fear. Liberal perspectives see a positive role for institutions in domestic conflicts, just as they do in international conflicts.

International institutions can help to rebuild domestic institutions. The United Nations and other organizations have been involved in most of the ethnic conflicts since the end of the Cold War. UN peacekeeping or observer missions were or still are present in Burundi, Democratic Republic of Congo, Sudan, Somalia, Lebanon, Kosovo, Macedonia, Afghanistan, and numerous other places. In 2007, the UN had 100,000 military and civilian personnel deployed in over seventeen countries at a cost of $5.6 billion per year. The EU keeps the peace in Bosnia, and NATO is involved in Afghanistan and supports peacekeepers from the African Union in Darfur. The objective of outside intervention in these cases is, first, to separate the belligerents; second, to feed the war-ravaged populations; third, to mediate the disputes; and fourth, to reconstruct in some fashion common institutions and leadership to overcome divisions. These efforts range from simple monitoring and reporting about arms and militia movements to reconstruction and nation-building; however, they generally stop short of democracy promotion or regime change. The hope, characteristic of liberal perspectives, is that behavioral habits learned through daily and ongoing contact in common institutions will suffice eventually to surmount antagonistic identities.

According to liberal perspectives, **elite manipulation** of ethnic differences and historical memories are major factors in ethnic conflicts. Leaders exploit people's fears to advance their own personal and group interests. Slobodan Milosevic in Serbia, for example, incited violence to massacre Bosnian Muslims and later stood trial for these acts in The Hague (he died suddenly in captivity in 2006). Other Serbian leaders in

Spotlight on
failed states and institutions

Spotlight on
UN peacekeeping activities

elite manipulation
leaders' exploitation of people's fears to advance their own personal and group interests; the principal cause, according to liberal perspectives, of ethnic conflicts.

Bosnia, such as Ratko Mladić and Radovan Karadžić, are still being hunted for similar war crimes. Violence in Yugoslavia was not inevitable. The borders of the Yugoslav republics had been drawn in the 1940s and 1950s on the basis of extensive negotiations and consultations, unlike many borders in Africa. Most republics had mixed populations that lived peacefully side by side. Some 3 million people, out of a population of 22 million, were the products of ethnically mixed marriages or were themselves married to someone of a different ethnicity.[21] So, violence had to be incited, liberal perspectives contend. But once violence begins, it is self-perpetuating; people grow fearful where before they were tolerant. The extent to which elites incite or respond to mass fear is hard to pin down and ultimately depends on judgment. But the fact that animosity and conflict foster thuggish behavior is undisputed. Look at the behavior of African leaders such as Mobutu in the Democratic Republic of Congo or Robert Mugabe in Zimbabwe.

International interventions try to stop and reverse destructive elite behavior. Peacekeeping forces have kept the peace in Bosnia and Kosovo, with minor flare-ups, since 1995. They have also stopped the butchery in Sierra Leone and Liberia. Where fighting continues, as in the Darfur region of Sudan or eastern part of the Democratic Republic of Congo, the problem is usually that there are not enough peacekeeping forces. Once fighting stops, international institutions undertake **post-conflict reconstruction** activities that resettle ethnic groups back into the areas from which they were expelled, rebuild infrastructure and homes destroyed in the conflict, and mediate political processes of reconciliation and power sharing. In the Democratic Republic of Congo, for example, UN mediators facilitated a cease-fire agreement in 1999. Although fighting continued, all parties eventually signed a power-sharing agreement in 2003. Rival leaders hold various posts in a shaky transition government in Kinshasa, while rival tribes, Lendu and Hema, continue to clash far from Kinshasa in the Ituri region along the Ugandan border. A 17,000-strong UN force tries to keep the peace. But the area is filled with thousands of refugees, and the fighting is gruesome. Many of the combatants are youths and even children. They are often high on drugs. They rape, hack people to death, and indulge in primitive rituals such as pulling out the hearts of enemies and wearing women's wigs and dresses to ward off death in battle.

Thus, international interventions are no panacea either. First, international peace-keeping forces are usually ill-trained and insufficiently supported to carry out their missions. For example, when Serbian forces entered Srebrenica in 1995, Dutch UN forces fled in front of them. The Serbian troops actually wore UN uniforms and fooled Muslim inhabitants into cooperating. Second, UN officials and troops may be corrupt. Reports found that UN peacekeeping forces in the Democratic Republic of Congo were involved in drugs and rape, often abusing their positions of power over local populations.[22] Third, there are limits to international interventions. The further international institutions get into the process of nation-building, the more difficult it is for them to remain neutral. Inevitably, domestic groups, particularly minority ones, seek to use international institutions to back their own narrow interests. International institutions get caught between a rock and a hard place. For example, if the UN, which is trying to mediate a long-term solution in Kosovo, presses for independence, the Serb minority and Serbia strongly resist. If it advocates autonomy, the majority Albanian population in Kosovo resists and threatens to secede and form a greater Albania. When Kosovo declared independence in early 2008 backed by a number of western states, Serbian nationalists backed by Russia protested violently, burning the U.S. Embassy. As identity perspectives would argue, lasting solutions depend on nation-building and

post-conflict reconstruction
activities to resettle and rebuild areas ravaged by ethnic conflict.

the reconstruction of ethnic identities, not just peacekeeping and the reconstruction of physical facilities.

Identity Solutions—Nation-Building

How do various ethnic groups acquire a sense of nationhood? This is a central question from an identity perspective. **Nationhood** involves reordering the priority of manifold identities held by individuals. At any one time, people feel loyalty to family, local communities, religious organizations, and a national community. In strong states, individuals may identify with their ethnic or religious group in private life, but they tend to associate more with the nation or state in public life. As *Financial Times* columnist Krishna Guha writes, "ethnic and religious identity may define values, but citizenship must define attitudes to law and political process."[23] Citizenship involves a **civic identity,** as opposed to an ethnic one, and means that people are willing to submit to the laws of a common government rather than those of separate ethnic or religious groups. They entrust their physical safety to a set of institutions that go beyond their specific group and that they consider to be legitimate.

A key determinant of group identity, therefore, is the authority that people turn to and consider legitimate to make and enforce the law. Which group or institution has this legitimate authority and can use force against the people if they break the law or can use force on their behalf if some other group attacks the people? When threats emerge, do people turn to their ethnic group to defend them or to a local or national government? This is a life-wrenching choice. For example, at the outbreak of the American Civil War, General Robert E. Lee was asked why he had joined the Confederacy even though he was a West Point graduate and believed the Union was right on the question of preserving national unity. He said it was because he could not draw his sword against his own family and state of Virginia. At that moment, he was saying that his family and regional ties were stronger than his national ones. Family or ethnic ties are always strong. If the nation is to be constructed or preserved, however, national memories and allegiance need to be stronger. Bosnian Serbs and Croats need to see themselves as more distinct from the Croats in Croatia and the Serbs in Serbia than from the Serbs, Croats, and Muslims living inside Bosnia. Chechens eventually have to trust Moscow more than their own provincial leaders. Non-Arabs in Sudan have to look to the capital, Khartoum, for help rather than to their own tribal leaders. Protestants in Northern Ireland have to trust Dublin more than London, and ethnic Chinese have to rely more on the Indonesian or Malaysian governments where they reside to protect them than on the prospect of flight to Hong Kong or some other foreign refuge when trouble arises.

Setting out the requirements of nationhood in this fashion suggests how difficult it may be to achieve and why so many analysts are skeptical of **nation-building.** Still, this is the process throughout history by which ethnic groups have evolved toward nationhood and, in some cases, such as the EU, beyond nationhood. It is a long-term process. It may be important to start people moving in a collective direction without knowing the exact destination, as liberal perspectives would emphasize. But eventually people have to figure out where they want to wind up. What kind of people do they want to be? Do they want a religious or secular state? Do they want a democratic or authoritarian government?

For many who view ethnic conflict from an identity perspective, democracy promotion becomes the goal and long-term solution to ethnic conflict. Indeed, as politi-

nationhood

a status acquired by states strong enough to protect their borders and command the loyalty of their citizens.

civic identity

identity constructed when people are willing to submit to the laws of a common government rather than those of separate ethnic or religious groups.

Spotlight on construction of identities

nation-building

process by which ethnic groups evolve toward nationhood.

cal scientist Amitai Etzioni argues, ethnic separation is justified only in cases where ethnic groups are fighting against oppression: "Only when secessionist movements seek to break out of empires—and only when those empires refuse to democratize—does self-determination deserve our support."[24] From an identity perspective, the moral or normative claim to democracy may be the only way to adjudicate ethnic conflicts. Liberal perspectives are more skeptical. As Raymond C. Taras and Rajat Ganguly argue, "liberals may sympathize with the motives and moral claims [such as democracy] that separatist movements embody, but they insist that other ways are available to satisfy their demands short of recognizing their right of secession."[25]

This is a classic case of a difference in judgment between identity and liberal perspectives looking at ethnic conflicts. An identity perspective emphasizes the importance of ideational forces over institutional ones and justifies ethnic secession if it leads to more democracy. The liberal perspective emphasizes processes within existing institutions despite separate moral claims and expects to find ways to accommodate moral differences short of secession.

causal arrow

Thus, international interventions to deal with ethnic conflicts through the reconstruction of identities also have their limits. At some point, unless all outside parties share similar political values, they will disagree about the political form nation-building should take. Russia, for example, is skeptical of democracy in the Balkans and in Iraq. China is equally skeptical of democracy in Taiwan and in North Korea (for example, through unification with a democratic South Korea). Some African countries are fragile and vulnerable. One-party rule based on the dominant ethnic group may not be democratic, but it is potentially more stable, especially in countries where ethnic and family ties are stronger than national ones. The Kikuyu tribe, which ruled Kenya since its independence in 1963, maintained stability but in the process alienated the minority Luo and other tribes, which ignited violence in late 2007 after disputed elections. Constructing new identities is as political as it gets. Little wonder that talk about regime change, especially by force, sparks controversy. But even softer versions of regime change trigger widespread disagreement. It may seem self-evident to Americans that a multiethnic society is to be preferred over a partitioned society and that democracy is the best, perhaps only decent, way to construct a multiethnic society. But it is certainly easy to understand why communist societies saw that goal for many years as objectionable and why fundamentalist and deeply divided societies today find it not only dangerous but immoral.

Critical Theory Perspective

David Campbell offers us an example of a critical theory perspective on ethnic conflict. Campbell is a deconstructivist; as he writes, "deconstructivist thought calls for an ongoing political process of critique and invention that is never satisfied that a lasting solution can or has been reached."[26] Notice that deconstructivism as a critical theory denies the possibility of objective analysis and causal solutions. Rather, it envisions an endless process of inquiry and critique designed to open up space for alternative points of view, particularly for minority voices.

Spotlight on deconstructivism

In the case of the ethnic conflict in Bosnia in the early 1990s, Campbell describes the problem as a clash of two narratives, or ways of interpreting reality. The international community brought to the conflict a narrative of national identity and territorial integrity that forced participants to think in terms of exclusive and separate ethnic states. The idea of demarcated territories and fixed identities was central to the system of sovereign nation-states. But it was completely antithetical, Campbell argues, to the historical narrative of Muslims in Bosnia, who had lived for centuries under a deterritorialized concept of identity. "In the Ottoman empire," he explains, "there existed a communal form that embodied the idea of multiculturalism as the pluralization of the possibilities of being on the same territory." [27] People lived in communities that shared a common religion but not a common language, territory, history, or ethnicity. They treated ethno-religious differences the same way they treated differences between men and women or rural and urban dwellers. In other words, ethno-religious differences were not the basis of separation but of pluralization.

From this critical theory perspective, the intervention of the international community in the Bosnian conflict was destructive because all the mainstream perspectives envisioned by the international community mandated territorialized identities. Realist perspectives advocated separate ethnically defined territorial states; liberal perspectives emphasized building a single institutionalized territorial nation integrating multiple identities; and identity perspectives called for assimilation to national, as opposed to ethnic, identities to facilitate the cohesion of a territorial state. No perspective envisioned the possibility of a nonnationalist alternative that resisted both exclusiveness and assimilation. Campbell's purpose, like that of other critical theorists, is to open up space for these alternative political ideas. In the case of Bosnia, he applauds the work of many Bosnian NGOs, such as the Forum of Tuzla Citizens and Circle 99 in Sarajevo, which tried to articulate other narratives but were ignored by international institutions.

Iraq—What Is the Solution?

Iraq illustrates many of the classic features of ethnic and religious conflict, including the struggle to define a national identity. It has a proud history that evokes memories of past self-governance and grandeur. As we learn in Chapter 2, Baghdad was the center of the Abbasid dynasties that ruled Islam at the peak of its golden age. Subsequently Iraq was part of the Ottoman Empire, where Turkish dynasties served as the last caliphates of the Muslim world. Iraq also experienced colonialism. During World War I, Britain encouraged the Arabs to revolt against the Ottoman Turks, who were aligned with Germany. When the Ottoman Empire dissolved after the war, Britain secured a League of Nations mandate to create and administer Iraq. The new territory was an artificial agglomeration of Kurdish and Arab ethnic groups and of Sunni and Shiite religious sects. Sunnis, who dominate in most Arab countries, were a minority in the new Iraq. Shiites, whose religious center was outside Iraq in the neighboring, non-Arab, Persian territory of Iran—also a British mandate—were the majority. Kurds, who are mostly secular, had more in common with Turkish tribes in Turkey, Syria, and Iran than with the Sunni or Shiite Arabs in Iraq. In 1932, Iraq became formally independent under a Hashemite king, but it was never stable. After a series of military coups, it became a republic in 1958 and then in 1968 fell under the rule of the Baath Party, an Arab Sunni group that advocated secular nationalism. Saddam Hussein took control of the Baath Party in 1979 and proceeded to fight wars with Iran (1980–1988), Kuwait (1990), the United Nations (1991), and the United States (2003).

What was the cause of Iraq's discontent? Take your pick. Maybe realist perspectives have it right. The country straddled ancient divisions and perhaps hatreds among Arab, Turkish, and Persian ethnic groups speaking different languages—Arabic,

Turkish, and Farsi—and practicing different versions of the Islamic religion. On the other hand, institutional structures, both domestic and international, were weak and episodic. The territory experienced oppressive rule under various imperial and then militant nationalist governments. Elites manipulated tribal and sectarian resentments. Sunni Arabs, who make up only 20 percent of the population of Iraq, dominated the government from early on and systematically excluded and persecuted Kurdish and Shiite participants, who made up about 20 and 60 percent of the population, respectively. Outside powers intervened frequently and decisively, imposing mandates, creating governments, supporting Iraq in the war against Iran and then opposing it in the war against Kuwait, sanctioning Iraq to rid the country of WMDs, and then deposing Saddam Hussein to start all over again with a new government. Throughout it all, as identity perspectives emphasize, Iraqis have struggled to find a national identity. Arab nationalism excluded the Kurds; Shiite nationalism threatened to align with Iran; and Kurdish nationalism clamored for an independent state that would absorb portions of Turkey, Iran, and Syria, as well as Iraq.

Can anything be done? A great experiment testing different perspectives is underway today in Iraq. The United States and its coalition partners that successfully invaded and then occupied Iraq in 2003 are betting that they can construct a new national or civic identity based on constitutional processes and the rule of law. Skeptics, including those countries and international organizations that opposed the war, are betting that the identity, or democratic, gambit won't work, especially because it is being attempted without the participation and legitimacy of the world community. The best we can hope for, the skeptics argue, is a government of oligarchs who will divide up the spoils of Iraq's oil and maintain stability under the loose supervision of international institutions. This outcome re-creates the status quo before the invasion, in which the international community maintained inspectors to prevent the development of WMDs, supervised the distribution of oil export revenues, and worked diplomatically to resolve the Arab-Israeli territorial conflict.

Spotlight on civil war

Some realist observers think even that is expecting too much. They see a future in which civil war is inevitable. Shiite militia in the southern part of the country operate death squads and secret prisons to avenge past wrongs at the hands of their Sunni oppressors. Sunni insurgents in the center and west of the country switch sides as needed to arm themselves and prepare for future conflicts. Initially, they teamed up with outside *jihad*ist forces from other Muslim lands to battle U.S.-led occupation forces. When the United States poured additional troops into Iraq in 2007, Sunnis cooperated and joined the Iraqi police and army. They are now armed, and should political reconciliation stall between Sunnis and Shiites, the new weapons, as liberal perspectives fear, may fuel renewed sectarian violence. Kurdish forces, meanwhile, exercise de facto sovereignty in the northern part of the country and engage in a kind of reciprocal process of ethnic cleansing. Saddam Hussein encouraged the settlement of Arabs in the north to reduce Kurdish autonomy. Now Kurds seek to reduce the number of Arabs in cities such as Kirkuk to enhance the prospects for Kurdish independence. From a realist perspective, there are two possible outcomes—either the country splits apart, a solution that Kurds and Shiites, who control most of the country's oil, might favor, or one group again asserts its dominance, an outcome Sunnis have traditionally preferred because they have no significant oil resources in their areas.

What do you think will happen? Which perspective will prove to be right? You, too, have to decide. Here are some pertinent facts to keep in mind, but remember that facts don't easily decide the matter, although the more facts you can gather the better informed your final judgment will be.

The first year of occupation was chaotic. Widespread looting and sabotage occurred. Critics charged that the United States and coalition forces were insufficient to secure the country, and the occupation authority, known as the Coalition Provisional Authority (CPA), initially dissolved the Sunni-dominated Iraqi army to purge supporters of Saddam Hussein. The occupation inspired the insurgency and drew thousands of radical fundamentalists from outside the country to fight the occupying infidels. Iraq became the training ground for Al Qaeda that Afghanistan had been.

Nevertheless, in June 2004, the CPA turned over control of the government to an interim Iraqi government under a Shiite prime minister. The interim government organized elections of an interim parliament in January 2005. Sunnis boycotted the elections and threatened the participants, but the turnout—58 percent of registered voters—was impressive and showed the potential power of democratic freedom. The interim parliament wrote a new constitution, which was ratified by referendum in October 2005. This time, Sunnis participated, and the turnout reached 63 percent. Elections for a permanent parliament followed in December 2005; the turnout reached 68 percent. Some observers, inclined to look at these developments from a liberal perspective, might conclude that the political process was beginning to coopt the dissidents. Despite extremely difficult conditions, international election monitors did not find any evidence of major fraud.

The new constitution is deftly drafted both to protect the rights of ethnic and sectarian groups and to postpone critical issues for later decision by the parliament. For example, the constitution could have been defeated by a two-thirds vote in any three of Iraq's eighteen provinces. Thus, provinces where Sunnis and Kurds are in the majority were assured that their consent was necessary for the constitution to go into effect. The constitution declares Islam to be *a* basic source of law but not *the* source, as many Shiite leaders preferred. What role Islam plays will be decided by the parliament. And the constitution provides a personal status law, which protects women's rights, although it allows for women to choose religious law in matters of marriage, divorce, and inheritance if they wish. In an unprecedented move for a Muslim country, the constitution also reserves 25 percent of the seats in the new parliament for women.

Spotlight on constitutional government

The government that was finally formed in 2006 after six months of negotiations was still fragmented largely along ethno-sectarian lines. Of the 275 total seats in the new parliament, a coalition of Shiite parties held 128 seats, Kurdish parties 53, and a Sunni coalition 44. Secular parties combining Sunnis and Shiites won 25 seats or fewer, suggesting that cross-sectarian alliances remain weak. The Shiite coalition, known as the United Iraqi Alliance, included the Supreme Islamic Iraqi Council, which has close connections with and strong support from Shiite-dominated Iran, and a militant Shiite group under the control of the firebrand cleric, Muqtada al-Sadr, suspected of revenge killings against Sunnis in southern Iraq. The various factions periodically boycotted the parliament. Nevertheless, in early 2008, the government passed legislation to hold provincial elections and allow Sunnis who were members of the Baathist Party under Saddam Hussein to serve in various government posts. Other key pieces of legislation, for example, proposals to share oil revenues among the provinces, are still pending.

The process of building trust has just begun, and there is a race going on between ethnic tensions pulling Iraq apart and inhibiting political reconciliation and economic reconstruction, domestic institutional processes promoting reconciliation and compromise, and identity factors dividing loyalties between ethno-sectarian and national feelings. Some see international interventions helping the process; others see them as hurting the process. What do you think? The box on page 263 examines one judgment of the facts. Do you agree?

National and Territorial Conflicts

Today, the principal actors in contemporary international affairs identify with nations. How did nations come about? In some cases, national identities are ethnic identities writ large. As we have noted earlier, the first nations evolved from interlocking ethnic groups and a gradually expanding central administration or state. In these cases, ethnic (feudal) and state (aristocratic) identities came first and eventually forged a common identity among the people or nation at large.

But other nations had spiritual or sectarian origins, as well as ethnic ones. Arab, Jewish, papal Italian, and orthodox Russian nations derived from communities of faith as well as blood and were less affected in their early stages by bureaucratic centralization. They emerged from religious ideas as well as ethnic roots. Still other nations emerged from conquest and power struggles. Empires molded new nations in Russia, China, Japan, and Turkey; and colonialism invented new nations in Africa and Latin America. Finally, immigration defined new nations in the United States and Australia. In some cases of nation-building, such as the United States and Israel, ideas came first and created institutions and power. In other cases, such as the colonial empires, power came first and molded ideas and institutions. In still other cases, such as the early European states and China, central institutions came first and drove the development of power and ideas.

causal
arrow →

As we learn in Chapters 2 and 3, nationalism was an ideology that sprang out of the French Revolution and profoundly affected the development of international affairs. It created myths of common origins where none may have actually existed—for example, the myth of Aryan descent in Nazi Germany—and galvanized cultural and historical groups to unite on ideological grounds. Perhaps most important, nationalism associated ethno-national elements of identity with specific territories and governments. Nations, unlike ethnic groups, acquired distinct borders and territorial interests. As political scientist Anthony Smith explains, territory is the defining element of national groups and conflicts:

Spotlight on
identity
construction

> By definition the nation is a community of common myths and memories, as in an *ethnie* [ethnic group]. It is also a territorial community. But whereas in the case of *ethnies* the link with territory may be only historical and symbolic; in the case of the nation, it is physical and actual: nations possess territories. In other words nations always require ethnic "elements." These may, of course, be reworked; they often are. But nations are inconceivable without some common myths and memories of a territorial home.[28]

The link between territory and government gives the modern nation its unique character. Feudal government was not associated with contiguous territory. Prince Metternich, a nineteenth-century Austrian statesman, grew up in the Austrian Netherlands, a region under Hapsburg authority but geographically separated from the Hapsburg government in Vienna. The Hapsburg emperors themselves originally came from Swiss territory, also physically separated from Austria. Cardinal de Richelieu, the French cardinal and foreign minister under Louis XIII, changed this feudal setup by incorporating neighboring Hapsburg and German territories into a cohe-

Using the Perspectives to Read

→ **Between** ←
the Lines

Solutions to Iraq

John Deutch, a former deputy secretary of defense and director of the CIA under President Clinton, wrote an op-ed piece entitled "Time to Pull Out, and Not Just from Iraq." Let's look at his op-ed to see how he sorts out the realist, liberal, and identity perspectives on resolving ethnic conflicts in Iraq, but also in other places.

First, Deutch rejects identity solutions, especially imposed by military force:

> America embarks on an especially perilous course . . . when it actively attempts to establish a government based on our values in another part of the world. It is one matter to adopt a foreign policy that encourages democratic values; it is quite another to believe it just or practical to achieve such results on the ground with military forces. . . .

Second, Deutch doubts realist solutions, particularly that military force is very effective except in short-term interventions for humanitarian purposes or when used by mature local forces in their own self-defense:

> We should not shirk from quick military action for the purpose of saving lives that are in immediate danger. For example, the decision not to intervene early to prevent mass murder in Rwanda was a major failure. But we should not be lured into intervention that has as its driving purpose the replacement of despotic regimes with systems of government more like our own. . . .

When, after the fall of Baghdad, the decision was made to disband the Iraqi army, an impossible security situation was created: a combination of hostile ethnic factions supported by demobilized, but armed, military and security units with surrounding nations actively supporting them.

The insurgency cannot be overcome easily by either United States military forces or immature Iraqi security forces. Nor would the situation be eased, even if, improbably, the United Nations, NATO, our European allies, and Japan choose to become seriously involved.

Third, Deutch advocates liberal solutions—diplomacy and economic cooperation:

> If we want to influence the behavior of nations, we would be better served by combining diplomacy with our considerable economic strength. . . . Politically the United States should declare its intention to remove its troops and urge the Iraqi government and its neighbors to recognize the common regional interest in allowing Iraq to evolve peacefully and without external intervention. . . . Economically, we should define what amount of assistance we are prepared to extend to Iraq as long as it stays on a peaceful path. It would be best if this aid was but one facet of a broader set of economic initiatives to benefit Arab states that advance our interests.

sive French state. France then became known more by its contiguous boundaries than its feudal (Capetian or Valois) or sectarian (Catholic) origins. Later, after the French Revolution, the entire French nation identified with these territorial borders.

An early criterion for statehood, therefore, was the capacity to acquire and defend territorial boundaries. Nationalism, or the ideologically based component of the

Spotlight on territory (geography)

nation, became an important instrument to achieve and secure a national homeland. Napoleon mobilized, for the first time, the citizens of the entire nation to defend and expand the state. Later in the nineteenth century, Otto von Bismarck and Count Camillo Benso di Cavour used nationalist sentiments to unite German and Italian territories, respectively. The nation-state became synonymous with territorial integrity and with what became known as geopolitical or national interests. From a realist perspective, at least, such interests are primarily physical—geographical and resource factors that largely determine a nation's foreign policy. Island nations (Great Britain) have different interests than continental ones (France), mountainous ones (Switzerland) have different interests than flat ones (Poland), and so on.

Subsequent conflicts during the age of nationalism were often, perhaps mostly, about territorial issues. As Kalevi Holsti tells us, "the international politics of nineteenth-century Europe revolved around questions of territory, state creation, balance of power, alliances, and colonial rivalries."[29] Nations consolidated and traded territory as the principal stake in international affairs. Border disputes, the desire for more living space or *Lebensraum,* acquisition of natural resources, and simply conquest motivated territorial expansion, including the European struggle for the balance of power; colonial expansion in Asia, Africa, and the Middle East; and America's expansion across the North American continent. Hypernationalism then spawned racism and class warfare, which linked territorial identities with still deeper physical determinants of identity such as biology (race) and forces of economic determinism (class).

Nationalism was also the incubator of liberal and romantic ideas. Liberal nationalism in Great Britain and the United States promoted democratic development. But this development also involved issues of territory. Slavery was a key issue in the westward expansion of the United States. Do these territorial elements still matter? Is territory still a defining feature of modern nationalism? Some argue that nationalism is on the wane. Liberal perspectives that emphasize modernization see resources and territory as less important in an information age. Identity perspectives that emphasize democracy, human rights, or Marxist-Leninism see ideologies transcending nationalism and territory. Realist perspectives, on the other hand, observe the continuing relevance of nationalism in international affairs. They point to a number of contemporary disputes where territory remains a primary motivation of national behavior.

Let's look first at how the different perspectives interpret and react to these nationalist conflicts (the box on page 265 lists selected national disputes). Then we examine in more detail two of the most serious conflicts today that revolve around nationalist sentiments and territory: the China-Taiwan conflict and the Israeli-Palestinian conflict.

Realist Solutions—Balancing Power

Realist perspectives argue that the best way to cope with nationalist, especially territorial, conflicts is by balancing power. Thus, they advocate arming Taiwan to deter China; an alliance among the United States, Japan, and South Korea to deter North Korea; balancing power between India and Pakistan; and defending the security of Israel. Balancing power does not necessarily resolve issues, but it stabilizes them. Once stabilized, conflicts can be negotiated. From a realist perspective, a big problem in the Middle East is the power of extremists, especially states that reject the existence of Israel or Israeli groups that reject the existence of Palestine. These extremists are strong enough to torpedo any negotiated settlement, as they did the Clinton-mediated settle-

Spotlight on nationalism

Selected National Conflicts Around the World

China-Japan	Historical disputes over Japanese atrocities during World War II and worship of war criminals by Japanese leaders at the Yasukuni Shrine and over conflicting territorial claims to the Diaoyu (Chinese)/Senkaku (Japanese) islands off the southeast coast of China.
Japan-South Korea	Historical disputes over Japanese occupation of Korea from 1905 to 1945 and rival claims to the Dokdo (Korean)/Takeshima (Japanese) islands in the Sea of Japan.
Japan-Russia	After World War II, Russia occupied four Japanese islands, known as the Kurile Islands, off the northern coast of Japan and still holds them.
South Korea-North Korea	Divided since World War II, North Korea is a closed, totalitarian society seeking nuclear weapons that China supports with vital food and fuel supplies, while South Korea is a modern, young democracy aligned with the United States but sharing the memories and myths of Korean unity going all the way back to the ancient kingdom of Koguryo.
South China Sea	China claims 80 percent of the region, including the Spratly Islands, believed to be rich in energy reserves, which Malaysia, the Philippines, Taiwan, Vietnam, and Brunei also claim.
India-Pakistan	Two nations—one Hindu, one Muslim—formed from British colonies and possessing nuclear weapons fight over Kashmir, a mountainous province in the north, which India retains but whose people are predominantly Muslim.
Latin America	Border disputes still smolder between Colombia and Venezuela, Venezuela and Guyana, and Bolivia and Peru. Interstate wars occurred in the past thirty years between Ecuador and Peru, El Salvador and Honduras, and Argentina and Great Britain (over the Falkland/Malvina Islands). Class-based nationalism in Venezuela, Bolivia, Cuba, and Ecuador protests against U.S. dominance.

ment of 2000–2001. Realists from the power transition school—who believe that conflicts occur when power is moving toward balance and hence advocate dominance rather than just balancing—prefer Israeli dominance to protect the status quo, but those from the classical or balancing school support a two-state solution that divides territory and preserves stability by a spheres-of-influence policy.

Liberal Solutions—United Nations Diplomacy and Sanctions

Liberal perspectives worry that arming squabbling nations only increases insecurity. They prefer negotiations and, if necessary, international intervention to sanction aggressors and prevent the proliferation of arms, especially nuclear arms. They also advocate economic cooperation to divert attention from zero-sum territorial disputes. Thus, liberal perspectives support an aggressive diplomacy to mediate the Taiwan, North Korea, Kashmir, and Middle East disputes. They support multilateral institutions, such as the IAEA, and the use of sanctions to prevent the spread of nuclear weapons. From this perspective, the United Nations has multiple advantages. It encourages great power cooperation, as well as facilitating and monitoring cease-fires. In the Middle East conflict, the UN separated the belligerents after the 1956 war and passed crucial resolutions after the 1967 war. UN Resolution 242 spelled out balanced, albeit ambiguous, terms for territorial compromise, calling for the Israeli withdrawal from occupied territories—but not specifying all territories or exactly which boundaries—in return for security guarantees.

During the Cold War, UN intervention in the Middle East avoided U.S.-Soviet intervention and the potential escalation of superpower conflict. After the Cold War, UN conferences started peace talks that led to the Oslo Accords and the mutual recognition of Israel and the Palestinian Authority. Liberal perspectives stress the U.S. role as honest broker in the talks—which many European and Arab countries, of course, doubt—and often fault American diplomacy rather than extremists for failure to make progress. Extremism grows because the Arab-Israeli dispute persists. Notice that liberal perspectives see the failure of negotiations as fueling extremism, whereas realist perspectives see extremism as preventing the implementation of any negotiated solution even if it can be achieved, as happened with Clinton's mediation. Realist perspectives see stability as a prerequisite for negotiations and worry that forcing antagonists to negotiate before they feel safe only increases instability. Liberal perspectives see negotiations as a way to increase trust and create the stability that facilitates disarmament and feelings of safety. These are differences in judgment which the facts often equally support.

causal arrow

The United Nations may have to play a similar role in the Indian-Pakistani dispute. Both India (since the 1970s) and Pakistan (since the 1990s) have nuclear weapons. Thus, Kashmir is a territorial dispute, like Berlin during the Cold War or Korea today, which is overshadowed by a potential nuclear confrontation. Some realist perspectives believe that nuclear deterrence stabilizes such conflicts because neither side would risk an armed intervention.[30] But liberal and some identity perspectives judge the risks to be too high, given the diplomatic and bureaucratic difficulties of managing nuclear weapons, especially in nationalistically oriented developing countries.

Spotlight on deterrence

Identity Solutions—Democracy

Identity perspectives settle for neither stability nor perpetual negotiations. They seek to change the ideas and motivations fueling nationalist conflicts by reforming domestic institutions. President Bush said in 2005 that, for thirty years, the United States had sought stability in the Middle East at the expense of liberty. To defend Israel and the status quo, the United States collaborated with many authoritarian governments—Saudi Arabia, Egypt, Jordan, and others. In the end, Bush argued, the United States achieved neither stability nor freedom. Now it would try a different way; it would seek to spread democracy in the region. Eventually, more open and moderate governments in the region would redefine the situation. Military balances would matter less, extremists on both sides of the conflict would be marginalized, and negotiations would be facilitated and backed up by trust engendered by a democratic peace. According to studies of democracy and war, free nations trust one another more and are more open to outside scrutiny as well as internal accountability. Transformed political identities would bring negotiations and peace, rather than stability leading to negotiations or negotiations achieving stability.

Spotlight on democratic peace

For other identity perspectives, regime change is anathema. The objective is tolerance and basic human rights, not western-style democracy. Cultures are more durable than politics, and all cultures need to be accepted and respected. Hence, international intervention should occur only when all nations agree. The United Nations is the primary source of legitimacy and norms in the world community because it represents everyone.

Spotlight on universality

China-Taiwan Conflict

One of the most dangerous nationalist conflicts in Asia is between China and Taiwan, with the United States caught in the middle. China has ambivalent feelings toward western powers in the region. It remembers its colonization in the nineteenth century at the hands of western powers and advocates anti-hegemonism, a code word meaning reduced American influence in Asia. China seeks to reclaim lands lost to colonialism as well as territories it perceives as culturally related to China. So it seized Tibet in 1949, a territory never colonized by the west but often romanticized by western folklore. The Dalai Lama, the religious head of Buddhism, fled to India, and some western groups support his claim to regain independence for Tibet. Whenever western governments receive the Dalai Lama, as the United States did in 2006, China strongly protests. In 1997, China recovered both Macao from Portugal and Hong Kong from Britain, and now it focuses on the most important piece of colonial territory still outside its control—Taiwan, an island separated by the Taiwan Strait from the southeastern coast of China.

Taiwan is the flashpoint of contemporary Chinese nationalism. Occupied by Japan after the Sino-Japanese war in 1895, Taiwan was taken over after World War II by Chinese Nationalists fleeing the communist victory on the mainland. Until the opposition Democratic Progressive Party was elected in 2000, successive governments in Taiwan proclaimed the island to be the authentic government of one China, while the communist government in Beijing asserted the same claim from the mainland. Although indigenous Taiwanese have different ethnic roots and were only loosely part of the mainland Qing dynasty from the late seventeenth to the late nineteenth centuries, the China-Taiwan conflict is not primarily between two rival nationalities but between rival interpretations of the same nationality.

During the Cold War, the United States defended Taiwan against Beijing. When the United States recognized mainland China in 1979, however, it abrogated its defense treaty with Taiwan. It continued to sell arms to Taiwan and to call for a peaceful resolution of the "one China" dispute. Matters became more complicated when Taiwan became democratic in the 1990s. The military government transferred power to a civilian government in 1990, and in 2000, opposition parties, which did not draw political support from the military, took control of the government for the first time. The democratic government was more sympathetic to local Taiwanese desires for independence and advocated referenda to establish eventual independence from Beijing. China subsequently warned that it would never permit Taiwan to become independent and announced that it would use force if Taiwan declared independence or delayed a resolution of the issue for too long.

Both China and Taiwan continue to arm against one another, and the United States seeks to deter the use of force. It maintains a policy of so-called strategic ambiguity, acknowledging that Taiwan is part of China but keeping forces in the region to assist Taiwan if China tries to resolve the dispute by force. In 1996, the United States sent two aircraft carrier task forces into the area when China fired short-range missiles into the sea next to Taiwan. And in 1998 and again in 2005, Chinese generals made pronouncements that China might use nuclear weapons against the United States if it interfered in a China-Taiwan conflict. China has only a couple dozen intercontinental ballistic missiles that could hit the United States, but it deploys hundreds of short-range missiles that target Taiwan and spends somewhere between its official estimate of $50 billion a year and upper estimates of $70–100 billion a year to modernize its military,

Spotlight on decolonization

making China's defense budget the third largest in the world, behind the United States and Japan.

Spotlight on
balance of power

What should be done? Observers taking a realist perspective worry more about preventing China from using military force to conquer Taiwan than about gradual independence for Taiwan. If China uses force successfully, it will destabilize relationships throughout the Asian region. Assuming America did nothing, Japan and other U.S. allies would have reason to doubt America's commitment to stand up to China in future situations. China would now control vital sealanes through which Japan imports most of its oil. Would America resist if China then used Taiwan to extend its control over oil routes? How would South Korea react? While it has no stake in the China-Taiwan conflict, South Korea depends on U.S. military forces to defend against a powerful military in North Korea, potentially armed with nuclear weapons. Would both Japan and South Korea seek their own nuclear weapons, as South Korea tried to do under an earlier military government in the 1970s? The important strategy, then, from a realist perspective is to sell arms to Taiwan to match China's buildup in the Taiwan Strait and to keep the U.S. Pacific fleet on call to intervene as necessary and deter a Chinese attack.

Spotlight on
diplomacy

Observers taking a liberal perspective worry more about Taiwan avoiding or delaying indefinitely negotiations with the mainland. They emphasize the cross-strait talks to forge greater economic contacts and tourism between Taiwan and the mainland. They downplay the utility of the arms buildup and believe that aggressive diplomacy is the best way to deter China from using force or Taiwan from declaring independence. In this case, no one advocates multilateral or UN intervention. China, because of the colonial legacy, strongly objects to such intervention and argues that the issue is an internal Chinese matter. China, taking a more realist view, hopes to alter the military status quo to force negotiations on its terms.

Spotlight on
shared or relative
identities

Observers taking an identity perspective emphasize neither the military nor diplomatic aspects of the dispute but aspects of discourse and democracy. Some might focus on the emerging democratic identity of Taiwan and note that, as in the case of South and North Korea, the conflict is increasingly defined by diverging regime types as well as by territorial claims. This complicates the resolution of the dispute. Either mainland China democratizes or demonstrates, as it did in the case of Hong Kong, that it can tolerate different political systems under the umbrella of Chinese national unity or Taiwan grows more estranged from China and impedes diplomatic solutions, perhaps hardening the military confrontation. Some other identity perspectives might urge for that very reason the continuing need for dialogue and discourse to find new terms of reference that prevent the rivalry from degenerating into an enemy relationship. Nationalist conflicts may just take an inordinately long time to resolve.

Israeli-Palestinian Conflict

ethno-national communities

groups of people in which ethnic and national identities overlap substantially.

Perhaps no conflict illustrates better the continuing importance of national (territorial) issues in international affairs than the conflict between Israel and the Palestinians. Both peoples constitute **ethno-national communities** that searched for centuries for territorial homelands. Although both have ancient claims to Palestine, neither had established a national home there prior to 1948. After World War I, Britain promised in the Balfour Declaration to work for a Jewish homeland in Palestine. After World War II and the Holocaust, international support for a Jewish nation increased. In 1948, the United States backed a UN resolution that partitioned Palestine between Arabs and Israelis. But the participants in the conflict could not agree, and war ensued.

Indeed, six full-scale wars ensued, the first in 1948 and the last one in 1982 when Israel invaded Lebanon. In a war in 1967, Israel occupied large portions of Palestinian territory as measured by the original partition, including the West Bank (bordering on Jordan), Gaza (bordering on Egypt), and the Golan Heights (bordering on Syria). Since 1982, the region has been afflicted by repeated smaller conflicts, such as Israel's battle with Hezbollah in 2006, and uprisings or *intifada*s, such as the one that torpedoed the Camp David agreement in 2001. Palestinian militants launch terrorist attacks and suicide bombings in the occupied territories. Israeli forces impose rigid police controls, establish Jewish settlements in the occupied territories, and destroy Palestinian homes and neighborhoods to suppress terrorist activities.

The most prominent issue is territory. The Palestinians demand a homeland, but some also want to eliminate Israel. Israelis demand secure borders, but some also want to annex the occupied territories and eliminate Palestine. Where the borders will be drawn; how Jerusalem, which both sides claim as their capital, will be managed; and what will be done with millions of Palestinian refugees who fled the occupied territories—these are the obstacles to a final settlement. By 2005, after almost continuous negotiations since the beginning of the conflict, both entities, Israel and the Palestinian Authority (created during the Oslo negotiations in the 1990s to bring together the various Palestinian factions), accepted a two-state solution, but extremists, supported by Iran, Syria, and, before 2003, Iraq, continued to reject it.

What should be done? Observers taking a realist perspective worry most about stability in the area. The Middle East is a strategic piece of real estate, not only because of oil but also because of its location between Europe and Asia and between Christianity and Islam. Great powers have historically intervened and competed in this area. So, the top priority from a realist perspective is to preserve the status quo both regionally and in terms of outside intervention. That was clearly the thrust of U.S. policy during the Cold War. Preventing great power clashes was more important than the negotiation of a final Arab-Israeli settlement or the reform of authoritarian governments in the region. Stability is still the priority goal for realist observers and caused many of them to object strongly to the war against Iraq in 2003, precisely because it threatened to increase extremism and to endanger fragile governments in the region.

Observers taking a liberal perspective worry most about negotiations to achieve a final Israeli-Palestinian peace settlement. President Clinton gave these negotiations top priority in 2000, even though the military initiative was slipping into the hands of hard-liners in both Palestine (the *intifada* began in September 2000) and Israel (the more hard-line Likud Party replaced the Labor Party in February 2001). To secure this agreement, the United States and other sponsoring governments were ready to pump in large amounts of foreign aid. The judgment was that peace would strengthen moderates to reform corrupt governments in the region. Instead, unreformed extremists torpedoed the agreement.

Observers taking an identity perspective worry most about reforming oppressive political regimes in the region. Palestinians are unable to accept negotiated compromises or restrain their military forces until they have stronger and more accountable leadership. Arafat, the Palestinian leader, confessed that, had he signed the 2000 agreement, he would have been dead within a few weeks. He controlled neither the minds nor the might of his own people. Nor was the Likud government in Israel in a position to compromise. It was beholden to settlers who demanded the annexation of the occu-

Spotlight on stability

Spotlight on negotiations

Spotlight on authoritarian governments

pied territories. Thus, as some identity perspectives see it, negotiations and stability awaited democratic reforms to succeed. And opportunities for negotiations and stability improved when Arafat died in 2004 and Ariel Sharon, Israel's prime minister, faced down extremist settlers and removed some 8,000 of them when Israel withdrew from the Gaza Strip in 2005. But then democratic elections in the Palestinian Authority in 2006 brought the militant group Hamas to power. Hamas immediately split away from Fatah, the more moderate Palestinian group, took control of Gaza, and initiated daily rocket attacks against Israel. Will moderates or extremists win the race, and does democratic reform help or hurt the peace process?

Summary

The terrorist attacks of 9/11 renewed the century-old debate about how to manage international conflicts. Liberal perspectives urged international cooperation to hunt down nonstate terrorist actors and remove the diplomatic and economic sources of discontent. Realist perspectives saw a bigger threat defined by potential alignments among rogue states, nonstate actors, and rising powers and urged global war to preempt or counterbalance these threats. Identity perspectives worried about reforming or changing autocratic governments and transcending clashes between civilizations.

At the regional and local levels, ethnic and religious conflicts are as old as recorded history. Blood ties divided groups in Mesopotamia and ancient China. Primitive beliefs in sundry gods and then in the Buddhist (600 BCE), Confucian (600 BCE), Christian (0 CE), and Islamic (600 CE) religions compounded ethnic differences. Some ethnic groups amalgamated to form early states in Europe and unified kingdoms in China and the Americas. States then mobilized national groups united by culture, language, and common memories. Other national groups, such as Russia and Germany, emerged from conquest and common cultures to forge unitary states and then empires. Today, ethnicity and nationalism continue to fragment the human family. In some places, such as Iraq, ethnic and sectarian groups struggle to find a sense of nationhood. In other places, such as China and the Middle East, nationalities seek to recover lost territories or establish new homelands.

Ethnic and national conflicts tend to make many other problems in the world more difficult. Fighting reduces food supplies and interrupts distribution. It produces refugees who leave the land uncultivated and destroy the environment by scavenging for resources and limited animal life. Conflicts spread diseases, such as AIDS, and contribute to trafficking in drugs and human beings. In short, ethnic and national conflicts compound environmental damage.

We look at these environmental problems in Chapter 14. Some of them divide the world, but others also have the potential to bring the world closer together to save the common heritage of humankind regardless of ethnic, religious, or national differences.

Key Concepts

civic identity 257
constitutional solutions 252
elite manipulation 255
ethnic cleansing 254
ethnic groups 250
ethno-national communities 268

federalism 252
global war on terror 239
madrassas 249
nation-building 257
nationhood 257
partition 254

post-conflict
    reconstruction 256
religious sects 251
Shiites 247
Sunnis 247
Wahhabism 248

Study Questions

1. Which perspective responds to terrorism as war, which responds to it as crime, and which responds to it as a clash of civilizations? Explain.

2. What are the differences between Sunnis, Shiites, and Wahhabists?

3. Why does the critical theory perspective reject mainstream realist, liberal, and identity perspectives?

4. What are the main causes and solutions to ethnic conflicts from the liberal, realist, and identity perspectives?

5. What are the limitations of partition, peacekeeping, and nation-building for resolving ethnic conflicts?

6. How do ethnic and national conflicts relate to one another? What is the principal difference between ethnic and national communities?

7. What are the main ethnic and religious groups in Iraq? Can institutional measures such as elections and federalism overcome the differences among these groups? What ideas other than ethnicity and religion might form the basis of an Iraqi national identity?

8. If a two-state or realist solution is the answer to the Israeli-Palestinian conflict, why is it not also the answer to the China-Taiwan conflict? How do the two situations differ in terms of ethnicity and religion? How are the two situations similar in terms of opportunities for economic interdependence and political reform?

Globalization and the World Economy

Part II

The chapters of Part I focused on international conflict and war. The chapters of Part II now give equal attention to globalization and the world economy. No one can understand international politics today without understanding international economics. Students sometimes fear economics—too much math and too many graphs. Well, the economics presented here is student-friendly. You learn not only about the history and debates about globalization but also in straightforward terms how globalization works—the economic policies that affect currency values and trade imbalances. When you finish, you may want to refer back to these chapters when you take your economics courses. These chapters will help you keep the big picture in mind as you work your way through the graphics and illustrations.

Recorded history began 5,000 years ago. But a world economy involving trade and finance across the entire globe began only 500 years ago. For the first four and a half millennia, people lived primarily on the land and produced everything they needed in local villages and communities. Worldwide, almost all economies were hand-to-mouth, or subsistence, economies with no excess production to invest. Phoenician seafarers around 1000 BCE and Roman merchants through the fifth century CE developed early trading communities in the Mediterranean. Later, Europe and the Middle East exchanged gold and silver, and caravans from China plied the Silk Road through central Asia to bring silk, spices, and jewels to the Middle East and Europe.

By the turn of the first millennium CE, therefore, it was still anyone's guess as to which part of the world would develop a modern economy first. China had more advanced technology—gunpowder, paper, printing, and ship rudders (a crucial invention enabling long-distance sailing expeditions). Islam was experiencing its Golden Age and, as Bernard Lewis, the well-known Middle East historian, writes, "medieval Europe was a pupil and . . . a dependent of the Islamic world."[1] Then, suddenly, Europe's economy—its trade and technologies—rapidly exploded, and European nations colonized the world, creating and leading the global economy ever since.

Chapter 8 explores, from the three perspectives, why this happened and how subsequently Britain and the United States organized the world economy under the gold standard before World War I and then the Bretton Woods institutions after World War II and a single global economy after the Cold War.

273

Chapter 9 examines the mechanisms that make globalization work—the domestic and international policies, institutions, and security arrangements that knit global markets together and create the prosperity and crises of a globalized world.

Chapters 10 through 12 look at specific mechanisms in more detail. Chapter 10 treats trade, investment, and the financial instruments of contemporary world markets. These instruments come together in the so-called balance of payments, a concept that is as central to the world economy as the balance of power is to world security.

Chapters 11 and 12 explore development policies. Chapter 11 compares the relative success of Asian and Latin American countries; Chapter 12 examines the relative lack of success in sub-Saharan Africa and in the Middle East and North Africa.

Chapter 13, which is new to this edition, also represents something of a departure from the way the rest of the book is organized in that it looks at globalization and development almost exclusively from a critical theory perspective. Here we flesh out the important downsides of globalization, issues that are not always accounted for by the mainstream theories. The chapter looks at the historical phenomena of imperialism and colonialism and the critical theory ideas of dependency and world systems meant to address them; at the labor-related inequalities that exist under globalization; and at the marginalization of indigenous peoples and women worldwide.

The realist, liberal, identity, and critical theory perspectives inform our discussion of economics, just as they did the discussion of security. The realist perspective sees markets and economic activities as another element of power and, hence, views differences in economic capacities as a function of the relative distribution or balance of power among states. Policymakers seek domestically and internationally to steer and dominate markets so that they gain relatively with respect to other players even if all players gain absolutely. The realist perspective puts heavy emphasis on running surpluses in the balance of payments, accumulating wealth to add to military and security needs. Known as mercantilism or economic nationalism, this approach aims to increase a country's relative power by accumulating trade surpluses and technological advances. Thus, mercantilism promotes exports, limits imports, screens foreign investment and the transfer of new technologies to prevent the export of militarily significant or dual-use civilian technologies, and uses foreign aid and lending to cultivate security ties. Trade and investment are promoted primarily with allies or in situations of hegemony where the hegemonic country sets rules that preserve and extend its dominance.

The liberal perspective sees economic activity as separate from and potentially a substitute for military or balance of power rivalries. It advocates open markets to expand trade, investment, and financial activities, increasing mutual wealth and diverting attention away from zero-sum military and territorial disputes. Known as laissez-faire economics, this approach calls for common rules and institutions to manage balance of payments imbalances and disputes. Surpluses and deficits are neither good nor bad but work to encourage greater efficiency and development, spreading rather than concentrating benefits (as in the case of mercantilism). Over time, a mutually beneficial economic system reduces the significance of relative power and makes alliances and hegemony increasingly irrelevant and unnecessary. Cooperation, not the struggle for dominance, is the eventual outcome of economic exchanges and interdependence.

The identity perspective sees economic activity as an expression of the ideas or identities of various groups or states. Traditional societies favored barter or tribute economies, which respect and preserve social customs. Democratic societies value private property and individual rights to trade, invest, lend, and borrow in an open market economy. Liberal trade policies follow from these democratic (that is, ideological) convictions, not from some general desire to displace military competition or cultivate allies and exploit hegemony. Not all hegemons, for example, practice free trade; the Soviet Union did not. It depends on the identities of the actors. Marxist societies pursue class-based economics, not free trade. They centralize control of markets and redistribute property away from capitalist classes of management and entrepreneurs toward worker cooperatives and labor unions. Developing countries often prefer neo-Marxist economics at the global level. They seek to escape colonialism and reverse dependency through global commodity and technology agreements and foreign aid. Fascist societies employ mobilization economies. They centralize resources to pursue aggressive ideological or military aims. The extent of global economic activity depends on the convergence or divergence of these various identity-based perspectives. Under Britain and the United States, open market economies—laissez-faire and embedded liberalism—flourished. Under Napoleon and the Soviet Union, mobilization and class-based economies prevailed.

Critical theory perspectives depict the global world economy as an historical fabrication that cannot be easily broken down into its constituent parts. It is the product of long centuries of domination and exploitation. Today's world economy is rigged against the interests of the poor and powerless. Trade and comparative advantage have not been ordained by nature; they have been created by power. Developing countries, for example, were systematically tied to the needs of colonial powers. They produced cash crops such as tobacco and rubber for advanced markets rather than food for their own people. These patterns persist today. An African country such as Mauritania produces only 30 percent of the food it consumes. Thus, the first countries to suffer from global food shortages or higher prices, such as the world was experiencing in early 2008, are the poorest ones. From a critical theory perspective, the situation cannot be changed by a new trade round or foreign aid; the causes are too multiple and deep seated. Some critical theory perspectives call for revolution or complete separation of poor countries from the global economy. Others simply call for listening to the poor and giving them a voice in the process and learning from them as much as teaching or developing them.

---

1. Bernard Lewis, *What Went Wrong? Western Impact and Middle East Response* (Oxford: Oxford University Press, 2002), 7.

History of Globalization
Mercantilism, Pax Britannica, and Pax Americana

Globalization juxtaposes the old and the new. China has demolished more than thirty McDonald's signs because they clashed with traditional architecture, such as Drum Tower in Beijing, shown here, where in the 1400s drums were beaten to mark the end of each day.

Globalization has evolved through three historical phases. In his best-selling book *The World Is Flat*, Thomas Friedman[1] characterized the three phases:

- **Globalization 1.0** lasted from 1492 to 1800 and "shrank the world from a size large to a size medium." This was the age of mercantilism and colonialism. The driving force was brawn, not brains—"how much muscle, how much horse-power, wind power, or, later, steam power—your country had and how creatively you could deploy it." Remember Paul Kennedy's "ships and fire power" from Chapter 2?

- **Globalization 2.0** ran from 1800 to the mid-twentieth century; it was ended by World War II. It "shrank the world from a size medium to a size small." This was the age of Pax Britannica. The driving force was new institutions, particularly the emergence of global markets and multinational corporations (MNCs). Global megacompanies exploited the dramatic drop in transportation and then communications costs to weave the world together into a seamless web of global products, capital, and labor.

- **Globalization 3.0** arrived during the second half of the twentieth century and "is shrinking the world from a size small to a size tiny and flattening the playing field

globalization 1.0
one of three periods of globalization; it lasted from 1492 to 1800 and was characterized by mercantilism and colonialism.

globalization 2.0

one of three periods of
globalization; it lasted from 1800
to 1950 and was characterized by
the emergence of multinational
corporations and institutions.

globalization 3.0

one of three periods of
globalization; it started in the
second half of the twentieth
century and continues into the
twenty-first and is characterized
by the flattening of the global
playing field and reliance on the
knowledge economy more than
on military power or big
institutions.

<u>causal</u>
arrow ➞

at the same time." This is the age of Pax Americana, and the driving force is the Internet, "the newfound power for *individuals* to collaborate and compete globally." Individuals now communicate, innovate, form groups, conduct business, and move money worldwide just the way MNCs do. Brains, not brawn or institutions, shape the world economy. And that world is now increasingly flat, meaning that every country and civilization can take part. China, India, and, potentially, Muslim countries—"every color of the human rainbow"—can participate in the globalization chat room. Neither power disparities nor institutional advantages matter as much as the ability to think creatively.

Notice how Friedman's three versions of globalization can be understood in terms of our three perspectives on international relations. In globalization 1.0, physical power mattered most (the realist perspective). In globalization 2.0, multinational institutions drove the process (the liberal perspective). And in globalization 3.0, innovations and ideas matter most (the identity perspective). But Friedman, of course, is making judgments. Maybe the ships and firepower of globalization 1.0 were the products of Protestant ideas, which gave a divine blessing to the acquisition of wealth. Or maybe the MNCs that drove globalization 2.0 were simply artifacts of Britain's dominant power or of Enlightenment ideas embracing free markets and private property. And perhaps globalization 3.0 is not about brains and flattening but about *American* brawn and imperialism or the spread of western democracy and its global validation of individual rights and creativity. Friedman sees technological change as the rocket booster behind all three versions of globalization. And he sees the impact of technological change as leveling or flattening the playing field for all individuals and all civilizations, regardless of ideological differences. In all these respects, his perspective on globalization is quintessentially liberal.

Causes of Globalization

Let's look more systematically at the arguments about how globalization evolved. Why did Europe become rich after 1500 while other civilizations—Islamic, Chinese, Mayan, and so on—fell behind? Why did Columbus discover the Americas by crossing the Atlantic, while Wang Chin, a Chinese explorer, did not do so but might have by crossing the Pacific? Why did Britain and France go on to colonize the Middle East, while Islam failed to conquer Europe when it besieged Vienna in the mid-seventeenth century? These are more of those big questions in history about which there is no agreement. As we observe in this chapter, the three mainstream perspectives and the critical theory perspective answer these questions differently. We examine the critical theory perspective in more detail in Chapter 13.

Once again, there are basic historical events you will need to remember. The parallel timeline on page 293 offers a bird's-eye view of these events and makes one (not the only possible) suggestion as to which perspective might emphasize the different events.

Realist Explanations

Realist explanations of globalization emphasize the relative distribution of power. They see trade and economic activities flourishing only under favorable security conditions, and favorable security conditions depend, in turn, on the relative distribution of power. The two most favorable security conditions are alliances and hegemony or imperialism. As Joanne Gowa tells us, "free trade is more likely within than across political-military alliances; and . . . alliances have had a much stronger effect on trade in a bipolar than in a multipolar world."[2] The reason is that free trade, exploiting comparative advantage, enhances economic efficiency and that economic efficiency frees up resources for military purposes. Another country, if it is not a permanent ally (and alliances are seldom permanent), may use the gains from trade to enhance its military power and threaten to harm the first country. Thus, according to realist logic, world economic expansion should be least robust in a multipolar world where countries cannot be sure of stable alliances, more robust in a bipolar world because alliances are more predictable, and most robust in a unipolar or imperial world because there is no significant challenge to the military power of the dominant power.

For historical evidence to support their argument, realist perspectives point to four periods: (1) the age of mercantilism and colonial competition before the first industrial revolution, when Europe was multipolar and mostly protectionist in its approach to trade; (2) the period from the industrial revolution to World War I when England dominated the world economy and liberalized trade unilaterally—the **Pax Britannica**; (3) the interwar period between World Wars I and II when Europe was multipolar and the world economy experienced a deep depression; (4) the period after World War II when the United States dominated first the free world economy and then, after the Cold War ended, the entire world economy and led the multilateral liberalization of trade—the **Pax Americana.**

Age of Mercantilism and Colonial Expansion

As we have learned in Chapter 2, the Holy Roman Empire reached its pinnacle around 1500, creating, as realist logic expects, a hegemonic environment that launched the age of discovery epitomized by Columbus's discovery of America. Thereafter, however, the multipolar state system emerged in Europe and weakened the central authority of the Holy Roman Empire. The territorial state consolidated jurisdiction over local markets and superseded the merchant-based city-states and city leagues of southern and northern Europe, such as Italy and the Hanseatic League, that flourished under the Holy Roman Empire.[3] This was the age of Richelieu and *raison d'état*, the consolidation of state authority under the rule of absolute monarchs. It was also the age of Jean Baptiste Colbert, the French official who advocated high tariffs and introduced the economic system of **mercantilism,** in which the central objective of state policy was to increase the state's wealth relative to that of other states in a zero-sum struggle for material advantage.

Mercantilism dominated trade in the sixteenth through eighteenth centuries. Each state sought to export more goods than it imported. States paid for excess exports in gold or silver and used these precious metals to buy bigger and better military contingents and capabilities. A favorable balance of exports over imports translated directly into a favorable balance of military power or dominance. High tariffs, or **Colbertism,** characterized the trade policies of all states and made the pursuit of wealth in this preindustrial period largely a zero-sum rather than non-zero-sum game.

Pax Britannica

British hegemony before World War I during the second period of globalization.

Pax Americana

American hegemony after World War II during the third period of globalization.

mercantilism

an economic philosophy that holds that the central objective of a state's policy is to increase the state's wealth relative to that of other states and to pursue that economic development independently, in a zero-sum struggle for material advantage.

Colbertism

an economic policy based on high tariffs; named after seventeenth-century Frenchman Jean Baptiste Colbert.

Pax Britannica

Beginning in the latter part of the eighteenth century, England began to emerge as the dominant country in Europe and, indeed, in the world. It mined more coal, manufactured more textiles, deployed more net tons of commercial shipping, and produced more manufactured goods overall than most of its competitors combined (France, Prussia/Germany, and the United States). With its domination of the seas, England set about to create the first genuine, albeit colonized, world economy in history that spanned the globe from east to west. It did so, according to realist logic, because it faced no significant military challenger, especially on the high seas, and therefore did not fear that economic gains by others might be used to harm England. It was free to pursue efficiency and expand global, not just national, wealth because its interests were global, while those of other countries were only local or regional.

HEGEMONIC STABILITY THEORY. Economist Charles Kindleberger wrote the classic book explaining why hegemons or dominant powers are necessary to create global markets.[4] Subsequent studies developed his ideas into **hegemonic stability theory.**[5] According to this realist theory, a hegemonic power is necessary to support a highly integrated world economy. The reasoning is as follows. As long as power is evenly distributed among several great powers, no single power can influence the system as a whole. Therefore, no single power takes the lead to organize the world economy. At the extreme, where there are many powers that are equally competitive, the world economy approaches the model of a perfect market. Because no single actor exerts significant influence on other actors, each acts to maximize its own national self-interests. In a perfect market, such self-interested behavior results in higher gains for all because competition maximizes efficiency.

But in a perfect market no one shoots anyone. That's because a hegemon, such as a domestic government, deploys a police force to provide safety in the market place. In the international system, there is normally no such hegemon or police force. Thus, numerous competitive nations have to fear that someone may shoot them. This is the multipolar world that Joanne Gowa spoke about in which nations cannot be sure about alliances and therefore hedge their economic activities against the possibility that another state may use its economic gains to harm them militarily. Even in a bipolar world where alliances are more stable, two great powers, such as the United States and the Soviet Union after World War II, have to worry about one another. Thus, the United States and the Soviet Union developed separate and autonomous "half-world" economies, which did very little trade with one another.

A hegemonic power overcomes these obstacles and provides common services that allow for the intensive development of international economic relations. As we learn in Chapter 1, these services constitute what liberal perspectives call collective goods. These are indivisible goods that cannot be provided selectively to some and not to others, and their consumption by one nation does not diminish the benefits available to other nations. But notice that from the realist perspective, hegemony is a prerequisite to providing collective goods. The distribution of power precedes and causes the existence of collective goods. The hegemon supplies these goods because it is the only power whose interests coincide with the system as a whole. Other nations with more parochial interests become **free riders** and seek to avoid paying for goods that will be supplied anyway. The hegemon offers **side payments** such as security assistance or foreign aid—in effect bribes—to get smaller nations to cooperate. Obviously, the hegemon expects to gain more from the global economy than it pays out. It believes its spe-

hegemonic stability theory

the theory that a hegemonic power is necessary to support a highly integrated world economy.

free riders

states that allow another to pay the costs of a particular transaction while at the same time receiving the benefits of that state's actions.

causal arrow

side payments

offers made by a hegemon (in effect, bribes) to get smaller nations to cooperate.

cific policies—for example, Britain's free-trade policies or the Soviet Union's command economy policies—will preserve and perhaps extend its dominance. Or, if it loses relative power, it expects to gain commensurately from cooperation with other nations because they too benefit from the global system.

The hegemon provides four collective goods: security, markets, common currency, and loans. For example, Britain dominated the seas by 1850 and provided security for traders and their investments. Britain's presence on the high seas encouraged traders to undertake long-term economic commitments in global markets. In effect, Britain superintended global peace, and that's why the era of the nineteenth century became known as the Pax Britannica.

Second, the hegemonic power provides a large market for the exports of other countries. When power is fragmented and stability is not guaranteed, every country scrambles to maximize exports and minimize imports. But a country that dominates the system is not afraid of competing powers and can be more generous. It opens its markets in the expectation that, as countries export more to its market, they will also buy and import more from it. After all, the hegemonic power has the most advanced technology and products in the world.

Thus, Britain opened its markets in the latter half of the nineteenth century, repealing the Corn Laws, which protected agriculture, and reducing other tariffs. It undertook **unilateral trade liberalization,** lowering or eliminating tariffs without asking other countries to reciprocate. Some countries—Denmark, Holland, and Turkey—followed suit. From 1750 on, Britain and other European powers also imposed free-trade or low-tariff policies on their colonies. They compelled colonies to buy products only from them, often at higher prices than the colonies might pay elsewhere, and to sell products only to them, often at lower prices. These colonial trade treaties were "unequal." The most notorious were the British navigation acts requiring the American colonies to import British products and use British shipping and the unequal treaties imposed on China during the Opium Wars (1839–1842) to allow the tariff-free import of opium.

Spotlight on collective goods

unilateral trade liberalization
one county's lowering or elimination of tariffs without asking other countries to reciprocate.

The opening of global markets has sometimes involved the use of force, as shown in this engraving of British East India Company ships destroying Chinese war junks in the First Opium War of 1841.

Not all countries joined the free-trade parade, especially land-based powers that depended less on peripheral world markets. France, with its tradition of Colbertism, retained high tariffs, and Germany and Italy, newly united in this period, were eager to develop their own national industries and protect them from more advanced industries in England, Holland, Denmark, and elsewhere. Another continental power, the United States, also protected its market. Before the Civil War, the United States was divided on this issue. The agricultural South favored low tariffs so it could import manufactured goods cheaply; the industrial North favored high tariffs to protect indigenous industries. The North won the Civil War, and U.S. tariffs went up and remained at high levels until after 1910.

Third, the hegemonic power supplies a dominant currency in which international transactions can be conducted. Imagine a fragmented world, in which trade is conducted in numerous currencies. Not only is such trade inefficient (if you've exchanged dollars into foreign currencies, you know the generous percentage banks deduct for their services), it is unstable because countries worry about the value of each currency and hedge against devaluation risks. By contrast, a single currency provided by a large country reduces the costs and risks of trading. The country is so large and economically dominant, there is no fear that its currency may lose value. Other countries are willing to hold the currency, assured that they can redeem it for gold, other currencies, or goods in the market of the dominant country.

Thus, in the nineteenth century when Britain converted to gold from a bimetal system of gold and silver and became dominant, other countries also embraced the gold system. Now countries that exported more goods than they imported were paid in gold. That gold eventually wound up in private banks—few countries had central or government banks yet—that used it to make more loans to local merchants. More loans created more local demand, which in turn generated more imports and fewer exports because resources were diverted to producing domestic goods. Fewer exports and more imports corrected the balance of payments. The opposite happened in countries that imported more goods than they exported. Their banks paid out gold and made fewer loans, resulting in fewer imports and more exports and a correction in its balance of payments. This system of international payments was known as the **gold standard.** Gold, fixed in price with respect to local currencies, was the conveyor belt by which countries settled and corrected balance of payments accounts.

gold standard

a pre–World War I system of international payments based on gold, which was fixed in price with respect to local currencies.

Fourth, the hegemonic country supplies loans to the world economy. That's how its currency comes into circulation in the first place. To finance expanding trade and investment, there has to be a larger and larger supply of global financing. The dominant country provides this financing through loans denominated in its currency. It can do so because it exports more than it imports, at least at the outset. It recycles its excess receipts in loans to foreign borrowers. Other countries are willing to hold the dominant country's currency because they know they can buy goods or invest in assets in the dominant country's market. Thus, another service that a hegemonic country provides is a large and deep capital market in which other countries can conduct sophisticated investment and hedging activities. London became the world economy's financial center in the nineteenth century and was replaced by New York only after the United States became the dominant country in the twentieth century.

THE FIRST ERA OF GLOBALIZATION. Under Pax Britannica, world exports and foreign investment soared. This expansion affected North Atlantic trade in the first instance but also trade with Latin America. After gaining their independence in the early nineteenth century, Latin American countries made their own policies, more or less, and avoided the direct effects of unequal treaties imposed on colonial territories. Trade with Australia and South Africa also expanded, but trade with developing countries in Asia and Africa lagged.

Capital flows, such as loans and foreign investments, also rose dramatically during this period, again primarily in the North Atlantic area, South America, South Africa, and Australia. As the leading power, Britain invested heavily in agriculture and infrastructure in other countries. From 1870 to 1913, British foreign direct investment—that is, not just loans but investments in physical facilities in foreign areas—increased 250 percent. By World War I, nearly half of British assets, other than land, were invested overseas, almost 90 percent in primary product areas such as agriculture and commodities.[6]

The world economy achieved levels of interdependence prior to World War I that would not be seen again until the 1970s. So pervasive was this early globalization that, as we note in Chapter 3, authors such as Norman Angell decreed that war was obsolete because it would be too expensive to interrupt economic ties. Indeed, international bankers generally opposed the policies that culminated in World War I. Globalization in this earlier era, however, was more fragile and less complex than it later became. Most exports and investments involved **interindustry trade,** that is, trade between separate industries such as manufactured goods for agricultural and raw materials. Lending involved mostly direct investment in resources and infrastructure. Financial investments in stocks, bonds and banking certificates, and short-term currency and hedging transactions were far less extensive. Later, globalization after World War II involved much more **intra-industry trade,** that is, trade of component parts within the same industry, for example, wiring assemblies for engines, all within the same automobile industry. And it entailed broader and more extensive financial markets involving short-term currency and financial investments that dwarfed direct investments and trade.

Table 8-1 summarizes the causes of Pax Britannica from the various perspectives and levels of analysis. It covers the realist causes just discussed and the liberal, identity, and critical theory perspectives discussed subsequently in this chapter.

Spotlight on interdependence

interindustry trade
trade between separate industries, such as manufactured goods for agricultural materials.

intra-industry trade
trade of component parts within the same industry.

Interwar Period

World War I drastically weakened the British economy and left Britain with large outstanding loans to its colonies. These colonies made up the so-called sterling area, in which the British currency, known as the pound sterling, was used. Britain abandoned and then struggled unsuccessfully to return to the gold standard. To do so, Britain had to squeeze domestic demand to generate exports and pay off the sterling debt. But Britain was no longer strong enough to bear this domestic cost. Meanwhile, the United States grew in economic power. But, after failing to ratify the League of Nations, it withdrew into political isolationism. Thus, the world economy lost its hegemon and, as realist perspectives would expect, the world economy shrank and fragmented. Mercantilism returned in the form of reparations and beggar-thy-neighbor policies involving competitive currency devaluation and trade protectionism. As Charles Kindleberger writes, "part of the reason for the length, and most of the explanation for the depth of the world recession [in the interwar period], was the inability of the British to continue their role as underwriter to the system and the reluctance of the United States to take it on. . . ."[7]

After World War I broke out, Britain and other European countries went off the gold standard. Currencies and the price of gold floated. Prices of goods generally rose

Table 8-1

The Causes of Pax Britannica: By Perspective and Levels of Analysis

Level of analysis		Realist perspective	Liberal perspective	Identity perspective	Critical theory perspective
Systemic	Structure	British hegemony creates collective goods for robust world economy	Industrial revolution ignites world trade and investment	British classical liberal ideas out-compete European and U.S. protection-ist nationalist ideas	Capitalist system emerges in which core states colonize and exploit peripheral states
	Process	Alliances restructure to form less multi-polar system more conducive to free trade	—	Spread of classical liberal economic policies supports stable environment for growth of trade and investment	—
Foreign policy		—	British leaders overcome domestic protectionism and repeal Corn Laws to initiate laissez-faire policies	—	—
Domestic		British export interests seek wider world markets	Britain develops decentralized institutions first, enabling institutional innovations in property rights and finance	Early religious and political revolutions in England create environment for laissez-faire policies	—
Individual		Aggressive British merchants exploit foreign markets	—	Adam Smith and David Ricardo discover and disseminate free-trade ideas	—

as governments placed enormous demands on their economies to meet wartime exigencies. After the war, reconstruction efforts continued to pressure prices. Vast areas of continental Europe needed rebuilding, and soldiers needed civilian employment. Without the discipline of gold, countries inflated their money supply, printing money to produce more goods even if it resulted at the same time in higher prices. Reparations, unstable currencies, and the beggar-thy-neighbor policies added to economic instability.

reparations

large fines in the form of payments levied against an aggressor (in the case of World War I, Germany) to help rebuild nations affected by war (for example, Britain and France).

REPARATIONS. The Versailles Treaty imposed severe **reparations** on Germany to rebuild war-torn Europe. Reparations involved large payments by Germany to help rebuild Britain, France, and other countries. To make these payments, Germany had to export, squeezing resources from domestic reconstruction. It was naturally reluctant to do so and therefore expanded both domestic and export production, severely inflating the German economy.[8] Inflation, which means higher average prices for all goods and assets, is always a tool that debtors use to reduce the real value of their debts. They pay back their debt in currency that is worth less. And Germany used inflation to reduce the value of the reparations it owed. Other countries resisted. Recall how France occupied the Ruhr industrial region of Germany in January 1923 precisely to seize German industrial assets and generate the exports needed to make reparation payments. Eventually, American and British central banks worked out a plan (called the Dawes Plan, after the American banker Charles Dawes) to lend Germany the money to pay its reparations over the longer term. From 1924 to 1929, Germany paid a total of $2 billion in reparations to European powers and another $1 billion in principal and interest on U.S. loans.[9]

DEMISE OF THE GOLD STANDARD. When England abandoned the gold standard, there was no longer a stable common monetary unit. As long as the price of gold and, hence, currencies fluctuated, the world economy lacked a stable basis to foster trade and investment. Banks and individuals were reluctant to lend overseas. (Think about it: if you did not know today with some degree of assurance what the exchange rate or price of the dollar would be in three or four years, would you lend that dollar to someone overseas? If the price of the dollar went down, you would be repaid in principal that was worth less, potentially substantially less, than the original loan.) Great Britain called a conference at the League of Nations in Genoa in 1922 to restore the gold standard. But Britain had drawn down much of its gold and foreign exchange holdings. The United States was now the major surplus country, that is, the country with a net export surplus that resulted in the import of gold and the ability to lend money back to other countries. By 1926, the United States held 45 percent of the world's gold supply. The role of the leading economy had passed from Great Britain to the United States. But the United States was not present at Genoa; it had declined to join the League of Nations. It worked informally to support Britain's return to the gold standard in 1925. As previously mentioned, it helped finance the Dawes Plan and became the principal lender in the world economy by issuing dollar-denominated bonds on behalf of foreign governments and corporations. And, indeed, the system stabilized for a brief period in the late 1920s. But domestic priorities eventually led the United States in 1928 to raise interest rates to slow the boom on Wall Street. When it did so, the international lending and payments system creaked and then crashed.

Higher interest rates made investments in the United States worth more than investments overseas. Capital flowed back into the United States, and net U.S. lending abroad effectively stopped in the second half of 1928. The hegemon was no longer willing to finance the system. When the Great Depression hit in 1929, the world had two choices to adjust to reduced U.S. lending and still maintain currency and gold prices: renegotiate reparations and other loans, or squeeze domestic prices further in Europe to increase exports and reduce the need for U.S. loans. Neither choice was politically palatable. Germany was sliding toward national socialism under Adolf Hitler, and domestic production in Europe and the United States was already starting to drop precipitously. From 1929 to 1932, U.S. industrial production plummeted 48 percent and German production 39 percent. Unemployment reached 25 percent in the United States and 44 percent in Germany. (Remember that when we complain today about unemployment under 10 percent.) World prices dove 47.5 percent, and the volume of world trade went down 25 percent. In twenty-four advanced countries, 25 million workers lost their jobs, and the total income lost in 1932 alone equaled the total income in 1929 of all twenty-four advanced countries for which statistics are available, save the United States and United Kingdom.[10]

A massive infusion of new money not backed by a fixed price of gold was the only thing that might have avoided the severity of the Great Depression, but this was totally contrary to economic thinking at the time. As identity perspectives might emphasize, ideas constrained material and institutional options. Most economists thought that monetary expansion was a problem that would lead to higher inflation, not a solution that would lead to higher production and output. And monetary expansion would have required an unprecedented degree of international cooperation in a world that was being torn apart by larger political and geostrategic forces (which realist perspectives would emphasize). The answer, instead, was *sauve qui peut*—every country would fend for itself. In 1931, Britain suspended gold convertibility, and in 1933 after the election of Franklin Roosevelt, the United States devalued the dollar (eventually requiring $35 instead of $20.67 to obtain an ounce of gold, each dollar now being worth less in terms of gold). Governments convened the London Economic Conference in June 1933 to try one last time to salvage the system. This time the United States attended. But the most significant international economic meeting to date failed completely, not least because the U.S. delegate to the conference delivered the message that the United States would not rejoin any scheme to reinstate fixed prices for currencies.[11]

Beggar-Thy-Neighbor Policies. The 1930s came to represent the worst possible model for international economic relations. Countries engaged in unrestrained, competitive policies to reduce imports and increase exports. Everyone wanted to sell, and no one wanted to buy. With all countries doing the same thing, they succeeded only in reducing export demand and shrinking world markets. One country after another reimposed high import tariffs. The most famous case was the Smoot-Hawley Tariff passed by the U.S. Congress in 1930. Smoot-Hawley raised U.S. tariffs to levels—60 percent of the value of dutiable imports—not seen since the Tariff of Abominations in 1828 (which almost provoked the South to secede and start a civil war thirty years early).[12] Countries also devalued their currencies, made them cheaper, in a self-destructive effort to lower prices for their exports and trade their way out of depression. In anticipation of such exchange rate changes, capital flowed rapidly into or out of countries, destabilizing external accounts even more. Such competitive policies to reduce imports and the value of currencies became known as **beggar-thy-neighbor policies.**

Old-style mercantilism had called for export surpluses that could be converted into gold for military purposes. Mercantilist incentives to buy military equipment increased as war clouds gathered during the 1930s. But a new kind of social mercantilism also fanned protectionism. Countries sought surpluses to revive their economies and create jobs. But, with everyone trying to export and no one willing to import, surpluses could not be achieved. Even seventeenth-century mercantilism was better than the interwar beggar-thy-neighbor policies. In the case of mercantilism, the amount of gold for which mercantilist states competed remained constant or perhaps even grew a bit through new discoveries. But in the case of interwar policies, the amount of imports or the size of the world market for which countries competed shrank even as countries tried to expand exports. Countries were chasing exactly the exports they were in the process of destroying by reducing imports.

After 1931, the world economy splintered into a bewildering array of conflicting regional and bilateral markets. The main regional markets were a U.S.-led western hemispheric system based on gold (with the United States going back on the gold standard in 1934 at $35 per ounce), a UK-led colonial commonwealth market based on the pound sterling, and a Nazi Germany–led continental European system based on the Reichsmark and direct government control of currencies, trade, and investment. Trade

beggar-thy-neighbor policies

competitive economic policies to reduce imports by raising tariffs and to increase exports by lowering the value of currencies, with the net result that global markets shrink.

markets became increasingly bilateral and discriminatory. Unwilling to run trade deficits and unable to achieve trade surpluses, countries sought to balance trade through **quotas,** or specific limits on goods that could be imported or exported.

Pax Americana, or globalization 3.0, followed the interwar period and emerged in two phases: globalization 2.5 was the Bretton Woods system that organized economic activities among the western countries and lasted from 1950 to 1973; globalization 3.0 was the information age that accompanied the revival and dominance of U.S. and western economies as the Cold War ended and created the single global market of western, eastern, and developing countries that prevails today.

Pax Americana: 1950–1973

After World War II, the United States finally accepted its role as the leading world economic power. It led the effort to provide for postwar security, first through the United Nations and then through NATO; it rescinded Smoot-Hawley and opened its markets for imports; it fixed the dollar in terms of gold; and it made generous loans through the Marshall Plan to kick-start the reconstruction of war-torn economies abroad.

The United States was now clearly the dominant power among western countries. It accounted for 60 percent of GNP among industrial (OECD) countries, 33 percent of trade, and two-thirds of all gold supplies. Already during the war, it had initiated discussions with Great Britain and other countries to design a more stable postwar international economic system. In July 1944, the United States convened the largest world economic conference in history. The conference at Bretton Woods, New Hampshire, reached agreements that gave the postwar economy its name, the Bretton Woods international economic system.

BRETTON WOODS. The Bretton Woods agreements drew on the experience of the world economy to date. The pre–World War I gold standard suggested the power of stable exchange rates and open markets. But the interwar period demonstrated both the domestic employment costs of maintaining stable exchange rates and the destabilizing effects of uncontrolled and speculative capital flows. The Bretton Woods agreements sought a happy middle ground between these two experiences. They placed the objective of opening trade markets at the top of the postwar economic agenda. But they struck a compromise between rigidly fixed and floating exchange rates and between domestic policy discipline and external finance.

FIXED EXCHANGE RATES AND THE DOLLAR/GOLD STANDARD. Bretton Woods fixed exchange rates just as the gold standard did, but it fixed the rates in terms of the dollar rather than gold. The United States was the only country that had an obligation to redeem dollars in terms of actual gold (at $35 per ounce). The currency system, because it relied mostly on dollars, became known as the **dollar standard** or, to acknowledge the U.S. gold obligation, the dollar/gold standard. Bretton Woods also permitted countries to change their exchange rates under specified circumstances, or what was called fundamental disequilibrium, if the other members approved. Hence, the system was not as rigid as the old gold standard. The United States, on the other hand, could not change the price of gold. If it did, the rest of the world might lose confidence in the system and no longer be willing to hold dollars. Countries might then scramble to buy gold, and gold supplies would not be sufficient to satisfy them all. The system would implode.

quotas
quantitative limits on imports or exports regardless of price.

dollar standard
the fixed exchange rate system established by Bretton Woods, that pegged the U.S. dollar to gold and other currencies to the dollar.

Thus, the United States could devalue, or lower the price of, the dollar only by convincing other countries to revalue, or raise the price of, their currencies. Generally, countries in surplus on their external accounts need to revalue (to lower exports and raise imports). But they face less pressure to change the value of their currency than deficit countries do because surplus countries are accumulating foreign reserves. Deficit countries, by contrast, are losing foreign exchange reserves and need to borrow. At some point, deficit countries have to devalue or they go bankrupt. Surplus countries can accumulate gold indefinitely. As we'll see, the reluctance of surplus countries to revalue became one of the Achilles's heels of the Bretton Woods system.

MULTILATERAL TRADE. In addition, the Bretton Woods system established a mechanism for **multilateral trade liberalization,** in contrast to unilateral trade liberalization under Pax Britannica. The United States had initiated bilateral trade liberalization already in 1934 under the Reciprocal Trade Agreements Act; it now promoted multilateral liberalization at Bretton Woods. Nations would negotiate reciprocal tariff reductions and apply the **most-favored-nation (MFN) principle,** that is, apply the same low tariff to all nations that they offered to the most-favored nation, meaning the nation that paid the lowest tariffs. MFN treatment avoided the discrimination among countries that had chewed up export markets in the 1930s. Agriculture and commodities such as copper were excluded. Few Latin American countries participated (the exception being Chile) because they exported mostly agriculture and commodities and saw few benefits. Some Asian countries, such as Singapore and South Korea, did participate, but most developing countries were still colonies. Thus, subsequent trade negotiations under the initial postwar trade organization known as the General Agreement on Tariffs and Trade (GATT) dramatically lowered tariffs only on manufactured products traded mostly among the industrial countries.

PUBLIC FINANCING AND PRIVATE CAPITAL CONTROLS. Finally, anticipating larger trade flows, Bretton Woods provided public financing to give countries more time to reduce imports and increase exports if they were running trade deficits. Prior to Bretton Woods, financing of trade deficits was ad hoc and negotiated from private banks. Bretton Woods made such financing systematic and available beforehand through public institutions such as the IMF. The IMF and other international economic institutions such as the World Bank were expected to provide adequate external financing to encourage countries to change domestic policies to correct trade imbalances. The Bretton Woods agreements did not liberalize private capital flows. Countries were still allowed to control foreign investment and private banking transactions. The bad experience with speculative capital flows in the interwar years was very much in the minds of negotiators. Restricting capital flows reduced the prospects of large and sudden shifts in external balances and gave deficit countries more leeway to pursue domestic policies that did not reduce jobs. But capital controls also discouraged foreign direct investment, obstructed the development of private international financial markets, and generally reduced the availability of world savings.

The Bretton Woods system succeeded beyond anyone's expectations. Economists refer to the period right after World War II as the "Golden Age." [13] From 1950 to 1973, growth averaged more than 8 percent per year for the OECD countries (twenty-five industrial nations) and over 15 percent per year for developing countries, such as Hong Kong and South Korea, that participated in international trade. Exports among

multilateral trade liberalization

a Pax Americana trade system in which nations negotiate reciprocal tariff reductions rather than one nation reducing tariffs unilaterally.

most-favored-nation (MFN) principle

the principle in trade agreements by which nations that negotiate tariff reductions offer the same low tariff to all nations that they offer to the most-favored nation, meaning the nation that pays the lowest tariffs.

Table 8-2

The Causes of Pax Americana, 1950–1973: By Perspective and Levels of Analysis

Level of analysis		Realist perspective	Liberal perspective	Identity perspective	Critical theory perspective
Systemic	*Structure*	• Bipolar U.S.-Soviet confrontation creates better environment than multipolar interwar system for free trade • American hegemony after World War II overcomes beggar-thy-neighbor policies among western countries	United Nations creates Bretton Woods institutions to overcome weaknesses of laissez-faire system	U.S. conservative Chicago School ideas compete with British and European aggressive Keynesian ideas	Social construction of embedded liberalism creates Bretton Woods consensus (shared ideas) of international free trade and domestic government interventionism
	Process	The seven sisters, or western oil companies, develop oil markets to rebuild Europe and Asia	Multilateral trade negotiations create expanded global markets that grow through spillover from trade to finance	—	—
Foreign policy		—	—	Embedded liberalism trades off liberalization of international markets for government intervention in domestic markets to provide a social safety net	—
Domestic		Export interests in the United States overcome isolationist forces and seek world markets	—	—	—
Individual		—	—	Karl Polanyi and Friedrich Hayek popularize socialist and conservative economic ideas, respectively	—

OECD countries went up nearly sixfold. By the mid-1970s, trade flows had returned to levels generated under the gold standard before World War I.

Table 8-2 summarizes the causes of Pax Americana (1950–1973) from the various perspectives and levels of analysis. It can help you follow the realist view of the causes just discussed and the liberal, identity, and critical theory perspectives discussed later in this chapter.

Pax Americana: 1970s to Present

However, in the 1970s, America's relative power declined, and the Bretton Woods system collapsed. The Soviet Union appeared to extend its power, projecting military forces into Afghanistan, Southeast Asia, and parts of Africa just as the United States withdrew from Vietnam. In addition, the oil-producing developing countries provoked two oil crises and dramatically altered the power relationships between advanced countries (generally referred to as the North) and developing countries (labeled the South). From a realist perspective, the precondition of hegemonic power waned, and the global economic system slowed in train and entered a period of stagflation, or slow growth accompanied by rising prices. The oil-rich Organization of Petroleum Exporting Countries (OPEC) and the rest of the developing world called for a New International Economic Order (NIEO) to replace the Bretton Woods institutions. And OPEC's success suggested a new ideology of interventionist rather than open-market policies. Power shifts necessitated institutional and ideological changes. Notice again how realist perspectives do not ignore institutional or ideological factors but see them as ultimately being caused by changes in relative power factors.

<u>causal</u>
arrow →

But in the 1980s, American power rebounded; and when the Soviet Union collapsed in 1991, a single power, for the first time in history, straddled the entire globe. From a realist perspective, American *global* preeminence is what makes globalization 3.0 different from both globalization 2.0 and 2.5. British dominance in the nineteenth century under globalization 2.0 centered mostly on the high seas. American dominance under Bretton Woods and globalization 2.5 covered only the western countries. Under globalization 3.0, America dominates a single world economy as no country has ever done before.

COLLAPSE OF BRETTON WOODS. The success of the Bretton Woods system shifted power relatively to Europe and Japan. By the early 1970s, the United States accounted for only one-third of world industrial production, compared to one-half in 1945, and U.S. gold reserves were only a fraction of the total dollars held abroad that countries might choose to redeem in gold. The decline in relative U.S. power meant that it could no longer provide the collective goods of security, currency, markets, and loans to preserve the hegemonic world economy. Confidence in each of these areas declined.

France challenged U.S. security leadership. In the 1960s, President Charles de Gaulle withdrew France from the military command in NATO and launched a policy of détente with the Soviet Union. France was particularly eager to reduce the privileged role of the U.S. currency. As trade expanded, the world needed more and more dollars to finance external accounts. The United States supplied these dollars by spending more abroad for imports and investments than foreign countries spent in the United States. Foreign countries accumulated and held excess dollars, in effect lending them to the United States. De Gaulle objected to this arrangement and sought to reduce the role of the dollar both by redeeming dollars for gold and by advocating the creation of an international reserve currency independent of the dollar, known as Special Drawing Rights (SDRs). To stem the outflow of dollars, the United States needed to lower the price of its currency relative to those of Europe and Japan; other countries would then find a cheaper dollar less attractive to hold. But under the Bretton Woods rules, the United States could not change the price of gold. So, the only way it could lower the value of the dollar was for Europe and Japan to raise the prices of their currencies. Europe and Japan resisted because they enjoyed the fact that their undervalued currencies made their exports cheaper and fueled national economic prosperity.

Trade rules also discriminated against U.S. interests, reducing its willingness to maintain open markets. When the United States provided Marshall Plan assistance to strengthen western security, it encouraged European countries to cooperate with one another. The **European Payments Union,** a predecessor to European integration in the 1950s, allowed European countries to settle their import and export accounts first with one another and then with the United States. This arrangement discriminated against U.S. imports and exports. Later, European integration reinforced this discrimination by reducing tariffs to zero in a European Common Market on industrial products, which excluded the United States, and by creating a Common Agricultural Policy and increasing European production, which reduced agricultural imports from the United States. Similarly, Japan was a latecomer to industrial free trade. It did not join the GATT until the 1960s and practiced strategic trade, which not only limited imports but targeted exports. Government directives channeled subsidies and loans to Japanese industries to build up a competitive, as opposed to comparative, advantage in a particular product such as semiconductors and to exploit that advantage on foreign markets (more about this later in the chapter and in Chapter 10).

Finally, the United States lost its role as dominant lender in the Bretton Woods system. Lending by banks based in Europe gradually exceeded lending by U.S. banks. As trade expanded, companies invested more in Europe, both to take advantage of lower labor and transportation costs and to invest inside the Common Market, where they paid no tariffs on exports to other member countries. The first wave of MNCs, mostly American, washed ashore in Europe in the 1960s to exploit the zero tariffs of the Common Market. U.S. companies could not transfer dollars directly to Europe because the Bretton Woods system controlled capital flows. Hence these companies borrowed dollars accumulating in banks based in Europe. This borrowing created what became known as the unregulated offshore or Eurodollar market. The U.S. government periodically tried to stem this capital outflow, but, as realist perspectives see it, it was no longer dominant enough to do so.

All these factors weakened America's commitment to maintaining sound domestic policies that supported the price of gold. In the late 1960s, the United States switched from moderate to aggressive Keynesian policies (a change in economic ideology, which identity perspectives emphasize; see later discussion). Large budget deficits, loose money, and domestic wage and price controls, spurred by the need to finance the Vietnam War and social welfare programs of the Great Society, eventually tripled inflation between 1961–1967 and 1968–1974. Inflation cheapened the dollar because countries holding dollars now had to pay higher prices for U.S. products and assets, and countries rushed to redeem their dollars in gold. At Camp David in August 1971, the United States suspended the convertibility of dollars into gold. In December 1971 and again in February 1973, it devalued the dollar. But nothing could save the dollar at this late date and, within a few weeks after the second devaluation, the dollar floated loose completely, and its value sank.

The Bretton Woods system was dead, well before the first oil crisis in October 1973. The world economy went to a floating exchange rate system. Within ten years the dollar depreciated from $35 per ounce of gold to more than $800 per ounce. Ouch! Imagine if you had trusted the United States and continued to hold dollars instead of gold during this period. You would have been on the losing side of one of the greatest devaluations of a currency in market history.

European Payments Union a predecessor to European integration in the 1950s that allowed European countries to settle their import and export accounts first with one another and then with the United States, thus discriminating against U.S. imports and exports.

OIL POWER. From a realist perspective, oil and resources are central elements in the struggle for power. Western governments colonized the Middle East and put western companies in charge of oil development. The Middle East was home to two-thirds of the world's known oil reserves. After World War II, Saudi Arabia and the newly independent oil-producing states fought back. The oil crises of the 1970s saw the balance of oil power shift decisively from the western oil companies to the **Organization of Petroleum Exporting Countries (OPEC),** a cartel of the oil-producing states led by the major Middle East oil-reserve countries.

Private companies had spearheaded the development of oil in the last half of the nineteenth century. The most famous was the Standard Oil Company, founded by John D. Rockefeller. Western companies discovered Middle East oil in the interwar period, when the area, except for Saudi Arabia, was still under colonial control. English, Dutch, French, and American companies divided up oil concessions under the so-called Red Line Agreement. Standard Oil of California (one of the spin-off companies formed when Rockefeller's empire was broken up in 1911) and Texaco formed the Arabian-American Oil Company, known as Aramco. Standard Oil of New Jersey (Exxon) and Standard Oil of New York (Mobil) joined Aramco after World War II. These four companies, along with Royal Dutch/Shell, British Petroleum, Gulf, and the French firm CFP, controlled the production and distribution of Middle East oil. The firms, minus CFP, came to be known as the **seven sisters.**

After World War II, Middle East countries looked for ways to renegotiate the oil concessions. The United States, concerned about Soviet influence in the region, viewed such independent or nationalist initiatives as communist-inspired and used covert operations in 1953 to prevent the overthrow of the western-oriented shah of Iran. The United States and local governments also clashed over the Arab-Israeli dispute. During Arab-Israeli wars in 1956 and 1967, Arab countries tried to embargo oil to supporters of Israel. In this period, crude oil sold for about $2 per barrel. Supplies were plentiful and temporary shortages had little impact on the market; these early embargoes did not work. As time went on, however, world growth accelerated and oil-producing countries acquired technology and learned the oil business from the seven sisters. Influence shifted to the oil-exporting countries. In September 1960, four Middle East countries—Saudi Arabia, Kuwait, Iraq, and Iran—plus Venezuela established OPEC. At the time, these countries controlled 80 percent of the world's crude oil exports. Throughout the 1960s, they pressured the seven sisters for higher oil revenues and ownership participation in production decisions.

By 1973, given the sustained growth and now inflationary pressures building up in the world economy, oil markets were much tighter. When another Arab-Israeli war broke out in October, the oil weapon proved more effective. At a meeting in Kuwait City on October 16, OPEC officials announced a 70 percent increase in the price of crude oil, from $2.90 to $5.12 per barrel. It was the first time OPEC, not the seven sisters, set the world oil price, and Ahmed Zaki Yamani, the Saudi oil minister, reflected on the event: "This is the moment for which I have been waiting a long time. . . . We are masters of our own commodity."[14] The next day, the oil ministers from Arab countries alone (the Persian Iranian representative having left) announced an embargo of oil, cutting production by 5 percent each month and specifically targeting the United States for the most severe cuts. Targeting the United States did not work because the oil companies were able to redistribute supplies from other sources without shipping Arab oil directly to the United States. But the cutbacks supported higher prices. In December, OPEC doubled prices once again to $11.65 per barrel. Oil prices had quin-

Evolution of World Economy from Different Perspectives

Realist		Liberal		Identity		Critical theory	
Age of mercantilism	1500s–1600s			Renaissance and individual creativity	1300s–1400s	Colonialism and imperialism	1500s–1800s
				Reformation and the Protestant ethic	1500s		
				Religious and economic revolutions in England	1600s		
		Industrial revolution	1700s	Laissez-faire ideas of Adam Smith and David Ricardo	1700s–1800s		
Britain dominates high seas—Pax Britannica	1800s	Unilateral laissez-faire trade rules	Early 1800s				
Gold standard emerges	Late 1800s	Trade and investment boom—first era of globalization	Late 1800s	Ideas of economic nationalism; ideas of Marxist socialism	Late 1800s	Historical dialectic between capitalism and socialism	1900s
Britain declines and the United States hides	1930s	Breakdown of free-trade—beggar-thy-neighbor policies	1930s	Keynesian economic ideas	1930s		
United States dominates after World War II—Pax Americana	Second half of 1900s	Bretton Woods institutions create multilateral free trade	Mid-1900s	Chicago School of neoclassical economic ideas	1950s	Dependency, neocolonialism	1950s–1960s
		Information revolution	1970s				
				Washington Consensus	1990s	World systems	1990s

Group of 77 (G-77)
originally a collection of seventy-seven developing countries, organized to champion cartels and the regulation of other world resource markets.

New International Economic Order (NIEO)
A set of economic proposals put forward in the 1970s by the Group of 77 developing nations that challenged the Bretton Woods system.

Group of 7 (G-7)
starting in 1975, an annual process of economic summits among the heads of state and governments of the United States, Great Britain, France, Germany, Japan, and, after 1976, Canada and Italy.

stagflation
slow growth accompanied by high inflation.

petrodollar recycling
the recycling by private banks in Europe and the United States of dollars deposited by oil exporters through loans to oil-importing countries.

tupled in three months and would stay there or go even higher after the oil embargo ended in March 1974.

Inspired by OPEC, developing countries organized the **Group of 77 (G-77),** a collection of developing countries that now numbers one hundred and thirty countries, to champion cartels and regulation of world resource markets. At meetings of the United Nations Conference on Trade and Development (UNCTAD), the G-77 put together its proposals for the **New International Economic Order (NIEO).** These proposals advocated a Commodity Import Program (CIP) to set prices and supplies of raw materials other than oil, such as bauxite, aluminum, and copper; a Generalized System of Preferences (GSP) to provide special and differential treatment for developing countries' manufacturing exports; codes of conduct to expedite the transfer of technology and regulate MNCs; and generous programs of aid and subsidized loans to promote development. NIEO posed a direct challenge to the Bretton Woods order. As realist perspectives expect, developing countries were pushing back against the free-trade policies and MNCs of the United States and its western allies.

The advanced countries fought back. They too created new institutional mechanisms. In the wake of the first oil crisis, five principal industrial countries met at Rambouillet, France, in November 1975 and started an annual process of economic summits among the heads of state and government. The process became known as the **Group of 7 (G-7)**—the United States, Great Britain, France, Germany, Japan, and, after 1976, Canada and Italy. The G-7 may have helped stave off the worst consequences of the oil crises, especially, as liberal perspectives see it, preserving the open trading system, which might have collapsed under the weight of volatile capital movements and protectionism as happened in the 1930s.[15] The advanced countries also established the International Energy Agency (IEA) to coordinate importing-country policies toward OPEC and initiated a Conference on International Economic Cooperation (CIEC) with OPEC countries to counter the more revolutionary proposals being propounded under NIEO.

The oil crisis threw the world economy into its worst condition since the 1930s. **Stagflation,** slow growth accompanied by high inflation, crippled industrial economies, while volatile exchange rate and capital movements discouraged trade and foreign investment. Oil-importing developing countries were hit particularly hard. Except for a few Asian countries that based their development on exports, most developing countries, especially in Latin America, pursued import substitution policies—building up domestic industries to substitute for imports (discussed in Chapter 11). They had little capacity to increase exports to pay for higher-priced oil imports and thus needed foreign loans. The IMF and government aid could no longer meet this need. Hence, private banks in Europe and the United States stepped in to fill the gap. They undertook what became known as **petrodollar recycling.** They recycled the dollars that oil exporters deposited with them by making loans to oil-importing countries. From 1973 to 1982, the debt of six principal Latin American countries soared from $35 billion to $246 billion.

The world economy, then, was already in bad shape when the second oil crisis hit in 1979. The price of crude oil doubled once again from roughly $15 per barrel in 1978 to $35 per barrel in 1981. The proximate cause was the revolution in Iran. This time, unlike in 1953, the revolution succeeded in unseating the shah. Disruptions cut oil supplies and caused another price panic. But the underlying causes were the widespread inflation, protectionism, and rapid financial expansion of world markets in the 1970s. From 1973 to 1979, annual inflation among sixteen advanced countries averaged 9.4 percent and among a representative group of Latin American and Asian developing countries it averaged 95.0 and 14.6 percent, respectively.[16] In the United States, inflation hit 13.5 percent in 1980, and unemployment reached around 10 percent in 1975–1976, levels not seen since the immediate postwar years of 1946–1947.

UNITED STATES REBOUNDS AND WINS THE COLD WAR. Why didn't the United States use force to prevent the oil price hikes? Realist accounts say because it was weakened by its withdrawal from Vietnam in 1973 and subsequent Soviet interventions in Africa, Indochina, and Afghanistan. Through a domino effect, the U.S. failure in Vietnam led to power shifts elsewhere, and the Pax Americana seemed to be on its way out. Pax Sovietica or Pax OPEC was about to replace it.

But in the 1980s the United States and other western countries rebounded. Power shifted back to the United States and industrial nations as Soviet imperialism burdened the Soviet economy and the oil-importing developing countries confronted mountains of OPEC-generated debt that they could not repay. Inflation came down, and so did oil prices, weakening OPEC's clout. The United States powered ahead, exploiting the information revolution before anyone else did and, eventually, burying the Soviet Union, as President Reagan predicted in 1982, "on the ash-heap of history."[17]

How did the United States do it? Realist perspectives see power shifting by competition and struggle, so they give considerable credit for the rebound to the policies by Ronald Reagan in the United States and Margaret Thatcher in Great Britain to rebuild military defenses and strengthen free markets in the Cold War struggle with the Soviet Union. Actions from the domestic level of analysis increased western power. Reagan and Thatcher introduced policies to reduce inflation, stimulate savings and investment, deregulate labor and capital markets, and liberalize trade. The United States, for example, was the first advanced country to deregulate the airline industry (already in the late 1970s) and break up the monopoly of AT&T in the telecommunications sector. And the United States and Britain acted more or less unilaterally (domestic level) or competitively (systemic process level) to pull other countries along with them, as realist accounts would expect, rather than acting cooperatively on the basis of common institutions or shared consensus (systemic structural level), as liberal and identity perspectives would expect.

causal arrow

Policies to reduce inflation inevitably raise interest rates. Why? Because inflation entails too much money chasing too few goods. As a result, the prices of goods go up. The demand for money therefore has to be reduced. The way to do that is to raise the price of money. And the price of money is the interest rate. Tighter money in the United States and Great Britain sent short-term interest rates soaring through the roof—over 20 percent in the United States. The increase was larger than it would have been if the U.S. government had not also increased its budget deficit, reducing taxes and raising defense spending. The budget deficit increased the demand for money even as higher interest rates sought to reduce demand.

Germany's Chancellor Helmut Schmidt complained to President Reagan at the G-7 economic summit in Ottawa, Canada, in July 1981 that Germany now had "the highest interest rates . . . since the birth of Jesus Christ."[18] Let's just assume he had a good memory. But what did German interest rates have to do with U.S. interest rates? Well, when the United States raised interest rates, short-term money flowed from foreign banks to U.S. banks to capture the higher yield. Capital markets were now increasingly open, and commercial banks did more and more international lending. The capital inflow increased the demand for dollars and raised the price of the dollar. Measured against the currencies of eleven other industrial countries, the dollar soared from an index of 90–110 in the 1970s to over 160 in 1985.[19] Correspondingly, the price of German and other European currencies went down. Why didn't European governments accept this decline? After all, it made their exports cheaper. True, but it also made their imports more expensive, and European governments too were worried about inflation. So, they raised interest rates to match U.S. increases and preserve the value of their currencies. The United States acted as the world's self-appointed central banker and led the world toward lower inflation.

Doesn't sound like a very international approach, right? The developing countries screamed even louder than Chancellor Schmidt. Remember they had accumulated huge loans to pay off their external deficits from the oil crises; now the interest rates on those loans dramatically increased. How were the developing countries going to service these loans? They could no longer cover the repayment of principal, let alone the interest due. In August 1982, Mexico suspended the interest payments on its $80 billion debt acquired before Mexico became a significant oil producer. Brazil and Argentina followed suit that fall.

The debt crisis plagued North-South relations throughout the 1980s. Eventually, the IMF increased lending again, helping to pay off, or "bail out," private banks. In return, banks rescheduled, or "stretched out," the developing countries' loans, reducing interest rates and increasing the number of years to repay the loans. The IMF also promoted structural reforms to wean developing countries from import substitution policies and encourage them to export more. The United States extended major loans to Mexico to underwrite the North American Free Trade Agreement (NAFTA; see Chapter 10). The cost of adjustment was high. From 1980 to 1986, the major Latin American countries averaged a negative 1.6 percent annual growth rate.

The U.S. economy, by contrast, rebounded vigorously. From 1983 to 1989, real growth in the United States (that is, adjusted for inflation) averaged 4.3 percent per year. After a mild recession in 1990–1991, the economy grew again from 1992 to 1999 at an average rate of 3.6 percent a year. Inflation dropped from over 10 percent in 1980 to under 4 percent by 1990 and stayed at 2 percent or less throughout the 1990s. Annual productivity growth doubled from the 1970s to the 1980s and then went up another 50 percent in the 1990s. No other country matched the performance of the United States. Thus, when the Soviet Union disappeared in December 1991, the United States sat supreme astride the world economy. And U.S. policies were emulated everywhere, particularly in the former communist countries and heavily indebted developing countries.

Thus, as realist perspectives see it, globalization 3.0 is a direct consequence of America's rebound from the economic malaise of the 1970s and its subsequent victory in the Cold War. When the Soviet Union disappeared, the United States became the world's only military and economic superpower. The global system was now unipolar in a way it had never been under Pax Britannica or the previous incarnation of Pax Americana (which, recall, until 1973 was only western-based).

FUTURE OF PAX AMERICANA. A third oil crisis hit in 2003. Oil prices averaged around $20 a barrel throughout the 1990s. Then, beginning in early 2003 and coincident with the war in Iraq, oil prices moved up steadily. By mid-2008, oil prices reached levels over $135 a barrel. This time, however, the U.S. and world economies weathered the impact much better. After a recession in 2001–2002 that was milder than the one in 1990–1991, the U.S. economy roared back and grew at a rate of more than 3.5 percent per year for the next ten quarters, a streak not accomplished since the late 1940s. The world economy also maintained solid growth—rising at unprecedented rates of 5 percent per year from 2003 to 2007. America's preeminence opened up the world not only for technology and the Internet but also for the spread of free markets and democracy. Former communist countries—from the Soviet Union and eastern Europe—and previously protectionist, developing countries—China, India, Mexico, Brazil, and the like—flocked to join the world economy. China grew three times and India twice as fast as the United States. Oil-producing countries, which now included Russia and Mexico, also benefited from another bonanza of petrodollars. From 1998 to 2005, oil-producing states earned an estimated $1.3 trillion, about half going to Saudi Arabia and the Persian Gulf states. Despite soaring oil demand, a war in the Middle East, and bitter controversy over free-market economic policies, the world economy thrived.

By mid-2008, however, the United States appeared to be slipping into a recession, and the outlook for the global economy was less certain. Critics of U.S. policy blamed U.S. budget and current account deficits and warned, as they had during similar downturns in the past, that the dollar would have to depreciate significantly and eventually undermine American preeminence. Indeed, the dollar did decline after 2002 by some 40 percent against the euro. Was Pax Americana finally coming to an end? For some realist perspectives, those of the power balancing school, preeminence or hegemony can never last forever. Hence, counterforces are already developing to push back American power and potentially limit globalization. Terrorists exploit the Internet to disrupt global trade and financial centers; populist leaders in Cuba, Venezuela, Bolivia, and Malaysia resist American power; and China and Russia control the Internet and repress nonstate actors to limit foreign influences. From a realist perspective, power struggles continue to shape globalization and determine the evolution of technology, institutions, and ideas.

Thus, realist perspectives see trade and ideology (democracy) as following the flag, or the rise and fall of power of respective countries. Interdependence and identity are not the cause but the result of power shifts. The four historical periods of mercantilism, Pax Britannica, interwar years, and Pax Americana show that the ebb and flow of international markets are largely determined by the ebb and flow of the distribution of power. Global markets flourish under a dominant power and decline under competition among many powers. But liberal perspectives question whether power balances satisfactorily explain historical outcomes. In each of the four periods, the world economy was very different. What explains the growing role of technology and international institutions from one period to the next? And what explains the fact that the United States exploited its economic hegemony after, but not before, World War II?

<— *causal arrow*

Table 8-3 summarizes the causes of Pax Americana from 1973 to the present from the various perspectives and levels of analysis. It covers the realist perspectives discussed here and the liberal, identity, and critical theory perspectives discussed in the rest of this chapter.

Liberal Explanations

Liberal accounts explain the evolution of the global economy primarily in terms of technological change, specialization, trade and increasing interdependence, and the strengthening of global rules and institutions. From this perspective, the most important historical events driving globalization are (1) the agricultural and industrial revolutions that launched the modern world, (2) the discovery of market institutions and

Table 8-3

The Causes of Pax Americana, 1973–Present: By Perspective and Levels of Analysis

Level of analysis		Realist perspective	Liberal perspective	Identity perspective	Critical theory perspective
Systemic	Structure	Decline and then rebound of America's dominant power	• Complex interdependence creates multiple issue areas and restrains the use of force in oil crises of 1970s • New International Economic Order (NIEO) fails to replace Bretton Woods	Conservative Hayekian ideas win out over communist and socialist ideas	Deepening contradictions as American imperialism exploits the rest of the world
	Process	OPEC states form cartel to shift balance of power in oil sector	• Outbreak of the information revolution • Spillover of trade to financial sectors	—	—
Foreign policy		—	—	—	—
Domestic		Rise of conservative political parties in U.S. and UK	—	U.S. and British free-market reforms reverse stagflation	—
Individual		—	—	Reagan and Thatcher lead free-market revolution	—

free-trade rules that propelled Pax Britannica, (3) the Bretton Woods institutions and their spillover or path-dependence effects that characterized the first phase of Pax Americana, and (4) the Internet or information revolution that extended Pax Americana to include the communist and developing worlds.

Agricultural and Industrial Revolutions

According to liberal accounts, the agricultural and industrial revolutions of the seventeenth and eighteenth centuries did far more than add a new element of economic power to the workings of the old military balance of power, as mercantilism implies. The revolution in machinery to increase human productivity, first on the farm and then in the factory, transformed domestic and international relationships and created many new actors in world affairs, especially nongovernmental ones. Not surprisingly, as liberal perspectives see it, the emergence of the world economy dates precisely from the onset of the agricultural and industrial revolutions.

The agricultural revolution began in the sixteenth and seventeenth centuries. Technological change increased farm output dramatically, allowing land holdings to be consolidated and farming to become more specialized. Western Europe specialized in animal husbandry and became a source of meat for eastern Europe, while eastern Europe specialized in grain and became a breadbasket for western Europe. As farms modernized, peasants gained bargaining power over the landowners. Peasants who worked in bondage to landowners exploited the revolution in property rights that occurred at the time. They became tenant farmers who paid rent and eventually yeoman farmers who owned their own farms outright. Farmers moved into towns where commerce and cottage industries such as handicrafts and textiles sprang up to absorb the surplus labor. For various reasons (having to do with power struggles, realist perspectives would say, or political ideas and the Enlightenment, as identity perspectives see it), this development went further in England, Holland, and northern France than in Spain, Portugal, and eastern Europe. Whereas Spain and Portugal had led the age of mercantilism, economic leadership now shifted from southern to northwestern Europe, to England, the Netherlands, and France. As we have learned in Chapter 2, France fought the Spanish Hapsburgs in Italy and elsewhere, England destroyed the Spanish Armada in 1588, and the Netherlands gained its independence from the Hapsburgs via the Treaty of Westphalia in 1648. Overseas trade also expanded as European colonizers followed the explorers, exploiting the revolution in shipping and transportation technologies. All these developments were interrelated and their relative significance disputed. As we discuss in Chapter 13, the key debate was and remains the extent to which early European modernization was internally generated or dependent on the enslavement and exploitation of the colonial world.[20]

The industrial revolution began in England in the second half of the eighteenth century and changed economic and social life unalterably. The factory created the modern manufacturing economy. The step-level change was not immediately noticeable to the people of the time. Factories sprang up initially in isolated areas, and the transformation from agriculture to manufacturing took a hundred years or more before teeming cities and bustling cosmopolitan travel became the earmarks of modern life. But the breakout of the modern economy dates almost exactly from the time of the industrial revolution, confirming from the liberal perspective, the crucial role of technological change.

The eighteenth century produced a welter of new inventions—chemical combustion, cotton gin, steam engine, and chemical fertilizers, to name just a few. The key to this revolution was the harnessing of mechanical power to the production of goods. Prior to the eighteenth century, human and animal power limited output. Now machines multiplied human and animal labor. Indeed, productivity, which becomes a major marker of modern economies, is precisely the ratio or multiplier between human and material input and the eventual output of goods. With machines, labor could produce three, five, or ten times more products in a given period of time than before. Thus, machines in large textile plants began to do the spinning and weaving that had previously been done in homes or small cottage industries, displacing for the first time, but not the last, thousands of workers in small shops. Steam engines magnified the power available to pump water from mines or to turn equipment in factories. Mills and plants no longer had to be located near river streams to exploit natural waterpower. Steam ships, railroads, and eventually cars harnessed mechanical power and replaced sailing ships (dependent on natural wind) and horses as more efficient means of transportation. The telegraph and telephone revolutionized communications.

Market Institutions and Laissez-Faire Trade Rules

Prior to the eighteenth century, markets were merchant exchanges, usually in seaports or river towns, where traders sold precious metals, spices, and other exotic goods. Most rural communities were self-sufficient, producing locally all the goods they needed to survive. Industrialization drastically changed this picture. Communities began to spe-

Spotlight on
stagflation

Spotlight on
finance

Spotlight on
regional trade

causal
arrow

**laissez-faire or
free trade**

the economic model based on the
idea of comparative advantage,
calling for a country to reduce
tariffs and specialize in products
that it produces most efficiently
while importing products that
other countries produce more
efficiently.

cialize and trade products through more sophisticated markets that sprang up in cities where factories were increasingly located. To accommodate the expanded markets, trade rules changed almost precisely in line with the industrial revolution. Starting in the 1820s before it was clearly dominant, England began to lower tariffs on imports. Notice how in this liberal interpretation trade relationships and rules change before and indeed cause power shifts. Britain's policy of **laissez-faire** or **free trade** flew in the face of mercantilist trade practices. Mercantilism emphasized self-sufficiency (few imports) and export surpluses to accumulate gold. Laissez-faire trade emphasized new rules based on comparative advantage. A country reduced tariffs and specialized in products that it produced most efficiently while importing products that other countries produced more efficiently. In this way, each country grew faster, creating more output with the same input. On the strength of its industrial development, Britain was ahead in manufactured goods. But other countries had more land and better climates and produced more efficient agricultural products. So, as we have already noted, Britain repealed the Corn Laws in 1846 and by 1850 removed virtually all other British tariffs and restrictions on manufactured as well as agricultural products, with the exception of a few revenue duties. Britain moved decisively from a zero-sum mercantilist system to a non-zero-sum laissez-faire policy.

The growth of trade required a more stable means of financing. The dual monetary system of gold and silver was not very efficient or stable. If central banks—then mostly large private, not government, banks—set prices for gold and silver that were inconsistent with available supplies, there might be a flood of one type of metal and a scarcity of the other. This happened in England in the eighteenth century, eventually driving it to adopt the gold standard. Similar pressures moved other countries toward a single standard. When Germany unified in 1871 and switched to gold, France, the Netherlands, Belgium, Switzerland, and the Scandinavian countries did so as well. Even the United States, which remained divided between eastern bankers who favored gold and western ranchers who favored silver, effectively went on the gold standard in 1879. Notice how sequential and path-dependent interactions, not British power or ideas, tend to do the heavy lifting in liberal explanations of economic change.

causal
arrow

From a liberal perspective, however, pre–World War I economic rules and institutions were weak and potentially fragile. As noted earlier, not all countries liberalized trade, and acting unilaterally did little to exploit negotiations and lock in commitments. As the economic historian Angus Maddison notes, "there were no international organizations . . . to 'manage' a world 'system', and no equivalent of the World Bank, UN agencies, or indeed bilateral aid 'donors' to direct capital flows in the light of developmental objectives."[21] As a result, the system faced repeated crises, such as the Baring Crisis in 1890, when a major British merchant bank made bad loans to Argentina and went bankrupt, and financial crises in the United States in 1893 and in Germany, Russia, France, and other countries in the first decade of the twentieth century.

**Spotlight on
international
institutions**

But, marking the first real beginning of a world economy, the new market rules and relationships generated greater and more widespread prosperity than ever before. The industrial revolution spread to the European continent (France, Germany, and Italy), the United States, Australia, Japan, and parts of the developing world such as Latin America. The results confirmed, in some measure, the famous notion of the invisible hand developed by the classical economist Adam Smith. The **invisible hand** meant that, if each nation acted in its own best interests, the common good would be served. Generally beneficial outcomes could be obtained from decentralized initiatives rather than centralized institutions. Realist perspectives emphasize the invisible

invisible hand

the economic theory that says
that, if each nation or individual
acts in its own best economic
interests, the common good
will be served.

hand within multistate alliances, but liberal perspectives see it applying more generally and believe that more comprehensive and centralized institutions reinforce, not reduce, overall benefits.

Bretton Woods Institutions

Thus, from the liberal perspective, the breakdown of the pre–World War I global economy and the chaos of the interwar period demonstrated the need for stronger international institutions. Bretton Woods created three major international economic institutions to administer the new system: GATT, the IMF, and the International Bank for Reconstruction and Development (IBRD) or the World Bank. We examine these institutions in their contemporary forms in Chapter 16.

The **General Agreement on Tariffs and Trade (GATT)** was a remnant of a more ambitious trade organization, the International Trade Organization (ITO). The ITO sought to liberalize not only industrial products but also agriculture and raw materials and to prescribe standards not only for open markets but also for full employment. However, the U.S. Congress was not ready to liberalize agriculture or accept interventionist policies to achieve full employment. It never ratified the ITO, and trade leadership devolved to another, much smaller organization. The GATT focused on liberalizing trade in industrial or manufactured products only.

GATT was an agreement, not an organization, and thus never required congressional approval. It was administered by fewer than five hundred civil servants, compared to thousands in the cases of the other Bretton Woods institutions. Nevertheless, it may have accomplished more than any other Bretton Woods institution. Concluded in 1947 while the ITO was being debated, GATT supervised multilateral trade negotiations to reduce tariffs and other trade barriers on manufactured goods. In the early years, it confronted and overcame a fierce battle between the United States, which favored global free trade, and Great Britain, which clung to regionalism with its preferences for trade with British Commonwealth or colonial territories. The United States prevailed on this issue. But concessions were made to allow regional liberalization efforts, such as the European Common Market, as long as these efforts reduced restrictions to zero within the region and did not raise tariffs on average toward countries outside the region.

Through eight major rounds of trade negotiations starting in 1948, GATT cut tariffs and quotas dramatically, and it did so on a nondiscriminatory or MFN basis. Average tariffs dropped from 40 percent to less than 4 percent among most industrialized nations. In 1994, when GATT completed its eighth round, known as the Uruguay Round, it became the WTO and took on organizational features more like its bigger Bretton Woods sister institutions. But the postwar world economy owes its existence to GATT. It was the proverbial "little engine that could." If GATT had not succeeded, the rest of the Bretton Woods agreements would have amounted to little more than table talk.

The **International Monetary Fund (IMF)** was perhaps the flagship Bretton Woods institution, even though its role until the 1980s was relatively small. The IMF supervised the system's fixed exchange rate system—a more flexible system than the earlier gold standard—and provided external loans to countries undergoing balance of payment adjustments. It reviewed domestic policies in member countries and approved when countries could change their exchange rates. It also monitored the gradual removal of controls that prevented currencies from being converted into other currencies at any

General Agreement on Tariffs and Trade (GATT) the Bretton Woods economic institution that supervised multilateral trade negotiations to reduce trade barriers.

International Monetary Fund (IMF) the international economic institution that supervises the exchange rate system, provides external loans to countries undergoing balance of payment adjustments, and reviews domestic policies in member countries.

Cape Verde Finance Minister Cristina Duarte speaks at an IMF meeting in 2007, drawing the attention of international institutions to the impact of globalization on Africa.

World Bank

the international economic institution set up to provide long-term financing for infrastructure development and basic human needs such as health and education; originally called the International Bank for Reconstruction and Development.

Marshall Plan

the U.S. post–World War II economic plan that provided loans for the reconstruction of war-torn economies in Europe.

spillover

the idea that, once interdependence starts down a certain path in one sector such as trade, it creates issues that can be resolved only by extending interdependence to other sectors such as finance.

Spotlight on

path dependence

exchange rate. Many countries had imposed such controls in the 1930s; by 1959, these controls had been dismantled, and currencies became fully convertible.

The **World Bank** was set up to provide additional long-term financing. Its original name, IBRD, suggested that it was intended to finance the reconstruction of war-torn countries as well as promote development. Many developing countries were still colonial territories, and the colonial powers were largely responsible for their development. But even the sums provided by the World Bank were inadequate to meet postwar reconstruction needs.

The **Marshall Plan** eventually supplied the bulk of postwar financing. Over seven years, the United States gave out $41 billion in foreign aid and $31 billion in gifts, or the equivalent today of over $300 billion. Without this aid, as a government report noted in 1954, "friendly countries would have been forced to restrict their purchases of American goods and services to such a degree that economic and political chaos might well have ensued abroad."[22] Marshall Plan aid thus served the U.S. geopolitical purpose of containment; it became the IMF for the more limited western world economy that replaced the Bretton Woods–designed global economy once the Cold War started.

The Bretton Woods institutions, as we noted earlier, did not include communist and most developing countries. But the success of the Bretton Woods institutions inevitably led, as liberal perspectives see it, to the expansion of globalization through path-dependent mechanisms such as emulation, spillover, and complex interdependence. Already in the 1960s, a group of developing countries known as the Asian tigers—South Korea, Hong Kong, Singapore, and Taiwan—began to emulate the success of the Bretton Woods system. They manufactured for export to global markets, particularly the U.S. market, and developed rapidly. Other developing countries— Thailand, Philippines, Indonesia, and others—followed later. Eventually, when the Cold War ended, the former communist countries joined the global economy. Whereas realist perspectives see the 1970s as a period of U.S. decline and a crisis of hegemonic power, liberal perspectives see it as a period of transition to an ever more globalized world.

Globalization Deepens: Spillover from Trade to Finance

Liberal perspectives emphasize interactions and path dependence. When the Bretton Woods agreements liberalized trade and trade expanded astronomically, it was inevitable that finance would have to be liberalized as well. High volumes of trade spilled over into high volumes of finance. **Spillover,** a path-dependent mechanism, means that, once momentum starts down a certain path of interactions, there is no going back to the starting point. The world economy may move forward or backward (spillback), but all the while, trade and financial markets deepen, and the world economy becomes more integrated than it was before. Today, more money passes through the world financial markets in a single day than passes through the trade markets in four months.

More trade required more finance. But, as noted earlier, Bretton Woods was stingy on finance and controlled capital flows. So the U.S. dollar filled the gap and accumulated in unregulated offshore Eurodollar markets in the 1960s. The first oil crisis popped the cork and liberated financial markets. The effect of oil price increases on domestic economies can be thought of as the equivalent of a tax increase. OPEC imposed a 300 percent tax increase on crude oil consumption in advanced and developing oil-importing countries. This tax not only raised prices of derivative domestic products; it reduced the amount of money available to spend on other things. Thus, the oil crisis caused higher prices and slower growth simultaneously, spreading the stagflation that already afflicted the United States and other advanced economies. Many importing countries responded by loosening their fiscal and monetary policies to generate more demand and compensate for the OPEC tax drag. That fueled (no pun intended) even further inflation and instability.

Spotlight on stagflation

Much of this instability resulted in volatile exchange rates. The dollar and other major currencies now floated, not because U.S. power had declined but because the world was awash in dollars. Prices for trade and investment became unpredictable, and the real economy, which deals with production, took a back seat to the financial economy, which deals with currencies and speculation. The Eurodollar market exploded, and more and more oil money went to developing countries to help finance their massive balance of trade deficits.

To accommodate this petrodollar recycling, financial markets had to be liberalized. The United States began by negotiating bilateral agreements to free up capital markets. The Bretton Woods restrictions on capital flows gradually disappeared. By the late 1980s, a massive new dimension had been added to world markets. Transactions on private capital accounts—bank loans, investments by MNCs, and transactions in stocks and bonds by mutual and hedge funds—soon dwarfed trade flows by a factor of 100 or more. The third age of globalization—globalization 3.0—was not only about the global Internet; it was also about global finance, which the Internet supported.

Spotlight on finance

Multilateral trade also expanded. The completion of the Uruguay Round in 1994 extended the principle of liberalization to agriculture and services, in addition to lowering further barriers to manufactured trade. It also addressed trade-related aspects of foreign investment (such as provisions requiring foreign companies to export so much of their production before they can set up a plant in a developing country) and intellectual property rights (such as requiring foreign companies to sell their patents or technology to local firms before they can invest). GATT was transformed into the WTO, with stronger procedures for settling trade disputes.

The multilateral approach to trade was accompanied by a flurry of regional and bilateral agreements. NAFTA established a regional free-trade area among Mexico, Canada, and the United States. The Asian Pacific Economic Conference (APEC) developed trade initiatives among Pacific-rim countries, and the Association of Southeast Asian Nations (ASEAN) created a free-trade area, which China, South Korea, and Japan are now seeking to expand. The most significant regional initiative, however, was the deepening of the European Community. In 1987, the EC implemented the Single European Market Act to dismantle all sorts of domestic regulatory as well as border restrictions on Community trade. In 1992, it created a common currency (the euro) and changed its name from European Community to European Union to suggest the spillover from a trading arrangement to a full economic union. In 1999, it created a full-scale monetary union, eliminating national currencies and creating the euro zone.

Spotlight on regional trade

Bilateral free-trade agreements also proliferated. The United States changed a decades-long policy of nondiscrimination to carve out privileged trading arrangements with Israel, Jordan, Morocco, and others. Japan and the EU followed suit. Some of these initiatives aimed to jump-start multilateral negotiations. But when the 1999 Seattle WTO round failed to launch a new round of multilateral trade talks, fears multiplied that the trading system was breaking up into preferential zones.

Eventually, the WTO launched a new multilateral round in Doha, Qatar, in 2001. This round placed the liberalization of agriculture at the top of the agenda. For the first time, developing countries participated in a significant way and stood to gain expanded markets for their agricultural products. In return, the advanced countries demanded greater access to the manufacturing and service markets in developing countries. The stakes were high. Protection of agriculture was deeply embedded in the European Union and in the United States, in temperate-zone products such as wheat and corn as well as in many tropical products such as cotton, peanuts, and rice. Because the stakes were high, progress was slow, and the outcome of the Doha Round was still in doubt in early 2008. Its outcome will decide whether multilateral trade continues to be the trademark of contemporary globalization and whether bilateral and regional trade arrangements are ultimately "building blocks" that lead toward freer global trade or "stumbling blocks" that disrupt and once again fragment global markets.

Internet and Information Revolution

Each version of globalization, as Friedman tells us, was driven by new technologies. For globalization 3.0, which began already in the 1970s, the new technology was information systems and the Internet. The **information revolution** produced lightning changes in computer, software, and communications technology that dramatically lowered the cost of processing and transmitting information—so much so that Friedman tells the story of his mother's calling him upset about playing a game of bridge on the Internet with three Frenchmen who annoyed her by constantly speaking French with one another.[23] Playing bridge across continents would not have been possible in 1900 or even 1970, although the players might have talked with one another on the phone at very high cost. It is the density (such as sending streaming video simultaneously with voice), speed, and cost of globalization that are new, not the fact of interconnectedness. If the price of automobiles had dropped as fast as the price of semiconductors—the automobiles of the Internet—cars today would cost about $5 apiece.[24]

Information technologies flattened, furrowed, and fertilized the earth. Flattening the earth made it possible for poor countries as well as rich ones to participate in global production. In globalization 2.0, MNCs and their rich parent countries had an advantage. They had worldwide contacts and resources to exploit production opportunities. They could produce components abroad, or offshore, and ship hard goods for assembly to any market. Most global trade was in manufactured goods and natural resources such as oil. Now information technologies gave service industries the same advantage. Businesses that produced delivery, news, financial, communications, engineering, software, insurance, data, tourist, research and development, and other information services and that were previously confined to home markets could engage in international trade. They could outsource an information activity previously done inside the firm, such as research or reservations, to overseas markets and tie the activity via the Internet back into the overall company's operations. They could send raw personnel and payroll data abroad to be returned the next day in the form of spreadsheets or paychecks. They

information revolution
the latest stage of the technological revolution that transforms the world economy through communications, digitization, and software management of data and voice transactions.

could send engineering or software problems abroad and get back, within a day or so, design solutions. Banks and financial institutions no longer had to do business primarily in local communities and home countries where they were known; they could advertise and offer their services worldwide with instantaneous access to markets and news around the world. Retail stores, previously boutique operations serving small communities, now operate globally. Wal-Mart, which has a presence in almost every country of the world, is the new poster child of the information age.

The flattened earth emphasizes brain power. Individuals anywhere with an education can participate in the world economy. Indian or Egyptian doctors and engineers no longer have to come to England or the United States to pursue their profession. They can stay at home and read x-rays on the Internet or design software in cyberspace. Major centers of research and development are sprouting up in Bangalore, India, and in Dalian, China. They are increasingly comparable to Silicon Valley in Palo Alto, California, or Route 128 in Boston, Massachusetts. Indeed, this aspect of globalization is frightening many white-collar or professional workers. Global trade no longer threatens just low-paying jobs; it also threatens high-paying jobs. And China and India are now training more scientists and engineers than the United States. Information technologies make human resources count more than natural resources, factories, or MNCs. These technologies have leveled the global playing field for developing countries in a way no previous technology has done—assuming, of course, that the developing countries can house, feed, keep healthy, and educate their enormous human resources.

Furrowing the earth means tying the world together with broadband fiber-optic cable and satellite transmissions. Furrowing magnifies exponentially the capacity to transmit information simultaneously, eventually allowing the virtual world to replicate in real time the physical world at any spot on the globe. In 1980, phone calls over copper wires carried one page of information per second. Today, one thin strand of optical fiber (and a normal cable contains multiple strands) carries 90,000 book volumes of information per second. What is more, the switching technologies, which transmit light through optical fibers faster and faster, improve yearly. It's like driving faster and faster on an interstate highway. More and more cars can use the same road (fiber) and in this case with rarely an accident (garbled or missing information). Webcams already facilitate visual telephone calls and video-streaming Internet transmissions. But teleconferencing, telecommuting, and other long-distance means of communications are only in their infancy. When they mature, they will make it possible to communicate electronically as easily as we communicate face to face. Practically all services, including medical care and education services, may be supplied by digital connections.

Fertilizing the earth means fostering through the Internet the emergence of all sorts of new international organizations, particularly transnational organizations or NGOs. The Internet is the admission ticket to world society for individuals and small groups. Individuals and groups can now hook up online from anywhere with anyone to conduct a conversation, explore a problem, or advocate a cause. The dramatic flowering of global networks and informal institutions is evident everywhere. Formally constituted NGOs numbered fewer than 200 before World War I. In 1970, they numbered 2,000. Today, they number more than 26,000. Now add to that the literally hundreds of thousands of bridge games, chat rooms, and other informal networks that exist on the Web. The citizens of the world have lost their chains. Just as flattening and furrowing the earth empower developing countries to do battle with industrial countries, fertilizing the earth empowers ordinary citizens to do battle with governments and MNCs.

Spotlight on nongovernmental organizations

Internet communities have emerged in virtually all areas of international life. They affect military, social, technological, economic, environmental, political, and cultural relationships. Terrorists troll the Internet for information about WMDs and sources of financing to carry out their terrorist plans. Some social movements organize to support women and orphaned children in developing countries, while others engage in drug and sex trafficking. Technological partnerships flourish on the Web. One of the biggest contemporary movements is open-source software development, which involves literally thousands of people online around the world collaborating to write a new operating system, such as Linux; or new Web server software, such as Apache; or a database, such as Wikipedia, the online encyclopedia. Economic liaisons proliferate, from institutes that support poor people doing business in informal sectors outside the legal system to hedge funds operating 24/7 in global markets that are open somewhere in the world at any time of the day. Environmental groups protest whaling expeditions and free-trade meetings. NGOs promote human rights in China and democracy in Ukraine and Russia. Cultural communities work through the Internet to preserve local languages and bring attention to isolated and dying cultural legacies.

From a liberal perspective, technologies such as the Internet are protean forces. They create a new world to which powerful groups and conventional ideas must adapt.

Complex Interdependence and Financial Crises

By the 1990s, then, the world was more densely and deeply interconnected than ever before. Interdependence made countries more sensitive and vulnerable to one another. **Sensitivity interdependence** meant that they were affected by what was happening in other parts of the world, whether they were directly involved or not. Bad effects such as financial crises could be transmitted as rapidly as good effects such as lower prices for consumer products. **Vulnerability interdependence** meant that countries had few choices if interdependence was cut and they could no longer get resources or capital. If oil or food supplies were cut off, there would be a global, not just a local, crisis. Countries worried about oil and food security at the same time that they benefited greatly from global supplies of oil and food.

Interdependence had become so extensive and intensive, it was called **complex interdependence,** a dense network of interconnections emphasizing horizontal rather than vertical relationships that benefited more and more countries but also exposed them to more and more risks. Complex interdependence created a world of separate and multiple issue areas that were relatively equal in importance, such as oil, finance, and trade. No one country controlled all of these issue areas, as OPEC demonstrated with its oil cartel. A hierarchy of military power was no longer dominant across all issue areas. Realist perspectives saw this decline of hierarchy or hegemony as detrimental to global growth; liberal perspectives saw it as making force less fungible—for example, making it more difficult for the United States to use force to resolve the oil crisis without creating numerous other problems—and broadening participation to include countries that had economic but not necessarily military power, such as the OPEC countries and the newly industrializing countries of Asia. Notice how in liberal perspectives interdependence restrains and diminishes the significance of military power.

These features of complex interdependence became transparent in the series of financial crises that marred the 1990s. First Mexico, then Russia, the Asian developing countries, and, finally, Argentina endured currency and major economic disruptions. The crises had similar patterns. In each case, a local currency came under pressure,

sensitivity interdependence situation in which a country is affected economically or politically by what happens in other parts of the world, whether it is directly involved or not.

vulnerability interdependence situation in which a country is put at risk if interdependence is cut and it can no longer get resources or capital from external sources.

complex interdependence a dense network of interconnections emphasizing horizontal rather than vertical relationships that benefits more and more countries but also exposes them to more and more risks.

causal *arrow*

either from slowing exports (as with Mexico) or burgeoning imports (as with Argentina). Investors sold out anticipating a depreciation of the currency. Eventually, the currency was devalued. Now local businesses and investors had to repay foreign debts with much larger amounts of local currency. Let's say you lived in Thailand and borrowed $100 from a foreign bank, which you converted into 1,000 baht, the local currency, at a rate of $1 : 10 baht. Then, the currency is devalued to a rate of $1 : 20 baht. When you repay your loan, you will need 2,000, not 1,000, baht to repay the debt—twice as much local currency as you originally received as a loan. And, of course, you still owe interest too.

In some countries, such as Mexico and Russia, domestic policies were the root causes of the crises. But many Asian countries, such as the Asian tigers, were pursuing sound domestic policies. They often tied their currencies to the dollar or a basket of currencies to ensure confidence and stability. Certain that the currency would not depreciate, international investors, some of them speculators, put large amounts of money into these countries to exploit higher short-term interest rates and longer-term investment opportunities. However, when the dollar appreciated in the 1990s due to America's good economic performance, the Asian currencies tied to the dollar went up too. That made their exports more expensive and less competitive. Now they exported less, and trade surpluses declined or trade deficits rose. Investors began to wonder whether the country could maintain the fixed exchange rate or would have to devalue. They began to unravel their investments. When nervous investors sold local assets for dollars, the government had to supply dollars from its foreign exchange reserves. As more investors did the same, the country's foreign exchange reserves dwindled. Eventually, investors panicked, fearing they might not get to the central bank before it ran out of foreign exchange. Panic turned into rout, and the crisis spread to other countries in similar situations. The Asian crisis started in Thailand in summer 1997, but it spread quickly to the Philippines, Malaysia, Indonesia, and South Korea.

The IMF stepped in to provide liquidity and help stabilize the situation. But now, critics argue, the IMF did the wrong thing. It imposed austerity, or tight monetary and fiscal policies, to free up domestic resources to increase exports and restore foreign confidence in the currency. That only compounded the problem, critics allege, because it drove local economies into serious recession.

The financial crises sparked a big debate about whether capital controls that existed under the original Bretton Woods system should be reinstated, especially on the most volatile, short-term capital flows, called "hot money." Some economists, even some who advocated free trade, felt that they should be;[25] but others felt they should not. The debate hinged on what analysts thought the underlying cause of the problem was. If it was speculative capital flows (systemic process level), then clearly controls provided an answer. But if it was an underdeveloped banking system in the Asian countries that encouraged excessive lending and borrowing by local and foreign investors, if it was a currency policy to maintain an exchange rate tied to the dollar, or if it was a domestic export structure that produced products already in surplus on world markets (all domestic level factors), then domestic policy changes were in order, not new constraints on international capital flows.[26] Notice here how levels of analysis considerations factor into a policy decision about what to do to resolve international problems.

Does complex interdependence, especially massive and interwoven financial markets, undermine and rob a state or culture of its independence and sovereignty? Look at the box on page 308 to see how one analyst sorts out the different causes and consequences of globalization. In this view, globalization advances neither western impe-

Spotlight on interdependence

← **causal** *arrow*

Globalization as Cultural Contamination, Not Cultural Imperialism or Clash of Cultures

Philosopher Kwame Anthony Appiah at Princeton University wrote an essay for the *New York Times Magazine* on January 1, 2006. Here is a summary of what he says about how cultures and globalization interact.

Appiah begins by describing the views of those who see globalization as attacking and destroying diverse cultures, noting that in their view:

> There is a world system of capitalism. It has a center and a periphery. At the center—in Europe and the United States—is a set of multinational corporations. Some of these are in the media business. The products they sell around the world promote the creation of desires that can be fulfilled only by the purchase and use of their products. They do this explicitly through advertising, but more insidiously, they also do so through the messages implicit in movies and in television drama. . . . Herbert Schiller, a leading critic of "media-cultural imperialism," claimed that "it is the imagery and cultural perspectives of the ruling sector in the center that shape and structure consciousness throughout the system at large."

Appiah rejects this imperialist (realist if we isolate power as the primary cause) or critical theory (if we emphasize center-periphery relations) perspective on globalization:

> Talk of cultural imperialism "structuring the consciousness" of those in the periphery treats people . . . as blank slates on which global capitalism's moving finger writes its message, leaving behind another cultural automaton as it moves on. It is deeply condescending. And it isn't true.

He then considers the views of those who see globalization in terms of competing universalistic ideas, such as Muslim fundamentalists who reject western culture:

> [Muslim fundamentalists] resist the crass consumerism of modern Western society. . . . [They] are building . . . what they call the *ummah,* the global community of Muslims, and it is open to all who share their faith. . . . [They] think there is one right way for all human beings to live. . . . If what concerns you is global homogeneity, then this utopia, not the world that capitalism is producing, is the one you should worry about.

Appiah also rejects this relative identity perspective because it is intolerant. Rather, he opts for a third view, which he calls cosmopolitan:

> Cosmopolitans believe in universal truth, too, though we are less certain that we already have all of it. . . . Cosmopolitans think that there are many values to live by and you cannot live by all of them. . . . [W]e should learn about people in other places, take an interest in their civilizations, their arguments, their errors, their achievements, not because that will bring us to agreement but because it will help us get used to one another. . . . [T]he larger human truth is on the side of contamination—that endless process of imitation and revision.

Notice how Appiah judges that cultures ultimately come to terms with globalization by getting used to one another through an "endless process of imitation and revision," a liberal perspective. They do not succumb to one another, either as a result of power (realist) or world systems (critical theory) domination. Nor do they engage in arguing to "bring us to agreement," a relative identity perspective. In the end, they share a process and mutual respect (reciprocity, a procedural norm), not shared or similar values.

rialism (realist or critical theory) nor western values (identity) but rather catches all countries in the flytrap of cosmopolitanism in which different cultures get used to and learn from one another based on mutual respect (liberal), not coercion or agreement.

Identity Explanations

Identity explanations of world economic relations emphasize the role of ideas, norms, values, and identities in spurring global material and institutional change. They see each period of global economic expansion as preceded by a revolution in ideas: (1) the Renaissance and Reformation, the flowering of art, literature, and religious freedom that spread across Europe in the fifteenth and sixteenth centuries, jump-started the new spirit of individualism and human adventure that created the age of discovery and mercantilism; (2) the Enlightenment two centuries later brought the startling discoveries in science and technology that launched the industrial revolution and provoked (caused) the new classical liberal ideas of individual property rights and free markets that formed the foundations of Pax Britannica; (3) new ideas of nationalism and Marxism arose in the nineteenth century to fuel the fascist, socialist, and communist movements of the twentieth century that emphasized government intervention and control to harness capitalist forces to collectivist aims; (4) Keynesian policies of full employment and Hayekian policies of neoclassical liberalism competed to establish the Bretton Woods system; and (5) the "Washington Consensus," a collection of neoclassical liberal ideas in the 1980s and 1990s, emphasized a reduced role for government and powered the recovery and expansion of the global economy and the advent of the information age.

Spotlight on ideas

    Here we look more closely at each of these clusters of ideas and how, according to identity perspectives, they shaped the institutions and power configurations of the world economy after 1500.

Renaissance and the Protestant Ethic

The Renaissance introduced the idea that individuals, initially noble elites, could criticize the church and develop artistic and cultural expressions of freedom celebrating human, not just divine, qualities. The Reformation marked an open rebellion against church authority and created the basis for individual thought and action applied to worldly affairs. To understand this period, Max Weber, the German sociologist, poses a simple question: How was it that pursuing worldly affairs through exploration and commerce became an acceptable undertaking in human affairs? Making money in the form of commerce existed long before the Reformation and in all parts of the world. But it was never looked on as a worthy calling. Religious, martial, and agrarian pursuits were considered to be superior vocations. Economic activities were suspect. For centuries, usury laws made it illegal to charge interest on loans. Using capital to make money, let alone devoting your life to making money, was considered simply unacceptable. Such activity violated every tenet of traditional and customary mores. With the Reformation, making money became acceptable. Vocation, not devotion, became the central focus and calling of a person's life. Something happened that justified this rational pursuit of wealth and overcame the stigma attached to money. That something was a change in ideas. From an identity perspective, ideas had to change before institutions could.

Protestant ethic

the Reformation idea, formulated by sociologist Max Weber, that each individual lives out God's will in a specific vocation and demonstrates his or her faith by the works of his or her vocation, an idea that ultimately justifies the rational pursuit of wealth.

The Reformation provided this change of ideas. As Weber argues, it created the **Protestant ethic,** the idea of a specific calling of the individual by God to a life task, a practical field of endeavor in which he or she was divinely inspired to work. The individual lived out God's will in a specific vocation and demonstrated his or her faith by the works of his or her vocation. The ascetic life of the pious monk in a monastery was not discarded but transformed into the disciplined life of a merchant in the marketplace or a clerk in the new state bureaucracy. Notice how this idea of worthiness preceded and now made possible specialization (not the reverse, as the liberal perspective would argue). Indeed, as Weber writes, "the emphasis on the ascetic importance of a fixed calling provided an ethical justification of the modern specialized division of labo[r]."[27] It made the vocation of the baker, butcher, and brewer, the famous trio that Adam Smith used to illustrate the division of labor, acceptable and vested such vocations with a purpose sanctioned by God. Human energy and discipline "now . . . strode into the market-place of life, slammed the door of the monastery behind it, and undertook to penetrate just that daily routine of life with its methodicalness."[28]

causal → arrow

Observe in Weber's argument how ideas influenced institutions such as specialization in the economic sphere (not the other way around) and how these ideas were not a rationalization of the existing power of the Catholic Church (in which case, the ideas may be what political scientists call epiphenomenal or secondary) but significantly altered the existing distribution of power that ultimately weakened the Catholic Church. He reaches the conclusion that religion inspired commerce and conquest. By contrast, Immanuel Wallerstein, another historian of the period, sees it differently:

> No doubt the passions of Christianity explain many of the particular decisions taken by the Portuguese and Spaniards, but it seems more plausible to see this religious enthusiasm as rationalization . . . not . . . as primary factors in explaining the genesis and long-term persistence of large-scale social action.[29]

Here again we observe how eminent scholars can look at the same events and reach diametrically opposite conclusions about the causes of these events.

Classical Economic Liberalism

Classical economic liberalism drew from the powerful ideas of individual freedom, open markets, and comparative advantage developed by Enlightenment philosophers, such as John Locke, Adam Smith, and David Ricardo. We examine comparative advantage in more detail in Chapter 10. However, it is useful to consider here how this idea revalued the elements and goals of relationships. Relationships facilitate specialization, but they do not necessarily direct it toward the production of wealth. For centuries, relationships involved specialization within a hierarchical or coercive context. Masters directed slaves to perform specific tasks. Or prelates and peasants had their specific functions within the hierarchy of the church and feudal institutions.

classical economic liberalism

an economic orientation that holds that parties have a right to own property and exchange goods in a relatively free and competitive marketplace without violence and coercion.

Classical economic liberalism introduced two new ideas. The first was the relative equality of the parties in a relationship. This was the political aspect of liberalism, developed by John Locke and others, and involved the notion of property rights. The baker, brewer, and butcher had title to the fruits of their labor and were roughly equal in status, unlike the master and slave or the cardinal, bishop, and monk. The second idea was that these merchants exchanged goods in a marketplace free of violence and coercion, a marketplace of free and competitive exchange. This idea was crucial because it ensured, through competition and relative equality of participants, the valuing of goods and services on the basis of economic price, not on the basis of inheritance or where an individual came from (path dependence, as emphasized by liberal perspectives) or on the basis of coercion and relative power (as emphasized by realist perspectives). Competition sorted out the **opportunity costs** of different uses of existing resources, that is, what alternative products or assets the money might buy, and hence what use of these resources would yield the highest return. Competition had to be relatively free; that is, no single party could dominate or affect the bargaining decisively. The question of whether markets are free or not is, of course, always the debate about markets. But assuming the protection of property rights and existence of competition, the two ideas of equal status and free exchange put a high value on efficiency and, hence, specialization. Specialization became a relationship in which parties maximized the efficiency and hence the value of resources, not a relationship in which slaves served masters or peasants served lords.

opportunity costs
the costs associated with using the same resources to produce one product compared to another.

From an identity perspective, England developed decentralized institutions and introduced laissez-faire policies first because it was the pioneer of political and economic liberalism. It had already had its political revolution—the Puritan revolution under Oliver Cromwell—in the 1650s, a full century before the revolution in France. This liberal experience and thinking were central to both the industrial revolution and the repeal of the Corn Laws. England liberalized not in response to negotiations with other countries (a liberal scenario) but unilaterally. Ideas not interactions spurred the change. And England started the process of liberalization well before it was dominant (as realist scenarios require). Moreover, as Angus Maddison notes, the gold standard functioned more or less autonomously without the help of international organizations. Thus, ideas drove development, not institutions or power.

←――― **causal**
arrow

Laissez-faire policies worked abroad because domestic policies supported them at home. Classical liberal policies prevailed, not economic nationalism or Marxist policies. Government intervention was discouraged, and market mechanisms worked more or less automatically.[30] For example, as we note earlier, the gold standard required that a country with a deficit in its external accounts pay off the difference in gold. The loss of gold reduced domestic consumption and diverted domestic resources to meet foreign demand. Governments had to allow for this reallocation of resources or the gold standard payments mechanism would not work. To make domestic adjustments most efficiently, advanced countries during this period favored low inflation, low taxes, restrained government spending, low regulations, and a strong reliance on market forces. Hence, the domestic policies underlying the gold standard in England and elsewhere were classically liberal or what we would call today conservative economic policies emphasizing small government, private entrepreneurship, and a relatively unrestricted private market place.

Economic Nationalism and Marxism

Classically liberal or conservative economic ideas were not accepted everywhere. As we note earlier, Germany and the United States pursued protectionist trade policies, which allowed for a larger government role in the domestic economy. In Germany, the economist Friedrich List advocated policies of national industrial development that protected domestic industries from low-cost British and foreign imports. The state imposed high tariffs on imports and then subsidized or, in some cases, assumed direct ownership of national industries. France adopted similar policies. This approach of assisting national industries to catch up and compete with more advanced foreign

economic nationalism

the approach of assisting domestic industries to catch up with and compete with more advanced foreign industries through protectionism, high tariffs, and subsidies.

socialism

big government policies that call for strong labor unions to match big corporations as well as state regulations and ownership to control substantial sectors of the economy.

causal
arrow

Keynesian economics

an economic model that calls for more activist government intervention to stimulate domestic growth, protect imports, and adjust exchange rates more frequently.

Chicago School of economics

an economic model that allows for fiscal and monetary policies to manage domestic demand, but sharply limits government spending and taxation and seeks to reduce tariffs and maintain relatively stable exchange rates to ensure more competitive and, hence, efficient domestic and international markets.

industries became associated with **economic nationalism.** The United States used this approach after the Civil War with its high tariff policies, although, like England, it relied more heavily than Germany or France on private rather than state industries. Later, after World War II, Japan and some developing countries used nationalist approaches that emphasized government targeting of industries and technology. Japan pioneered strategic trade policies, and many developing countries adopted import substitution policies, which we discuss in Chapter 10.

The period during which the gold standard prevailed also witnessed the rise of Marxism and socialism in Europe, as well as the progressive movement in the United States. Markets, Karl Marx argues, distributed wealth unevenly, concentrating economic and social power in the hands of bankers and corporations and exploiting the labor of workers and farmers. Marxism encouraged **socialism,** or big government policies that called for strong labor unions to match big corporations and for state regulations and ownership to control substantial sectors of the economy. The domestic and international struggle between liberalism and socialism divided domestic as well as international politics throughout the run-up to World War I.

After World War I, both economic nationalism and Marxist-Leninism, now known as communism, tore the world economy apart. The world economy went into decline and then depression and did not recover to the pre–World War I levels of interdependence for another fifty years. The reason had little to do with the fragmentation of power (as realist perspectives argue) or with weak institutions (as liberal perspectives argue). From the identity perspective, the clash of economic ideas and ideologies explains the course of world economic events better than weak institutions or the absence of a strong power.

Critical theory perspectives, which we examine in more detail in Chapter 13, reach the same conclusion—the world economy fragmented—but they do not attribute independent causal power to ideas. Critical theories argue that ideas, power, and institutions are all caught up in a historical process, or dialectic, that pits capitalist and proletariat forces against one another. This dialectic increases conflict and capitalist expansion, leading to global struggles among capitalist states. Communist states hoped to benefit from these internal contradictions of capitalism and lead the way away from a capitalist world economy to a new global economy based on communism.

Keynesian Economics and the Chicago School

After World War II, another confrontation took place between the neoclassical liberal economic ideas championed by the United States and the socialist or Keynesian economic ideas championed by Great Britain. **Keynesian economics** was developed in the 1930s by the famous English economist John Maynard Keynes. It became popular after World War II as a way to avoid another depression. Keynes called for more activist government intervention to stimulate domestic growth, protect imports, and adjust exchange rates more frequently. Keynesian policies rejected the automatic adjustment process of the gold standard. Instead of reducing domestic demand to correct trade deficits and maintain the gold standard, Keynesian policies called for maintaining domestic growth and achieving full employment while restricting imports and making exchange rates more flexible by getting rid of the gold standard. By contrast, the United States favored more free-market-oriented policies championed by economists at the University of Chicago. The **Chicago School of economics** allowed for fiscal and monetary policies to manage domestic demand, but it sharply limited government spending and taxation and sought to reduce tariffs and maintain relatively stable exchange rates to ensure more competitive and, hence, efficient domestic and international markets. It championed policies that were closer to classical liberal than to the later Marxist or socialist standards, and it became known as the neoclassical school of economics.

The policy debate between Keynesianism and the Chicago School mirrored a broader philosophical debate at the time between two other economists writing during World War II. Karl Polanyi and Friedrich Hayek outlined contrasting approaches to the postwar world economy. Polanyi supported more government intervention and called for "the great transformation" from market rationality to social regulation and planning, moving beyond the laissez-faire policies of the gold standard.[31] Hayek supported greater market competition to preserve basic economic and political freedoms and warned that the move toward social regulation and planning was "the road to serfdom."[32]

Two differing interpretations of the Bretton Woods system followed from this debate. One interpretation, echoing Polanyi, described the postwar system as **embedded liberalism.** According to this interpretation, governments accepted the discipline of free trade and relatively stable exchange rates in the international economy but "embedded" this liberalism in domestic economies through government commitments to intervene extensively to achieve full employment, control prices, and prevent disruptive capital flows. The second interpretation, echoing Hayek, described Bretton Woods as **neoclassical liberalism.** According to this interpretation, an international system of free trade and fixed exchange rates effectively limited the ability of governments to intervene in the domestic economy. Open international markets were at some point incompatible with extensive government intervention in domestic economies. Because governments could not impose tariffs or change exchange rates without international agreement, they had to correct trade deficits by domestic means. That meant, as in the case of the earlier gold standard, governments' policies had to encourage shifting resources from imports to exports and that meant, in turn, sound budgets, restrained monetary policies, and flexible market-based prices for labor and capital—in short, relatively limited government intervention. The difference was that the Bretton Woods system now allowed for somewhat more flexible exchange rates, which could be changed with the approval of the IMF.

EMBEDDED LIBERALISM: A SOCIAL CONSTRUCTIVIST VIEW. The embedded liberalism argument adopted a constructivist or constitutive view of the postwar world economy. According to political economist John Ruggie, who made this argument most effectively, no one specific country or factor caused the system.[33] Rather, the system gelled from an infusion of social purpose, political institutions, and economic power that underwrote the postwar international economic regime. America dominated that regime, but, as social constructivists see it, it was not American power that mattered most but a combination of its power, purpose, and politics. After all, hegemony defined the structure of the Soviet economic system as well, yet embedded liberalism did not mark the content of Marxist-Leninist economies. Soviet purposes and institutions were different.

Embedded liberalism emphasized the aspects of the Bretton Woods agreements that sided with Keynesian policies. Countries facing balance of payments deficits could alter their exchange rates, something that was not possible under the earlier gold standard. Moreover, they could control capital flows and started from positions where they already had high tariffs and quotas in place restricting trade. Although they committed themselves to removing these trade restrictions, trade rules provided generous pro-

embedded liberalism
an interpretation of the Bretton Woods system that held that governments accepted the discipline of free trade and relatively stable exchange rates in the international economy in return for "embedding" these liberal commitments in domestic government policies to intervene extensively to achieve full employment, control prices, and prevent disruptive capital flows.

neoclassical liberalism
an interpretation of the Bretton Woods system that held that an international system of relatively free trade and fixed exchange rates effectively limited the ability of governments to intervene in the domestic economy because such intervention would ultimately contravene commitments to keep markets open, inflation down, and exchange rates stable.

visions for so-called safeguards and exceptions. Keynes also wanted an international paper currency known as the bancor that could be created and expanded by the IMF to cover the trade balances of deficit countries without forcing them to restrict domestic demand. He preferred that surplus countries (those exporting more than they imported) adjust, which he expected the United States to be. Keynes lost the argument. He did not get either massive IMF financing or the scarce currency clause that would have required surplus countries to make more of their "scarce" currencies available. But the IMF and World Bank were the first international institutions ever to make loans for balance of payments and reconstruction purposes. So, the system certainly provided more liberal finance than any previous arrangement.

NEOCLASSICAL LIBERALISM. The conservative school of neoclassical liberalism interpreted the Bretton Woods system very differently. It emphasized the aspects of the Bretton Woods agreements that sided with Chicago School policies. Herbert Stein, an American economist who later served as chairman of the Council of Economic Advisers under President Nixon, developed this argument most effectively.[34] After World War II, he notes, two extreme economic views were thrown out. No one wanted to go back to the pure laissez-faire policies of the nineteenth-century gold standard. In that sense, a new social consensus had emerged that called for more government involvement in the domestic economy than had been the case before World War I. On the other hand, no one, especially in the United States, wanted to embrace socialist planning of the sort that some social democratic and communist countries were implementing in Europe. Extreme socialism—essentially communism—Hayek had warned, was about to repeat the mistakes of fascism and destroy the protection of private property and market-based exchanges that underwrite political and economic freedom, all in the vain pursuit of a planned utopia to eliminate human want.

That left two views in between, the moderate or conservative Keynesians, as Stein called them, and the aggressive Keynesians. **Moderate Keynesians** accepted some government intervention in the domestic economy to achieve high, but not necessarily full, employment. U.S. legislation in 1946 explicitly removed the term "full employment" from the bill, suggesting sharper limits on government intervention than those favored by more aggressive Keynesians in Europe. Otherwise, moderate Keynesians favored classical market policies of low inflation and sound money, deregulated or flexible labor and capital markets, and open international trade. **Aggressive Keynesians** favored more extensive intervention to achieve full, not just high, employment and were less averse to inflation, price controls, or other forms of government intervention in the domestic economy. Like Keynes himself, they did not want free trade and other international objectives to restrict domestic policies of maximum employment and high wages.

Now, as the neoclassical or Chicago school sees it, Bretton Woods came down in almost every respect on the side of the moderate, not aggressive, Keynesian approach. The commitments to fix exchange rates, open markets, and limit financing for trade deficits meant that domestic policies would have to adjust. As the economist Richard Cooper writes, "the IMF system . . . involved a combination of modest financing and main reliance on internal measures to correct imbalances, but with allowances in extreme cases for external measures."[35] If countries could not easily change exchange rates, impose trade barriers, or obtain abundant financing, they had to adjust mostly by shifting resources from domestic demand and imports to exports. That meant, in turn, domestic policies that limited budget deficits, inflation, and interventionist labor

moderate Keynesians
economists who favor accepting some government intervention in the domestic economy to achieve high, but not necessarily full, employment while still favoring the classical market policies of low inflation and sound money, deregulated or flexible labor and capital markets, and open international trade.

aggressive Keynesians
economists who favor more extensive government intervention to achieve full, not just high, employment and are less averse to inflation, price controls, or other forms of government intervention in the domestic economy.

and capital market regulations. Such relatively conservative policies were followed after the war, not only in the United States but in Germany under Ludwig Erhard and in other countries as well.

Notice how embedded liberalism and neoclassical liberalism consider the same facts surrounding the Bretton Woods system but judge them differently. These differences are important for understanding not only the origins of Bretton Woods but also its demise. When Bretton Woods collapsed in the 1970s, embedded liberalism advocates saw it as a consequence of contradictions in the system, such as insufficient gold and financing, that could be corrected by extending government intervention to provide a social safety net for international as well as domestic markets. The Chicago conservative school saw it as a consequence of changing ideas, such as the United States adopting more aggressive Keynesian policies in the mid-1960s that inflated the U.S. economy and caused the dollar to decline, motivating other countries to be less willing to hold dollars. The loss of confidence in U.S. economic policies, not insufficient quantities of gold or financing, brought the system down. Identity perspectives, especially ones that look at relative rather than shared ideas, illuminate some of the more interesting ideological controversies in international economics.

← *causal arrow*

Spotlight on
relative versus shared identities

Economic Battleground of the 1980s

When the Bretton Woods system collapsed in the 1970s, a furious struggle broke out between free market and interventionist policies. Some groups, labor unions and developing countries, argued for more stimulus and protectionism, both to absorb unused domestic resources and to redistribute international resources. Other groups, particularly business and conservative parties in Great Britain and the United States, argued for fighting inflation and liberalizing incentives and trade to foster new service and information industries. This time, more conservative views prevailed. As Angus Maddison reports,

> the economic consensus amongst the economic establishment (civil servants, politicians, academic pundits) moved sharply away from the Keynesian mode. Full employment was no longer an objective of policy, economic growth had become a secondary objective. The top priorities were to stop inflation and avoid payments deficits.[36]

Three economic policy movements emerged to replace aggressive Keynesian policies. One sought to revive rapid economic growth through private markets spurred by tax cuts and deregulation. The second championed the success of export-led growth and advocated a new idea of strategic trade. And the third sought to limit growth and make it sustainable through government intervention that took into account population, environmental, and resource constraints.

Margaret Thatcher, the Conservative Party leader elected in Britain in 1979, and Ronald Reagan, the Republican Party leader elected in the United States in 1980, led the **tax cut and deregulation movement.** They advocated policies that drove up interest rates to kill inflation, reduced taxes and deregulated markets to restructure investment incentives, and liberalized trade and capital markets to spur efficiency. They succeeded in good part; but, as critics argued, the costs were high in terms of a steep recession in 1980–1981 and fiscal deficits that stretched out into the 1990s. Nevertheless, the U.S. and world economies rebounded strongly. Supporters of Thatcher and Reagan argued that free-market policies paved the way for the information and service revolutions. If America and Britain had not rebounded, the information age would have

tax cut and deregulation movement
a set of policies advocated by Margaret Thatcher and Ronald Reagan that drove up interest rates to kill inflation, reduced taxes and deregulated markets to restructure investment incentives, and liberalized trade and capital markets to spur efficiency.

← *causal arrow*

Britain's Conservative Prime Minister Margaret Thatcher and France's socialist President François Mitterrand point in different directions in this 1987 photo, as they often did in the 1980s as they clashed over neoclassical liberal versus socialist prescriptions for the global economy.

Multi-fiber Agreement (MFA)

an agreement imposing direct quotas on the imports of textiles and apparel.

voluntary export restraints (VERs)

agreements in which exporting countries "voluntarily" (actually under pressure) agreed to limit exports of specific products.

newly industrializing countries (NICs)

another term for the Asian tigers (Japan, South Korea, Taiwan, Singapore, Malaysia, and later Thailand, the Philippines, Indonesia, and Chile, among others); the term focuses on their use of manufacturing to develop.

certainly progressed more slowly, and it is possible, if the Soviet Union had rebounded instead, that it would have looked very different under Soviet influence than under contemporary globalization. Policy ideas drove technological change and the Internet, not the other way around (as liberal perspectives see it). By the time Thatcher and the Republicans left office, globalization had taken off.

Export-oriented developing countries rode out the oil crisis in the 1970s better than other developing countries. They competed increasingly on an equal basis with advanced countries, and their success caught the attention of other countries. A second wave of Asian and other tigers emerged—Thailand, Philippines, Indonesia, and Chile, among others—and a second wave of MNCs spread to Asia (recall that the first went to Europe in the 1960s). MNCs produced and assembled products offshore—low-cost footwear, clothing, and consumer electronic products—and shipped them back to advanced countries' markets. Manufactured goods flooded world markets, and labor unions in advanced countries clamored for protection. Protectionism grew in various forms. Direct quotas, such as the **Multi-fiber Agreement (MFA),** limited imports of textiles and apparel. Voluntary agreements, called gray-area measures because they circumvented the application of existing trade laws, got foreign exporters to cut back shipments. Thus, Asian governments, under pressure from advanced countries, imposed **voluntary export restraints (VERs)** on the export of footwear, as Japan did on the export of cars. The tigers, or **newly industrializing countries (NICs)** and **newly exporting countries (NECs),** as they were alternatively called, complained that they were being cut out of global markets just as they were achieving competitive success.

The United States and advanced countries, in turn, accused Japan and the NICs of pursuing unfair trade policies that contravened comparative advantage. Following a combination of protectionist and free-trade policies known as **strategic trade,** these countries protected home industries in products such as cars and electronic products and then subsidized these industries to export once they had achieved efficient economies of scale. They developed so-called **national industry champions,** or domestic industries that first dominated home markets and then conquered world markets. This strategic trade approach created *competitive* advantage through government targeting of technology and capital rather than relying on *comparative* advantage derived from fixed land, labor, or raw material resources. We discuss strategic trade further in Chapter 10.

A third economic policy movement developed at the global level. It advocated **sustainable development** and drew its inspiration from the "limits to growth" and "small is beautiful" movements of the 1970s.[37] Worried that economic growth was outstripping energy and other resources as well as the environmental carrying capacity of the planet, this approach called for smaller-scale development that worked in harmony with resource, population, land and environmental constraints. Renewable energy technologies arrested resource depletion, smaller-scale communities avoided the overpopulation of cities, land conservation preserved forests and wildlife, and environmentally friendly growth policies reduced pollution and noise. The 1992 UN Conference on Environment and Development, or Earth Summit, in Rio de Janeiro,

Brazil, galvanized support for this approach, but many of the principal skeptics were developing countries, such as China, which saw sustainable development as a way to make countries that were developing now pay for the development sins of advanced countries that had developed earlier.

Washington Consensus

The rebound of the U.S. and western economies and the collapse of the communist economies seemed to settle some of the economic policy arguments that plagued the 1970s and 1980s. The tax cuts and deregulation movement inspired emulation in other western countries. At the G-7 summit in Williamsburg, Virginia, in 1983, industrial nations produced an annex of conservative economic policies—lower taxes and inflation, sound fiscal and monetary policies, deregulation (later called privatization), and freer trade—that went on to inspire the EU to deregulate industries under the Single Market Act in 1987 and to pass a Pact on Stability and Growth to keep budget deficits within certain limits.

Developing countries too followed suit, although more slowly. Latin American countries moved grudgingly away from import substitution policies to more efficient export-oriented policies. Mexico led the way, closing down its notoriously protectionist commerce ministry and joining the GATT in 1986. Throughout the developing world, more emphasis was placed on domestic policies, which generate most of the savings for development even in the poorest countries. The IMF, amid much controversy, encouraged indebted countries to deregulate markets, open up foreign investment, and discipline fiscal and monetary policies. Development specialists discovered the robust informal sector in many developing countries that generated growth outside the formal or regulated sector and called for eliminating the red tape and bureaucracy that stifled initiative and forced it into the underground economy.[38]

In one of the most important economic policy decisions in the 1980s, China entered world markets and adopted more market-oriented policies both at home and in the export sector. This decision may have had more to do with the triumph of global market policy ideas than anything else. No one could foresee at the time, of course, that China would sustain explosive growth for the next three decades. And that growth would not have been possible if the United States and other countries had not restored the health and vitality of world markets in the 1980s.

Thus, the policy movement toward market-oriented ideas was crucial, at least as identity perspectives see it. This movement, known in the 1990s as the **Washington Consensus,** received a big boost when the communist countries collapsed in the early 1990s. Marxist economics was now completely discredited. Eastern European countries and even Russia rushed to deregulate, sell off state-owned firms, and restructure their economies toward competitive prices rather than state planning and production quotas.

Daniel Yergin, a Pulitzer Prize–winning author, summarized the triumph of Hayekian conservative over Keynesian interventionist policies in the 1990s:

> In the postwar years, Keynes' theories of government management of the economy appeared unassailable. But a half century later, it is Keynes who has been toppled and Hayek, the fierce advocate of free markets, who is preeminent. The Keynesian "new economics" from Harvard may have dominated the Kennedy and Johnson administrations in the 1960s, but it is the University of Chicago's free-market school that is globally influential in the 1990s.[39]

newly exporting countries (NECs)
another term for the Asian tigers (Japan, South Korea, Taiwan, Singapore, Malaysia, and later Thailand, the Philippines, Indonesia, and Chile, among others); the term focuses on their use of exports to develop.

strategic trade
trade policies that rely on competitive advantage through government targeting of technology and capital, rather than comparative advantage derived from fixed land, labor, or raw material resources, to enter markets first and eventually dominate them where the economies of scale are so large that only one firm or country can make a profit.

national industry champions
industries that are protected and subsidized by the state so as to dominate home markets and gain an edge in world markets.

sustainable development
an economic approach that calls for smaller-scale development that works in harmony with resource, population, land, and environmental constraints.

Washington Consensus
the policy movement in the 1990s advocating market-oriented ideas for developing nations.

Economic Nationalism Survives

The clash of economic policy ideas was hardly over, however. Economic nationalism persisted in the form of the strategic trade policies of Japan and other Asian tigers. And the ideas of sustainable development gathered momentum, especially during the world recession of the early 2000s.

In the early 1990s, Japan and the Asian tigers seemed to be the miracle economies.[40] As we note in Chapter 6, the saying was that "the Cold War was over and Japan had won." Strategic policies, it was argued, were more advantageous than the free-market or communist alternatives. Advances in economic theory supported strategic trade concepts, suggesting that there were circumstances under which protectionism paid.[41] But two developments eventually undermined the appeal of strategic trade. First, the economists who originally validated the concept later concluded that strategic trade *could* work in theory but, as it turned out, *actually* worked only in very limited cases.[42] In general, free-trade concepts still made more sense. A second development was when, in the 1990s, Japan and the Asian tigers fell on hard times. Japan went into a decade-long slump, and the Asian tigers experienced a series of financial crises. Moreover, China, often seen as the latest Asian tiger, actually followed a different development strategy than the earlier tigers. Unlike Japan and South Korea, it practiced free trade not only in exports but also in foreign direct investment, attracting foreign companies to China rather than developing national champions to boost strategic trade.

Sustainable development and policies of government intervention got a big boost from the third and latest oil crisis in 2005–2008. Oil countries earned substantially higher revenues once again and used those revenues to advance a resource-based, rather than market-based, economic strategy. Latin American countries, in particular, experienced political blowback from free-market policies, and populist leaders looked for ways to develop that did not rely on multinational, particularly American, corporations. Leftist governments in Venezuela, Bolivia, Ecuador, and other countries used their swelling oil and gas revenues to assist peasant and rural development, renegotiate contracts with foreign oil companies, and oppose free-trade agreements such as the Free Trade Area of the Americas (FTAA) advocated by the United States. Russia also renationalized key industries, and China began to distribute foreign aid in the Middle East, Africa, and Latin America in return for agreements that guaranteed its access to local energy and commodity resources. Development economists drew attention to the billions of poor people left behind by the free-market policies of the IMF and World Bank and called for more foreign aid and limits on the activities and profits of MNCs.[43] The concern with global warming highlighted once again, as in the 1970s, the limits to growth and the need to move beyond fossil fuels and big energy companies to a world economy that does more to tax and regulate the polluters and profit-makers.

Summary

Realist versions of the causes of globalization stress the impact of American unipolar power at the systemic structural level of analysis, the competitive military and economic policies of the United States that won the Cold War at the domestic level, and the dynamic leadership of Ronald Reagan and Margaret Thatcher at the individual level.

Liberal versions emphasize the information revolution and complex interdependence at the systemic structural level, spillover of trade to finance and loss of national sovereignty at the systemic process level, the proliferation of nongovernmental groups at the domestic level, and the empowerment of individuals at the individual level.

Identity perspectives emphasize the contestation and construction of economic policy ideas. At the systemic structural level of analysis, British laissez-faire ideas and American conservative Chicago School ideas defeated their respective rivals. At the systemic process level, classical liberal policies spread to underwrite the gold standard, and embedded liberalism constituted the new social consensus that guided the Bretton Woods system. At the domestic level, religious and political revolutions generated the institutional innovations that enabled Britain to take advantage of the industrial revolution first. And at the individual level, great economic thinkers, such as Adam Smith and David Ricardo, and then Karl Polanyi and Friedrich Hayek, developed new ideas that captured the human imagination and motivated technological and economic advances.

Key Concepts

aggressive Keynesians 314

beggar-thy-neighbor policies 286

Chicago School of economics 312

classical economic liberalism 310

Colbertism 279

complex interdependence 306

dollar standard 287

economic nationalism 312

embedded liberalism 313

European Payments Union 291

free riders 280

General Agreement on Tariffs and Trade (GATT) 301

globalization 1.0 277

globalization 2.0 278

globalization 3.0 278

gold standard 282

Group of 7 (G-7) 294

Group of 77 (G-77) 294

hegemonic stability theory 280

information revolution 304

interindustry trade 283

International Monetary Fund (IMF) 301

intra-industry trade 283

invisible hand 300

Keynesian economics 312

laissez-faire or free trade 300

Marshall Plan 302

mercantilism 279

moderate Keynesians 314

most-favored-nation (MFN) principle 288

Multi-fiber Agreement (MFA) 316

multilateral trade liberalization 288

national industry champions 317

neoclassical liberalism 313

New International Economic Order (NIEO) 294

newly exporting countries (NECs) 317

newly industrializing countries (NICs) 316

opportunity costs 311

Organization of Petroleum Exporting Countries (OPEC) 292

Pax Americana 279

Pax Britannica 279

petrodollar recycling 294

Protestant ethic 310

quotas 287

reparations 284

sensitivity interdependence 306

seven sisters 292

side payments 280

socialism 312

spillover 302

stagflation 294

strategic trade 317

sustainable development 317

tax cut and deregulation movement 315

unilateral trade liberalization 281

voluntary export restraints (VERs) 316

vulnerability interdependence 306

Washington Consensus 317

World Bank 302

Study Questions

1. What are the differences among Tom Friedman's three versions of globalization—1.0, 2.0, and 3.0—and what perspective does each version reflect?

2. Explain what is meant by the flattening, furrowing, and fertilization of the world economy through globalization.

3. How do the realist, liberal, and identity perspectives explain the recovery of the world economy from the stagflation of the 1970s and the era of globalization that followed?

4. What are the Asian tigers, and how did globalization contribute to and complicate (for example, the financial crises in the 1990s) their development?

5. Does globalization destroy or empower individual and cultural diversity? How do the three perspectives answer this question?

How Globalization Works in Practice

The New York Stock Exchange, shown here, is now but one of many markets worldwide. Twenty-four hours a day, a stock market is open somewhere.

How does globalization actually work? What policies and institutions govern it? And how do the realist, liberal, and identity perspectives evaluate the role of these policies and institutions?

Too many textbooks and commentators write about globalization without knowing the actual economic mechanisms by which it works. They talk about trade deficits when they mean current account deficits.[1] Or they argue that government deficits lead to current account deficits even though Japan has had both government deficits and current account surpluses for decades. Sounds a bit esoteric, I know, but by the end of this chapter perhaps you will understand more economics than many sophisticated journalists.

Let's begin with a tale of globalization as it works out on an everyday basis. On tax day, April 15, 2005, Steven Pearlstein, a columnist for the *Washington Post,* gave us this account of how tax cuts in the United States reverberate through the world economy:

> The problem is that the global economy settled into an arrangement of mutually dependent economic pathology. It's complicated but the story goes something like this:
>
> With his tax cut American Joe buys a DVD player whose components are made in Taiwan and Singapore and assembled in China. But rather than spend their wages and profits, workers and companies in those countries put 40 percent of them in the bank.

The banks might have used the deposits to make loans so local companies could expand, but there is already too much capacity in most industries. So they do the safe thing and buy U.S. Treasuries and Fannie Mae bonds, knowing their central bank will minimize their currency risk by keeping it pegged to the dollar.

As it turns out all these purchases of U.S. bonds help push interest rates down to unusually low levels, sparking a housing boom and prompting Joe to refinance his home and take out some equity. He uses the proceeds to build a new family room and equip it with a flat-screen TV whose components are made in Taiwan and Singapore and assembled in China. . . .[2]

Did you follow all that? Well, let's break it down and observe the domestic and international policies and institutions at work behind the scenes. As we do so, look at the graphic illustrations in Figure 9-1 to help visualize the different policies and flows affecting the world economy. And then let's ask why Mr. Pearlstein is so upset with this kind of globalization. Notice that he calls it "an arrangement of mutually dependent economic pathology." For him, globalization is a sickness. What perspective is he applying?

Everyday Globalization

fiscal policies

policies affecting a government's budget; when revenues exceed expenditures, the budget surplus restrains the domestic economy; when expenditures exceed revenues, the budget deficit stimulates the domestic economy.

First, American Joe just got a tax cut. That means the U.S. government used its **fiscal policy** to stimulate the economy and get Joe to spend more money. What is fiscal policy? It's the U.S. government's (or any government's) budget, which accounts

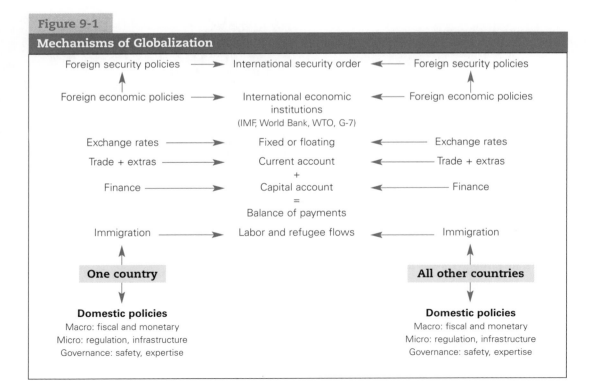

Figure 9-1

Mechanisms of Globalization

One country		All other countries
Foreign security policies →	International security order	← Foreign security policies
Foreign economic policies →	International economic institutions (IMF, World Bank, WTO, G-7)	← Foreign economic policies
Exchange rates →	Fixed or floating	← Exchange rates
Trade + extras →	Current account +	← Trade + extras
Finance →	Capital account = Balance of payments	← Finance
Immigration →	Labor and refugee flows	← Immigration

One country

Domestic policies
Macro: fiscal and monetary
Micro: regulation, infrastructure
Governance: safety, expertise

All other countries

Domestic policies
Macro: fiscal and monetary
Micro: regulation, infrastructure
Governance: safety, expertise

for roughly 18–20 percent of all purchases in the U.S. economy, and even more in most other countries. If the government wants to create more demand to make the economy grow, it does so by creating a budget deficit. It either spends more of its own money on government programs without raising taxes or gives the people a tax cut without cutting government spending, hoping to encourage them to spend more of their money. When the U.S. economy went into recession in early 2001, President Bush gave the people a tax cut. So American Joe now has more money to spend. And, assuming the government did not cut spending, it now has a fiscal or budget deficit.

American Joe buys a DVD player. The components come from Taiwan and Singapore, but they don't go directly to the United States. They are assembled in China. Apparently, it is cheaper to make DVD players in Asia and import them into the United States. Labor and other costs are less. **Trade policy** has lowered tariffs and other restrictions on goods and services such that companies can take advantage of these cost differences, or comparative advantage (as we learn in Chapter 10), and ship components and products around the world economy without encountering taxes or restrictions at every border. Because of freer trade, the United States may import more from China than it exports to China. If the United States imports more than it exports from all countries, it runs a trade deficit or, if we add net government transfers—for example, foreign aid—and net interest and dividend earnings from foreign investment, a **current account** deficit in its balance of payments. See, already how trade and current account deficits differ.

Third, workers and companies in Taiwan, Singapore, and China do not spend all their wages and profits from producing the DVD players. They put 40 percent in the bank. They may save the money because they already have everything they want, they can't get what they want, or they are culturally conservative and want to prepare for a rainy day. As Pearlstein notes, companies in China may already be investing as much as they can in most industries. They don't need or want to invest and expand their facilities any more. Workers may not have everything they want, even though China built four hundred large shopping malls in the last six years and already claims four of the ten largest shopping centers in the world. But workers may also be inclined for cultural reasons to save more than American Joe. The Chinese government does not provide generous pensions and health care for retired workers as the U.S. and European governments do. That's why American Joe, counting on Social Security and Medicare, may not feel the need to save as much and can't wait to spend his tax cut. So different countries have different **savings and investment policies.** In fact, as we'll see, if savings are greater than investment in a particular country, such as China, those savings have to go somewhere. In a globalized world economy, they go abroad. The outflow—or inflow for the other country—of those savings equals what we call the **capital account** of a country's balance of payments. This account includes **portfolio investment,** the transfer of money to buy stocks, bonds, and so on, and **foreign direct investment (FDI),** the building of factories or purchase of real estate. Since the 1980s, barriers to capital flows have been reduced, just like those for trade flows. Companies can now move whole factories to other countries without heavy fees or restrictions or invest easily in another country's stock or bond markets. As we discuss in Chapter 8, this is the distinctive feature of globalization 3.0.

The capital account and current account taken together constitute the **balance of payments.** In a system of floating exchange rates, the current and capital accounts more or less offset one another. If China exports a lot more than it imports and runs

trade policies

policies that affect the prices of goods and services when they cross borders by either taxing or subsidizing the price or restricting the quantity of those goods.

current accounts

the net border flows of goods and services, along with government transfers and net income on capital investments.

savings and investment policies

domestic economic policies that influence savings and investments.

capital accounts

the net flows of capital, both portfolio and foreign direct investment, into and out of a country.

portfolio investments

transfers of money to buy stocks, bonds, and so on.

foreign direct investment (FDI)

capital flows involving the acquisition or construction of manufacturing plants and other facilities to a foreign country.

balance of payments

a country's current and capital account balances plus reserves and statistical errors.

a current account surplus, it has to invest the excess foreign exchange earnings in foreign countries and run a capital account deficit.

Chinese banks can't invest locally all the savings their customers deposit, so they invest them in U.S. Treasury and Fannie Mae bonds. We know what U.S. Treasury bonds are—U.S. government securities sold to the public or other governments when the U.S. government borrows money. But what are Fannie Mae bonds? Well, Fannie Mae is the nickname for the Federal National Mortgage Association. It packages individual home mortgages into securities and sells them to the general public with government guarantees. Government guarantees raise demand for Fannie Mae bonds and thus lower their interest rates. In this way, Fannie Mae raises money to make low-interest loans to American homebuyers and encourage a specific sector of the economy, in this case housing. We call that **microeconomic policy.** China doesn't have a Fannie Mae. If it did, it might not have to buy so many U.S. bonds; it might invest more capital in its own housing market. So, microeconomic policies differ among countries and influence global economic flows.

Because capital markets are open, Chinese banks can easily use renminbi (or yuan, the local currency) to purchase dollars and buy U.S. bonds. They now hold securities valued in dollars. Aren't they worried that the dollar may go down in value? If that happens, they will get fewer renminbi when they sell their bonds and convert dollars back to renminbi. But they aren't worried because the Chinese government pegged the renminbi to the dollar. It goes up and down as the dollar goes up and down. At the time Pearlstein was writing, China had a fixed **exchange rate policy** that guaranteed dollar-denominated investments held by Chinese banks.

Next, if Chinese banks purchase a lot of U.S. bonds, as they have, they push up the price of U.S. bonds. More demand on anything, assuming supply cannot increase as rapidly, pushes up prices. When the bond's price goes up, the bond's interest rate—which is a fixed amount expressed as a percentage of the price of the bond—goes down. When interest rates go down, housing becomes a more attractive investment. Why? Because most people borrow money to buy a house in the form of mortgages, and if interest rates are low, they can afford to borrow and pay more for a house. So, lower interest rates usually spark an increase in housing demand and housing prices. If you already own a home, as American Joe does, an increase in the price of your home offers you a good opportunity to refinance your mortgage. That means paying off the old mortgage with its higher interest rate and getting a new mortgage at a lower interest rate. Because the interest payment on the new mortgage is lower, you might be able to afford a bigger loan. That's what Joe decides to do. He gets a new mortgage that is bigger than the old one but that has roughly the same monthly payment as before. He uses the extra amount from the new mortgage, after he pays off the old loan, to build a new family room and buy a flat-screen TV. And guess what? That TV comes from Taiwan, Singapore, and China, and the whole scenario starts over again.

Several other policies and institutions are at work behind the scenes. The U.S. Federal Reserve Board (or Fed, for short), is the U.S. central bank that controls monetary policy. **Monetary policy** seeks to control the supply of money by raising or lowering the price of money or short-term interest rates--rates that commercial banks charge one another for overnight loans. Taken together, monetary and fiscal policies are called **macroeconomic policies** because they affect the domestic economy as a whole, not a specific sector. In spring 2005, the Fed was raising short-term interest rates or tightening the money supply to cool off the U.S. economy. However, capital inflows from China made it more difficult to tighten money. How so? Well,

microeconomic policies
government policies usually taking the form of regulations, subsidies, price controls, competition or antitrust policies, and labor laws that apply to a specific sector, industry, or firm in the domestic economy, not to the economy as a whole as in the case of macroeconomic policies.

exchange rate policies
policies affecting the price of one country's currency in relation to another country's currency.

monetary policies
government policies that seek to control the money supply and affect the economy as a whole.

macroeconomic policies
fiscal and monetary policies that affect the domestic economy as a whole.

as short-term interest rates went up in the United States, investors abroad, such as Chinese banks, moved cash into U.S. banks to capture the higher interest rate. They put the money back into U.S. banks that the Fed was trying to take out. Second, the Fed raised short-term rates in the hope that long-term rates that affect mortgages—ten-, fifteen-, and thirty-year loans—would also rise. But, as we noted, Chinese bond purchases pushed long-term rates lower than they would have otherwise been. Thus, in spring 2005, long-term rates were going down in the United States as short-term rates were going up. Globalization makes it much harder for a central bank, such as the Fed, to run an independent monetary policy. It reduces national sovereignty in a critical economic policy area, even for the largest countries such as the United States.

Similarly, our scenario assumes that China has good ports, roads, electric power, and other **infrastructure.** Otherwise, companies would not locate production plants there. Asian countries generally have better infrastructure than African countries. One reason may be **domestic governance.** Asian governments are more stable and use resources more efficiently. There is generally less corruption (although that's a big and growing problem in China) and more bureaucratic expertise in government.

Various international institutions and great power groups, such as the G-7, provide **global governance.** The World Bank helps developing countries build infrastructure. The IMF helps them develop better budgeting, banking, and accounting procedures to manage fiscal and monetary policy. The WTO (and, before it, the GATT) facilitates the lowering of trade barriers and the free flow of components and finished products that enables American Joe to buy cheaper DVD players from Taiwan, Singapore, and China. The G-7 is a forum of finance ministers and heads of state and government of advanced countries that meets annually to discuss world economic and financial affairs, and the Group of 20 (G-20) is a similar forum for a group of advanced and developing countries. Pearlstein was actually writing his article to the G-7 finance ministers and central bankers gathering in Washington around the same time as tax day. We examine these international institutions and great power groups in more detail in Chapter 16.

Finally, Pearlstein is not happy with the mutually dependent globalization described in his scenario. Why? Two reasons. It's unsustainable, he argues, because China is not going to lend the United States its savings forever. When it stops, U.S. interest rates will rise, U.S. housing and growth will slow, American Joe's house price will go down, he won't have more money to spend, and companies may cut back production and employment. If he loses his job, he'll really be in trouble. Second, Pearlstein says it makes no sense and may even be immoral to take savings out of poor countries like China and give it to rich countries like the United States. The world is supposed to help poor countries grow, not help rich countries and American Joe indulge their insatiable consumer habits.

infrastructure
a country's ports, roads, electric power, and other basic facilities that provide the framework for its economy.

domestic governance
the domestic institutions and policies that govern the local economy.

global governance
the various international institutions and great power groups that help govern the global economy.

How Globalization Works from the Different Perspectives

Pearlstein acknowledges in his article that globalization is a "wonderful arrangement" for short-term growth that generates "spectacular growth in Asia" and "spills over" into Europe, Latin America, and the Middle East. So his concerns do not have to do

causal *arrow*

Spotlight on

economic independence and national competition

inward-first approach
an approach to international economic cooperation in which countries act first to fix their problems at home and then, if successful, push other countries toward compatible policies abroad.

causal *arrow*

Spotlight on

collective security and interdependence

outward-first approach
an approach to international economic cooperation in which countries agree first on common international policies and then change their separate national policies to conform to international agreements.

primarily with the distribution of power. Rather, he fears that globalization goes beyond the capacity of international institutions to sustain it, something the liberal perspective would worry about, and may be supporting the wrong values, such as consumerism, a concern of identity perspectives.

Realist perspectives focus on the great powers that control and benefit most from globalization. Great powers not only create the security framework for globalization, as we have learned in Chapter 8, they also provide the policy mechanisms to manage globalization. Thus, realist perspectives focus on competitive national policies to steer the world economy, not coordinated or common policies through international institutions such as the G-7 economic summits. Governments that perform most efficiently will set international standards, and other countries will converge toward policies that represent the "best practice." Generally speaking, if governments do what is best for their own national economies, the world economy will prosper, particularly among those countries that are allies and pursue common security interests.

Realist perspectives emphasize mercantilist policies—economic sanctions to punish adversaries, procurement policies to benefit independent defense industries, resource policies to secure oil and other essential commodities through government agreements or cartels, and trade and investment policies to strengthen allies. In general, realist perspectives are indifferent as to how other countries manage their domestic economic policies, such as fiscal or monetary policy. They expect individual countries to pursue different domestic policies based on different national cultures (for example, China saves more, the United States less) and prefer a process of competition among national policies to determine the most effective policies. They favor what political scientist Robert Paarlberg calls an **inward-first approach** to international economic cooperation, in which countries act first to fix their problems at home—hence, inward-oriented—and then, if successful, push other countries toward compatible policies abroad.[3] A good example of this inward-first approach was President Reagan's policies in the early 1980s. As noted in Chapter 8, he backed the Fed's effort to raise U.S. interest rates to bring down inflation and thereby pressure other countries to raise their interest rates and also bring down inflation.[4] Notice how in this example the causal arrows run from the domestic level of analysis (domestic policies to lower inflation) through systemic process interactions (international connections among interest rates) to systemic outcomes (lower inflation in other countries).

Liberal perspectives emphasize common goals and absolute benefits from globalization. They seek to separate security and economic policies. Economic sanctions may be needed from time to time, but they are seen as instruments of collective security that substitute for military actions and are applied multilaterally, not as instruments of national security policy that are backed by military force and applied unilaterally. Because liberal perspectives worry about the sensitivity and vulnerability of economic interdependence, they expect all national economic policies to be coordinated through international negotiations and institutions. They prefer what Professor Paarlberg calls an **outward-first approach** to international economic cooperation, in which countries agree first on common international policies and then change their separate national policies to conform to international agreements. The classic example of the outward-first approach was the 1978 Bonn economic summit where the United States agreed to cut back energy consumption and European countries agreed to stimulate domestic demand. Countries acted first internationally and then went home to persuade domestic groups to change policies in line with international agreements. Political scientists Robert Putnam and Nicholas Bayne, favoring the outward-first approach, lamented the fact that under Reagan: "national . . . measures were given priority over international . . . management. The motto—that each country 'put its own house in order'—was directly contrary to the ideal of international policy co-ordination" that characterized the Bonn Summit.[5]

Pearlstein's perspective also illustrates this liberal approach. He fears China might stop investing in U.S. bonds if the dollar declines or that the United States will impose protectionism and stop importing Chinese products if the dollar does not decline. From the liberal perspective, these policies are closely intertwined and must be coordinated through economic summits and the activities of international financial institutions (IFIs). The G-7 and IMF have to encourage the United States (American Joe) to consume less and save more, and China to export less and invest more. Liberal perspectives place a great emphasis on the function of international institutions to keep markets open—the role of the WTO—and to limit international payment imbalances, both current account deficits and surpluses, so that markets will not destabilize and throw globalization into reverse.

Identity perspectives worry less about who benefits from globalization and whether international institutions function effectively than about what substantive goals are being pursued and whether these goals are appropriate in given circumstances. Policy goals are decided through social discourse. In the former communist world, social goals encouraged tightly integrated economies under state management. These goals served the purposes of communist society but strangled growth and caused environmental damage. In the West, social goals favored more competitive, relatively open global markets. These goals maximized growth, but encouraged giddy consumerism and resource depletion. Identity perspectives evaluate globalization in terms of individual or social norms and values. What bothers Pearlstein from this perspective is the tawdry consumerism of American Joe, a goal that he does not want globalization to support.

Spotlight on social discourse

Thus, identity perspectives stress the substantive objectives or ideas behind national and international economic policies more than their coordination or relative material consequences. Free-market perspectives, for example, stress growth and efficiency. If that is achieved by fixed exchange rates, as it was under the Bretton Woods system, or by greater exchange rate and market competition, as it was after 1980, the method is less important than the outcome. One reason policies in the early 1980s did not advocate outward-first international coordination is that such policies were identified with inflation in the 1970s. Sustainable development perspectives, on the other hand, stress smaller-scale local development and a sound environment. If that can be achieved by market mechanisms, such as micro-credits and pollution emissions trading, or by international development and environmental aid, again, the method is less important than the outcome. Globalization need not lead to best practices, as realist and liberal perspectives encourage; it can also lead to diverse practices. Some identity perspectives see diversity as a more important goal than efficiency.

Now let's look at all these policies and institutions of globalization more systematically. This time, instead of discussing how globalization works from the standpoint of the various perspectives, we'll discuss how globalization works through various domestic and international policy mechanisms and institutions. Then we'll give examples along the way of how the various perspectives evaluate different policy mechanisms and institutions. The mechanisms of globalization are somewhat technical. So, it's important to understand them independently at the same time that we see what the different perspectives emphasize. Figure 9-1 can help you maintain an overview of the discussion in the rest of this chapter.

Domestic and Foreign Economic Policies

There are basically seven government policies that directly affect a country's relationship to the world economy: (1) macroeconomic policies, (2) microeconomic policies (including infrastructure such as airports, roads, and electricity), (3) governance policies (including cultural influences), (4) exchange rate policies, (5) trade policies, (6) policies about foreign capital investments and financial flows, and (7) policies about the flow of people (international immigration or labor policies). The first three policies are considered domestic economic or sometimes **behind-the-border policies,** meaning they affect all domestic goods, services, capital, and labor, whether traded or not. The second four are called foreign economic or **border policies,** meaning they affect goods, services, capital, and people only as they cross national boundaries.

These government policies and the policies of private-sector actors they affect, such as multinational companies, determine the price and quality of the products, services, assets, and people countries exchange with one another. The price and quality of exchanged items, in turn, affect what a country earns and spends in the international economy and how competitive it is. Next we look at how the balance of payments records the exchanges among countries in the international economy and then examine separately each of the seven government policies that affect the balance of payments.

Balance of Payments

Border flows of goods and services, along with government transfers and net income on capital investments, constitute a country's current account. Government transfers involve foreign aid and military expenditures. Income on capital investments includes the interest and dividends earned by one country on its foreign investments in all other countries minus the interest and dividends earned by all other countries on foreign investments in the first country. Notice that trade of goods and services is only one part of the current account. Merchandise trade is an even smaller part because it excludes trade in services, which in the information age is becoming larger. Thus, trade deficits and current account deficits are not the same thing. For twenty-five years after World War II, the United States ran trade surpluses that were large enough to offset foreign aid and military expenditures. But after 1970 this was no longer the case, and America's current account went into deficit and has stayed there ever since, except for seven years. American Joe has been borrowing from other countries for a long time, although only more recently from poor countries such as China. This borrowing (and lending for China) comes through the capital account and includes portfolio investments (stocks, bonds, and cash) and FDI (plants and other facilities). Taken together, the current and capital accounts make up the country's balance of payments account. People flows do not appear in the balance of payments, although any money that immigrants remit to their home country does. Table 9-1 shows the balance of payments for the United States in the calendar year 2006.

One way to think about the balance of payments is as your country's checkbook at a bank known as the World Economy. If you spend more than you earn, you have a deficit in your checkbook, a current account deficit, and have to borrow an equiva-

Table 9-1

U.S. Balance of Payments, 2006 (in billions of dollars)

Goods and services			Capital account		
Exports	1,127.4		Net capital transfers	−4.0	
Imports	−1,886.0		U.S.-owned assets abroad	−1,057.0	
(Subtotal)		−758.6	Foreign-owned assets in the United States	1,859.0	
			Net financial derivatives	28.7	
			Capital account balance		826.7
Income on investments					
Income	650.5		Reserve account	2.0	
Payments	−613.8		Statistical discrepancy	−17.2	
(Subtotal)		36.7	(Subtotal)		−15.2
Government transfers		−89.6			
Current account balance		−811.5	Capital account balance + reserves + statistical discrepancy		811.5
Balance of payments (current account balance + capital account balance + reserve account + statistical discrepancy)					0

lent amount, a **capital account surplus** or inflow, from the World Economy bank. If you spend less than you earn, you have a surplus in your checkbook, a current account surplus; if you don't draw it out, you in effect lend that amount, a **capital account deficit** or outflow, back to the World Economy bank, which pays you interest on your checking or savings account. Notice that any checkbook surplus is offset by a loan to the bank and any checkbook deficit by borrowing from the bank. Similarly, any current account surplus is offset by loans to other countries, or a capital account deficit. And any current account deficit is offset by borrowing from other countries, or a capital account surplus. The current and capital accounts are mirror images of one another with opposite signs (if one is negative, the other is positive). As Table 9-1 shows, after increases or decreases in foreign exchange reserves held by central banks and statistical discrepancies, the balance of payments equals zero. Like your checkbook, it's just an accounting device.

Nevertheless, realist perspectives often see a checkbook or current account surplus as desirable. In the mercantilist era, such a surplus meant that a country accumulated gold, and that was a good thing because gold could be used to buy the instruments of national military and economic power. In today's global economy, it means that a country accumulates loans to other countries. Is that good or bad? Realist outlooks say it's good because it's better to be a lender than a borrower. And they have a point. During financial crises in the late 1990s, Asian countries resented the policies that the IMF and United States imposed on their economies as conditions for new loans. Subsequently, they formed their own lenders' club, the Chiang Mai Initiative, to make loans to one another in future crises and avoid IMF **conditionality.**

But how big an advantage is it to be a lender? What if the borrower can't pay the loan back? You know the old saw: if I owe the bank $100 I'm in trouble; if I owe the bank $1 million, the bank is in trouble. Neither the IMF nor the United States could afford to let the Asian countries go bankrupt. So there is risk in international lending, just as in any other type of lending. Liberal perspectives tend to emphasize mutual

capital account surplus
the net amount that a country has to borrow from abroad when it imports more than it exports.

capital account deficit
the net amount that a country lends out to other countries when it exports more than it imports.

conditionality
a requirement by the IMF that, in exchange for balance of payment assistance, a country alter its policies to correct its balance of payment deficit.

In this 1998 photo, IMF Director Michel Camdessus (left) symbolizes the authority of international institutions as he watches Indonesian President Suharto sign an IMF agreement providing economic assistance to Indonesia in return for domestic policy reforms.

dependency between lender and borrower and see current account surpluses and deficits as normal and inevitable given the high levels of trade and capital flows. Chronic balance of payment and debt imbalances, however, are a problem because they threaten the sustainability of trade and capital flows.

Identity perspectives evaluate balance of payments in terms of the goals they serve. Growth-oriented identity perspectives see large accumulations of international loans or debts as acceptable if they aid growth but as unacceptable if they harm growth. In similar fashion, environmentally minded identity perspectives see imbalances as harmful if they promote consumerism but as beneficial if they promote the environment and sustainable development.

Exchange Rate Policy

The government policy that has the greatest immediate impact on the prices of a country's goods and assets is the exchange rate. The exchange rate is the price of one country's currency in terms of another country's currency. Change it and you have changed the relative prices of everything that moves across the borders between these two countries. Let's say we import a Chinese shirt today that costs 16 renminbi and we pay $2 for it because the exchange rate is $1 : 8 renminbi. Tomorrow the value of the renminbi goes up (fewer renminbi buy the same amount of dollars), or the exchange rate changes to $1 : 4 renminbi. The shirt still costs 16 renminbi, but we now pay $4 instead of $2 to import it. Notice how powerfully the exchange rate affects trade. A country can in effect subsidize all of its exports by maintaining an undervalued exchange rate. That's why exchange rates are so controversial and why the U.S. Congress in 2005–2007 threatened China with tariffs if it did not raise its exchange rate so U.S. consumers would pay more for Chinese imports and buy fewer of them. Consequently, exchange rates are often the first thing that governments have to coordinate when they want to create a stable world economy. If they don't, they get the conflict and chaos that marked the interwar period when every country tried to cheapen its export prices by devaluing its currency and no country succeeded because imports, which became more expensive as countries devalued, dried up.

What should the exchange rate be? Sometimes governments fix exchange rates, called a **fixed exchange rate system,** as under the Bretton Woods system after World War II. But how do governments know what the correct price should be? It's a tough call. Because many factors affect prices, such as unemployment and trade policy, it matters what the general conditions in a country are when the exchange rate is fixed. For example, employment was low and trade restricted in 1945 when exchange rates were set at Bretton Woods. As restrictions and other conditions changed, more than twenty countries, including Great Britain, had to alter their exchange rates in 1949. Economists talk about equilibrium exchange rates in terms of **purchasing power parity,** that is, what a general basket of goods in one country costs compared to the same basket in another country. This measure takes out the influence of different inflation rates on exchange rates. Often purchasing power parity rates are used to compare total output in one country to another. But using any particular measure to set exchange rates is not very reliable.

So maybe the best policy is to let the marketplace decide the exchange rate, just watch to see how much of the currency for a particular country is supplied and how much is demanded by all the exporters and importers in the world economy. To some extent, that's the system that exists now. Except for some developing countries such as China, which peg their rates either to the dollar or a basket of currencies, exchange rates float. That means, of course, they may be volatile because markets are sometimes volatile, especially if short-term capital flows are not restricted. And if rates are volatile, trade and investment become unpredictable, and then the world economy shrinks. So most governments today watch their exchange rates carefully, and sometimes they intervene to keep them from falling or going up too much. Japan did that in 2003 and early 2004 to prevent the yen from appreciating too much against the dollar. The government did not want a higher yen that would make Japanese exports more expensive just at a time when the Japanese economy was trying to recover. So governments intervene to keep their exchange rates within certain ranges or to have them go up or down gradually. Economists call this system a **managed float** or **dirty float** because governments often intervene secretly.

How do governments affect exchange rates? Central banks buy or sell their own currency in large enough quantities to affect its price. That's called **exchange market intervention.** Currency markets today are so deep, however, that even government purchases or sales amount to only a small proportion of the market and therefore may not have much effect. Thus, timing becomes very important. Central banks act secretly and try to catch the markets off guard. On other occasions, central banks may coordinate their interventions. If they all buy or sell a currency at the same time, chances are they will have a bigger impact. Even better is when central banks coordinate their short-term interest rates to support currency changes. If the United States is trying to weaken the dollar, it lowers its interest rates while European countries do not lower their rates as much or keep them the same. Now currency traders demand more of European currencies with higher interest rates and less of the dollar with lower interest rates. This is what the G-7 countries did in 1985 when they acted to bring the high dollar down. Now you know why investors and financial markets pay so much attention to G-7 meetings and what central bankers say. Often central bank officials try to affect markets just by what they say, knowing that the best way to affect

fixed exchange rate system
a system in which governments fix exchange rates to gold, another currency, or a basket of currencies.

purchasing power parity exchange rates
exchange rates that adjust for the local purchasing power of currencies recognizing that prices are generally lower in a developing than developed country.

managed or **dirty float**
exchange rates that are not fixed but are kept within certain ranges or go up and down gradually by governments intervening (sometimes secretly) in exchange markets.

exchange market intervention
the buying or selling by a government's central bank of its own currency in large quantities hoping to affect the currency's market price.

the market, given the small part that governments affect directly, is to get private actors to move in a certain direction. For example, in the 1990s a strong dollar was important to ease the Asian financial crisis. Why? Because a strong dollar encouraged U.S. imports and helped Asian economies export more. Thus, the U.S. Secretary of the Treasury, Robert Rubin, repeated over and over again during this period that a high dollar was in U.S. interests.

Intervening to alter exchange rates can change other policies, such as monetary policy. Let's say the New York Fed, one of the regional banks of the Federal Reserve System, acting under instructions from the U.S. Treasury Department—which has exchange rate authority in the U.S. government—sells dollars to keep the price from going too high. It acquires foreign currencies and puts them into its foreign exchange reserves. Now there are more dollars in circulation. In effect, the intervention has expanded the money supply. If the Fed does not want to expand monetary policy, it has to reabsorb those dollars. It does so by selling U.S. Treasury securities and sponging up excess dollars. That's called **sterilization.** Now the dollar supply is back to where it was before. But, if that's the case, the price of the dollar cannot be affected much, right? Well, maybe it can be affected in the short-term until the market figures out what the Fed is doing. But, generally, economists believe it is not possible to change exchange rates significantly through intervention unless monetary authorities are willing to let the money supply expand or contract, in other words unless they do not sterilize the intervention. In recent years when the Bank of Japan intervened to prevent a rise in the yen, it maintained an extremely loose monetary policy involving interest rates only fractionally above zero.

Liberal perspectives tend to favor G-7 coordination to maintain exchange rates within relatively narrow ranges, believing that exchange rate volatility encourages protectionism and capital flight. Realist perspectives tolerate greater exchange rate competition, believing that it is hard enough to get agreement on policy choices domestically, let alone among numerous countries internationally. And without underlying agreement on policies, coordination is, at best, a short-term fix and, at worst, a long-run inflationary threat because when politicians meet in public gatherings they like to cut rates, not raise them. Finally, identity perspectives are eclectic, favoring stable exchange rates if they serve the right goals but flexibility if they don't—for example, when the IMF mandates a fixed rate that forces a sharp contraction in the economy of a developing country and hurts the prospects of sustainable development.

Trade Policy

Trade policy affects the price of goods and services when they cross the border by either taxing or subsidizing the price or restricting the quantity. Taxes on goods and services crossing borders are called **tariffs**; the price of an import is increased by a certain percentage. Thus, as we have seen in Chapter 8, the highly protectionist Smoot-Hawley legislation in the United States in 1930 raised tariffs to an average of 60 percent of the price of imported products. If that tariff prevailed and we imported the Chinese shirt that we talked about before, we would pay an extra 60 percent, or 9.6 renminbi, on top of the price of 16 renminbi. Even if the exchange rate stayed the same ($1 : 8 renminbi), we would now pay over $3 for that shirt instead of $2. **Customs fees and duties** may also be added to the import price. Taxes (or tariffs) and subsidies can also be applied to exports. An **export tax** may be designed to keep products that are in short supply at home. In the 1970s, the United States placed an export

sterilization

central bank action to offset the increase or decrease of local currency in circulation caused by interventions to affect exchange rates.

Spotlight on perspectives

tariffs

taxes on goods and services crossing borders.

customs fees and duties

charges added to the import price of goods.

export taxes

taxes levied on exported goods, perhaps in order to keep products that are in short supply at home.

tax on soybeans. This was a mistake because U.S. soybean producers lost foreign markets to other suppliers, such as Brazil. **Export subsidies** reduce the price of exported products. The European Union applies subsidies to food exports, and Japan at one point subsidized many industrial exports to capture foreign markets.

Trade policy also involves **nontariff barriers (NTBs)** such as quotas and qualitative regulations. Quotas are quantitative limits on imports and exports regardless of price; recall that the Multi-fiber Agreement imposed quotas on textile trade from the 1960s to 2005. An **embargo** reduces imports or exports to zero; for example, the Arab OPEC states embargoed oil. **Qualitative regulations** involve restrictions on traded products to protect safety, health, labor standards, and the environment. Imported toys have to meet certain safety standards, agricultural products certain health requirements, imported clothing basic labor standards (for example, no slave labor), and car mufflers approved environmental standards. Trade policies also include domestic laws that allow companies to appeal for relief from import surges, dumping policies (a foreign producer's sale of a product abroad at a price below domestic production costs), subsidies, and other unfair trade practices by foreign producers. Sometimes governments use domestic trade laws to protect products through the backdoor. Trade disputes involve these trade laws as often as tariffs, quotas, and standards. For example, other countries often accuse the United States, whose tariffs are low, of using anti-dumping laws to restrict imports. Anti-dumping laws may be written to make it easy to prove that a foreign producer is dumping and thus to impose duties on imports that have the same effect as tariffs. One recent U.S. law that was declared invalid by the WTO, known as the Byrd Amendment, not only imposed duties on imports but gave the revenues to the U.S. industry competing with those imports, creating open-ended incentives for U.S. firms to claim foreign dumping as a way to pocket the duties if they win the cases. We talk more about trade in Chapter 10.

Realist perspectives favor trade policies that serve national security goals such as sanctioning adversaries or strengthening allies. Liberal perspectives support free-trade policies more unequivocally and favor stronger enforcement of trade agreements through international institutions such as the WTO. Identity perspectives favor fair trade policies, by which they mean trade among countries whose policies are similar. Countries that share similar political (for example, human rights), economic (higher wages), social (strong labor unions), and environmental institutions are more likely to benefit equally from trade, although this approach often disadvantages developing countries whose comparative advantage lies in cheaper labor or weaker environmental standards.

Policies Toward Foreign Direct Investment and Portfolio Capital

Policies at the border affect the flow of capital no less than trade. As we learn in Chapter 8, capital flows under Bretton Woods were controlled. Today, capital flows to most countries are liberalized, although China and some other developing countries still maintain strict capital controls.

Nevertheless, indirect controls persist on many capital flows, especially FDI. For example, countries may require foreign investors to export or import certain amounts—quotas—of the company's production, make certain commitments to transfer technology, or pay special taxes and other provisions that discriminate between foreign and national firms. Export-oriented developing countries, particularly in Asia, set up special export zones in which foreign industries operated as enclaves

export subsidies
reductions on the price of exported products.

nontariff barriers (NTBs)
policy instruments other than price, such as quotas and qualitative restrictions, designed to limit or regulate imports and exports.

embargoes
trade policies that effectively reduce imports or exports to zero.

qualitative regulations
restrictions on traded products to protect safety, health, labor standards, and the environment.

Spotlight on perspectives

trade-related investment measures (TRIMs)

the policies of a country that require foreign companies, before they can invest in the country, to export a large share of their production or source many of their inputs from local suppliers.

trade-related intellectual property issues (TRIPs)

the policies of a country that require foreign companies, before they can invest in the country, to share their technology to help local suppliers reach international standards.

national treatment

the treatment of foreign firms on the same terms as local firms.

short-term investments

investments of less than a year, typically volatile.

long-term investments

investments of more than a year, typically less volatile than short-term investments.

immigration

the movement of peoples across national boundaries.

separate from domestic markets. Governments wanted to earn foreign exchange and control the interaction between foreign and domestic companies. In many cases, they required foreign companies to export a large share of their production, source many of their inputs from local suppliers, and share their technology to help local suppliers reach international standards. These FDI policies distorted trade and became known as **trade-related investment measures (TRIMs)** and **trade-related intellectual property issues (TRIPs).**

Government defense policies also restrict capital flows. In 2005, CNOOC, a Chinese company, made a bid to take over Unocal, a major U.S. energy company. Amid considerable opposition from Congress and the U.S. government on national security grounds, CNOOC eventually withdrew its bid. Because local governments treat foreign and domestic firms differently, foreign firms and their governments often ask for **national treatment,** meaning treatment on the same terms as local firms.

Portfolio capital flows include investments in stock and bond markets—**short-term investments** of less than one year and **long-term investments** of more than one year. Stock exchanges are now open somewhere in the world twenty-four hours a day. If you operate a global mutual or hedge fund, you buy and sell in Japan on Sunday night (where it is Monday morning), in Europe on early Monday morning (6–8 hours ahead of the United States), and in the United States the rest of Monday, turning to Japan again on Monday evening (where it is now Tuesday morning). If you own any investments today, almost certainly some part of that investment is in foreign companies and governments. Generally, long-term portfolio investments are less volatile than short-term capital. But when economies slide into recession or a banking crisis occurs, you may lose confidence in that country and sell long-term as well as short-term investments. That's how a stock market crash in one country spreads to others. The world experienced this phenomenon in 2007–2008 when declining prices for housing in the United States sparked loan defaults on mortgages that had been packaged into securities and sold as bonds to investors all over the world. As those bonds became worth less, banks and other institutions holding them had to sell other assets to raise capital and cover their losses. That triggered interdependent stock and bond market declines around the world.

Short-term investments or capital flows are particularly volatile. If problems develop anywhere in a banking system, capital flight takes place immediately and often leads to panic. The Asian financial crisis witnessed such a panic, which exacerbated an already serious problem. Should short-term capital flows be controlled again? Realist perspectives that worry about the loss of national sovereignty and liberal perspectives that worry about instability might say yes. But some identity perspectives that seek free-market reforms might say no and urge instead that local banks become more efficient. As long as these banks are inefficient and corrupt, they encourage foreign capital speculation and do little to promote efficient domestic growth. Protecting them with capital controls will only make matters worse. If protection is not good for industry, why is it good for banking?

Policies Toward People Flows

The movement of peoples across national boundaries is a relatively new feature of globalization. **Immigration,** of course, has always existed, but people flows accelerated after the end of the Cold War and the adoption by developing countries, such as Mexico, of more open and market-oriented economic policies.

Most countries limit immigration. The United States is one of the most open. The European Union concluded the Schengen Agreement that opened borders within the EU but kept them restrictive toward immigrants from outside the EU, especially from Muslim countries. Other countries, such as Japan, control immigration to fill specific and usually less desirable jobs in the economy. Germany admits guest workers, principally from Turkey and the Balkan states that made up former Yugoslavia, but its laws make it difficult for guest workers to become German citizens.

German Muslims pray in a park in Freiburg, Germany. Can such communities assimilate into western society?

When people are free to move, wages are the principal economic factor driving them. Wages in the United States are some five times higher on average than in Mexico. This disparity drives labor north, so much so it comes in illegally as well as legally. Although the United States has admitted some 23 million immigrants since 1965, mostly from Latin America, another 11 million—3–4 million from Mexico alone—have slipped in illegally. How to treat these immigrants is a perennial and heated issue in U.S.-Mexican relations. But it is also a problem in many other countries. Immigrants make up 15 percent of the population in more than fifty countries worldwide, suggesting that flows of people are becoming as common as flows of goods and capital.

Skilled immigrants have become more important as globalization affects the information industries. Software engineers from India populate Silicon Valley and other high-tech centers in the United States. Skilled labor in the United States worries about the outsourcing of other service jobs to India and Egypt. With the Internet, people don't have to move. The jobs are brought to them. People located in India, not the United States, do data processing and customer service calls for companies located in the United States.

Realist perspectives tend to see population as an important ingredient of national power and are reluctant to liberalize immigration flows unless doing so offers relative national advantage. Liberal perspectives emphasize the opportunities to match labor skills and economic needs across national boundaries and seek common rules and standards to govern immigration flows. Identity perspectives tend to view immigration flows in the context of preserving cultural homogeneity or encouraging cultural diversity. They might also emphasize basic human rights and treat immigration issues largely as refugee problems.

Spotlight on perspectives

Macroeconomic Policies

Domestic fiscal and monetary policies provide the ballast for the world economy. Most economic activity still takes place inside a country. Trade in the United States and Japan constitutes only 20–25 percent of total production and considerably less in the EU taken as a whole. Domestic savings, even in the poorest countries receiving the most foreign aid, still account for over 90 percent of all savings. So the policies that affect domestic economies are crucial and constitute, so to speak, the ground floor of the world economy. The more open international markets are and, therefore, the more layers or floors added to domestic markets, the more important ground-floor policies become. They act like the foundation of a building supporting the upper floors.

Fiscal policy, as we have noted, is the national budget. If it is balanced, the budget's influence on the economy is neutral. If the budget is in deficit, however, the government is spending more in the economy than it is taking out in taxes or revenues. In that case, fiscal policy is stimulating the economy, creating more net demand. Keynesian policies call for such a stimulus whenever the economy has unused resources, that is, when unemployment and unused industrial capacity are high. As the economy then grows, in part due to the fiscal stimulus, production and employment increase, people and businesses earn and spend more, tax revenues go up, and the budget comes back into balance. If the budget is in surplus, the government is taking more resources from the economy by taxing than it is providing by spending. Thus, the government is contracting or slowing down the growth of the economy.

Monetary policy seeks to control the money supply. As noted earlier, central banks buy and sell government securities to create or absorb liquidity in the economy. If they buy securities, they push up the price of these securities and lower the interest rate. So creating money—the local currency the banks use to buy the securities—is associated with lowering interest rates and absorbing money is associated with raising interest rates. Lowering interest rates increases demand; raising them decreases demand.

Now, consider how fiscal and monetary policy interact with one another and with the world economy. If fiscal policy is stimulative, that is, in deficit, the government is borrowing from domestic savings. Domestic savings consist of what the government saves—public savings, which are negative if the government runs a deficit—and what private households and industries save after they finish spending and investing— private savings. If the government absorbs total private savings to finance its fiscal deficits, additional savings have to come from abroad. That creates an inflow or surplus on the capital account. Now, as we know, if the capital account is in surplus, the current account has to be in deficit. In this way, a budget deficit may lead to a current account deficit, and economists frequently speak, especially in the case of the United States, about the "twin deficits," namely the budget and current account deficits. Notice, however, that a budget deficit does not have to cause a current account deficit. If private savings are huge, the government can run a deficit and not have to borrow from abroad. The country can still run a current account surplus. That's exactly what Japan did throughout the 1990s; the government ran chronic budget deficits, but Japan continued to show a current account surplus. The government was able to finance its budget deficits entirely from domestic savings.

Now, what if in addition to a budget deficit the government is running a tight monetary policy? It is trying to absorb local currency, or liquidity, by selling bonds and raising interest rates. Higher interest rates attract foreign capital or savings. The bigger the budget deficit (loose fiscal policy) and the higher the interest rate (tight monetary policy), the larger the capital inflow. This inflow creates a capital account surplus and, as its flip side, a current account deficit. All of this assumes no change in private savings. But what if the budget deficit stimulates more consumption and business spending? After all, that's what it is designed to do. Private savings then also go down. Now the inflow of foreign savings has to be even greater to cover not only public spending but also private spending and investment. This describes the flow of for-

Spotlight on

fiscal and current account deficits

Spotlight on

interactions of fiscal and monetary policies

eign savings to the United States in the early 1980s, caused by U.S. fiscal deficits and tight money policy. No wonder German Chancellor Schmidt complained in 1981 about the highest interest rates since Jesus Christ. He meant the enormous squeeze that U.S. policies of big budget deficits and tight money were putting on capital resources (savings) and, hence, interest rates in Europe.

Often governments pursue a loose monetary policy with budget deficits. They are trying to revive an economy. Stimulating both fiscal and monetary policies creates two bangs for every buck—higher spending and more money. This combination of domestic macroeconomic policies, however, often generates inflation. Supply can't rise as fast as demand, prices go up, exports become less competitive (because they are now more expensive), imports more attractive (because they are now relatively cheaper than domestic goods), and the country incurs a growing current account deficit. If interest rates are low and inflation is rampant, it may be difficult to attract foreign savings. Indeed, capital may go in the opposite direction. Anticipating that the growing current account deficit may lead to a depreciation of the currency to correct the deficit, local investors may try to get their money out of the country. This scenario all too often afflicts poor developing countries that have lost control of domestic policies and offer few good opportunities to attract foreign investment.

Realist perspectives expect countries to pursue different macroeconomic policies and rely on competition and fluctuating exchange rates to coordinate or narrow differences in fiscal and monetary policies. This was the approach used by the United States in the early 1980s to drive interest rates and the dollar up, leading other countries to raise interest rates as well. Liberal perspectives urge the direct coordination of macroeconomic policies through international summits and institutions. In the preparations for the Tokyo Summit in 1986, the United States and other major industrial countries agreed to reduce interest rates together to bring the dollar down. If the United States had reduced interest rates unilaterally, the dollar might have gone down too rapidly; and if Europe or Japan had reduced interest rates without the United States, the dollar might have gone up and not down. Identity perspectives urge the adoption of similar macroeconomic policies by all countries. At the Williamsburg Summit in 1983, the G-7 countries agreed to pursue similar policies of sound money, disciplined spending, low inflation, and deregulation. This consensus spread throughout the 1980s and became known in the 1990s as the Washington Consensus, advocating low inflation and market reforms in developing as well as developed countries.

Spotlight on perspectives

Microeconomic Policies

Fiscal and monetary policies influence supply and demand, and supply and demand influence prices. So a big factor for any country is how well supply and demand structures respond to macroeconomic policy. That depends on domestic labor and capital markets and whether individual workers and firms are sensitive to price changes and market forces. A government's microeconomic policies have a lot to do with the flexibility of domestic capital and labor markets.

Microeconomic policies come in many forms. The principal ones are regulations, subsidies, price controls, competition or antitrust policies, and labor laws. These policies may apply to a specific sector of the economy, such as agriculture or telecommunications; a specific industry, such as steel or semiconductors; or a specific firm, such as Chrysler, which got a U.S. government loan in the early 1980s. As a rule, such policies do not apply to the economy as a whole, and that is how they are distinguished from macroeconomic policies.

regulations
standards that are established for health, safety, labor, and the environment that apply to all domestic, including traded, products through various qualitative restrictions.

Regulations establish health, safety, environmental, labor, and other standards for all domestic products and services. They apply to traded products through various qualitative restrictions or NTBs, such as the requirement that imported windshields for automobiles meet domestic crash standards. Obviously, a point of conflict arises when domestic and trade regulations differ. A big task of international trade negotiations is to narrow these differences. In the Single Market Act in 1987, the European Community rationalized domestic regulations among its member countries to create a single integrated market with compatible regulations, not just a customs union with zero internal tariffs. Although regulations serve good purposes, they also involve costs and, if excessive, reduce market responses and efficiency.

subsidies
grants and loans at below-market interest rates.

Subsidies come in the form of grants and loans at below-market interest rates. Boeing, the U.S. aerospace company, has long complained that the European Union subsidizes Airbus, the European aerospace company that competes with Boeing. The EU, on the other hand, argues that the U.S. government's procurement of defense weapons from Boeing amounts to the same thing because such purchases create a large guaranteed market for Boeing, which enables it to reduce costs for commercial aircraft. Japan and the Asian tigers subsidized domestic industries to jumpstart their development and then subsidized the exports those industries produced.

price controls
microeconomic policies designed to keep prices down.

price supports
microeconomic policies designed to keep prices up.

Price controls are used to keep prices down, and **price supports** are used to keep them up. The United States used price controls in 1973 to contain inflation, but at the same time it stimulated the economy with loose fiscal and monetary policies, which drove prices up. The government was heating up the economy—in effect, boiling steam—while freezing relative prices that might have redirected resources toward scarce supplies—allowing no place for the steam to go. Eventually, the economic kettle exploded. It produced goods that were not scarce and put unbearable pressure on the prices of goods that were scarce. Both stagnation and inflation resulted. The EU's Common Agricultural Policy (CAP) is a prominent example of the use of price supports. CAP sets domestic prices for agricultural products above market levels. It then uses import quotas to keep cheaper foreign products out and export subsidies to sell domestic surpluses abroad. Notice that all these microeconomic policies, like the macroeconomic ones, affect trade and hence globalization.

competition policies
policies that deal with monopolies by authorizing, deregulating, or privatizing them.

Competition policies deal with monopolies. Sometimes they authorize monopolies. For example, in former communist countries, practically all industries were state monopolies. Until the 1980s, the telecommunications sectors in many western countries were too; in the United States, it was a private monopoly known as AT&T. Today, utility sectors in most countries are still monopolies, although that's beginning to change.[6] For years, however, and particularly since the end of communism, governments have deregulated or privatized many monopolies. Antitrust policies in the United States broke up the Rockefeller Standard Oil empire in 1911 and AT&T in 1984. Eastern European countries sold numerous state monopolies in the 1990s. The EU investigated the U.S. firms Microsoft and Intel on charges of monopoly practices in computer operating systems and computer chips.

labor laws
microeconomic policies that set minimum wages and working conditions for factory and other workers.

Labor laws set minimum wages and working conditions for factory and other workers. Labor unions in advanced countries complain bitterly that these laws are so lax in developing countries, such as China where unions are forbidden, that these countries have unfair trade advantages. Immigrants from Mexico and other developing countries undermine labor laws more directly, taking jobs below minimum wage and working illegally in advanced countries. Unions, on the other hand, restrict layoffs and push expensive compensation packages that reduce competitiveness and cause companies to invest abroad or in equipment to save, rather than create, jobs at home. European countries have much stronger unions than the United States. They also have much higher—roughly twice as high—unemployment than the United States. European companies are reluctant to hire new workers because they can never get rid of them. On the other hand, many workers in the United States lose their jobs and, although they find new ones, often work at lower wages or with fewer benefits.

Microsoft founder and chairman Bill Gates defends his company in Brussels, Belgium, in 2003 against charges of monopoly practices brought by the European Union.

Domestic Governance

Economic policies do not exist in a vacuum. The domestic institutions that govern the local economy are critical. They include security or police forces to protect the safety of the marketplace; predictable political institutions to decide economic policies; relatively efficient and noncorrupt legal and administrative systems to implement policies; and a well-constructed and maintained infrastructure for energy, transportation, and communications. Often the problems of lack of growth, poverty, and inequality in a country are the consequence of poor systems of domestic governance. Yet these institutions go to the heart of sovereignty in a world of national governments. They are extremely sensitive topics, and for years the domestic policies of developing countries were off-limits in international discussions concerning growth and development.

Security is a prerequisite of the marketplace. Domestic governments monopolize the use of force and provide safety, just as hegemonic or great powers do in international markets. Countries engulfed in guerrilla or civil wars do not offer great investment opportunities. This was true in the United States during its civil war as well as much of Africa during the civil wars of the Cold War period. Military dictatorships are especially destabilizing. Although they provide security, as in South Korea and Spain after World War II, they also store up big problems that often lead to violent coups and scandal-ridden transitions. If domestic or foreign investors cannot predict the security conditions in a country beyond a couple of years, they will not undertake the long-term projects that take seven to fourteen years to achieve a return on investment. Instead, money will go into short-term speculative projects or the pet projects of political elites.

Even if safety is assured, **predictable domestic politics** is also essential to manage an effective economy. Countries that are held together by weak and unstable coalitions and that experience frequent changes in governments, such as Italy—fifty-eight governments in sixty years—do not grow as rapidly as countries with more stable two-party systems, such as Britain, Germany, or the United States. One-party systems, while predictable, tend to ossify and impede growth. Mexico had to end its one-party system to achieve sustained growth, and Japan endured a slow economy throughout the 1990s under entrenched one-party rule. Competitive and transparent political systems seem to do best. All major industrial powers today are democracies, suggesting that accountable government may be an important prerequisite for economic growth.

Spotlight on stability

security
the prerequisite for a stable domestic economy that a government not be engulfed in civil or guerrilla war.

predictable domestic politics
the prerequisite for a stable domestic economy that a government not be run by weak or unstable coalitions or experience frequent changes in leadership and policies.

corruption

violations of the rule of law on the part of government officials that divert public resources to private gain and create an unpredictable investment climate.

Spotlight on collective goods

Spotlight on perspectives

For defying Russia's political elites, Russian billionaire oil tycoon Mikhail Khodorkovsky was sentenced in 2005 to nine years in jail on fraud and tax evasion charges.

Corruption is a major problem in all societies, but especially in ones with poor governance. It is particularly pernicious in the legal system. A legal system establishes and protects property; if that system is arbitrary, investors, whether state or private entities, cannot be sure that their property will not be seized. In the early 2000s, the Russian government confiscated energy properties that had been sold off in privatization auctions in the 1990s. This action soured the investment environment in Russia.

Security and public trust are collective goods. So is public infrastructure such as roads, power plants, electricity grids, and telephone lines. Private companies may run some of these services, but the services must be widely available to support an efficient economy. The Chinese government today is investing massively in infrastructure, from dams to roads to subway systems. The more efficiently this is done, in line with market expansion—so that the roads are used and do not become "white elephants"—the more successful the Chinese economy will be. But it is difficult to manage these projects without politics and corruption intervening. Even advanced countries such as Japan and the United States have roads and bridges "built to nowhere" because the construction industry and local governments constitute powerful political lobbies.

Realist perspectives are generally indifferent toward the microeconomic and governance policies that countries pursue. These are matters of different cultures and domestic politics and can be best accommodated by more competitive realist processes in the international system. On the other hand, domestic infrastructure and institutions are the bread and butter of liberal perspectives. Hence, liberal perspectives pay a lot of attention to corruption and domestic institutional reforms. Domestic economic policies are part of nation-building, and liberal perspectives place a high value on nation-building in failed or divided societies. Identity perspectives make different assessments depending on the values they emphasize. Free-market advocates seek similar reforms across countries to deregulate and make economies more efficient. By contrast, advocates of sustainable development value diversity more and stress micro-structures and local regulations to integrate cultural, environmental, and economic incentives.

Mainstream and Critical Theory Perspectives

The box on page 341 gives an example of one explanation of international economic cooperation that emphasizes identity over realist and liberal factors. Take a look and see if you agree. Don't skip these boxes when they appear in most chapters. They illustrate the relevance of the perspectives and levels of analysis we develop in this book for everything that goes on in the real world of international affairs. Policymakers, newspaper reporters, op-ed columnists, scholars, and citizens all use the perspectives and levels of analysis, whether they realize it or not. The boxes demonstrate that point convincingly.

Notice in the box that even the most sophisticated scholars, after doing extensive research and data collection, still end up having to make judgments that weigh the evidence from the standpoint of the three main independent variables shaping international events: power,

An Explanation of Cooperation in International Economic Summits

As we note in this chapter, the economic summits of the heads of state and governments of the major industrialized countries—started in 1975 as the G-5 (United States, Great Britain, France, Germany, and Japan), then in 1976 as the G-7 (adding Italy and Canada), and most recently in 1999 as the G-8 (adding Russia)—are a principal mechanism through which globalization actually works. Which perspective best explains what drives or causes cooperation within this summit mechanism? Here are the conclusions of a leading study of the economic summit process from 1975–1987.

> Objectively speaking, the international distribution of power varied only slightly over the period between 1975 and 1987 . . . but the character and intensity of international co-operation varied substantially, and a constant cannot explain a variable.
>
> On the other hand, what we might call "subjective hegemony," that is, the readiness of the American administration to assert international leadership, . . . did vary markedly over this period, and those variations are correlated in an intriguing way with the intensity of summit cooperation . . .
>
> When American leadership within the summit context has faltered, no other country has been able to pick up the slack. In that sense, the "subjective" hegemonic theory of co-operation is confirmed.

In this passage, Robert D. Putnam and Nicholas Bayne conclude that "the international distribution of power," or the realist perspective, cannot explain the "character and intensity of international co-operation." But the "subjective hegemony" or ideas motivating America's power that make it willing or unwilling to "assert international leadership" may explain the varia-

tion in cooperation; so identity factors are more important than realist ones. What about institutional factors?

> The summit process takes place amidst a veritable alphabet soup of informal and formal regimes: IMF, OECD, . . . GATT, . . . and so on. . . . [W]hat are the effects, if any, of these regimes on co-operation in the summit context?
>
> In a number of important instances, summit co-operation was aided by the preparatory and follow-up activities in the conventional international organizations. . . .
>
> However, less congenial to this theory is the fact that comparable regime-linked negotiations were equally often the prelude to failed efforts at co-operation. . . .
>
> Thus, we see no simple correlation between regime strength and activity, on the one hand, and the waxing and waning of summit co-operation, on the other.

So the institutional factors that the liberal perspective emphasizes, like the distribution of power that the realist perspective emphasizes, don't help much either. What's left? We're back to identity factors; and sure enough, that's what the study emphasizes in its final conclusions:

> If our conclusions on the role of interests, power and regimes in explaining summit co-operation must be cautionary [meaning largely negative], our verdict on the role of ideas and learning is more positive. Both external . . . and internal evidence . . . makes clear how important, in accounting for co-operative behavior or its absence, are the reigning ideas and the salient historical lessons as interpreted by leaders in each era.

Source: Robert D. Putnam and Nicholas Bayne, *Hanging Together: Cooperation and Conflict in the Seven-Power Summits,* revised ed. (Cambridge, Mass.: Harvard University Press, 1987), quotations from 273–275.

<u>causal</u>
arrow →

institutions, and ideas. As scholars who employ causal methods, Robert D. Putnam and Nicholas Bayne are willing to conclude that the best way to predict or induce cooperation in the future is to have a U.S. hegemon that sees the value of cooperation and is willing to take the lead. Critical theory perspectives might be more skeptical about isolating a primary causal variable. They would see American power and ideas as well as the institutions themselves as more of a problem than a solution. American hegemony is deeply embedded. It is not only a function of the distribution of power and the various "alphabet soup" institutions that constitute international summitry, it is also a consequence of America's ideological dominance. As we discuss in Chapter 1, a Gramscian Marxist analysis would see this type of "subjective hegemony" as even more oppressive and difficult to uproot than an American hegemony based on just power or institutions. Critical theory perspectives see in the mechanism of international economic summits the very kind of neocolonial and western imperialism that marginalizes the rest of the world. Why is it even useful, they might ask, to study an institution that privileges the powerful countries and excludes the developing world?

Summary

Realist perspectives generally emphasize independent national actions or the role of the major powers in coordinating international economic policies and institutions. When the great powers are not involved, international institutions become irresponsible and irrelevant. They cannot implement their decisions, and they become talking shops without any real impact on international outcomes. Great powers have to lead these institutions, although one measure of their leadership is whether in the end they generate a wider consensus, bringing other countries along with them. For realist outlooks that anticipate power balancing rather than power transition, broader consensus is in the interest of great powers; consensus coopts countries that might otherwise counterbalance. For power transition realists, international institutions constrain rather than serve great power interests; it is better to run the world economy through national initiatives or smaller groups of major powers such as the G-5 or G-7.

Liberal perspectives see international economic institutions in a more favorable light and are more critical of the great power dominance of these institutions through rich country clubs such as the G-5 and G-7. Because they believe countries behave largely in terms of the way they relate to one another, they emphasize the networking and feedback effects of international institutions. Let's listen to economist Barry Eichengreen about the contemporary international monetary system. He calls the realist idea that countries act independently of one another in response to common external circumstances misleading; rather, countries act interdependently in response to benefits and externalities that can be generated only through networks. He uses the example of PCs. Once your neighbor uses an IBM computer, it is better for you to use an IBM too, not an Apple. Similarly, once your neighbor implements a certain kind of domestic or international economic policy, it is better for you to coordinate with rather than compete with that initiative.

> To portray the evolution of international monetary arrangements as many individual countries responding to a common set of circumstances would be misleading. . . . Each national decision was not, in fact, independent of the others. The source of their interdependence was the *network externalities* that characterize international monetary arrangements. When most of your coworkers use IBM PCs, you may choose to do like-

wise . . . , even if there exists a technologically incompatible alternative (call it the Apple Macintosh) that is more efficient when used in isolation. . . . Similarly, the international monetary arrangement that a country prefers will be influenced by arrangements in other countries. Insofar as the decision of a country at a point in time depends on decisions made by other countries in preceding periods, . . . the international monetary system will display *path dependence.*

Given the network-externality characteristic of international monetary arrangements, reforming them is necessarily a collective endeavor.[7]

Notice the emphasis by Eichengreen on networks, interactions, path dependence, and the need to respond collectively or cooperatively—all indicators of a liberal perspective. He rejects independent or competitive actions, which realist outlooks might emphasize. Eichengreen goes on to argue that countries rarely have the political leverage (that is, power) to compel other countries to tow the line—the so-called free-riding countries that benefit from cooperation but avoid contributing to it. In short, unlike realist outlooks, he doubts that great powers can work their will through independent actions and small group clubs, such as the G-5 or G-7. From his perspective, incremental cooperation along a path-dependent institutional trajectory, not international competition in a relatively unregulated international marketplace, is the best way to deal with global monetary issues.

Finally, from an identity perspective, the process and institutions of international economic cooperation are less important than the substantive outcomes. International cooperation may or may not help. For example, it did not help when the European Union established a Stability Pact to keep budget deficits in line. After the pact was negotiated, budget deficits among the member countries increased; more members were out of compliance afterwards than before. Alternatively, national competition is not always harmful. U.S. policies in the early 1980s to lower inflation were certainly controversial. But they did contribute to, or at least coincide with, the outcome of much lower inflation and more efficient growth, not only in the United States but eventually in much of the rest of the world as well. This outcome was not achieved cooperatively and perhaps could not have been—governments don't like to take the nasty medicine of reining in inflation by making public agreements. Nevertheless, lowering inflation was certainly worthwhile. Or so someone might argue from the identity perspective, which worries more about the substantive economic ideas that countries achieve than the relative capabilities they have or the role international institutions play.

Key Concepts

balance of payments 323
behind-the-border policies
    328
border policies 328
capital accounts 323
capital account deficit 329
capital account surplus 329
competition policies 338
conditionality 329
corruption 340
current accounts 323
customs fees and duties
    332
domestic governance 325
embargoes 333
exchange market
    intervention 331
exchange rate policies 324
export subsidies 333
export taxes 332
fiscal policies 322
fixed exchange rate system
    331

foreign direct investment
    (FDI) 323
global governance 325
immigration 334
infrastructure 325
inward-first approach 326
labor laws 338
long-term investments 334
macroeconomic policies
    324
managed or dirty float 331
microeconomic policies
    324
monetary policies 324
national treatment 334
nontariff barriers (NTBs)
    333
outward-first approach 326
portfolio investments 323
predictable domestic politics
    339
price controls 338

price supports 338
purchasing power parity
    exchange rates 331
qualitative regulations 333
regulations 338
savings and investment
    policies 323
security 339
short-term investments
    334
sterilization 332
subsidies 338
tariffs 332
trade policies 323
trade-related intellectual
    property issues (TRIPs)
    334
trade-related investment
    measures (TRIMs) 334

Study Questions

1. What are the seven basic government policies that influence a country's relationship to the world economy? Give an example of each type of policy.

2. What is the difference between the current and capital accounts, and how do these accounts relate to one another in the balance of payments?

3. What is the difference between an outward-first and an inward-first approach to international economic policy coordination, and why is outward-first a liberal approach and inward-first a realist approach?

4. What are the three types of public and private savings in any country? When do government budget deficits contribute to current account deficits, as in the case of the United States, and when do they not contribute to current account deficits, as in the case of Japan?

5. What are the differences between tariff and nontariff barriers, macroeconomic and microeconomic policies, and trade and current accounts?

Trade, Investment, and Finance

Engines of Growth

10

Filleting catfish in an export-processing zone in Vietnam. Are these women being dominated by multinational corporations from powerful countries (realist perspective), earning more than they previously did (liberal perspective), being empowered to play a more equal role in society (identity perspective), or being exploited by core countries in an oppressive world capitalist system (critical theory perspective)?

Trade and investment are the meat and potatoes of the world economy. When they function properly , the health of the world economy flourishes. Economists refer to trade and investment markets as the **real economy.** Finance is the wine or beverage of the world economy. It provides the liquidity to digest the meat and potatoes and constitutes what economists call the **financial economy.** It also mobilizes world savings to invest in the next meal of meat and potatoes. When trade and investment markets go bad, financial markets lose their anchor and slosh around with plenty of speculation and much instability. They act like diners who have had too much wine and too little meat and potatoes. When the financial economy is anchored to the real economy, however, diners mellow out and the world economy hums.

Imagine that you, as a resident of New Jersey, are allowed to transfer dollars to Mississippi but are not permitted to export or import goods and services or build a factory there. Given the import restriction, you will have to draw all your supplies and expertise from resources already located in Mississippi. And, because exports are barred, you will be able to take your money back out of Mississippi only in cash or stocks and bonds, not in goods and machinery. It might still be useful to invest in Mississippi if it has unused resources, but it will not be very efficient because the internal market will be small (again, because no

real economy

the trade and investment markets involving production activities.

financial economy

portfolio, financial, and currency transactions involving money exchanges.

345

exports are permitted), and you will have to work with the quality of resources that are available in Mississippi (no outside or "foreign" investment of expertise or equipment). That's what the world economy would be like if it favored portfolio, financial, and currency transactions more than trade and investment. Global markets would be vastly less efficient. When trade and investment suffer, the world economy suffers. Think of the 1930s, when protectionism shut down trade markets, and the 1970s, when inflation discouraged long-term investments. The issues of trade, investment, and finance, therefore, are crucial for understanding contemporary globalization.

So how do world leaders open trade and investment markets and avoid protectionism? President Ronald Reagan had a favorite question he would ask whenever someone suggested that the United States retaliate against another country that had imposed protectionist measures on U.S. trade: "If two fishermen are in a boat and one shoots a hole in the bottom, does it make sense for the other fisherman to shoot another hole in the bottom?" Reagan understood that protectionism was self-defeating, even though the political temptation to retaliate was great. He knew that free trade could "raise all boats" if self-destructive trade wars could be avoided politically. That, of course, is no small feat because trade and investment destroy some jobs and create other jobs as they increase productivity and growth. They redistribute jobs and are therefore politically controversial.

The controversy arises primarily because, as our fictional Mississippi example shows, trade and investment promote specialization, and specialization involves a division of labor among members of society. A division of labor, in turn, creates social categories—workers, farmers, managers, and so on—and social groups compete for political power and influence. Trade and investment extend this idea of specialization to the international economy. Called comparative advantage, specialization leads to a division of labor and different social categories in international affairs—poor (periphery), middle-income (semi-periphery), and rich (core) countries—and these groups compete for power and influence in international institutions. International politics therefore is never very far from international economics.

In the rest of this chapter, we look at the trade, investment, and financial markets sequentially and, along the way, discuss how the perspectives evaluate each activity.

How the Perspectives View Trade, Investment, and Finance

geoeconomics
the regional or global struggle for relative power and geopolitics through economic competition.

Realist perspectives see trade, investment, and finance as **geoeconomics,** another arena in which geopolitics and the struggle for relative power take place. Liberal perspectives see trade, investment, and financial activities as an opportunity for common or non-zero-sum gains and for the development of global institutions. Identity perspectives see them as a reflection of competing ideas—for example, capitalism versus socialism. And critical theory perspectives see them as the outgrowth of a neo-Marxist historical dialectic that generates a single world imperialist system.

Let's see if we can detect these different perspectives in one assessment of the options for dealing with international trade. In *Globaphobia,* the economist Gary Burtless and his colleagues outline three options and then their choice, a fourth option, for designing a "fair" trade policy for the world economy:

There are three, logically consistent, extreme responses to this call for fair trade. One is to trade only with similar countries, as open as the United States, with similar rules, regulations, wage levels, and labor standards. The second is not to negotiate any more trade deals, thus reversing the trend toward open borders and expanded international agreements and institutions. The third is to pursue aggressive "strategic" industrial and export policies, designed to promote American dominance in high technology and other critical sectors.

We believe that none of these policies makes sense. It is undesirable for nations either to be completely unconstrained or forced to be alike. With respect to strategic industrial policies, experience in the United States and abroad shows that governments have neither the wisdom nor the freedom from pressure-group politics to make anything but a botch of them.

The appropriate responses are more subtle and nuanced. Abroad, U.S. national interest lies in negotiating international rules and arrangements that lead to open markets, while still leaving scope for national autonomy. At home, it is essential to offer compensation and facilitate the adjustment of workers who are harmed by greater openness. The ideal is balanced global and national rules. . . .[1]

What do you think? Can you link each option that the authors discuss to one of the perspectives in this book? What about the first option to negotiate only with similar countries? That implies that countries have to have similar domestic ideas about economic policies and institutions before they can trade fairly. They have to be all capitalist or all socialist, or all capitalists and socialists of the same type. In short, they have to have similar political identities. Country identities determine whether or not trade can be fair. Can you see the identity approach in this option? What about the second option? The authors obviously reject the idea of not negotiating; this option would negate the possibility of exploiting comparative advantage and perhaps would appeal to a critical theory perspective advocating isolation or the rejection of the existing economic system. In fact, the option they actually choose, when you read further (the fourth option), is to continue to negotiate despite different countries and different policies. Negotiations eventually overcome international political and other differences, while "leaving scope for national autonomy" to compensate the workers who lose their jobs through free trade. Can you see the liberal perspective in this choice? Finally, the third option implies a strategy to achieve dominance, to use aggressive government policies to gain the upper hand in technology and other critical sectors. In this case, the pursuit of relative power drives trade relations. Can you see the realist or mercantilist perspective in this option?

Now, notice how the authors set up the options to make their judgment as to which option or perspective they wish to emphasize. They call the options they don't like "extreme responses." Analysts do this all the time when they make judgments. They want you to think that their judgment is the only reasonable one, so they label the other options extreme. But the authors don't really believe that similar ideas play no role in trade or that some countries don't pursue mercantilist policies. Most trade and investment today are conducted among democracies, and some democratic countries, such as Japan, are known for their pursuit of strategic or mercantilist trade policies. The authors know this, otherwise they would not be trying to persuade you not to imitate those countries. What they are arguing for is "emphasizing" negotiations—the liberal perspective—while also taking into account identity and realist factors. Notice how they call the negotiating, or liberal, approach "more subtle and nuanced." Those words are always a giveaway not only that analysts favor a particular approach but also that they are making judgments about relative emphasis among ideal types. They use

Spotlight on judgment

ideal types, just as we do in this book, to sharpen differences among coexisting realities and even call their own approach "ideal," as you notice in the last sentence of the quotation. But they are making judgments about "subtle" differences in emphasis, not mutually exclusive "extremes" or ideal types.

In the trade sections that follow, we examine more closely the key concepts of specialization and comparative advantage, the exceptions to free trade, the effect of trade on jobs, the way countries negotiate freer trade, and, finally, the benefits and drawbacks of regional as opposed to global free trade.

Trade

Seventeen seventy-six was an eventful year. For Americans, it was the year Thomas Jefferson wrote the Declaration of Independence—the inspiring manifesto of political freedom stating that all people are created equal. In the same year in London, however, Adam Smith published another manifesto, this one dealing with economic freedom. In his book, *An Inquiry into the Nature and Causes of the Wealth of Nations,* Smith traces the wealth of nations to the principle of specialization—the more specialized nations are, the wealthier they are. "The division of labour," he writes, "occasions, in every art [activity], a proportionable increase of the productive powers of labour. The separation of different trades and employments from one another . . . is generally carried furthest in those countries which enjoy the highest degree of industry and improvement."[2]

Specialization and the Division of Labor

Smith gives the example of the manufacture of pins. One person draws the wire, another straightens it, a third cuts it, a fourth points it, a fifth grinds it at the top for receiving the head, and so on. Altogether, making a pin in Smith's day involved eighteen distinct operations. As workers specialized, they became more proficient, saved time, and discovered easier and readier means to accomplish their individual tasks. They could specialize to make single or different products. Smith spoke about the butcher, baker, and brewer, each of whom could specialize and become more proficient in making a particular product. Then they could exchange their products and have more of everything than they would if they had produced each product for themselves.

Notice that, to specialize, workers must be free to exchange the products of their labor with one another. If the products are taxed or embargoed at each stage, specialization cannot increase returns. Thus, specialization brings with it the idea of unimpeded exchange or integration of economic activities, vertically within factories and horizontally within markets. Obviously, factories and markets may work under different rules. Communist economies organize factories and markets based on direct political control and government plans. Bureaucracies set multiyear production and consumption quotas and order direct exchanges of resources and final products. Capitalist economies organize production based on opportunity costs and market prices. Numerous independent managers calculate the alternative uses of resources based on competitive prices and decide to buy or sell based on the most efficient use.

If markets are truly competitive, meaning no one producer or consumer is large enough to influence price, specialization brings economic freedom and what Smith calls the "invisible hand." Producers and consumers interact, but cannot control one another or the marketplace as a whole. They act independently against competitive forces that are beyond their control, and the net result, through an "invisible hand," is an increase in the wealth and well-being of all participants. Smith does not believe that domestic or international government—the visible hand—is therefore unnecessary. He devotes one of the five parts of his treatise to the role of government. He sees defense and education as government tasks. He even anticipates the drudgery of factory work, or what he calls the "mental mutilation" induced by specialization—boredom from repetitive activities in a production process—and calls on the government to encourage public diversions.[3] But the government must leave the butcher, baker, and brewer free to exchange their products on a wider competitive basis so that they are not just dealing with friends, which restricts the size of markets, or being told what to charge, which distorts the productivity of markets. Specialized businesses needed access to a relatively free marketplace in which prices were determined by impersonal competition rather than friends or government connections and, hence, possibly corruption.

Specialization allows individuals to take advantage of their unique talents. Think of Tiger Woods, the professional golfer. His special talent is golf. If he had to spend time every day tailoring his shirts or growing his own food, he could not develop his specialty to the fullest and contribute as much to his profession. It pays for him to focus on golf, even if he is also very good at sewing and farming. His comparative advantage derives from the fact that he is better at golf than sewing or farming, not that someone else is better than he is at sewing and farming. The comparison is among his own talents, not between his talents and someone else's.

Comparative Advantage

The benefits of comparative advantage in international trade derive from this same principle of specialization and division of labor. Countries have different talents: resources, institutions, and people. They are better at doing some economic activities than other economic activities. Even if they are more advanced and better at doing everything—golf, sewing, and farming—they are still comparatively better at doing one of these activities than the others, as in the case of Tiger Woods and golf. If they could specialize, they could be more productive. Notice, again, **comparative advantage** is about relative talents or costs within a single country, not between them. As long as comparative advantage within one country differs from comparative advantage within another country, specialization and trade result in higher output for both countries. To specialize, of course, countries, like butchers and bakers, have to be free to exchange products. National marketplaces emerged in the sixteenth and seventeenth centuries only after states reduced or eliminated inland tariffs and river tolls. Similarly, an international economy emerged in the nineteenth century only after countries decided to reduce international barriers to trade and commerce. As we have seen in Chapter 8, Britain was the first country to do this systematically. It also did so unilaterally, recognizing that the benefits derived from relative advantages within a country, not only among countries.

In 1817, David Ricardo, another English economist, demonstrated Smith's principle of specialization for international trade. He took two countries, Portugal and England, and considered their relative talents in producing two goods: cloth and wine. As Table 10-1 shows, Portugal can produce both products more efficiently than England. It can produce a bolt of cloth in 90 days of labor, while England requires 100. And it can produce a barrel of wine in 80 days, while England requires 120. Portugal

comparative advantage
a relationship in which two countries can produce more goods from the same resources if they specialize and trade products rather than produce them separately.

has an **absolute advantage** in both products, meaning it can produce both products more efficiently than England. The benefits of comparative advantage are easier to show when each country is better at producing one product, but Ricardo wanted to take the hard case, when one country is better at producing both products.

At first glance, then, why should countries specialize and trade if they can produce both products more efficiently? But look again at Table 10-1. In Portugal, one bolt of cloth should exchange for 9/8 barrels of wine. Why? Because it takes exactly the same number of days of labor—or input—to make these two quantities. In England, one bolt of cloth will exchange for 5/6 barrels of wine. Thus, one bolt of cloth buys more wine in Portugal (9/8 barrels) than it does in England (5/6 barrels). Conversely one barrel of wine buys more cloth in England (1 1/5 bolts) than it does in Portugal (8/9 bolts). So if Portugal and England could trade cloth (where 1C stands for one bolt of cloth) for wine (where W stands for barrel of wine) at any ratio between 1C = 9/8W and 1C = 5/6W, both countries would gain. To see this, look again at Table 10-1. With 1,000 days of labor invested, half in each product, Portugal and England together produce 10 5/9 bolts of cloth and 10 5/12 barrels of wine. With 1,000 days of labor invested in only the product each produces more efficiently, England produces 10 bolts of cloth and Portugal 12 1/2 barrels of wine. They have not used more resources, yet they have produced almost the same amount of cloth (10 compared to 10 5/9 bolts) and 20 percent more wine (12 1/2 compared to 10 5/9 barrels). The reason is comparative advantage—Portugal is comparatively more efficient at making wine, even though it is better than England at making both products, and England is comparatively better at making cloth.

This is a simplified example. More is involved in making wine and cloth than labor, and exchange rates may distort costs and push the exchange ratios outside the range where trade is beneficial (in the example, between 1C = 9/8W and 1C = 5/6W). But the result holds even if we include other costs: land, capital, and know-how. Whatever

Table 10-1

Comparative Advantage		
	Days of labor required to produce	
	Cloth (1 bolt)	*Wine (1 barrel)*
Portugal	90	80
England	100	120
	1,000 days of labor without specialization produces	
	Cloth (500 days)	*Wine (500 days)*
Portugal	5 5/9 bolts	6 1/4 barrels
England	5 bolts	4 1/6 barrels
Total	10 5/9 bolts	10 5/12 barrels
	1,000 days of labor with specialization produces	
	Cloth (Portugal: 0 days; England: 1,000 days)	*Wine (England: 0 days; Portugal: 1,000 days)*
Portugal	0 bolts	12 1/2 barrels
England	10 bolts	0 barrels
Total	10 bolts	12 1/2 barrels

Source: Data in section entitled "Days of labor required to produce" from James C. Ingram and Robert M. Dunn Jr., *International Economics,* 3d ed. (New York: John Wiley, 1993), 29.

it takes to make a bolt of cloth, we compare that to the costs of making wine. Economists call these comparisons **opportunity costs.** What is the cost of the opportunity I forgo if I make cloth instead of wine, or vice versa? The more alternative uses of resources that are involved, meaning the more products and countries involved, the bigger the gains. Comparative advantage offers all countries the opportunity to create more wealth without using additional resources. Developing countries may be less competitive in producing all products, as England was in the example in Table 10-1. Yet they can benefit from freer trade because they always produce some products more efficiently than others. The comparison is among their own products, not between their products and those of advanced countries. Trade, in short, is a powerful multiplier of wealth for all countries, just like technology. (Critical theory perspectives see comparative advantage as coerced and exploitative, not free and mutually beneficial—see Chapter 13.)

opportunity costs
the relative costs associated with using resources to produce alternative products.

Exceptions to Unrestricted Trade. If unrestricted trade is so wonderful, we might ask, why then is it so disputed? Well, there are obvious limitations to liberalizing barriers to trade. One involves products critical to a nation's defense. A nation may wish to have **national security export controls** to limit trade in military and dual-use (having both commercial and military applications) products and technology. Adam Smith recognized this limitation, and all nations and economists since have drawn the line at liberalizing barriers if national security interests might be compromised. Similarly, some products (and technologies, when it comes to investment) are too vital for military purposes to depend on imports from abroad, at least in large quantities. Hence, countries impose national security limits on some imports. These include not only critical weapons, weapons parts, and weapons designs, but also, at some level of trade dependence, products crucial to the overall economy, such as energy, food, and potentially scarce resources, such as copper or bauxite.

national security export controls
limitations on the trade of military and dual-use (having both commercial and military applications) products and technology.

The difficulty with national security exceptions to free trade is where to draw the line. In some sense, every product may be involved in national security. As a rule, the limitation applies more to new products and technologies than to widely used ones and more to WMDs than to conventional weapons. Still, countries use the national security rationale to limit dependence on crucial imports. The United States frets about dependence on foreign oil, and Japan worries about excessive dependence on food imports. Diversifying suppliers of crucial imports and stockpiling reserves, such as the Strategic Petroleum Reserve in the United States, are alternative ways to minimize the national security risks of trade dependence.

A second exception to unrestricted trade is protection for **infant industries.** How do countries develop new products for international markets if they are wide open to imports in those same products? In other words, how do they get started if they start from far behind? Local industries may never emerge if they have to compete from the get-go against imported products. Thus, infant industries, it is argued, warrant initial trade protection until they develop the scale and experience to compete effectively with imports. This was the rationale for the **import substitution policies** of developing countries right after World War II. These policies sought to substitute domestic industries for imports—hence the term import substitution. Domestic industries in import sectors were infant industries that needed to be protected from imports until they could compete at world standards. As we discuss in Chapter 11, Latin American countries pursued such policies, as did late-developing industrialized nations like the United States, Germany, and Japan in the nineteenth century.

infant industries
developing industries that require protection to get started.

import substitution policies
policies developed in Latin America that substitute domestic industries for imports.

Infant industry protection seems logical enough. The problem, of course, is to know when the "infant" has grown up. Too often, protected industries get used to protection and never grow up. They compete only against local competitors, who are also infants, while industries in other countries that compete in foreign markets continue to advance and develop new and better products. Larger countries, such as Brazil, Argentina, and Mexico, are more tempted by import substitution strategies than small ones, such as the Netherlands or Singapore, because large countries have big internal markets for local industries to supply. But even large countries run into limitations and eventually shift to more open trade policies. The United States did so in the early twentieth century, Germany and Japan came around after World War II, and the large Latin American countries followed suit in the 1990s.

STRATEGIC TRADE THEORY. A more serious challenge to the theory of comparative advantage developed in the 1980s and 1990s. Until World War II, most international trade involved the exchange of complementary products, such as food products for manufactured goods. Trade was mostly interindustry trade, in which complementary products were exchanged from different industries and often from countries at different stages of development. In colonial regimes, imperial powers exported manufactured goods and imported agricultural products and commodities. Even as late as the early 1950s, two-thirds of all trade took place between advanced and developing countries. In this case, comparative advantage seemed to explain trade patterns quite well. Colonial territories were mostly southern countries with climate and population suitable for agriculture and mining. Advanced countries were northern countries with less arable land and more industry and technology. Each traded products that they produced relatively more efficiently.

After 1950, however, trading patterns began to shift. By 1990, three-quarters of all trade was among advanced countries and only one-quarter between advanced and developing countries. And the trade among advanced countries was in competitive, not complementary, products. Advanced countries shipped automobiles, aircraft, cameras, machine tools, and semiconductor chips to one another, not agricultural or raw material products. And they often shipped products to one another within a single industry; for example, some exported the semiconductor chips for computers while others shipped central processing units. Trade was mostly intra-industry trade in which components from the same product or industry were traded. What explained this type of trade? Did countries have different capabilities (i.e., talents) within industries (e.g., within the cloth industry) as well as between them (cloth and wine)?

Yes, in one sense, specialization had advanced now to differentiating tasks within an industry as well as between them. If Japan could specialize in semiconductor chips and produce them in sufficient volumes to cover the U.S. and European as well as Japanese markets, it could exploit **economies of scale,** whereby the larger the amount of anything produced, the lower the average cost of production. The United States might do the same in customized chips or sophisticated central processing units. OK, but what explains the fact that Japan specialized in computer chips and the United States in central processing units? Or that the United States dominated the international aircraft market? How did comparative advantage work in these cases?

It might be argued that the United States simply had more sophisticated workers in the computer processing and aircraft industry. But did it have more sophisticated workers because it already had a dominant share in computer and aircraft sales around the world? Which came first, the sophisticated workers or the dominant market share?

economies of scale

the larger the amount of a good that is produced, the lower the cost of production.

Toyota vehicles line up for export at Yokohama port, south of Tokyo. Japan has pursued a strategic trade policy of pushing exports and inhibiting imports in key sectors.

And did governments help their industries gain dominant market share? For example, the United States emerged from World War II with the largest and most sophisticated aircraft industry in the world. Did that happen largely because the government poured vast resources into this industry to build military aircraft during World War II and the industry then used that technology to create a comparative advantage in commercial aircraft?

Seeking to explain this conundrum, economists developed a new trade theory called **strategic trade,** starting from the premise that in markets for some products the economies of scale are so large that only one firm or country can make a profit in that product. If another firm enters the market, profits drop below cost and neither firm can gain. Thus, the firm that gets to the market first wins. It exploits what economists call **monopoly rents.** But it costs a lot of money to get into monopoly markets such as computer processors or aircraft. There are "high costs of entry," and governments may play a crucial role by subsidizing and protecting these industries to get them over the initial high costs or barriers to entry.

The U.S. government did that, in effect, with Boeing and perhaps with IBM. During World War II and afterward, the U.S. Defense Department supported research and development (R&D) in Boeing and provided Boeing with a large guaranteed market for its military aircraft—in effect offering protection from foreign competition by purchasing planes exclusively from Boeing. That helped Boeing surmount the large entry costs into the commercial aircraft market, even though the government did not directly support commercial aircraft development. Once Boeing started selling aircraft commercially, it quickly grabbed a dominant market share. Now dominant market share reinforced its strength in R&D and skilled workers. Boeing was an almost invincible force in the civilian aircraft industry. It is possible that the U.S. government's large defense expenditures for the development of computers had the same effect on IBM.

So this theory of trade assumed that comparative advantage did not just exist naturally to be exploited; it had to be created. And only governments had the deep

strategic trade

trade policies that rely on competitive advantage through government targeting of technology and capital, rather than comparative advantage derived from fixed land, labor, or raw material resources, and that emphasize getting into markets first and eventually dominating them when the economies of scale are so large that only one firm or country can make a profit.

monopoly rents

a firm's dominating a market and setting prices above what the market would ordinarily permit because of lack of market competition.

competitive advantage

a trade advantage created by government intervention to exploit monopoly rents in strategic industries.

patient capital

money invested by the government or government-directed banks over the long term to develop dominant industries for the future; common in Japan and other Asian economies.

Spotlight on
perspectives

pockets to create it. Thus, governments intervened in the case of strategic trade to create what became known as **competitive advantage.** Competitive advantage calls for governments to protect and subsidize key industries and technologies, whereas comparative advantage calls for governments to liberalize trade. Japan was thought to have a special advantage in strategic trade because it had a highly trained bureaucracy and a weaker parliament. Government could pick industries and technologies for the long term and not be besieged by special interests to promote this or that industry important to some legislator's constituency. Japan, it was said, had **patient capital,** that is, money invested by the government or government-directed banks over the long term to develop dominant industries for the future. By contrast, the United States was short-term oriented, with a Congress dominated by special interests and industries dependent on equity markets expecting earning results on a quarterly basis.

Similarly, the EU subsidized the development of Airbus, which is now a competitor to Boeing. And Microsoft, helped by defense contracts, dominated the operating software system for computers, some say with a system that was actually inferior to others, such as Apple's Macintosh. But Microsoft got its Windows system to the market first and captured monopoly rents. Now it is hard to challenge Microsoft. Recently, the EU moved to break up Microsoft's monopoly by demanding that it separate parts of the operating system before it can compete in European markets. Perhaps the best example of a product that illustrates what might be called first advantage—that is, the first company into a market dominates the market—is the typewriter and now word processor keyboard. The placement of the keys is neither logical nor efficient. But the so-called "QWERTY" keyboard became the standard. Everyone learned on it, and it has dominated the market ever since, carrying over into the computer age.

What about this new trade theory? Does it invalidate comparative advantage and call for governments to intervene in trade markets rather than withdrawing from them by lowering barriers to trade? Realist perspectives tend to favor strategic trade because they view markets as zero sum. Identity perspectives see it suggesting how different economic cultures—a more consensus-oriented Japanese culture versus a more individualistic American culture—distort and limit comparative advantage. Liberal perspectives emphasize that strategic trade itself has limitations.

As liberal perspectives see it, strategic trade theory, although theoretically valid, is very difficult to implement in practice.[4] The reasons? First, very few industries actually have the features that permit one company or country to dominate. And, second, if there are such industries, it is very difficult to know which ones are critical for the future. Bureaucrats may be good, but if they were that good they would have a better track record. Japan's Ministry of International Trade and Industry (MITI), now the Ministry of Economics, Trade and Industry (METI), made many choices about industry development in Japan that proved to be wrong, especially as Japan caught up with Europe and the United States.[5] And now that Japan is no longer catching up in world markets, its economy has slowed dramatically and its strategic trade model seems to offer no special advantages.

Identifying future technologies and industries and targeting them using government programs are easier to do when countries are catching up, as Japan was doing in the 1960s and 1970s. Then a government can look at competitive world markets and see where its industries are behind, subsidizing and protecting those industries until they achieve global competitiveness. In this situation, strategic trade theory is a form of the infant industry argument applied to catching up with world standards in high technology. But guessing which completely new industries will dominate the future is another matter. Nanotechnology, which exploits the property of materials at very small dimensions, is a new technology for the future. But its uses are vast and still in many cases unknown. Sorting out what aspects to focus on and particularly what aspects to develop first is difficult and best left to a competitive process of multiple participants and trial and error. Government policies for R&D and procurement still play a role, but this role is more one of developing support infrastructure (for example, funding multiple research projects and educating qualified engineers), similar to developing an efficient transportation and communications system, than of picking specific technologies and industries for special treatment.

Trade and Jobs

Does trade create jobs or destroy them? This is the biggest controversy related to trade. As we will see, it does both. It destroys relatively less skilled or low-wage jobs and creates relatively more skilled or high-wage jobs. In some sense, trade acts as a jobs escalator, moving people up to higher levels of skills and wages, assuming they can acquire the required training and education. On balance, trade creates *better* jobs but not necessarily *more* jobs. It increases more productive and efficient jobs through comparative advantage. But domestic economic policies and technological development are more important than trade for creating additional jobs. So trade and domestic policies work together to generate greater wealth; one without the other would be less efficient. Remember that trade enhances specialization and specialization uses resources more efficiently. We can get more growth out of the same resources. But if we also want resources to grow, an economy has to produce more and better-educated workers or generate higher domestic savings that can be invested in machinery and technology and so on. Appropriate domestic policies create resources; trade uses those resources more efficiently.

From a realist perspective, which emphasizes exports, taking in more imports than exports may be seen as substituting foreign jobs for domestic jobs. After all, any product imported in excess of exports involves a foreign job to service the domestic demand, not a domestic job. This is what led Latin American countries to embrace import substitution policies. They sought to substitute domestic jobs for the foreign jobs producing imports. Realists tend to see trade as a zero-sum game. But this reasoning, according to the liberal perspective, looks too narrowly at trade. It ignores broader interconnections (interdependence). Much more is going on in domestic policies and overall relations between importing and exporting countries than trade.

For example, more imports than exports also means that foreign countries are lending money to the importing country. Remember our discussion in Chapter 9 about the current and capital accounts; that's how the importing country pays for excess imports. Now, if that money goes into luxury consumption or corruption, it is wasted. But if it goes into productive uses, it helps the importing country develop and grow. Developing countries are expected to import more than they export, especially to import machinery or capital equipment to build new factories. Advanced countries such as the United States are expected to export more than they import in order to lend money to developing countries. But the United States imports more than it exports and thus borrows from developing countries like China. Remember, that's why Mr. Pearlstein in the previous chapter did not like globalization. But borrowing by the United States is not necessarily bad for growth or for the world economy. It depends on what the United States uses the borrowed money for. If it invests the for-

Spotlight on realist perspective

Spotlight on liberal perspective

Spotlight on domestic policies

eign money to develop new service and high-tech industries, where it has a comparative advantage, it contributes to U.S. and world growth. Whether the United States or any other net-importing country actually uses capital inflows for these purposes is a function of its domestic policies, not its trade policies.

Identity perspectives emphasize the ideas governing domestic policy more than net exports (the realist perspective) or the interconnections driving trade policy (the liberal perspective). For example, a developing country may pursue domestic policies that encourage elites to import luxury goods, not machinery. Import substitution policies generally had this effect. Although they allowed some imports of industrial machinery, they also encouraged imports of luxury products because these products were not available locally. Or, as another example, the United States might be pursuing inflationary domestic policies, as it did in the 1970s. Higher prices encourage imports for consumption, not investment, because consumers buy now before prices go up while industries wait to invest until prices stabilize. Thus, domestic policies that regulate local industry and foreign investment (microeconomic policies) or encourage inflation (macroeconomic policies) are more fundamental than trade policies for influencing growth and jobs. If domestic policies encourage savings and investment rather than inflation-driven consumption, a trade deficit does not cost jobs but, instead, creates the right kind of jobs. Developing countries need to import more than they export because they are developing. They need foreign capital to industrialize and grow.

What about trade with low-wage countries? If such trade doesn't cost jobs, doesn't it lower wages and reduce standards in advanced countries if they want to compete? An economic theory known as the **Hecksher-Ohlin theory** suggests it might. Over time, trade will equalize prices for products from different countries. That's the effect of creating a single world market. But economists Hecksher and Ohlin argued that it will also equalize prices eventually for labor and other inputs or factors of production. As prices for final products become more competitive through trade, so will prices for inputs such as labor. Thus, some critics of free trade worry that, with unlimited supplies of labor in developing countries, trade will eventually drive wages in advanced countries down to levels prevailing in developing countries. After all, in the late 1990s, the average worker in manufacturing in China cost only $730 per year, while the average worker in Germany cost $35,000 per year and in America $29,000 a year.[6]

The critics are right that wages for low-skilled jobs will move down in advanced countries, at least relative to higher-skilled wages in advanced countries. But they are wrong that wages in developing countries will never move up relative to wages in advanced countries. Wages in developing countries are lower because productivity is lower. A worker in a developing country takes longer to do a job because of lesser skills and poorer health. So, that worker in China who makes $730 a year produces annually only $2,900 of value-added (that is, the difference between inputs to and outputs from that worker), while the German worker who is paid $35,000 a year produces $80,000 of value-added and the American worker paid $29,000 produces $81,000 of value-added.[7] For trade to drive wages down, productivity would have to go down. Yet, as we have learned in this chapter, trade increases efficiency and hence productivity in both advanced and developing countries. Thus, if trade equalizes wages, it does so at higher, not lower, levels in both countries.

The data in Figure 10-1 suggest that, as imports from developing countries increase, wages in developing countries move up toward levels in advanced countries. In 1960, developing countries that traded with the United States paid their manufacturing workers only 10 percent of the wages paid to American workers. By 1992, that

Spotlight on identity perspective

Spotlight on macro- and micro-economic policies

Hecksher-Ohlin theory
the theory that over time trade will not only equalize the prices for products from different countries but also the prices for labor and other inputs or factors of production.

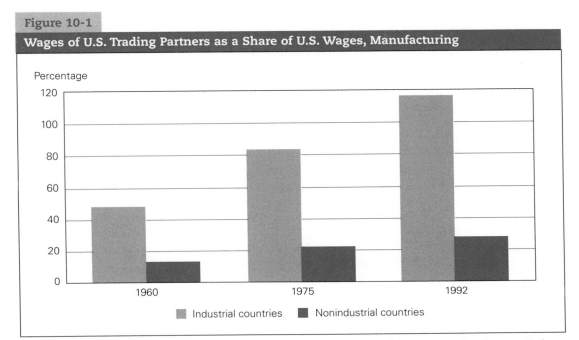

Figure 10-1

Wages of U.S. Trading Partners as a Share of U.S. Wages, Manufacturing

Percentage

■ Industrial countries   ■ Nonindustrial countries

Source: Gary Burtless, Robert Z. Lawrence, Robert E. Litan, and Robert J. Shapiro, *Globaphobia: Confronting Fears About Open Trade* (Washington, D.C.: Brookings Institution, 1998), 69. Used with permission.

figure had jumped to 30 percent.[8] Wages for workers in industrial countries that trade with the United States rose even faster, exceeding U.S. wages in 1992. Productivity and, hence, wages in manufacturing go up, not down, as developing and industrial countries trade more with one another.

So, if manufacturing wages are converging, as the Hecksher-Ohlin theory predicts, they are converging toward the top, not the bottom. Moreover, trade with developing countries permits advanced countries like the United States to shift employment to the high-tech and service sectors, where more than two-thirds of the workforce is employed. These sectors dominate U.S. exports, and export jobs pay 5–15 percent more than the national average.[9]

Thus, trade shifts jobs from lower productivity and wage levels to higher ones. This movement is, after all, the story of industrialization and development. Map 11-1 in the next chapter shows this story as told by employment or jobs data. In the nineteenth century, before the industrial revolution took off in the United States, 80 percent of the American people still earned their living on the land. Today, less than 2 percent are engaged in agriculture; jobs moved into the manufacturing sector. By 1950, more than 40 percent of American workers were employed in manufacturing. Then, the next phase of the industrial revolution began. Jobs moved into the service sectors. Today, less than 10 percent of American workers are employed in manufacturing, while over two-thirds are employed in service sectors. Jobs moved into retail, transportation, banking, financial, marketing, and other information-related activities. United Parcel Service (UPS), a major U.S.-based delivery service, for example, adds on average several hundred thousand jobs a year to its workforce. We read about the loss of steel and automobile jobs, but seldom do we hear about the creation of new jobs in service

Spotlight on technological change

industries, such as UPS. This is another reason we need to know more about international events than just what newspapers tell us.

Think about this statistic. In 2005 in the U.S. economy, just over 29 million jobs were lost and 31 million jobs were created.[10] Jobs are churning every day. Why don't we read about that? What perspective or special interest is driving the news coverage? Jobs changing on a massive scale is the mark of a growing and robust economy. The former communist countries tried to save jobs by not participating in free international trade—and they did save jobs. They saved the same old jobs in the same old industries that eventually became obsolete and uncompetitive and the entire economy went bankrupt. Then everyone lost and had to change jobs. By contrast, throughout the cycles of job loss and creation over the past century, per capita incomes in the United States rose. And during the periods of greatest prosperity in this century—before World War I and after World War II—trade markets were open and expanding. In the interwar period when trade was restricted, the country suffered a severe depression. Certainly no one would argue that U.S. citizens are worse off today than they were a century ago. Developing countries also gain from trade if they pursue sound domestic policies and world markets remain open to their products.

Opponents of free trade say, yes, but trade involves job losses by the least-skilled workers in a society, those least capable of finding new jobs. These workers become marginalized and inequality increases. And the critics are right. As we have learned, trade shifts jobs from activities in which countries are less efficient into those in which they are more efficient. That means the less efficient or least-skilled workers are displaced. (By reporting only jobs lost, the media are clearly acting as advocates for these workers.) This happens in both developing and advanced countries. Think of the enormous displacement going on today in the Chinese countryside. Millions of Chinese laborers are no longer needed on the farm, where machinery and better farming know-how are increasing production with less labor. They migrate to the cities, a strange and disorienting environment for people used to a traditional rural culture. Today, 40 percent of China's people live in cities, compared to 18 percent in 1978. Some 13 million make the shift every year. They are the least educated and the most vulnerable. Similarly, high school–educated steel and automobile workers in the United States, whose families have worked in these industries and lived in the same community for generations, suddenly lose their jobs and have to move to new and unfamiliar areas.

These are serious issues, and past remedies have been inadequate. Many countries offer trade adjustment assistance in the form of cash benefits or programs to retrain workers displaced by trade. But these programs often discourage the search for new jobs by paying workers what they earned before and do little to overcome the psychological effects of losing a job and moving a family. Newer plans call for wage insurance that would encourage displaced workers to take new jobs at whatever level of pay. Insurance then makes up the difference between the old and new wages. But is a remedy pegged specifically to jobs lost through trade the answer, or should the problem, like an excess of imports over exports, be viewed in a broader perspective? Data show that job loss for workers without high school diplomas is just as great in industries that are not affected by trade as in those that are.[11] Something larger is going on.

From a liberal perspective, the fundamental cause of change in jobs is not trade but technological development. Farmers in China and steel workers in America lose jobs primarily because new machinery does their old job more efficiently, not because trade takes place. Technological development is a function of education and domestic eco-

Spotlight on liberal perspective

nomic policies. So, doing a better job generally of educating and retraining workers and of pursuing domestic policies to sustain healthy growth may be more important than specific trade assistance programs. Domestic policies, in short, play a bigger role than trade policies. One thing is certain. Stopping trade ends the possibility of using resources more efficiently and, thus, stops or at least reduces growth. On the other hand, neglecting displaced workers creates powerful forces to stop trade. So, dealing with the transition of the least-skilled workers displaced by technology and trade in both developing and advanced countries is part of the global effort to continue and spread the benefits of growth.

Finally, what about **unfair trade**? A catch-all complaint is that countries at different stages of development cannot trade with one another because their standards are too different. Identity perspectives are particularly concerned about this aspect of trade. It is not just that wages are lower in developing countries but also that labor, environmental, health, and other regulatory standards that reflect different values are lower. Think about the controversy that arose in the United States in 2007 about the import of toys from China that failed to meet U.S. safety standards. Some 4 million toys from China sold as Aqua Dots were recalled because children swallowed beads in the toys containing a dangerous chemical.[12] If industries can export products that are unsafe, that are produced with child labor or with few concerns for pollution and the health or safety of their own workers, and that are subject to lower taxes or higher subsidies, their exports are not fairly priced and therefore undercut the higher labor, environmental, and other standards in the importing countries. As Table 10-2 shows, numerous trade rules exist in domestic legislation and international agreements to safeguard against these abuses. But differences will always exist unless countries become identical to one another. In that case, however, there would be no basis for comparative advantage and mutually beneficial trade. Managing regulatory differences

unfair trade

trade by a firm or government that violates an international trade agreement or trade practices by a firm or government not covered by agreements and that are unjustifiable, unreasonable, and discriminatory.

Spotlight on
identity perspective

Table 10-2

Various Trade Rules to Provide Relief from Imports	
The principal measures for trade relief from imports include:	
Escape clauses	Companies are allowed to petition for relief or protection if imports surge or can be shown to cause serious injury to domestic firms.
Countervailing duties	If a foreign government gives a subsidy to a particular exporting industry or firm, the domestic firm affected by imports from this foreign industry or firm can petition its government to impose a countervailing duty equivalent to the size of the subsidy.
Anti-dumping laws	If a foreign industry or firm exports a product below prices charged at home or if it exports most of this product below prices charged in third countries, a domestic firm that suffers material injury may petition for an offsetting duty to compensate for the price discrimination.
Trade adjustment assistance	If firms are injured or workers lose jobs as a result of import competition, they are eligible for trade adjustment assistance consisting of financial aid and retraining benefits designed to help them move into new, more competitive jobs.
Unfair trade practices	If foreign firms are shown to violate an international agreement or engage in practices that are unjustifiable, unreasonable, and discriminatory, the government of the importing country may seek appropriate remedies. Special rules may apply to products that are not yet subject to adequate international agreement, such as intellectual property rights and trade in services.

Source: I. M. Destler, *American Trade Politics,* 3d ed. (Washington, D.C.: Institute for International Economics with the Twentieth Century Fund, 1995). Reproduced with permission of the Institute for International Economics with the Twentieth Century Fund via Copyright Clearance Center.

by rules that meet minimal levels of fairness and raise standards as countries develop is probably the best way to proceed. As we see next and in Chapter 16, that's increasingly the job of the international trade organization, the WTO.

Trade Negotiations

In the nineteenth century, Great Britain, as we note in Chapter 8, applied free trade policies unilaterally. It simply removed tariffs on corn (grain) imports and proceeded to reduce barriers on other imports as well. Why didn't farmers resist? They lost jobs as agricultural products from abroad flooded British home markets. Moreover, because Britain was liberalizing trade unilaterally, export interests did not immediately gain. So why did Britain do it? The realist answer is that farmers were simply too weak politically to stop the free-trade movement. Technology had shifted the advantage to manufacturing activities. Exporters had gained the upper hand earlier by shipping manufacturing goods to colonial territories. Now, once other industrializing countries such as France and the Netherlands followed Britain's lead to liberalize unilaterally, manufacturing exporters gained access to industrial markets as well.

In the 1930s, when the United States took the lead in trade negotiations, it did not liberalize imports unilaterally but reduced barriers through bilateral negotiations. It negotiated so-called reciprocal trade agreements; each country lowered tariffs and opened markets. Now, although importers lost, exporters in the same country gained. As long as export interests dominated, free-trade agreements went forward. Consumers gained because of lower prices and workers gained new jobs in the export sector. But lower prices and export jobs did not help those who lost jobs in import-competing sectors, generally those who did not qualify for higher-skilled export jobs. So the politics of trade liberalization depended on whether export interests outweighed import-competing interests. Consumers are usually not a significant factor in trade politics because they are affected only indirectly—through incremental price increases on imported products—and do not organize nationally as labor unions do.

Protectionism dominated through World War II. In 1947, over two hundred bilateral quota agreements limiting imports by specific amounts carved up markets in Europe. The liberalization process to reduce these barriers was slow. Gains from bilateral trade agreements between just two countries were not enough to generate much enthusiasm. Moreover, the United States applied the MFN principle to these agreements. As we have learned in Chapter 8, the MFN principle gave all countries, including those who did not participate in the negotiations, the same benefits as the countries participating. Some way had to be found to get more countries involved directly in negotiations if trade liberalization was to become more significant.

This was the rationale for the initiation of **multilateral trade rounds,** in which multiple countries negotiated simultaneously. GATT, which dealt only with manufactured goods, organized the first such round in 1947. There was no consensus to lower trade barriers on agriculture, foreign investment, or commodities, although tariffs were generally low on unprocessed raw materials. At the outset, GATT had only twenty-three member countries. Countries negotiated bilaterally on specific commodities but circulated these offers among all participants. They then decided on an overall set of agreements. The first round lowered tariffs by an average of 20 percent. Even among twenty-three countries, however, these negotiations went slowly. As more countries joined GATT, the process became more difficult still. The next four rounds accomplished less,

---

Spotlight on

unilateral trade liberalization

Spotlight on

most-favored-nation (MFN) principle

multilateral trade rounds

trade negotiations in which multiple countries participate and reduce trade barriers simultaneously.

although free trade moved forward in the OEEC (the Marshall Plan) and the European Common Market.

By the sixth round in the 1960s, known as the **Kennedy Round,** a broader approach was undertaken, called across-the-board trade negotiations. Countries agreed to lower tariffs by a certain average across all manufactured products, rather than product by product. The Kennedy Round reduced tariffs on average by about 35 percent. This was the first round in which the EC countries negotiated as a group. They had consolidated their common market in 1962 and now had a common external tariff toward outside countries. GATT required that all trade liberalization be applied in a nondiscriminatory fashion. Notice the liberal character of this MFN rule, which included all countries and treated them equally. But why would countries negotiate tariff reductions and then give these lower tariffs to countries that did not negotiate? Well, they selected their products carefully. Countries formed negotiating groups based on **major suppliers.** All countries that were major suppliers of a particular product traded offers to lower tariffs. Once they reached an agreement, lower tariffs affected their trade the most because they were the major suppliers. Minor suppliers might benefit, but they would not be the primary beneficiaries. Developing countries fell into this group. As we have noted before, few participated in the GATT rounds, and few of the products, such as agriculture and commodities, for which they were major suppliers were included. Nevertheless, some developing countries in Asia that emphasized exports exploited the MFN principle to get a foothold in advanced country markets.

The participation of developing countries began to change in the next two rounds. The **Tokyo Round** in the 1970s moved trade liberalization forward even as developing countries challenged the GATT and other Bretton Woods institutions through the NIEO (see Chapter 8). The Tokyo Round accepted a proposal from UNCTAD, the developing countries' preferred trade organization, to grant developing countries tariff preferences. Known as the **Generalized System of Preferences (GSP),** these preferences violated MFN rules by applying tariff reductions discriminatorily. For approved products, GSP granted exports from developing countries duty-free access, while similar exports from advanced countries faced a tariff. Developing countries were also not required to reciprocate. GSP, however, was severely limited by restrictions. Many exports did not qualify, such as textiles, steel, and footwear. As we note in Chapter 8, these products were being increasingly restricted by quotas—the most notorious being the Multi-fiber Agreement—and GSP exports lost duty-free access if they exceeded a *de minimis* level, which was usually set fairly low. Nevertheless, the Tokyo Round recognized the need to bring developing countries increasingly into the world trading system. Overall, the Tokyo Round lowered tariffs on average by another 30–35 percent. Tariffs were now so low that other restrictions or NTBs, such as domestic regulations, were becoming more important, and attention was shifting to product sectors that GATT was never intended to address, such as services, agriculture, and investment.

The **Uruguay Round** was the first round to bear the name of a developing country and involve significant participation by developing countries. Initially, developing countries blocked the round. They broke up a GATT ministerial meeting in Geneva in 1982 because they feared that a new focus on services and investment would divert attention from their concern with manufactured goods, especially the quota restrictions on textiles in the Multi-fiber Agreement, and other low-technology exports. Domestic reforms in the 1980s changed their mind. Countries such as Mexico and India shifted toward more market-oriented policies and followed Asian countries to

Kennedy Round
the sixth round of trade talks under which across-the-board trade negotiations took place, reducing tariffs by an average of 35 percent; this was the first round of talks in which EC countries negotiated as a group.

major suppliers
countries that produce a great deal more of a product than other countries; a criterion for negotiations during trade rounds that called for countries that were major suppliers of a particular product to offer to lower tariffs, primarily to the benefit of those same countries.

Tokyo Round
the seventh round of trade talks, which moved trade liberalization forward by reducing tariffs further across the board and, among other means, granting developing countries tariff preferences.

Generalized System of Preferences (GSP)
a proposal to grant developing countries tariff preferences in violation of MFN rules.

Uruguay Round
the eighth round of trade talks and the first to bear the name of a developing country; it extended the principle of free trade to services, investment, agriculture, and intellectual property.

focus more on exports. The Uruguay Round was finally launched in 1986 and ended successfully in 1994.

The Uruguay Round lowered tariffs further, but its big accomplishment was to extend the principle of free trade beyond manufactured goods to services, investment, agriculture, and intellectual property. A new General Agreement on Trade in Services (GATS) was signed and steps were taken to convert agricultural barriers to tariffs for future liberalization and to create common rules for investment and intellectual property. The widened agenda for liberalization was incorporated into the WTO, which superseded GATT as an organization. GATT continued as a part of the WTO, along with GATS and other agreements. Advanced countries agreed to remove quantitative restrictions on textiles and other products. The infamous Multi-fiber Agreement, which had existed since the 1960s, terminated over the next ten years, ending in early 2005. And developing countries looked ahead to the next round, which would deal for the first time with the liberalization of agricultural products, an area of potentially enormous benefit for large and small developing countries alike.

The ninth round commenced in Doha, Qatar, in November 2001. As in the Uruguay Round, the first attempt to launch the **Doha Round** in Seattle in 1999 also failed. Hundreds of NGOs turned out to protest the spread of free trade. Under labor union pressure, President Clinton called for making free trade conditional on developing countries' adopting higher labor and environmental standards. The new round continues to disappoint many activists. But, known as the Developing Country Round, it does put key objectives at the top of the agenda that benefit developing countries: reducing agricultural subsidies in the European Union and United States, liberalizing patents for high-priced medical drugs for AIDS and other diseases in the third world, and strengthening trade capacity-building infrastructure and procedures in the most vulnerable developing countries. At the same time, the Doha Round also calls for further measures that benefit advanced countries, such as lower barriers on industrial, service, and investment flows.

Doha Round

the ninth and most current round of trade talks, which has as its goal to aid developing countries with respect to agricultural subsidies, more favorable systems for the manufacture and distribution of medical drugs, and the improvement of infrastructure, while still lowering barriers for advanced countries on industrial, service, and investment flows.

Members of the World Trade Organization gather in 2001 in Doha, Qatar, to launch another round of global trade negotiations (liberal perspective) that participants hope will override military (realist perspective) and ideological (identity perspective) differences.

Regional Trade

Multilateral trade rounds are complex and difficult to manage. Free trade on an MFN basis is a collective good. All countries can enjoy it even if they don't contribute to it. In these circumstances, many countries become free riders; they wait to see what other countries will contribute, thereby hoping to get the benefits without contributing much.

When GATT started, only 23 countries were involved; in 2008, the WTO had 151 members. Recall that GATT and WTO operate on a one-country, one-vote basis, unlike the IMF and World Bank, which have weighted voting. Decisions in trade areas require consensus, a time-consuming process. The Uruguay Round took eight years to complete. In 2008, the Doha Round was already in its seventh year. Countries become impatient and seek alternative trading arrangements at the bilateral or regional level, even though such trade is theoretically less beneficial than global trade.

Article 24 of the GATT makes an exception to the MFN principle for discriminatory regional trade blocs that agree to reduce their internal tariffs to zero. This was the basis for the creation in the 1950s of the European Common Market and the European Free Trade Area (EFTA). A **common market** involves a common external tariff as well as zero internal tariffs. A **free-trade area** involves only zero internal tariffs; members retain different external tariffs. Imports come into the free-trade area usually through the country with the lowest external tariffs and then are transshipped within the free-trade area duty-free. To get their fair share of tariff revenues, countries have to track imports carefully or create a common external tariff and become a common market. The countries that founded EFTA eventually joined the European Union. Many developing countries also tried regional trade arrangements. Examples included the Central American Common Market (El Salvador, Nicaragua, Costa Rica, Guatemala, and Honduras), Andean Common Market (Peru, Bolivia, Ecuador, Colombia, and Venezuela), the East African Common Market (Kenya, Tanzania, and Uganda), and the Latin American Free Trade Association (LAFTA).

Through the Tokyo Round, however, the emphasis remained on global trade liberalization. Then, in the early 1980s, the United States, frustrated by its failure to launch a new global round in 1982, turned more to bilateral and regional arrangements. If countries were not willing to move forward as a whole, the United States decided it would move forward with those that were willing. It signed bilateral trade agreements with Israel and Canada. Then it negotiated NAFTA, bringing Mexico into the U.S.-Canadian bilateral agreement. President Clinton extended this idea to a free-trade area, the FTAA, which included most of the countries of South America. But major countries such as Brazil and Argentina objected, and the FTAA stalled. Brazil and Argentina had formed their own regional trade organization, known as Mercosur, fearing dominance by a North American trade block. The United States negotiated a smaller regional pact with five Central American countries plus the Dominican Republic, known as the Central American Free Trade Agreement (CAFTA), and concluded further bilateral agreements with, among others, Chile, Morocco, Australia, Colombia, Panama, Peru, and South Korea.

Regional agreements also proliferated. ASEAN initiated regional trade arrangements in Asia. Then in the late 1980s, Australia and, subsequently, the United States launched APEC. Bringing together the countries of the Pacific Rim, APEC is a consultative mechanism rather than a free-trade area. Nevertheless, it reflects the enormous growth of trade in the Asian region, especially since China became a member of the

common market
a transnational market system that reduces internal tariffs to zero and establishes a common external tariff.

free-trade area
a market that reduces internal tariffs to zero, but whose members retain different external tariffs.

WTO in 1999. China, South Korea, and Japan also pursue the "ASEAN plus three" forum, which excludes the United States. And Japan and China have concluded their own bilateral trade agreements with countries in Southeast Asia. The EU too has special regional trading arrangements with Mediterranean countries and the so-called Lomé countries in Africa.

By mid-2007, the WTO reported the existence of 205 regional trade agreements in the world and projected as many as 400 by 2010. Most of these agreements were small and insignificant. But, as regional and bilateral trade arrangements proliferated, a big debate erupted as to whether these arrangements were "stepping stones" or "stumbling blocs" to global free trade. Regional arrangements inherently give preference to members. Although external tariffs are applied on an MFN basis, zero internal tariffs apply only to members. The increasing number of regional blocs therefore increases discrimination and reduces the benefits compared to global trade. On the other hand, bilateral and regional ties spark emulation. Brazil lowers tariffs with its neighbor Argentina to better compete with the United States, which lowers tariffs with its neighbor Mexico. Countries compete to lower tariffs, albeit within competitive regional blocs. As long as bilateral and regional agreements move in a liberalizing direction, they may develop momentum that might recharge negotiations at the global level.

Thus, more recent bilateral and regional pacts are not like the protectionist pacts of the 1930s. Then, countries competed to raise tariffs and devalue currencies (which raised import prices further); today, countries compete to set up free-trade agreements. But current bilateral and regional free-trade arrangements add to the complexity of international trade, what a WTO report called a "spaghetti bowl" of deals that distort investment by creating incentives to get behind the external tariff walls of regional common markets.[13] And, as countries narrow their focus to regions, they may become more alienated politically. Global free trade still offers greater benefits, and the completion of the Doha Round remains the test of whether regional pacts have stimulated global liberalization or substituted for it.

Investment

As we note in Chapter 9, FDI involves transfer of physical assets or facilities to a foreign country (factories, warehouses, real estate purchases, back-office activities such as accounting, and the like). It may be accomplished by mergers and acquisitions across borders in which a foreign firm takes over an existing local firm or by so-called greenfield investments in which a foreign firm builds a new facility on an open "green field." FDI is usually long-term and brings into play what is now a major nonstate international actor—the MNC, such as IBM or Royal Dutch Shell.

Spotlight on perspectives

Realist perspectives regard international investment from the standpoint of access to resources and markets and of protection of defense capabilities to safeguard national military and economic security. In March 2006, Dubai Ports World, an Arab company in the United Arab Emirates, tried to purchase a British company providing services for five U.S. ports. The attempted takeover raised an enormous outcry from Congress as well as the broader public over control of U.S. ports to combat terrorism. Eventually the takeover was withdrawn, as was an earlier bid by a Chinese oil company, CNOOC, to take over an American oil company, Unocal. Countries resist foreign investment in security areas and use them in economic areas to gain critical supplies, such as energy, or to pressure other countries to follow their foreign policy wishes.

China has aggressively used foreign aid to woo countries throughout the world, such as Venezuela, Iran, Sudan, Gabon, Nigeria, and others, to supply oil and gas resources on favorable terms, while Russia uses gas pipeline investments running through Ukraine and other countries to threaten or actually cut off gas supplies if these countries stand in the way of its foreign policy goals.

Liberal perspectives acknowledge the security and economic dependence created by foreign investments but prefer broader measures to diversify investments and strengthen international rules to protect national interests. They support the liberalization of manufacturing and service-sector investments as well as portfolio investments. And they hope these links will become so intense that states will no longer contemplate the use of military force.

Identity perspectives see problems with unlimited investment flows. They worry that powerful capitalist corporations and banks use liberalized capital markets to dominate and exploit developing-country cultures. Some advocate sharp limits on private international capital flows and urge more foreign aid and public or government sources of international financing. Critical theory perspectives see FDI as one of the principal tentacles by which core countries maintain their stranglehold on the developing world.

Resource-Based Foreign Investments

Until 1960, most FDI went into resource-based industries (mining and agriculture) and infrastructure (roads, railroads, public utilities, and so on). In the last quarter of the nineteenth century, British firms invested heavily in mines, public utilities, and railroads in North and South America, India, Australia, and South Africa. American firms followed with major investments in plantation crops in Latin America: tobacco, cotton, sugar, coffee, bananas, and fruit of all sorts. During and after World War II, American firms accelerated their overseas development of critical raw materials such as copper, tin, and bauxite, often with the encouragement of and subsidies from the U.S. government.

Resource-based foreign industries were often oligopolies, or concentrations of a few firms that were integrated both vertically (that is, they did their own shipping, processing, and marketing, as well as production) and horizontally (that is, they produced raw materials, as well as agriculture). Oligopolies were highly profitable. At one point before World War I, returns on FDI supplied about 10 percent of Britain's national income.[14] This early FDI took place within colonial empires or along North-South lines and left a legacy of exploitation and ill will (more on this in Chapter 13).

For host countries, abundant resources often proved to be a mixed blessing. In fact, economists call this phenomenon the **resource curse.** Where resources were abundant, corruption was easy and local elites fought one another to grab resources, sometimes leading to civil wars. Diamonds in Angola and oil in Nigeria produced serious conflicts. Moreover, resource-based extraction often did little to develop the interior of the country and sometimes ravaged the landscape and environment. Resource demand was cyclical and, over time, declined compared to manufacturing. This caused wide price fluctuations and overvalued exchange rates, which discouraged diversification. Foreign demand for resources drove up the value of the local currency, which then cost more than it should and discouraged foreign investment and exports in nonresource areas. In Saudi Arabia, for example, oil still makes up 45 percent of GDP, 90 percent of export earnings, and 75 percent of government revenues. After more than 50 years of

resource curse

a phenomenon that occurs when an abundance of natural resources prevents development by encouraging overvalued exchange rates, corruption, and lack of diversification into industry.

development, the non-energy-related manufacturing sector remains miniscule. Foreign resource firms also exercised significant influence over the host nation's government and foreign policy. When some Latin American countries expropriated U.S. firms after World War II, Congress passed the **Hickenlooper Amendment** that called for the United States to cut off all foreign aid if U.S. company property was seized without adequate compensation.

Resource-based MNCs have considerable leverage when they first begin operations in a country. Local governments are eager to attract these companies to develop their resources, and only the MNCs have the capital and technology to do so. The companies pretty much set the terms of investment. Once in the country, however, foreign companies become more hostage to local government influence. It is now easier for governments to impose taxes and other regulations. Firms with a lot already invested cannot pick up and leave the country as easily as they entered it. In addition, host countries gradually learn the technology and business of the MNCs and then nationalize the firms. In this way, OPEC members slowly took control away from the big seven sister oil companies and now dominate oil markets through their own cartel. In recent years, nationalist governments in Venezuela and Bolivia imposed new taxes and nationalized some parts of foreign companies that were developing oil and natural gas in those countries.

The rapid development of China and India has added enormous new pressure on the development of natural resources in the Middle East, Africa, and Latin America. With a fifth of the world's population, China now consumes half of the world's cement, a third of its steel, and over a quarter of its aluminum. And Chinese firms are scouring the world from Canada to Indonesia to Kazakhstan to secure additional resources. In late 2007, the Congo government announced that Chinese state-owned firms would invest $12 billion to build or refurbish railroads, roads, and mines throughout the African country in return for the right to mine copper ore of equivalent value. The size of the deal is the equivalent of Congo's entire foreign debt, three times its annual budget, and ten times the amount of foreign aid the country receives. China is also guzzling oil and investing in the oil-rich states of the Persian Gulf to secure oil imports. In 2007, it imported 3.5 million barrels of oil per day, a figure that is expected to rise fourfold over the next twenty years.[15] China's growing influence promises to make MNC expansion into resource development increasingly important in world politics, reviving the role that resource development played in the colonial era of western expansion.

Hickenlooper Amendment

post–World War II legislation that called for the United States to cut off all foreign aid to a country if U.S. company property was seized without adequate compensation.

Chinese President Hu Jintao (left) visits Zambia in 2007 and inspects a model plan for Chinese investments in the country. Chinese firms have pursued development in numerous other African and developing countries as well. Is China the next imperialist (realist perspective), market (liberal perspective), ideological (identity perspective), or systems dynamic (critical theory perspective) power that will drive the global economy?

Manufacturing Foreign Investments

By the mid-1950s, however, resource-based investments were less significant than booming manufacturing investments. Some manufacturing companies became multinational long before World War II. The Singer Sewing Company had set up operations in Europe already in the late nineteenth century, and Ford and General Motors established factories in Europe during the interwar period. FDI in manufacturing, however, did not expand in a big way until the late 1950s and 1960s. Recall that Bretton Woods did not liberalize foreign investment and other capital flows across national borders. But, as we discuss in Chapter 8, U.S. current account surpluses in the 1950s led to the accumulation of dollars abroad. These dollars sitting in European banks financed the first real breakout of U.S. manufacturing investments in Europe. If American companies could not send dollars abroad to build factories, they would borrow them in the Eurodollar market to do so.

By the late 1960s, American MNCs were a strong presence in western Europe, concentrated in growth sectors and under the control of a relatively few American companies. U.S. firms, for example, accounted for 25–30 percent of the automobile market, 60–70 percent of the aircraft and tractor markets, 65 percent of the computer market (industrial computers; there were no personal computers as yet), 30 percent of the telephone market, and 25–30 percent of the petroleum products market. Only three companies—Esso (now Exxon Mobil), General Motors, and Ford—accounted for 40 percent of all U.S. investments in France, Germany, and Britain, and only twenty-three firms controlled two-thirds of all U.S. investments in western Europe.

These investments sparked an early political controversy among advanced countries.[16] Europeans complained that U.S. companies, concentrated in high-tech sectors, exerted undue influence over critical European R&D resources and preempted European industries' development in advanced technology. This so-called **technology gap** controversy sparked new interest in the causes of FDI. Did investment flows increase efficiency as trade flows did? If so, should FDI, and perhaps capital flows more generally, be liberalized as GATT was liberalizing trade flows?

PRODUCT LIFE CYCLE. Theoretically, investments should flow to countries that provide the highest rates of return. And returns should be higher where capital is scarcest and in greatest demand. That suggests that investments should flow primarily from advanced countries to developing countries. But they don't. As Figure 10-2 shows, the bulk of FDI inflows go to advanced, not developing, countries. In 2005, $540 billion, or 59 percent, of global direct investment went to advanced countries; $330 billion, or 36 percent, went to developing ones; and $37 billion, or 4 percent, went to the CIS.[17] Developed countries invest in one another more than they do in developing countries. In 2006, 53 percent of total U.S. foreign investment around the world was located in Europe, three times more than U.S. corporate investment in all of Asia and more than double the U.S. investment in developing nations.[18] Why is this so?

One explanation was developed by economist Raymond Vernon.[19] Known as the **product life cycle,** it argues that high-tech product development went through various stages. In the first stage, when the product was first produced, companies operated close to home, where R&D were located and new products could be tested and adapted to consumer needs. American firms had an advantage at this stage because U.S. research and consumer markets were highly advanced. Thus, U.S. firms produced at home and exported to other advanced markets where there was a demand for sophisticated products. In the second stage, as the technology matured and other costs—labor and shipping—became more important, it was advantageous to shift production to European markets. Once the European Common Market existed, tariffs were lower inside Europe, and producing the product closer to the final consumer avoided paying the external tariff and forestalled local competition. Finally in

technology gap
the feared dominance of high-tech U.S. companies in Europe in the 1960s, limiting critical European research and development resources and preempting independent European technological and industrial development.

product life cycle
a theory that argues that high-tech product development goes through various stages, explaining why foreign direct investment most often goes to advanced, not developing, countries.

Figure 10-2

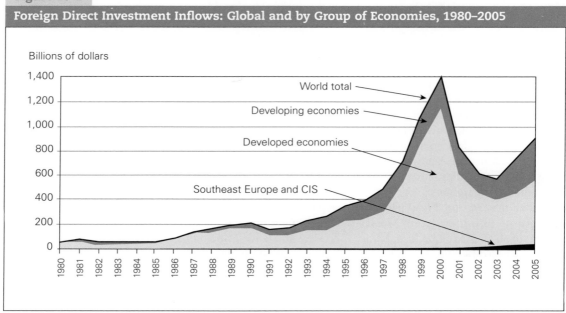

Foreign Direct Investment Inflows: Global and by Group of Economies, 1980–2005

Billions of dollars

Source: From UNCTAD, based on its FDI/TNC database (www.unctad.org/fdistatistics). UNCTAD, *World Investment Report 2006: FDI from Developing and Transition Economies: Implications for Development* (New York and Geneva: United Nations, 2006), 36; available at: www.unctad.org/en/docs/wir2006_en.pdf.

the third stage, when production had become fully routine, production shifted to developing countries, which had the lowest labor costs. Developing countries then exported the product back to the United States and Europe. Thus, the expansion of U.S. investments to Europe in the 1960s reflected the second stage of the product life cycle, when FDI displaces exports in advanced markets; and the expansion of MNCs to Asia in the 1970s and 1980s reflected the third stage, when FDI moves to developing countries, which export back to more advanced countries. According to the product life cycle theory, FDI seemed to follow demand (consumers) more than supply (labor), and thus most of it went to advanced countries where demand was high and changing.

Initially, few developing countries welcomed FDI in manufacturing. As we note in previous chapters and again in Chapter 11, Latin American countries were intent on developing their own industries through import substitution policies, and many newly independent developing countries feared neocolonial influences from the MNCs. They advocated technology transfer without the accompanying capital and management, but that approach was neither accepted by MNCs nor terribly effective for mastering new technologies.

Some Asian developing countries bucked the trend, however. The four tigers— Taiwan, Hong Kong, South Korea, and Singapore—focused on exports and welcomed FDI. As the product life cycle predicted, investments began to flow to these countries in labor-intensive and standardized technology products. A second wave of MNCs expanded to Asia, this time including European as well as American companies. The success of the Asian tigers encouraged emulation, and other Asian nations opened up to FDI: the Philippines, Thailand, Indonesia, Malaysia, and later

China and India. Some Latin American and African countries, such as Mexico and Tanzania, did so as well.

GATT did not deal with investments. So the expansion of MNCs was negotiated on a country-by-country and, often, contract-by-contract basis. Bilateral investment treaties proliferated, much the way bilateral trade agreements had in the 1940s. These treaties were often discriminatory and involved numerous restrictions that affected trade. As we noted earlier, investing firms might be required to export a certain percentage of production or source their imports from specific countries. Developing countries set up **free-trade export-processing zones** as separate industrial areas in which they gave foreign companies profitable concessions, such as low or no taxes, lenient labor laws, and duty-free imports, as long as these companies produced for export. Foreign investors found such zones attractive for importing components and assembling final products for export. However, export zones produced limited local benefits. Often the value-added to production (the difference between the value of the inputs and the value of outputs from these zones) was relatively small, and while foreign firms employed local workers, they created enclave communities rather than linking up with internal markets and developing local resources. In some ways, manufacturing export zones resembled the natural resource enclaves of earlier resource-based multinational investments.

Proliferating export zones and the oil crisis accelerated interest in liberalizing capital flows. In the 1970s, the United States began to negotiate bilateral investment treaties that contained clauses requiring national treatment. As we discuss in Chapter 9, national treatment meant that, rather than offering special treatment for FDI in selective export zones, host countries treated foreign investors the same as local or national investors throughout the entire economy. This reduced the discrimination inherent in export zones. GATT began to discuss and negotiate rules to govern investment and technology restrictions that distorted trade, the TRIMs and TRIPs. GATT also discussed a Multilateral Agreement on Investment (MAI), and the WTO acquired jurisdiction over investment as well as trade issues when it superseded the GATT in 1994.

free-trade export-processing zones
separate industrial areas established within developing countries that give foreign firms profitable concessions as long as these companies produce goods primarily for export.

Spotlight on national treatment

Service-Sector Foreign Investments

As technological development quickened and FDI became freer, the product life cycle collapsed. That is, countries had very little time between developing a product and shifting production overseas to recoup their R&D costs. Investments spread simultaneously to many markets at once. It was essential to be invested in all these markets from the outset and to develop comparative advantage in high technology by encouraging networks of universities, entrepreneurs, and financiers to create new products. Strategic trade theory suggested that comparative advantage was no longer based on fixed factors, such as lower labor costs, but depended increasingly on getting to all markets first and dominating those markets as quickly as possible. Once a company had a large market share, it could reap monopoly profits or rents and recoup development costs.

The next, or fourth, wave of MNC expansion reflected this emphasis on investing in the most advanced markets simultaneously. First Japan in the 1980s and then European countries in the 1990s invested massively in the U.S. market. Some developing countries—Brazil, Mexico, and South Africa—also developed their own MNCs and opened operations in both Europe and Asia. Some countries are friendlier to FDI than others. FDI in Japan, for example, remains a small share of the value of total sales or employment compared to the United States or Europe. Overall, however, FDI spread, and world markets became intensely competitive. Companies were now truly global, often decentralizing to run operations from regional headquarters abroad rather than from the home countries.

A further step in this evolution became visible in the early 2000s. Companies expanded abroad not just to manufacture products but also to provide services. Historically, services were more home-bound enterprises catering to local cultures, languages, and tastes. But advances in transportation and communications now shrank the service world. Financial companies—banks, insurance companies, mutual, pension, and hedge funds—set up operations overseas. Retail (for example, Wal-Mart and McDonald's), telecommunications (AOL and Google), and entertainment companies (Disney and Bertelsmann) did so as well.

outsourcing

sending in-house payroll, software, and data processing tasks to other, often foreign, firms for execution via the Internet, requiring no transfer of physical production facilities.

The latest expansion of multinational service industries comes in areas of data processing, back-office accounting services, software development, and call centers. This phenomenon is known as foreign **outsourcing.** Whereas in earlier expansions MNCs continued to do payroll, data services, and R&D activities at the home headquarters, they now exploited the Internet to outsource these tasks to foreign firms. Payroll and other forms of accounting and data processing could be sent to firms in India or China for completion and shipped back via the Internet to the home company the next day or week. Even research tasks could be outsourced. An R&D firm in Dahlian, China, might be asked to develop a new software program for a cell phone chip. The task could be done entirely online, without the need to transfer physical facilities.

offshore investment

the production of the components of a product overseas, followed eventually by the assembly of the components abroad as well.

Textile and steel workers and their unions have long decried foreign investment in manufacturing. In this case, it was called **offshore investment** and involved the transfer of production facilities to make components of a product overseas, followed eventually by facilities to assemble the components abroad as well. More recently, highly skilled labor has raised similar concerns about outsourcing. Silicon Valley software operations are being outsourced to Egypt, India, and Ireland, where engineers work for much less pay. FDI, like trade, involves job displacement, and job displacement is disruptive. But the issue is also what the alternative might be. If foreign outsourcing is banned, companies will become less competitive or have to invest in more advanced technology at home. The latter, too, results in job losses, as machines replace labor. More textile jobs have been lost in the United States by modernizing local plants than by trade or offshore investments.

Perhaps the next service that will be outsourced is education. Training by corporations as well as instruction by universities may be done online from distant locations. Professors will lose their jobs or at least have to compete as instructors abroad specialize and teach online courses in specific topics. Then we'll get a chance to see how much professors and especially economists really favor free trade.

Are Multinational Corporations Too Big?

In 2005, world sales of foreign affiliates totaled $22.2 trillion, up from $2.7 trillion in 1982. World exports, by comparison, equaled only $12.6 trillion, up from $2.2 trillion in 1982. The gross product of foreign affiliates—the sales of foreign affiliates minus the cost of production, or the value-added—totaled $4.5 trillion compared to world GDP of $44.7 trillion.[20] Thus, in 2005, foreign affiliates, some 770,000 worldwide, accounted for about 10 percent of world production, while their total sales were almost twice as large as world exports. Moreover, MNCs themselves accounted for over 33 percent of world exports. FDI has integrated the world economy far more than trade. Since two-thirds of all FDI takes place among advanced countries, this integration is more extensive among advanced countries than between them and developing countries.

If we use total sales as a measure, in 2000, MNCs made up fifty-one of the world's one hundred largest economies. But this measure compares the total sales of MNCs with the GDP of countries, and recall that GDP is measured by total sales (output) minus total costs (inputs), or value-added. When corporations are also measured in terms of value-added, only twenty-nine companies appear among the top one hundred economies, and only two of these—Exxon Mobil at forty-five and General Motors at forty-seven—rank in the top fifty.[21] Still, that is a large number. Few developing countries appear in the top one hundred economies. So, twenty-nine MNCs are much larger than the economies of many developing countries, certainly of the poorest countries.

Doesn't this give them enormous clout? Yes and no. Yes, they control large amounts of capital and labor, and, as realist perspectives point out, that gives them real power. But, no, they also must compete, and recipient countries can play them off against one another, certainly more so than fifty years ago when MNCs were fewer in number and highly concentrated in specific sectors such as resources.

MNCs usually pay higher wages than local firms but not as high as they pay in their home countries. Yet international human rights groups find numerous instances of labor abuses, especially among sweatshops in export-processing zones. That wages and conditions can be improved is beyond doubt, but applicable standards need to be proportionate. Workers in developing countries are less productive. If they were paid the same wages as workers in developed countries, no firm would invest or trade with developing countries. The relevant standard is what they were paid before they went to work for foreign firms. In almost all cases, workers do better where MNCs are present, especially women and children. Most women are unemployed before the MNCs arrive; children work because parents often require it, and they would be working anyway if they stayed on the farm. Children also worked during the early stages of development in advanced countries; at that time, abuses occurred and had to be corrected. The same holds true today in developing countries. For a dissenting view on the impact of MNCs, see the critical theory perspective developed in Chapter 13.

Finance

Since the liberalization of financial markets in the early 1980s, finance, including currency transactions, has become by far the biggest component of global markets, dwarfing trade and FDI. In 2006, capital flows crossing national borders, including loans, equity, and FDI, equaled $8.2 trillion ($1.23 trillion of that being FDI). This amount almost equaled total world exports or trade.[22] But this figure does not include the derivatives and currency markets.

The **derivatives market** involves the exchange of financial claims against future earnings by households, corporations, and financial institutions. An example of a derivative is a stock option. You buy an option, or right to purchase or sell a stock at a given strike price within a given time period. You may be hedging against the rise or fall of a stock that you own, or you may just be speculating against price changes. Derivatives can be created for any asset: commodities; loans, including mortgages;

derivatives market
the market that exchanges existing loans and financial assets and hedges them as derivatives against future prices, earnings, or interest.

insurance policies; and so on, Parties in global financial markets often swap or package financial assets to spread risks. They don't create new wealth, as in the case of new loans, equity investments or FDI, but they take existing loans and financial assets and hedge them as derivatives against future prices, earnings, and interest changes.

The derivatives market has grown phenomenally and was behind the financial market crisis that began in 2007. In 2006, the notional value of the derivatives market was $477 trillion. That's more than thirty times the size of U.S. GDP, which was around $15 trillion, and roughly three times the size of all global financial assets, which, measured as the market value of all publicly traded equities, bank deposits, and government as well as private debt securities in the world, totaled $167 trillion in 2006. This market was not only huge, but because it was new it was also largely unregulated by international and, in many cases, national authorities.

Now, add to these totals the financial transactions that take place in currency markets. **Currency markets** involve transactions that swap one currency for another. This amount equals roughly $3 trillion per day or $1 quadrillion per year.

Can you count that high? The size and dynamics of global financial markets raise new issues in global economics and bring into play major nonstate actors in a big way, including now multinational banks; investment houses, such as Deutsche Bank and Goldman Sachs; and the largest mutual and hedge fund companies, which move literally billions of dollars per day through world markets. Some major new state actors are also involved, such as sovereign wealth funds (SWFs; see later in the chapter).

The expansion of financial markets was inevitable once trade and FDI were liberalized. As liberal perspectives see it, spillover or path dependence occurred on a global scale. If corporations operated worldwide, so must banks; insurance companies; investment houses; pension funds; mutual and hedge funds; and stock, bond, and currency exchanges. After all, companies have to borrow, invest, and work in multiple currencies. They have to insure trade and financial transactions, hedge against currency and interest rate risks, and diversify their assets across country markets.

Meanwhile banks and financial institutions mobilize world savings and make them available for investment opportunities worldwide. Overall, this financial intermediation function is good for everyone. If global financial institutions did not exist, countries that saved more than they invested would have to bury the extra savings in the ground. No country could invest more than it saved. Local resources and opportunities would simply be wasted. In terms of our earlier discussion, China, which saves roughly 40 percent of its national income, would have to bury most of those savings in the Gobi Desert or, in our earlier example of investing in Mississippi, someone in New Jersey could not even send money to Mississippi, let alone move factories there or import and export from Mississippi. Local economies would be even further isolated and impoverished.

But open financial markets also bring global problems. Whereas capital flows in the earlier Bretton Woods system came largely from governments and intergovernmental institutions, such as the IMF and World Bank, private sources (commercial banks, investment banks, pension funds) now provide the bulk of capital flows in world markets. These flows are not only large, they are volatile. From 1990 to 1996, net private capital flows to emerging market economies jumped from $40 to $329 billion. Then, in the Asian financial crisis of 1997–1998, they dropped sharply from $329 to $144 billion.[23] These are huge sums and shifts. Short-term capital flows are particularly volatile. As we have seen in the previous chapter, some economists advocate restricting short-term flows. Others believe the problem lies in weak banking systems in developing

currency markets

the market that involves transactions that swap one currency for another.

Spotlight on
liberal perspective

countries and advocate reforms to make local banks more competitive. The liberalization of capital markets raises issues of both the international regulation of foreign banking activities and the improvement of domestic banking and financial institutions in developing countries.

The financial crisis of 2007–2008 illustrated both problems. The crisis started in the so-called subprime mortgage markets in the United States.[24] During the housing boom from 2000 to 2007, mortgage companies made home loans to less-qualified investors at low or subprime interest rates. To recoup the initial subsidy, the lenders reset the interest rates to rise to higher levels in future years. The loans were then packaged into securities and sold worldwide to banks and other investors. When the resets kicked in, many homeowners defaulted. The original loans were now worth less. Institutions holding the loans lost money. Once the housing bubble burst and home prices started to decline, the homes underlying these loans also were worth less. One estimate puts the total amount of risky mortgage loans at $2.5 trillion. Not all homeowners will default, but enough may that the securities containing these mortgages will sell only at higher interest rates (meaning lower prices for the securities or bonds) or may not sell at all (if no one wants to buy them). Banks and other institutions holding these loans have to recognize losses—what is called mark to market—and raise capital to cover these losses. To do that they will sell equities and other good assets, which will drive the stock and bond markets down. The financial crisis spreads. Spillover or path dependence affects markets when they collapse just as it does when they expand.

Now the derivatives market comes into the picture. Mortgage securities called collateralized debt obligations (CDOs) had been broken down into tranches, with the riskier tranches bearing higher interest rates. These tranches went bad first, but then investors began to fear that the good parts were also worth less. Rating agencies that give grades to different types of bonds downgraded the less risky securities. Banks had bought and sold many of these securities through so-called structured investment vehicles (SIVs). Normally, when banks lend, they have to back up some percentage of outstanding loans by cash or capital reserves. But SIVs were set up off the balance sheet precisely to avoid such capital requirements. Banks could make virtually unlimited loans and get a fee for each transaction. Business was good until some of the loans, now held by thousands of global investors, started going bad. Not knowing exactly who held the loans, how much was bad, and what the real price of these assets were, the markets panicked and lending essentially froze up. Central banks in the United States, Britain, and other countries had to step in and make cash available to banks to keep them afloat. Not only commercial banks were involved. For the first time, the Federal Reserve Bank intervened to keep an investment house from going under. Bear Stearns, a Wall Street investment company, was taken over by JPMorgan Chase, a large commercial bank, with substantial financial assistance from the Federal Reserve Bank.

Here is a classic case of how global markets sometimes outpace the capacity of both national and global governments to manage them. Who regulates the derivatives market? Even inside countries, these markets are relatively new. In the United States, regulations are dispersed among a whole series of alphabet-soup agencies, including the Fed, the U.S. Treasury, and the Securities and Exchange Commission (SEC). In the midst of the subprime crisis, the U.S. Treasury Department unveiled a comprehensive proposal to revise and restructure banking and financial regulations. International institutions did the same; at its spring 2008 meeting, the IMF reviewed a report by the Financial Stability Forum, a commission of banks and regulators from the major

Spotlight on path dependence

Spotlight on global governance

industrial countries, which recommended the strengthened surveillance of banking and derivative markets.

SWFs are also new, unregulated actors in contemporary financial markets. **Sovereign wealth funds (SWFs)** are state-controlled investment companies that manage large chunks of central bank foreign exchange reserves in capital-surplus countries such as United Arab Emirates, China, Singapore, Kuwait, Norway, Canada, and Russia. Some analysts worry that these financial institutions, particularly because they lack transparency, may conceal the foreign policy or even national security objectives of their governments. If SWFs can roam the world and invest secretly, they may pose national security threats to some countries. The largest fund, the Abu Dhabi Investment Authority, controls almost $1 trillion. That compares to $1.5 trillion for all hedge funds, $3 trillion for all SWFs, and over $50 trillion for all pension and endowment funds.[25] Some of the SWFs made significant investments in 2007–2008 to shore up major U.S. and European banks during the subprime mortgage crisis. The Swiss bank UBS got $11.9 billion from GIC, Singapore's SWF; Citi Group, the U.S. banking conglomerate, got $7.5 billion from ADIA, Abu Dhabi's SWF; and Morgan Stanley, the U.S. investment bank, received $5 billion from China's SWF.[26] These investments by foreign-government-controlled investment funds in private banking operations illustrate the new players, both public and private, that now shape global financial markets.

More regulation seems to be in the cards. But bear in mind that, if regulations become too tight, banks and other financial institutions will reduce lending. If they reduce lending, they take in fewer deposits. And if private and public institutions cannot put their savings in the bank, they have to bury them in the sand. So banking is not a rogue activity, although some banks may engage in rogue activities. Banking is an essential activity that lubricates expanding international trade and investment markets and makes sure that the meat and potatoes of the world economy, namely trade and investment, stay on the table, not just for the next meal but for future ones as well.

Perspectives on the New Global Markets

What are we to make of this globalization of international trade, investment, and financial markets? Critics of global markets see many problems. From a realist perspective, which emphasizes the relative distribution of wealth, MNCs, banks, investment companies, and SWFs are now bigger than many nations. They undermine the sovereignty of governments and dominate labor and consumer groups in world markets. They take advantage of poor countries and, especially, of women and unorganized workers and accelerate the race to the bottom that trade initiates (more on this in Chapter 13). They also destroy jobs in home countries, including highly skilled jobs such as software development. Last, they subvert democracy and the environment, dominating global institutions such as the WTO to expand profits and consumer materialism. If the MNCs that dominate world markets come from your country, their power may reinforce national security. But, even then, national governments have to be vigilant to ensure that global markets strengthen allies and not adversaries.

Liberal perspectives emphasize the growing complexity and competitiveness of international markets. They seek to overcome institutional deficiencies, both the

sovereign wealth funds (SWFs)

state-controlled investment companies that manage large chunks of central bank foreign exchange reserves in such countries as United Arab Emirates, China, Singapore, Kuwait, Norway, Canada, and Russia.

lack of international regulations to hold private market institutions accountable and the weak governmental institutions in developing countries that collude with foreign firms. When foreign commercial actors make exorbitant profits, they usually do so in cahoots with local government elites. Local governments offer generous tax subsidies and protection to foreign firms. That kind of arrangement between local governments and foreign firms can be very lucrative for both parties (for example, in Argentina, foreign companies could assemble TVs and sell them locally for two to four times more than the price on world markets, and government officials could take bribes or sell licenses to authorize this business). But foreign companies and banks gain in this case because local governments help them, not because foreign companies simply take over. Large corporations are not saints, but neither are host governments. From a liberal perspective, what protects smaller governments and consumers best is competition and, when necessary, regulation. International regulation and competition are both growing. If local governments do their homework, run sound economies, and solicit the help of international institutions such as the World Bank, they can exploit this competition. The Asian tigers and now others, such as China, that have opened their markets to FDI demonstrate the value of working with foreign commercial and financial institutions rather than banning them.

Identity perspectives fear the erosion of distinctive developing country policies and cultures by global trade, investment, and financial markets. Export-processing zones, for example, lead to competition to lower taxes and other incentives, depriving host countries of needed revenues. Many countries, such as China, have multiple export zones. Local officials who control these zones run "beauty contests" to attract FDI. This competition is particularly destructive. However, these drawbacks are due to local government policies as much as MNC management. Developing countries, with help from the World Bank and elsewhere, are getting smarter in how they structure these zones and link them to the development of the internal economy.

From an identity perspective, foreign companies and banks also raise concerns about the loss of jobs in advanced countries, especially at the lower end of the labor structure. Growth requires job change, and job change in turn brings cultural change. Advanced countries such as France lose their culture of small farms and rural life. However, a no-change economy in the end does not preserve jobs, as the former Soviet Union learned. Eventually, traditional cultures adapt, or they go under. Moreover, banning offshore and outsourcing investments destroys the jobs created by offshore and outsourcing investments from other countries. In 2004, for example, FDI in the United States, that is, offshore or outsourcing investments by other countries and thus actually *insourcing* investments for the United States, accounted for over 6 million jobs. If the United States banned outsourcing, other countries would do so as well.

Finally, one answer from an identity perspective for influencing and controlling global investment is democracy. In democracies, MNCs exercise influence over government policies, but so do numerous other interest groups, such as labor and environmental organizations. Competition among these groups limits the influence of any one group and usually results in improved economic policies and conditions. Democracies encourage pluralism, and strong NGOs ensure checks and balances between regulation and competition. Many NGOs have become as powerful as MNCs. We look more closely at some of these organizations in Chapter 15.

Summary

Trade, investment, and finance create the opportunity for specialization and comparative advantage in the global economy. All other things being equal, comparative advantage results in the more efficient use of resources; with the same input, countries can produce more output. In the real world, however, all other things are seldom equal. Thus, trade and investment advantage some workers and industrial sectors while disadvantaging others. The least-skilled workers and sectors lose benefits; the most-skilled gain them. To preserve the benefits of trade, investment, and financial markets, therefore, ways have to be found, both domestically and internationally, to smooth the transition from less- to more-skilled workers. Better education; wage insurance; and the accountability of MNCs, banks, and local governments are necessary or the backlash from the less-skilled sectors may shut down trade, investment, and banking activities. If nothing is done, nations may be bypassed or collapse, as the outdated workers and industries in communist countries were.

Realist perspectives raise important questions about who gains and who loses, relatively, from international trade and investment. Liberal perspectives raise equally important questions about competition, accountability, and institutional arrangements to achieve better outcomes at the domestic and international levels. And identity perspectives focus on the changes in policy ideas and traditional cultures that are inevitable whether growth occurs or not. Change is a constant that alters identities. That fact becomes even more evident as we turn in the next two chapters to a discussion of the development process in Asia, Latin America, Africa, and the Middle East.

Key Concepts

absolute advantage 350

common market 363

comparative advantage 349

competitive advantage 354

currency markets 372

derivatives market 371

Doha Round 362

economies of scale 352

financial economy 345

free-trade area 363

free-trade export-processing zones 369

Generalized System of Preferences (GSP) 361

geoeconomics 346

Hecksher-Ohlin theory 356

Hickenlooper Amendment 366

import substitution policies 351

infant industries 351

Kennedy Round 361

major suppliers 361

monopoly rents 353

multilateral trade rounds 360

national security export controls 351

offshore investments 370

opportunity costs 351

outsourcing 370

patient capital 354

product life cycle 367

real economy 345

resource curse 365

sovereign wealth funds (SWFs) 374

strategic trade 353

technology gap 367

Tokyo Round 361

unfair trade 359

Uruguay Round 361

Study Questions

1. What is the difference between absolute and comparative advantage? Give examples of each using the scenario of wine and cloth discussed in the book.

2. Does trade increase, decrease, or shift jobs? Which jobs gain and lose from trade? What are the remedies for job losses? Is trade or technology the most important cause of job shifts?

3. Which perspective emphasizes the following approaches to trade and why: multilateral trade rounds; trade and investment conditioned on the same environmental, labor, and other standards; and strategic trade?

4. In what sequence did the following types of FDI evolve: resource, manufacturing, and service-sector investments? Which perspective is reflected in each of the following approaches to FDI: national security export controls, reducing TRIMs and TRIPs, and requiring all MNCs to meet the same wage and regulatory standards throughout the world economy?

5. Which is greater in the world economy, trade and FDI or portfolio and currency transactions? Describe what the world economy (read, Mississippi) would look like if, first, trade and FDI were banned, and, second, portfolio and currency transactions were banned?

11

Miracle and Missed Opportunity
Development in Asia and Latin America

As evidenced by this photo of highway construction in Mexico City, Mexico is booming, growing sevenfold from 1993 to 2005. Is it because of NAFTA (liberal perspective), democratic political reforms (identity perspective), or American money and capitalism (realist perspective)?

East Asian Miracle
a period of unprecedented economic growth and development in East Asia between 1965 and 2005.

Asia has been the most successful developing region since World War II, far more successful than Latin America, which is the next best performing area. Even after Asia experienced a severe financial crisis in 1997–1998, which was expected to hobble it for at least a decade, the region grew by 9 percent per year through the year 2005, doubling the wealth of the region and lifting millions of people out of poverty.[1] A World Bank report in 1993 documented the origins of this **East Asian Miracle.** "From 1965 to 1990," it notes, "the twenty-three economies of East Asia grew faster than all other regions of the world." Most of the gains, it points out, were "attributable to seemingly miraculous growth in just eight economies: Japan; the 'Four Tigers'—Hong Kong, the Republic of Korea [South Korea], Singapore, and Taiwan, China; and the three newly industrializing economies (NIEs) of Southeast Asia, Indonesia, Malaysia, and Thailand."[2] These eight countries grew twice as fast as the rest of Asia, three times as fast as Latin America and South Asia, and five times as fast as sub-Saharan Africa. In the last decade of the period covered by the World Bank, the two biggest countries in Asia joined the miracle growth parade. From 1980–2000, China and India, where 40 percent of the world's population resides, grew by 10 and 6 percent per year, respectively. No country in the world grew as fast as China, and no country with the same poverty rates and population, except China, grew as fast as India.

Why did East Asia grow three times faster than Latin America? And why are China and India growing so much faster today? These are the questions we address in this chapter. Asia and Latin America make a good contrast because Asian countries pursued export-oriented development strategies that exploited economic competition in open international markets, while Latin American countries, for the most part, adopted inward-oriented, import substitution strategies for development. Both regions learned something from these different experiences. By the turn of the millennium, Latin American countries moved toward more outward-oriented strategies, while some Asian countries questioned the value of completely open markets, especially for short-term capital flows. Meanwhile, sub-Saharan African and Middle Eastern countries followed a separate and much less successful path of development, largely divorced from world markets—except for the oil exporters—and geared largely to resource exploitation rather than industrial diversification and development. We look at their experience in the next chapter.

What Is Development?

Wealth is unequally distributed in the world. Map 11-1 shows the distribution of national income measured by gross domestic product (GDP) per person in purchasing power parity, which takes account of the fact that goods are cheaper in poorer countries and a dollar buys more there than elsewhere. North America, western Europe, Japan, Australia, and New Zealand are the only areas of the world with incomes over $25,000 per person. By contrast, many countries in Africa have incomes of less than $1,000 per person. A few additional countries—such as Portugal, Hungary, Slovakia, the Czech Republic, South Korea, and Saudi Arabia—have incomes over $10,000 per capita, while the majority of countries in Latin America, the Middle East, and Asia fall well below $10,000.

Map 11-1 also shows the employment side of development. Influenced by technological change, development involves the movement over generations of the bulk of jobs from agriculture to manufacturing and eventually to high-skilled service activities. The least advanced countries still have most of their population employed in agriculture (or in low-skilled service jobs in tourism or government). More developed and industrializing countries have a substantial proportion of their workforce employed in manufacturing. Some, such as France and Germany, are downsizing jobs in manufacturing and moving them into services; others, such as China, are increasing jobs in manufacturing and moving them out of agriculture. The most advanced countries, such as the United States, have completed the transition from manufacturing to services. They have entered the information age. Their workforce is employed predominantly in high-skilled service activities, such as finance, telecommunications, software, consulting, and so on. This employment transition does not mean that the most advanced countries lose the manufacturing or agricultural sector. The United States remains a leader in both sectors, and manufacturing output in the United States today equals the same share of GDP that it did fifty years ago—between 20 and 25 percent. It's just that U.S. companies produce manufactured and agricultural goods with far less labor than they used to. The United States needs less than 2 percent of its workforce in agriculture and less than 10 percent in manufacturing to produce these products.

Other development indicators, such as population, human resource development, democracy, knowledge resources, and economic incentive structures, are important and appear in maps in Chapters 12, 14, and the Conclusion. Population is both a plus and minus for economic development and has global implications, which we explore

Map 11-1 **World Development as Country GDP (PPP) Per Capita and Employment by Sector**

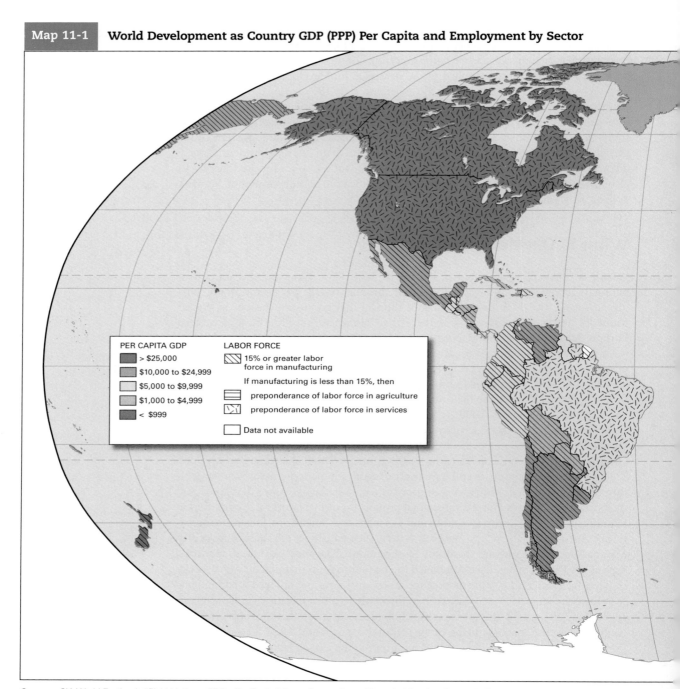

PER CAPITA GDP
- > $25,000
- $10,000 to $24,999
- $5,000 to $9,999
- $1,000 to $4,999
- < $999

LABOR FORCE
- 15% or greater labor force in manufacturing

If manufacturing is less than 15%, then
- preponderance of labor force in agriculture
- preponderance of labor force in services
- Data not available

Sources: CIA World Factbook, "Field Listing—GDP—Per Capita," https://www.cia.gov/library/publications/the-world-factbook/rankorder/2004rank.html; and "Field Listing—Labor Force—By Occupation," https://www.cia.gov/library/publications/the-world-factbook/fields/2048.html. Accessed May 6, 2008.

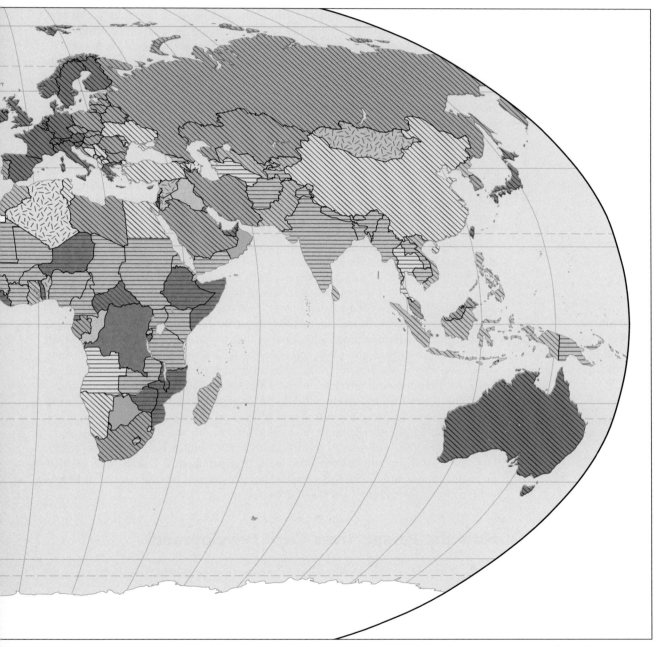

Note: Data for gross domestic product (GDP) and percent labor force by occupation come from different years, but most are from within the past ten years. GDP is expressed in terms of purchasing power parity (PPP) per capita. For labor force data, agriculture, fishing, forestry, and mining are considered agriculture. Government, public works, construction, trade, tourism, commerce, utilities, and so on are considered services. Any processing of raw materials beyond agriculture, mining, fishing (for example, food processing, oil refining, or canning tuna) are considered manufacturing. In cases where employment in manufacturing is less than 15%, that country is classified according to which other sector claims the greatest share. Data are not available for some countries; those countries are not shaded.

in Chapter 14. Human resource development measures the education, housing, and health status of the country's workforce. Democracy measures political development, knowledge resources measure higher education and research capabilities, and economic incentive structures measure market characteristics in different countries.

In Chapter 13, we ask the question, how did global inequality arise? We take a critical theory perspective on development, recognizing that the analysis of and debate about specific policies may not matter much if world development is the consequence of world systems dynamics and capitalist oppression. In this chapter and the next, however, we assume that development has specific causes that we can discover from the past and apply to the future. We ask what the advanced world and the poorer countries themselves can do to make development happen.

causal ⟶
arrow

Most analysts agree that the wealth disparities cannot be ignored, especially in an age of globalization. But is the goal perfect equality? Or is the goal maximum freedom, a solid floor for everyone and then space for individual, community, and national achievement and differentiation through competition? In some countries, such as Russia, people assume that if their neighbors get ahead they must be corrupt. Hence, fewer incentives exist for individuals to take the initiative and get ahead. In other countries, such as Haiti, elites do take the initiative and get ahead, but then forget about their neighbors. What is the right mix of incentives to help yourself and to help others? Without individual initiative, development does not occur, as many communist countries learned. And without social solidarity, communities divide and development becomes oppression, as many failed states experience.

development

the process of material, institutional, and human progress in a particular country or region.

What do we mean by development? In general **development** involves material, institutional, and human progress. It involves the growth of material resources, which enables people to consume more and enjoy better lives—better nutrition, housing, sanitation, and health. It involves advances in specialization, technology, and institutions that permit people to relate to one another across greater distances and coordinate more complex production activities in modern institutions, such as factories, cities, MNCs, and now cyberspace communities. And development involves improvements in human and social welfare, including better health and education, more work-related and professional choices, greater creative opportunities for the arts and leisure, and more satisfying communities and natural environments. It is easy to see that development is a multifaceted process, and our perspectives on international relations tend to emphasize different aspects of this process.

How the Perspectives View Development

Realist perspectives see development in mercantilist or relative terms, that is, who gains more even if all gain some. Development is not just about growth but also about control of resources because resources serve larger social and political goals, such as national security. Governments set these goals and foster development primarily among allies and friends. Liberal perspectives view development in terms of specialization, competition, and markets. Development fosters interdependence, which in turn fosters cooperation and the building of international regulations and institutions, from which all can gain. Identity perspectives view development in terms of political and social objectives. Does development cultivate NGOs; human rights, especially for women; and democracy? Does it lead to sustainable growth that conserves resources and the environment? Does it contribute to human, not just

causal ⟶
arrow

economic, development; better health; education; and protection of life and property for the least advantaged?

Economists and other analysts disagree about what causes development. The perspectives help us sort out these disagreements. The 1993 World Bank study that documented East Asian development successes talks about two views of what causes development: the neoclassical view and the revisionist view. The neoclassical view reflects a liberal perspective; the revisionist view reflects a realist one. Overall, Asian countries pursued the former and Latin American countries the latter.

According to the World Bank study, the neoclassical view holds that "the market takes center stage in economic life and governments play a minor role." It stresses that all of the Asian high-performing countries, in contrast to Latin American countries, pursued policies that disciplined the government's role or used government policies to enhance market competition, not to override it. According to this view, development works best on the basis of decentralized markets that subject economic decisions to the costs and benefits of alternative resource use. Investors look at the opportunity costs and decide to use resources in one area over another because the first area promises higher returns on their investment. Notice that development in this view depends on specialization and comparative exchange. It assumes a decentralized distribution of resources but not a struggle for power that might curtail specialization, as in a mercantilist approach. Countries pursue common non-zero-sum, not self-interested zero-sum, goals; and governments seek to reduce the need to interfere in the free exchange of specialized products. As one neoclassical advocate puts it, the high-performing Asian economies "greatly benefited from decisions and policies that limit government's role in economic decision making, and instead allow markets—notwithstanding their imperfections and shortcomings—to exercise a decisive role in determining resource allocation."[3]

> **Spotlight on markets and opportunity costs**

One of the imperfections of markets, of course, is inequality in the distribution of resources. Monopolies may exist and distort resource allocation. As we note later in the chapter, realist perspectives understand and emphasize this possibility, just as they recognize and focus on the monopolies of imperialism or hegemony in military relations. However, realist perspectives differ on whether inequalities last—the power balancing versus power transition schools. Liberal perspectives generally assume that inequalities do not last, that wealth spreads rather than concentrates benefits. Governments can anticipate and accelerate this redistribution of resources by investing in education and infrastructure and maintaining a sound macroeconomic policy environment. But in the long run governments do best if they work with, rather than try to override, the forces of the marketplace.

> **Spotlight on inequalities**

The revisionist view of development takes a more realist perspective on markets. It worries about the relative distribution of gains from development and doubts that governments pursue policies that spread wealth unless they are confident that the growth in wealth serves their existing interests and allies. Market forces may enrich others, but they inevitably serve the objectives of those who already possess wealth. Thus, governments that start behind internationally or challenge traditional interests domestically have to override markets to ensure development.

> **Spotlight on relative power and government intervention**

Accordingly, revisionist views of development stress government intervention to protect against or correct market forces. Domestic subsidies and foreign aid play a significant role. In Latin America, revisionist policies called for import substitution. Governments imposed barriers on imports and licensed domestic firms to produce these products. In Asia, from the realist perspective, revisionist policies also existed.

They emphasized all the different ways Asian high performers intervened in the marketplace to "govern" development.[4] Starting with Japan, they protected home markets, subsidized domestic industries, and targeted export markets. They did not adjust to market circumstances to get prices right; they overrode market circumstances to get prices "wrong," that is, to distort prices in their favor. Thus,

> the experiences of Japan, Korea, and Taiwan, China, provide evidence that governments can foster growth by "governing markets" and "getting prices wrong" and by systematically distorting incentives in order to accelerate catch-up—that is, to facilitate the establishment and growth of industrial sectors that would not have thrived under the workings of comparative advantage [that is, under the workings of the market].[5]

As one revisionist scholar puts it, "economic expansion depends on state intervention to create price distortions . . . [and] is necessary even in the most plausible cases of comparative advantage, because the chief asset of backwardness—low wages—is counterbalanced by heavy liabilities."[6]

In its 1993 report, the World Bank essentially took the side of the neoclassical view of development. It acknowledged a role for governments, but that role was to support, not distort, markets. "In general," it concludes, "governments have been unsuccessful in improving economic performance through attempts to guide resource allocations by other than market means."[7] The World Bank was reinforcing the Washington Consensus, which, as we have learned in Chapter 8, was dominant in the early 1990s. The World Bank came under severe criticism for this view, especially after the Asian financial crisis, which seemed to tarnish the record of the Asian high performers.

In a more recent report, the World Bank has backtracked and articulated a third view of development policy. This third view takes into account many aspects of the neoclassical or market approach, but recasts them into a neoliberal approach that stresses institutions over markets and the sensitivity of domestic institutions and policies to country- or culture-specific characteristics. In the language of this book, we might say this third approach is heading in the direction of an identity perspective, one that emphasizes the unique institutional and cultural heritage of each country. Here's how the World Bank describes the new policies:

Spotlight on
identity perspective

> They confirm the importance of macro-stability, of market forces governing the allocation of resources, and openness [neoclassical factors]. But they also emphasize that these general principles translate into diverse policy and institutional paths, implying that economic policies and policy advice must be country-specific and institution-sensitive if they are to be effective [liberal and identity factors]. . . .
>
> [T]here is no unique universal set of rules [notice the backtracking from a purely liberal perspective, which would emphasize collective rules for all]. Sustained growth depends on key functions that need to be fulfilled over time: accumulation of physical and human capital, efficiency in the allocation of resources, adoption of technology, and the sharing of the benefits of growth. Which of these functions is the most critical at any given point in time, which institutions will need to be created for these functions to be fulfilled, and in which sequence, varies depending on initial conditions and the legacy of history. Thus we need to get away from formulae [read: the Washington Consensus] and the search for elusive "best practices" [read: advances through market competition], and rely on deeper economic analysis to identify the binding constraints on growth. . . . This much more targeted approach requires recognizing country specificities [identity factors], and calls for more economic, institutional, and social analysis and rigor rather than a formulaic approach to policy making.[8]

Compared to the 1993 report, the shift in emphasis is away from markets to institutions, path dependence, sequencing or timing of policies, and ultimately to country-specific variables, including social (and, we might add, cultural) variables. The emphasis is no longer on factors emphasized by market forces but more on those emphasized by country-specific institutional and identity variables. The development process is multifaceted and historically contingent, not the consequence of a single global market or a single universal culture. In fact, the 2005 report debunks the notion that Asian countries succeeded because they more or less mimicked the western market culture. It recognizes that other countries did well that did not follow western market formulas. Of the 117 countries studied in the 2005 report, 18 sustained growth rates that allowed them to close the per capita income gap with industrialized countries. Of those eighteen, only seven were East Asian countries (China, Indonesia, South Korea, Laos, Malaysia, Thailand, and Vietnam). Five were South Asian (Bangladesh, Bhutan, India, Nepal, and Sri Lanka), three were sub-Saharan African (Botswana, Lesotho, and Mauritius), two were Middle Eastern and North African (Egypt and Tunisia), and one was Latin American (Chile). Although Asian countries still loom large in the sample, there is no longer an East Asian miracle or model. Development success is widespread and occurs in communist countries (China, Vietnam, and Laos) as well as countries with domestic unrest (Sri Lanka, Nepal, and Bhutan). And development is more difficult than it seemed to be based on the phenomenal growth of the Asian tigers. Almost one hundred countries, although growing in fits and starts, are still falling further behind the industrialized world.

Spotlight on culture and identity

We can wonder if the World Bank overcompensated for the market-friendly approach of its earlier report. The 2005 report certainly comes out with more diplomatic results. Many countries resented the East Asian countries' being singled out for their development achievement, and other countries wanted to restore an emphasis on foreign aid as well as markets. But the report also loses its impact. Now it seems that any country can develop and with just about any sequence or combination of policies it might choose. The 2005 World Bank report wants to emphasize everything from governments (the realist perspective) to institutions (the liberal perspective) to societies (the identity perspective). It has something for everyone and therefore, at least potentially, nothing for anyone. If we have no idea of the direction in which the causal arrows run, we have no idea of what to do to change the status quo. We may be trapped in a deeply embedded historical process, as critical theory perspectives emphasize, and policy adjustments are not likely to help much.

Spotlight on overdetermined outcomes

causal arrow ←

Yet a World Bank update in April 2008 continued to note the crucial importance of sound economic policies. Identifying ongoing challenges, it concludes that:

> the region's investment in sound macroeconomic policies and structural reforms over the last decade has added economic resilience and flexibility that will help deal with these challenges over the next year or two. Foreign exchange reserves are at all time highs, non-performing loans of banks have been steadily lowered, external and public debt burdens are at acceptable levels, most governments have unused fiscal space, the real economy has momentum, and diversification of trade and financial flows provides some flexibility in adjusting to the impending global slowdown.[9]

It may be diplomatic to conclude that everything is important for development, but this conclusion offers little guidance as to which policies matter more and where scarce resources should be spent to achieve development objectives. These questions of strategy and priority are the stuff of development debates. And they confirm the role that the different perspectives play in the development arena no less than in security or globalization debates.

Measuring Development and Inequality

One objective of development, as we have noted, is the growth of material resources, income, and consumption. Careful studies show that there is a strong relationship between income growth and poverty reduction.[10] In China and India, rising incomes reduced the number of people living on less than $1 per day by 48 and 20 percent, respectively. But is this enough? Some developing countries have a rising production of goods and services, or **gross domestic product (GDP),** and even a rising average income (GDP per capita), but the situation of the poor remains unaffected. You know the old saw about averages: put one hand on a hot stove burner and the other in an ice bucket, and you are now at room temperature. Well, maybe, but you've also just lost both hands. So, considerations of distribution and equality are important in evaluating development. While economists and economic institutions make much use of per capita income and other averages, they also measure inequality (using something called the Gini coefficient) and certain minimum prerequisites for growth or basic human needs, such as clean water, housing, health, and education.

Measures of inequality can be tricky. For example, in the late nineteenth century, the average income of the world's richest country (that is, the average over a number of years) was roughly ten times that of the world's poorest country. Today, that ratio is closer to sixty times greater. This ratio of inequality between the top and the bottom country increased sharply after 1980. But, if we take into account the population of countries, the data show a trend toward a decline in income inequality between countries since the mid-1970s.[11] In the example from the 2005 World Bank report, eighteen developing countries, including China and India, actually closed the per capita income gap with the advanced countries. Thus, inequality in per capita income may be declining while inequality in average country incomes may be increasing.

Increasingly, economists also measure what might be called the "floor" of development, the absolute level of the poorest people, not just the degree of inequality between them and others. The World Bank reports that from 1990 to 2004 the number of people living on less than $1 per day went down by 278 million, and by 150 million in just the last five years of that period.[12] But some economists note that the number living on less than $2 per day went up in the 1990s, from 2.7 to 2.8 billion.[13] Not surprisingly, critics of policies pursued in the 1990s point to the latter number, while supporters point to the first number.

Even then, numbers alone do not tell the whole story of development. What about the quality of life? Many people in advanced countries complain about stress and a polluted environment. In developing countries, these conditions are even worse. Listen to one visitor's description of the environment in major cities like Shanghai and Hong Kong:

> Last winter in Shanghai, nearly everyone I met had hacking, never-ending coughs that are partly caused by the gray, sooty air that blankets the city like split pea soup. In heavily industrialized northeastern China, city aquifers are filled with heavy minerals. Even Hong Kong, by far the wealthiest part of the country, now frequently suffers from such horrific air pollution that its breathtaking skyline is almost totally obscured on some days.[14]

gross domestic product (GDP)

the quantification of a country's production of goods and services at home.

What about a sense of community? Development uproots people from traditional communities in the countryside and dumps them with little preparation into big cities, where they are vulnerable to exploitation and other forms of impoverishment: prostitution, crime, child labor, and so on. An estimated 150 million Chinese citizens live on the margins of big cities, looking for work and a place to live. Barrios, or slums, are commonplace around all major Latin American cities. Alienation sets in, not only in relationship to big-city life but also, after a while, to the home village. Young adults returning to the countryside in China have less and less in common with their parents.

Spotlight on identity

Let's keep this big—or, at times, small—picture of the lives of individual human beings in mind as we look now at the different experiences of development. We'll use the basic policies (seven of them) developed in Chapter 9 to compare these experiences. Review in particular Figure 9-1, which shows how these policies interact to influence a country's performance in the global economy. As we go along, we will spotlight certain concepts from Chapters 9 and 10 to illustrate how policy developments in the real world reflect these concepts. Remember too that in this chapter, as in others, we show a causal arrow whenever the discussion deals with the interaction of perspectives or levels of analysis. This feature illustrates how scholars and policymakers make judgments among the perspectives and levels in real-world debates. Thus, the discussion that follows here (and in the next chapter) is organized in four policy areas:

1. Security and political development (alliances and global governance).
2. Domestic economic policies and institutions (macro- and microeconomic policies).
3. External economic policies (currencies, trade, investment, finance, and refugees).
4. Sociocultural equality and development (domestic governance).

Asia—The Development Miracle?

The tigers of East Asia—Hong Kong, Singapore, Taiwan, and South Korea—pioneered export-led development and achieved a development status that, for all practical purposes, put them in the same class as developed countries. With a per capita income over $20,000, South Korea, for example, became a member of the OECD, the economic organization of industrial countries. The tigers were followed by a second wave of NICs in Southeast Asia: Malaysia, Philippines, Thailand, and Indonesia. These countries now boast per capita incomes around $4,000–$10,000 per capita, roughly halfway between developing and industrialized countries. The most recent wave of Asian export tigers includes China and India, countries that alone account for 40 percent of the world's population and 80 percent of the world's poor people. On the basis of purchasing power parity, China now has a per capita income of approximately $6,500 and India of $3,400.[15]

What is more, these countries not only grew, they witnessed a dramatic reduction in inequality. In the 1970s and 1980s, Indonesia, Malaysia, Singapore, and Thailand reduced the percentage of people living below the poverty line by 25–40 percentage points. As noted earlier in this chapter, China and India achieved similar reductions in the 1980s and 1990s. The four tigers and three of the four NICs (Malaysia is the exception) had relative inequality ratios (that is, the ratio of the income share of the top 10 percent, or decile, of the population to that of the bottom decile) of less than 10, well below that of almost all other developing countries. In short, development in Asia did not increase domestic inequality. One reason may be that Asian countries did not extract resources and savings from the countryside to promote urban development, as other developing countries did. Rather, Asian developers invested substantial resources in the countryside. For example, Korea, Thailand, and Indonesia invested as much in sanitation in rural as in urban areas, while Latin American countries, as we see later, invested less than 50 percent. Agricultural incomes rose faster, by almost a full percentage point per year, than in Latin America or Africa.[16]

North or East (sometimes called northeast) Asia includes China, Hong Kong (now part of China), Taiwan (claimed by China), the two Koreas, and Mongolia; it also includes Japan, which is, however, an industrialized country. Southeast Asia includes the ten nations that make up ASEAN. South Asia includes India, Pakistan, Bangladesh, Afghanistan, and the small island or mountain states of Sri Lanka, Bhutan, and Nepal. And central Asia refers to the former republics of the Soviet Union: Kazakhstan, Kyrgyzstan, Turkmenistan, Tajikistan, and Uzbekistan. Together these countries have about 3.5 billion people, or 55 percent of the world's population, and about one-third of world's GDP. (See Map 11-2.)

If development continues in this part of the world, the future for humanity looks much brighter. South Korea, a country of almost 50 million people living in an area less than the size of California, started in the 1950s with a per capita income under $500. It raised this level fortyfold while living through a devastating war and its aftermath, remaining a divided country, and participating in an Asian economic environment that did not encourage integration like the European Union did in Europe. East

Map 11-2   Asia's Regions

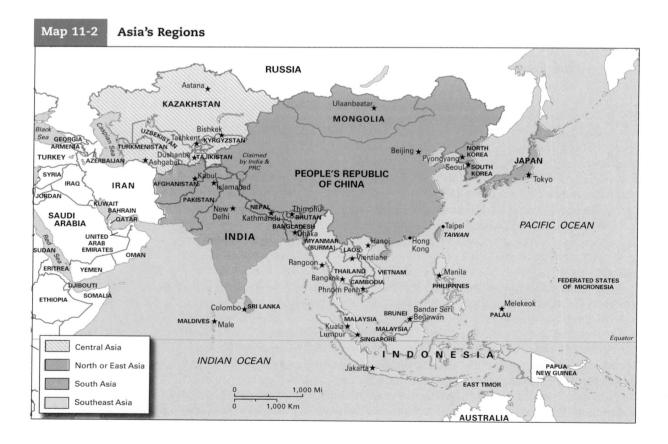

Asia holds important clues about what it takes to develop, even if Asia's experience may not translate directly into the circumstances of other developing countries, especially those in Africa.

Stable Governments and Unstable Region

Political stability, we have noted, helps development. And Asia had political stability in spades. After World War II, authoritarian or stable one-party governments (as in Hong Kong) held power for long periods throughout the region. Once Mao seized power in China in 1949, domestic unrest was not a significant factor influencing economic prospects, as it was in Latin America—but international unrest was. Two of the major wars fought after 1945—Korea (1950–1954) and Vietnam (1961–1975)—took place in Asia. Korea was and remains a divided country, long after the reunification of Germany in Europe. And China continues to reunify its territory—at least as China defines it—peacefully in the case of Hong Kong and Macao but increasingly with threats and a buildup of military force in the case of Taiwan (and a Chinese police force in Tibet). North Korea pursues nuclear weapons and could start another war of major proportions in the region with a million men and thousands of artillery pieces positioned within range of Seoul, the capital of South Korea.

So, it is hard to argue that overall stability, taking into account the international as well as domestic environment, is the secret to Asian development success. What is more, democracy has spread in Asia, particularly since the mid-1980s. And democracy, while it aids development in some ways, often brings with it greater political disputes, scandals, and uncertainties that also impede economic policy.

Military governments in South Korea repressed labor groups for three decades, including violent crackdowns that remain issues in South Korean politics today. In 1987, the military finally turned the government over to civilian leaders, but the con-

Election officials in Seoul, South Korea, count ballots in April 2008 from the elections that transferred power peacefully from the liberal to the conservative political party in the parliament. Elections in December 2007 did the same for the presidency.

servative political party that initially controlled the government was still supported by the military. It was not until ten years later that the liberal opposition party not beholden to the military won office. In 2007–2008, the government (both presidency and legislature) switched back again to the conservative parties, reflecting a peaceful rotation of parties in power that even Japan has not yet achieved to the same degree (experiencing a rotation of parties only once since 1955, and then for only a few months in 1993). Today, South Korea has a robust multiparty system and wrestles with the legacy of past authoritarian governments (complete with trials of former presidents and military leaders) as well as the delicate problem of living side by side with North Korea without starting another devastating war.

Taiwan, too, is now a democracy that rotates power peacefully between opposition parties, complicating the issue of reunification with the mainland, which remains an authoritarian communist country. A civilian government supported by the military took power in 1987. Then in 2000, a liberal opposition party not identified with the military won the presidential elections and, in 2001, a plurality in the legislature as well. In 2007–2008, power rotated back to the conservative parties. Taiwan's parties differ on relations with mainland China. The conservative Kuomintang, or Nationalist Party, accepts the notion of "one China" and supports eventual unification with China. The liberal Democratic Progressive Party leans more toward national self-determination and independence for Taiwan. Because Taiwan's economic life is closely tied up with trade and investment on the mainland, these political differences add uncertainty to economic policies.

Democracy also made inroads in Southeast Asia. In 1986, the Philippines ousted the dictator, Ferdinand Marcos. Thailand held competitive elections in 1988. And Indonesia held its first parliamentary elections in thirty years in 1999 and its first direct elections for the presidency in 2004. All these democracies are weak. The Philippines remains vulnerable to military coups (six attempts from 1986 to 1992 alone and the most recent attempt in early 2006). Thailand too suffered military coups, most recently in September 2006. Indonesia lost one province in 1999 when East Timor separated from it violently, and it faces secessionist struggles in other provinces such as Aceh, the scene of the tsunami disasters in 2005.

What is more, unlike the situation in Europe, Asian democracies still live with totalitarian neighbors. Three of the four remaining communist governments in the world—China, Vietnam, and Laos—are in Asia (Cuba is the fourth). Brutal military governments rule in North Korea, Bhutan, and Myanmar (formerly Burma). Even successful small states, such as Singapore (which separated from Malaysia in the 1960s) and Malaysia, have repressive governments. Democracy in Hong Kong is slowly being squeezed by Beijing since its reversion to China in 1997.

The bright spot in South Asia is India. The largest but also poorest democracy in the world has recently opened up to trade and foreign investment. Its growth prospects now rival China's. But India, too, has hostile and unstable neighbors. India and Pakistan possess nuclear weapons and face off against one another over the disputed province of Kashmir. India and China have border disputes. Pakistan has an unstable government and fights alongside the United States against Taliban terrorists in Afghanistan. Afghanistan fights for its modest democratic life surrounded by right-wing theocrats in Iran and military generals in Pakistan. Bangladesh and Sri Lanka struggle against separatist movements. Maoist guerrillas toppled the Nepalese monarchy in 2008.

What about Asia's colonial legacy? Britain ruled Hong Kong, Singapore, Malaysia, Burma, and India—including present-day Pakistan and Bangladesh—for a hundred years. The Netherlands colonized Indonesia. Spain and then the United States colonized the Philippines. Portugal colonized Macao. And France colonized Indochina— Cambodia, Laos, and Vietnam. Japan occupied Taiwan, South Korea, Manchuria, and parts of Southeast Asia for various periods from 1895 to 1945. More recently, China occupied Tibet and fought border wars with India and Vietnam. Thailand, like Saudi Arabia in the Middle East, escaped colonialism.

Colonial rule was harsh and left lasting grievances. China resents western and American hegemony. South Korea and China harbor bitter memories of Japanese occupation. French colonialism in Indochina spawned the Vietnam War and left lingering communist governments in Laos and Vietnam. Nevertheless, colonialism did not cripple development in Asia to the extent that it may have in Latin America, Africa, and the Middle East. Why? Some might say, from a realist perspective, because Asia was farther from the western powers than Latin America, the Middle East, or Africa. Or because Asia benefited from Cold War conflicts that poured American aid money into South Korea and Taiwan. Others might say, from a liberal perspective, because the region was more central to commerce and shipping than landlocked countries in other regions (countries close to the Suez and Panama Canals being exceptions). Still others might argue, from an identity perspective, because Asia had a more unified and resilient regional culture in Confucianism, or what people today call "Asian values."

← causal arrow

Altogether Asia has probably had a more politically unpredictable past than Europe or Latin America. Yet it has experienced unparalleled development. How do we explain this success? Maybe it has to do with the economic and social factors that we examine next: sound economic policies, export-led development, the limits of export development, and cultural and social cohesion.

Sound Economic Policies

Here's how the World Bank describes the domestic economic policies of the eight high-performing Asian economies (HPAEs) that it studied in 1993:

> Fundamentally sound development policy was a major ingredient in achieving rapid growth. Macroeconomic management was unusually good and macroeconomic performance unusually stable, providing the essential framework for private investment. Policies to increase the integrity of the banking system, and to make it more accessible to non-traditional savers, raised the level of financial savings. Education policies that focused on primary and secondary schools generated rapid increase in labor force skills. Agricultural policies stressed productivity and did not tax the rural economy excessively. All the HPAEs kept price distortion within reasonable bounds and were open to foreign ideas and technology.[17]

First, notice that the assessment stresses macroeconomic and microeconomic (including sectoral policies such as education, banking, and agriculture) policies, which, as we learn in Chapter 9, provide the deep foundation for a country's position in the global economy. Second, notice how different these policies are compared to those in Latin America, which, as we note later, involved large fiscal deficits, high inflation, and low savings. For the thirty years prior to 1993, inflation in the high-performing Asian economies was only one-tenth as great as in other developing countries and only one-twentieth the levels in Latin America. Because inflation rates remained under control, interest rates were more stable and real interest rates, which subtract out inflation, stayed positive, encouraging long-term savings and investments. Postal savings systems in South Korea, Taiwan, Singapore, Malaysia, Japan, and China solicited sav-

Spotlight on macroeconomic policies

ings. Postmen not only delivered mail; they also picked up monthly savings checks. Asian countries had savings and investment rates that were twice as high as other developing countries—40 percent compared to 20 percent. Money stayed at home rather than fleeing into foreign currencies, as happened so often in Latin American countries. One reason inflation stayed low is that governments restrained fiscal policy and kept fiscal deficits in line. The average annual budget deficits in South Korea as a share of GDP ran one-fifth the levels of many Latin American countries. Although other countries such as Thailand and Malaysia ran higher deficits, they financed these deficits through higher domestic growth and savings, avoiding undue dependence on foreign debt.[18]

Spotlight on microeconomic policies

land reform
domestic policies to redistribute land for the purposes of equity and development.

Microeconomic policies focus on land reform, primary education, small enterprises, and housing and health services.[19] Indonesia and Thailand traditionally had widespread land holdings, but South Korea and Taiwan, as well as Japan, instituted **land reform** after World War II. Taiwan seized land from landlords and compensated them with shares in state enterprises. In South Korea, U.S. occupation forces redistributed land confiscated from Japanese landowners; and then the South Korean legislature, after lengthy debate, seized the properties of Korean landlords, paid them nominal compensation, and parceled out the properties to 900,000 tenants. Hong Kong and Singapore had no agricultural sector. Land reform in the Philippines and elsewhere lagged behind and so did economic development.

Land reform created a sense of participation on the part of rural areas and formed the basis for a successful education program. Asian governments poured money into public education. Although other developing countries did this as well, Asian governments concentrated on primary and secondary education. South Korea, for example, put 85 percent of its investment into basic education and only 10 percent into higher education and universities. Venezuela, by contrast, put 45 percent into higher education. Education in Asia served the masses, not just the elites. South Korea and Taiwan developed an educated labor force, which then took jobs in the urban and industrial sectors. An educated workforce, in turn, developed a demand for higher education, which was supplied in good part by private universities and capital.

Asian governments absorbed an educated labor force by supporting small- and medium-size enterprises. In all economies, these firms account for most of the employment. As government policies stimulated the broad economy, specific programs provided preferential credits and specific support services for smaller companies. In Taiwan, as a result, small enterprises make up 90 percent of all enterprises in most sectors and 60 percent of the export enterprises as well. South Korea initially relied more on conglomerates, known as *chaebols,* but beginning in the late 1970s, it also expanded the small-enterprise sector. From 1976 to 1988, employment in small businesses rose from 37.6 to 51.2 percent of total employment.

Why didn't Korean and Taiwanese peasants coming to the big cities to find jobs wind up, like Latin American peasants, living in slums on the outskirts of affluent neighborhoods? A big reason is the investment that Asian governments made in housing and health services. Hong Kong and Singapore, besieged by migrants from China and Malaysia, built massive public housing projects. By 1987, more than 40 percent of the population in Hong Kong and 80 percent in Singapore lived in public housing. Most of the inhabitants owned their own units. South Korea and Indonesia had similar public housing programs.

For decades, Asian labor was not free. Governments suppressed radical activity in the labor sector. But the political discontent was managed and did not result in coups or revolutions, as often was the case in Latin America, because the governments pro-

Shown here, on either side of an overpass, is a public housing project in Singapore, representing microeconomic policy. Eighty-four percent of Singapore's population live in public housing.

vided generous education, housing, and other benefits, such as land reform, that sustained a sense of participation in national prosperity.

Export-Led Development

Throughout the region, therefore, governments played a crucial role in Asian development. The issue was not the government's role per se, but what kind of government role. Did government provide incentives to support market-oriented and competitive development, or did it seek to create industrial and technological establishments that substituted for, or leapfrogged, market characteristics? The debate intensified between supporters of the neoclassical liberal, or Chicago School, perspective on economic development that urged reliance on markets and supporters of the realist or revisionist school that emphasized government intervention to create market advantages. This was the same debate, now in the development arena, that divided advocates of comparative advantage and advocates of strategic trade in the trade arena (discussed in Chapter 10).

    One point is certain. Asian high performers geared their development toward foreign markets. They relied on export-led development, not import substitution policies. They created export zones for selected industries, usually industries at the lower end of the technological spectrum where the countries possessed a labor cost advantage. Thus, the Asian tigers first produced and exported toys and handicrafts and then produced textiles, shoes, radios, and black-and-white television sets. Eventually, they graduated to the heavy manufacturing industries, including steel, chemicals, and shipbuilding, and thereafter to more sophisticated components and consumer products such as semiconductor chips, automobiles, computers, and electronic games. They did so, as the World Bank study documents, by

← *causal arrow*

Spotlight on
strategic trade

targeting and subsidizing credit to selected industries, keeping deposit rates low and maintaining ceilings on borrowing rates to increase profits and retained earnings, protecting domestic import substitutes, subsidizing declining industries, establishing and financially supporting government banks, making public investments in applied research, establishing firm- and industry-specific export targets, developing export market institutions, and sharing information widely between public and private sectors.[20]

The key point, then, is that Asian governments took their development signals from international markets even as they intervened in domestic markets. They developed domestic industries, not on the basis of import substitution determined by elite consumption patterns at home but on the basis of international competition determined by underlying comparative advantage. They then boosted comparative advantage by protecting domestic markets to give their firms an assured level of demand—Japan was notorious for such protection. The objective from the beginning, however, was to become competitive as soon as possible in export markets, not just to service protected home markets. This strategy required a disciplined bureaucracy. Here Asia had another advantage over Latin America. By tradition, the best and the brightest went into government service in Asia, and government bureaucrats were motivated more by technical expertise than by political or personal gain. Governments were not immune to scandals and corruption, as democratic politics in Japan, South Korea, and Taiwan has subsequently uncovered. And bureaucrats were often closely connected to business interests, leaving government posts at some point to take up second careers in the corporate sector. But the process was motivated by a sense of national pride and duty, not the rent-seeking and resource-stripping policies that afflicted many elitist Latin American governments.

Spotlight on
domestic governance

Later studies showed that Asian development was not necessarily a result of greater efficiency or productivity. It was mostly a consequence of investing more capital and labor to achieve higher output, rather than getting higher output out of the same level of capital and labor inputs.[21] Asian countries did a better job than other developing countries in other regions of mobilizing more savings (capital) and a well-educated, healthy workforce (labor). A part of the secret at least was the sound underlying domestic policies that created stable prices and exchange rates to guide and sustain resource mobilization. At some point, however, growth by accumulation involving the addition of more and more labor and capital resources to achieve higher output reaches its limits. Greater efficiency is needed to get more out of the same inputs, and that requires innovation and industrial restructuring toward higher technology or value-added industries.

Limits to Export-Led Growth

Asian export-led development reached its limits in three areas. The first was the rapid expansion of international markets. By the late 1990s, more and more countries were pursuing export-led growth. Recall that the end of the Cold War brought the former communist countries into world markets. Trade markets were becoming increasingly crowded. Countries had to run faster to stay in place. Before Japan had mastered the shipbuilding industry, South Korea was building ships and taking away market share. And before South Korea had mastered that industry, China was building ships. As suppliers multiplied, and each sought to protect its own home market, consumers relatively dwindled. In a small way, export-led development, after many countries adopted it, replicated the market squeeze that occurred in the 1930s when everyone wanted

Spotlight on
strategic trade

to export and no one wanted to import—export markets became saturated. By the mid-1990s, Asia was awash in excess production capacity for electronic products, steel, automobiles, and shipbuilding.

The second area limiting export-led performance was that, as Japan and other Asian high performers caught up, it became less apparent where they should invest their resources. Taking cues from world markets was a good strategy for catching up to world standards. But once a country reached the frontiers of the high-tech and new service industries, it had to spend more on innovation and trial and error to develop future markets. Asian bureaucracies were better at administration than those in some other developing countries, but they were not necessarily better at inventing and creating the future. As one critic noted, "funding concentrated on a 'catch-up' targeting of known technologies was much easier than having to push out along an unknown technological frontier." Once a country caught up, "it was no longer clear where and how to spend the money since future technologies by definition did not exist. . . ." [22]

Much of Asian development also depended on a single market, the United States. In 1999, the United States still absorbed 24 percent of Hong Kong's exports, 31 percent of Japan's, 30 percent of the Philippines's, 21 percent of South Korea's, 25 percent of Taiwan's, and 22 percent of Thailand's. [23] As the dollar soared in the 1990s, so did the currencies of a number of Asian countries, such as South Korea and Hong Kong, which tied their currencies to the dollar. So, currency appreciation also hurt export performance. Finally, protectionism in the United States was growing. As country after country, including now the titan of China, exported its way to growth through the U.S. market, Congress called for protection. In a real sense, the open U.S. market gets a good deal of the credit for the success of Asian development strategies, and now for development strategies in Mexico and elsewhere. But, like export markets overall, the U.S. market reached a saturation point, at least in the political sense of being willing to absorb more and more foreign imports.

The third limit on the Asian export-led model was in the financial area. Finance or banking was the sector in Asian countries that held back improvements in efficiency and industrial restructuring. As we have noted, governments dominated the credit markets in Asian countries. Government postal systems collected savings, and government banks disbursed loans, usually in line with government industrial and technological development plans. There was little competition in the banking sector. Equity markets, where companies might raise money from the private sector, were marginal in most Asian countries. As a result, the allocation of loans became routine and hard to change. Banks and companies developed cozy relationships, in what subsequently became known as **crony capitalism.** Banks invested in the same companies, companies invested in the same industries, and industries built up excess capacity. They built new steel or automobile plants when none was needed or more roads and bridges when existing ones were not being used. Many of these loans later went sour.

So-called nonperforming or simply bad loans accumulated and drained capital from more efficient uses. While Asian countries needed to restructure into higher value-added industries and ultimately services, such as financial services and retail distribution, they stuck with manufacturing and slowly lost ground to new competitors such as China. In the effort to protect home industries, some countries, such as South Korea and Japan, restricted long-term foreign investment. Thus, foreign money flowed into less productive areas such as real estate opportunities or short-term loans to local banks eager to borrow with their overvalued exchange rates, which went up with the dollar in the 1990s. International banks happily provided such loans, assured that the

Spotlight on currency appreciation

Spotlight on protectionism

Spotlight on finance

crony capitalism noncompetitive lending and investment relationships between financial institutions and industry, such as between government banks and private manufacturing companies.

IMF and other international institutions would not allow countries to go bankrupt, with the Mexican bail-out of 1994–1995 proving their point. When exports slowed, foreign exchange reserves dwindled; and the stage was set for the Asian financial crisis in 1997–1998.

The Asian financial crisis focused attention back on domestic markets in Asia. As international markets soured, obstacles to growth in the domestic economy loomed larger. The IMF and other international institutions called for structural reforms to increase domestic demand and imports, reverse the 1930s-like drift toward more exports and less imports, and clean up the bad loans and crony banking systems. These reforms were more urgent than ever because new big suppliers, such as China and India, were entering and crowding world markets.

China pursues policies similar to the earlier Asian fast growers. It bases its growth on exports, it channels loans to industry largely through state banks, and it maintains an undervalued exchange rate to gain a foreign market advantage. But, there is one major exception. Unlike Japan and South Korea, which initially discouraged FDI, China welcomes it. In 2006, FDI inflows into China totaled $69 billion.[24] The accumulated stock of FDI in China totals more than $500 billion. In addition, China saves an enormous percentage of its GNP, around 40 percent in 2006. China therefore is not dependent on foreign capital, although it does need the foreign expertise that comes with FDI. Indeed, it exports capital, using the surpluses generated on current account to buy U.S. treasury bonds and finance the twin deficits of the United States discussed in Chapter 9.

The problem in China is massive inefficiency. It is accumulating bad loans at an astonishing rate. It uses four to five times more energy to produce a unit of output than the industrialized countries. Although it has privatized many sectors, it maintains large numbers of inefficient state enterprises to preserve the jobs they provide. And it wrestles with the rural and urban disruption that moves 13 million people per year from the farm to the cities, looking for work. At the moment, investment in transportation, energy, and business infrastructure takes precedent over housing and health care. But we may wonder why China is unwilling to use its large domestic savings to build housing and health services and thereby coopt the working classes, the way Hong Kong, Singapore, and Taiwan did. If China did for its people what Fannie Mae has done for U.S. homeowners, the chances of averting national discontent would be considerably improved. As we have learned in Chapter 9, microeconomic policies such as housing policies can have a powerful effect on international capital flows.

India is probably twenty years behind China, but it is moving in the same direction. While China has reduced average tariffs from 35 to 13 percent and its trade—exports plus imports—accounts for 70 percent of GDP, India still has average tariffs above 28 percent and its trade accounts for only 45 percent of GDP. India is much less open to foreign investment, with a total FDI stock of $30 billion compared to China's $500 billion. Illiteracy in India tops 35 percent, against just 6 percent in China. In 1999–2000, only 47 percent of children passed through five years of primary school in India, while 98 percent did in China. In India 59 percent of the people still live in the countryside, in China 45 percent. Industrial activities employ less than 10 percent of the labor force in India, but 20 percent and rising in China.[25]

Spotlight on domestic reforms

Spotlight on foreign direct investment

Spotlight on microeconomic (housing) policies

Cultural and Social Cohesion

Successful Asian societies are more ethnically homogeneous than Latin American or African countries. China is mostly Han, with a small but restive Muslim population in the western part of the country. Japan, except for miniscule Korean and indigenous minorities, is, as Edwin Reischauer, Harvard professor and one-time U.S. ambassador to Japan, observed, "the most thoroughly unified and culturally homogeneous large bloc of people in the world, with the possible exception of the Northern Chinese."[26] Both North and South Korea are ethnically unified, although the peninsula was divided historically into three separate regional kingdoms. South and Southeast Asian countries are more diverse. Overseas Chinese constitute a majority in Singapore and significant minorities in Malaysia, Indonesia, and other countries. The overseas Chinese often dominate commercial life, which creates resentment among indigenous populations, for example, among the Malays and Indonesians. Four major religions divide the region: Islam in Pakistan, Bangladesh, and Indonesia; Hinduism in India; Buddhism in China, Tibet, and Japan; and Shintoism in Japan.

Was cultural homogeneity the key to Asian development? Identity perspectives might be inclined to think so. Asia's success sparked a debate about **Asian values.** Was it widespread Confucian values that contributed to domestic stability and motivated bureaucratic and commercial success? Confucianism offers a different basis for social and economic life than western values. Authority takes precedence over individualism. Nowhere in Asia is individualism celebrated as it is in the United States; instead authority patterns infuse all levels of society—in the family, business, and the state. This authority is patrimonial, personalized, and less institutional or accountable than authority in the west. It creates extended family ties that infiltrate formal institutions and are difficult to penetrate, especially for foreigners. Overseas Chinese business circles play a large role in tying together markets and corporations in Asia. *Quanxi* is the Chinese word for these close personal relationships and connections. Japanese business practices are also notoriously exclusive and discriminatory. Authority is collective and invisible, rather than individual and subject to legal transparency. While much of this is changing, Asian societies are comparatively more cohesive. As Lee Kwan Yew, the former prime minister and elder statesman of Singapore, expressed it, "the main object is to have a well-ordered society" and "What a country needs to develop is discipline more than democracy."[27] Mohammed Mahathir, the former president of Malaysia, put it more bluntly, "the group and the country are more important than the individual."[28]

Asian values might account for the prevalence of authoritarian governments in Asia and the closed character of Asian business practices and culture. They may also help to explain the less formal nature of economic integration in Asia and the continued political divisions that make Asian international affairs more unstable. There is no common market in Asia, as there is in Europe. APEC is a forum, rather than a legal institution like the European Union. To be sure, integration is growing. China, as we have noted, is more open to FDI than Japan or South Korea. Nevertheless, much of this integration is a function of the relocation of investments from Southeast Asia and Hong Kong to mainland China, where products are assembled from imported components and shipped to the United States and other world markets. Asian integration is still more vertical and outward-oriented than European integration, which is more horizontal—competitive—and inward-oriented. The European Union, for example, exports only 10–15 percent of its trade outside Europe, whereas Asian countries, as we have noted, depend heavily on U.S. markets.

Asian values may also explain the greater rivalry that permeates the Asian region. Because Asian societies are ethnically insulated from one another, especially in East Asia, they have been less willing to forgive and forget wartime or historical wrongs.

Spotlight on culture and identity

Asian values
the Confucian ideas that motivated economic success in Asia; based on cultural/ethical principles such as the privileging of authority—family or community—over the individual.

Development in Asia: Key Factors

Relative domestic stability

Recent colonialism and regional wars (Korea, Vietnam)

Export-led growth, but domestic industrial and state banking concentration

Low budget deficits and inflation

Land reform

Primary and secondary education

Relative cultural cohesion (Asian values)

Bitter memories linger between Japan and China and between Japan and South Korea, breaking out periodically in ugly violence, such as anti-Japan demonstrations in China in spring 2005. Cultural homogeneity strengthens development within a country, but it impedes integration among countries or gives this integration a less institutional and stable character. Reconciliation lags well behind that in Europe, where a common European culture of multilateral institutions and law is slowly supplementing national cultures. China's looming dominance may also deter integration in Asia, whereas the EU developed among relatively equal partners.

The box to the left summarizes the key features of Asian development, which we now contrast with Latin American development.

Latin America—A Lost Decade?

Spotlight on import substitution

Latin America's development experience contrasts sharply with that of Asia. Except for Chile, Latin American countries deliberately opted out of the GATT free-market trading system after World War II and based their development strategies on import substitution rather than export-led growth. This model facilitated some initial industrial development in Brazil, Argentina, Mexico, and other countries, but it actually made Latin America more, rather than less, vulnerable to international markets. Industries served domestic markets only and did not stay competitive in the absence of foreign competition. They developed little export capacity to finance vital imports. When the oil crisis hit in the 1970s, Latin American countries had to borrow heavily to finance higher-priced oil imports; and when interest rates went up in the 1980s, they could no longer service their loans. Latin America experienced a *lost decade*, while East Asia experienced an economic miracle.

Latin America encompasses one country in North America (Mexico), seven in Central America, and twelve in South America. Strictly speaking not all are "Latin" (or Spanish and Portuguese)—some are English, Dutch, and French—and eight small Caribbean countries also belong to the developing countries of the Western Hemisphere (see Map 11-3). Together these twenty-eight principal countries account for about 556 million people, or 8.55 percent of the world's population. Coincidentally, they also account for about 8 percent of world gross national income (GNI)—at purchasing power parity exchange rates, that is, exchange rates that take out differences between countries in inflation rates.

From 1950 to 1973 Latin American countries grew on average by 2.5 percent per year in real GDP per capita. This performance was slightly below the average for all developing countries (2.7 percent per year) but less than half the growth rate in South Korea and Taiwan and one-third the growth rate later in China and Thailand. Brazil and Mexico did best, growing at about 3.8 and 3.1 percent per year, respectively. These were the years of inward-oriented policies in Latin America, and the performance was not that bad. So, it is incorrect to say that protectionist policies never pay. Notice, however, that these policies paid off mostly in big countries, such as Brazil and Mexico, that had large domestic markets to support import substitution industries.

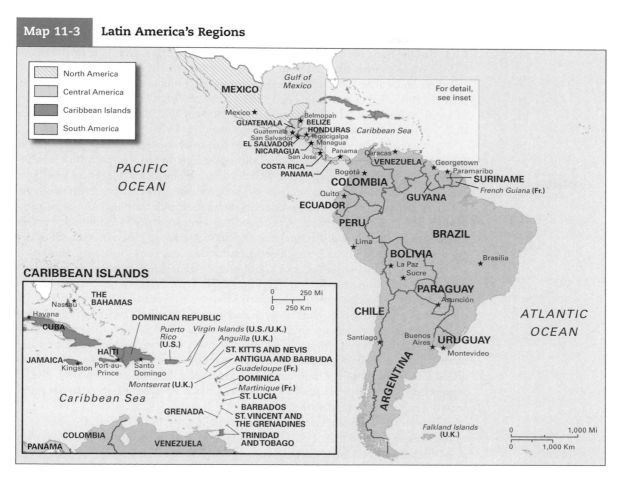

Map 11-3   **Latin America's Regions**

The issue is, at what price do such policies pay? The next decade and a half, from 1973 to 1987, suggested the price was pretty high. Known as the **lost decade,** this period saw average real per capita growth in Latin America plummet to 0.8 percent per year. It held up best in Brazil at 2.2 percent, dropped dramatically in Mexico to 0.9 percent, and was negative for the entire period in Argentina at –0.8 percent. What happened? Well, Latin America went through a very difficult transition period occasioned in part by oil crises, which ran up Latin America's external debt. The debt of six major countries—Argentina, Brazil, Chile, Colombia, Mexico, and Peru—increased from $35 to $248 billion in less than a decade. But import substitution policies also played a role. They fueled inflation and did nothing to reduce inequality. Inflation rates soared to an average over 100 percent per year, compared to 20 percent in the earlier decades, ten to thirty times higher than inflation rates in Asia and the industrialized countries. In addition, the disparity of incomes between the top 10 percent of income earners and the bottom 20 percent was twice as high in Latin America as in Asia and the industrialized countries.[29] Chile was the only country to weather the oil crises and continue to grow, and it was also the only country that followed export-led rather than import substitution policies.

Starting in the late 1980s, almost all Latin American countries undertook market-oriented policy reforms. Following the Washington Consensus, they stopped accommodating inflation, liberalized domestic markets, and opened trade and investment

lost decade

economic stagnation in Latin America brought on by domestic policies, the oil crises, and high debt, lasting from the early 1970s to the late 1980s.

Spotlight on
debt and finance

ties with foreign firms. As the World Bank reports, "policies were better in nearly *every* country in Latin America in 1999 than they were in Chile in 1985."[30] And remember Chile had the most liberal policies in 1985. At first, expected economic growth did not follow. While growth accelerated in the early 1990s—reaching 7 percent in 1992—it tailed off badly after 1995, when Mexico underwent a financial crisis, and slumped to zero in 1998, where it stayed through 2002.[31] After 2002, however, Mexico and the rest of Latin America rebounded smartly. From 2003 to 2007, the region grew by more than 5 percent per year, the best record since the early 1970s.[32]

causal arrow →

Was this belated performance the result of free-market policies finally paying off, or was it a consequence of soaring oil, agricultural, and commodity prices, which benefited Latin American energy producers such as Mexico and Venezuela and beef producers such as Argentina? As the box on page 401 suggests, the answer depends on your perspective. Some analysts see it as a product of colonialism and continued American intervention and dominance (realist). Others see it as a consequence of insufficient market interdependence and weak national and regional institutions (liberal). And still others see it as an outcome of conflicting ideologies and class and ethnic warfare (identity).

The World Bank suggested four "syndromes"—that's diplomatese for "causes"—associated with Latin America's continuing struggle to match the better performance of Asian developing countries: (1) governments that are elite-dominated, are unstable, do not protect property rights, and engage in corruption; (2) macroeconomic policies that cause inflation, fiscal deficits, volatile exchange rates, and high debt; (3) external policies that restrict trade and investment; and (4) financial systems dominated by state-owned banks and legal institutions that do not enforce contracts. The World Bank also added a fudge factor—bad luck; this covers geography (landlocked countries), disease susceptibility, and being "cursed" by resources (remember from Chapter 10 the problems of resource-based industries?).[33]

Spotlight on relative wealth

Whatever the syndromes or causes, here are the results. In 1800, Argentina had a per capita income equal to that of the United States; today, its per capita income is less than one-fifth that of the United States. Similarly, in 1800, Brazil, Mexico, Chile, and Peru had per capita incomes at 40–50 percent of the U.S. level. Today, Chile is at U.S. levels, but all the others are at levels of one-fifth or less.[34] Let's look more closely at the four "syndromes" associated with this dramatic divergence in living standards between the United States and Latin America. (For a summary of the discussion that follows, see the box to the left.)

Development in Latin America: Key Factors

Relative domestic instability

No recent colonialism or regional wars

Import substitution-based growth

High budget deficits and inflation

Little land reform

University (elite) education

Cultural friction (large, disenfranchised black and mestizo minorities)

Unstable Governments and Stable Region

Colonized by European powers after 1500, Latin America had already secured its independence in the early nineteenth century. After that, South American countries, such as Brazil and Argentina, remained largely free of outside interference—with a few exceptions, such as British intervention in the Falkland Islands in 1833. But Mexico, the Caribbean, and Central American countries endured American expansion and periodic intervention for the next one hundred years. Mexico lost roughly half of its territory to American conquest, and American troops occupied Cuba, Nicaragua, Honduras, the Dominican Republic, and other neighbors for extended periods of time. In most

Using the Perspectives to  Read

 Between ←

the Lines

A View of Development from Latin America

Juan Tokatlian, director of political science and international relations at the Universidad de San Andrés in Argentina, reflected on the process of development in Latin America in an article that he contributed to the *Financial Times* on March 10, 2006. His main point in the article is that Latin America "needs stronger, more competent and legitimate political institutions rather than . . . corrupt courtesan states. . . ." This point, we might say, reflects a liberal perspective (a focus on domestic institutions) from a domestic level of analysis.

But, now, how does Latin America reach this goal, considering the crucial role of the United States? Let's look at his views of U.S. foreign policy:

> Washington has no imaginative strategy to deal with contemporary U.S.-Latin American relations. . . . Adding to this is the resurgence of a strongly ideological perspective in the Bush White House; during the cold war, the threat was communism, now it is radical populism. . . . the temptation to tolerate, or even promote, "benevolent" coups was noticeable in Venezuela in 2002, Haiti in 2004 and Ecuador in 2005. . . . In short, U.S. behavior remains fixated on myopic unilateralism and coercive diplomacy.

Notice how he rejects the "strongly ideological perspective" toward Latin American reforms, our identity perspective, and "the temptation to tolerate, or even promote, 'benevolent' coups," our realist perspective. So what does he advocate? You guessed it, a more liberal perspective:

> The region and the U.S. need to concentrate on what could be called an agenda of "four Ds": democracy, debt, development and drugs—all of which can be handled with creativity and effectiveness. It is urgent to revitalize, politically and materially, the Organization of American States [OAS], as the key forum to tackle these issues. Washington should accept a mode of concert diplomacy with leading, intermediate Latin American powers . . . [and] stimulate "citizen diplomacy"—people to people—around the Americas.

Notice that, although the agenda includes democracy, the "key forum" to achieve democracy is the OAS, even though some key members, such as Venezuela, may not be democratic. This is the hope of many liberal perspectives, that "concert" and "citizen" diplomacy, not direct democracy promotion or coups and power politics, will eventually lead to democracy.

Source: Excerpts from Juan Tokatlian, "America Should Look More Often in Its Own Backyard," *Financial Times,* March 10, 2006, 13. Excerpts used with permission of *Financial Times.*

cases, the pretext for intervention was instability and the threat of interference by outside powers, principally the former European colonial powers. In 1823, the United States warned European countries in the Monroe Doctrine (named for James Monroe, who was president at the time) that it would not accept any new European colonies, transfer of colonies, or reversion of independent nations to colonial status in the Western Hemisphere. The Western Hemisphere, in short, was America's sphere of influence. Thus, while Latin American countries, unlike other developing countries, escaped early from direct colonialism, they labored under the continuing presence and sometimes direct intervention of the "colossus to the north." Puerto Rico and the Virgin Islands, of course, became and remain American territories.

dependency theory

theory developed by Latin American economists that explains the lack of growth in terms of external or colonial exploitation and oppression.

The colonial experience, although lighter in Latin America than in other regions, nevertheless cut deeply. As we discuss further in Chapter 13, Marxist scholars in Latin American studies developed **dependency theory,** which blames external forces for the lack of growth. This theory holds that Latin American countries needed foreign capital to develop but that this capital came from American imperialist interests, and imperial interests exploited and drained local resources. Foreign companies carved out enclaves in Latin America to extract resources at low cost and market their manufactured goods at high profits—they essentially took more out of the economy than they put in. Fear of such foreign exploitation played a big role after World War II in the decision by Latin American countries to follow import substitution policies. Unfortunately, as already noted, those policies may have contributed to Latin America's continued dependency. With no or only a small external sector, Latin American economies became more vulnerable and, when the oil crises hit, had no export capacity to pay for higher-priced oil.

Military rule and political instability characterized Latin American politics throughout much of the nineteenth and twentieth centuries. Interruptions of constitutional power were common. In the seventy-five years after 1900, only Colombia and Costa Rica had fewer than ten years of nondemocratic rule. All the other countries clocked at least two decades of dictatorial rule. Some, such as Argentina, Brazil, Ecuador, Bolivia, Mexico, the Dominican Republic, and all of the Central American countries except Honduras, clocked four decades or more. A few, such as Haiti, never experienced a peaceful transfer of power from one party to another. The only exceptions to this experience of authoritarian rule are the small English-speaking islands of the Caribbean.[35]

Today, most Latin American countries, with the exceptions of Cuba and Venezuela, are democracies. But they are weak democracies. Although elections take place, the continuous, stable transfer of power between opposing political parties is less common. Instead, Latin America has experienced waves of democratization and then reversals. After World War II, democracy spread to all countries except five: Paraguay, El Salvador, Honduras, Nicaragua, and the Dominican Republic. By 1954, however, this process had been reversed; only four countries remained democratic: Uruguay, Costa Rica, Chile, and Brazil.[36] Then, in 1964, Brazil succumbed to a military coup; Chile did likewise in 1973. Critics blamed U.S. policies for this rollback. Fearing communist governments in the region, U.S. intelligence agencies assisted coups in Guatemala (1954) and Chile (1973) and fought to prevent Castro from taking power in Cuba (1959). Also recall, from our discussion of the Cuban Missile Crisis in Chapter 5, the CIA attempts after 1959 to invade Cuba and assassinate Castro.

Another wave of democratization began in 1978. Some thirty elections occurred over the next sixteen years in fifteen countries that had previously been under authoritarian rule. Half of these elections represented second, third, or fourth elections, and four-fifths of them involved peaceful transitions to opposing parties.[37] Latin America seemed to be on the way to a more stable pattern of pluralist politics. Mexico's democratic turn in 1997 provided further encouragement. Opposition parties took control of the National Assembly for the first time, and a center-right party, the National Action Party (PAN), won the presidency in 2000, taking that office for the first time from the Institutional Revolutionary Party (PRI), which had ruled Mexico for seventy years. The PAN retained the presidency in elections in 2007. Nevertheless, Latin America also endured some reversals. A dictator, Alberto Fujimori, ruled Peru for a decade before he was driven into exile in Japan. Venezuela succumbed to the populist military dictator Hugo Chavez. Colombia and Ecuador fought debilitating civil wars against drug lords and guerrillas. Bolivia experienced riots, threats of secession by individual provinces, and unstable governments. Argentina flirted with a populist and potentially extra-constitutional regime. And Cuba, even after Castro stepped down in 2008 in favor of his brother Raúl, remained an outpost of authoritarian and quixotic rule in the region.

Political instability is undoubtedly a major cause of the disappointing economic performance in Latin America. It is also a reason why governments tend to centralize and control economic policies and institutions. When political power is unstable, economic resources become a major stake in the

Colombian President Alvaro Uribe (right) walks a fine line in the civil war between anti-government guerrillas, shown here surrendering their weapons, and renegade paramilitary forces supporting the government outside the law.

political game. Governments pursue dirigiste or neo-Marxist policies to keep economic resources under tight political control and thereby marginalize the opposition. The only way for the opposition to gain economic advantage is to seize political power; there is no independent marketplace of any significance. Realist considerations trump institutional (market) and ideological factors.

← causal *arrow*

Import Substitution Policies

Latin American countries were the "poster children" for import substitution policies. Remember from Chapter 10 that such policies called for developing local industries to substitute for imports. Even before World War II, elites in Brazil, Mexico, and other Latin American countries found such centralized economic policies congenial to their political control. Import substitution policies meant protected and, hence, highly profitable domestic markets. The government doled out licenses to political supporters, who then ran companies either as state-owned enterprises or as private companies with generous state subsidies.

State policies encouraged a massive and rapid reallocation of capital from agriculture and rural areas to industry and urban areas. State marketing boards bought and sold major food products. They set food prices very low to feed the urban population, in effect, extracting savings from the rural sector by not paying market prices for agricultural output. Economists call this policy **financial repression,** forcing savings from rural areas at below-market rates of return. State entities also controlled and developed natural resources, such as oil, selling these products at subsidized prices at home and profiting from their export abroad. Pemex, the state-owned oil company in Mexico, dominated all aspects of energy supply, including electricity. State-run or state-dependent banks made loans at subsidized interest rates to establish industries. During World War II, Brazil created state companies in steel, iron ore, airplane engines, tractors, trucks, automobiles, soda ash, caustic soda, and electricity. Other licenses went to private companies. These companies then lobbied to limit competition. They were

financial repression
a system in which states extract savings from one sector, usually agriculture, by not paying market prices for the goods produced by that sector.

rent-seekers

firms that lobby to limit competition, extracting monopoly rents by producing at low costs while selling at high prices.

what economists call **rent-seekers,** hoping to exploit monopoly rents from markets that had limited or no competition. If the markets were large enough to support significant volumes of output, as they were in Brazil and other big Latin American countries, companies could make high profits. They achieved low costs from economies of scale while setting high prices in the absence of competition. Best of all, they faced no foreign competition and could get cherished import licenses, if needed, to purchase foreign equipment or technology that was not available locally.

Governments controlled the commanding heights of the economy. To finance industrial development, they extracted savings by tapping natural resources and holding wages down. Extraction worked as long as labor and natural resources remained plentiful and local industries expanded. From 1940 to 1982, the large Latin American countries grew at rates of 6–8 percent per year. But the government budgets were always under strain; the tax base of the economy was small, and industry absorbed more taxes in the form of government subsidies than it paid. Savings and natural resources eventually became more difficult to extract. Meanwhile, expenditures soared, mostly to accommodate privileged elites and to build infrastructure—universities, hospitals, and electrical power—that catered to urban needs. Budget deficits became chronic, and monetary policies expanded to accommodate government deficits. Central banks, controlled by finance ministries, printed money to pay the bills. Too much money chased too few goods, and inflation soared and encouraged debtors, who repaid loans in currency that was worth less. By 1986, the per capita debt in Latin America was three times as high as in Asia.[38] Inflation also encouraged **capital flight**; money moved out of the local currency and country. If you're holding a local currency that is declining in value daily due to inflation, it makes sense to convert it into a foreign currency that is appreciating.

Spotlight on

macroeconomic policies and currency devaluation

capital flight

moving money out of the local currency and country because of inflation and economic or political instability.

External shocks ended the party. The oil crises of the 1970s hit oil importers such as Brazil hard, although they benefited oil producers such as Mexico and Colombia and were fairly neutral for self-sufficient oil producers such as Argentina, Chile, and Peru. The real crunch came from higher interest rates in the 1980s. The one thing someone in debt does not want is higher interest rates. When Great Britain and the United States decided to attack the inflation of the 1970s by raising interest rates, Latin America's debt mountain creaked and then collapsed. With massive debt burdens, high interest rates raised dramatically the debt-servicing costs. Because most of the debt was in dollars, Latin America had to export more. But import substitution policies had done little to develop exports. Latin American exports in 1986 were only 13 percent of GDP, compared to 22 percent in 1929.[39] Exports had gone backward. Thus, Latin American countries first paid the interest and rolled over the principal. Then they could not pay the interest either, and they defaulted altogether. Mexico was the first to do so in 1982, and others followed. The next decade was spent rescheduling debt and trying to reverse domestic policies that had reached a dead end.

Opening Markets

Chile was the first Latin American country to try export-led development policies. Under a repressive but stable military government, which the United States helped to bring into power, Chile moved in the late 1970s toward more competitive market-oriented policies. Following the Hayekian or Chicago School of economic policy, Chile attacked inflation by disciplining the growth of the money supply, reduced fiscal deficits, converted a portion of foreign debt into equity (an early form of privatiza-

Spotlight on

neoclassical liberal ideas

tion), deregulated the domestic economy, and opened markets to foreign trade and investment. Such sweeping changes had its costs, but Chile weathered the lost decade better than other Latin American countries and became the model for more market-oriented policies throughout Latin America in the 1990s.

Mexico made the decisive breakthrough. In the late 1980s, it abandoned 150 years of **economic autarky,** or a closed domestic economic system; shut down the notorious citadel of Mexican economic nationalism, the Ministry of Commerce and Industry; and joined GATT and the world trading system. It reduced tariffs and joined NAFTA. Over the next decade, Mexico abolished 700 of its 1,200 state enterprises, introduced more realistic market prices for previously subsidized commodities, made large cuts in bloated public-sector bureaucracies, and established an independent central bank and more competitive private banks. Mexico also became a major oil exporter and contemplated, although it has not yet done so, opening up the nationalized energy industry to FDI and competition.

economic autarky
a closed domestic economic system based on protectionism and state-owned industries.

The returns were not immediate or spectacular. The Mexican economy overheated, and Mexico suffered another financial crisis in 1994. It devalued the peso, reallocating resources from domestic use to exports. The devaluations squeezed domestic demand and hurt small consumers and entrepreneurs. Nevertheless, Mexico bounced back quickly. It paid off its emergency loans sooner than required. On balance, as the World Bank concludes, NAFTA "had positive effects on trade, foreign direct investment, technology transfer, and growth, and is also associated with productivity improvements in manufacturing."[40] As the picture caption at the beginning of this chapter notes, Mexico grew sevenfold from 1993 to 2005, more than doubled its ratio of trade to GDP, and absorbed more FDI than any other Latin American country.

Other Latin American countries followed suit. Argentina, Colombia, Costa Rica, El Salvador, Guatemala, and Nicaragua lowered tariffs by 10–20 percent, and exports and imports soared 1.5–2 times as a ratio of GDP. Brazil and Argentina formed a free-trade community of their own in 1991, known as Mercosur, which Paraguay and Uruguay also joined, and Chile and others became associate members. Again, the transition was not smooth. Argentina's experience suggests the risks of opening markets when domestic institutions are weak. The central government lost control of fiscal policy, and Argentina's provinces went on a spending spree and issued dollar-denominated bonds to finance debt. External obligations mounted until the currency collapsed in 2002. Argentina defaulted on its debt, and it signed new agreements with the IMF to reform its fiscal policy. But, in the meantime, it reached an agreement with most of its private foreign bank creditors to forgive three-quarters of its debt. Uncertainty and lack of compliance with IMF targets, however, bedevil Argentina's future access to credit.

The business climate in many of these countries improved, not just for foreign investment but, more important, for domestic investment as well. Microeconomic policies impede local as well as foreign investment. Unreliable infrastructure (ports, roads, phones, and so on), legal problems with contract enforcement, crime, bribes, and regulations add 15 percent to the costs of doing business in Brazil, and upward of 25 percent in other countries. Over 40 percent of Brazil's roads, which transport 60 percent of all cargo in the country, are essentially unusable because of large potholes.[41] Fifty percent of Brazilian firms lose money, and 40 percent express a lack of confidence that the courts will uphold their property rights. In Guatemala, 70 percent of businesses express the same concern. Regulations ensnare entrepreneurs in red tape. In Brazil, it takes 152 days to register a new business; in Haiti it takes 203. Chile is the best, requiring only 27 days. As a result, entrepreneurs operate outside the law. The

Spotlight on microeconomic policies

informal sector

business activities that take place outside the legal system of a country and that involve no legal titles or tax payments.

informal sector in many Latin American countries, in which businesses operate without legal documents and pay no taxes, is huge. In Mexico, it accounts for about 30 percent of GDP and in Peru over 50 percent.[42] In urban areas alone throughout Latin America and the Caribbean, 56 percent of all jobs are in the informal sector.[43]

Mexico privatized commercial banks in 1991, after nationalizing them in 1982. While privatization was considered a technical success, subsequent bank lending to politically powerful groups contributed to the financial crisis in 1994. After the crisis, Mexico permitted foreign banks and investment firms to enter and increase competition. But banking and financial markets in other countries remain underdeveloped, largely because of a lack of competition and foreign expertise. Most loans still go to close connections rather than to the most profitable ventures. Equity and bond markets, where firms can raise money independently of government influence, are weak.[44] Nevertheless, in the 1990s, many governments established independent central banks. By the end of the decade, Brazil, Chile, Colombia, Peru, and Mexico had taken away the printing presses that finance ministries used to finance debt and fuel hyperinflation.

From liberal perspectives, market-oriented reforms clearly moved Latin American countries in the right direction. Exports not only grew but diversified away from commodities, for which prices were declining, and toward manufactured goods, for which prices were rising. For Latin America and the Caribbean as a whole, the share of manufactured exports to total exports tripled from 15.4 percent in 1970 to 46.6 percent in 2000.[45] From realist and identity perspectives, however, trade and other reforms did not measurably reduce inequality, although they did not increase it either. Unlike China and India, Latin America did not see a reduction in the number of people living below the poverty line.

Spotlight on perspectives

Stubborn Inequality

Inequality in the mainly middle-income Latin American region is among the highest in the world, with the richest 10 percent of the population receiving 41 percent of total income and the poorest just 1 percent. Poverty reduction has stagnated in recent years, leaving 47 million people in the region—more than 8 percent of the population—mired in extreme poverty.[46] Why is inequality in Latin America so resistant to change? Is it culture and the long history of oppression of native populations by European (Spanish and Portuguese) elites, as identity perspectives might argue? Is it the unholy alliance between U.S. foreign policy interests and local elites that maintains political stability; exploits Latin American resources; restricts Latin American exports, such as textiles and agricultural products; and floods Latin American markets with U.S. manufactured exports, as realist perspectives contend? Is it the failure of social and economic reforms that fuels populist and revolutionary resentment and creates the damaging cycle of political revolution and instability that defeats sustained economic growth, as liberal perspectives might see it? It is probably all these things and more. But, in comparison to Asian countries, three factors stand out: the absence of large-scale land reform, the relative lack of primary education, and a culture of paternalism and clientelism. Let's look at them in sequence.

causal arrow

In Latin America, some 5–10 percent of the population, depending on the country, own 70–90 percent of the land. Yet over half the population still earns its living in the countryside. There have been periodic attempts at land reform. Mexico redistributed some land to peasants under the ***ejido* system,** but the plots were owned collectively, not individually, and depended on government development banks for financing. The

ejido system

Mexican land reform project that redistributed some land to peasants; however, the plots were owned collectively, not individually, and depended on government development banks for financing.

U.S. aid program in the 1960s known as the Alliance for Progress pushed land reform, and nearly 1 million peasant families acquired plots. But another 10–14 million families did not and continued to work the land as tenant farmers.[47] In Colombia, which is torn by the narcotics trade and crime, large landowners rule whole tracts of the countryside as feudal fiefdoms and even employ paramilitary forces to protect their territories. In Ecuador, 45 percent of the people live on the land, while 86 percent of the land is owned by the wealthiest 20 percent of the population.[48] Nothing contributes more to the inequality of income in Latin America than the absence of land reform. The richest 10 percent of the people control almost twice as much wealth in Latin America as in the United States, 47 percent compared to 28 percent.

Basic human needs—such as education and health care—have improved steadily in Latin America. But primary and elementary school education still lag behind other regions. Much of the problem lies in the fact that so many people still live in the countryside or in urban slums on the edge of monstrous cities such as Sao Paulo in Brazil. In Haiti, for example, 80 percent of the population lives outside the urban areas. They lack access to basic sanitation, housing, and health care. Children are needed to scratch a living from the land. In some cases, they are drafted into drug gangs and criminal activities that contribute to the general political discontent and violence affecting the Latin American landscape. Discrimination also plays a role. Large portions of the population in Latin American countries are black (in Brazil, 50 percent, and in Colombia, 29 percent) or mestizo, mixed European and American Indian ancestry (Colombia, 50 percent; Guatemala, 60 percent; Venezuela, 70 percent; Ecuador, 40 percent; Paraguay, 76 percent; Bolivia, 71 percent; Chile, 70 percent; and Peru, 42 percent).[49] These groups do not receive the same opportunities for education and employment as those of European ancestry. The problems are interconnected. The education problem is part of the land reform problem, which in turn is part of the problem of industrial development, which might spur education and employment of the rural masses.

Industrial development in Latin America is held back by a patrimonial and clientelist culture in which family and fraternal ties suffocate initiative and entrepreneurship. Individual initiative is not lacking; that's evident in the robust informal sectors in most Latin American countries. But economic and political institutions do not welcome individual initiative and entrepreneurship. A tradition of **paternalism** prevails, grounded in part in the Catholic Church, which dominates the region. At one point, the church owned 60 percent of the land in Latin America. The heavy weight of the church on society led some Catholic priests and laity to rebel and fight the state openly. They preached a hard-left type of liberation theology and allied with Marxist guerrillas to fuel many of the rebellions in Latin American countries during the Cold War. When institutions stifle the masses long enough, revolutions follow. Democracy is caught in the middle, a desirable but dangerous alternative, as President Kennedy said, if it entails the prospect of populism or communism, as we see today in Venezuela and Cuba.

Spotlight on domestic governance

paternalism

institutions such as the church or state providing for the needs of individuals or groups but without granting them real rights or responsibilities, thus stifling individual initiative and entrepreneurship.

Indigenous Indians in Bolivia occupy unused land seized from a giant soy plantation by the government of President Evo Morales as part of land reform efforts.

Summary

Development, or the spread of material, institutional, and human progress, is necessary but not easy. Poorer countries start from different traditions and historical legacies. But the record suggests that progress is possible and countries are not doomed by colonialism or oppression. Asian countries experienced more recent colonialism and more frequent regional wars than Latin America. Yet they grew faster over the past fifty years than Latin American countries, and today China and India, the two most populous countries in the world, are leading the development competition. The reasons for their outperformance of the Latin American countries are multiple, but open world markets and responsible domestic policies played a key role.

The boxes on pages 398 and 400 contrast the policies of the two regions. Asian countries pursued export-oriented strategies supplemented by selective government interventions to redistribute land, promote primary and secondary education, and maintain sound macroeconomic policies. Latin American countries, except for Chile, pursued domestic-oriented policies to promote import substitution industries, encourage large land holdings and agricultural operations, educate an elite population, and finance growth by fiscal deficits and inflation.

By the turn of the millennium, the results were clear. Asian countries fared much better and joined the global middle class. But development debates continued. Latin American countries turned toward more outward-oriented policies but, in line with identity perspectives, sought to adapt policies and institutions to more country-specific characteristics rather than a single Asian or western global market model. Asian countries confronted the limits of export-oriented development and experimented with liberal reforms of financial institutions and other service sectors. China welcomed FDI from the outset but retained an oppressive government that viewed development in nationalistic or realist terms. Venezuela pioneered an even more populist or independent approach to development in Latin America. And the nationalistic approach remains popular in sub-Saharan Africa and the Middle East and North Africa as well. Those regions are the subject of our discussion in the next chapter.

Key Concepts

Asian values 397	East Asian Miracle 378	informal sector 406
capital flight 404	economic autarky 405	land reform 392
crony capitalism 395	*ejido* system 406	lost decade 399
dependency theory 402	financial repression 403	paternalism 407
development 382	gross domestic product (GDP) 386	rent-seekers 404

Study Questions

1. What are the different meanings of and ways to measure development?

2. Contrast the different perspectives on development. Which perspective emphasizes the following factors: market forces, culture and democracy, and monopolies or rent-seekers? Explain why.

3. What were the main differences in policies pursued by Asian and Latin American countries? What were the strengths and weaknesses of each approach?

4. How would you describe China's approach to development? What elements of its approach follow from the liberal, realist, and identity perspectives? If China succeeds, what are likely to be the consequences for the United States from the different perspectives? For example, would a realist, identity, or liberal perspective expect China to become more friendly, more hostile, or just different?

5. Compare the external environment for development in Asia and Latin America after World War II. What was the history of each region with respect to colonialism, democracy, and Cold War alliances? What is the relative importance of external versus domestic policies in development? Could Asia have developed without world markets? Was Latin America justified in ignoring world markets?

12

Foreign Aid and Domestic Governance
Development in Africa and the Middle East

Africa's first elected woman president, Ellen Johnson-Sirleaf of Liberia, is sworn in on January 16, 2006. Does she represent a new Africa of gender equality (the identity perspective) and political reforms (the liberal perspective) or an old Africa of customs imposed by imperialist powers (the realist perspective—Liberia was founded by freed American slaves)?

Africa and the Middle East stand apart for several reasons. They possess abundant resources, and indeed the Middle East has developed oil resources to become the world's dominant supplier of energy. Those resources, of course, were first developed under colonial rule. Western intervention is a fact of life in these two regions, more so than in parts of Asia—such as Japan—or most of South America. Africa and the Middle East are also the poorest regions of the world, with the largest youth populations and the most deeply embedded discrimination against women. In some Muslim countries, women are largely banned from public places, let alone public life, although change is coming. In 2005, Liberia elected the first woman ever as African head of state, Ellen Johnson-Sirleaf, and several Arab countries, such as Morocco and Jordan, now mandate a number of seats for women in national parliaments. Parts of the Middle East are oil rich but industrially poor. Heavy dependence on oil discourages the development of manufacturing and services, and economic fortunes rise and fall with world oil demand. Meanwhile, the fortunes of Africa, which has little trade or foreign investment, are largely divorced from the world economy. Not surprisingly these two parts of the developing world face massive obstacles to achieving sustained industrial growth and human development.

Although we speak informally of Africa and the Middle East, what we actually have are two regions divided by the Sahara Desert, which stretches across the upper third of the African continent. Thus, sub-Saharan Africa (SSA) refers to the forty-eight states that are located south of the Sahara Desert; and the Middle East and North Africa (MENA) refers to the band of African countries along the Mediterranean and Red Seas, the countries of the Arabian Peninsula and Persian Gulf, the countries of the Levant (Israel, Lebanon, Syria, and Jordan), and Turkey (see Map 12-1). SSA is non-Arab and draws deeply from earlier African civilizations with indigenous, Muslim, and, after colonization, Christian religions. MENA is largely Arab—Israel, Iran, and Turkey are the main exceptions—and draws deeply from the cultural and spiritual legacies of ancient Egypt and the Golden Age of Islam.

Perspectives on Development: Resources, Governance, and Democracy

Realist perspectives emphasize the struggle over resources and strategic advantage in the development of SSA and MENA. The struggle for resources, especially oil, but also diamonds and other raw materials, takes place at all levels of analysis—foreign intervention, government monopolies, and ethnic and civil wars in which resources play a key if not dominant role, for example, diamonds in Angola. The Middle East is also a vital strategic area, constituting the traditional crossroads between European and Asian societies and a crucial geopolitical prize during colonial and Cold War struggles. Because of the central role of governments, realist perspectives stress foreign aid, particularly security assistance. Western powers and the Soviet Union showered weapons on the region, and today the United States and Europe provide massive amounts of aid to influence a Middle East peace settlement, while Russia and China sell arms for oil in the region. Struggles among local elites compound the divisions and conflicts and, until resolved, strangle development.

Liberal perspectives focus on the prospects for better governance and market reforms. The lack of development in SSA and the concentration of development in MENA on one resource (such as oil) puts a premium on control of the government, which is the sole source of wealth. Domestic groups compete for this prize, corruption follows, economic policy governance suffers, and aid is largely wasted or siphoned out of the country. Liberal perspectives support aid but link it to market reforms that might begin to decentralize the production and control of wealth. They encourage diversification through trade and foreign investment, a prospect in MENA, although even wealthy countries such as Saudi Arabia have done relatively little to develop manufacturing and service industries. But many SSA countries are landlocked, transportation is poor and expensive, and international restrictions on agricultural trade inhibit exports. Thus, liberal perspectives advocate the liberalization of agriculture in the Doha Round and see better domestic governance as a prerequisite for more foreign investment and access to international export markets.

Identity perspectives focus on the culture of oppression and modernization. They argue that ethnic conflicts, corruption, bad governance, and lack of opportunity for foreign trade and investment are not the causes of poverty but the consequences. The causes are discrimination against women, the abuse of human rights, and the failure of the world community to listen to different voices among the poor. Answers lie in greater freedom for the poor but also in greater understanding by the rich. The poor

**Spotlight on
levels of analysis**

**Spotlight on
foreign aid**

**Spotlight on
domestic governance**

**Spotlight on
human rights**

Map 12-1 Sub-Saharan Africa (SSA) and the Middle East and North Africa (MENA) Regions

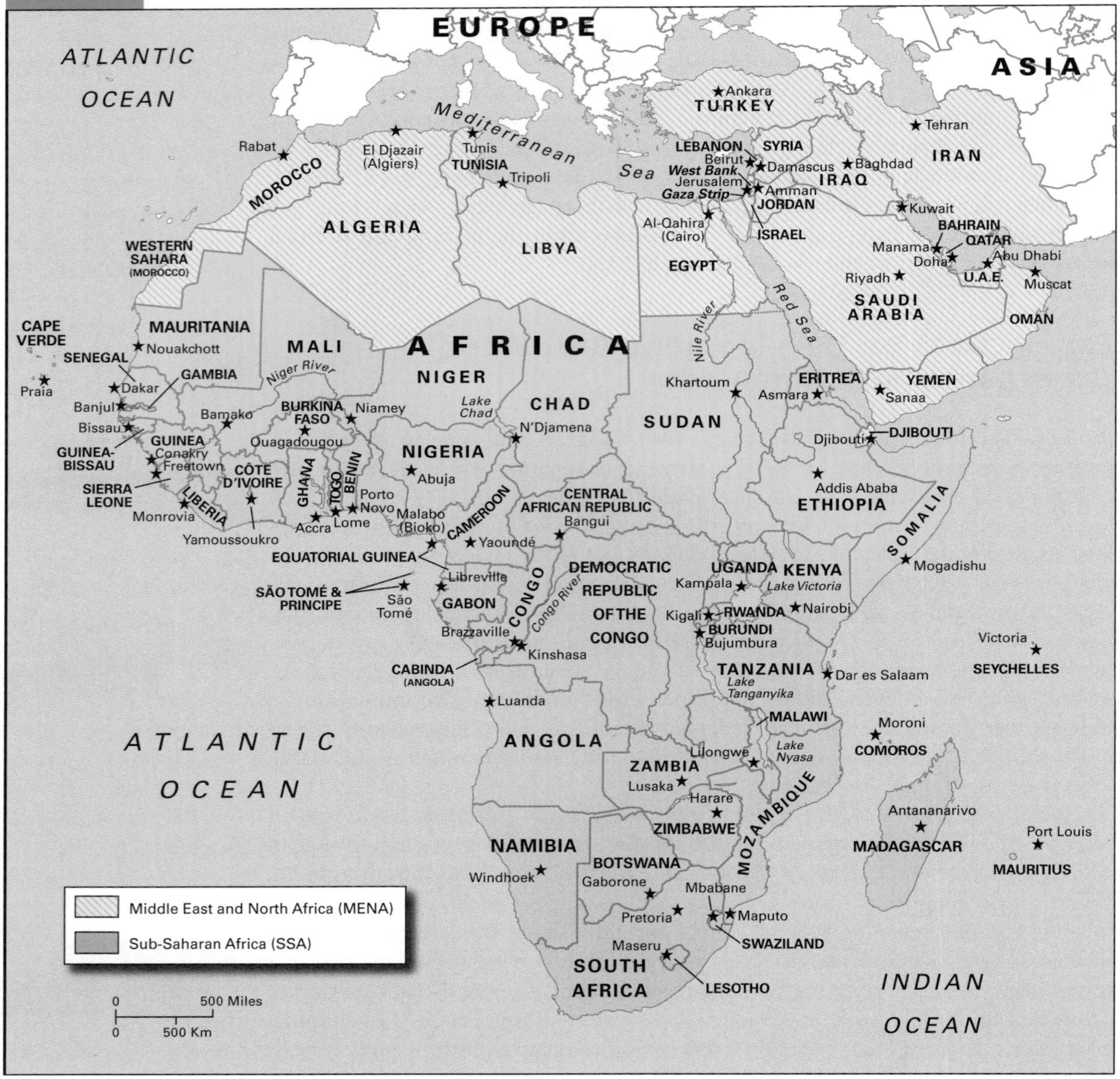

are not blank vessels; they have ideas and assets. And development should strengthen those ideas and assets, not replace them.[1] Whether aid or a new mentality comes first is debated. Some analysts advocate massive foreign aid, roughly $250 billion per year, or ten times current levels.[2] As the box on page 413 suggests, other analysts advocate listening first to local entrepreneurs. In MENA, societies face a confrontation with modernization—how to grow, modernize, and liberate women without losing the rich traditions of their ancient Arab and Islamic heritage. A 2004 report by Arab analysts notes that "freedoms in Arab countries are threatened by two kinds of power: that of undemocratic regimes, and that of tradition and tribalism, sometimes under the cover

Using the Perspectives to Read Between the Lines

A View of Development in Africa

William Easterly, a professor at New York University and former World Bank economist, wrote an op-ed piece in the *Washington Post* about development in Africa. Let's use our perspectives to investigate what he said.

First, he notes how world leaders at the G-8 meeting in Great Britain in 2005 called for

> "a big, big push" to end poverty—to be financed by an increase in traditional foreign aid. The G-8 agreed to double foreign aid to Africa, from $25 billion a year to $50 billion, and to forgive the African aid debt incurred in previous years to fund previous (unsuccessful) "big pushes." Rock celebrity Bob Geldof assembled well-known bands—virtually none from Africa—for "Live 8" concerts in nine countries around the world to urge G-8 leaders to "Make Poverty History."

Easterly is clearly skeptical of realist approaches to development that emphasize great power plans at G-8 meetings:

> As G-8 ministers and rock stars fussed about a few billion dollars here or there for African governments, the citizens of India and China (where foreign aid is a microscopic share of income) were busy increasing their own incomes by $715 billion in 2005.

He is apparently more optimistic about liberal approaches, like those in India and China, that relied on markets and trade. He identifies two African entrepreneurs, a university educator teaching young Africans to think for themselves and a founder of a telecom company that employed four hundred workers until the Kenyan government shut it down, who were not heard at the G-8 meetings. Yet, as he writes, portraying a priority identity bias, "Africa's true saviors are the people of Africa."

> Everyone, it seems, was invited to the "Save Africa" campaign in 2005 except for Africans. They starred only as victims: genocide casualties, child soldiers, AIDS patients and famine deaths on our 43-inch plasma screens.
>
> Yes, these tragedies deserve attention, but the obsessive and almost exclusive Western focus on them is less relevant to the vast majority of Africans—the hundreds of millions not fleeing from homicidal minors, not HIV-positive, not starving to death, and not helpless wards waiting for actors and rock stars to rescue them. . . .
>
> Development everywhere is homegrown. . . . Economic development in Africa will depend—as it has elsewhere and throughout the history of the modern world—on the success of private-sector entrepreneurs, social entrepreneurs, and African political reformers. It will not depend on the activities of patronizing, bureaucratic, unaccountable, and poorly informed outsiders.

of religion."[3] The report confidently predicted that Arab countries desire freedom and modernization no less than other countries. Turkey (not an Arab country) is the Muslim country most advanced toward freedom.

In the rest of this chapter, we examine the conditions in the SSA and MENA regions. Once again, we use the policy tools of Chapter 9 and our spotlight and arrow features to compare four aspects of development in each region: political or gover-

Table 12-1

Comparing Development Experiences	
Sub-Saharan Africa (dependence on aid)	**Latin America (independence)**
Little trade	Little trade—import substitution
Bad governance	Better governance
Lots of economic aid	Less aid
Middle East and North Africa (dependence on oil)	**Asia (interdependence)**
Resource trade mostly	Lots of trade
Oppressive governments	Good governance
Lots of political aid	Least aid

nance reforms; domestic economic policy reforms; foreign aid, trade, and investment; and human, especially women's, development. SSA is, so to speak, where the rubber of development policy hits the road. It's the poorest region of the world, far behind South Asia, Latin America, and East Asia. MENA, meanwhile, is considerably better off where oil exists (for example, in Saudi Arabia), but only slightly better off overall than the next poorest region, South Asia.

To help you follow this discussion and maintain an overview of the development experience in all four regions, Table 12-1 provides a brief comparison. Notice that the regions that do best do so with more trade, better domestic governance, and, ultimately, less aid. The secret to development may lie not in independence (import substitution) or foreign aid but in domestic policies that balance growth through trade with equity through investments in rural development, housing, health, and education.

Sub-Saharan Africa

They approached each other like gladiators in a Roman arena. They came for battle, a battle over the issue of how to eradicate poverty in Africa, the poorest continent of the world. The situation seemed so desperate that the topic was not how to develop African states but how and why African states fail to develop. The two gladiators—well, O.K., they are just economists—were Jeffrey Sachs, professor at Columbia University, and Arye Hillman, economist at Bar-Ilan University in Israel. They faced off at World Bank headquarters in Washington, D.C., in spring 2004. The auditorium was full with people as well as anticipation. Here's an excerpt from the battle.

Sachs began, speaking with such passion he often failed to complete his sentences:

> The idea that African failure is due to African poor governance is one of the great myths of our time. They can't get out of the hole on their own. If we don't take a different approach, we will see certain collapse; we will see a catastrophic downward spiral of violence.
>
> If you go to rural Ethiopia, Burkina Faso or Mozambique and try to figure out how to solve the problems of crushing disease burden, lack of cooking fuel—they're living on dung as cooking fuel. They lack access to basic medical care. We have not begun to take this problem seriously. What will it take for villages with no access to anti-malarial drugs, where 10 percent of the population is HIV-positive and has depleted soils because they can't afford fertilizer? If you have another idea of how they're supposed to do all this by themselves, let me know.

Hillman responded somewhat conciliatorily but soberly:

> We all have the same objective. We all want to help the poor. But billions of dollars have been spent in Africa over the course of two decades. Someone has to show us that throwing more money at the problem will solve it. All the problems you [Sachs] pointed to are the responsibility of the government. Most of these problems are resolved in civil societies. It's a problem with culture here. We all know there are political elites in poor countries that do very well.[4]

Who's right? Is failed or delayed development primarily a consequence and responsibility of local elites and cultures, or is it the fault and responsibility of the international community? Can local elites succeed without the aid of the international community? Sachs says no; but China was no big recipient of foreign aid when it started development, and it succeeded. Or can the international community succeed without the cooperation of local governments and their willingness to adopt responsible policies? Hillman says no; but the international community opposed the apartheid policies of white South Africa and eventually succeeded in turning that country away from apartheid. The better answer, of course, is that both are needed: an involved international community and responsible local governments. But what's the relative emphasis and, more important, what's the link between foreign aid and domestic governance?

Is the answer a new culture, as identity perspectives argue, and, if so, from which level of analysis—reform of local culture or adoption of universal economic principles and human rights? Is the answer better governance and more interconnection with the world economy, as liberal perspectives advocate, and, if so, from which level—better policies by international institutions or by local governments? Or is the answer the need for a decisive economic success model for the two regions—such as a reformed South Africa or a democratic and modernized Turkey—that lead the way, like the Asian tigers, to better governance and human development? And if so, do such elites emerge from foreign intervention (at the systemic level of analysis) or from domestic or individual level forces? The easy answer, of course, is all of the above. But remember that's pie in the sky. We can't do or have everything at once. Resources are limited, and we have to select priorities. For one effort to sort out priorities, read again the box on page 413.

causal arrow ←

Aid Is Not Enough

Every week in the developing world—mind you, not month or year but week—190,000 children under five years of age die from disease and 10,000 women lose their lives in childbirth.[5] In SSA alone, some 23 million people live with AIDS and more than 1.5 million die each year, and the number is rising steadily, with 2 million contracting the disease every year. Africa accounts for about 70 percent of all AIDS cases, and AIDS reduces life expectancy by up to twenty years, effectively eliminating all the gains in life expectancy made in the twentieth century. AIDS orphans make up 5–10 percent of the population in the most afflicted countries, such as Zambia and Kenya. Some 50 million children in Africa and more than 100 million worldwide are not in school. The largest number of these children who are not receiving an education are girls and young women in rural areas. Two hundred million people have no access to health care, and 300 million have no access to safe water.[6] Deaths from malaria are up 60 percent in the last thirty years from 107 per 100,000 people in 1970 to 165 per 100,000.

neocolonialism

the post-colonial domination of the developing world by multinational corporations.

In the 1950s and 1960s, the causes of the problems were seen as largely external, as the consequences of colonialism. Aid was considered the principal contribution that the international community could make. Beyond that, outsiders were expected not to criticize or even discuss domestic policies. After all, colonialism had dictated domestic policies; developing countries were now free and could run their own domestic policies however they wished. Moreover, they and the international community had to remain alert to a new form of colonialism, the **neocolonialism** of MNCs. Most newly independent African nations did not welcome foreign trade or investment; opening markets was seen as just another way to open countries to new forms of imperialism. Thus, the North-South development dialogue, particularly in the 1970s, was limited to little more than increasing aid and establishing a new international economic order (remember NIEO from Chapter 8) to limit and regulate foreign trade and investment.

By the 1990s, the debate had shifted. From the 1960s to the 1990s, African countries had regressed, not progressed. The per capita income in 1987 dollars dropped from $546 to $525 and, if we leave out South Africa, the richest country on the continent, from $525 to $336. Meanwhile, comparable ratios went up 50 percent in Latin America, 90 percent in South Asia, and 450 percent in East Asia. Yet Africa received by far the most foreign aid, averaging 9 percent of GDP for the typical poor country, equivalent to almost half of public spending and far higher than countries in other regions.[7] Altogether, aid accounted for two-thirds of all capital inflows, and Africa absorbed 30 percent of total international aid. What is more, aid did not stimulate domestic savings but seemed to substitute for it. Domestic savings in Africa, unlike Asia, dropped substantially, from 20.7 percent of GDP in 1970 to 16.6 percent in 1997. And genuine domestic savings (which subtracts out the depletion of natural resources) was only 3.4 percent of GDP in Africa, far below that of any other region, with South Asia being the next worse region at 7.1 percent. So foreign money was coming in but domestic savings and growth were going down. Maybe it was time to talk about domestic policies and the role of foreign trade and investment.

Millennium Initiative

That was the backdrop to the Sachs-Hillman face-off and the larger development debate that began in the 1990s. The discussion eventually led to a new consensus that focused on both enhanced international aid and better governance policies in developing countries. That consensus was expressed in the Millennium Declaration signed at the United Nations in September 2000 by 189 countries, including 147 heads of state. The declaration outlined the Millennium Development Goals. These goals were very ambitious. By 2015, the international community pledged to eradicate extreme poverty and hunger; achieve universal primary education; promote gender equality and empower women; reduce infant mortality; improve maternal health; combat HIV/AIDS, malaria, and other diseases; ensure environmental sustainability; and develop a global partnership among governments, private companies, and NGOs to increase aid, employment, trade opportunities, debt relief, and affordable medicines for developing countries.

The Millennium initiative stressed the link between international aid and local policies. This link was considered crucial. Too often in the past, it was argued, aid did not influence domestic spending patterns. Governments, for example, did not use aid for health services to improve rural conditions where the majority of poor lived but, instead, continued to finance urban priorities, such as state-of-the-art hospitals, which involved heavy administrative costs and often poor and corrupt implementation. On the other hand, aid-donating countries or multilateral agencies attached so many restrictions to projects that there was no sense of ownership by local elites and institutions; local governments felt left out. The Millennium approach stressed country-owned and -led poverty reduction strategies. These strategies aimed at both overall growth and growth of the poorest populations and regions. Multilateral development banks, donor countries, and NGOs were asked to coordinate their aid with country-specific poverty plans. We might argue that the Millennium initiative adopted the third view of development strategy discussed in Chapter 11, a country- and culture-specific approach that channels policies and resources through the prism of local elites and institutions and holds them accountable to reach the Millennium targets by 2015—for example, to achieve universal primary education by that year.

Spotlight on
domestic governance

A Poor and Divided Continent

The Millennium initiative addressed developing countries as a whole, but it gave special attention to SSA. Real income in SSA is one-third less than in South Asia, the next poorest region. SSA's total income is just a little more than that of Belgium, and its median income (half the countries are below and half above this level) is the equivalent of the output of a town of 60,000 people in a rich country. Forty percent of the people live below the poverty line of $1 per day.

But SSA is not only the poorest continent; it is also one of the most divided. It consists of forty-eight countries with 165 borders, thirteen countries with fewer than 5 million people, and six more with fewer than 1 million people. Many of these small countries are landlocked and far too small to develop independently. Nigeria with about 140 million people is the most populous country by far, having more than double the population of the next largest states, Ethiopia and the Democratic Republic of Congo (hereafter, DR Congo to distinguish it from the Congo, which is a separate, much smaller country west of DR Congo; see Map 12-1 on page 412). The other major countries by population include South Africa, Tanzania, Kenya, Sudan, and Uganda. Among the smallest are Cape Verde, Comoros, and Seychelles. The wealthiest country by far is South Africa, with four times the purchasing power parity GNI of Nigeria. (Look back at Map 11-1 in the previous chapter for the distribution of wealth in sub-Saharan Africa.)

Africa was completely colonized, and only Liberia and Ethiopia escaped western intervention. The boundaries in Africa were drawn by colonialists in Europe with little regard for ethnic or cultural homogeneity. Arguably, it may not have mattered. Africa is home to so many tribes and ethnic groups that it may have been impossible to create coherent states. Some 2,000 tribes exist throughout the continent. They speak some 750 different languages. Only four states can claim ethnic homogeneity: Botswana, Lesotho, Somalia (although it is divided by clans), and Swaziland. By contrast, DR Congo alone has 75 distinct languages. Thus, the continent sags under the triple legacy of unfavorable geography, colonial rule, and indigenous divisions.

Since the countries of SSA became independent in the 1950s and 1960s, fighting has been incessant somewhere on the continent. In 2001, civil and interstate wars raged in west Africa, central Africa, and east Africa. In west Africa, Sierra Leone was caught up in a savage conflict between local elites in cahoots with Lebanese diamond miners and a rebel force known as the Revolutionary United Front (RUF) under Foday Sankoh.

Spotlight on
ethnic differences

| Map 12-2 | **Human Development: Basic and Advanced Measures** |

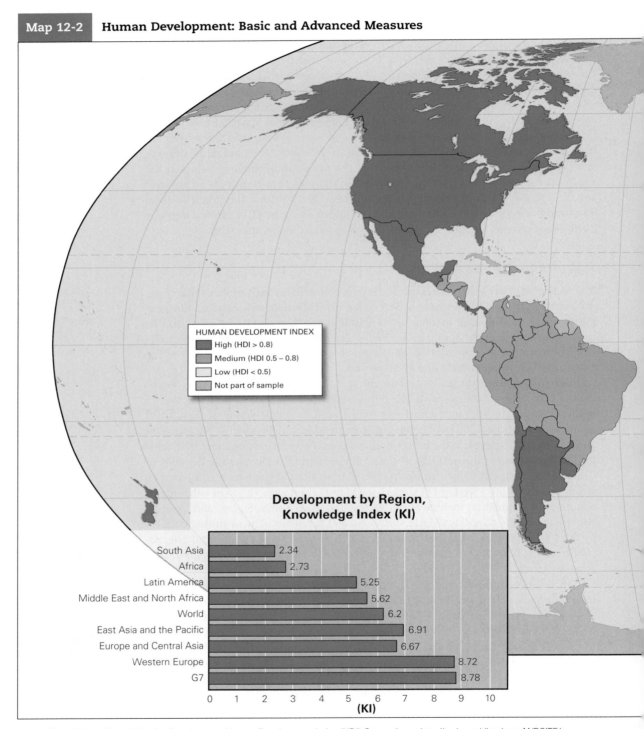

HUMAN DEVELOPMENT INDEX
- High (HDI > 0.8)
- Medium (HDI 0.5 – 0.8)
- Low (HDI < 0.5)
- Not part of sample

**Development by Region,
Knowledge Index (KI)**

Region	KI
South Asia	2.34
Africa	2.73
Latin America	5.25
Middle East and North Africa	5.62
World	6.2
East Asia and the Pacific	6.91
Europe and Central Asia	6.67
Western Europe	8.72
G7	8.78

(KI)

Source: World Bank's Knowledge for Development Human Development Index (HDI) Categories at http://web.worldbank.org/WBSITE/
EXTERNAL/WBI/WBIPROGRAMS/KFDLP/EXTUNIKAM/0,,contentMDK:20584353~menuPK:1433284~pagePK:64168445~piPK:64168309~
theSitePK:1414721,00.html. Accessed May 6, 2008. The World Bank's "Knowledge for Development" at http://web.worldbank.org/WBSITE/
EXTERNAL/WBI/WBIPROGRAMS/KFDLP/0,,menuPK:461238~pagePK:64156143~piPK:64154155~theSitePK:461198,00.html. Accessed
May 6, 2008.

Note: The World Bank's Human Development Index (HDI) tells us how countries are doing at the basic end of development, measuring average
achievement in three fundamental dimensions of human development: a long and healthy life (measured by life expectancy at birth), knowledge

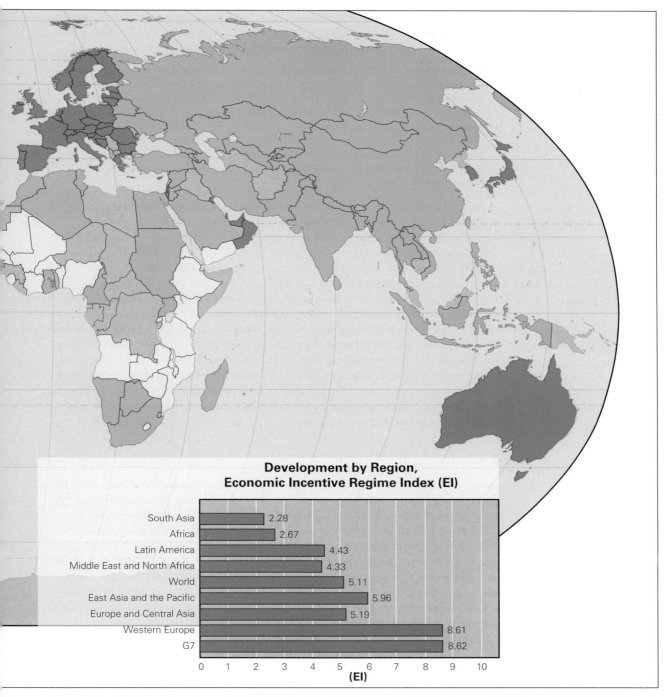

**Development by Region,
Economic Incentive Regime Index (EI)**

Region	EI
South Asia	2.28
Africa	2.67
Latin America	4.43
Middle East and North Africa	4.33
World	5.11
East Asia and the Pacific	5.96
Europe and Central Asia	5.19
Western Europe	8.61
G7	8.62

(EI)

(measured by adult literacy rate and gross school enrollment ratio), and a decent standard of living (measured by GDP per capita [PPP U.S.]). These values are shown in the map. Not all countries were included in the World Bank's sample; those countries excluded are indicated in gray.

   The inset bar graphs show two different development indicators. The World Bank's Knowledge Index (KI) measures a region's ability to generate, adopt, and diffuse knowledge. This is an indication of overall potential of knowledge development (innovation, etc.) in a given region. Thus, it tells us how a region is doing at the high end of development. A region's economic incentive regime index (EI) is a kind of policy variable showing its economic incentive structure or its policy regime. Thus, we get a glimpse of how that area might do in terms of development in the future.

Sankoh, supported by then leader of neighboring Liberia, Charles Taylor, set new standards for butchery. Listen to one description of the horror of this conflict, which eventually claimed an estimated 75,000 lives and displaced another 4.5 million people:

> The RUF often gave their victims a choice. Farmers could either rape their own daughters or have both hands cut off. Young girls could either have their fathers shot or their mothers and sisters burned alive. The mass butchery . . . is most startling because children perpetuated most of it. High on cocaine, children as young as six wielded machetes, following orders to chop off fingers, hands, arms, legs, and ears. In the January 1999 invasion of Freetown—known as Operation No Living Thing among the RUF—the rebels first killed all the patients in the hospitals to make room for their own injured. They then slaughtered an estimated six thousand civilians, raped thousands of women, and hacked off the limbs of thousands more.[8]

In central Africa, a civil war in the Congo eventually drew in Rwanda and Uganda in the eastern part of the country and Angola and Namibia in the southern part. The war claimed 3 million lives over five years and continues to simmer on the eastern border, where Rwanda intervenes periodically to attack Rwandan rebel sanctuaries and loot the rich mineral resources in the region. In east Africa, Rwanda and Burundi fought wars that culminated in the genocide of the Tutsi tribe in 1994; a Muslim-dominated government in Sudan remains locked in conflicts with Christian rebels in the south and non-Arab rebels in Darfur in the west; and the Ugandan government battles rebels in the border area with Sudan led by a self-proclaimed messiah, Joseph Kony, and his Lord's Resistance Army (LRA). Next door to Darfur, Chad has been destabilized. The war in southern Sudan has cost some 2 million lives and displaced 4 million more people over the past twenty years. In west Africa, Côte d'Ivoire erupted in civil war. Charles Taylor, from his exile in Nigeria, threatened to return to Liberia, but Nigeria and international authorities cooperated to seize him and send him off to stand trial for crimes against humanity.

Political Reforms

Unlike Latin America, SSA experienced no waves of democracy and then reversals. There was simply no democracy to speak of. Before 1990, only five countries had ever held free elections with competing parties—Botswana, Gambia, Mauritius, Senegal, and Zimbabwe; and in only one, Mauritius, did free elections result in a peaceful transition of power from the governing to the opposing party. The norm after independence in the 1950s and 1960s was not democracy but one-party rule under strong men, such as Kwame Nkrumah in Ghana, Mobutu Sese Seko in Zaire (now DR Congo), Jomo Kenyatta in Kenya, Felix Houphouet-Boigny in Côte d'Ivoire, and Julius Nyerere in Tanzania. These leaders manipulated ethnic loyalties much the way colonial powers had and maintained stability by brute force. In the process, they became fabulously rich and used state resources to build vast networks of clients. In most cases, their particular ethnic group dominated, but they also built alliances across ethnic groups by lavishing cash awards and other benefits on cooperative groups. Governments were rife with corruption, and ethnic divisions seethed beneath the surface. The United States and Soviet Union, as part of their Cold War rivalry, lavished foreign aid on client states and reinforced corrupt and authoritarian rule.

The end of the Cold War brought the first real outbreak of democracy in Africa. From 1989 to 1997, forty-four of the forty-eight SSA countries held competitive elections—the exceptions being Nigeria, Somalia, Swaziland, and DR Congo. As you might

Spotlight on
domestic governance

imagine, many of the elections left much to be desired, given the weakness of political institutions and civil society, such as a free press and independent courts. Of some fifty-four elections between 1990 and 1994, only thirty were considered free and fair by international election standards. Nevertheless, eleven involved a peaceful transfer of power from an incumbent to an opposing party, something only Mauritius had achieved prior to 1990. The most important peaceful transfer took place in South Africa, the wealthiest and most controversial African country, at least during its apartheid days. This transition was remarkable and stands as a testament to the way democracy begins even in the most difficult racial or ethnic circumstances. Other peaceful transitions took place in Benin, Burundi, Cape Verde, the Central African Republic, Congo, Madagascar, Malawi, Niger, São Tomé and Príncipe, and Zambia. Three other countries—Lesotho, Mali, and Namibia—installed new governments through elections but no incumbents chose to run.

Elections in fifteen additional countries from 1994 to 1997 were disappointing. None met international standards. Eleven were boycotted by the opposition and only one, in Sierra Leone, involved a peaceful transfer to an opposing party, although no incumbent ran. In most cases, ruling military leaders ran as civilians, which testified to the growing need to legitimate power by at least nominally going to the people. But subsequent military coups in Burundi, Sierra Leone, DR Congo, Gambia, and Niger reversed election results before second elections could be held. Sierra Leone and DR Congo descended into civil war, as we have noted, and fragile governments exist in these countries today under precarious cease-fire arrangements monitored by UN peacekeeping forces.

Second elections in seventeen new democracies from 1995 to 1997 also yielded disappointing results. In only two countries did power change hands—in Madagascar and Benin—and, in Zambia and Mali, incumbents rigged the elections. Kenya remained under one-party rule until the early 2000s when fragmented opposition groups, mostly based on ethnic ties, came together to unseat the long-reigning Kenya African National Union (KANU) party of Kenyatta and his successor, Daniel arap Moi. Ghana and Senegal followed similar courses to end one-party rule. Uganda remains under one-party rule, although its leader, Yoweri Museveni, is considered by some observers to be progressive.

Since the turn of the millennium, Africa's democratic fortunes remain troubled. Nigeria, the continent's most populous country, held elections in 1999, 2003, and 2007, but each was "less fair, less efficient and less credible" than the one before.[9] Kenya defeated a referendum in 2005 to expand the powers of the long-ruling government, but disputed elections in 2007 left the country in turmoil under a fragile power-sharing arrangement worked out by Kofi Annan, the former UN secretary-general. Museveni in Uganda overturned constitutional restrictions to stay in power, as did governments in Ethiopia, Eritrea, Cameroon, and Rwanda. Some countries such as Ghana, Sierra Leone, and Liberia made progress in recent years, but, as one student of democracy in Africa reports, "the political struggle in Africa remains very much a conflict between the rule of law and the rule of a person."[10]

Perhaps the most egregious example of bad government in Africa is Zimbabwe. A former British colony—once known as Rhodesia—it inherited a thriving agricultural economy when it became independent. The largely white landowner community stayed on. For a time, Zimbabwe's future looked at least hopeful, but today the country is desperate. The strong man leading the country, Robert G. Mugabe, systematically routed the white landowners out of the countryside and indeed the country, redis-

A man buys groceries in Zimbabwe in March 2008 with an armload of Zimbabwe dollars, 25 million of which equal one U.S. dollar, reflecting the chaos of the economy under the presidency of tyrant Robert Mugabe.

Spotlight on perspectives

tributed the land to squatters, and ruined a thriving commercial agricultural sector. Lack of exports and hence foreign currency sent the exchange rate plunging—from a ratio of 55 Zimbabwe dollars per U.S. dollar in 1999 to a ratio of 150,000 per U.S. dollar in 2005—encouraging inflation and capital flight. By 2008, Zimbabwe had the world's highest official rate of inflation at 100,500 percent per year.[11] Almost everything is in short supply. In 2006, Mugabe, whose staple political trick is to find someone else to blame for Zimbabwe's troubles—mostly former colonialists—turned on street merchants operating in the informal sector, blaming them for the short supplies. Although defeated by opposition groups in early 2008, Mugabe refused to give up power and initiated a campaign of intimidation against the opposition, accusing them of trying to return the country to British colonialists. African neighbors and the international community have criticized Mugabe, but have taken no action to end his reign of ruin.[12] South Africa's leader, Thabo Mbeki, collaborated with Mugabe and even refused to attend a regional conference to pressure Mugabe to step down.

Is democracy the right formula for development under the circumstances that prevail in Africa? It's a fair question because democracy opens up political competition to all groups and, if these groups identify with opposing ethnic backgrounds and have little else in common, competition can easily lead to open conflict. Maybe strong man rule, if it is progressive, is a better approach. Perhaps. But what ensures that it is progressive? It certainly isn't in Zimbabwe. Even if it is, what gives one ethnic group the right to rule over another? As realist perspectives might argue, if it's just a matter of who can use force more brutally, why speak of a country at all? Let the various groups establish their own governments and eventually achieve some kind of a balance of power, as states do internationally. This is basically the situation that prevails today in Somalia among various clans. That might mean, of course, as liberal perspectives warn, many more small African states that are more uneconomical and dysfunctional than the existing ones. So democracy, identity perspectives insist, may offer a better way. Even in primitive form, electoral politics compels diverse groups to take one another into account. Over time, or so the cosmopolitan moral view argues, groups in any culture can find ways to reconcile differences through competitive but peaceful means under the rule of law.

Thus, political stability in Africa remains elusive. It is without doubt one of the major reasons for the lack of economic progress. Nevertheless, stability begins with small steps. And compared to the situation before 1990, SSA on the whole has been moving in the right direction. Political change has created an opening for economic reforms, and some African countries are seizing the opportunity.

Economic Reforms

Since 1980 only five SSA countries have achieved a real per capita growth rate above 2 percent per year: Botswana, Cape Verde, Mauritius, Seychelles, and Swaziland. Notice that, except for Swaziland, these are the same countries that score high on political stability and accountability. Botswana has the best record, comparable to that of some East Asian high performers—8 percent per year GDP growth from 1965 to 1990. But the same party has won every election in Botswana since 1965, and Botswana and the other four countries are extremely small. They hardly qualify as representative of the whole of Africa.

Since the mid-1990s, more countries have exceeded 2 percent per year real (taking out inflation) per capita growth rates. Over the past ten years, some eighteen countries, including Ghana, Mali, Mozambique, Tanzania, and Uganda, grew at average rates of more than 5.5 percent per year, more typical of Asian rather than African countries. But another twenty countries remained trapped in poverty.[13] Oil-producing countries, such as Angola, Cameroon, Chad, DR Congo, Equatorial Guinea, Gabon, and Nigeria, enjoyed the best performance. DR Congo used oil-price increases to boost public investments in electricity consumption and school enrollments. But the narrow focus on oil led to a failure to develop other non-resource-based sectors and left the country exposed to a fall in world oil prices. By 2000, real per capita income in the DR Congo had dropped to $900, from $1,000 in the mid-1980s. Sustained growth requires productivity improvements—that is, improving efficiency or getting more output from the same inputs—and those have been uniquely lacking in SSA.[14]

Nevertheless, macroeconomic policies have improved. Except in Zimbabwe, where it reached 100,000 percent in 2008, inflation in SSA is at historic lows. In 2000–2003, only six countries—Angola, Eritrea, Liberia, Nigeria, Zambia, and Zimbabwe—reported inflation rates over 10 percent a year. Fiscal policies have seen less improvement. The IMF works with countries to improve the transparency of their fiscal spending. In most countries, few people have access to reliable information about the government budget. And much of the data that are available are not reliable. Weak fiscal constraints facilitate both graft and waste. In Nigeria under military rule, it is estimated that some $40 billion was siphoned off from the fiscal budget, much of it leaving the country. Chronic fiscal shortages then increase pressures to print money and weaken monetary control. Few countries in SSA have independent central banks; South Africa is one that has an independent central bank, and its economic performance ranks among the best.

Spotlight on macroeconomic policies

Microeconomic policies in Africa, as in Latin America, constrain growth. The electricity supply is unreliable. Losses from power interruptions average 6–7 percent of sales in Ethiopia and Zambia, and 10 percent or more in Eritrea, Kenya, and Senegal. Because of red tape, starting a company costs over five times more in SSA than in South Asia and thirty times more than in industrialized countries. According to World Bank surveys of the investment climate in various countries, sixteen of the twenty countries with the greatest regulatory obstacles are found in SSA.[15] To transfer a piece of property takes more than a year in Ghana and Rwanda. In Senegal, the costs of transfer equal one-third of the property's value. Courts too are slow and expensive. To enforce a commercial or loan contract, creditors have to take more than thirty steps and pay more than 43 percent of an average person's annual income. Small businesses in the informal sector, which provide in many cases 70 percent of the nonagricultural jobs in SSA countries, are simply squeezed out of the picture.

Spotlight on microeconomic policies

Labor laws in SSA countries are among the strictest in the world. In Burkina Faso, for example, companies have to hire people permanently unless the job is seasonal. If you cannot lay off workers, you do not hire them. The minimum wage in Burkina Faso is also $54 a month. That's 82 percent of the value the worker adds to a product and

microlending

small loans made to individual
farmers and merchants who
would not otherwise have access
to credit.

**Spotlight on
trade and
investment**

**Spotlight on
agricultural
protectionism**

**Spotlight on
Doha Round**

the third highest minimum wage in the world. High mandated wages also discourage employment. Only a few SSA countries have credit bureaus to screen private borrowers. Hence, lending to the private sector is rare outside a few countries such as Mauritius and South Africa. Multilateral institutions and foreign aid try to fill this gap with what is called **microlending.** Such lending involves small loans to individual farmers and merchants, especially women, who would not otherwise have access to credit. Microlending is important, but alone it cannot override numerous other restrictions on businesses.

Trade and investment played a small role in African development through the mid-1990s. SSA countries' share of world trade dropped by two-thirds—from 2.1 percent in 1975 to 0.7 percent in 1995.[16] The small foreign investment that occurred went mostly into resource extraction—mainly oil—and did little to develop other sectors of the economy. Three major obstacles impeded SSA access to world markets. The first was geography; with so many landlocked countries and conflicts, access across national boundaries was prevented. The second was local government policies that discriminated against agriculture in favor of urban priorities. African governments made generous use of marketing boards that monopolized the purchase of agricultural products in the countryside and sold food to the urban population at subsidized prices and on world markets to enhance tax revenues. (Remember the policies of financial repression from Chapter 11?) Farm income suffered badly, precisely in the areas where poverty was most concentrated.

The third and most inexcusable obstacle was the policies of the industrialized countries, which protected their agricultural markets. The United States, Japan, and particularly the European Union, through its Common Agricultural Policy, not only imposed barriers on agricultural imports but also subsidized the domestic production of food products at much higher prices. Farmers in developing countries suffered, but so did consumers in industrial countries, who paid far more for food products than they would have otherwise. To top it all off, the industrialized countries then sold their surpluses of food products, generated by the artificially high domestic prices, on world markets at subsidized prices or gave away food as foreign aid, keeping the world market prices lower than they would have been otherwise. Thus, developing-country marketing boards got less for their exports than they should have. Farmers and governments in developing countries lost, as did consumers in industrial countries and their governments that paid out the high subsidies. The only winners were the already well-off farmers, usually large ones, in the industrialized countries.

This sham may be about to change. In the Uruguay Round in 1994, the international trade community agreed to convert quotas and other NTBs on agricultural trade to tariffs that might then be lowered through trade negotiations. Liberalizing agricultural tariffs is the top agenda item of the new Doha Round that began in 2001 and was still ongoing in early 2008. Resistance from farm communities in the industrialized countries is fierce. Globalization opponents of the WTO and other international institutions rightly criticize the hypocrisy of industrialized countries on farm policy. But many of them also oppose trade liberalization and the Doha Round, which might end this hypocrisy. The World Bank estimates the gains from a successful Doha Round would be more than $250 billion per year by 2015. One-third to two-fifths of these gains would accrue to developing countries and would raise GDP growth in SSA countries alone by 1.3 percent per year. These are gains far in excess of foreign aid to SSA countries, which amounted to around $25 billion in 2007 and, often in the past, added little to sustained growth in low-income countries.

Developing countries have higher trade restrictions on manufactured than agricultural goods. Industrial countries have higher trade restrictions on agricultural than manufactured goods. If they could bargain lower agricultural barriers in industrialized countries for lower industrial barriers in developing countries, a huge opportunity to exploit comparative advantage would emerge. Because trade barriers have been coming down since 1995, developing-country exports are already rising. Even SSA countries have increased their share of world trade from 0.7 percent in 1995 to 0.9 percent in 2003. Once trade flows more freely, foreign investment follows because MNCs often locate abroad, at least initially, to service other foreign, rather than local, markets. With proper governance, a good climate for foreign investment translates into a good environment for domestic investment. Obviously, much work needs to be done on the business climate, as we have noted. But competition among MNCs, many now from developing countries such as Brazil and India, is much greater today than in the era of import substitution. Developing countries have greater bargaining leverage than they did when MNCs were concentrated in a few advanced countries and interested primarily in resource extraction.

Spotlight on comparative advantage

Human Development, Especially for Women

Africa is at the beginning stages of industrial development. As Map 11-1 (see Chapter 11) shows, two-thirds of the people still live and work in the countryside. That's also true in India and China, but there it is changing rapidly. More and more people are moving into cities and industry. By contrast, two-thirds of the people in Latin America already live in cities, although often in squalid slums on the outskirts of big cities. Thus, while human deprivation exists in all poor countries, Africa deals with it at its rural roots. The biggest problems are disease and health more generally and discrimination against women, especially in education.

In 2007, 33 million people lived with AIDS, roughly half of them women (adjusted down from an earlier estimate of 39 million),[17] and 2.1 million died (some 25 million total have died since the outbreak of the disease). An additional 2.5 million became infected in the same year. Children accounted for 2.5 million of the infected, and some 12 million children have been orphaned by the disease. Two-thirds of all these cases exist in the SSA countries. One in every fourteen adults in Africa is affected by AIDS, one in three in South Africa. In nine SSA countries, life expectancy has dipped below forty years of age due to AIDS.[18]

There are numerous obstacles to dealing effectively with AIDS, but three stand out. The first is catching the disease early in high-risk populations, such as sex workers and intravenous drug users, before it spreads, often by roving militia, to the broader community. A few countries in SSA, such as Senegal, have done well in this regard. Others, such as South Africa, have not done as well. For a time South Africa's president, Thabo Mbeki, refused to acknowledge the disease, and precious time was lost. Once the disease has spread, the main defense is education involving forthright national leadership, widespread public awareness campaigns, and intensive prevention programs, including advocating the use of condoms and abstinence. Uganda has had notable success in this regard, reducing HIV among pregnant women from 13 to 5 percent of the pregnant population. Botswana, Ethiopia, and Kenya have also stabilized the spread of the disease in urban areas. By contrast, outside SSA, India, China, and Russia are doing less well in confronting the disease.

Spotlight on microeconomic policies (health)

Spotlight on
pharmaceutical MNCs

The third obstacle is treating existing HIV/AIDS cases. For this, expensive anti-retroviral drugs are needed. Here, the global pharmaceutical companies come in for heavy criticism. Some of this criticism is justified; some is not. These companies do an enormous amount of research, which is very expensive. They generally develop new drugs for advanced markets and introduce them in developing markets only after the drugs have been tested and approved for use and sale in advanced countries. They seek to recoup their large and growing research expenses by demanding patent protection, which delays competition and results in high prices for medicines. Indeed, if they could not charge high prices for a time to recoup investment costs, they would stop the research altogether—then there would be no new drugs, unless governments and NGOs picked up the research, manufacturing, and marketing costs. Companies survive on profits, meaning they finance their operations by retaining earnings in the form of profits or by borrowing funds, which they have to repay with future earnings. So it is probably unjustified to criticize their need for profits, unless we are opposed to profit-making organizations altogether.

Spotlight on
NGOs

Where the companies go too far is exploiting monopoly circumstances when they face no counterbalancing forces. If they own a patent, of course, they face no direct competition, although other companies always produce similar products. So, it seems appropriate that governments and NGOs exercise some scrutiny over company operations and assist them if they wish companies to move faster toward the production of cheaper generic drugs or offering their drugs at discounted prices. Partnerships are emerging in this area. Government commitments to fight AIDS have gone up from $400 million in the late 1990s to an estimated $6 billion in 2005. Some 3 million people received drug treatments in 2007. Even more important, new donors have joined the fight. The Global Fund to Fight AIDS, Tuberculosis and Malaria assists countries throughout the developing world. The Global Alliance for Vaccines and Immunizations, created and funded by billionaire Bill Gates, supports the search for an AIDS vaccine, as well as vaccines for other killers such as malaria. The Global Alliance is also encouraging major pharmaceutical companies, such as Wyeth, GlaxoSmithKline, and Merck, to develop drugs specifically for developing-country diseases, breaking the pattern of developing drugs first for developed and then for developing markets. By December 2004, the Global Alliance had disbursed over $500 million for vaccines, and one of its top priorities was a vaccine for rotavirus that causes severe diarrhea and kills 500,000 children every year in poor countries.[19]

Water sanitation and broader health services remain critical deficiencies in SSA countries. Bad water and poor sanitation are responsible for 90 percent of the diarrheal diseases and as much as 8 percent of all diseases burdening poor countries. Ghana, Senegal, South Africa, and Uganda have improved clean water supplies and sanitation services. A key problem is developing sanitation services that can be sustained. They have to be paid for by taxes or user fees. Experiments in Senegal, and also India, have demonstrated that on-site sanitation facilities run by local communities and financed by user fees do more to improve sanitation facilities on a sustained basis than municipal-run toilets that rapidly deteriorate and cannot be maintained.

Spotlight on
women's rights

Education is another major deficiency, particularly for women. In SSA countries, enrollment of girls in primary level schools is still less than 90 percent that of boys, and the completion rate for girls is 15 percent below that for boys. Girls and women endure inequalities in families, tribes, and villages that stem from centuries-old traditions and superstitions. In some countries, girls are subjected to the painful and often life-threatening mutilation of female organs, and village women in Malawi, Zambia, and Kenya submit to a ritual when their husband dies that requires them to sleep with one of their husband's relatives to break the bond with their dead husband's spirit. Conflicts in Africa often involve widespread rape and humiliation of women. Many of these practices contribute directly to the spread of AIDS.

The biggest constraint in dealing with many of these health and educational problems is insufficient and inadequately trained teachers and health-care providers. Money can help this problem but not quickly. Many of the practices that discriminate against education for all, especially women, would have to be changed to create a larger pool of people who might then be trained for such services. And often training is not relevant to the conditions in the countryside. Physicians still serve predominantly urban areas. In Ghana, for example, 66 percent of the people live in rural areas, but only 15 percent of the physicians practice there. The loss of trained people is another serious problem. Of 489 students who graduated from Ghana Medical School in 1986–1995, 61 percent left the country, one-half going to Great Britain and over one-third to the United States.

Despite the obstacles, some African countries have made notable progress as of 2008. Ghana, Mozambique, Tanzania, and Uganda accelerated growth and reduced poverty; Malawi achieved particular success in boosting agricultural productivity; Ghana, Kenya, Tanzania, and Uganda increased primary school enrollment; Niger, Togo, and Zambia made progress in combating malaria; Senegal and Uganda increased access to water and sanitation; Niger promoted reforestation; and Rwanda achieved an impressive recovery from conflict.[20]

Spotlight on emigration

Foreign Aid

Our discussion of development in SSA countries clearly suggests that foreign aid can help local development. Just consider the successful effort that effectively eradicated smallpox in the world or the revolution in agricultural technology, called the Green Revolution, which developed all sorts of new varieties of seeds, pesticides, and fertilizers that greatly increased the yield and efficiency of third-world agriculture. However, the discussion also makes clear that these improvements will benefit only a very few, or perhaps no one at all, if local leadership and policies are not up to the task of delivering these advances to the people.

Official development assistance (ODA), or aid from governments, is rising. In real terms, aid to SSA countries was higher in 2007 than it was in 1990 and represented a higher percentage of total worldwide aid (about one-third). Most of this aid is in grants that do not have to be paid back, while the multilateral development banks provide highly **concessional loans,** or loans at subsidized interest rates. Some donors, such as the United States, want the banks to switch to grant aid only, but the banks fear that this step may deplete their resources and that they may not get timely and adequate replenishments. The United States provides the major share of aid to SSA (20 percent). The International Development Association (the so-called soft or concessional loan window of the World Bank) is the next largest provider of aid, followed by France and the European Union.

The IMF has assistance programs in eighteen SSA countries, and twenty-two of the twenty-seven countries involved in the IMF's Heavily Indebted Poor Countries (HIPC) Initiative at the end of 2004 were in SSA. **Debt relief** involves rescheduling loans and stretching them out over longer periods of time or forgiving loans altogether. It is probably best applied to the poorest countries that do not yet depend

official development assistance (ODA)
aid from advanced governments to developing nations.

concessional loans
loans made to developing nations at subsidized interest rates.

debt relief
the rescheduling of loans to developing nations to stretch the loans over longer periods of time or forgiving the loans altogether.

on private bank financing. Once countries start borrowing from private banks, debt relief can be just as harmful as it is helpful because private banks are reluctant to lend to countries that have previously defaulted; Argentina, which defaulted on its private debt, is having difficulty obtaining future bank loans. Moreover, relieving the debts of even the poorest countries requires care because doing so when corruption is high and local leadership is lacking only encourages more fraud and waste.

The Millennium initiative estimates that SSA countries will need another $75 billion to $100 billion of total aid per year to meet the projected Millennium Development Goals in 2015. That is four times the current level of official aid and, realistically, is not likely to be reached. It is roughly the amount that developing countries could gain by that date from trade if the Doha Round succeeds. Still, we could make the case that the time for aid has never been better. Whereas before 1990 aid was provided largely without a willingness on the part of the donor or recipient communities to consider seriously the quality of domestic policies, today the global community is focused on domestic policies. Development success in Asia and elsewhere has made it unmistakably clear that countries cannot succeed unless they have a local leadership that is committed to clean and fair government, growth through sound economic policies, a better investment climate for both domestic and foreign entrepreneurs, and poverty reduction that gives all groups a stake in national prosperity.

In the end, therefore, everything still depends on how well resources are used, and that depends in turn on the quality of local institutions and policies. The Millennium initiative recognizes this fact by advocating local ownership of development strategies and asking donors to coordinate their external efforts better to support these strategies financially. We'll have to see if this approach keeps the development community on the right track. It is hard to argue that in recent years the development community has not moved in the right direction. As Map 12-2 on page 418 suggests, while many SSA countries remain in the lowest range of human development indicators, some, such as Ghana and Uganda, have moved into the middle range. Now the task is to sustain that direction even if all the goals laid out by the Millennium initiative are not met immediately or fully. (See Table 12-1 for a summary of SSA development factors.)

The Middle East and North Africa

MENA is a paradox. On the one hand, the region is very rich in resources, young people, and aid. Oil flows abundantly in many, although not all, the countries. The workforce is highly educated, compared, for example, to the population in SSA. And countries such as Egypt and Jordan receive large amounts of aid because of the Arab-Israeli conflict. On the other hand, the region is very poor in jobs, skilled manufacturing and service industries, trade, foreign investment, and technology. Compared to other developing countries, the manufacturing sector is small, about half the size of other lower-middle-income countries; and the share of non-oil merchandise exports in GDP is only 6 percent on average, compared to 20 percent for East Asia and the Pacific. In a sense, the entire region suffers from what we call in Chapter 10 a resource curse—the abundance of oil diverts attention away from non-oil investments, contributes to an overvalued exchange rate, and discourages the development of non-oil investments and exports.

The region also constitutes a strategic piece of real estate and has been convulsed in invasions and conflicts for millennia. As we have learned in Chapter 2, the Philistines and Greeks, Sparta and Athens, Rome and Carthage, Israelites and Babylonians, Catholic and Orthodox Christians, Christians and Muslims, and European colonialists and the Ottoman Empire have fought over this land for centuries. The Middle East was Europe's gateway to China and India (the latter through the Suez Canal), Russia's outlet to the Mediterranean, and Asia's destination on the old trading route known as the Silk Road. More recently, the region was a hot spot in the Cold War between the United States and the Soviet Union, and today it is a seedbed of division and terrorism—torn between Arabs and Israelis, Arabs and Persians (Iran), secular and sectarian governments, and government elites of one branch of Islam and mass publics or minority groups of a dissident branch.

On top of it all, since the 1920s, the area has been the richest source of oil and natural gas deposits in the world. The Gulf countries—Iraq, Iran, Saudi Arabia, Kuwait, Bahrain, Qatar, United Arab Emirates (UAE), and Oman—are the oil titans of the region. The Levant countries—Israel, Jordan, Syria, and Lebanon—and the Palestinian Authority (still a nonstate entity until a final Arab-Israeli settlement) have no oil. Their borders and development fortunes center inextricably around Israel, the only modernized state in the region. Of the remaining countries—Morocco, Algeria, Tunisia, Libya, Egypt, Yemen, Djibouti, and Turkey—a few (Libya and Algeria) have oil, but most rely on exports of agricultural and light manufacturing products to Europe. Apart from Israel, Turkey is the most advanced country, with a population of 65 million, about the same as Egypt and Iran, but a per capita income twice that of Egypt and 15 percent higher than that of Iran. Map 12-1 shows the geographic layout of the region; Map 12-2 shows the economic development.

Except for its strategic location and resources, MENA would probably not be considered a separate region, certainly not on a scale with SSA, Latin America, or Asia. It contains only 5 percent of the world's population and accounts for 2 percent of the world's income. And in terms of development, as we note earlier in this chapter, it ranks at the bottom with SSA and South Asia. From 1980 to the early 2000s, per capita income grew annually at a slower rate (0.9 percent) than that of SSA.[21] Since 2000 and the explosion of oil prices, the region has done better, with output growing at over 5 percent per year.[22] Per capita income increased to 4.2 percent in 2006, still only 75 percent of the rate attained by other developing regions.[23] But inflation is rising rapidly, and some of the region's major economies, such as Egypt and Saudi Arabia, are fragile. The exception, of course, is Israel, but its economy too suffers from heavy defense expenditures and the political uncertainties of the region. The geopolitical significance of the region attracts global attention, both for good and bad. Constant turmoil and intervention breeds cautious and defensive governments in the region. They lack confidence to alter the status quo, fear foreign trade and investment, and seem paralyzed by the enormous pressures building up in labor markets, where a growing pool of unemployed people who are young and better educated clamor for economic opportunities and political participation.

If development takes place, it will require three ingredients: domestic political reforms and regional peace settlements, an opening up of MENA markets to greater foreign trade and investment, and a more egalitarian and tolerant social order that resolves the religious issues constraining modernization and women's participation in society. Let's look more closely at each of these three areas.

Spotlight on
military intervention

Political Reforms and Regional Peace Settlements

For decades, Cold War rivalries and the Arab-Israeli conflict focused attention on diplomatic and alliance arrangements in the region and neglected, comparatively, domestic reforms. Political settlements and security were considered to be a prerequisite for MENA economic development, as the realist perspective might predict. In the 1990s, however, attitudes shifted in line with the broader change in development thinking, giving more importance to domestic policies. Peace existed between Egypt and Israel after 1979, and it might be expected from liberal perspectives that economic interdependence would follow. But in fact little economic cooperation occurred. Instead, as the peace process accelerated in the early 1990s under the Oslo Accords, economic development seemed to go in the opposite direction. Oil prices declined in the 1990s, cutting into public revenues, and countries in the region had few alternative private-sector activities to fall back on. Clearly something else was holding back development besides the political turbulence of the region (realist) and economic volatility of oil (liberal).

That something else was poor domestic governance (identity). World Bank studies documented that "when compared with countries that have similar income and characteristics . . . , the MENA region ranks at the bottom on the index of overall governance quality." [24] MENA countries have a lower quality of administration in the public sector than would be expected from their incomes, and they measure particularly low on the index of public accountability, which assesses the openness of political institutions and participation, respect for civil liberties, transparency of government, and freedom of the press. By available measures, no government except Israel reaches even the middle of the scale of democratic features. All the others are lumped together at the authoritarian end of the spectrum. Eleven of these regimes are autocratic republics; and nine are monarchies ruled by kings or emirs. All feature strong executives, corrupt public administrations, nonexistent (Qatar, UAE, and Saudi Arabia) or very weak parliaments (the strongest ones are in Morocco and Bahrain), fragile and in some cases politically dependent courts, and a civil society that is underdeveloped and largely disenfranchised by lack of political and media competition. The result is a development process heavily dependent on inbred political elites, unresponsive to domestic and international markets, and yoked to the price and volatility of oil, as well as worker remittances from abroad and foreign aid. When oil prices soared from 1970 to 1985, the region grew, albeit very wastefully. When oil prices tanked between 1985 and 2000, growth shriveled. Today, higher oil prices again offer hope, and some reforms are under way. But without a fundamental restructuring of domestic institutions, the MENA region is stuck in a poor governance trap.

MENA countries suffer from arbitrary policy making, corrupt administration, and poor public services. The transparency of government is minimal. In some countries, detailed budget information is not available at all, and in most, the absence of a free press means that the numbers are discussed only inside the government. Tax assessments are ambiguous, and tax collectors, unchecked by parliamentary or civil society groups, exercise virtually unlimited powers.

Corruption is endemic at all levels. Bureaucrats can help you find your land title but then explain that this will take a lot of time and unfortunately they will not be compensated for the extra work, a hint that they expect a tip.[25] Nepotism is also widespread. Public officials dole out jobs and other government favors to ethnic and tribal relations. Favoritism in contracts and tax evasion are highest in Saudi Arabia, Lebanon, Jordan, Egypt, and Tunisia.[26]

Poor governance means that public services are often deficient. Phones, roads, and power facilities are lacking. MENA countries tend to do pretty well in providing access to water and sanitation services—90 percent of urban and 71 percent of rural areas have safe water, and 96 and 73 percent, respectively, have improved sanitation facilities. But electric power is in short supply and often interrupted. Each year, according to World Bank estimates, MENA countries lose 13 percent of national output due to power losses. Electric power is unavailable for as much as three months out of the year in some countries, for example, Algeria, Morocco, and Yemen. Telephone service has improved. MENA countries now have twice as many phone lines as in 1980. But the ratio of unsuccessful phone connections is still extraordinarily high—35 percent in Tunisia, 50 percent in Lebanon, 57 percent in Morocco, and 60 percent in Jordan. The region is way behind Asia in the deployment of mobile phones.

Opening Trade and Investment Markets

Economic policies are often another casualty of poor governance. They are shaped to extract rents from state-owned resources and government-awarded licenses. Political leaders and bureaucrats channel resources to state-owned enterprises and political clients in the private sector. They set exchange rate, trade, and investment policies to protect these groups. A system of entrenched interests develops and prevents any flexibility. The economy rides up and down on the exogenous fluctuation of oil prices. Social programs appease a disenfranchised civil society but create growing financial burdens and debt, especially when oil or export prices decline. The economy never diversifies, and the MENA countries develop an increasingly educated workforce that finds few jobs or opportunities. Skilled labor leaves the country for Europe or the United States or works in wealthier Gulf oil states and sends back remittances to sustain family members. Foreign aid fills the financing gap rather than stimulating self-sustaining investments and jobs.

Spotlight on monopoly rents

Over the past three decades, virtually all the MENA countries followed either de facto or formal fixed exchange rate regimes. Their exchange rates, determined by the reliance on resource exports, were significantly overvalued—by 30 percent in the early decades and by more than 20 percent in the last decade. Oil and resource exports are less sensitive to overvalued exchange rates because they are priced globally and do not face immediate substitutes. But manufactured exports are highly sensitive. If the exchange rate is overvalued by 25 percent, manufactured exports cost 25 percent more than they should. The result, in the case of MENA countries, is a loss of export competitiveness. The ratio of manufactured exports to GDP fell by 18 percent per year. Manufactured exports averaged 4.4 percent of GDP during the previous three decades; they would have averaged 5.2 percent without the overvaluation.[27] This is an enormous albatross around the neck of economies that need to diversify from resource-based to more highly skilled manufacturing and service industries. Why do countries follow such policies? Again, their focus is on resource exports, not manufactured exports. Few domestic interests benefit from exporting manufactured goods; many, especially the state, benefit from exporting oil. An overvalued exchange rate also contains inflation by making imports cheaper and offsetting high import tariffs and restrictions. And MENA countries maintain very high restrictions on imports. Indeed, in order to retain this advantage of an overvalued exchange rate, Kuwait switched in 2007 to an exchange

Spotlight on exchange rates

Spotlight on

trade

Spotlight on

microeconomic
policies

Spotlight on

foreign direct
investment

Spotlight on

immigration

rate pegged to a basket of currencies rather than to the dollar; the dollar's decline was dragging the Kuwaiti currency down with it.

Trade protection in MENA countries is higher than in any other developing region besides Latin America—the poster child of import substitution policies. Thus, it is very profitable to produce manufactured goods for the domestic market but not for export. If a manufacturer gets a license from the government, which favors its supporters, he (not many women own businesses) can charge very high prices for domestic products without having to worry about competition from imports. Consumers bear the cost. They buy inferior goods at higher prices. There are no Wal-Marts or dollar stores. Those in power have no incentive to change the system, and those out of power have no influence to change it.

Without competition, the business environment is abysmal. In Egypt, it takes seventeen procedures and 202 days to register a business, even after you get the license. In Jordan, it takes three months. In Lebanon, it takes 721 days to enforce a contract through the court system, in Syria 596 days, in UAE 559 days, and in Algeria 387 days.[28] For the average business, it costs 62 percent of the average person's annual income to register and enforce a business contract. Is it any wonder that many business people don't bother or just pay off a public servant to avoid the courts?

The domestic business environment is also the environment for FDI. In 2000, FDI accounted for only 5 percent of gross capital formation in the MENA countries, compared to 26 percent in Singapore. Again, despite peace between Israel and Egypt for more than twenty-five years and enormous sums of foreign aid given to these countries, no significant trade and investment take place between them. Obviously, peace is necessary to ignite widespread development in the region, but this alone is not enough. Domestic policy reforms are also necessary.

And some reforms are under way. Tunisia and Morocco started trade reforms in the 1980s, including export-processing zones for light manufacturing such as textiles and garments. Jordan cleaned up its fiscal mess and signed a trade agreement with the EU in 1997 and with the United States in 2002. Lebanon ran up huge reconstruction deficits after the civil war ended in 1990, but is now reforming (albeit in the face of renewed violence from Hezbollah). Algeria, Iran, Yemen, and Syria reformed later and more sporadically. The six Gulf Cooperation Council (GCC) countries—the oil titans of Saudi Arabia, UAE, Qatar, Bahrain, Kuwait, and Oman—are the most integrated into the world economy, having developed sophisticated financial systems to manage their investments around the world. They also encourage large inflows of skilled and unskilled workers to service the domestic economy. But the largest one, Saudi Arabia, is still poorly diversified, using its oil revenues to protect a large, inefficient, domestic non-oil sector that is largely publicly owned. Although Saudi Arabia finally joined the WTO in 2005, it faces the need for continuing reforms to liberalize trade, privatize state companies, and increase FDI.

Empowering Women in Society

MENA countries have made major improvements in social services, from access to safe water and sanitation to primary and secondary school education to significantly reduced rates of infant mortality. Women have benefited from many of these services, but they remain far behind the standards prevailing in other countries, with the exception perhaps of those in SSA. Saudi Arabia is the only country in the world that denies women the right to drive.[29]

Four factors impede the full entry of women into MENA development and politics. First, the family rather than the individual constitutes the main unit of society. The centrality of the family is considered a cultural asset and implies that women will marry early and devote themselves to children and household affairs. Second, the man is still seen as the sole breadwinner, and the idea of a two-income household is unwelcome. Third, a modesty code shields the reputation of women, on which family honor rests, and restricts the opportunities for women to enter the workplace and other public spaces. And fourth, family religious laws dictate a radically unequal balance of power between men and women in the family. These cultural and religious factors, more than legal factors, limit employment possibilities.

Spotlight on
women's rights

Women are becoming better educated. The average number of years of schooling for women increased from 0.5 in 1960 to 4.5 in 1999. The literacy rate among women went up from 16.6 percent in 1970 to 52.5 percent in 2000. Female gross enrollment in schools generally is now 90 percent that of male gross enrollment, up from 75 percent in 1980. Women make up 49 percent of the population, but they make up 63 percent of university students.[30]

The difficulty is that women are being better educated but not more widely employed. Females make up only 28 percent of the workforce in MENA countries. That's up by 50 percent since 1960 but still well below what we would expect from the education levels, fertility levels, and age structure of women. If employment reached those levels, household earnings would increase by 25 percent. As the World Bank notes, "these increased earnings are the ticket to the middle class." [31] Because women and many young people (men and women) are unemployed, one working person supports more than two other people, the highest ratio in the world and slightly above that for SSA.

Female Muslim students study at Da'wi College in the Gaza Strip, but they will likely struggle to find jobs after graduation in the impoverished Palestinian economy.

Six of ten people in the region are under twenty-five years of age. This is the time bomb awaiting MENA governments—young people, including women, are being better educated and prepared to contribute to society, but the countries' and region's economies cannot employ them. Interestingly, the resource-poor countries, such as Egypt and Lebanon, do slightly better at employing women than resource-rich ones, such as Algeria and Iran. The reason for this, aside from gender discrimination, is that the focus on resources distorts incentives to favor capital-intensive rather than labor-intensive activities where more women workers might benefit.

Women are also underrepresented in the political system. Only 6 percent of parliamentarians in MENA legislatures are women, compared to 14–15 percent in SSA and Asia. In local governments, only 14 percent of representatives are women, the second lowest percentage in the world. Times are changing but slowly. In 2002, Bahrain set aside 5 of the 30 seats in its Shura council for women. Jordan has 6 of its 110 seats in parliament reserved for women. And in Morocco in 2002, 35 women entered the parliament after political parties agreed on a 10 percent quota. (See Table 12-1 for a summary of MENA development factors.)

Summary

In this chapter, we have looked at the two poorest regions of the world—sub-Saharan Africa and the Middle East and North Africa. We have considered the factors that influenced their history and development. Both regions suffered from historical oppression. SSA was thoroughly colonized, except for Liberia and Ethiopia, as was MENA, except for Saudi Arabia. After colonization, it might be argued MENA endured too much external attention and intervention, while SSA received too little.

But MENA also had an enormous advantage—oil. Or was it a curse? Oil squeezed out manufacturing and service development. MENA remains in a time warp, dependent on resource prices, worker remittances, and foreign aid. It educates a growing young population, including more women, but offers them few professional jobs or opportunities.

SSA focused on state-building. Strong men fostered patronage and one-party rule amid massive ethnic diversity. The economies depended on resource extraction, including diamonds, copper, and oil, and foreign aid; little industrial trade or investment took place. MNCs dominated resource development and drug distribution. Ethnic divisions ignited civil wars, exacerbated by superpower rivalries during the Cold War and indigenous elites after the Cold War. In the past decade, however, SSA has taken a new turn. More governments welcome trade and investment and demand that advanced countries open their agricultural and textile markets. Better governance is yielding higher growth, but success is still partial and tentative. SSA is the continuing test for local and world leadership to address extreme poverty.

Key Concepts

concessional loans 427   neocolonialism 416

debt relief 427   official development

microlending 424   assistance (ODA) 427

Study Questions

1. In what ways are sub-Saharan Africa (SSA) and the Middle East and North Africa (MENA) distinguished from Asia and Latin America?

2. How do the three perspectives view development in SSA and MENA? Which perspective emphasizes the culture of poverty, poor governance, and natural resources? Explain.

3. What are the advantages and disadvantages of abundant resources and foreign aid?

4. What are the obstacles to the empowerment of women in SSA and MENA? Are they the same in each region?

5. Why have trade and foreign investment played such a small role in SSA countries and, at least in manufacturing and service sectors, in MENA countries? How do exchange rates, the local business environment, and macroeconomic policies affect trade and foreign investment?

13

Global Inequality, Imperialism, and Injustice

A Critical Theory Perspective

An indigenous Indian family scrapes out an existence in the Chiapas region of Mexico.

W e began this section of the book with the observation that, while world history based on recorded sources is about 5,000 years old, the world economy by contrast is only about 500 years old. Let's circle back to the question that this fact begs: What happened around 1500 that suddenly drove the world together and produced modern-day globalization?

Mainstream Perspectives

As we observe in Chapter 8, the mainstream perspectives on international relations have some answers. The identity perspective attributes the rapid development of Europe relative to the rest of the world largely to Renaissance, Reformation, and Enlightenment ideas that inspired the Protestant ethic of scientific, technological, and commercial achievement. As Max Weber, the well-known German sociologist, points out, prior to the Reformation, the activity of invention and making money was not looked on as a worthy calling in Europe or anywhere else in the world.[1] Protestantism made it acceptable. Not surprisingly, from this perspective, Protestant—not Catholic, Muslim, or Confucian—countries led the process of modernization. Britain launched the industrial revolution, and the United States, its offspring, later pioneered the information revolution.

The realist perspective attributes Europe's ascendance primarily to demography, geography, and the decentralized distribution of power. Europe's population dipped in the tenth and eleventh centuries as a result of the Viking and other invasions and dipped again in the fourteenth century as a result of the Black Plague. But thereafter Europe's population grew vigorously. It fanned out to find more space to grow grain and raise animals. China's agriculture, by contrast, was based on rice and required less space. Thus, China had less motive to expand. According to Pulitzer Prize–winning author Jared Diamond, Europe had a number of environmental advantages over other continents: larger choice of wild plants and animals available for domestication, which enhanced food production and released people to pursue the kinds of specialty crafts that help develop technology; denser population more conducive to the development of resistance to virulent germs; and orientation of its continental axes predominately from east to west rather than north to south, which accelerated the spread of food production and other technologies.[2] Another favorable factor, emphasized by Paul Kennedy, was the decentralized competition for "ships and fire power."[3] When Columbus sought resources to sail around the world, he was turned down by one monarch after the other. After many years, the Spanish monarchs, Ferdinand and Isabella, finally supported him. By contrast, when a Chinese explorer, Wang Chin, applied in 1479 to explore the Indochinese kingdom of Annam (now Vietnam), he was turned down by the Chinese emperor and had no other monarch to go to. Separate powers—the pope and holy Roman emperor, initially, and later multiple states—always struggled to control Europe. Rivalry among the many European monarchs and states spurred progress and enabled Europe to colonize and exploit more centralized, less dynamic empires in other parts of the world.[4]

Spotlight on anarchy and competition

The liberal perspective traces western success to technology, specialization, and institutional innovations, such as the modern factory, markets, and domestic and international bureaucracy. Technology was an exogenous factor that multiplied the output of human and animal labor. Its impact, although initially disruptive, was generally progressive over the longer run. As we discuss in Chapter 10, specialization, or the division of labor in which two parties specialize to make common or different products, offered unique advantages. From a liberal perspective, which emphasizes relationships and repetitive interactions, such specialization meant that workers became more efficient. They produced more by concentrating on only one product or component than by trying to make them all. It also meant that workers could exchange products on a relatively open basis. Specialization became the basis for the emergence of more sophisticated systems of exchange or markets. By contrast, realist perspectives see specialization more in terms of hierarchy and control of exchanges through domestic bureaucracies (e.g., factories) and the international structure of power, while identity perspectives emphasize the ideologies, such as capitalism and Marxism, that motivate specialization.

Spotlight on repetitive interactions

← **causal arrow**

Trade institutionalized the practice of specialization at the international level and created the attendant need to lower transaction costs. According to the economic historian Douglass North, increasing specialization and trade raised the transaction costs of exchanges. **Transaction costs** involve additional expenses incurred to find appropriate buyers and sellers and establish appropriate prices. When trade takes place over longer distances, people do not know one another, as they did in villages. They have to spend more money to find out who owns a particular piece of property, what a fair price for that item might be, and how they might ensure its delivery. From the fifteenth century on, state and international institutions emerged in part to handle these tasks

transaction costs

the expenses incurred in long-distance exchanges or large markets in which people do not know one another personally, namely the costs of finding appropriate buyers and sellers, establishing appropriate prices, and enforcing contracts.

and lower the transaction costs of long-distance trade. As a result, Europe developed "more complex forms of organization" than the traditional exchanges in the Middle East (the *suq* or bazaar) and Asia (the caravan trade).[5]

When and what kind of state institutions took shape also mattered. Countries started on a certain path and accumulated advantages or disadvantages along that path. Recall how liberal perspectives emphasize path dependence. England, for example, got an early start toward decentralized institutions when English lords forced King John to sign the Magna Carta in 1215. It passed these institutions on to the United States. By contrast, Spain, when it united, adopted Castile's centralized bureaucratic system rather than Aragon's decentralized merchant system, and France compounded already centralized Capetian institutions with policies of economic nationalism advocated by Jean Baptiste Colbert in the seventeenth century. Out of their decentralized institutions, England and the United States went on to create innovative societies that started the industrial and information revolutions. A more centralized France developed later and never quite as efficiently, while Spain and its colonies in Latin America developed even more centralized, patrimonial institutions, such as a large, land-owning church, which were less friendly to change and innovation.

A Critical Theory Perspective

What's wrong with these mainstream answers to the question why the West developed faster than the rest? Remember that the purpose of mainstream perspectives is to understand objectively, that is, independent of the observer or scholar, how the world works by designing propositions or hypotheses about what causes events and then testing these hypotheses against the facts. If the propositions are not falsified, mainstream perspectives abstract this knowledge from the past and seek to apply it to improve or predict the future.

Now comes the rub. Think for a minute about what mainstream conclusions imply when they are applied to future world development. They establish the West and its experiences as the standard for thinking about and shaping the future of other societies. First, according to identity perspectives, if other countries want to become modern, they have to adopt western ideas of the Renaissance, Reformation, and Enlightenment. Second, according to realist perspectives, they may not be able to develop independently because geography and demography appear to favor the western countries. To the extent that they can develop at all, they may have to do so under the hegemonic rule and stability offered by western powers. Third, according to liberal perspectives, developing countries have to implement the western rules and institutions of specialization, comparative advantage, MNCs, open markets, and pluralist political systems. In short, the mainstream perspectives suggest that development is a universalistic process that follows a single course initially set by western ideas, power, and institutions.

Critical theory roundly rejects this conclusion. It contends that western development is not a product of internal western ideas, institutions, and competition that can serve as models for future development. Rather, western development is a consequence of the systematic **exploitation** of other countries. This exploitation involves military **imperialism** and **colonization,** which began around 1500 and continues to the present day. It further involves the cultural **marginalization** of foreign societies, creating two categories of countries: advanced countries, which are western, and all the rest, which are non-western, undeveloped, primitive, savage, and uncivilized. In addi-

---

Spotlight on path dependence

exploitation
extracting profits from the use of resources or workers in an unjust way.

imperialism
the forceful extension of a nation's political authority by territorial conquest establishing economic and political domination of other nations.

colonization
the establishment of outposts or colonies within a foreign population with the intention of dominating resources and indigenous peoples.

causal arrow

marginalization
the social process of making unimportant or powerless certain groups within a society especially indigenous peoples and women.

tion, it imposes the economic institutions of capitalism, in particular the unique oppressive mechanism of the factory and now multinational corporations (MNCs), which extract profits from local labor to finance the cosmopolitan consumerism of elite classes. Most of all, western development was achieved on the backs of women and minorities, who were literally slaves in the colonial era and remain figuratively so today—oppressed and disenfranchised in the sweatshops and squalid slums spawned by globalization.

What is more, this exploitation was not carried out piecemeal by individual countries such as Spain and England acting independently or through isolated forces such as western ideas, institutions, and military forces causing specific outcomes. It was carried out through systemic and historical processes deeply rooted in the structures of particular eras. What made the globalization of the world economy so encompassing and relentless was the fact that it stemmed not just from material circumstances but from cultural, social, institutional, and even spiritual conditions of capitalism. Karl Marx marveled at the power of the bourgeoisie movement that ignited globalization. As John Micklethwait and Adrian Woolridge observe:

> In less than a hundred years, Marx argued, the bourgeoisie had "accomplished wonders far surpassing Egyptian pyramids, Roman aqueducts and Gothic cathedrals"; had conducted "expeditions that put in the shade all former exoduses of nations and crusades"; and had "created more massive and more colossal productive forces" than all the preceding generations put together.[6]

Thus, as critical theory perspectives see it, globalization is driven by a totalistic (not sequential) logic that cannot be steered or stopped. But it can be understood within historical parameters. As Robert Cox, a respected critical theorist writes, "positivism [that is, mainstream perspectives] can be useful but only within 'defined historical limits.' "[7] Critical studies unpack global development to reveal the contradictions and conflicts of specific historical periods. They examine these conflicts to locate marginalized voices, and most of all, they demonstrate that another future is possible. Critical theory does not see the future in the past, constructed from a set of propositions tested in the past and applied to the future. Rather, it sees a future without the past or other than the past. That future is one in which marginal and minority voices are emancipated, global inequities are lessened, and inclusive institutions prevail. Such a future must be imagined, and therein lies the utopian element of critical theories.

Spotlight on Marxism

Colonialism and Imperialism

From a critical theory perspective, it is hardly a coincidence that western development began at the same time as western imperialism and colonialism. European voyages to discover and colonize other parts of the world began in the fifteenth century. Portugal led the way, capturing Cueta on the northern coast of Africa across from Gibraltar in 1415. By the end of that century, Portuguese explorers had worked their way down the western coast of Africa and initiated voyages around the Cape of Good Hope to the Far East, reaching India and China in the early decades of the sixteenth century. Along the way, they established bases in the Persian Gulf and Malacca, on the west coast of the Malay Peninsula.

Meanwhile, Spain carved out an empire in another direction. Columbus's voyage in 1492 opened up the Americas, initially the various islands of the Caribbean and then the vast interiors of Central and South America. It was not that western technology or ideas were that superior to those of the countries colonized. Chinese navigating techniques were as advanced as Portuguese techniques, and western ideas that brought slavery and the righteous wrath of Christianity were hardly those of the Renaissance or Reformation. Rather, from a critical theory perspective, it was historical happenstance and the unusual cunning of western adventurers that made the difference. When Spain joined Portugal to contest foreign lands, the two monarchies literally divided the world into two parts rather than fight one another over its boundless resources. At the Treaty of Tordesillas in 1494, they drew a straight line south of the tip of Greenland (370 leagues west of the Cape Verde Islands) across the middle of the Atlantic Ocean, hiving off the easternmost section of South America, which is today Brazil. Portugal took the territories east of this line, which included Brazil. Spain took everything west of the line, including the rest of the Americas. The audacity of partitioning the then-known universe was but the first instance of a western imperial mindset that came to dominate international affairs.

As the English and Dutch, under the impetus of the Reformation, revolted against Spain and the Hapsburg empire in the sixteenth and seventeenth centuries, these two sea powers challenged and eventually supplanted Spain and Portugal. France, too, although more of a land power, joined the colonization effort. The later colonial powers transformed the character of colonization. Whereas Spain and Portugal conquered in the name of their monarchs, England and Holland did so in the name of commercial companies, the East India companies, that presaged the age of MNCs. In all cases, however, the motive and method of conquest were the same. Early colonizers bought cotton cloth in India, exchanged it for slaves in Africa, shipped slaves to Central and South America to mine gold and silver, and used gold and silver to purchase spices and silks in the Far East. The imperialists ransacked the gold and silver in colonial territories and enslaved the human population to work the mines and later the plantations—sugar, cotton, tobacco, and rubber—that did the plundering. Altogether, some 10 million slaves were transported from Africa to the New World. Untold millions more died en route or in the local wars among rival tribes in Africa that supplied the slaves.

The devastation done to the cultures and institutions of the local societies was severe and long lasting. At the core, according to critical theory perspectives, was the phenomenon of exploitation. Growth was not a process of mutual benefit and gain, a non-zero-sum game; rather it was a zero-sum game, a process by which a dominant country or class systematically exploited a subordinate country or class and drew that class into a tight system of global interconnections from which it was impossible to escape. These connections made it possible to strip the subordinate class of its just returns and transfer these returns systematically to the dominant center. With the coming of the industrial revolution, the phenomenon of exploitation took on even more sinister dimensions. It led subsequently to the developments of dependency and world systems dynamics that continue to characterize the world economy to the present day.

Dependency

From a critical theory perspective, colonialism was not just a historical phenomenon. It cut deeply into the fabric of local societies and established patterns of dependency and integration that permanently yoked those societies to the objectives and needs of the advanced world. The inequity and indeed brutality of these patterns were best expressed by one of the leading colonizers of Africa, the Englishman Cecil Rhodes, who founded the colony of Rhodesia (today, Zimbabwe) and endowed one of today's top prizes for academic achievement, the Rhodes Scholarship (notice how colonialism continues to influence and distort contemporary life):

> We must find new lands from which we can easily obtain raw materials and at the same time exploit the cheap slave labor that is available from the natives of the colonies. The colonies would also provide the dumping ground for surplus goods produced in our factories.[8]

Here, as critical theorists see it, are the trading and political patterns that characterize globalization today. Comparative advantage is not some God-given distribution of resources that confers advantages on each country that it can then exploit in free and uncoerced trading relationships. Rather, it is a pattern of historically determined and dominant relationships shaped by colonial governments and raw power.

Spotlight on comparative advantage

Colonial powers not only stripped the colonies of precious metals and other material resources; they also converted and reorganized resources to produce cash crops that paid off handsomely year after year. Agriculture became another large "mine" that colonial powers exploited. In Gambia, colonizers replaced rice farming for local consumption with peanut plantations for European consumption. In Ghana and other parts of the Gold Coast of West Africa, local foodstuffs were replaced by cocoa; in Liberia by rubber plantations; in Uganda by cotton; in Dahomey and Nigeria by palm oil; and in Tanganyika (now Tanzania) by sisal. The same patterns prevailed in Asia. Under French rule, rice became the dominant export crop in Indochina, rubber in Malaysia, and coffee in Indonesia. And the great fruit companies, along with other agricultural and mining conglomerates, replicated these patterns in Central and South America. Plantations became the first multinational "factories" in colonial countries, diverting production from local to foreign demand; usurping the best infrastructure, such as land and water, for commercial purposes; and forcing the peasantry onto marginal soil or into work at slave wages in the new enterprises servicing metropole markets.

One consequence of this coerced allocation of comparative advantage was that developing countries lost the capacity to feed themselves. As Frances Moore Lappé and Joseph Collins note, "colonialism destroyed the cultural patterns of production and exchange by which traditional sectors in 'underdeveloped' countries previously had met the needs of their people."[9] To this day, global trade incentives favor western agriculture, which dumps surpluses generated by domestic protectionist programs on to global markets and undercuts prices for agricultural products from developing countries. Another consequence of coercive comparative advantage was to force most local enterprise and production activity into the informal sector, that is, the part of the economy in developing countries that flourishes outside the protection of law and the subsidies and other privileges that flow to the formal sector, which is globalized. Local production in both agriculture and industry is marginalized and can never get hooked up in a beneficial way with the globalized economy, which dashes further and further ahead.

Spotlight on informal sector

So indelible and enduring were these patterns of plundering that critical theorists developed a more elaborate dependency theory, drawn from the experience of Latin America. Latin America actually had the earliest and least recent encounters with colonialism. By the mid-nineteenth century, most of Central and South America was independent. The Bolivarian revolutions of the early part of that century severed colonial

Spotlight on dependency theory

ties with Europe and brought independence to Latin America a century or more before it arrived in Asia or Africa. Yet Latin America's experience is relevant, critical theorists believe, because it reveals the long-lasting effects of colonialism. Despite the hundred years or more since colonialism, Latin America still showed the deep-seated scars of dependency.

According to dependency theory, the advanced country or metropole relates to the developing colonial country or satellite in the same way that a city relates to the countryside. The **metropole,** like the city, organizes the satellite, or countryside, to serve its social and political purposes. The metropole becomes an all-encompassing center of economic, social, and political life and in the process also becomes an all-encompassing center of exploitation. The exploitation derives from five factors.

First, the metropole is independent, but the satellite or dependent country never becomes independent. It is permanently subordinated. The proof of this point for dependency theorists is the experience of the great metropolitan areas of Latin America such as São Paulo and Buenos Aires. These metropolitan areas enjoyed nominal independence in the nineteenth and twentieth centuries. They grew significantly during this period but still at the end of the twentieth century remained largely dependent on the outside metropolis—first, Great Britain and, then, the United States.

Second, Latin America's experience suggests that the satellite grows fastest when it is isolated from the metropole. The greatest industrial development in Argentina, Brazil, Mexico, and other countries such as Chile occurred precisely during those periods when Europe and the United States, the metropoles, were weak and hence less dominant in the international economy. These periods included the European wars of the early seventeenth century, the Napoleonic Wars, the First and Second World Wars, and the Great Depression of the 1930s. In each of these periods, large Latin American countries enjoyed significant economic growth.

Third, this autonomous development of satellite regions is choked off the minute the metropole recovers and reasserts its oppressive role in the world economy. For example, British-led economic liberalism in the eighteenth and nineteenth centuries undercut incipient manufacturing development in Latin America. Foreign investment destroyed local competition, the export economy absorbed the best lands and other resources, and **systematic inequality** increased both between rural and urban areas and between metropole and satellite countries.

Fourth, the plantation or hacienda (*latifundium*) is a direct result of metropole-satellite relationships. It is not a reflection of the natural stage of agricultural development that subsequently leads to industrial development, as in the evolution of feudalism to capitalism in Europe. Rather, it exists and survives solely at the will of the metropole. Plantations produced products for the metropole country, which in turn supplied food to the satellite country. The development of agriculture did not produce food for industrial and urban development in the satellite country.

Fifth and finally, the proof of this dependence lies in the fact that, as industrialization proceeds, the demand for agricultural and raw material products relatively declines. The terms of trade—what is paid in exports for imports—turned against the satellite countries. Because the metropole spends more on industrial goods and less on foodstuffs and raw materials, the satellite economy produces products of declining relative value and slowly dries up. This pessimistic view of the capability of world markets to provide the demand that could spark development in the satellite regions led Latin American countries after World War II to reject export-led growth strategies and turn to strategies based on developing local industries to substitute for industrial imports. In

metropole
the metropolitan (political, commercial, and military) centers of imperial powers.

**Spotlight on
economic autarky**

systematic inequality
deep-seated disparity in the distribution of wealth and/or power generated by colonialism and dependency.

**Spotlight on
import substitution**

effect, this strategy was an attempt to break completely with the world economy in which the ancient patterns of colonial exploitation were so irreversibly embedded.

World Systems

Other work by critical theorists formalized dependency theory into a world systems model. Building on Marxism, world systems analysts emphasized the totality of social and economic phenomena in the world economy. Consistent with critical theory perspectives, they rejected the idea of sequential or rationalist causation. As Georg Lukacs, a Marxist, once wrote, "it is not the primacy of economic motives in historical explanation that constitutes the difference between Marxism and bourgeois thought, but the point of view of totality."[10]

The world economy—globalization—must be seen as a whole. It is a system or total structure whose unifying metric is the division of labor. Firms and workers existed long before the world economy expanded in 1500. But they did not exist in a total system of multiple states and a global market. The capitalist world system dates from that moment when multiple states and a global market came together for the purpose of accumulating capital. The system, as Marx made clear, is driven by the desire for more profit and capital. This desire persists today, for example, in the television commercial featuring a stock broker who says he never thinks about how well he has done on the last trade, only about how he can do better on the next trade. The accumulation of profits and capital, raw greed, is the *raison d'etre* of the system.

Ideally, all individuals or countries in the global marketplace would prefer to have a monopoly because a monopoly generates the greatest differential between the sales price and the cost of production. However, multiple actors/states make perfect monopolies difficult. Still, larger or leading actors/states can create quasi-monopolies using patents and other market restrictions. Quasi-monopolies last long enough to accumulate considerable profit, but they are eventually challenged by other actors/countries and become less profitable. Once innovations arrive in the trailing states, the profits are far less. (There are some similarities here with the product life cycle discussed in Chapter 10, but, according to mainstream perspectives, developing countries eventually catch up, as Japan did after World War II and the East Asian tigers such as South Korea did thereafter.)

Thus, the world systems dynamic creates a **division of labor** between leading sectors that generate high profits and lagging products that generate little or no profits. Large and leading countries constitute the **core states** of the world economy; they produce most of the leading or quasi-monopoly products. Smaller and less-developed countries constitute the **peripheral states,** which produce most of the low-profit or lagging products after their monopoly qualities have been lost. Some countries fall in between. They are **semi-peripheral states,** which produce a nearly even mix of monopoly and competitive products.

The global economy is thus stratified and fixed. Core states have a permanent advantage in producing quasi-monopoly products and use their clout in global markets to protect patents and other privileges that produce disproportionate profit. Peripheral states are at a permanent disadvantage because the dynamic of global markets makes available to them only those products for which competition has lowered the available profit. Semi-peripheral countries have the greatest difficulty. They struggle to keep from falling back into the peripheral zone while using government intervention (protection,

Spotlight on
Marxism

division of labor
division of world markets into core, peripheral, and semi-peripheral areas.

core states
large and leading countries that produce most of the leading or quasi-monopoly products.

peripheral states
smaller and less-developed countries that produce most of the competitive or lagging products after their monopoly qualities have been lost.

semi-peripheral states
states that produce a nearly even mix of monopoly and competitive products.

subsidies, and so on) to advance into the core group. Unless they are of substantial size, like India, Brazil, or China, they have little chance of succeeding.

According to world systems theorists, therefore, a global division of labor is inevitable and largely static. There will always be the need for a division of labor. And while some countries may rise in the hierarchy of core and peripheral states, others will fall. The advantages lie with already developed countries. Thus, as critical theory perspectives see it, global divisions and inequalities persist. Whereas earlier the industrial countries produced textiles, the developing countries now do so. The same is true of steel, automobiles, consumer electronics, and so on. Yet industrial countries retain their lead by producing an endless stream of new products fueled by the profits of earlier products and the protection of patents and other market restrictions. Meanwhile, peripheral states industrialize and some even make it into the semi-peripheral class of states, but they can never leap forward far enough financially and technologically to reverse the capitalist world order. Indeed, in return for exports of competitive (low- or no-profit) products to core countries, peripheral countries must continue to accept the exports of core countries in quasi-monopoly products. At the heart of Doha Round trade negotiations today, for example, is a trade-off between, on the one hand, advanced (core) countries seeking to reduce barriers to trade in developing countries for their highly profitable products in the high-technology, pharmaceutical, and service industries and, on the other hand, developing (peripheral) countries receiving in return reduced barriers in advanced countries for their lower-profit agriculture and low-technology products.

Spotlight on
Doha Round

Multinational Corporations and Exploitation of Labor

A large reason for the frozen economic hierarchy of global markets is the MNCs. Like the trading and plantation corporations during the colonial era, the MNCs internalize the division of labor and structure global markets to perpetuate the advantages of the core states. Because of global dependence, states are no longer effective agents that control the MNCs. The states lose a measure of autonomy and cannot reverse the dynamics of capitalist world systems. MNCs hold "sovereignty at bay" and make it more difficult for states to accomplish their domestic and foreign policy objectives.[11]

Although protected by the law, MNCs, it is argued, operate outside the law. They circumvent laws in advanced countries by relocating factories in developing countries. And they circumvent the laws in developing countries by exploiting the desperate conditions of the local poor. If MNCs don't violate the laws directly, they frequently do business with local enterprises and entrepreneurs who are little more than common criminals. The most egregious offenses are child labor and discrimination against women.

An oft-cited example is a brave young Pakistani boy named Iqbal Masih. Iqbal was indentured to work in a locally run carpet factory at age four for a payment, essentially a loan, of $16 to his parents. Shackled to a loom for twelve hours a day, seven days a week, Iqbal earned so little that at the end of six years his parents owed $400 rather than the $16 for his original servitude. At age ten, Iqbal, learning that **bonded labor** was no longer permitted, stole away one day to attend a rally sponsored by an NGO known as the Bonded Labour Liberation Front. He returned to the factory to free his

bonded labor
a form of unfree or indentured labor, typically a means of paying off loans with direct labor instead of currency or goods.

fellow laborers, infuriating the factory owner, and then became a spokesman on behalf of more than 100 million children under the age of fifteen who worked in peripheral countries in 1994 essentially as slaves. Three years later, he was killed, many suspect by henchmen of the Pakistani carpet industry.[12]

Through Iqbal's efforts and NGOs such as the college student organization United Students Against Sweatshops, corporate codes have improved labor conditions in a range of low-tech developing-country industries such as textiles, apparel, footwear, forest products, coffee, and toys. RugMark, a consortium of carpet manufacturers and exporters in India, Nepal, and Pakistan, inspects factories and certifies with the RugMark label rugs that are made without child labor. Reebok, Nike, and other apparel firms developed similar codes. Abuses continue and, from some critical theory perspectives, abound. From this perspective, exploitation lies at the heart of the global development process and when confronted in one area, such as slavery, pops up again in another area, such as child labor.

Spotlight on NGOs

From the point of view of mainstream perspectives, abuses by MNCs can be corrected and even abolished. From a critical theory perspective, however, MNCs are not the primary cause. There is no single cause; the global system itself is at fault. Competitive processes compel all states to remain open, including core states. Consider the following. If countries want to survive in a highly competitive global economy, they can't tax their MNCs more than other countries, impose pension and welfare costs that disproportionately burden their industries, or pile up regulations that prevent their firms from adapting to rapid changes in technology and other market conditions. If they do, the MNCs will cut back operations at home and relocate them abroad where costs and regulations are less onerous. The system, in short, gives MNCs *carte blanche*.

← causal arrow

Countries also lose control of fiscal and monetary policies. They may expand government spending to create jobs and exploit resources, but if they import a large percentage of their consumption, as many developing countries do, much of this added domestic spending goes into imports. It leaks out, in effect, to foreign firms and does not increase domestic jobs. So, domestic spending has to be increased even more to create jobs. Thus, profligate spending and fiscal deficits in developing countries are not the consequences primarily of bad governance, corruption, or incompetent leaders; they are the consequence of world system constraints. Local government officials have to pump more and more fiscal gas into the domestic economic car because the gas line of the car is leaking out to foreigners on its way to the engine. Or consider monetary policy. As we have noted in earlier chapters, governments raise interest rates to slow money growth. But raising interest rates more than other countries only attracts capital from abroad, requiring local central banks to raise interest rates still more by selling bonds (reducing bond prices and raising interest rates) to absorb the excess money coming in from abroad.

Mainstream perspectives focus on only specific aspects of this phenomenon of globalization. Liberal perspectives, for example, which emphasize interactions rather than power or ideology, conclude that, because of spillover, governments have

Iqbal Masih, the 12-year-old boy who won international acclaim for highlighting the horrors of child labor in Pakistan, was shot dead in 1995, allegedly because of his campaign against child labor.

Spotlight on
spillover

no choice but to integrate monetary policies and coordinate fiscal policies, as EU members, for example, are doing today. Their only other alternative is to leave their countries at the mercy of the biggest central banks and government spenders in the global economy—today these are the United States and EU. The effect of expanding the reach of globalization to more and more sectors, however, is ultimately beneficial. The scope of governance expands, and global society as a whole becomes more like domestic societies.

But from the critical theory perspective, the situation is actually much worse and cannot be easily corrected by any one measure. There is no way to escape the dependence and relentless division of labor that lies behind these global inequities. The effects of globalization are total. They go well beyond economic policies and weaken the psychological and political will of peripheral countries. Countries lose control of their national media and entertainment industries and, indeed, of their local languages and cultures. Small countries, in particular, are defenseless. McDonald's golden arches descend on these countries, and Hollywood movies and music dominate their airwaves. Slowly, local language broadcasts and artistic opportunities dwindle. Ancient languages disappear. Cultural diversity is the victim, and the whole world is the loser.

Spotlight on
culture (identity)

Except perhaps for the big countries. America, Japan, and the MNCs of the advanced world may be the winners. As Thomas Friedman explains, the Lexus drives out the olive tree. "Olive trees," Friedman writes, "represent everything that roots us, anchors us, identifies us and locates us in this world—whether it be belonging to a family, a community, a tribe, a nation, a religion or, most of all, a place called home."[13] The Lexus built for export with ultra-modern robots, on the other hand,

> represents all the burgeoning global markets, financial institutions and computer technologies with which we pursue higher living standards today. The biggest threat today to your olive tree is likely to come from the Lexus, from all the anonymous, transnational, homogenizing, standardizing market forces and technologies that make up today's globalizing economic system.

Friedman, however, is a mainstream analyst, seeing the world, as we have noted previously, largely from a liberal perspective. Unlike some critical theory perspectives, he can imagine that globalization has a liberating side.

> There are some things about this system that can make the Lexus so overpowering it can overrun and overwhelm every olive tree in sight. . . . But there are other things . . . that empower even the smallest, weakest political community to actually use the new technologies and markets to preserve their olive trees, their culture and identity.

Witness the upsurge of ethnicity, nationalism, religion, local pride, and interest in personal roots that belie the notion that globalization homogenizes culture. Maybe, as Friedman concludes, the Lexus and the olive tree need one another.

That's the mainstream view of globalization, that it benefits, not destroys, national sovereignty and culture. Countries choose to join the global economy, and globalization gives them more options. No country has developed in isolation. The communist countries were the last to try, and they did not preserve their sovereignty and cultures but eventually lost them. Modernization has been going on for a long time, yet people have retained their identities, their homes, and their communities. Technology benefits local languages and arts by making people aware of diversity and, through the Internet and other information technologies, better able to defend their cultural heritage.

The box on page 447 analyzes one recent book that critiques conventional ways to think about social movements in the contemporary world. Western thinking,

Using the Perspectives to Read
→ Between ←
the Lines

Searching for a New Paradigm for Globalization

Kevin McDonald, a sociologist at the University of Melbourne, argues as follows:

> An older international context, where social life largely took place within the borders of nation-states, and where states were the main actors on the international stage, is increasingly giving way to a context involving new global actors, from NGOs, organized crime, or terror networks, and with it, to a whole series of debates attempting to interpret the nature of this emerging global world.

OK, so far, he seems to be rejecting a realist interpretation of the new global world ("states were the main actors") and embracing a liberal perspective. But let's read on.

> We need to grapple with forms of sociality transforming the relationship between individual and collective; with grammars of movement that are better understood in terms of cultural pragmatics . . . and personal experience . . . than organization building and collective identity; with new forms of complexity and fluidity . . . ; with civilizational grammars shaping ways-of-being and acting in the world. . . .

He's being very abstract, to be sure, but notice the shift to a focus on language ("grammars of movement" and "civilizational grammars"), which is now more important than "organization building" (liberal perspective)

and "collective identity" (identity perspective). All right, maybe he is still a constructivist. After all, they emphasize language and discourse.

But soon McDonald gives away that he wants to go beyond the mainstream perspectives. He wants to "rethink our understandings of action in terms . . . [that] point to limits of the autonomous secular subject . . . [and] confront us with forms of public experience that do not correspond to understandings of deliberative, rational, disembodied public spheres. . . ." Notice that he is rejecting the rationalist methods used in mainstream perspectives. He goes on to advocate "a radical paradigm shift" that emphasizes "embodiment and the senses." Instead of action among separate or disembodied groups, in which one group encounters or confronts another, he wants to talk about actions that resonate among groups and reinforce them such as we experience when we encounter "dance, music, drumming, bicycle riding, experiences of vulnerability. . . ." These experiences, he writes, "allow us to break out of often repeated debates framed in terms of individual versus the community. . . ." He then studies protest and religious groups (NGOs), such as the Falun Gong movement in China, that are searching for more fluid and resonating ways to deal with global differences that do not automatically separate people into disembodied and, hence, antagonistic groups.

Source: Excerpts from Kevin McDonald, *Global Movements: Action and Culture* (London: Blackwell, 2006), 3, 4, 18. Used with permission.

Professor Kevin McDonald argues, leads us to analyze social movements, such as protest groups or religious sects, in terms of antagonistic relationships, dialectical processes, and individuals versus the collectivity. He is looking for another paradigm that does not follow the rationalistic western (including Marxist) mode. And he goes beyond constructivism because he does not seek to apply the past to the future, as most constructivists do. Rather, he hopes to find a radical alternative that liberates oppressed groups in the future but does not threaten other groups—the alternative of resonance, where groups that are different feed off of one another rather than conflict with one another. The rhetoric of critical theorists is sometimes abstract, but perhaps it needs to be because they are trying to outline something in the future that we are not familiar with in the past. See what you think.

Marginalized Minorities: Global Injustice

From a critical theory perspective, nothing is more evident from the assault of globalization than the marginalization of indigenous peoples and women. Colonialism, imperialism, and then open world markets ran roughshod over native peoples and forced women into what are in effect ghettos. Think of the plight of the native Americans, who fell like weeds beneath the scythes of white men expanding across the American continent. Land, the most cherished possession of indigenous peoples, was systematically appropriated or, more accurately, stolen from them. Indigenous tribes were stripped of their livelihood and, even worse, of their culture, identity, and dignity. They were dismissed as primitive, uncivilized, and uneducable. The indigenous natives of Latin America and Asia suffered no less. And the legacy of such material and moral looting goes on to the present day.

Spotlight on exploitation

Let's listen to Subcomandante Marcos, a leader of indigenous people in the southeast Mexican state of Chiapas, as he talks about his eviscerated homeland:

> Chiapas loses blood through many veins: . . . petroleum, electricity, cattle, money, coffee, banana, honey, corn, cacao, tobacco, sugar, soy, melon, sorghum, mamey, mango, tamarind, avocado, and Chiapaneco blood all flow as a result of the thousand teeth sunk into the throat of the Mexican southeast. These raw materials, thousands of millions of tons of them, flow to Mexican ports, railroads, air and truck transportation centers. From there they are sent to different parts of the world—the United States, Canada, Holland, Germany, Italy Japan— . . . to feed imperialism. . . .
>
> In 1989 these businesses took 1.2 trillion pesos from Chiapas and only left behind 616 million pesos worth of credit and public works. More than 600 million pesos went to the belly of the beast.
>
> In Chiapas . . . Pemex [the Mexican state oil company] has eighty-six teeth sunk into the townships of Estacion Juarez, Reforma, Ostuacian, Pichucalo, and Ocosingo. Every day they suck out 92,000 barrels of petroleum and 517 billion cubic feet of gas. . . .
>
> Chiapas also bleeds coffee. Thirty-five percent of the coffee produced in Mexico comes from this area. . . . 53 percent is exported abroad. . . . more than 100,000 tons of coffee are taken from the state to fatten the beast's bank accounts: in 1988 a kilo of pergamino coffee was sold abroad for 58,000 pesos. The Chiapeneco producers were paid 2,500 pesos or less.
>
> Three million head of cattle wait for middlemen . . . to take them away to fill refrigerators in Arriasga, Villahermosa, and Mexico City. The cattle are sold for 400 pesos per kilo by the poor farmers and resold by middlemen and businessmen for up to ten times the price they paid for them.
>
> The tribute that capitalism demands from Chiapas has no historical parallel. Fifty-five percent of national hydroelectric energy comes from this state, along with 20 percent of Mexico's total electricity. However, only a third of the homes in Chiapas have electricity. . . .
>
> The plunder of wood continues in Chiapas' forests. Between 1981 and 1989, 2,444,777 cubic meters of precious woods, conifers, and tropical trees were taken . . . to Mexico City, Puebla, Veracruz, and Quintana Roo. . . .

The honey that is produced in 78,000 beehives in Chiapas goes entirely to the United States and European markets.

Of the corn produced in Chiapas, more than half goes to the domestic market.... Sorghum grown in Chiapas goes to Tobasco. Ninety percent of the tamarind goes to Mexico City and other states. Two-thirds of the avocados and all the mameys are sold out of state. Sixty-nine percent of the cacao goes to the national market, and 31 percent is exported to the United States, Holland, Japan, and Italy. The majority of the bananas produced are exported.[14]

The indictment is total. And Chiapas is but one example. In the Philippines, indigenous peoples totaling 16–18 percent of the population, mostly Muslims, face expulsion from their native lands to accommodate forty-nine major new hydroelectric dams. The proposed energy supply is to encourage foreign investment not local entrepreneurs. In Peru, Columbia, and elsewhere in Latin America, landless peasants join guerrilla movements to reclaim land and natural resources. In Cuba and Venezuela, Fidel Castro and now Hugo Chavez champion a new revolutionary-style politics to empower the poor and indigenous peoples. In southern Africa, the Sari, an indigenous people, were evicted from land that became the Central Kalahari Game Reserve (CKGR), one of the largest such reserves in the world.

Altogether, the United Nations estimates that some 370 million indigenous peoples live in over seventy countries around the world. Through efforts by NGOs, the Africa Commission on Human Rights, and the United Nations International Decade of the World's Indigenous People (1995–2004), the United Nations adopted in September 2007 a landmark Declaration on the Rights of Indigenous Peoples emphasizing their rights to culture, identity, language, employment, health, education, and other benefits and outlawing discrimination against them. Canada, Australia, New Zealand, and the United States voted against the declaration, arguing that the language was unclear and the negotiating process had not been transparent.

Women are the other main victims of marginalization. Globalization has marginalized women in four principal ways: through low wages to fuel export zones, neglect of the informal economy where most women work, increased unpaid labor by women in the household sector, and damage to the environment where most women live.

Women staffed the globally oriented trade activities imposed by the colonial legacy on many postcolonial developing countries. Export sectors had to maintain low wages to service metropole markets, and women were the cheapest source of labor and filled most of the jobs in export-processing zones throughout the developing world. Today, women constitute approximately 90 percent of the workforce in such export zones. They assemble garments, electronics, and other items that require tedious and repetitive manual skills. Women, it is argued, have the natural dexterity and nimble fingers to carry out repetitive tasks at very high rates of speed. In export zones, women work 50–80 hours a week and earn less than a $1 per hour, generally 30–40 percent less than men are paid for comparable work. They enjoy few basic job or social protections and are often subjected to physical and sexual abuses. The recruitment and housing of the women needed to work in these industries led in some cases to kidnapping and prostitution rings. Women were lured to fill jobs and then forced into prostitution either directly or indirectly to pay off loans. A sex trade developed in emerging countries, often associated with other low-wage service industries such as tourism and hotels.

A similar pattern, on a smaller and less exploitative scale, affected women in industrialized countries. In these countries, the employment of women was concentrated in the garment and low-wage sectors, and these sectors were usually the first affected by

Spotlight on free-trade export-processing zones

Migrant Bangladeshi women and children haul stones in a quarry in the northeastern Indian state of Assam, earning less than $1 per person per day.

Spotlight on
informal sector

job losses when markets opened up to accommodate the still cheaper garment and toy imports produced by women in developing countries. When jobs were lost in advanced countries, women, families, and sometimes whole regions were devastated.

Exploited and then just as quickly neglected by the global economy, women work mostly in the informal sector of developing countries. They do jobs that mimic housework, such as cleaning, sewing, and cooking, and are paid far less than even the low wages they would get in the formal sector. For this reason, some mainstream perspectives argue that the formal, or export-centered, global economy is still a step up for women. But critical theory perspectives emphasize the few opportunities that women have to move up in or break out of the export-oriented global economy. Women in developing countries and among the poor in advanced countries are either exploited by the global (modern) economy or left to work in a ghettoized informal economy where there is little support in the form of credits (loans), child care, educational incentives, or health care. As in the case of developing countries more broadly, the patterns of global dependency and world systems do not involve a dynamic that lifts individuals, especially women and minorities, from the bottom to the top but rather exploits them for the benefit of those who are already at the top.

Globalization further deemphasizes the valuable work that women do in the home, even in the most advanced economies. By stressing modernization and the transformation of traditional tasks and communities, globalization values home care even less than traditional societies do. Bearing children and caring for them, maintaining a household that often takes care of elderly members, and sustaining village and community relations are all tasks that are invaluable, indeed priceless, for any society. Yet they are unacknowledged and unpaid in a modern globalized world. The United Nations estimates that the unpaid work that women do in the home in a year amounts to about $11 trillion, or practically the size of the entire U.S. economy. Even that estimate seems unpersuasively low because the value of raising healthy educated children cannot really be measured.

Finally, globalization has a devastating impact on the environment in which most women live. As Manisha Desai points out,

> whether it is the destruction of the rain forest in Latin America, the falling of trees in the Himalayan Mountains in India, desertification in Africa, or toxic dumping in the United States, the environmental desecration caused by global economic policies has led to increasing material and cultural hardships for women.[15]

Women, who have the primary responsibility for home care, have to work harder to fetch wood, find drinking water, feed cattle, and care for children afflicted by poisons and deprivation. Most of all, women have to do all these tasks with less and less help because globalization not only strips the environment of natural resources but also the village of husbands and children. These vital human resources are drawn increasingly from the countryside into the urbanized and globalized economy. This movement of human beings from rural to urban areas (13 million each year in China alone) creates transient and often impoverished communities where criminal organizations lure young men and women into sex industries and drug trafficking.

Persisting Global Inequality

Despite all the development of the past five hundred years, why do all these shocking inequalities still exist? Mainstream perspectives answer this question in separate parts.

From a realist perspective, for example, the key question is, who gains most? Does globalization spread economic benefits or concentrate them? Does the hegemon stay on top, or do other countries—China, India, and oil-producing states—gain more and counterbalance the hegemon? Or, at the individual and domestic levels of analysis, do individuals and minorities eventually work their way up the income ladder? Or are workers and minority groups stuck at the lower end and capitalist managers and financiers ensconced at the upper end?

← *causal arrow*

As we've noted, realist perspectives don't always agree with one another. The power transition school believes hegemons endure because moves toward balance are dangerous and bring war. They agree, in effect, with critical theory perspectives that some kind of hierarchy is necessary to promote development. But power transition realists do not necessarily believe that this hierarchy is rigid or static. The same hegemons, classes, or individuals do not endure. Realist perspectives allow for the rise and fall of powerful countries or, at the individual and domestic levels, of powerful classes and individuals. Nevertheless, global development is greatest when hegemons rule, because that hegemonic stability favors growth, as we recounted in Chapter 8. So, inequalities are inevitable from this power transition perspective, even if the winners and losers in inequality change.

Spotlight on **power transition**

The balance-of-power realist school sees it differently. It expects other states or classes and individuals to rise eventually and counterbalance the hegemon. It sees inequalities as dangerous and destabilizing. Thus, at the individual, domestic, and systemic levels of analysis, power balancing realists accept, if they don't seek, relative balance or equality as the norm. They see markets and politics as competitive exercises and trust that increasing equality will stabilize and maximize benefits in the same way that perfectly competitive markets maximize growth. They assume, however, that a

Spotlight on **power balancing**

balancing of military capabilities preserves stability and peace. If not, power balancing realists favor a world that discriminates between friendly and enemy states. Development is pursued to reduce inequalities among friends, but development is a zero-sum game and not recommended in relations with adversaries.

Liberal perspectives don't have a single answer either. Let's listen first to economists who fear that globalization increases inequalities. According to Joseph Stiglitz, a Nobel Prize–winning economist:

> A growing divide between the haves and the have-nots has left increasing numbers in the Third World in dire poverty, living on less than a dollar a day. Despite repeated promises of poverty reduction made over the last decade of the twentieth century, the actual number of people living in poverty has actually increased by almost 100 million. This occurred at the same time that total world income increased by an average of 2.5 percent annually.
>
> In Africa, the high aspirations following colonial independence have been largely unfulfilled. Instead, the continent plunges deeper into misery, as incomes fall and standards of living decline. The hard-won improvements in life expectancy gained in the past few decades have begun to reverse. While the scourge of AIDS is at the center of this decline, poverty is also a killer. Even countries that have abandoned African socialism, managed to install honest governments, balanced their budgets, and kept inflation down find that they simply cannot attract private investors. Without this investment, they cannot have sustainable growth.[16]

On similar grounds, economist Dani Rodrik agrees and notes that globalization is leading to a new "digital divide, . . . a deep fault line between groups who have the skills and mobility to flourish in global markets" and groups that don't, "such as workers, pensioners, and environmentalists."[17]

But now let's listen to an economist who sees globalization as reducing inequalities. According to Martin Wolf, a distinguished economist and journalist at the *Financial Times* in London:

> Between 1980 and 2000, India's real GDP per head more than doubled. . . . China . . . achieved a rise in real income per head of well over 400 percent between 1980 and 2000. China and India, it should be remembered, contain almost two-fifths of the world's population. . . . Never before have so many people—or so large a proportion of the world's population—enjoyed such large rises in their standards of living. Meanwhile, GDP per head in high-income countries (with 15 percent of the world's population) rose by 2.1 percent a year between 1975 and 2001 and by only 1.7 percent between 1990 and 2001. . . . the incomes of poor developing countries, with more than half the world's population, grew substantially faster than those of the world's richest countries.
>
> What . . . has this progress to do with international economic integration? . . . the World Bank divided seventy-three developing countries . . . into two groups, the third [or twenty-four countries, including China, India, Brazil, Bangladesh, Mexico, the Philippines, and Thailand, which alone make up 92 percent of the population of the twenty-four countries] that had increased ratios of trade to GDP since 1980 by the largest amount, and the rest. . . . The average incomes per head of the twenty-four globalizing countries rose by 67 percent . . . between 1980 and 1997. . . . the other forty-nine countries managed a rise of only 10 percent . . . over this period. . . . the notion that international economic integration necessarily makes the rich richer and the poor poorer is nonsense.[18]

Are these economists talking about the same planet? Some see more people living in poverty than ever before; others see more people climbing out of poverty than ever before. Can both be right? Well, yes, they can. It depends on which statistics they use and what they emphasize. The absolute number of people living on less than $1 per day did go up between 1990 and 1998. But, as a ratio of total population over a longer period of time, this number has gone down from 50 percent in 1950, to 32 percent in 1980, to 24 percent in 1992.[19] Thus, Wolf looks at ratios, a longer time period, and the populated countries of India and China. Stiglitz and Rodrik focus on absolute numbers, the most recent period, and the poorest countries of Africa. Reality is different depending on how you slice it.

Measuring inequality is also very tricky. Are we talking about inequality between countries or within them? For example, between 1820 and 1980 global inequality increased among countries but inequality actually went down within countries.[20] So from 1960 to 1997, the ratio of incomes of the 20 percent of the world's population living in the richest countries to that of the 20 percent living in the poorest countries went up from 30 : 1 in 1960 to 74 : 1 in 1997, while it increased from 7 : 1 to only 11 : 1 in the previous era of globalization before World War I (1870–1913).[21] During the same period, however, a burgeoning middle class reduced income differences within countries, ending the appeal of class warfare ideologies such as Marxism and communism. Are we talking about ratios or absolute numbers? From 1980 to 2000, Chinese average real income per head rose by 440 percent; U.S. income per head rose by 60 percent. But the absolute per capita income gap between China and the United States increased from $20,600 to $30,200 per head. China grew faster than the United States but from a much smaller base. It would have had to grow thirty, not seven, times faster to reduce the absolute gap.[22] Closing relative gaps thus takes time and accelerates only toward the later phases of catch-up. Moreover, are we talking about just incomes or the quality of life, which includes life expectancy, education, and health care? Life expectancy and other measures of the quality of life in most developing countries grew steadily from 1950 to 2000, even as incomes grew less in some countries or stagnated in others.

Spotlight on methods

What governs these interpretations and methodological preferences among economists who largely view the world from a liberal perspective of increasing mutual gains? Perhaps their views are determined not just by wealth and markets (relational or liberal aspects of reality) but also by substantive or ideational issues such as what they consider to be the rate of sustainable development, the preferred quality of life, or the best mechanism for political life—redistributive versus decentralized political practices. In short, identity factors may trump liberal or realist factors. Is it ideologically acceptable if some people remain poor and perhaps even get poorer, at least relatively, as long as more (other) people get richer? Is it acceptable that some people become many times richer than others as long as others still also get richer? For example, is it immoral for Bill Gates to make billions while average middle-class incomes have gone up much less? Should limits be applied to multiples of wealth until every individual, group, or state in the world has reached a certain minimal level of development? If so, what is that minimal level for all participants, what is the multiple limit that must be enforced until that level is reached, and how do we know what degree of redistribution of resources is still consistent with sustained growth that, over the long run, is the only way to increase overall wealth rather than just redistribute the wealth that already exists? These are not easy questions to answer. Or they are questions that can be answered only from different ideational, material, institutional, or critical perspectives.

Spotlight on perspectives

Summary

Critical theory perspectives remind us that such questions may not be answered at all given the totality of the world in which all participants, including scholars, are trapped. Our perspectives and preferred methods (including levels) of analysis are themselves a product of the realist, liberal, and identity aspects of the social reality that we seek to examine. Those realities today are a legacy of deep and powerful historical forces that emerged around five hundred years ago and produced a developed world economy dominated by western European institutions (states), ideas, and power. An understanding of development and the world economy cannot be pursued apart from this legacy because that history represents only one of other possible alternatives that privileged western peoples and that colonized and marginalized nonwestern peoples. It cannot be applied to the future without perpetuating the legacy of western dominance. From a critical theory perspective, we need to search continuously for other alternatives by listening to additional narratives and voices. The purpose of scholarly research has to be not problem solving in terms of applying existing perspectives to present and future issues but a broader, more holistic understanding of the historical structures that have brought us to the present point. That understanding will direct us to the marginalized groups that have borne the brunt of historical imperialism and bring them into the dialogue, emancipating them to participate and lead the world toward future policies of greater global justice and harmony.

Key Concepts

bonded labor 444	exploitation 438	peripheral states 443
colonization 438	imperialism 438	semi-peripheral states 443
core states 443	marginalization 438	systematic inequality 442
division of labor 443	metropole 442	transaction costs 437

Study Questions

1. How do critical and mainstream perspectives differ on the causes of and solutions for globalization? How do they see the past as it relates to the future?

2. How has colonialism affected today's trading patterns among advanced and developing countries in the agriculture and high-tech industrial sectors?

3. What perspective does the following analysis reflect?

   The mercantilists compelled their subjects to sell many goods only to them, paying the colonies less than world market prices for crops and raw materials. . . . Mercantilist policy also required the colonies to buy many products from the mother country, ensuring that the homeland could sell to its subjects at above world market prices.[23]

4. In what ways are multinational companies like the raw material plantations of the colonial era? How have they marginalized indigenous peoples and women?

5. Has global inequality increased or decreased? And what is the difference between changes in inequality within and between countries?

Global Forces for Change

The world changes slowly, but it does change. In Parts I and II, we have seen how the world changed through ancient and modern history and have examined the array of military and economic issues that affect our present-day world. In Part III, we look at issues that portend change in the future. The contemporary state system is experiencing two major cross-cutting developments. Underneath the nation-state system or level, some forces are fragmenting international society and potentially pushing the world toward even more decentralized structures. Above the nation-state level, other developments are potentially unifying and globalizing international life.

Above the level of the contemporary nation-state, some concerns are compelling individual states to unify; chief among them are environmental concerns. All states recognize that they share one planet and have a common responsibility to preserve it. Despite continuing disputes over global warming, progress has been made on dealing with the depletion of the ozone layer. And the world is also pulling together to confront the scourge of disease. Pandemics are not new, but because of increased population and interconnectedness, they can now become global within weeks rather than years. Governments and international organizations are increasingly coordinating their efforts through specialized agencies such as the World Health Organization in order to combat and in some cases eradicate the world's most debilitating diseases. Chapter 14 addresses the manifold issues of population, pollution, and pandemics.

Underneath the state system (that is, inside individual countries), institutions and actors are proliferating. NGOs populate national and world affairs as never before. People live in local and regional as well as global communities, and they are asserting the right to exercise more indigenous control of their lives and cultural identities. They need to feel comfortable at home before they can participate effectively in global society abroad. The explosion of NGOs offers encouraging evidence of local initiative and pluralizing forces. The Internet is empowering more and more individuals and small groups to play on the same level as MNCs and state governments. This pluralization of world politics creates a global civil society to go along with nation-states and intergovernmental or international institutions. Whether this pluralization ultimately divides or unites the peoples of the world depends on a consensus in the global civil society. The old nation-state system reflected a global consensus among states on sovereignty. Today's world envisions increasing limitations on sovereignty, especially when it comes to the physical abuse of minorities. Will the new NGO-dominated system reflect a global consensus among NGOs on basic human rights? Those are the topics and questions we address in Chapter 15.

Perhaps most encouraging of all, at the level above the nation-state, there is the slow but steady progress toward the consolidation of political authority. The European Union, with all of its faults, is one of the shining symbols of a new world order in which larger geographical entities emerge, governing via the rule of law rather than the threat or use of force. Asia and Africa, which need more integration, are taking note. Recently, the African Union changed its name to mimic the EU. Regional integration alone cannot solve the problem of continuing global fragmentation, but it surely cannot be wrong to aspire to consolidate political authority at the regional and global levels—as long as that authority is not despotic and serves the interests of both large and small participants. Chapter 16 examines the European Union and the United Nations, as well as other international institutions that envision greater global political unity.

Finally, the Conclusion to this book examines one of the most hopeful, perhaps utopian, visions of future global society, the democratic peace. While it may be ethnocentric for us in the West to envision a world with an increasing number of democracies, it is also true that the number of democracies is increasing and that they do seem to behave more peacefully, especially toward one another. We don't yet know the exact reasons for this phenomenon. So, the Conclusion helps us understand the various explanations using the tools of perspectives and levels of analysis that we have developed in this book.

Notice, however, how these visions of a pluralizing and perhaps unifying global universe depend on qualifying caveats. Nongovernment (NGOs) or non-despotic means that governments do not control everything or most things. Equal respect means treating large (MNCs) and small (individual) participants alike, and the democratic peace implies the prevalence of democracy. These caveats reflect the continuing relevance of perspectives as we examine global society in the future. Realist perspectives may be the most skeptical about global integration. They fear the lack of constraint or counterbalancing as institutions become larger and larger. Who will control more centralized institutions, and will there be sufficient competition to protect regional and local rights and initiatives? Liberal perspectives are perhaps the most hopeful. They count on institutions and the habits of routine interdependence to narrow ideological differences. They expect that the best attributes of each society will cross-pollinate and that in a world of diversity and equality no human being will feel left out or oppressed. Some identity perspectives might agree, as long as the discourse that brings diverse people together respects the norms of human rights, gender equality, and social community. But other identity perspectives might wonder if evil ideas can realistically be purged permanently from the human family and whether future communications will depend, as in the past, on an understanding and perhaps even clash of competing ideas and a ceaseless struggle to define the human good.

14

World Environment
Population, Pollution, and Pandemics

Yanomami Indians in Brazil clear farmland in the Amazon and progressively destroy rain forests larger than western Europe. The rain forests act like "the lungs of the world," except in reverse, absorbing carbon dioxide to reduce greenhouse gases and producing oxygen that nurtures 30 percent of the planet's animal and plant species.

The world has many players but only one stage. And that stage is planet Earth. The environment—the materials below the Earth's surface, and the atmosphere and space above it—is the world's common home. It is perhaps the best example of a collective good. It will be preserved for all peoples, or it will be preserved for none. It is indivisible. And one person's ability to enjoy it does not subtract from another's enjoyment. It is non-appropriable; that is, it can't be converted from public to private consumption. Thus, the environment is or should be a force unifying the people and nations of the world.

The world's environment or ecosystem is complex. It starts with population and crowding that limits land to cultivate crops, exhausts resources such as energy and water, and threatens the diversity of animal and plant life. It is compounded by industrial and agricultural growth that pollutes the atmosphere and waterways, damages the ozone layer, and arguably warms the Earth. And the ecosystem is the medium that transmits deadly diseases and pandemics and causes natural disasters such as hurricanes and earthquakes. These natural disasters, in turn, contribute to massive refugee movements that catalyze trafficking in sex, drugs, and human beings.

In this chapter, we look at each of these components of the global ecosystem. Science and technology play a large role in the environment—analyzing problems such as global warming, causing problems such as industrialization and fossil fuel use, and solving problems such as the eradication of smallpox. But like facts and reasoning in other areas, such as the study of war or globalization, science and technology do not substitute for the role of perspectives. People see the perils and promises of the environment from different perspectives. And so we start with an overview of how the different perspectives approach the topics of the environment. Then we examine individual environmental issues—population, resources, pollution and global warming, and pandemics—and observe how the perspectives agree and disagree about the severity of these issues and their solutions.

Identity View—Environment as Globalist Ideas

Identity perspectives, especially social constructivist perspectives, tend to see environmental problems as deeply embedded in human societies and values. As one study suggests, "environmental threats are the product not only of population growth and ignorant or careless individual actions, they are deeply embedded in our religious, cultural, economic, and social systems."[1] Today, they are embedded in the nation-state system. And from a social constructivist perspective, this system cultivates the wrong self-images. It encourages governments to think only of the interests of their own people and ignore or transfer the costs of transnational problems such as the environment to other people outside their own borders. As Professor John McCormick writes, "the modern industrial state may have improved the quality of life of many of its citizens, but it has done so at the expense of encouraging people to think of themselves as competing citizens of individual states rather than as cooperating members of the human race."[2] What is needed to cope with environmental problems is a new idea "based on the belief in the notion of globalism, where institutions and ideals other than the state attract the loyalty of humans."[3]

International institutions among the nation-states are not sufficient because they are accountable only to states and have no influence over problems on which states cannot agree. They are also one step further removed from the people who often suffer the consequences of international neglect of environmental problems. A better arrangement is to shift responsibility to international NGOs and networks that represent people outside the formal structures of government and that cultivate actions and goals that transcend governments. Constituting a new **global civil society**, NGOs have flourished in the environmental area, numbering some 2,500 in 2001, and increasingly influence public opinion and governments to address environmental problems.

NGOs grow out of the concepts of citizen responsibility and activism. Thus, behind the development of a global civil society is democracy, the idea of individualism and freedom to assemble, organize, and influence public opinion. Collectively held ideas inspire grassroots initiatives and groups interact in a spirit of tolerance and pluralism. What if some governments do not permit activist NGOs? Russia requires all foreign NGOs to register and follows their activities closely. China disallows any NGO, foreign or domestic, that is not officially sanctioned. So identity perspectives that call for transformative ideas and identities to deal with environmental problems assume that these governments, at a minimum, do not prevail at the international level. Ideas trump power and institutions. Openness and access to political and economic resources are the *sine qua non* of globalist NGO approaches to the problems of the world environment.

NGOs develop epistemic communities, or groups of people who have similar expert-

global civil society
the international network of nongovernmental organizations that seeks to influence governments and intergovernmental organizations in numerous issue areas such as development and the environment.

causal arrow

sustainable development

an economic approach that calls for smaller-scale development that works in harmony with resource, population, land, and environmental constraints.

ise and share substantive knowledge about how to approach a problem. One substantive globalist idea that many identity perspectives favor is **sustainable development.** Sustainable development seeks to balance economic and environmental concerns. The brainchild of NGOs, this idea was popularized by the Brundtland Report, a 1987 study by the World Commission on Environment and Development, chaired by Gro Harlem Brundtland, the prime minister of Norway. Sustainable development calls for meeting the needs of human beings, especially the essential needs of the world's poor, without compromising the ability of future generations to meet their needs. It implies limitations on growth such that resources are not used more rapidly than they are replenished and pollution emissions are no greater than the carrying capacity of the environment. In some ways, social identity perspectives call for a radical rethinking of the model of industrialization and competitive, decentralized nation-states that has characterized international politics since the eighteenth century. This model is inherently incapable of dealing with the deep-seated cause of the environmental problems that the world faces today and needs to be replaced by ideas that transcend divisive borders.

Liberal View—Environment as a Common Task

Liberal perspectives also embrace NGOs and ideas of pluralism and sustainable development as ways to cope with environmental problems, but their emphasis shifts to managing collective goods through traditional international institutions. From this perspective, environmental problems are less the consequence of deeply embedded values of modernization that need to be changed than of the familiar problem of managing collective or public goods. Many activities that affect the environment remain private goods. Resources are better used and renewed through competition rather than centralized management, as the experience of the planned economies in communist countries certainly demonstrated. Water and other resources may be provided by private as well as public companies. What is needed is better coordination and regulation of these activities through international institutions and regimes.

Spotlight on collective goods

Spotlight on free riders

International institutions solve the problems of collective action. First, they include everyone, so that there are no free riders. Recall that free riders are participants who think that others will solve the problem for them; they go along just for the free ride. Institutions in which everyone participates overcome this problem. Developed and developing countries alike not only comply with international regimes but influence them as well. Second, common institutions facilitate side payments to encourage small countries to comply. International institutions such as the World Bank and the numerous UN specialized agencies provide foreign aid and technical assistance to help smaller and poorer countries meet the required regulations. Third, common institutions focus on non-zero-sum solutions from which everyone gains. They don't limit growth, which hurts poor countries that need to grow, or redistribute existing resources, which hurts rich countries that innovate and invest.

Spotlight on side payments

Liberal solutions seek broader scope and participation to solve environmental problems regardless of national differences. One example of broadening the scope of a problem is suggested by flu epidemics. Many infectious diseases that afflict human beings originate in animals. Avian flu, a potential epidemic that the world is watching warily, is thought to originate in domestic birds even though it is spread by migratory birds and has yet to spread, except in one case, from one human being to another. A typical liberal approach calls for addressing such diseases by instituting programs aimed at animal as well as human health. Animals, such as gorillas and chimpanzees in central Africa, may have no immunity to common human diseases, and human beings may have no immunity to animal-borne diseases. Thus health-care systems and information need to encompass both animal and human diseases and to treat diseases on both sides of the human-animal barrier before a pathogen breaches that barrier. Liberal solutions seek holistic approaches that include all aspects of the problem and all participants, "based on the understanding that there is only one world—and [in the case of human beings and animals] only one health." [4]

Realist View—Environment as a Resource

Realist approaches to the environment stress circumstances and scarcity rather than institutions or ideas. The most prevalent circumstance facing the world is competition. Human beings compete for physical security and economic prosperity. They use resources and the environment as instruments in that competition. While some collective problems, such as pollution and natural disasters, have the characteristics of collective goods, they also require private resources to resolve. The countries that control the resources call the shots. Cooperation and even institutions may be helpful in certain cases; but, if the scope and participation of these efforts are too broad, nothing gets done. Including everyone and every issue, as liberal perspectives advise, is often a prescription for inaction. It is better to act on a decentralized basis than not act at all. Thus, realist solutions often favor indirect market rather than direct institutional measures to deal with environmental issues. If pollution is a problem, tax it and internalize the external costs. Or if regulations are necessary, set an overall cap on pollution but then let individual countries trade **pollution rights** (credits toward meeting the overall cap) and promote new technologies to achieve better results. Above all, from a realist perspective, do not prescribe a single set of standards or rules, which means that one rule or group has to dominate, and do not limit growth except through prices that signal scarcities and increase incentives to produce alternatives. In environmental affairs, realist solutions seek to avoid a hegemony of rules, institutions, or ideas, just as in military affairs the balance of power seeks to prevent the dominance of a single power.

Thus, realist thinking about the environment is not selfish as much as practical. The environment, like security, may be a collective good. But can one kind of environmental regime or security arrangement satisfy all countries? Probably not. Realist perspectives resist one-size-fits-all solutions, just as they resist one-power-fits-all solutions, or hegemony. Take, for example, protection against a pandemic. If a flu epidemic occurs, and there is an insufficient amount of vaccine to inoculate everyone, who gets it? Who is responsible for the distribution? You can be sure there will be an investigation after the epidemic. Now who bears the responsibility? Will international institutions be held accountable? Realist solutions argue no because people look to the most capable and accountable institutions for security from disease (as well as from military attacks) and these institutions are still nation-states. International institutions may be useful, but they are not necessary, and utopian ideas that ignore the reality of decentralized power may be immoral. They delude people into thinking that common goals serve all countries, when they may actually serve mostly the few most powerful ones.

A good example is the problem of greenhouse gas emissions, such as carbon dioxide, which may cause global warming. These emissions come from industrialization and burning fossil fuels. Advanced countries are far and away the worst offenders. Now

> **Spotlight on anarchy**

pollution rights
a country's credits toward meeting the overall cap on pollution emissions; when an individual country exceeds the cap on pollution emissions, it may trade for credits with another country that has not exceeded its cap.

Spotlight on
power balancing

they propose global standards to curb greenhouse gases, just as developing countries are beginning to industrialize and need fossil fuels to grow. Developing countries might be excused for rejecting a single standard or common idea solutions. They argue that advanced countries should clean up the environment while the poor countries develop and get rich. When the poor countries are rich, they will join the effort. Realist perspectives, emphasizing the impulse of the weak to align against the strong, can serve the interests of small countries as well as large.

Our three perspectives capture legitimate differences in the way various groups interpret and react to world environmental problems. Let's see how these differences emerge over specific environmental issues.

Population

The world's human population lies at the center of the world's environment. Land constitutes about 30 percent of the Earth's surface. As the human population increases, the land becomes crowded; resources are exploited, including animal and plant life; and nutrition and health suffer. Already in the eighteenth century, Thomas Malthus, a British economist and clergyman, predicted that population would outstrip the Earth's ability to feed itself and famine and disease would follow. Malthus was living through the early days of the industrial revolution and might be forgiven for not seeing the potential of technology. Industrialization brought new ways to increase the food supply, but it also added new burdens on the environment. Industrial processes consumed raw materials in large quantities, not only minerals such as iron ore and copper but, most important, energy resources such as coal and, later, oil and gas. By spewing chemicals into the air, the human population began to exhaust or destroy other natural resources such as clean air and protective ozone layers in the Earth's atmosphere. Many Malthusians since Malthus have worried about human activity creating environmental burdens that will go beyond the carrying capacity of nature and have called for a limit to human population and industrial growth.

Spotlight on
sustainable development

Today there are some 6.5 billion people in the world, and the population is still growing. It is expected to reach 9 billion by 2050 and stabilize thereafter, although some estimates go as high as 15 billion and climbing. Even if it stabilizes, however, population changes will be unevenly distributed around the world. Almost all of the population growth will take place in the developing countries and in already crowded and polluted urban, rather than rural, areas. What is more, because of the way population size changes as living standards improve, most of the population increase will take place in the poorest parts of the developing world, creating throngs of young people with no education, jobs, or future. Youth bulges in the Middle East and Africa will add to political instability, while population declines and aging in the industrialized world may slow growth and create a declining global economic pie. This age gap could build up intolerable tensions and, like an electrical discharge across a voltage gap, spark new streams of immigrants and refugees across national borders, disrupting trade and other global economic activities.

demographic transitions

periods of accelerating population growth as living standards increase because death rates decline faster than birth rates.

Demographic transitions are periods of accelerating population growth even as living standards increase. Death rates decline first as food supplies increase and access to health care expands. Birth rates change only later as people leave rural areas where more kids are needed, the workforce becomes better educated, and the status of women improves. During the interim transition, which can last 50–150 years, the population continues to increase. Only when lower birth rates eventually catch up with lower death rates do population increases stabilize at a lower level.

Industrial countries completed this transition a century ago and now face declining population trends. Developing countries fall into two groups. Some started the transition 40–50 years ago and are beginning to see a significant decline in birth rates. But others are just starting the transition and face rapid population growth in the near term. East and Southeast Asian nations such as South Korea, Taiwan, Thailand, and, increasingly, China fall into the first group. SSA (782 million people), South Asia (India, Pakistan, Bangladesh; 1.5 billion people), and, to a slightly lesser extent, MENA (311 million people), fall into the second group. The second group, the poorest countries, except for some rich oil states in the Middle East, will experience the most rapid population increases. India's population, for example, was 1.1 billion in 2006, up from 358 million in 1950. It is expected to increase to 1.3 billion, or by about 20 percent, by 2015. Pakistan's population is expected to swell by more than 20 percent, from 160 million in 2006 to 195 million.[5] In the next fifty years, Ethiopia's population is expected to increase by 120 percent from 77 to 170 million.[6] The outcome under these conditions is likely to be demographic disasters, either by starvation, disease, or both. For example, even though Botswana enjoys economic growth, the AIDS epidemic in Botswana, which affects about 25 percent of the adult population, has reduced life expectancy from sixty-one years in 1990 to forty-four years in 1999 and, if it continues, to a projected thirty-nine years in 2010.

What is worse, in terms of international implications, population increases in the developing world will be largely among young people, while populations in industrialized nations and some late-transition countries, such as China and Russia, will shift disproportionately to older people. As the Map 14-1 shows, the **youth bulge** is already present in Africa and the Middle East. Many countries have 30–50 percent of their population under fourteen years of age. The **graying population** of the industrial world is also apparent. In Europe, for example, the number of working-age people will decline over the next twenty-five years by 7 percent, while the number older than sixty-five will increase by 50 percent. This divergence between age groups in industrial and developing countries may both weaken growth and increase violence. Industrial countries may not be able to sustain growth as a larger percentage of their people leave the workforce. And Middle Eastern and African youths who have no jobs may migrate to cities or neighboring countries where they stir up unrest and violence.

Studies show that youth bulges are associated with increases in civil and ethnic conflicts. In the 1990s, three demographic factors correlated closely with the likelihood of civil conflict in a country: a youth bulge, rapid urban growth, and exceptionally low levels of cropland and/or freshwater per person.[7] Population imbalances thus spawn conflicts, which in turn induce immigration flows that spread unrest to developed nations. In the early 2000s, legal and illegal immigrants accounted for more than 15 percent of the population in more than fifty countries. Between now and 2015, several million migrants are expected to move annually to North America from Latin America and Asia, to Europe from North Africa and the Middle East as well as eastern Europe, and to richer developing countries from poorer ones. What is more, immigration and refugee flows often mix easily with drug, sex, and human trafficking. Population problems, therefore, are a highly mobile and degrading factor for the quality of human life everywhere.

What do we do about population problems? Realist perspectives tend to see population as a factor contributing to national power. Increasing population means more

youth bulge
the demographic pattern in which a substantial percentage of the population in a given country is young, typically below the age of fifteen.

graying population
the demographic pattern in which a substantial percentage of a country's population is growing progressively older than sixty-five.

Spotlight on
realist perspective

Map 14-1

A View of the Global Environment: Population, Pandemics, and Pollution

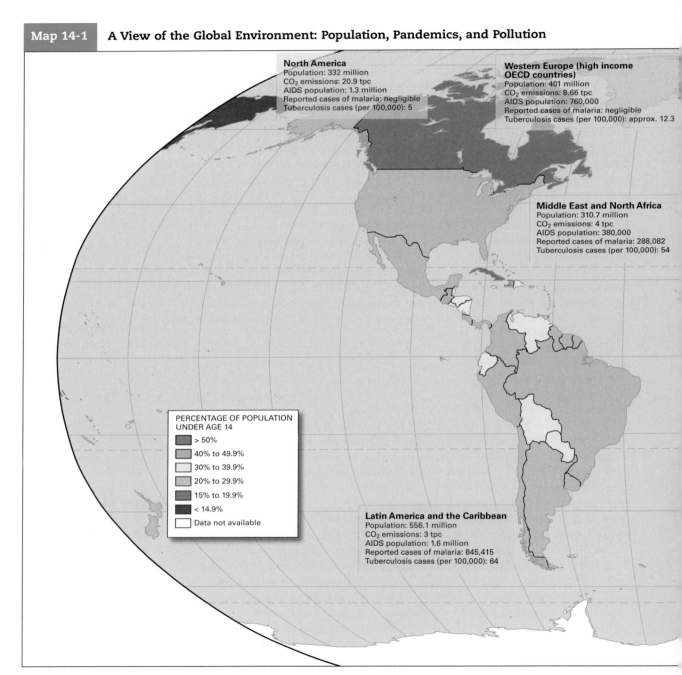

North America
Population: 332 million
CO$_2$ emissions: 20.9 tpc
AIDS population: 1.3 million
Reported cases of malaria: negligible
Tuberculosis cases (per 100,000): 5

Western Europe (high income OECD countries)
Population: 401 million
CO$_2$ emissions: 8.66 tpc
AIDS population: 760,000
Reported cases of malaria: negligible
Tuberculosis cases (per 100,000): approx. 12.3

Middle East and North Africa
Population: 310.7 million
CO$_2$ emissions: 4 tpc
AIDS population: 380,000
Reported cases of malaria: 288,082
Tuberculosis cases (per 100,000): 54

Latin America and the Caribbean
Population: 556.1 million
CO$_2$ emissions: 3 tpc
AIDS population: 1.6 million
Reported cases of malaria: 845,415
Tuberculosis cases (per 100,000): 64

PERCENTAGE OF POPULATION UNDER AGE 14
> 50%
40% to 49.9%
30% to 39.9%
20% to 29.9%
15% to 19.9%
< 14.9%
Data not available

Source: Age data: *CIA World Factbook,* "Field Listing—Age Structure," https://www.cia.gov/library/publications/the-world-factbook/fields/2010 .html. Accessed May 23, 2008. Other data compiled from the Organization for Economic Co-operation and Development, the World Bank, the *CIA World Factbook,* and the World Health Organization. All data are for the most recent year available.

Notes: tpc = metric tons per capita; OECD = Organization for Economic Co-operation and Development.

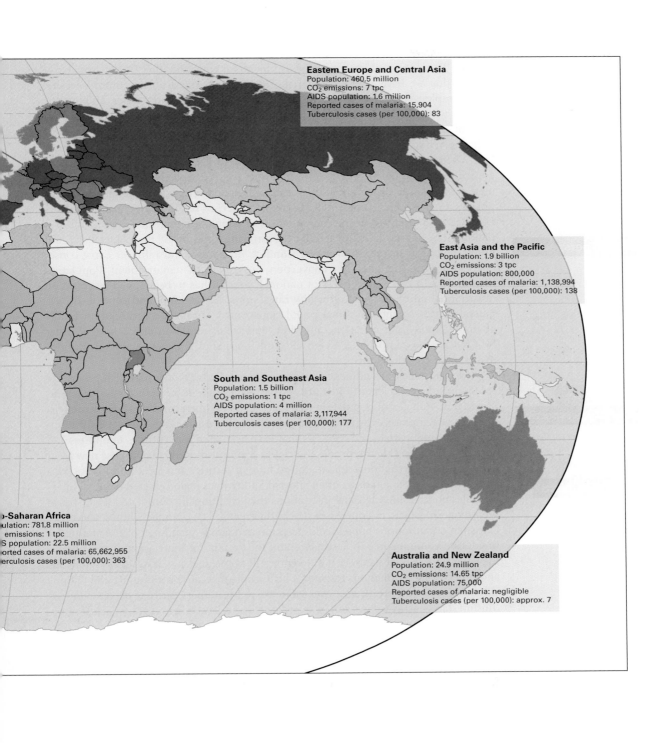

Eastern Europe and Central Asia
Population: 460.5 million
CO_2 emissions: 7 tpc
AIDS population: 1.6 million
Reported cases of malaria: 15,904
Tuberculosis cases (per 100,000): 83

East Asia and the Pacific
Population: 1.9 billion
CO_2 emissions: 3 tpc
AIDS population: 800,000
Reported cases of malaria: 1,138,994
Tuberculosis cases (per 100,000): 138

South and Southeast Asia
Population: 1.5 billion
CO_2 emissions: 1 tpc
AIDS population: 4 million
Reported cases of malaria: 3,117,944
Tuberculosis cases (per 100,000): 177

⊃-Saharan Africa
ⲟulation: 781.8 million
emissions: 1 tpc
S population: 22.5 million
ⲟrted cases of malaria: 65,662,955
ⲉrculosis cases (per 100,000): 363

Australia and New Zealand
Population: 24.9 million
CO_2 emissions: 14.65 tpc
AIDS population: 75,000
Reported cases of malaria: negligible
Tuberculosis cases (per 100,000): approx. 7

people to work on farms, toil in industries, and fight in armies. In contrast to Europe, for example, the United States has a growing population because it allows freer immigration. Thus, one well-known realist commentator concludes that "it is reasonable to assume that we have only just entered a long era of American hegemony" because "demographic trends show the American population growing faster and getting younger while the European population declines and steadily ages."[8] Large poor countries, of course, might see it differently. China, for example, has pursued a determined policy to reduce population by enforcing, ruthlessly at times, a one-child-per-couple law. Whether national interests dictate an increase or decrease of population, national governments bear the principal responsibility, as realist perspectives see it, because population is a critical factor in national competition and one-size-fits-all institutions or policies, such as China's one-child-per-couple policy, do not fit all national situations.

Liberal perspectives see the consequences of population increases spilling out over national boundaries and threatening the carrying capacity of the planet itself, not unlike pollution in the atmosphere. Conflict, migration, and refugees carry consequences around the globe like convection currents in the environment. Population growth therefore is a collective, not national, good. It has to be stopped by common institutional efforts to reduce fertility rates, improve nutrition, and control disease. Liberal causes champion global population control through contraception, family planning, and, when necessary, abortion. Planned Parenthood and a host of other NGOs lead the campaign. Foreign aid and international development institutions make major contributions.

However, policies to influence fertility rates rapidly become a part of the world of conflicting ideas and identity. Identity perspectives ask about the ideas that inform policies to deal with global population problems. Classical liberal and social constructivist perspectives emphasize the emancipation and role of women. They suspect institutions such as the nation-state and churches that have been used for centuries to oppress and control women and their reproductive rights. Feminist movements propose new ideas to restructure international affairs around human security and local or domestic violence, where women are more often affected, rather than male-centered national interest states and the international institutions they traditionally dominated. Faith-based identity perspectives, of course, see it very differently. The Catholic Church and other Christian organizations oppose contraception and family planning policies and prefer to educate young people in abstinence and the sanctity of marriage and conception. Ideologically oriented states see it differently still. Some, such as China, justify abortions and other stringent methods to enforce birth control because communist and nationalist ideology takes precedence over women's rights. Others, such as deeply religious Muslim states, justify oppression in terms of religious law. Religious law (*sharia*) subordinates women to imams, who are exclusively men, and takes precedence over democratic or social constructivist ideologies calling for equal rights for women.

Resources, Food, Energy, Water, and Biodiversity

Population and industrial pressures exhaust croplands and food, consume limited energy and water supplies, and destroy animal and plant life.

People need about 600 square meters or 0.06 hectares of land per person—about the size of a hockey rink—to feed themselves. When this level is not met, countries import food or people move. In Bangladesh, for example, overcrowding in the late

1970s, accompanied by several years of flooding, reduced croplands and forced massive migration across the border into India. By 1990, over 7 million Bangladeshis had made the trek, swelling the population of the Indian state of Assam by over 50 percent and causing land shortages and conflicts throughout the border regions. If the population of Ethiopia triples, as is currently projected, cropland will be reduced to about 0.04 hectares per person, 33 percent below the bare subsistence level. We can anticipate large flows of refugees in East Africa, which, as we note in Chapter 7, is already rife with ethnic conflicts. In Pakistan, people flock to urban areas, such as Karachi, and become tinder for popular unrest, violence, and terrorism against local as well as distant governments. Urban sprawl further reduces the availability of needed croplands.

Poor people scavenge the Earth for wood to cook their food, and rich nations devour the world's energy resources, especially fossil fuels, to keep their industries going. The loss of forested land contributes to global warming; but equally as important for those who live close by, it reduces the capacity of the land to hold water and contributes to desertification. The Sahara Desert, which stretches across the northern half of Africa, expands annually as many of the world's poorest people strip wooded areas to eke out a paltry existence. Rich countries, of course, don't need wood for fuel, but they still harvest trees for commercial purposes. And, more important, they mine and burn fossil fuels and use other mineral resources in enormous magnitudes to fire the engines of industrialization.

The principal raw materials for industrialization are fossil fuels, iron ore, copper, nickel, zinc, tin, bauxite, platinum, manganese, and chromium. **Fossil fuels**—coal, oil, and natural gas—have the largest consequence for international affairs because they provide 95 percent of world energy consumption and are unevenly distributed. As we have learned in Chapter 8, oil and gas reserves are concentrated in the Middle East, a strategic and unstable part of the world; on the other hand, industrialized countries use 80 percent of all oil and natural gas resources. So international trade of oil and gas is enormous and vital. And energy use continues to grow. In 2007, the world consumed an estimated 86 million barrels of oil per day, and consumption is expected to grow to more than 116 million barrels per day by 2030.[9] Consumption of natural gas—the cleanest burning fossil fuel—is expected to grow even faster, doubling by 2015. Trade in natural gas will create a whole new network of tanker and port facilities to transport liquefied natural gas. Oil and gas development, as well as other resource mining, scars and damages the environment, causing periodic oil spills in lakes and oceans and interfering with wildlife in parkland and natural habitats. As Figure 14-1 shows, between 2003 and 2030 total energy consumption (in BTUs, British thermal units) will more than double in developing (non-OECD) countries while increasing another 30 percent in advanced (OECD) countries. Altogether world energy consumption is predicted to increase by nearly 72 percent.

Other resources are more evenly distributed, although Japan and Europe are generally more dependent on mineral imports than the United States. South Africa controls three-quarters of the world's supplies of manganese and chromium. When it was a pariah in the international community because of its apartheid practices, interest developed in mining manganese and other minerals from the ocean's deep seabed out beyond the territorial claims of littoral states. The Law of the Sea Treaty, negotiated in the 1980s, called for an International Seabed Authority, which would mine manganese and other deep seabed resources on behalf of all nations. But interest declined after South Africa abandoned apartheid, and early enthusiasm for global commodity agreements to regulate raw material production and trade waned. Resource scarcities were

fossil fuels
coal, oil, and natural gas.

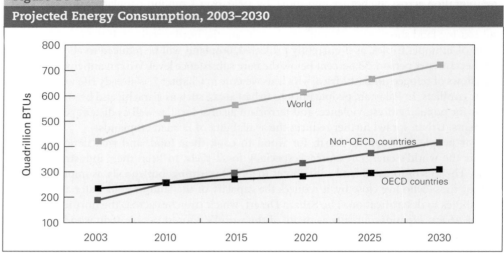

Figure 14-1

Projected Energy Consumption, 2003–2030

Source: Data from the U.S. Department of Energy, Table A1, "World Total Energy Consumption by Region, Reference Case, 1990–2030 (Quadrillion Btu)," available at www.eia.doe.gov/oiaf/ieo/pdf/ieoreftab_1.pdf.

a big concern at the height of the oil crises in the 1970s and have continued to flare up periodically since then.

Water is an old and new resource concern. Civilization began close to rivers and shorelines. Today water disputes are escalating. Water use grew twice as fact as the population during the past century. So, water became more valuable as it became increasingly scarce. One-fifth of the world's population does not have safe drinking water, and 40 percent has no sanitation. Some of the problem is due to nature and the distribution of water. But some is also due to mismanagement. Water is often subsidized in the same countries where it is scarce.[10] Eighty or more countries suffer water shortages. **Water tables,** or aquifers under the Earth's surface, are sinking, especially in heavily populated countries. In parts of China, water levels are falling by five feet per year and throughout India, by three to ten feet per year. India uses water twice as fast as it accumulates. Once the underground aquifers are depleted, the use of water will have to be cut to the recharge rate, or by 50 percent. That could reduce harvests dependent on irrigation by as much as one-fourth.

More than one-half of the world's land surface consists of river basins shared by more than one country, and more than thirty nations get one-third of their water supply from outside their borders. In the Middle East and Africa, rivers are a major source of disputes. The Euphrates River originates in Turkey and runs through Syria and Iraq. Turkey diverts water for various uses, which Syria and Iraq oppose. And Syria diverts water, which Iraq opposes. The Jordan River sparks similar disputes among Syria, Lebanon, Israel, and Jordan. In 1964, Israel attacked dams that Syria and Lebanon had built to divert the Jordan River and captured the Golan Heights in 1967, in part to control the upper reaches of the Jordan River. Egypt, Sudan, and Ethiopia fight over water from the Nile River.

Biodiversity refers to the multiple species of plant and animal life in nature. Population growth and resource use reduce biodiversity in two ways. First, they lead directly to overhunting, overfishing, and transplanting species where they don't belong. And, second, they contribute indirectly by eliminating the natural habitats of

water tables
the aquifers below the Earth's surface that supply freshwater.

biodiversity
the multiple species of plant and animal life found in nature.

During a multiyear drought in the early 2000s, women in a village in the Indian state of Gujarat fetch water from a murky water hole shared with animals.

various plant and animal life, principally through the destruction of rain forests, pollution of rivers and streams, and elimination of agricultural lands, especially wetlands, to accommodate urban sprawl and commercial development. Because the preservation of biodiversity is more location-specific, national governments exercise greater control. For example, the United States restricted logging in the U.S. Northwest to save the natural habitat of the northern spotted owl.[11] But international agreements also seek to regulate biodiversity. UN treaties and conventions regulate trade and the natural habitats of endangered species. Some environmentalists are particularly concerned about whales and dolphins. The International Whaling Commission sets quotas for hunting certain types of whales, but Norway, Japan, and other countries periodically flout the agreement. Efforts to protect dolphins also affect tuna fishing, restricting fishing methods that catch a lot of dolphins in tuna fishing nets. Under laws to prevent this, the United States banned tuna from Mexico and Venezuela, which reduced Venezuela's tuna fleet to less than one-third of its original size. Mexico and Venezuela took the United States to the WTO, arguing that the tuna ban was discriminatory. The WTO agreed, sparking a loud outcry from environmental groups who see the free-trading system running roughshod over environmental concerns.

How do the different perspectives view resource and biodiversity concerns?

Realist perspectives adopt competitive practices toward resources. If material resources are physically limited, states compete for those resources through territorial acquisition or government agreements. As we have learned in earlier chapters, resource competition was a significant factor in wars during the nineteenth and twentieth centuries. And government agreements spawned the original multinational oil companies and then cartels such as OPEC that wrested control of oil production from western countries. From realist perspectives, such competition is unlikely to lead to despoliation because decentralized systems such as nation-states or markets—if they are not overregulated—price resources based on scarcity. Resources in this economic sense are not strictly limited. As they become scarce at some price, demand declines and new supplies are discovered or become economical to develop. Governments may embar-

Spotlight on realist perspective

go some countries, to be sure, but they can always sell their supplies to someone else, and because markets are fungible (that is, goods are freely exchanged among many actors), these supplies will be available for purchase elsewhere in the marketplace. Because realist perspectives worry about relative power and who controls resources, they prefer either to dominate supply, if that's possible, as with the seven original oil companies, or fragment it so that no one controls it. Hence, realist solutions often advocate market mechanisms or the private-sector supply of certain resources, such as water and electric power. This is an especially appealing option, of course, if countries have strong private companies to provide these services.

Liberal perspectives prefer cooperative approaches to resource scarcity, both to prevent the overuse of supplies and to allocate them more fairly. They see resources, especially water and biodiversity, as common property that has to be managed for the collective good. They fear that decentralized mechanisms, particularly markets, will sacrifice the collective for the private good. More is involved than just security or commercial undertakings, they contend, and institutions that include everyone are needed to represent the common interest. Thus, liberal perspectives hail the successes of international institutions, such as the International Rice Research Institute that pioneered the **green revolution,** to develop new and more productive varieties of crop seeds, pesticides, and fertilizers. They urge similar solutions to develop alternative energy sources and to manage resource exploitation to conserve natural habitats, parklands, and endangered species. As political scientist Karen Mingst observes, while "realists and radicals . . . fear dependency on other countries because they diminish state power and therefore limit state action, liberals welcome the interdependency and have faith in the technological ingenuity of individuals to be able to solve many of the natural resource dilemmas." [12]

Some identity perspectives go one step further and see the root cause of resource scarcity and despoliation in the excessive consumerism of modern society. As we have already noted, they call for sustainable development, which means, if necessary, limits on industrial growth to bring resource use back in line with the carrying capacity of the planet and the needs of future generations. In the 1970s, when resource concerns reached a peak, globalist environmental perspectives advocated **limits to growth** to slow consumption, conserve resources, and preserve natural habitats and wildlife. [13] Social identity perspectives, in particular, tend to see the valuing of industrialism and commercialism as the cause of resource depletion and to urge a more communitarian approach.

Critical theory perspectives take a more holistic point of view. Feminist perspectives, for example, locate the problem deep in the structure of an international society that discriminates against women. They call for self-sustaining development as opposed to competitive, market-oriented globalization. Development should not focus solely or primarily on growth and profits, which are individualistic measures of performance, but also on non-market, volunteerist activities that value the home, village, community, and environment, where women have been historically employed and have contributed so much to the continuity and quality of human life. [14]

Pollution and Global Warming

Pollution of the world environment comes in many forms. First, there is **smog,** the belching bile of factories that chokes industrial cities and damages the health of urban residents. While the United States and Europe have curtailed this form of pollution, it

---

**Spotlight on
liberal perspective**

green revolution
international research that led to new and more efficient varieties of crop seeds, fertilizers, and pesticides.

**Spotlight on
identity perspective**

limits to growth
limits on industrialization proposed in the 1970s to slow consumption, conserve resources, and preserve natural habitats and wildlife.

**Spotlight on
critical theory perspective**

smog
air pollution, especially as a result of industry.

is only starting in the developing world. As one visitor writes, "smog in Beijing, Shanghai, and other cities reduces visibility most summer days to less than half a mile: when you drive along the elevated highways that cut through Shanghai, office and apartment towers emerge sporadically from the haze and then dissolve away."[15] Second, there is **acid rain,** which results from pollutants that travel in the upper atmosphere and descend in rain, despoiling distant lakes and the plant and wildlife that live in them. Canada complained for years about acid rain from the United States. Eventually, the two countries signed an agreement, but acid rain persists and afflicts numerous other areas. Third, there is **river and ocean pollution.** Industrial effluents, garbage and human sewage, and run-off from agricultural pesticides and fertilizers kill fish and plant life in streams and estuaries, and even in large bodies of water. The Great Lakes and Chesapeake Bay in the United States were badly polluted for years, although they are somewhat improved today; the Mediterranean Sea is still severely polluted.

Toxic and hazardous wastes constitute the fourth and growing source of pollution. Over 70 percent of China's rivers and lakes are reportedly contaminated with toxic pollutants. In 2005, a petrochemical plant in Jilin, China, northeast of Beijing, exploded and dumped one hundred tons of chemicals into the Songhua River, which then flowed north as a fifty-mile-long toxic slick through other Chinese cities and into Russia.[16] The 1986 nuclear accident at Chernobyl in the former Soviet Union created radioactive pollutants that reached Italy and Sweden and made an entire region in what is now Ukraine uninhabitable for a decade or more. The Aral Sea in the former Soviet Union, now bordering on Kazakhstan and Uzbekistan, shriveled up by 50 percent because a massive Soviet agricultural project to grow cotton diverted and polluted the inland rivers that flowed into the Aral Sea. Environmentalists have given up on reclaiming it; it was once the fourth largest inland sea in the world.

Altering the outermost blanket of the Earth's atmosphere is the fifth and perhaps most serious form of pollution. Two threats exist. One is destruction of the **ozone layer,** which protects the Earth from harmful solar radiation. The second is contami-

acid rain
condensation-borne pollutants that may be transported through the upper atmosphere over long distances.

river and ocean pollution
waterway contaminants from industrial and agricultural run-off, garbage, and human sewage.

toxic and hazardous wastes
pollutants from the disposal of petrochemicals, nuclear waste, and other dangerous materials.

ozone layer
the outer layer of the Earth's atmosphere that protects the planet from solar radiation.

A sea-going vessel is grounded on the sandy bottom of what was formerly the Aral Sea. Once the fourth largest lake in the world, the Aral Sea has been destroyed by the Soviet Union's diversion of its water sources for irrigation, shrinking the lake and increasing its salinity, plus the runoff of pesticides and other chemicals from upstream agricultural projects in Kazakhstan when it was part of the former Soviet Union.

global warming
the heating up of the Earth's atmosphere due to greenhouse gases.

causal → arrow

chlorofluorocarbons (CFCs)
chemicals that break down the ozone layer.

Montreal Protocol
an agreement reached in 1987 that set the specific goal of reducing chlorofluorocarbons by 50 percent by 1998.

greenhouse gases
emissions from fossil fuels and other sources that can cause climate change.

Kyoto Protocol
an agreement reached in 1997 that set deadlines of 2008–2012 for industrial countries to cut their greenhouse gas emissions.

nation of the Earth's atmosphere with greenhouse gases, principally carbon dioxide, which trap heat and, assuming we can control for all the other factors affecting climate, cause **global warming.** The two threats tell different stories. The world community, including top corporations, pulled together to establish a common approach to dealing with ozone depletion. The liberal and perhaps identity perspectives seemed to prevail, reflecting common regimes and perhaps a new global civil society of corporations and NGOs demanding more accountability. By contrast, the world community is still badly divided over the causes and solutions to global warming. Developing countries, such as China and India, see it primarily as an advanced-country problem, and the United States is unwilling thus far to risk its economic growth to reduce greenhouse gases that may not be the primary cause of global warming. Let's look at these threats more closely.

The ozone layer is depleted by certain chemicals used by industrial countries in refrigeration and aerosol sprays. These chemicals, primarily **chlorofluorocarbons (CFCs),** rise to the top of the atmosphere and interact with ozone, breaking it down and reducing the ozone layer. The thinning of the ozone layer leads to more human diseases, such as skin cancer, and disruptions in plant and animal life. For a time, the evidence linking CFCs to ozone depletion was disputed, but the costs of doing something about CFCs were far less than eliminating greenhouse gases. Thus, by the mid-1980s the world community, including major MNCs such as DuPont and Dow Chemical, began to move toward consensus and action. In 1985, they adopted the Vienna Convention for the Protection of the Ozone Layer, which provided a general framework for the adoption of more substantive protocols. In 1987, twenty-two states negotiated the **Montreal Protocol,** which set the specific goal of reducing CFCs by 50 percent by 1998. In 1990, the timetable was accelerated, and eighty-one states agreed to eliminate all CFCs by 2000. When it was discovered in the early 1990s that an actual hole in the ozone layer had emerged above Antarctica, the timetable was accelerated once again. The advanced countries agreed to phase out CFCs by 1995 and to provide aid to third-world countries to do the same by 2010. Advanced countries met the deadline and gave more than $1 billion in the 1990s to developing countries. Whether the latter will meet the 2010 deadline is unclear, but even the reduced levels of CFCs continue to break down the ozone layer. The real verification of the science linking CFCs and ozone depletion won't come until ozone depletion actually begins to recede in line with the elimination of CFCs.

The science and costs of global warming are considerably more controversial. The problem first received widespread international attention in the 1980s. The United Nations invited the UN Environmental Program, which had been created in 1972, and the World Meteorological Organization to form the Intergovernmental Panel on Climate Change (IPCC), a gathering of some 2,000 climate experts to investigate the problem. The panel reported in 1990 that the Earth was indeed gradually warming and that human activity or the production of **greenhouse gases** from burning fossil fuels—mostly carbon dioxide, the rest methane, CFCs, and nitrous oxide—was the contributing cause. The UN Conference on the Environment and Development took up the issue in Rio de Janeiro, Brazil, in June 1992. It launched the UN Framework Convention on Climate Change, which called for holding emissions of greenhouse gases to 1990 levels. Meeting later in Japan in 1997, the participating countries adopted the **Kyoto Protocol,** which set deadlines of 2008–2012 for industrial countries to cut average emissions per year by 5 percent below 1990 levels. The developing countries were exempted. The United States, which accounts for about 35 percent of industrial-country emissions, initially signed but then withdrew from the protocol. Today, the protocol is in effect, after Russia ratified it and the signatories reached the required limit of accounting for 55 percent of all greenhouse gases produced by industrialized countries.

Since the late 1990s, the IPCC has stated its conclusions with increasing confidence, reporting in 2007 that human activity or the increase in greenhouse gases was "very likely" (90 percent confidence level) the principal cause of global warming.[17] Nevertheless, the United States has led the opposition to the Kyoto Protocol. The arguments against the protocol are twofold: the scientific evidence contains many uncertainties and the solution of reducing greenhouse gases to 1990 levels is too costly and will be ineffective if it excludes developing countries. The evidence that the Earth is warming is accepted, and the increase in greenhouse gas emissions is also well documented. The scientific dispute is about the link between the two factors. In the case of the depletion of the ozone layer, as the physicist Lisa Randall tells us, "chemists were able to detail the precise chemical processes involved in the destruction of the ozone layer, making the evidence that chlorofluorocarbon gases (Freon, for example) were destroying the ozone layer indisputable." But, in the case of global warming, she writes, "even if we understand some effects of carbon dioxide in the atmosphere, it is difficult to predict the precise chain of events that a marked increase in carbon dioxide will cause."[18] The Earth's climate has warmed and cooled for centuries. It was cooling, for example, before 1970. And, although it is clearly warming today, the ice pack around Antarctica is growing and set a record maximum for coverage in 2007 while the ice pack in the Arctic is shrinking.[19]

Spotlight on methods

The climate system is extraordinarily complex. According to a report by the nonpartisan Council on Foreign Relations, uncertainties in climate science include the role of clouds, some of which warm the environment while others cool it; the many natural processes that cycle carbon between its different forms (for example, carbon sinks such as rain forests absorb carbon dioxide and then release it when they are destroyed); the still rather coarse resolution of computer models that assign the same temperature to large areas; the possibility of abrupt changes due to feedback effects such as alterations in the circulation of the oceans; and, finally, the weighing of human factors, such as politics, law, and institutions, that involve trade-offs with future generations and the costs of losing species.[20] Many scientists admit that computer climate models are still very crude, yet they believe that the dangers are sufficient to warrant action.[21] The uncertainties divide industries as well as governments. Exxon Mobil, like many energy industries, opposes an abrupt shift away from fossil fuels. But Royal Dutch Shell and British Petroleum support heavy investments in alternative fuels.[22]

Even if science demonstrates the link, at least in the judgment of many scientists, the second issue concerns the relative cost we are willing to pay to solve the problem. On the basis of purely economic costs and benefits, one panel of leading world experts ranked the probable dangers of global warming below that of other critical problems such as HIV/AIDS, malaria, and lack of sanitation.[23] Compared to current growth priorities, China and India decided that dealing with global warming was not worth any cost for them at the present time. They refused to join the protocol because they saw the problem, as future generations might see it, as a way of permitting existing generations to impose costs on them for the sins of their predecessors, in this case the industrialized countries. The United States also worries about the economic costs of the Kyoto targets and advocates voluntary measures and technological innovation to address the problem. The United States accounts for about the same percentage of the

Spotlight on opportunity costs

world's GDP as its share of greenhouse gases, and in the past decade, it provided more than half of the increase in growth of the world economy. So, if the United States cuts way back on greenhouse gases and slows its economic growth, will other countries grow faster? And if poorer countries like China and India do, will they pollute even more because their technology is older and more polluting? To include the developing countries exempted from the Kyoto Protocol, in 2005 the United States formed the Asia Pacific Partnership on Clean Development and Climate. This partnership brings together China, India, South Korea, Japan, and Australia to focus on developing, deploying, and transferring cleaner, more efficient technologies for energy production.

The Kyoto Protocol expires in 2012, and negotiations began in Bali, Indonesia, in 2007 to replace it. The United States agreed to join the talks, although it prefers to negotiate with the major countries, including developing countries, that are the biggest emitters of greenhouse gases. It is not clear that some participants, such as the European Union and Japan, will meet the existing Kyoto targets. So the large UN gathering has its work cut out for it.[24]

Global warming illustrates the complexity of integrating scientific knowledge and social preferences. If the Earth warms up significantly, the consequences could be catastrophic. Ice caps will melt; ocean levels will rise; whole island complexes, such as the Maldives, whose highest point is only eight feet above sea level, could disappear; gulf streams will shift and affect temperatures; crops and wildlife will be decimated across wide swaths of existing continents; and weather patterns will change, causing more frequent and violent hurricanes and other storms. But the probability of these events is smaller than the likelihood of pandemics, wars, or other natural and human-created catastrophes. It would be nice to safeguard against every danger, but the world of policy making, no less than the world of understanding international relations, requires priorities, selection, perspective, and judgment. The box on page 477 illustrates how different judgments yield different conclusions about global warming and what to do about it. For the moment, the United States and a few other industrial countries prefer a more competitive or realist approach to confronting the dangers of global warming, while their critics seek a more institutionalized, liberal approach and, in some cases, a new identity perspective that would create a culture of development that turns away from fossil fuels to renewable and more sustainable sources of energy.

Pandemics

Diseases are closely interconnected with the human and natural environment. There are about 1,500 known infectious diseases. Sixty percent of them affect both animals and humans. The rest infect animals only, but carry the potential to affect human beings and to eventually mutate so that they can be passed on from human to human. AIDS, which is now transmitted by human sexual activity, originated among primates in Africa, and the avian flu virus originated in domestic birds and has infected human beings.

The world has long battled infectious diseases. The World Health Organization (WHO), a UN specialized agency, was established in 1948 and led postwar campaigns to eradicate small pox, polio, and tuberculosis. Tuberculosis has since made a comeback. Each year almost 9 million people contract the infection and 1.5–2 million people die. Malaria kills another million people a year and causes 500 million new cases and close to 5 billion episodes of clinical illness.[25] A vicious outbreak of Ebola virus occurred in Africa in 2005. AIDS has already killed 26 million people, orphaned

Using the Perspectives to **Read Between the Lines**

The Debate About Global Warming

Let's compare two judgments about global warming, one by a leading economist and another by a leading political commentator. Neither is a scientist, so their expertise on this topic, we could say, is roughly comparable.

Economist Paul Krugman says in the *New York Times*:

[T]here's now overwhelming scientific consensus that the world is getting warmer, and that human activity is the cause.... So how have corporate interests responded? ... as the scientific evidence became clearer, many ... oil companies like BP and Shell ... conceded the need to do something about global warming. Exxon ... decided to fight the science.... [Its] lavish grants have supported a sort of alternative intellectual universe of global warming skeptics.... But the fake research ... gets picked up by right-wing pundits ... because it plays perfectly into the he-said-she-said conventions of "balanced" journalism.[1]

Political commentator George F. Will writes in the *Washington Post*:

Time magazine ... exhorted readers to "Be Worried. Be Very Worried" ... about global warming.... The National Academy of Sciences says the rise in the Earth's surface temperature has been about one degree Fahrenheit in the past century.... Never mind that one degree might be the margin of error when measuring the planet's temperature.... [thirty years ago, we were] told to be worried, very worried, about global cooling.... *Science Digest* (February 1973) reported that "the world's climatologists are agreed" that we must "prepare for the next ice age".... [S]uppose the scientists and their journalistic conduits, who ... were so spectacularly wrong so recently, are now correct.... Are we sure that there will be proportionate benefits from whatever climate change can be purchased at the cost of slowing economic growth and spending trillions?[2]

Krugman sees the science of global warming as clear-cut and blames profit-based corporations, right-wing pundits, and "balanced" journalism for misleading the public. Will sees the science as uncertain and blames media hype for misleading the public—in the 1970s toward global cooling, today toward global warming. Krugman's world is one in which experts dominate (the liberal perspective) and profits (the realist perspective) and ideology (the identity perspective) obfuscate. Will's world is one in which experts sometimes err because they have ideologies or value preferences too (the identity perspective) and, even if they get it right (the liberal perspective), cannot resolve issues of resource trade-offs between climate change and growth (the realist perspective).

15 million children, and infected another 33.2 million others, two-thirds of them in Africa. Severe acute respiratory syndrome (SARS) infected 8,000 people in 2003 and killed 10 percent of them. It spread to five countries within twenty-four hours and to thirty countries on six continents over several months.

In 2004, a new variety of influenza, known as the H5N1 Z+ bird flu virus (or the avian flu virus), killed 11 million chickens in Vietnam and Thailand and spread there-

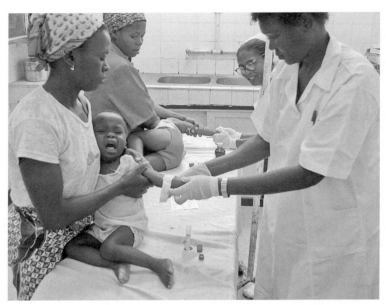

Children are tested for HIV/AIDS in a clinic in Mozambique in 2005. Few of those infected have access to life-prolonging drugs.

pandemics

diseases such as AIDS, the avian flu, and SARS, which spread or threaten to spread worldwide.

after by migratory birds to Africa, Europe, and the Middle East. It is 100 percent lethal in lab mice. As of January 2007, the avian flu virus had infected 265 human beings in ten countries, killing 159 of them. There was one documented case of human-to-human transmission in Thailand in late 2004, indicating that the virus could mutate at any time and spread by human contact.[26] Map 14-1 shows the prevalence of various diseases around the world.

Pandemics are not new. The Black Plague killed 25 million people, or one-third of the European population, in the fourteenth century. In 1918–1919, the Spanish flu killed 40–50 million people in eighteen months, with some estimates going as high as 100 million. That's far more than the number of people who died in the fighting in World War I. It's easy to see why pandemics may qualify as national security threats. Two lesser flu epidemics in 1957–1958 and 1968–1969 killed 70,000 and 34,000 people, just in the United States. One institute estimates that a mild bird flu epidemic as virulent as the flu epidemic in 1968 will kill 1.4 million people and cost $330 billion; an epidemic as severe as the 1918 flu will kill 142 million people and cost $4.4 trillion.[27]

Each year, a WHO committee decides which flu strains should be included in the annual flu vaccine. More than a dozen international drug companies are researching new vaccines, but only a limited number of companies currently produce vaccines. The number has shrunk from two dozen in 1980 to a handful today. In 2005, when the British government suspended the license of Chiron Corporation due to contamination problems, there was a shortage of flu vaccine. NGOs, such as the Global Alliance for Vaccines and Immunization, sponsored by the Bill and Melinda Gates Foundation and others, have stepped up efforts to develop new vaccines and drugs, especially for diseases prevalent in developing countries.

MNCs also contribute. Drug and biotechnology companies have launched some sixty projects in recent years to develop new treatments.[28] Merck, the U.S. pharmaceutical giant, donated drugs to eradicate river blindness, a scourge that affected tens of millions of Africans living near rivers (the disease is caused by parasitic worms that work their way through the skin behind the eyes and blind the victims). GlaxoSmith Kline, AstraZeneca, and Novartis have built new research centers focused on neglected diseases. MNCs have made large research investments. They spend millions of dollars to develop drugs but then, not surprisingly, file patents and charge high prices to recoup costs. But high costs for treatments, such as anti-retroviral drugs to combat AIDS, often deny help to millions of poor people in developing regions. WHO and NGOs such as the Treatment Action Campaign (sponsored by Oxfam, Africa Action, and others) lobbied drug companies to reduce prices. Brazilian and Indian companies also introduced cheap generics. Prices went down, but tensions persist. Drug companies can't operate without profits and fear the additional liability associated with manufacturing vaccines. For example, when the United States faced a swine flu scare in 1976, Congress asked companies to manufacture vaccines in haste. Companies, in turn, asked Congress to assume liability, and Congress wound up paying claimants who received the vaccine some $90 million for alleged side effects. Congress decided never to assume such liability again. Yet MNCs do not feel it is their sole responsibility to do so either. Manufacturers have never made more than 400 million doses of vaccine in any single year. If avian flu became an epidemic, some 5–6 billion doses might be needed.

Here we come again to the role of perspectives. Who should pay and be responsible for controlling such epidemics? Liberal perspectives count heavily on international institutions. WHO is one of the largest and most technical international institutions. It has laboratories all over the world and works closely with the Food and Agriculture Organization (FAO), another UN specialized agency, which monitors flu epidemics in animals and advises governments on culling infected flocks and on vaccinations. But can expertise suffice, or will an epidemic involve major political stakes? The World Health Assembly, WHO's main decision-making body, has three delegates from each country—one from the scientific community, one from a professional organization, and one from the nongovernmental community. These delegates then select thirty-two members to sit on the executive board. By convention, the board is supposed to include at least three members from the UN Security Council, not necessarily from the veto powers. Thus, WHO comes close to a pure technical institution that tries to pay as little attention to power and politics as possible. It succeeds in part, but it also remains relatively small. Its budget runs about $2 billion a year, compared to $1.2 billion for the New York City Department of Health alone.

But are expert groups, such as the delegates of WHO, up to the task of leading the world in dealing with a major epidemic? Realist perspectives doubt it. They believe that countries, threatened by a major epidemic, will put the interests of their own people first. The countries will isolate those who become infected and quarantine visitors who might spread the disease. Such measures will likely close borders and interrupt trade. If vaccines are in scarce supply, individual countries would treat their own people first. Today, Tamiflu, the only anti-viral drug available against the avian flu virus, is being hoarded by some groups and was manufactured in 2005 by only one company in Switzerland. And there might be shortages of other supplies, such as mechanical ventilators, respiratory protection masks, and even hospitals. As Laurie Garrett points out, "in the event of a deadly influenza pandemic, it is doubtful that the world's wealthy nations would be able to meet the needs of their own citizenry—much less those of other countries."[29] The reality, according to realist perspectives, is that pandemics are now, in terms of the numbers of dead that might be involved, the equivalent of military attacks. They are matters, therefore, of the highest national security concern and cannot be entrusted to international institutions any more than the nation's defense might be.

Identity perspectives lament the fact that this national security picture is precisely the problem. People continue to see themselves divided into separate nation-states and ignore the larger reality that they are affected by what happens in other countries and cannot solve these problems by barricading themselves off from one another. Poor nations are especially at risk. If nothing else, national security interests have to be recast to address collective security issues. Nations need a sense of common human purpose and destiny and have to reconstitute their loyalties to take into account

Spotlight on liberal perspective

Spotlight on realist perspective

Spotlight on identity perspective

human, not just national, security. The instinct is certainly laudable, but on the basis of which ideas do common institutions decide? Do they decide on the traditional basis of "one nation, one vote," regardless of how much individual nations contribute or whether they govern in a manner accountable to their citizens? Or do they decide on the basis of "one person, one vote," which would require more accountable and transparent governments? When the SARS epidemic broke out in China, Chinese officials concealed vital information, which impeded a rapid response to the epidemic. In a nondemocratic society and a world of separate nation-states, who disciplines this kind of behavior?

Critical Theory Perspective

What does a critical theory perspective on the environment look like? James Gustave Speth, a long-time leader in the environmental movement, gives us one example.[30] According to Speth, the current environmental crisis is not a consequence of national or international policy failures. Rather, it is "a result of systemic failures of the capitalism we have today." This capitalism, driven by MNCs, aims for higher perpetual growth and in the process "generate[s] ever-larger environmental consequences, outstripping efforts to manage them." He rejects the mainstream argument that it is possible to work within this system. "Working within the system," he writes, "will . . . not succeed when what is needed is transformative change in the system itself."

Notice that Speth rejects piecemeal change. We can't change the system by more competitive solutions (realist), national or international institutional initiatives (liberal), or more democracy (identity). Although it is the best we can expect, American democracy is too "weak, shallow, dangerous and corrupted" to offer a solution. In short, he indicts all mainstream suggestions to fix the system. The system itself must go.

Now how does that happen? Like many neo-Marxist approaches, Speth's argument is better at diagnosis than prescription. He should call for revolution and the confidence that an historical conveyor belt that we can neither see nor control objectively will take us forward into a new and better world. Instead, he calls for a profound change in personal and collective values. We need a "post-growth society" that no longer seeks to accumulate resources but, instead, seeks to sustain and achieve an ecological balance between human activity and resource depletion and pollution. He wants a different set of ideas, but suggests no way that those ideas might come about. If the system of capitalism is so relentless, what hope is there that new ideas might emerge that could revolutionize the system? He has some doubts himself. While individuals may have personal conversions, he asks "can an entire society have a conversion experience?" Probably not, unless he tells us how to fix our educational system or our media sector, and, if he does that, then we are back on the turf of mainstream perspectives.

Summary

The environment should be the classic, collective goods issue driving the world toward common solutions and outcomes. Population pressures no longer affect only isolated poor countries. As advanced countries age and developing countries experience a youth bulge, population trends create a global imbalance that could slow economic growth and increase immigrant and refugee flows. Industrial pressures on natural resources now come from rapidly developing countries such as China and India, as well as from advanced countries, and accelerate the world's dependence and interdependence on oil and gas trade. Pollution further integrates the world community, despoiling the air, rivers, lakes, and even the oceans. Most important, chemicals released by human activity deplete the ozone layer and arguably warm the planet, creating a threat to planet Earth equivalent to an invading extraterritorial force. Add to that the growing prospects of pandemics as large as the 1918 Spanish flu, which killed more people than the fighting in World War I, and the planet has ample reason to address its future cooperatively if it is going to survive.

Still, tensions persist, not because of ill will or stupidity but because the problems are complicated, knowledge about them is uncertain if possible to determine at all, and people's perspectives diverge. Much is being done collectively, as liberal perspectives urge. Smallpox and polio, dreaded diseases for centuries, have been eradicated, and the Montreal Protocol may still succeed in saving the planet's ozone layer. Nevertheless, as realist perspectives predict, differences persist about the science behind and political urgency of global warming, and nations prepare for pandemics wondering who will be held responsible for allocating limited vaccines and other supplies. People identify with nations as well as nature, identity perspectives remind us. A key question is how they sort out these multiple identities when they confront environmental issues. Critical theory perspectives doubt that it matters much, unless there is an unforeseen ecological shock. It may be that the threat to the planet, like the nation, has to be catastrophic before the people respond with unity and resolve. And whether a threat appears to be catastrophic, of course, is always subject to interpretation from various perspectives. One thing is certain. The planet is the world's common home. At some point, that reality becomes undeniable; if we destroy the Earth, we know the enemy is us, not someone else.

Key Concepts

Study Questions

1. In what ways are environmental issues examples of collective goods? In what ways are they not?

2. In what sense are natural resources, energy, and raw materials exhaustible? Which perspectives emphasize markets, regulations, and ideology as the sources and solutions of resource use?

3. How are aging trends, the youth bulge, and immigration patterns related?

4. What are the differences between the problems of ozone depletion and global warming and between the steps proposed by the Montreal Protocol and Kyoto Protocol to resolve them?

5. Reflect on the following aspects of pandemics and suggest which perspective would emphasize each aspect and why: scarcity of vaccines, interconnection between animal and human diseases, and the limitations of national loyalties.

15

Global Civil Society

Nonstate Actors and Basic Human Rights

Eleanor Roosevelt, an early activist for human and women's rights, holds a copy of the UN's Universal Declaration of Human Rights shortly after its 1948 adoption.

J ust as state and then national societies and governments emerged several centuries ago, is it possible that a truly global society and government might emerge in the decades and centuries ahead? Perhaps anarchy need not be the permanent state of affairs, and the world can be organized such that one day a global civil society and structure of governance take precedence over national governments and interests. In other words, could the most important locus of political power one day be found beneath and beyond the nation-state rather than at the national level? Intergovernmental and eventually global institutions might supplant national ones, and a new social consensus might form that privileges basic human rights for all peoples rather than sovereignty for national rulers and elites.

Global Civil Society and Global Governance

The forces beneath the nation-state that might drive such a change and eventually stand in for current institutions and regimes are the plethora of nonstate or nongovernmental actors (that is, the NGOs) that already influence international relations directly through transnational activities such as commerce, foreign assistance, media relations, human rights advocacy, religion, party politics, and professional associa-

Spotlight on nongovernmental organizations

483

tions. NGOs, including MNCs and environmental groups, are organizations that are not directly or closely controlled by governments. They constitute what political scientists call civil society, an arena of activity for groups and individuals that is relatively independent of and, to some extent, protected from government interference. To be sure, NGOs operate internationally within global frameworks shaped by governments, just as civil society functions at the domestic level within the framework of national institutions. Some national governments, such as Russia and China, control civil society more closely than others. But global institutions are generally less developed than national ones, and governments often find themselves chasing global developments initiated by NGOs beneath the nation-state rather than guiding them. For example, private actors are spreading the Internet abroad before governments can decide how the Internet should be managed and regulated. NGOs, in short, exert disproportionate power at the international level because national regulations do not easily apply and international regulations are relatively weak.

Spotlight on intergovernmental organizations

To cope with global forces breaking out *beneath the nation-state,* governments establish intergovernmental organizations (IGOs) *beyond the nation-state.* IGOs include international conventions, treaties, alliances, and other institutions that govern international relations among governments as well as between them and international civil society. Examples today include the United Nations Security Council, which governs international security relations through cooperation among the great powers, and the international economic institutions such as the IMF and WTO, which regulate the activities of banking and industrial NGOs. These IGOs set the broader rules for security as well as commercial relations. But, as we have already noted, IGOs in the contemporary world are still relatively weak compared to national governments. NGOs operating internationally create new realities, and IGOs adapt to those realities. For instance, corporations invest abroad and, although generally observing the rules of both their home and host governments, often find lots of slack between those rules to shape new international practices. Mercenary forces that protect MNCs may or may not follow national and international laws, even if such laws exist. Human rights and media groups expose foreign atrocities and create problems and tensions among governments.

In short, forces beneath and beyond the nation-state interact vigorously with one another. Today, many people argue that globalization, or global civil society, is outrunning global governance and that corporations, in particular, dominate the global sphere. But others worry that the wrong kind of global governance may be advocated to rein in globalization and that global institutions may not respect individual human rights and the rights of corporations and other groups to own property and protect themselves from overweening central governments.

The growth and interaction of NGOs and IGOs constitute the central arena of emerging global governance. In this growth and interaction major issues arise, similar to those raised by governance and civil society at the national level. Here are some of them.

What is the appropriate size and role of global government compared to national or local governments? In the United States, for example, the federal government runs trade policy, while the state and local governments, for the most part, run schools and educational policy. What is the appropriate division of tasks at the global level?

Should global government be centralized or decentralized? The UN is a centralized institution with its headquarters in New York. Should it be more decentralized with stronger regional counterparts and headquarters?

What is the appropriate balance among unitary, federal, or confederal (most decentralized) principles of government? Think of the debates and even civil war that this question provoked in the history of the United States. Today, the United States divides central institutions (those that make and administer the law) by functions (legislative, executive, judicial, and so on), by region (for example, federalism), and by powers (for example, president is commander-in-chief but Congress appropriates money for the military) to ensure a system of checks and balances. Does a global government decide human rights issues on a unitary basis for all regions, or are such issues better left to regional or local institutions? As we see later in the chapter, Asian and Islamic societies may have a different take on human rights than western societies.

What role and how big a role should global civil society play? Should private civil society or nongovernmental institutions be independent and protected from the centralized government? Or should they be strongly regulated, even run, by central authorities? Markets are an important component of civil society. How free or regulated should they be? National governments that try to control all or most of civil society are called **totalitarian governments.** Communist or radical religious governments such as Iran, for example, do not permit private organizations; government and political party or religious officials penetrate and command all sectors of society—commercial, religious, educational, and so on. Governments that reserve a large space for civil society to act independently are called **constitutional governments. Authoritarian states** fall somewhere in between, but usually restrict civil rights and control key sectors of society such as political parties and the media. The United States has a very large and independent civil society, but China and Russia impose significant restrictions on independent groups. Which model applies at the global level?

What role should international and especially constitutional law play in global governance? Traditionally, international law protects the rights of states; constitutional law protects the rights of individuals and groups in civil society. Democratic governments not only encourage local and private organizations, they protect them constitutionally from interference by the government. These protections are called **civil rights,** or rights for participants in civil society; and in many countries, such as the United States, they are regarded as existing before government and inalienable (that is, can't be infringed upon) by governments. Constitutions sometimes provide a formal bill of rights for private individuals and groups, as in the United States, while in other countries, such as England, customary law guarantees similar rights. The Bill of Rights and independent courts (a separate branch of government) protect civil liberties in the United States. Should the UN Universal Declaration of Human Rights and International Court of Justice perform the same function at the global level?

In short, how should the arrows of authority run between government and civil society in the international system? Do global institutions dominate national and local ones? When, for example, do UN decisions take precedence over U.S. government decisions? Or do global institutions dominate global civil society? When, for example, do rules of the WTO take precedence over national laws affecting the behavior of MNCs?

Let's consider first the various *forms* or organizational structures of global governance that might emerge at the international level and then the various *norms* or substantive principles that might guide these structures.

totalitarian governments
governments that try to control all or most of civil society.

constitutional governments
governments that reserve a large space for civil society to act independently.

authoritarian states
states that typically restrict civil rights in key sectors of society such as political parties and the media but allow some independent activities in commerce and other areas.

civil rights
rights for participants in civil society, regarded in democratic societies as existing before government and as inalienable by governments.

The Forms of Global Governance: Role of Civil Society

What kind of government will emerge at the global level? Where will it fall along the spectrum of totalitarian, authoritarian, and constitutional governments? What role should NGOs and civil society play? To whom should NGOs be accountable? How should IGOs be set up? Should key officials be elected internationally or appointed by national governments? Should IGOs grant NGOs the same access and influence as they do national governments? Does global governance require a global parliament to ensure political control and accountability of a global bureaucracy?

Figure 15-1 organizes some of the alternative forms of governance that might be envisioned at the international level. In the case of each alternative, the figure describes the relationships that exist among governments and then between governments and civil society. At the far left side of the spectrum, we can envision a world hierarchy in which a unitary government controls most of civil society, and NGOs and individuals are largely responsible to central institutions. Ancient and more recent colonial empires, as well as the seventh-century Islamic caliphate that Muslim fundamentalists seek to restore, approximate this model. The causal arrows of authority run strongly from governments to civil society.

Spotlight on collective security

Moving toward the right, the next alternative might be a world authority that centralizes some important functions such as security while allowing independent local governments to decide other functions. An example is collective security. An international organization centralizes the function of security, while state governments decide either unanimously (League of Nations) or in terms of relative power (United Nations

Figure 15-1

Forms of Global Governance

	World hierarchy	World authority	World anarchy	World constitutionalism		
IGOs *Relationship between central, state, and local governments*	Centralized unitary government *Example: Communist, fascist, colonial, or Islamic (caliphate) empires; Iran at national level*	Collective security *Example: United Nations (some hierarchy, such as Security Council); League of Nations (no hierarchy, unanimity)*	Balance of power *Example: Westphalia state system*	Pluralist *Example: Council of Europe, Democratic Peace*	Federalist *Example: European Union*	Parliamentary *Example: No international example but Germany and other parliamentary democracies at national level*
	↓	↓ ↑	↑	↑	↓	
NGOs *Media, corporations, universities, etc.*	No independent civil society NGOs or groups	No significant role for NGOs except within individual constitutional states, such as the United States	No significant role for NGOs except within emerging constitutional states, such as Britain	Civil society recognized among decentralized states	Strong civil society protected by guarantees from above and participation from below	

Note: Arrows depict direction of authority. The length of the arrow depicts the strength of authority.

Security Council) all matters related to international security. Many states continue to control all elements of civil society, while some constitutional states give more freedom to the nongovernmental sector. But the world authority does not recognize a legal role for global civil society. No part of the world authority is elected or accountable to global civil society; state governments are the only legally empowered entities. The causal arrows of authority still run strongly from top to bottom but slightly less so than in the case of world hierarchy.

The next governance model toward the right side of Figure 15-1 might be the traditional balance-of-power system. Global authority is highly decentralized, and independent states control all functions of government, including security. Global governance is minimal. The system operates on the basis of the "invisible hand," as in the case of the eighteenth-century balance of power, or a loose concert of great powers, as in the case of the Concert of Europe in the nineteenth century. States might differ in terms of how much independence they give to civil society groups and individuals. But the global balance-of-power system generally regards nongovernmental actors, where they exist, as subordinate to national actors. National governments protected by sovereignty dominate both IGOs such as international treaties and NGOs such as trading companies and multinational corporations. The causal arrow still runs from top to bottom, but it is now considerably weaker than in the case of a world authority or hierarchy.

Spotlight on
balance of power

Further models, on the right side of Figure 15-1, accord more explicit legal authority and protection to civil society. The causal arrows of authority begin to run more strongly from the bottom to the top; the world moves toward models of governance that are more centralized but also more constitutional and democratic. Leaders are accountable to civil society, and government institutions emphasize separation of powers to restrain central authority, first within governments and then between government and civil society. Such constitutional governments may be pluralist, federalist (presidential), or parliamentary.

A world pluralist government recognizes a significant role for civil society not only within states but among them. The Council of Europe, for example, empowers civil society across multiple states and expects governments to live up to constitutional standards on human rights whether they are democratic (like Germany) or authoritarian (like Russia). More generally, in a pluralist world, NGOs form multiple, relatively informal structures of global governance within specific sectors without a clear hierarchy of power among them. One such organization coordinates international bank settlements, while another allocates orbital slots for satellites. Professor Francis Fukuyama calls this type of structure "a world of multiple competing and partially overlapping international institutions . . . that could provide both power and legitimacy for different types of challenges to world order." He argues "not for a single, overarching, enforceable liberal order [along the lines of a single world authority such as collective security] but rather for a diversity of institutions and institutional forms to provide governance across a range of security, economic, environmental, and other issues."[1] Professor Anne-Marie Slaughter takes it one step further and calls for pluralizing intergovernmental as well as nongovernmental institutions by creating "a world of government networks [that] would be a more effective and potentially more just order than either what we have today or a world government in which a set of global institutions perched above nation-states enforced global rules."[2] These views reflect some disillusionment with the collective security or UN model of global governance, which tends toward authoritarianism and ineffectiveness, in favor of a more open-ended, competitive model that respects diversity but also limits hierarchy.

A federalist world government protects civil society by dividing powers by regions and institutions, as the European Union does today, while a parliamentary world government unites the executive and legislative branches of government as a potential EU might do when and if the European Parliament acquires the right to constitute and dismiss the European government, namely the European Council and Commission. We deal further with these intergovernmental structures of governance in Chapter 16.

In which governance direction is the world moving? After five centuries of balance-of-power governance (the middle of Figure 15-1), is it being pulled toward the right side of Figure 15-1 and more constitutional and perhaps democratic governance, or is it being pulled toward the left side and more authoritarian forms of governance? In the United Nations (to the left side of anarchy), for example, no official such as the secretary-general or body such as the General Assembly is elected by the people or responsible to them; the states are the only legal actors. The UN Human Rights Commission (now called a Council) provides little protection for individual rights or the rights of NGOs and civil society as a whole. On the other hand, to the right side of anarchy in Figure 15-1, the European Union has a constitutional form of government (even though it does not have a formal constitution; the people rejected one in 2005) in which a parliament elected by the people has increasing although not yet equal powers with the European Commission and Council, in which no officials are elected by the people. The European Union, when it was established in 1993, adopted and now implements the Council of Europe's Convention on Human Rights, which does give individuals and NGOs standing before the European Court of Human Rights. Thus, the European Union and the United Nations constitute two very different directions in which the forms of world governance may move in the future.

How do we influence the direction in which world governance moves? Not surprisingly, the perspectives differ in response to this question. Realist perspectives worry about who controls global governance because that determines which institutions are set up and which ideologies they implement. Power conditions the prevailing institutions and ideas. Liberal perspectives emphasize the inclusiveness and intensity of interdependence of global governance because they assume that repetitive interactions will narrow ideological differences and reduce the significance of power disparities. Woodrow Wilson expected that the League of Nations would increase the number of constitutional democracies. He was wrong, at least in the short run, but, from his liberal perspective, institutions would mold ideas and override power. Finally, identity perspectives focus on the social and cultural norms that support international governance. Do global institutions support the norms of the most powerful states? Do they support procedural norms of reciprocity and universality or inclusiveness? Or do they emphasize substantive norms of basic human rights or democracy? Identities guide power and inform institutions. Critical theory perspectives worry that none of these perspectives is adequate because they do not recognize that all governance is an exercise of power by some people for some purpose. Critical theorists seek to unmask that power and emancipate minority voices that are not being heard in the prevailing discourse. No objective cause or solution is possible, but a better dialogue is.

causal arrow

The Norms of Global Governance: Basic Human Rights

The models tell us about the forms of governance but not necessarily about the substance or the norms and ideas that infuse the forms. In constitutional models, where civil society is strong, much depends on the substance of the rights and rules that civil society advocates for governing. If civil society is democratic, a pluralist government will look very different than if civil society is fascist or Islamic. Indeed, in some cases, civil society may demand top-down authority, as was the case in Nazi Germany (to the extent that the people voted for the Nazis) and may be the case today in authoritarian Russia or in the Palestinian government in Gaza formed by Hamas. A democratic civil society, however, demands permanent restraints on government and permanent protections for civil rights. A democratic model of world governance, therefore, might involve relatively small, or at least restrained, institutions at all levels of governance and a robust civil society that is self-restrained by common beliefs in liberty and equality for all individuals and groups regardless of their national, ethnic, or religious background. The democratic peace, for example, is a form of pluralist world government (no hierarchy of power) informed by the substantive norms of liberal democracy—namely, freedom and equality for all individuals to participate in the making and implementation of laws. We examine the democratic peace more closely in the Conclusion of this book.

As we discuss in Chapter 2, the state system did not emerge until a consensus developed around the global norm of sovereignty. Sovereignty privileged actors with power to control territory (realist) and with a commitment to reciprocity or mutual recognition of other states (liberal). Sovereignty did not imply substantive or ideological agreement on the rules of government (identity). In fact, sovereignty emerged to accommodate substantive *differences* between states that were both Protestant and Catholic, Roman and Orthodox. True, all European states were Christian, and in that sense there was a common identity element underlying the early state system. But it was minimal and did not preclude deep differences over religious doctrine.

Today global governance may be moving toward a more substantive, secular consensus that restricts the sovereign rights of states. The world of nation-states is no longer just Christian. It includes peoples and states that profess Muslim, Buddhist, Shinto, and other religious faiths. But, increasingly, all states acknowledge the existence of a set of basic human rights that, at a minimum, guarantee the protection of all people worldwide from physical abuse and genocide. They disagree, as we will see, about how these protections are defined and whether these rights go beyond physical abuse and include economic, social, and political rights. But, if this trend continues, it implies a shift in the focus of international governance away from the rights of states to the rights of individuals. At least in some substantive areas, states will no longer be sovereign to do whatever they want to their own people as long as they control their territory, that is, do not let instability spill over to other states, and respect other states. If national governments were to mistreat their own people in areas of basic human rights, they would be subject to sanctions or intervention by global institutions. Global institutions would hold national institutions accountable for more than just control of their territory and mutual respect for sovereignty.

Thus, increasing authority for global institutions raises the corresponding question: To what norms will global institutions be held accountable? Remember that the rise of the *nation-state* in Europe triggered all kinds of versions of nationalism, in effect different norms to guide the consolidation of governing authority at the domestic level: fascism, communism, liberalism, and the like. The growing importance of the *global-state* is likely to trigger similar disputes today about different norms to guide the consolidation of governing authority at the global level. The norms that ultimately prevail may be substantive, as human rights were, or they could be procedural, as sovereignty was. For example, **regionalism** is a procedural norm that privileges neither

Spotlight on norms and beliefs

Spotlight on sovereignty

Spotlight on basic human rights and genocide

regionalism

a norm of global governance that tolerates different substantive ideologies based on regions rather than on states or universality.

nationalism (sovereignty) nor universalism (human rights) but advocates a more intermediate or regional basis of norms of global governance.[3] Some states are moving ahead on regional models of global governance. The European Union and the Council of Europe champion multilateralism and universal human rights, while Asian states promote a regionalism that emphasizes bilateralism, ethnic-based business practices, and strategic capitalism. What kinds of institutions will emerge at the international level, and under what ideological banner will they protect or not protect basic human rights? For a skeptical view of global governance, see the op-ed piece from the *New York Times* in the box on page 491.

In the rest of this chapter, we examine the civil society of the emerging international system. We look at the institutional forms of civil society, namely the international NGOs, and civil society groups that operate domestically *beneath* the nation-state and transnationally across nation-states outside the direct influence of governments; and we look at the substantive norms of civil society or the evolving debate and possible consensus about basic human rights. In the next chapter, we examine the forms and norms of intergovernmental institutions of the emerging international system, namely the IGOs and government actors that operate *beyond* the nation-state and forge new regional and global authorities. In both chapters, we highlight the crucial areas in which these two elements of the global system interact.

We start with a brief history of how nongovernmental institutions evolved from a system of sovereign states and how these institutions operate in the current international system. Then we look at the evolution of the norm of basic human rights in the context of the UN, EU, and briefly other regions, such as the Asian and Islamic regions.

Sovereignty

Sovereignty defined the state as the principal actor in international affairs, and the state retains that status to the present day. Sovereignty meant simply noninterference in the internal affairs of other states. States could decide for themselves how to organize their domestic life and treat their own people. At the beginning, the state meant the monarch and the divine right of kings. Later, it meant peoples or nations and the right of self-determination. Today, it means governments and the right of national self-defense. Article 2 (7) of the UN Charter stipulates that "nothing contained in the Charter shall authorize the United Nations to interfere in matters which are essentially within the domestic jurisdiction of any state." And Article 51 states that "nothing in the present Charter shall impair the inherent right of individual and collective self-defense."

Notice that the emphasis is on the autonomy of the state, not its anatomy or what its constitution may be. The state is sovereign whether it is organized by democratic, despotic, or doctrinal and religious rules. Governments could define themselves in any way they chose—Protestant or Catholic, Orthodox or Roman, authoritarian or pluralistic—and that was nobody else's business. The substance or *anatomy* of the actor mattered less than the independence or *autonomy* of the actor. Sovereignty concealed the question of who or what is the sovereign. Is it a monarch, an aristocracy, a class of merchants or workers, or an elected and representative government of the people as a whole? This was a substantive question that became more important as nationalism and the idea of democracy spread. Sovereignty portrayed the state more as an institutional shell than as a substantive commitment.

Using the Perspectives to Read

 Between

the Lines

A View Against Global Governance

Columnist David Brooks wrote the following in the *New York Times*:

> The people who talk about global governance begin with . . . the belief that a world of separate nations, living by the law of the jungle, will inevitably be a violent world. Instead, these people believe, some supranational authority should be set up to settle international disputes by rule of law. . . .
>
> [T]his vaporous global-governance notion is a dangerous illusion, and . . . Americans, like most other peoples, will never accept it. . . .
>
> [F]irst, because it is undemocratic. It is impossible to set up legitimate global authorities because there is no global democracy, no sense of common peoplehood and trust. . . .
>
> Second, . . . because it inevitably devolves into corruption. The panoply of UN scandals flows from a single source: the lack of democratic accountability. . . .
>
> [T]hird, because we love our Constitution and will never grant any other law supremacy over it. . . .
>
> Fourth, [because] these mushy institutions liberate the barbaric and handcuff the civilized. Bodies like the UN can toss hapless resolutions at the

> Milosevics, the Saddams or the butchers of Darfur, but they can do nothing to restrain them. Meanwhile, the forces of decency can be paralyzed as they wait for "the international community." . . .
>
> Fifth, [because] all the grand talk about international norms is often just a cover for opposing the global elite's bêtes noires of the moment— usually the U.S. or Israel. . . .

Notice, first, the comparison between a liberal world of global governance and a realist world of separate nations. The former is rejected, mostly because it is undemocratic, unaccountable, and conflicts with superior national ideas such as the American Constitution—all identity factors. But it is also rejected because it is impotent ("toss hapless resolutions") and generally serves as a cover to oppose or constrain the United States and its allies—all realist factors. Brooks prefers a world of separate nations in which America espouses its values "loudly" and carries "a big stick." Relative identity and power trump global governance even though this may mean "living by the law of the jungle" but not "inevitably . . . a violent world."

Transnational Relations

As Stephen Krasner argues, sovereignty in this sense of autonomy was always violated in practice.[4] Sovereignty was compromised by transnational relations, which involve international exchanges that take place outside the direct supervision or control of governments and derive from interdependence and domestic politics. Countries trade with one another, and populations move across state boundaries. Although sovereigns might control their borders, they can never control them perfectly. Smuggling and illegal migration always take place.

> Spotlight on
> interdependence

As technology advanced and the industrial revolution broke out, interdependence accelerated. In addition, the Reformation and Enlightenment brought new ideas that liberated individuals and created opportunities for more domestic groups to become active in politics. States could not always control these domestic groups (think of Cromwell's rebellion in England in the mid-seventeenth century), and nonstate actors gained a wider latitude to act independently of states (for example, the Protestant elites conspiring against a Catholic king to invite the Protestant king, William of Orange, to become the sovereign of England).

Today, all kinds of nonstate or nongovernmental elites are active within the sovereign domain of states. They create transnational or cross-national groups and institutions that weaken state influence. Some NGOs, such as terrorist groups, seek to destroy state authority directly. On the other hand, other NGOs act in support of state interests. They project, not weaken, state power. Rogue states, for example, sponsor terrorism to advance their national interests. And some MNCs operate under government instructions or, in the case of nationalized industries, under direct government control to secure energy and raw materials for national security. The activities of such state-controlled NGOs raise concerns, as we have noted in Chapter 10 in the case of Chinese resource companies or the sovereign wealth funds of other countries.

Let's look more closely at the transnational NGOs that challenge state sovereignty. In a later section, we look at the social norm of basic human rights, which may be creating a new basis for limiting the role of sovereignty.

Transnational Nongovernmental Organizations

Transnational nongovernmental organizations (TNGOs) are by far the most numerous actors in international affairs. By some estimates, there are as many as 30,000 such organizations, excluding MNCs, which number separately another 78,000 entities. That compares to fewer than 200 nation-states and some 250 or so IGOs.[5] TNGOs are extensions of the nongovernmental or private life of individual states into the public life of international affairs. Nongovernmental domestic actors take up international activities and become known as transnational actors because they are neither governmental nor intergovernmental organizations.

Liberal perspectives tend to see this phenomenon as a normal development of technology and specialization expanding the expertise and scope of institutions. Realist perspectives, because they emphasize the role of governmental (not nongovernmental) actors, tend to be more skeptical. They see NGO activities as either extensions of government policies or unaccountable to anyone and, hence, disruptive of international order. Most countries, for example, expect their MNCs to operate abroad in ways consistent with their home country's security and economic interests. In turn, they are wary of NGOs from other countries because these NGOs may act in ways contrary to their national interests.

The United States, for example, worries about NGOs that campaign to eliminate land mines or threaten to use the new International Criminal Court to punish American military personnel overseas because these NGOs do not answer to governments and may interfere with U.S. or UN military missions abroad. Identity perspectives point out that NGOs may be unique creatures of democratic governments. Nondemocratic governments see NGOs simply as extensions of foreign influence and disallow them. Myanmar and North Korea, for example, do not permit NGOs to operate domestically. They effectively ban international NGOs from entering the country even when disasters strike, such as the cyclone in Myanmar in 2008 or periodic famines in

North Korea. China persecutes religious groups, such as the Falun Gong, and Russia has clamped down harshly on independent media and other activities, particularly in political areas, where NGOs support the promotion of democracy in Russia. Pakistan and authoritarian Muslim countries do not control many of the NGOs within their own borders, particularly radical fundamentalist groups and Muslim schools, which pose direct threats to their authority as well as terrorist threats to western governments. In 2006, President Pervez Musharraf, at that time Pakistan's authoritarian leader, called madrassas (Muslim schools) supported by transnational fundamentalist groups the largest NGO in the world.[6]

Is the existence and role of NGOs, then, largely a western phenomenon and related to the development of constitutional and then democratic states? Critical theory perspectives may think so. The Reformation empowered individuals to participate in commerce and politics. In non-European cultures, especially Asian and Islamic societies, individuals mattered less; groups and religious communities mattered more. Authoritarian and theocratic states foster monolithic NGOs, such as madrassas; democratic states foster independent NGOs.

Democracies not only recognize but promote NGOs and civil society as a fundamental component of political society. From an identity perspective, the spread of NGOs in the world today owes as much to the spread of democracy as to the acceleration of technology and interdependence. Notice the judgment here that ideational or identity factors may be more important than institutional ones in facilitating the growth of NGOs. If the international community became less hospitable to democracy, NGOs might become less important even if interdependence remained at high levels.

Spotlight on
critical theory perspective

⟵ **causal arrow**

Even today in a world where nondemocracies remain strong, NGOs are not always independent and tend to be concentrated. A few large NGOs dominate most issue areas, and many do not function on the democratic principles of representation, accountability, and transparency. For example, eight large NGOs account for more than half of the money going into world relief work, and few NGOs provide detailed information about their personnel, operations, budgets, and funding sources.[7] This reality is not surprising, at least from the point of view of some identity perspectives, because many of the states today that spawn these NGOs are also not transparent or democratic.

NGOs exist across the broad spectrum of activities and functions that make up modern life—economics, environment, development, law and human rights, disarmament, politics, society, and the military. Their activities vary in effectiveness, but a number of them have received Nobel Prizes for their work, among them the International Campaign to Ban Landmines (1997) and, most recently, Doctors Without Borders (1999). Let's look at a few of them and how the different perspectives assess their significance. The box on page 494 identifies some of the biggest and best-known global NGOs, suggesting the functional areas in which they operate and sometimes overlap.

A plainclothes police officer wrestles a female Falun Gong practitioner to the ground in China after she took part in a protest in Beijing's Tiananmen Square in May 2000.

A Sampling of Transnational NGOs, by Field or Mission Focus

Development	Health	Women's rights	Children's rights	Human rights	Foreign aid	Environment	Anti-corruption
Bill & Melinda Gates Foundation	Amnesty International				International Crisis Group	World Wildlife Fund	Transparency International
Ford Foundation	Pathfinder International		Catholic Relief Services	Human Rights Watch	Ford Foundation	The Nature Conservancy	Partnership for Transparency Fund
Open Society Institute	International Association for Maternal and Neonatal Health			Oxfam		Greenpeace	Open Society Institute
MacArthur Foundation	Doctors Without Borders	International Alliance for Women	Coalition to Stop the Use of Child Soldiers		ActionAid	Global Witness	
Forest, Trees, and People Program	Carter Center	Global Alliance Against Traffic in Women	International Save the Children Alliance	Carter Center	MercyCorps	The Jane Goodall Institute	International Initiative on Corruption and Governance

Economic Nongovernmental Organizations

Many MNCs (or transnational corporations, TNCs) are bigger than whole countries. They are also more numerous. Some 78,000 MNCs now operate with over 780,000 affiliates around the world. In 2006, these foreign affiliates generated an estimated $5.2 trillion in value-added, employed some 72 million workers, and exported goods and services valued at more than $4.7 trillion.[8]

While competition among MNCs from different countries is growing, the concentration of MNCs in a few parent countries remains significant. Five countries (France, Germany, Japan, the United Kingdom, and the United States) account for seventy-three of the top one hundred firms, while fifty-three firms come from the EU countries taken together. Heading the list of the global top one hundred nonfinancial TNCs are General Electric, Vodafone, and Ford, which together account for nearly 19 percent of the total assets of these one hundred companies. The automobile industry dominates the list, followed by pharmaceuticals and telecommunications. Here is a case, realist perspectives would note, where the distribution of power matters more than ideologies. It is estimated that only 1 percent of MNCs account for half of the total existing foreign investments. The vast majority of MNCs still originate in industrialized countries, where most FDI is done.

Nevertheless, five companies on the list of the top one hundred MNCs come from developing economies, all with headquarters in Asia and three of them state-owned: Hutchison Whampoa (Hong Kong, China), Petronas (Malaysia), Singtel (Singapore), Samsung Electronics (Republic of Korea), and CITIC Group (China). In addition, Russia, Brazil, Mexico, Chile, South Africa, India, and the OPEC countries have, or are developing, significant MNCs of their own. In 2004, MNCs from developing countries accounted for total sales of $1.9 trillion and employed 6 million workers. In 2006, they constituted 16 percent of global FDI, up from 6 percent in the mid-1980s. In recent decades, privatization created many new MNCs, especially in the former communist countries.

MNCs establish their own global NGOs to facilitate trade and commerce. The private cartel of the seven major western oil firms (the seven sisters) ran the oil markets until the 1970s, when the government cartel of OPEC took over. A cartel headed by the Belgian De Beers Corporation still dominates world diamond markets. Moody's Investors Services and Standard & Poor's set the global standards for rating international loans and equities. The RugMark label ensures quality controls for the international marketing of carpets (and child-free labor, as we note in Chapter 13). MNCs collaborate to establish codes of conduct and good citizenship standards for their operations in foreign countries. They sponsor international conferences, such as the annual World Economic Forum in Davos, Switzerland, to promote information sharing and policy discussions. And they react, often under pressure from other NGOs and IGOs, to situations and events, for example, opposing apartheid in South Africa and fighting AIDS in sub-Saharan Africa. A notable case of MNC cooperation was the strong support of Dow Chemical and Dupont, the producers of CFCs that deplete the ozone layer, for the 1987 Montreal Protocol that called for phasing out CFCs. By contrast, many energy MNCs joined the Global Climate Coalition to lobby against the 1997 Kyoto Protocol to reduce carbon dioxide emissions that contribute to global warming.

Corporations often find themselves in an uncomfortable position between host governments and international NGOs. One example is the Canadian energy company Talisman and its operations in Sudan. Talisman Energy invested in oil and gas development in Sudan in 1998 during the civil war in the southern part of that country. The government of Sudan provided protection for the oil fields, and human rights NGOs, including Amnesty International, accused Talisman of conspiring with the government to displace residents around the oil fields and use the oil field security infrastructure (for example, helicopter landing areas) to wage the civil war. Talisman officials met repeatedly with the Sudanese government and reported that it saw no evidence of aggressive uses of oil field infrastructure. It issued regular corporate social responsibility reports detailing its efforts to meet NGO criticisms. Nevertheless, opposition to its operations in Sudan continued to build. Eventually in 2003 Talisman withdrew from the Sudan. A Chinese partner in the project remained and continued to work with the Sudanese government.[9] A precarious peace agreement was reached in 2005, but fighting continues in the area.

The different perspectives view such situations differently. Liberal perspectives are generally suspicious of MNCs and their corporate responsibility efforts at self-regulation. They want MNCs to be more accountable to intergovernmental agreements for foreign investment and technology transfer. Realist perspectives are more forgiving if MNCs support national security and economic goals, and dominate markets or operate in competitive markets that no one can dominate. After all, when Talisman left, other MNCs continued their operations. Notice once again the realist concern for the distribution of power and competition, both in security areas and in markets. Identity perspectives would like to see MNCs serve more worthy goals than merely fair play or national interests, such as sustainable development and fighting AIDS. Perhaps companies should never enter situations such as Sudan. A similar situation exists today in the oil-rich delta areas of southern Nigeria. Guerrilla bands attack oil platforms, companies hire mercenary forces to protect installations, and the fighting intensifies. Should the oil companies with massive investments just leave and let the country do without the oil revenues until the civil war is resolved?

Spotlight on
perspectives

Environmental Nongovernmental Organizations

NGOs abound in environmental areas. Some of the earliest were the Society for the Protection of Birds in 1889 and the Sierra Club in 1892. The Society for the Preservation of the Wild Fauna of the Empire was the first international environmental NGO set up in 1903. The Commission for the International Protection of Nature (now the International Union for the Conservation of Nature) followed in 1913. Interest in the environment blossomed in the 1960s. Rachel Carson's *Silent Spring* and Jacques Cousteau's *The Living Sea* inspired numerous environmental movements. The World Directory of Environmental Organizations now lists over 20,000 umbrella groups, domestic as well as international. Earthwatch, Environmental Defense, The Nature Conservancy, World Wide Fund for Nature, Conservation International, World Wildlife Fund, Rainforest Action Network, Greenpeace, and Earth Island Institute are but a few. Some 250 environmental NGOs attended the 1972 UN Conference on the Environment, and over 1,400 attended a similar UN conference in Rio de Janeiro in 1992.

Environmental NGOs lobby to influence governments and international organizations. Many have become increasingly assertive. Greenpeace, for example, sails ships into fishing fleets to protest whaling activities or ties its members to bridges to protest shipments of toxic waste. However, most environmental NGOs undertake the daily, mundane tasks of research, information exchange, raising money, influencing the media, and challenging various rulings by international organizations. In the international arena, they face significant obstacles. There is no international legislature where they can lobby their causes. They cannot easily access and present their briefs to international bureaucracies such as NAFTA or the WTO. There is no formal mechanism for them to bring suit before the World Court. As we note later in the chapter, some have consultative status with various UN agencies, but the UN agencies run by governments decide such status. And NGOs themselves are not accountable to a visible international public constituency or regulated under anti-racketeering laws or other international legislation that might hold them accountable. There were numerous complaints during the tsunami and earthquake disasters in 2005 that NGOs did not account properly for their use of funds.[10] Realist perspectives worry most about this lack of accountability on the part of NGOs. Liberal perspectives are generally sympathetic and seek to improve NGO access and transparency at international institutions such as the World Bank and WTO. Most identity perspectives seek to cultivate new norms such as sustainable development that point NGOs and other international actors in the same direction.

Spotlight on perspectives

The World Wildlife Fund (WWF) offers one example of how environmental NGOs operate. It is the largest multinational conservation organization in the world with activities in one hundred countries and 5 million members globally.

WWF invented and pioneered the use of the debt-for-nature swap. Such a swap enabled indebted developing nations to avoid cutting back on essential environmental projects. Here is the way a debt swap worked. Often debtor developing nations were asked by the IMF and other donors to reduce domestic expenditures to free up resources to repay their debts. One of the first expenditures they cut was for environmental projects. If a developing country agreed not to do this, WWF would purchase some of that country's foreign debt at a discount from a commercial bank or other originating source and transfer the title of the debt to the developing country. The developing country would then convert the purchased debt into local currency and use the proceeds to continue to fund essential environmental projects.

WWF carried out its first debt-for-nature swap in Bolivia in 1987. From that year through 2003, WWF negotiated some twenty-two debt-for-nature swaps in ten countries across four continents. Altogether it purchased debt worth around $55 million at a discount price of $23 million, which was then converted into the equivalent of $46 million for conservation purposes. Bolivia developed training programs to better manage lowland forests, Costa Rica purchased land for national parks, Madagascar developed conservation programs to manage protected areas such as natural forests, the Philippines developed training and infrastructure for national parks, and Poland funded programs to study and develop river basin resources.[11]

Law and Human Rights Nongovernmental Organizations

One study lists 325 international human rights NGOs and found that more than one-fifth of them started after 1979.[12] Some of the best known include Amnesty International, Human Rights Watch, the International Commission of Jurists, and the Lawyers Committee for Human Rights. These organizations monitor human rights in practically all countries, reporting abuses and mobilizing criticism. Amnesty International won the Nobel Prize in 1977 and makes available information that governments themselves could not or would not collect. Human Rights Watch started out as Helsinki Watch in 1978, part of U.S.-Soviet détente arrangements to monitor human rights in communist countries in eastern Europe. Today it monitors human rights worldwide. These organizations take on individual cases, such as efforts to track down abuses of military regimes in Argentina and Central American countries, and cases of group discrimination, such as Human Rights Watch's campaign to focus attention on caste violence and child labor abuses in India.

Amnesty International (AI) is among the most famous human rights NGOs. It was founded in 1961 by an English lawyer, Peter Benenson. Sitting on a train one day in 1960, Benenson read about two Portuguese students sentenced to long prison terms for criticizing Portugal's then dictator Antonio Salazar. He resolved to do something about it and founded AI. AI is headquartered in London and has offices in eighty countries. Its members include over 2 million people organized into more than fifty sections from around the world. The members are crucial to AI's survival and growth. Individual donations make up the bulk of its income, which in 2007 totaled more than 35 million British pounds (nearly $70 million). Of this amount, only about 1.5 percent came from other sources such as investments. AI also accepts money from "carefully vetted" businesses, but it is unique in so far as it never takes money from governments or political parties.[13]

AI focuses on eight global goals:

1. Reform and strengthen the justice sector; that is, end the imprisonment of prisoners of conscience, unfair political trials, torture, unlawful killings, and so on.
2. Abolish the death penalty, both in particular countries and internationally.
3. Protect the rights of defenders; that is, those who work on behalf of human rights.
4. Resist human rights abuses in the "war on terror," which AI believes has caused "a widespread backlash against human rights."
5. Defend the rights of refugees and migrants.
6. Promote economic, social, and cultural rights for marginalized communities, with a focus on fighting forced evictions such as those that took place around Africa in 2006. Other marginalized communities include various indigenous peoples, Roma (gypsy), and other groups subject to extreme poverty and government apathy.

During a rally in Bangkok, Thailand, in October 2007, an activist from Amnesty International holds a placard calling for release of political prisoners.

7. Stop violence against women, notably rape and domestic violence.
8. Protect civilians and close the taps that fuel abuses in conflicts in places such as Sudan, Israeli-occupied territories, and Lebanon.

When AI received the Nobel Prize in 1977, the Nobel Committee cited AI's work on behalf of prisoners of conscience, noting that of the 6,000 prisoners that AI "adopted" from 1972 to 1975, 3,000 had been released by 1977. It praised in particular the way AI mobilizes thousands of individuals locally to "adopt" and develop close relationships with prisoners, reassuring them that they have not been forgotten. At the time, AI volunteers wrote letters to officials asking about the prisoners and letting governments know that someone was aware of the situation. To remain apolitical, AI assigned prisoners to adoption groups within specific Cold War regions: East, West, and third worlds.[14]

In the early years, neither the UN nor governments welcomed AI's initiatives. But its grassroots and practical approach scored big. Today, it unmasks human rights abuses in China, Somalia, Congo, and the United States, being out in front condemning U.S. practices at places like Guantanamo and Abu Ghraib.

Basic Human Rights

Spotlight on social constructivism

According to social constructivists, state behavior is a consequence of common norms and identities, constructed over time at the systemic structural level of analysis by a constitutive process of mutual, rather than sequential, causation. Over the past century, the fundamental norm that emerged in the international system after the Treaty of Westphalia in 1648—that states did not interfere in the domestic jurisdiction of other states—has steadily weakened. Especially after the end of the Cold War, the world community moved toward a consensus that, under specific conditions, international intervention in the domestic affairs of other states was justified to defend the basic human rights of indigenous people endangered by violence, especially the right to survive free of physical deprivation and torture. This consensus was based on fundamental human rights, not the specific political institutions and values of democracy. Intervention protected people from arbitrary violence and starvation, but did not impose a specific political regime on the country. All political regimes, democratic and nondemocratic, could accept humanitarian norms, as they did in the UN and European Conventions on Human Rights, even as they continued to differ in political and economic ideologies.

As we have learned in Chapter 7, UN interventions in failed states raise controversial issues of sovereignty and basic human rights. What does the international community do if events in failing states involve the prospects of genocide, as in Rwanda in 1994? Can the international community breach the global norm of sovereignty in order to implement a new global norm of basic human rights? In 1999, Kofi Annan, the UN secretary-general at the time, spelled out the issues in stark form:

If humanitarian intervention is, indeed, an unacceptable assault on sovereignty, how should we respond to a Rwanda, to a Srebrenica—to gross and systematic violations of human rights that offend every precept of our common humanity? . . . surely no legal principle—not even sovereignty—can ever shield crimes against humanity.[15]

Many developing countries, not to mention Russia, China, and other authoritarian states, are reluctant to go along with such broad interpretations of basic human rights. Russia opposed UN intervention in Kosovo, forcing the United States and other countries to act through NATO. It also opposed Kosovo's declaration of independence in 2007, fearing that granting autonomy or independence to minority groups inside a country (in this case, the Kosovar people inside Serbia) might strengthen separatist demands in Chechnya and other parts of Russia to break away from the Russian state. China feared similar separatist demands in Taiwan, Tibet, and its western province of Xinjiang. Russia, China, and France also opposed U.S. intervention in Iraq; regime change, they believed, went too far and interfered in the sovereign affairs of another state.

If there is no consensus, is the use of military force without UN approval illegitimate? Many thought so in the case of Iraq, where the United States acted without NATO or UN authorization. But many thought not in the case of Kosovo, where NATO acted without UN authorization. If the world can act only with the agreement of all great powers, how often will it act? And what if some great powers, such as Russia and China, do not defend human rights as vigorously as others? Won't basic human rights be compromised? On the other hand, if human rights are defined by selective countries that have similar values, intervention becomes a prescription for regime change and for imposing the political ideologies of those particular countries. Annan asked an International Commission on Intervention and State Sovereignty to come up with an answer as to when intervention was justified. The commission came up with a rather complicated set of threshold criteria. The UN could intervene in cases of:

> large scale loss of life, actual or apprehended, with genocidal intent or not, which is the product of deliberate state action, or state neglect or inability to act, or a failed state situation; or large scale "ethnic cleansing," actual or apprehended, whether carried out by killing, forced expulsion, acts of terror or rape.[16]

It is not surprising that states continue to disagree about whether large-scale loss of life is apprehended, meaning anticipated, or whether a given state is unwilling or unable to act against it. Procedural norms of international life are changing. Sovereignty is no longer sacrosanct. But what *basic human rights* or *genocide* means is still disputed. The United States called the Darfur violence in Sudan genocide, but it did not apply the same label to Rwanda, Kosovo, or the killing fields of Cambodia where the communist Khmer Rouge government killed as many as 1.7 million people—one-fourth of the country's population.

Evolution of Human Rights

For centuries empires considered their own people (mostly just the elites) to be civilized and the rest of the world to be barbarians. That changed when the Westphalian states began to recognize one another as equals rather than superiors or subordinates. But mutual recognition of sovereignty extended only to other white Christian societies inside Europe. Black people were enslaved by Europeans as well as by Arabs, and outside Europe, colonialism or empire subjugated non-European peoples to European

Spotlight on **partition**

Spotlight on **legitimacy**

Spotlight on **genocide**

rule. Intervention was justified to protect colonialists and Christians—for example, Russia's interventions in the nineteenth century to protect Christians in the Balkans—but not blacks or Muslims.

Further normative change occurred in the nineteenth century. States abolished the slave trade and then eventually slavery itself. States and empires no longer had the right to enslave their subjects. The Geneva Convention of 1864 and subsequent elaborations in the 1920s and 1940s mandated humane treatment for captured military personnel during war and established certain protections for civilians as well, and the International Committee of the Red Cross, a Swiss NGO, began its long history of visiting and monitoring treatment of prisoners around the world.

Spotlight on
norms

The Covenant of the League of Nations was silent on human rights, and the United States opposed incorporating the principle of racial equality advocated by Japan. But the League itself developed refugee and other assistance programs that promoted human rights. The United Nations Charter was the first treaty in world history to recognize universal human rights. In Article 1, the Charter states that one of the purposes of the United Nations is "to achieve cooperation in solving international problems of an economic, social, cultural or humanitarian character, and in promoting and encouraging respect for human rights and for fundamental freedoms for all without distinction as to race, sex, language, or religion. . . ." The United Nations had legally binding authority to act only in security areas, however, although the Security Council later recognized the possibility that violations of human rights might lead to security crises, as in the cases of racism in South Africa and Southern Rhodesia (now Zimbabwe). Security was being interpreted increasingly in terms of the consequences for individual human beings. The objective was the human security of people, not just the national security of states. After World War II, special tribunals tried and executed war criminals in Germany and Japan. And the Holocaust during World War II led to the UN Convention on the Prevention and Punishment of the Crime of Genocide. Decolonization after World War II effectively eliminated the right of states to govern foreign subjects, replacing it with the right of *self*-determination.

Spotlight on
human security

Universal Declaration of Human Rights

Universal Declaration
of Human Rights

a UN declaration approved in
1948 prescribing the obligations
of states to individuals rather
than of individuals to states.

Gradually, the emphasis was shifting from the rights and responsibilities of states to the rights and responsibilities of individuals and groups within states. In 1948, the United Nations adopted the **Universal Declaration of Human Rights.** A nonbinding declaration, this document covered the panoply of rights long advocated by western states: political participation and civic freedom; entitlements to adequate food, clothing, shelter, and health care; and freedom from fear of bodily harm. The Soviet Union, however, voted against the declaration, and it was not until twenty years later in 1966 that the UN codified these rights in two binding treaties: the International Covenant on Economic, Social and Cultural Rights (ICESCR) and the International Covenant on Civil and Political Rights (ICCPR). Together with the Charter, these documents constitute what amounts to an international or global bill of rights, identifying certain common obligations all states have toward civil society or their individual citizens.

More specific conventions followed for racial discrimination, women's rights, torture, and children's rights. Regional bodies, such as the European Commission on Human Rights and the European Court of Human Rights, set even higher standards for human rights, including the political rights to assemble and vote. These documents and institutions increasingly prescribed the obligations of states to individuals rather than just of individuals to states.

States disagree about which rights were more fundamental. Authoritarian states such as China emphasize social and economic rights; liberal democracies, such as the United States, emphasize civil and political rights. China never ratified the Covenant on Civil and Political Rights; the United States never ratified the Covenant on Economic, Social and Cultural Rights. Saudi Arabia never reversed its vote against the Universal Declaration of Human Rights. The ICCPR set up a Human Rights Committee that monitors the Covenant and can consider individual cases. The ICESCR receives only state reports.[17]

Still, as consensus grows to protect the most basic rights such as freedom from physical abuse, torture, and genocide, implementation shifts increasingly from national to international institutions such as the permanent International Criminal Court established in 1999. The latter, as we examine in Chapter 16, has the right to accept cases brought by individuals or global citizens, not just by states or national governments.

Implementing, let alone enforcing, these norms has not been easy. Realist perspectives might say this is because powerful states, such as China and the United States, simply ignore them. Liberal perspectives might say this is because international institutions are not yet strong enough. In the past, countries such as Cuba, Libya, and Sudan chaired the UN human rights committees and made a mockery of the law. Nevertheless, identity and liberal perspectives point to some significant successes. UN sanctions worked against apartheid South Africa to bring down that regime. And human rights discussions under the auspices of the Helsinki Accords in 1975 opened up eastern Europe and the Soviet Union to political reforms that ended communism in Europe.

Let's look more closely at the success and controversies of implementing basic human rights through the UN Universal Declaration of Human Rights, the European Convention on Human Rights, and the Asian and Islamic human rights regimes.

Spotlight on perspectives

United Nations Human Rights Regime

During the Cold War, the United Nations intervened in military or humanitarian conflicts only with the consent of the rival superpowers and often of the local authorities as well. When the Cold War ended, numerous internal or intrastate conflicts erupted— in Somalia, Cambodia, and Bosnia, to name a few. The UN Security Council expanded its definition of what constitutes a threat to international peace and security under Chapter VII to include these conflicts. As human rights specialist David P. Forsythe points out, it implied more than once that "security could refer to the security of persons within states, based on human rights, and not just to traditional military violence across international frontiers."[18] The office of the secretary-general became more active. Supported by developing nations that became new members of the United Nations after decolonization, Secretary-General Boutros Boutros-Ghali appointed the first UN high commissioner for human rights in 1993. The idea was to broaden the attention focused on human rights.

Human Rights Commission/Council

The traditional center of UN diplomacy on human rights was the **UN Human Rights Commission.** Prominent in drafting the Universal Declaration of Human Rights, the

UN Human Rights Commission
the commission that drafted and implements the Universal Declaration of Human Rights, passed by the UN as a nonbinding resolution in 1948.

UN Economic and Social Council (ECOSOC)
a major organ of the UN General Assembly; among other things, until 2006 it elected the members of the UN Human Rights Commission based on geographic representation.

commission consisted of representatives of states elected by the **UN Economic and Social Council (ECOSOC),** a major organ of the UN General Assembly (see Chapter 16). Initially, because it represented states, it avoided specific claims about human rights abuses. But after the late 1960s, under pressure from developing countries, the commission began to discuss human rights abuses in Israel, South Africa, Haiti, and Greece. Based on resolutions passed by ECOSOC, the commission was also able to consider complaints from NGOs not just states. However, ECOSOC decides which NGOs have consultative status in the UN, that is, can attend meetings and submit documents to the commission. ECOSOC denied consultative status to some legitimate human rights NGOs. As Professors Margaret Karns and Karen Mingst point out, delegations feared that NGOs might eventually weaken or eliminate the monopoly of states in global decision making.[19] In addition, ECOSOC elects commission representatives on the basis of equitable geographic representation. This provision, along with the fact that many UN members are still authoritarian or even, in some cases, totalitarian regimes, severely politicized the Human Rights Commission. Cuba, which approximates a totalitarian regime, was elected to the commission, and at one point Libya, an oppressive monarchy, became president of the commission.

UN Human Rights Council
the 2006 successor of the UN Human Rights Commission.

Eventually, the commission was disbanded and replaced in 2006 by the **UN Human Rights Council.** Members of the council are elected by a majority of UN members voting by secret ballot and taking into account "the contribution of candidates to the promotion and protection of human rights." Seats are still apportioned by geographic area, but the General Assembly can suspend membership in the council by a two-thirds majority vote if a member "commits gross and systematic violations of human rights." The United States had sought a two-thirds vote to elect members, rather than to suspend them, and wanted to identify specific human rights violations that would disqualify a candidate. But in the interest of moving ahead, the United States accepted the compromise. Thus far, the Human Rights Council has continued to be polarized and ineffective.[20]

The United Nations human rights regime includes other conventions. Two important ones are the UN Convention on the Elimination of All Forms of Discrimination Against Women (CEDAW) and the UN Convention on the Rights of the Child (CRC).

Convention on Women's Rights

UN Convention on the Elimination of All Forms of Discrimination Against Women (CEDAW)
a 1979 UN convention broadly prohibiting all discrimination against women to which 185 members are parties and 8 (including the United States) have yet to ratify.

CEDAW was developed by the Commission on the Status of Women, initially a subcommission of the UN Commission on Human Rights. Passed by the General Assembly in 1979, the **UN Convention on the Elimination of All Forms of Discrimination Against Women (CEDAW)** prohibits all discrimination against women, defined as

> any distinction, exclusion or restriction made on the basis of sex which has the effect or purpose of impairing or nullifying the recognition, enjoyment or exercise by women, irrespective of their marital status, on a basis of equality of men and women, of human rights and fundamental freedoms in the political, economic, social, cultural, civil or any other field.[21]

One hundred eighty-five countries are parties to the convention. They elect a committee of twenty-three experts in the field of women's rights to receive and investigate reports from the member states submitted every four years.

Member states have submitted numerous reservations to CEDAW. Muslim countries, for example, do not recognize provisions of the convention inconsistent with religious law, or *sharia*. Saudi Arabia emphasizes the harmony and complementarities between men and women but not equality. The United States is one of eight countries yet to ratify the convention. Ratification has been stalled since 1980 in the Senate, where critics argue that the convention infringes on U.S. sovereignty, promotes abortion, interferes with the notion of family, and will legalize prostitution.

In 2000, the CEDAW adopted an optional protocol that permits an individual woman or women's groups to submit complaints. Less than half the member parties subscribe to this protocol, reflecting the reluctance of states to give women the right to appeal to an international body over national authorities if they feel their country is not respecting their rights.

Rights of the Child

The **UN Convention on the Rights of the Child (CRC)** was adopted by the General Assembly in 1989. It seeks to protect the rights of children, defined as anyone under eighteen years of age unless adult status has been attained earlier under national law, to life, to freedom from abuse, and to food, shelter, education, conscience (including religion), and participation in the community. It too developed initially out of the Universal Declaration of Human Rights, and like CEDAW, functions through a committee of experts (in this case, eighteen) elected by 193 member parties. Member parties are required to report to the committee of experts every five years.

CRC does not have provisions to hear complaints from individual children or their representatives. Optional protocols seek to prevent children from being used in warfare or subjected to sale, prostitution, or pornography. The United States has not signed CRC, arguing, as it has in other cases, that the convention does not bind oppressive countries that abuse the rights of not only children but adults and that U.S. law provides greater real protection for children's rights than the laws of any other country.

The United Nations is clearly hampered by the fact that there is still no clear consensus on the substance of basic human rights. Are basic human rights universal or are they cultural? Is the UN human rights regime just another form of western cultural imperialism? Countries such as Cuba, Libya, and Zimbabwe contend that the United States and other western countries violate the human rights of blacks, Muslims, the poor, and other minorities. The basic right to health care and education, they claim, is more essential than political or civil liberties, and the western nations, through their control of MNCs and wealth, systematically deprive developing nations of the most basic human needs. The United States and European countries counter that these charges are merely a smokescreen for repressive regimes that not only deny their people the freedom to acquire property and wealth but systematically bleed their country of resources and capital through a hemorrhage of corruption and favoritism. Perhaps human rights are best managed at the regional level, where countries may be expected to share greater cultural affinity.

European Human Rights Regime

The development of a human rights regime has progressed furthest in Europe, perhaps suggesting that cultural affinity may be necessary to support common practices and institutions in the human rights area. This development has been led by the **Council of Europe (CE),** created in the late 1940s before economic integration began under the

UN Convention on the Rights of the Child (CRC)
a UN convention adopted in 1989 to protect the rights of children, defined as anyone under eighteen years of age unless adult status has been attained earlier under national law, to life, to freedom from abuse, and to food, shelter, education, conscience (including religion), and participation in the community.

Council of Europe (CE)
the oldest (founded in 1949) and broadest (forty-seven member countries) organization working for European integration, focusing on legal standards and the protection of human rights, democratic development, and the rule of law in Europe.

European Convention on Human Rights and Fundamental Freedoms

the convention adopted by the Council of Europe in 1950 that establishes basic protections that block governments from violating citizens' rights to due process (legal rights, trial by jury, and so on) and political participation.

European Court of Human Rights

the court, established under the European Convention on Human Rights and Fundamental Freedoms of 1950, that enforces compliance with the convention's stipulations.

European Coal and Steel Community. The early treaties of the European Communities did not mention human rights, but the Maastricht Treaty in 1992, which transformed the European Communities into the European Union, committed the EU to respect the rights guaranteed by the Council of Europe. The European Court of Justice (ECJ), which we examine in Chapter 16, administers EU law.

The centerpiece of Europe's human rights regime is the **European Convention on Human Rights and Fundamental Freedoms** adopted by the Council of Europe in 1950. Drawing on the UN's 1948 Universal Declaration of Human Rights, the convention establishes basic protections that block governments from violating citizens' rights to due process (legal rights, trial by jury, and so on) and political participation. The convention is enforced by the Council of Ministers (usually foreign ministers) and by the **European Court of Human Rights** located in Strasbourg, France. In 2008, forty-seven countries belonged to the Council of Europe.

The novelty of the European Convention on Human Rights was not only to create an intergovernmental body to monitor the behavior of governments but also to allow for the right of private petition. This right gave private parties, such as individuals, NGOs, and associations of people, not just governments, the opportunity to petition the court. Originally, a separate European Commission of Human Rights screened these private petitions and represented the petitioners if the case went forward to the Court of Human Rights or Council of Ministers. But subsequent changes enabled private parties to appear directly before a special chamber of the court.

This move to give individuals, not just states, legal standing in international human rights proceedings was controversial. First, after ratifying the convention, member

Judges from the European Court of Human Rights attend a hearing in Strasbourg, France, in June 2007 to decide whether a seven-year-old girl from the United States, taken to France by her mother, should be returned to the custody of her father in the United States.

states still had the right to accept or reject the jurisdiction of the European Court of Human Rights as well as the option of allowing private parties from that state to petition the court. Eventually, all member states accepted these provisions. But for many years the Commission of Human Rights approved very few of the petitions that it screened, and states as a rule did not often choose to take one another to court over human rights. Only eight cases had been brought to the court by states as of 2005. By contrast, the number of private petitions continued to increase, despite the early rejection rates, and the commission began to approve a larger percentage of them. To improve efficiency, the commission was eventually replaced by a chamber of the court made up of several judges. Private parties could now go directly to the Court of Human Rights for preliminary hearings. The number of private petitions reached 13,858 in 2001.

Of private cases pending before the court in April 2008, one concerned the complaint of a couple from Slovenia that their son died in a hospital in 1993 as a result of medical negligence. After eleven years of legal proceedings, Slovenian courts had rejected their claim. The couple brought the case to the European Court of Human Rights, and in June 2007, the court ruled that it would hear the case. The plaintiffs alleged that the legal proceedings in Slovenian courts were excessively lengthy and unfair. They relied, in particular, on Articles 2 (right to life), 6 (right to a fair hearing), and 13 (right to an effective remedy) of the European Convention on Human Rights.

A second case concerned a group of Turkish nationals who contested a decision by Turkish courts to declare a parcel of land that the plaintiffs said had been in their family for three generations as belonging to the state forest. Relying on Article 1 of Protocol No. 1 (protection of property) to the European Human Rights Convention, the applicants contended that the Turkish courts' decision constituted a disproportionate interference with their right to the peaceful enjoyment of their possessions. A third case involved a television station in Norway that aired commercials for a political party despite a Norwegian law that prohibits political commercials on TV. The television station was fined and, after losing an appeal to Norway's Supreme Court, brought the case to the European Court.[22]

These cases suggest how deeply European law is reaching into the domain of national law. Remember that the states that belong to the Council of Europe are for the most part liberal democracies. Why are their citizens petitioning a European court for rights that presumably their national courts ensure? Well, one reason is that national laws are not in all cases fully democratic and, even among democracies, may differ in the degree to which they protect human rights. Russia, for example, is a member of the Council of Europe but hardly qualifies as a liberal democracy. And, a different example, rights in the United Kingdom are fully protected but by custom and not by formal laws. In 1997, UK citizens brought four hundred petitions to the European Court of Human Rights. More generally, the experience of the European Court of Human Rights suggests that people are becoming more comfortable identifying with regional as well as national authorities to protect their basic rights. As one human rights expert notes, "even with liberal democracy at the national level, there [is] still a need for regional monitoring of human rights—there being evident violations by national authorities."[23]

Do states comply with the European court judgments? As a rule, yes. But there are still instances of noncompliance. Earlier, Britain and Italy were the most frequent violators of court decisions. By 2005, the bulk of violations were by Turkey and Russia. In case of noncompliance, the Council of Europe Council of Ministers can order that compensation be paid. But, unlike the case in domestic courts, there is still no European police to arrest violators.

The Council of Europe has passed other human rights conventions. The European Social Charter, originally developed in 1961, was revised in 1996 and as of early 2008 had been accepted by nineteen members. This is less than half the number participating in the human rights convention. The Social Charter covers basic rights to housing, employment, health, education, legal and social protections, movement, and nondiscrimination. As such, it is more expansive and intrusive on national prerogatives. Social rights cannot be adjudicated by the Court of Human Rights, although there is some talk about making social rights part of the European Convention on Human Rights in the future. Nevertheless, from 1996 to 2005 the European Committee of Social Rights, charged to implement the Social Charter, received twenty-six petitions from collective private parties, such as trade unions and human rights groups, heard twenty-three of them, and ruled against states in sixteen cases, including child labor cases in Portugal, discrimination on the basis of disability in France, and protection of children against corporal punishment in Ireland and Belgium.

In 1986, the Council of Europe also passed the European Convention for the Prevention of Torture and Inhuman or Degrading Treatment or Punishment. All members ratified this convention. It is implemented by a committee of uninstructed (meaning independent of government) individuals who can make ad hoc visits to detention centers with minimal advance notice to investigate prison treatment. In recent years, the committee has ruled against France for abuse of a suspected drug dealer and Turkey and Russia for a variety of abuses. The fact that European states are accustomed to monitoring one another on the treatment of detainees may explain their outrage at the U.S. abuses of detainees at Guantanamo, Abu Ghraib, and secret CIA detention centers around the world, some in Europe. The United States does not participate in such regional human rights regimes and, hence, is not accustomed to such oversight.

Other Regional Human Rights Regimes

Latin America and Africa have human rights regimes that are similar to those in Europe, but numerous states in these regions have systematically violated the standards of basic human rights. Asia has no such regime, nor do the Arab and broader Islamic worlds. The limits of the acceptance of basic human rights remind us that the world is still not yet a community of common humanity, if we understand this to mean a consensus on basic human rights.

Latin America's human rights regime is centered in the Organization of American States (OAS). The OAS has a regional convention for the protection of human rights and an Inter-American Commission and Court of Human Rights to implement it. The **American Declaration on the Rights and Duties of Man** dates from 1948, the **Inter-American Convention on Human Rights** stems from 1969, and the **Inter-American Court of Human Rights** was set up in 1979. Although the declaration and convention have content similar to that of the European regime, only twenty-one of thirty-five states in the region accept the jurisdiction of the Inter-American Court of Human Rights. As a result, the court's caseload is small, and only forty-five binding and seventeen advisory opinions had been handed down as of 2004.[24]

Only the Inter-American Commission appointed by states and the states themselves can bring cases to the court. Nevertheless, in 1998, Brazil and Mexico, two of the

---

American Declaration on the Rights and Duties of Man
the world's first international human rights instrument of a general nature, adopted by the nations of the Americas in April 1948.

Inter-American Convention on Human Rights
an international human rights instrument adopted by the nations of the Americas in 1969; its purpose is to report, investigate, and conduct diplomacy to protect and promote human rights in Latin America.

Inter-American Court of Human Rights
the court charged with implementing the Inter-American Convention on Human Rights.

region's most important states, accepted the court's jurisdiction. The United States still does not, for fear that membership will subject U.S. defendants to all sorts of frivolous lawsuits.

Africa too has a Charter on Human and Peoples' Rights, which went into force in 1986. But Africa's charter sets up only an advisory commission to implement its provisions; until 2004, there was no court to hear cases. In that year, the African Court on Human and Peoples' Rights was created, and in 2006 it elected its first judges. But only states can bring cases, unless they explicitly accept the right of individual petition. Few are expected to do so.

Asia drafted its first human rights charter in 1998. But it was drafted by nongovernmental, not governmental, organizations, and it has yet to be embraced by governments. Only nine Asian states subscribe to the International Covenants on Civil and Political Liberties and Economic and Social Rights. By contrast, dozens of states subscribe to the UN CEDAW and CRC.

The rights of oppressed groups, such as minorities, indigenous groups, peasant and working-class groups, and the disabled, and rights to political participation are not widely recognized by Asian states. Asian states see these rights as a threat to state interests and sovereignty. Most of them view rights as being granted by the state rather than being protected from the state. Thus, social stability and the preservation of the state take precedence over the enforcement of human rights. Some states, such as China, Singapore, and Malaysia, argue unabashedly for Asian values that give priority to society rather than to individuals.

The Arab and broader Islamic worlds have similar disregard for basic or—as they see them—western human rights. The Arab League has a Human Rights Commission that focuses largely on what it perceives to be Israeli atrocities in occupied territories; and the Organization of the Islamic Conference (OIC), which consists of fifty-seven Muslim countries spread across four continents, has no human rights institutions whatsoever. Indeed, for the past decade, it has campaigned at the UN Human Rights Commission/Council to restrict the rights of freedom of expression, urging the council to report on instances, such as public statements against the Islamic religion, where freedom of expression involves religious discrimination. As the International Humanist and Ethical Union (an umbrella NGO for human rights organizations advocating a humanist not a religious or democratic definition of human rights) lamented, the OIC's position "would turn the Council's mandate on its head." Instead of promoting freedom of expression, the Council "would be policing its exercise." [25]

Spotlight on Asian values

Enforcing Basic Human Rights

Since the end of the Cold War, interventions to enforce basic human rights have become more frequent. As Martha Finnemore writes, "humanitarian claims now frequently trump sovereignty claims." [26] When the international community does not intervene, as in the case of genocide in Rwanda in 1994, states feel the obligation to explain why. Bill Clinton, for example, visited Rwanda in 1998 and apologized to the Rwandan people for the failure of the United States and international community to stop the Hutu rebels who slaughtered almost a million of their Tutsi neighbors.

Interventions are also shifting from unilateral to multilateral. Based on data compiled by Finnemore, thirty-four military interventions took place during the four decades of the Cold War, twenty-one of which were unilateral. Thirteen took place in just the first decade after the end of the Cold War, ten of which were multilateral.

Increasingly, interventions are considered legitimate only if they are carried out multilaterally. The near universal outcry against America's unilateral intervention in Iraq offers some evidence for this point.

Spotlight on
perspectives

Realist perspectives might argue that the shift from sovereignty to multilateralism was due to a shift in the structure of power from bipolar to unipolar. The United States and Soviet Union no longer competed in the world system and therefore had less at stake in international interventions. Also, the United States won the Cold War, and its multicultural humanitarian values naturally dominated world affairs. Liberal perspectives might see the hand of collective security at work; after the Cold War ended, the UN was free to assume its originally intended role. Social constructivists might argue that a constitutive change in norms came first, before power and institutions shifted, to move the consensus in humanitarian directions.

According to identity perspectives, common humanitarian norms may explain the world's reaction to terrorism better than power or institutions. The great powers did not react to 9/11 in a traditional fashion and take opposing sides. Confucian powers did not cooperate with Islamic powers, as Huntington hypothesized. Instead, the great powers cooperated in an unprecedented fashion, and they did so without formal UN involvement. The United States and Russia worked together outside the UN Security Council to establish a ring of U.S. military bases in former Soviet republics in central Asia that were used to root out the Taliban government in Afghanistan. Imagine such a scenario fifteen years earlier, when Russia was still engaged in a bloody and unsuccessful war to claim Afghanistan for its own! China also accepted U.S. bases in Tajikistan, which borders China. Cooperation faltered, to be sure, when the war expanded to Iraq. But that illustrated condemnation of U.S. unilateralism more than it did traditional competition among great powers.

causal
arrow

Spotlight on
human security

The entire civilized world felt threatened by random acts of violence against innocent civilians. All people were now human beings, whether white, black, Muslim, or Christian, and should be protected from such violence. There were no more barbarians, except perhaps the terrorists themselves. The global consensus on basic human rights seemed to be stronger than national, ideological, or religious ties. And it had an effect on outcomes even when UN institutions did not take the lead. In fact, those institutions were themselves sometimes involved in justifying terrorism. Arab states, for example, repeatedly used the UN to denounce Israel and condone acts of terror against it. Thus, for social constructivists, it was the emergence of a stronger common conception or norm of humanity that isolated terrorist groups such as Al Qaeda and explained the world's response to terrorism, not the actions of international institutions themselves or shifts in the distribution of power toward unipolarity.

causal
arrow

Summary

Nonstate actors and global civil society constitute one pillar of global governance in today's world. Spawned by the Enlightenment and industrial revolution, NGOs populate a large space in global affairs across many sectors—commercial, environment, human rights, and others—and increasingly affect relations with and among governments. NGOs in this space also increasingly agree on basic human rights and urge all governments to respect them. But the meaning of basic human rights differs at the global and regional levels. The UN human rights regime under the Human Rights Council remains polarized and ineffective, while the EU human rights regime under the Council of Europe's Convention on Human Rights grants individuals and groups an effective means to protect their rights even against their own governments. Elsewhere, Asian and Islamic countries continue to regard state interests and sovereignty as overriding basic human rights as defined by western law. Global civil society is still fractured, and it is unclear whether the world is moving toward more authoritarian or more constitutional forms of global governance.

Key Concepts

American Declaration on the Rights and Duties of Man 506

authoritarian states 485

civil rights 485

constitutional governments 485

Council of Europe (CE) 503

European Convention on Human Rights and Fundamental Freedoms 504

European Court of Human Rights 504

Inter-American Convention on Human Rights 506

Inter-American Court of Human Rights 506

regionalism 489

totalitarian governments 485

transnational nongovernmental organizations (TNGOs) 492

UN Convention on the Elimination of All Forms of Discrimination Against Women (CEDAW) 502

UN Convention on the Rights of the Child (CRC) 503

UN Economic and Social Council (ECOSOC) 502

UN Human Rights Commission 501

UN Human Rights Council 502

Universal Declaration of Human Rights 500

Study Questions

1. How do the different perspectives evaluate the role of NGOs in global governance?

2. Rank the UN and EU human rights regimes in terms of protection of basic human rights.

3. What are the different forms by which global civil society relates to global governance? Give examples of each in today's world.

4. What are the major differences between the human rights regimes of the UN and EU, on the one hand, and those of the Asian and Islamic regions on the other?

5. How has the enforcement of basic human rights changed over the past two centuries?

16

Global Governance
International and Regional Institutions

The headquarters of the United Nations in New York City flies the flags of all 192 nations of the world community in 2008.

**Spotlight on
liberal perspective**

International institutions and international law potentially exert a powerful unifying influence on international relations. Just as feudal actors consolidated power, sovereignty, and identities at the state level four centuries ago, is it possible that state actors may someday consolidate power and law beyond the nation-state at the level of international institutions? Global governance can finally provide the world with the kind of framework that domestic governments offer: common law-making processes, a body of codified laws, courts to adjudicate disputes, police to enforce laws, and prisons to punish offenders.

The liberal perspective has always envisioned this possibility. Its advocates are impressed by the steady advance of common institutions, from expert or functional international organizations such as the WHO, to regional integration institutions such as the EU, to IGOs such as the UN, to international legal and human rights activities such as the Universal Declaration of Human Rights and International Criminal Court (ICC), and finally to the plethora of TNGOs that advocate environmental, human rights, development, and other causes as part of a burgeoning global civil society, which we examine in the previous chapter.

The realist perspective acknowledges the existence of multiple strands of global governance, but it is less sanguine that it represents something novel. International, like domestic, institutions have to be run by specific groups. The key questions, therefore, are who controls international institutions and will they behave differently than state institutions. After all, state institutions replaced feudal city-states and leagues, and yet the struggle for power persisted. International and transnational organizations may only constitute new arenas for the pursuit of power and, if they increasingly consolidate into unified institutions of global governance, that pursuit becomes more, not less, deadly because so much is now at stake and there are fewer decentralized ways to correct mistakes made by centralized and unaccountable global bodies.

Identity perspectives say the future of global governance depends on the ideas and identities that constitute it. Secularists see a future for global governance if pluralism, tolerance, and respect for fundamental human rights prevail. Democracy advocates support global institutions if they become as accessible, open, and democratic as national democracies and increasingly educate the rest of the world in the mechanisms and mores of democracy. Religious advocates want global institutions to reflect spiritual values and, in the case of religious fundamentalists, subordinate public life to the laws of the Bible, Koran, Torah, or other holy books. Environmental enthusiasts want global institutions to put the common heritage of planet Earth first—the resources, biodiversity, and common atmosphere that we all share and must preserve. From an identity perspective, consolidation of governance is less a matter of strengthening institutions or fighting over their control than of establishing legitimacy based on some set of common norms, values, or beliefs.

Critical theory perspectives see global governance as a form of elite hegemony that is not desired and must be resisted. Elites in core countries, especially in the great powers, use international institutions and law to consolidate their hegemony. These institutions penetrate the peripheral countries and co-opt them such that they absorb the changes, such as free trade, that are consistent with hegemonic control. From this perspective, hegemony is more than power. It is power, ideas, and institutions all wrapped up into one that colonize not only the resources but the mind and institutions of peripheral countries. There is little possibility to resist such hegemonic governance directly. Critical theory perspectives call for resistance at the national and local levels that eventually shapes a new consciousness and creates a counter-hegemonic movement from the bottom up. Revolutionary action remains a necessary aspect of international relations.

In this chapter, we look at the principal means for consolidating global governance beyond or above the nation-state. We start with a discussion of state institutions, how and why they evolved. Then, we examine IGOs, such as the UN, and their reform and the evolution of international law and courts. Finally, we examine regional institutions transcending the nation-state, such as the EU. Along the way we take note of the different views toward these institutional and legal developments taken by mainstream and critical theory perspectives.

State

Why did the state emerge in the seventeenth century? Was it because it performed functions more efficiently than city-states or city-leagues, as the liberal perspective avers? City-states were too small to defend against new technologies, particularly gunpowder and the professionalization of the military; and city-leagues based around the Baltic and Mediterranean Seas lost prominence as the development of interior waterways, such as the Rhine River, opened up the vast expanse and resources of continental landmasses. Or was it because monarchs finally achieved the upper hand over the

**Spotlight on
realist perspective**

**Spotlight on
identity perspective**

**Spotlight on
critical theory
perspective**

pope and holy Roman emperor, as realist perspectives argue? Monarchs, such as Louis XIII and his foreign minister, Cardinal de Richelieu, established borders and defended them, compelling the respect and recognition of other states. Or did the concept of state sovereignty finally become appropriate after years of accumulating practice in which convention or custom replaced calculation and gradually constituted the norm of mutual recognition, as social constructivists might argue? No monarch gained the upper hand, but eventually they all relented and decided to let each become sovereign in his or her own domain. Or, last, did the state emerge to serve the hegemonic ambitions of the capitalist elites, as critical theory perspectives contend? After all, the state dates from the era of the rise of the bourgeoisie, and it served the purpose of military and economic expansion among western elites, eventually consolidating western hegemony through the international institutions and structures that constitute contemporary global governance.

As technology advanced, states, of course, could not dominate all aspects of their external environment and had to enter into interstate or intergovernmental relationships to cope with external exigencies. They met at conferences such as Osnabrück and Münster and concluded treaties such as the Treaty of Westphalia. In the nineteenth century, states convened more conferences, signed more treaties, and established intergovernmental bureaucracies to administer many of them. The Concert of Europe in 1815 created the first expectation of a regular conference process, and the Universal Postal Union in 1874 put in place one of the first expert or functional international institutions to facilitate interdependence, in this case the delivery of mail. Between 1848 and 1919, states signed treaties that filled 226 thick books. Between 1920 and 1946, they filled 205 more volumes. And between 1946 and 1978, they filled another 1,115 volumes.[1] IGOs grew in numbers and significance. They codified laws and practices, which interfered in the domestic jurisdiction of states.

To be sure, states run IGOs, unlike NGOs. Yet IGOs, too, develop a life and often independence of their own. They define issues that governments may initially ignore, such as the environment, and they gain a legitimacy that makes it difficult for governments to circumvent them. Today, some worry that international bureaucracies, such as the UN Secretariat, operate outside the guidelines and wishes of the member states. They lack accountability either to governments or NGOs from the member states. The world of organizations above the nation-state gradually eludes the grip of domestic sovereignty.

In recent decades, states, particularly great powers, have tried to regain some control over international institutions by establishing less formal "steering committees" of big countries, such as the G-7, G-8, and G-20. These **great power groups** meet on a regular basis to influence the international agenda and set directions and tasks for international institutions. As a rule, the great power groups are less formal or bureaucratic. They bring world leaders together for face-to-face talks and try to coordinate the many international organizations, both governmental and nongovernmental, that are involved in areas such as foreign aid, global finance, the environment, and drug trafficking. However, from some liberal perspectives these groups lack the legitimacy of universal organizations. Debate persists as to which countries should be included in these groups. The G-7 included only democratic countries until Russia became a member and the G-7 became the G-8. China, Brazil, and India are further aspirants to the G-8, and smaller developing countries belonging to the G-77 complain that they are insufficiently represented in the G-20, which includes the bigger developing countries. Do countries gain membership by virtue of power (realist), equality (liberal), or

Spotlight on IGOs

great power groups

assorted informal groupings of the major economic and financial powers that supplement formal international institutions in managing global economic affairs; examples are the G-7, G-8, and G-20.

G-8 leaders meet in Germany in 2007 for direct talks about the world's political and economic situation. Seated at the table, clockwise from left foreground, are German Chancellor Angela Merkel, U.S. President George W. Bush, British Prime Minister Tony Blair, Italian Prime Minister Romano Prodi, European Commission President José Manuel Barroso, Japanese Prime Minister Shinzo Abe, Canadian Prime Minister Stephen Harper, French President Nicolas Sarkozy, and Russian President Vladimir Putin.

ideology (identity)? Or are these informal great power groups simply additional tools of core-country hegemonism, as critical theory perspectives assert?

Over the years, states have also merged and fragmented. They have voluntarily or involuntarily ceded sovereignty to higher, supranational, or to lower, subnational authorities. The Prussian state, for example, transferred its sovereignty to the German state. The Czechoslovakian state gained its sovereignty from Austria-Hungary, only to cede it later to the separate Czech and Slovak states. So, new actors are part of the changing landscape of international affairs. Today, the EU is a new sovereign and independent actor in many sectors, such as trade and monetary policy, and regional organizations in general are gaining greater influence and attention. A big question is whether this process of merger and dissolution of states simply leads to new actors that are just like states, but now larger or smaller, or whether institutions like the EU are new institutions that behave differently than traditional states. Will the world of organizations *above* the nation-state eventually lead to institutions that go *beyond* and are different from the nation-state?

Intergovernmental Organizations

IGOs serve many purposes. First, they promote the interests of the member states, especially the great powers. Alliances, for example, defend the territory of member states, and the UN Security Council projects the influence of the veto powers on matters of international peace and security. Second, they address specialized problems that require expertise to solve. The WHO brings physicians and health experts together to eradicate disease. Third, they address common or collective problems that no one country or group of countries could manage on its own. The International Telecommunications Union and the International Seabed Authority (part of the Treaty on the Law of the Sea, which the United States has yet to ratify) seek to manage airspace and deep-sea ocean resources considered to be the "common heritage of mankind." Fourth, they help countries do things more efficiently. The WTO collects and standardizes data on tariffs and other trade restrictions, which facilitates multilateral trade negotiations.

Because states create and control IGOs, realist analysts doubt their autonomy. IGOs are merely extensions of states, especially the most powerful states, and are not regarded as independent actors in international affairs.[2] On the other hand, IGOs acquire their own personnel, budgets, and organizations to implement their tasks. As liberal perspectives see it, they may influence outcomes in ways that member states did not originally intend.[3] For example, the UN recognized the right of the Palestinian people to statehood long before the United States, one of its founders and most powerful members, did. In addition, IGOs stand for different principles or ideas, as identity perspectives emphasize.[4] To be a member of NATO or the EU, a country has to be a democracy. To be a member of the UN, it just has to be recognized as sovereign. From a critical theory perspective, IGOs perpetuate the status quo, reproducing the power, institutions, and ideas of a capitalist world system.

Spotlight on perspectives

Functional Organizations

When IGOs function in highly technical areas, they acquire even more independence from member states. The World Food Organization (WFO), for example, employs many nutritionists and other professional staff from all over the world. Even state delegates to WFO meetings are often experts. Together these professionals know more about the problem of food than any single member state. Potentially, this expertise gives the IGO more clout than the state in making decisions.

After World War II, David Mitrany, an English scholar, developed a way of thinking about IGOs working in specific functional areas that gave them a primary role in international affairs.[5] Called **functionalism,** this approach argues that expert IGOs grow in significance as they solve practical problems, such as food and health. By removing one problem after another from state competition, these organizations will gradually marginalize the political considerations that states emphasize. It will matter less which country sold more food to the world's poor as the number of poor people in the world goes down. Functional areas will be removed from the calculations of power politics. International politics, as it is traditionally understood, especially in realist perspectives, will become irrelevant and wither away.

functionalism
an approach that argues that states will decline in significance as expert intergovernmental organizations solve practical problems.

Expert or Epistemic Communities

Mitrany may have been too utopian, but his ideas live on today in what political scientists call expert or **epistemic communities.** Communities of experts work within IGOs and informal transnational networks to develop data and define problems that become more self-evident and accepted by all political groups. They apply the scientific method to problem solving and test their conclusions against real-world conditions, learning which solutions achieve the best results. The assumption of many of these experts is the same as that of Mitrany—once people have enough food, health, and other material benefits, they will pay less attention to politics. Science will replace politics.[6]

IGOs not only solve problems; they increase the efficiency of interstate interactions.[7] They reduce transaction costs. Just think how difficult it would be to conduct

epistemic communities
groups of experts who share and are motivated by the same set of scientific ideas and training.

bilateral negotiations to reduce trade barriers with the 151 WTO members. The WTO facilitates the formation of coalitions that make negotiations more efficient. Second, IGOs provide more information and make it less costly and, therefore, more widely available. The IMF, for example, publishes regular reports on the domestic economic policies of member countries; this helps countries anticipate problems that may arise from the domestic policies of other countries. Negotiations are often inhibited by lack of information. The WTO publishes lots of information to help countries, especially small ones, understand trends in trade relations. Think about our old prisoner's dilemma story. If the prisoners knew more about one another, they might be able to cooperate and achieve better outcomes.

Scholars talk about these problems in terms of coordination and collaboration. A **coordination problem** might be deciding on which side of the road cars should drive. Which side of the road does not really matter to the participants, but unless they coordinate and develop common information and rules, the roads will be a mess. A **collaboration problem** might involve settling a territorial dispute. This problem is more difficult and resembles the prisoner's dilemma—how do you share enough information to build mutual trust? A third way IGOs improve the efficiency of interstate relations is by reducing uncertainty. Institutions, as we have pointed out in earlier chapters, provide a "shadow of the future." They offer assurance that there will be negotiations again tomorrow and that today's negotiations are not the last move. That reduces uncertainties. Studies show that if participants know negotiations are ongoing they are more likely to cooperate.[8]

Perspectives on Intergovernmental Organizations

Realist approaches assume that IGOs do not exert direct effects on actors' interests and identities. IGOs serve the interests of states; they do not transform them and create new actors. Liberal perspectives see IGOs helping states communicate and, in the end, compromise interests so that they can achieve better outcomes. Just like the actors in our old prisoner's dilemma story, IGOs enable countries to achieve first- and second-best outcomes rather than settling for third-best outcomes.

Identity perspectives see IGOs as eventually transforming state interests by shaping new state identities. Functional IGOs, according to Mitrany, make states irrelevant. States simply fade away when they have no more functions to perform. But a later development called **neofunctionalism** envisions IGOs changing state loyalties and identities directly. In this approach, championed initially by the European Coal and Steel Community (ECSC), innovative leadership by a commission representing community interests proposes ways to upgrade and transform state interests, rather than simply serving state interests (the realist perspective), compromising them (the liberal perspective), or bypassing them (the functional perspective).

Notice again that the difference between functionalism and neofunctionalism is a matter of the direction of causal arrows. In functionalism, institutional problem solving simply removes issues from the competition among states. States retain their national identities but become less and less relevant. In neofunctionalism, institutional processes actually change the identities of states. Elites become less loyal to national governments and more loyal to European institutions. To the extent that institutions precede and cause identity changes, neofunctionalism is a liberal perspective. Identity perspectives, such as social constructivists, place more emphasis on the substantive discourse rather than just the problem-solving procedures of international institu-

---

Spotlight on
transaction costs

Spotlight on
prisoner's dilemma

coordination problems
problems that can be resolved by informal means rather than institutional cooperation.

collaboration problems
problems that can be resolved only when parties cooperate, usually through institutional means.

neofunctionalism
an approach that argues that intergovernmental organizations, such as the institutions of the European Community/Union, transform state loyalties and identities directly.

causal arrow

tions; shared ideas, not just shared practices, ultimately change identities and international norms.

Next, we look at the United Nations, which consists of both general-purpose institutions such as the Security Council and General Assembly, and specialized or functional IGOs such as the international courts and economic institutions. Then, we look further at the EU and the neofunctional institutions and logic that shaped the European integration process.

United Nations

United Nations (UN)

the principal general-purpose intergovernmental organization that deals with collective security, economic and social development, and international law and human rights.

The **United Nations (UN)** is the principal general-purpose IGO in contemporary international affairs. It deals with all three major international issues: collective security and peace, economic and social development, and international law and human rights. The UN Security Council has primary responsibility for peace and security. The UN General Assembly coordinates economic and social issues through its Economic and Social Council (ECOSOC). And the International Court of Justice (ICJ) serves as the primary judiciary organ. The UN Secretariat, with a staff of about 9,000 people under its regular budget, provides administrative support led by the secretary-general. A Trusteeship Council set up to administer colonial or non-self-governing territories after World War II is now defunct, although it still exists on the books. In 2008, the UN had 192 members.

Let's look at the security, economic, and human rights responsibilities of the UN.

Peacekeeping and Humanitarian Intervention

As we have learned in earlier chapters, the UN was intended to provide muscular collective security under Chapter VII of the UN Charter. The five permanent members of the Security Council with veto rights were to cooperate to enforce UN decisions. The Cold War between the United States and Soviet Union ended that expectation. Prior to 1990, the Security Council used Chapter VII only twice to enforce mandatory sanctions against Southern Rhodesia in 1966, when the white minority declared independence, and South Africa in 1977 in an effort to end apartheid. The UN sent forces to Korea in 1950, but the General Assembly authorized that action when the Soviet Union boycotted the Security Council because the UN refused to seat the new communist government in China.

Spotlight on **peace-enforcement activities**

Nevertheless, as we discuss in Chapter 5, UN forces did play a key role during the Cold War under Chapter VI of the Charter, which regulates the peaceful settlement of disputes. In conflicts in the Sinai Peninsula, Cyprus, Golan Heights, Lebanon, and other areas, UN forces played a peacekeeping, not peace enforcement, role to supervise cease-fires and mediate negotiations. They intervened to separate combatants, to observe and monitor cease-fire lines, and to maintain or restore civil order. All parties consented to these interventions, and UN forces acted neutrally. UN forces had no choice but to leave when asked. In 1973, the Egyptian government, before starting another war with Israel, requested that UN forces leave the Sinai Peninsula. They did, and war followed. Even with these limitations, however, UN peacekeeping forces are generally credited with preventing these conflicts from escalating into confrontations between the superpowers.

Spotlight on **peacekeeping activities**

After 1990, the requirements for peacekeeping activities escalated. As we have learned in Chapter 6, numerous conflicts erupted in Somalia, Cambodia, former

Yugoslavia, Haiti, Congo, East Timor, and elsewhere. For a brief period, it was thought possible to reconstruct the UN as a great power peace enforcement mechanism under Chapter VII. But that hope faded when U.S. soldiers acting under UN auspices died in Somalia and the U.S. withdrew. Peacekeeping proved to be more difficult in civil or intrastate conflicts than in interstate border wars. It was not so easy to separate combatants, and efforts to feed civilians inevitably involved international forces in local fighting. Without cease-fire agreements, UN forces were subject to attack. When Bosnian Serbs entered Srebrenica, for example, they simply overwhelmed the Dutch forces protecting Muslims in a so-called UN safe haven. The UN secretary-general appealed for more muscular capabilities. But UN peacekeeping forces remain stretched and inadequate; and they suffer from lack of proper training and oversight. UN forces and civilian workers in the Congo and elsewhere have been accused of rape, spreading AIDS, corruption, and other human rights abuses.[9]

Peacekeeping and Terrorism

Not just humanitarian concerns but terrorism also raises questions of intervention in the affairs of sovereign states. Terrorism and WMDs pose a new threat. Without any warning or visible buildup before an attack, a terrorist cell can detonate an atomic weapon and blow up a major city, killing millions of people. Should one state intervene in another if it suspects that state of harboring terrorists or possibly providing them with WMDs? That was the question raised by U.S. intervention in Iraq in 2003. The UN could not reach an agreement. When the Security Council deadlocks, the only other justification for the use of force under the UN Charter is self-defense (Article 51). Some countries, such as the United States and Great Britain, concluded that Iraq was seeking WMDs and might provide them to terrorists. They undertook a preemptive war as an act of self-defense, arguing that such action is justified when it appears imminent that one country is about to attack another. Others concluded that the links to terrorism and WMDs were unconvincing and accused the United States of waging a preventive war, a much more controversial act of self-defense mounted against a threat that is not yet evident, or *imminent,* but presumed to be coming, or *immanent,* in the future.

Spotlight on preemptive and preventive war

Kofi Annan, then UN secretary-general, convened another panel, the High-Level Panel on Threats, Challenges and Change, to consider the criteria for legitimate intervention in the face of the new threat of terrorism. The panel identified five criteria: (1) a sufficiently clear and serious threat to warrant the use of force; (2) a primary purpose to stop the threat, not other motives such as regime change; (3) the use of force as a last resort; (4) the use of proportionate and minimum necessary force; and (5) the consequences of using force are unlikely to be worse than no action.[10] Although the UN report acknowledged for the first time that there were threats that the international community had to address before they became imminent, there is still plenty of room in these criteria for disagreement. Realist perspectives are generally going to see a bigger threat sooner; liberal perspectives will insist on maximum participation in the decision, which means Security Council or General Assembly approval; and identity perspectives will distinguish between interventions on behalf of globalist ideas, such as genocide, and those on behalf of purely national interests, such as access to oil. Critical theory perspectives see such interventions as extensions of core-country hegemony to preempt counter-hegemonic challenges.

Spotlight on perspectives

Economic and Social Council

After World War II, the Bretton Woods institutions, nominally UN agencies but largely independent of it, had primary responsibility for economic development. Today, the World Bank, IMF, and WTO, guided by the G-7 and other great power groups, continue to take the lead (see sections later in the chapter). Nevertheless, the UN General Assembly plays a general oversight role in the economic and social area. It operates through six committees of the whole (in which all members participate): disarmament, economic, humanitarian, decolonization, budget, and legal.

The Second Committee oversees ECOSOC, the UN's principal economic organ. ECOSOC has fifty-four members elected to three-year terms by the General Assembly. It usually includes the veto powers, with the exception of China. ECOSOC oversees a bewildering array of specialized agencies and commissions. First come the seventeen specialized UN agencies, including WHO, FAO, IAEA, and the Bretton Woods institutions. Then come the ten functional commissions—for Social Development, Human Rights, Status of Women, Sustainable Development, Population and Development, and so on. There are also regional commissions for economic affairs—Europe, Asia, Latin America, and Africa. The UN Economic Commission for Latin America (ECLA) led the opposition against free-market policies to create UNCTAD in 1964. In UNCTAD, developing countries formed the G-77 (now actually 130 countries) to lobby for a New International Economic Order (NIEO) to replace the Bretton Woods system. Still further UN programs and funds exist, such as the UN Environmental Program (UNEP) and World Food Program (WFP).

Even if it had the power, ECOSOC could not oversee such a sprawling bureaucracy—and it has few powers. It can only issue recommendations and receive reports. It has no control over agencies' budgets or secretariats. For years, some members, especially the United States, which pays the largest share of the UN budget, complained about UN expenditures. The United States withdrew from the UN Education, Science and Cultural Organization (UNESCO) in 1984 because of corruption and withheld funding from the UN general budget. In this case, Washington was sharply criticized for impeding UN activities. But the United States argued that there was no other way to enforce accountability. Realist perspectives raise pointed questions about who provides the oversight of such international institutions. The UN bureaucracy, unlike domestic bureaucracies, is not subject to the immediate scrutiny of parliaments and NGOs. Nondemocratic UN members face no such scrutiny at all, even at home.

Liberal perspectives urge reforms to improve accountability but only at a pace that involves multilateral participation and consent. The UN adopted some reforms in the 1990s, but then the oil-for-food scandal revealed continuing widespread corruption. In administering sanctions against Iraq, UN officials were accused of influence-peddling, taking kickbacks, and other criminal offenses. Another investigation uncovered some $298 million of UN funds lost through fraud and mismanagement of UN peacekeeping operations.[11] Some identity perspectives lament the weakness of international norms governing the behavior of civil servants. Others point out, however, that these norms may be no weaker than in national bureaucracies, where corruption and scandals are also frequent occurrences.

Spotlight on perspectives

International Court of Justice and International Criminal Court

The ICJ sits in The Hague. It has fifteen justices elected for nine-year terms by the Security Council and General Assembly. It has no powers to force parties to appear before the court or to enforce its decisions. Only states, not individuals or NGOs, can bring cases to the court. States can accept ICJ decisions as compulsory, but when Nicaragua accused the U.S. government in 1984 of mining its harbors, the United States rejected the court's ruling and terminated its acceptance of compulsory jurisdiction. In fifty-five years, the ICJ considered only 107 cases and made 52 judgments. It issued another 24 advisory opinions. None of these dealt with major issues, although the ICJ helped developing countries resolve a number of border disputes, for example Cameroon and Nigeria, and issues related to fisheries and continental-shelf jurisdiction.

Ad hoc tribunals were created after World War II to deal with war criminals in Germany and Japan. Atrocities committed during civil wars in the former Yugoslavia and Rwanda revived interest in such panels. Today, ad hoc international tribunals try war criminal from these conflicts in The Hague and Arusha, Tanzania. These tribunals respond to individual, not just state, complaints.

The desire to make ad hoc tribunals permanent led to the creation in 1998 of the ICC. The ICC has both compulsory jurisdiction over states and jurisdiction over individuals. It considers four types of crime: genocide (killing people because of their race, ethnicity, or religion), crimes against humanity (forcible transfer of populations, torture, enslavement, and murder), war crimes, and crimes of aggression (left undefined). Anyone can bring a case to the ICC. The ICC acts as a court of last resort, however, only if national courts prove unwilling or unable to act.

The United States, China, and India, among others, refused to join the ICC. The United States, reflecting realist concerns, argued that the ICC could prosecute U.S. soldiers, saying that U.S. courts were unwilling to do so. A case in point might be the treatment of prisoners by the U.S. military in Guantanamo Bay. Yet the United States, more than any other country, has soldiers deployed around the world to protect international peace and security. Anyone who opposed U.S. actions could try its soldiers, even its president, before the ICC. The U.S. supports an amendment making the ICC subject to the Security Council. In the meantime, because the ICC has already gone into effect, the United States negotiates so-called Article 98 agreements with other countries, committing them not to send Americans to the ICC for prosecution.

Spotlight on international law

United Nations Reforms

Changing threats, globalization, and scandals led to widespread calls for UN reforms. The principal reforms include expanding the Security Council; trimming down the bureaucracy; coping with new threats such as state collapse, WMDs, and terrorism; and getting serious about human rights and development.

The proposals include expanding the Security Council from fifteen to twenty-four members. Brazil, Germany, India, Japan, Egypt, and either Nigeria or South Africa are likely candidates for permanent seats and, hence, the veto. But China opposes Japanese membership, and the United States has expressed skepticism about German membership, which would give the EU three seats on the Council. Adding veto members to the Security Council would make it more representative but not necessarily more efficient. An alternative is to give the new members semi-permanent status, elected to four-year renewable terms instead of the two-year terms for current nonpermanent members. The secretary-general's office would gain more powers and responsibility over budgets, and some bureaucracies would be eliminated. The Human Rights Commission, chaired in recent years by some of the worst human rights offenders, such as Cuba, Libya, and Sudan, would be replaced by a Human Rights Council, elected by a majority of the UN Assembly. The council would meet for more extended periods of time. It was set up in 2006.

The reforms are controversial and reflect continuing differences among the perspectives. Realist perspectives seek greater accountability by great powers. Liberal perspectives seek wider and fairer representation. Identity perspectives seek stronger democratic norms, particularly in the human rights area. When the new Human Rights Council was set up, the United States wanted members to be elected by two-thirds of the Assembly membership, giving democratic nations blocking power. But the majority of members, still nondemocratic, insisted on a simple majority vote.

International Economic Institutions

The most important institutions of global governance in the present world economy are the international economic institutions. We met these institutions initially in Chapters 5–7. They were created at the Bretton Woods conference in July 1944 and then reformed after the oil crises of the 1970s. Let's look a little more carefully at how these institutions are run. Who has control? In what way, if any, are these institutions accountable and democratic? And how do the different perspectives evaluate these institutions?

International Monetary Fund

In 2008, the IMF had 185 member countries. Each country has a representative on the Board of Governors, usually the minister of finance or central bank chairman. The board meets once a year but is too unwieldy to exercise daily control. It designates policy overview to the International Monetary and Finance Committee (IMFC). The IMFC consists of twenty-four governors from individual or groups of countries and meets twice a year. The IMFC designates, in turn, daily responsibility to the Executive Board. The Executive Board consists of twenty-four executive directors from the IMFC countries who are assigned to permanent duty in Washington, D.C., the headquarters of IMF. The IMF staff totals about 2,700 civil servants, led by a managing director and three deputy managing directors. By convention, the European members select the managing director, although that could change as members seek more equitable representation for developing countries.

Voting in the IMF is based on quotas, and quotas in turn are based on a country's economic power, including its GDP, current account transactions, and official reserves. An **IMF quota** represents the maximum amount of money a country provides to the IMF for lending to correct balance of payments problems. When a country enters the IMF, it pays 25 percent of this quota in SDRs (the international paper currency that has been issued in small amounts) or a major currency such as the dollar, yen, or euro. It pays the remaining 75 percent in its own currency. IMF resources totaled $338 billion in September 2007.

Not surprisingly, the United States has the largest vote, 16.8 percent (slightly less than its quota of 17.1 percent because all countries start with a base of 250 votes). The top five countries—the Group of 5 (G-5)—have 38.4 percent of the vote, and the G-7 countries, which add Canada and Italy, have 44.5 percent of the vote. The G-5 countries are the only members with permanent representatives on the Executive Board. The other nineteen countries share representatives. So, the IMF is run by the major

IMF quotas

the maximum amounts of money that countries provide to the International Monetary Fund for lending to correct balance of payment problems. A country's vote in the IMF is based on its share of total quota contributions.

financial countries. They provide the bulk of the financial resources, and they call most of the shots.

IMF quotas are recalculated every five years. Increasing and redistributing quotas are controversial steps that require an 85 percent majority vote. Notice that the United States can block a quota increase or reform. Of the thirteen quota reviews since the IMF began, seven increased total IMF funding by anywhere from 30 to 60 percent each. The last two reviews in 2003 and 2008 did not increase the quotas. The IMF needs fewer resources because it plays a smaller role in funding current account deficits; private banks do more of the financing. The U.S. quota has declined as its relative share of global wealth has declined. At the last quota review in 2008, China, South Korea, Turkey, and Mexico received ad hoc quota increases totaling 1.8 percent. Further ad hoc increases are anticipated to recognize the increasing role of fast-growing emerging countries in the world economy.

The principal task of the IMF is to encourage sound domestic economic policies to support global growth and economic stability. It conducts annual surveillance studies of member countries' policies; discusses these studies with the authorities in each country; and provides technical assistance to improve fiscal, monetary, exchange rate, banking, and statistical capabilities. If a country requires balance of payments assistance, the IMF lends the country money. But it does so on the condition that the country alter its policies to correct its balance of payments deficit (for example, reduce fiscal deficits to reduce domestic demand and hence foreign imports). This conditionality is the most controversial aspect of IMF activities. An international organization run by the major powers, in effect, dictates domestic policies for countries running balance of payments deficits. What is worse, the United States never has to borrow from the IMF because it can always print dollars to pay its current account deficits. Other countries are willing to hold those dollars and, in effect, lend them back to the United States, as long as these countries have confidence that the U.S. economy is strong and they can invest these dollars in bonds or other U.S. assets. On a few occasions in the past, when the United States ran short of foreign exchange reserves in other currencies, it arranged financing with other countries outside the IMF. Although the IMF criticizes U.S. policies, it has no leverage over U.S. policies through lending, as it does with developing countries.

Spotlight on conditionality

Critics charge that IMF policies serve primarily the interests of advanced countries. Like bankers, the G-7 or the G-10 countries (actually eleven countries, adding Belgium, the Netherlands, Sweden, and Switzerland to the G-7) care most about getting their money back. IMF conditionality squeezes developing countries to pay debts, which reduces resources for domestic growth. Developing countries have to keep borrowing, debts accumulate, and the pernicious cycle persists. For the first time in 1995, the IMF and World Bank set up a program to reduce the debts of heavily indebted poor countries (HIPCs). The HIPC program targeted forty-one deeply distressed developing countries for debt relief. As of 2008, thirty-three countries, twenty-seven in Africa, received debt relief totaling $49 billion. In 2005, the G-8 countries supplemented the HIPC program with the Multilateral Debt Relief Initiative (MDRI). MDRI cancels 100 percent of the debt owed to multilateral institutions, such as the IMF and World Bank, as countries fulfill their obligations under the HIPC program.

In 1999, the G-7 began holding a larger meeting involving some developing countries. Known as the G-20, this meeting included key developing countries such as China, India, Indonesia, Brazil, Mexico, Argentina, Turkey, South Korea, South Africa, and Saudi Arabia, as well as Russia, Australia, and the EU. The G-20 promotes dialogue on key aspects of the world economy, such as trade, transparency, fiscal stability, money laundering and terrorist financing, and reform of the global institutions. Although the G-7 and G-20 meet separately, they provide in parallel a better balance between advanced and developing countries in global economic decision making. Still, the great power groups have no formal authority, unlike the IMF.

Whatever its faults, the IMF has nurtured phenomenal growth in developing countries since 1945. The Asian tigers benefited from IMF programs, and despite criticism of the IMF during the Asian financial crisis of the 1990s, many stricken countries (for example, South Korea and Thailand) bounced back quickly from that crisis. The IMF was particularly effective in guiding India through a balance of payments crisis in the early 1990s and helping that country make an historic turn toward more open and market-oriented policies. The result is that India, along with China, has joined the world economy, and these two countries (with more than a third of the world's population) are now among the fastest growing economies in the world.

World Bank

The International Bank for Reconstruction and Development (IBRD), or World Bank, is the main global institution for promoting development and alleviating poverty. It is part of the World Bank Group, which consists of four other associated institutions: International Development Association (IDA), International Finance Corporation (IFC), Multilateral Investment Guarantee Agency (MIGA), and International Centre for Settlement of Investment Disputes (ICSID). While the World Bank makes loans to middle-income countries (some $12.8 billion in 2007), IDA focuses on the world's eighty-one poorest countries (loans of $11.9 billion in 2007). IFC invests in private enterprises in developing countries. MIGA guarantees FDI in developing countries against noncommercial or political risks, such as expropriation or war. ICSID helps to settle foreign investment disputes and thus encourage private investment.

In 2008, the World Bank, like the IMF, had 185 member countries; a country has to be a member of the IMF to join the World Bank. The Bank is run by a structure similar to the IMF, with a Board of Governors and a smaller (twenty-four-member) Board of Executive Directors. Bank voting is based on the size of a country's economy. Again, the United States has the largest share of votes—16.41 percent; the G-5 countries control 37.4 percent, and the G-7 countries control 43 percent. The Bank has almost 10,000 employees and is run by a president traditionally selected by the United States.

Members pay an initial subscription to the World Bank just like the IMF. IDA increases subscriptions (called replenishments) every four years. But the World

A World Bank loan finances the construction of the $750 million Bujagali Dam in Uganda that will supply electrical power to boost growth.

Bank itself, unlike the IMF, raises most of its money by selling World Bank bonds on private financial markets. Because governments back World Bank bonds, these bonds have the highest security rating and therefore sell at a higher price or lower interest rate. The World Bank passes on these lower interest rates to developing countries. If the latter borrowed directly from private financial markets, they would have to price their bonds at lower levels and pay much higher interest rates.

The World Bank and IDA make loans for development purposes, from infrastructure projects (dams, roads, ports, and so on) to basic human needs (food, health, education, housing, and so on) to sustainable energy and environmental programs. In 2008, the World Bank was involved in some 1,800 projects in virtually every developing country. The projects included providing micro-credit in Bosnia and Herzegovina, raising AIDS-prevention awareness in Guinea, supporting the education of girls in Bangladesh, improving health-care delivery in Mexico, and helping East Timor and India rebuild after civil strife and natural disasters. Increasingly World Bank programs have focused on the needs of the poorest people around the world, some 1.2 billion people living on less than $1 per day.

The World Bank faces fewer criticisms of the sort that plague the IMF because it is explicitly focused on poverty. Nevertheless, World Bank projects are faulted for catering to large-scale rather than micro projects (which benefit the poor more directly); tolerating, even facilitating corruption; being ineffectively coordinated; damaging the environment; and ultimately failing to reduce inequality. The World Bank's staff is also criticized as being bloated and overpaid. World Bank officials travel around the world in comfortable style and earn relatively high bankers' salaries that are exempt from income tax in the United States, where World Bank headquarters is located.

World Trade Organization

The WTO succeeded the GATT in 1995. It had 151 members in 2007 (GATT started with 23) governed by a Ministerial Conference, which meets at least once every two years. Below the Ministerial Conference is the General Council, which meets several times a year at the headquarters in Geneva, Switzerland. The General Council also meets as the Trade Policy Review Body to critique the trade policies of member countries and as the Dispute Settlement Body to resolve trade disputes. Below the General Council are councils for trade in goods (essentially the updated GATT), services (governed by the GATS), and intellectual property (governed by the TRIPs agreement). The latter two agreements came out of the conclusion of the Uruguay Round in 1994. WTO still has the smallest bureaucracy of the old Bretton Woods institutions, around six hundred personnel. A director general selected by consensus leads the organization. The director general has come from a developing country in the past, although the director general in 2008–2009 is a Frenchman.

The WTO, unlike the IMF and World Bank, operates on the basis of one country, one vote, not a quota system based on a country's size or, in this case, share of world trade. Voting is by consensus, which makes WTO politics more cumbersome than that of the IMF or World Bank. In the case of expert panels to resolve trade disputes, however, the consensus rule has been modified. Under the GATT, one government could block indefinitely a decision by a dispute panel; a consensus was needed to approve a panel decision. Under the WTO, a consensus is needed to block a decision. Thus, one country, particularly the country on the losing end of a panel decision, cannot thwart the entire dispute-settlement procedure. An appeals process was instituted whereby the losing country could challenge the decision on legal grounds. But once the appeals process was completed, the panel decision had to be implemented. The losing government had three choices: change its offending law, compensate the winning country by mutually agreed trade concessions in some other area, or accept retaliation or imposition of equivalent trade barriers by the winning country.

These WTO dispute-settlement provisions were very controversial. For the first time, an international institution could enforce a decision against an advanced country and specifically against the United States. Many members of Congress objected. But notice that the WTO cannot force the United States to change its laws. The United States has two other choices. In practice, however, the United States usually changes its laws to comply. It did so in a famous case (well, OK, not so famous that you would have heard about it) when the WTO rejected U.S. legislation that allowed U.S. firms to set up export companies in the Caribbean to avoid federal taxes. Overall, the WTO dispute-settlement process has worked well. The WTO settled some three hundred cases in its first eight years, while the GATT settled three hundred in its entire lifetime.

Spotlight on international law

Regional Organizations

regional organizations organizations whose members come from and are limited to a specific geographic region of the world.

The state, subnational, and transnational NGOs and the IGOs compete for the institutional loyalty of actors in international affairs. Increasingly, so do **regional organizations.** Regionalism, in fact, may be, according to some scholars, a stronger force in contemporary international affairs than nationalism (states), fragmentation (NGOs), or globalization (IGOs).[12] Regional organizations proliferate. During the Cold War, many regional organizations took the form of alliances—NATO, Western European Union (WEU), Warsaw Pact, Rio Pact, Central Treaty Organization (CENTO, in the Middle East), and SEATO (in Southeast Asia). Others were more economic in nature—the European Common Market (now the EU), Council for Mutual Economic Assistance (COMECON, in the Soviet economic bloc), Latin American Free Trade Agreement (LAFTA), ASEAN, and Central American and Andean Common Markets. Still others constituted regional diplomatic organizations—the OAS, CSCE (now the OSCE), and Organization of African Unity (now the African Union)—or politically inspired institutions, such as the Council of Europe and its promotion of human rights and democracy in Europe. In the last decade or so, further regional organizations have sprouted, especially in trade and financial relations—NAFTA, APEC, CAFTA, and various versions of ASEAN, such as ASEAN plus 3 (which adds China, Japan, and South Korea).

Spotlight on regionalism

Neofunctionalism

No regional organization has achieved greater significance in contemporary international affairs than the EU. How did this happen, and what can it tell us about how and what kind of new actors might emerge in the world system in the future? As we have discussed, a body of scholarship known as neofunctionalism built on the functionalist thinking of David Mitrany but went a step further.[13] It postulates that working on functional activities such as food and health will not only solve problems and make political loyalties less relevant but will also eventually change political loyalties directly. As regional institutions succeed, participants will shift their loyalties (identities) from state institutions to higher-level supranational institutions. This will happen through a combination of institutional processes such as spillover, as envisioned by the liberal perspective, and creative leadership, as envisioned by identity perspectives. Recall that spillover means that resolving one common problem leads to the need to resolve additional ones. Thus, creating a common market, which the European Community did in 1958 by reducing internal tariffs, created additional needs to reduce NTBs and eventually unify national currencies, which the EC did in the late 1980s and early 1990s. Creative leadership means establishing **supranational institutions,** such as the European Commission, that initiate proposals from the standpoint of common rather than national interests, compelling national governments to reassess their separate interests and upgrade or integrate them at a higher level. As time went on and more issues were subjected to this process, member states identified more and more with the supranational (rather than national) authorities.

Regional integration studies were eventually absorbed by interdependence and globalization studies.[14] Interdependence studies put more emphasis on the increasing number of horizontal interactions among regional and global actors rather than the transforming or vertically integrating character of regional institutions such as the European Community. In terms of our perspectives, we might say that liberal factors, which emphasize repetitive interactions, became more important than identity factors, which emphasize ideas and the construction of new political identities. Indeed, interdependence studies became known as neoliberal approaches because they focus almost exclusively on institutions, not on values or identities as in earlier classical liberal approaches. But Europe continued to integrate and eventually debated the idea of a European constitution. The constitution, although still disputed, sought to define a common political identity at the European, rather than national, level.

Other regions also emphasized regional institutions. The Organization of African States changed its name to the African Union to mimic the EU and put greater emphasis on a common African identity. Asian states talked about regional relationships not just in terms of efficiency, as liberal perspectives emphasize, but also in terms of Asian values, or what became known as "the Asian Way," as identity perspectives emphasize.

Most regional integration studies adopted rationalist rather than constructivist methods. They hypothesized that creative institutional leadership by actors such as the European Commission *caused* the shift of political loyalties to supranational institutions. Social constructivist studies came later and, although they too were concerned with how political identities changed, they paid little attention to regional integration studies. Why, we may ask? One reason may have been that social constructivist studies employ constructivist, not rationalist, methods. They see identities *constituting*, rather than causing, one another and are more interested in cumulative verbal discourses than in novel institutional devices such as the supranational European Commission. Constructivist studies drew their inspiration more from the sociological literature than from the political science literature. Here is an example of how studies of international relations differ because they adopt different methodological approaches.

Let's look more closely at European integration. It represents one of the most novel developments in post–World War II international relations. It can sensitize us to the interplay of states (power), institutions, and ideas in the study of international behavior.

supranational institutions

institutions above the level of the state that are motivated by common, rather than state-specific, goals; for example, the European Commission in the EU.

← _causal arrow_

European Union

The **European Union** began as a functional activity inspired by postwar leaders in Europe who were determined to end European wars. Jean Monnet, a French technocrat, was the principal architect of postwar European integration. He envisioned a process that would integrate the coal and steel sectors of France and Germany, taking a vital war-making industry out of the hands of nationalist rivals. As functionalist theory predicts, once these sectors were removed from rival state institutions, political divisions would recede. Monnet convinced Robert Schuman, then French foreign minister, to adopt this idea. In 1951, Schuman proposed the ECSC. As we discuss in Chapter 5, the ECSC inspired further integration plans—a proposed European Defense and Political Community (EDPC) that ultimately failed, and the European Atomic Energy Community (Euratom) and European Economic Community (EEC), or Common Market, that subsequently succeeded. The EDPC used a direct intergovernmental approach to integrate state interests. It was clearly premature. Wartime adversaries such as France and Germany were not ready to integrate their defense capabilities. But the neofunctional approach used by the ECSC concentrated primarily on economic interests and worked better. Euratom, the EEC, and ECSC attacked separate but interrelated functional activities under a common legal framework established by the Treaties of Rome. Most important, the Treaties of Rome framework created the supranational leadership organs known as commissions that were given exclusive rights to initiate legislation. This arrangement put community-minded officials in charge of designing policies that integrated and went beyond national interests, pushing separate nation-states toward common solutions.

SPILLOVER. The Common Market succeeded spectacularly by creating a common industrial market, which reduced internal tariffs to zero and established unified external tariffs, and a Common Agricultural Policy (CAP), which subsidized and protected European farmers. In 1967, in a further demonstration of spillover, the commissions of the three communities merged to form a single Commission of the European Communities (EC, no longer EEC). And starting in 1973, the EC expanded five times to include a total of twenty-seven members by 2007.

The EC also deepened as well as widened. Starting in 1987, the Single Market Act reduced regulatory barriers and converted the common market into an economic union. Once tariffs were reduced to zero, different internal regulations became the principal barriers to trade. In a classic example of spillover, the common market had solved one problem (tariffs at the border) and exposed another (regulations that restricted trade internally). One means of dealing with the differing internal regulations was the principle of **mutual recognition**—a product standard, say for automobile safety glass, recognized in one country would be recognized in all countries. In other cases, say pollution controls, member countries adopted minimal standards that all countries had to meet but allowed countries to go beyond those standards if they wished. Or members harmonized regulations, adopting a single standard for all countries. Finally, in 1992, the EC took the unprecedented step toward monetary union. Because tariffs and regulations were now liberalized, the costs of exchanging currencies were the biggest obstacles to trade. Once again, spillover required widening the EC's jurisdiction. The Maastricht Treaty created the Economic and Monetary Union (EMU) and set in motion the adoption of a single currency, the euro, which was introduced in 1999.

The Maastricht Treaty also created two additional pillars of cooperation, the Common Foreign and Security Policy (CFSP) and common policies on Justice and Home Affairs, and merged them with the EC to form the European Union (EU). The new pillars continued to make decisions by traditional intergovernmental mechanisms rather than supranational authority. But forty years after the failure of the European Defense and Political Community, foreign policy and domestic law were brought under the umbrella of the new EU, setting the stage for full integration in the future.[15]

STRUCTURE OF THE EUROPEAN UNION. EU institutions consist of the Commission, the Council of the European Union, European Parliament, and European Court of Justice; the European Central Bank (ECB) is the most important specialized institution. The Council, Commission, and Parliament meet in Brussels, although the Parliament also meets in Luxembourg and Strasbourg (France). The Court of Justice sits in Luxembourg. The ECB has its headquarters in Frankfurt, Germany.

The **European Commission** is the unique organ of the EU. A supranational body, it has the exclusive authority to initiate legislation and pursue the goals of an ever-closer union. It provides (although not always) the creative leadership envisioned by neofunctionalism. In areas where policies have been integrated, such as trade in goods, the Commission represents the EU. Nonmember countries, such as the United States, negotiate with the Commission, not individual EU member states. In 2008, the Commission had twenty-seven commissioners, one from each member state. Member states select the president of the Commission, who then, in consultation with member states, chooses the other commissioners. Notice that Parliament does not select the Commission, let alone establish the government, which includes the European Council (see next paragraph); in this sense, the European Union is not a parliamentary democracy. But Parliament interviews each commissioner and then votes on whether to approve the Commission as a whole, not the individual commissioners. The Commission serves for five years coincident with elections for the European Parliament. The Parliament can dismiss the entire Commission by adopting a vote of censure. Although it has never done so, the threat to do so in 1999 led a scandal-ridden Commission to resign. Some 25,000 civil servants work in the Commission bureaucracy.

The **Council of the European Union** represents the member states. One minister from each state attends. The subject matter of a meeting determines the specific minister. So, agricultural ministers deal with agriculture, finance ministers with finance, and so on. Up to four times a year, the prime ministers and/or presidents of the member states meet in summit meetings called the **European Council.** Summit meetings deal with overall issues that cut across ministers' jurisdictions and resolve issues that are blocked at lower levels. Until the Treaty of Lisbon signed in December 2007 goes into effect (see later in the chapter), the president of the Council rotates every six months among the member states. The Council has its own secretariat, known as the Committee of Permanent Representatives, which often competes with the Commission bureaucracy.

The Council is both an intergovernmental and supranational body. It represents national governments as an IGO but acts as a supranational body in the context of European treaties. Someday, for example, it might become something akin to the senate of a United States of Europe, representing the separate nation-states of Europe just as the U.S. Senate represents the fifty states of the United States. One major supranational feature of the Council is **qualified majority voting (QMV).** On some, not all, issues, decisions are made by a majority vote, not by consensus or veto. Member states vote

European Commission
the organ of the European Union that has the exclusive authority to initiate legislation and pursue the goals of an ever-closer union.

Council of the European Union
the assembly bringing together the member states of the European Union.

European Council
summit meetings of the Council of the European Union, involving heads of state and government, to deal with issues that cut across jurisdictions and resolve issues that are blocked at lower levels of the organization.

qualified majority voting (QMV)
the principle that decisions are made by majority vote, not consensus or great power veto; this is how some decisions are made today in the European Union.

both individually and on the basis of a certain number of votes allocated to each state. After Romania and Bulgaria joined the EU in 2007, QMV required a majority of member states (14 out of 27), 75 percent of allocated votes (258 out of 345), and at least 62 percent of the EU's total population. The system is complex to make it impossible for big countries to act alone or to block decisions by a majority of other countries.

European Parliament
the principal legislative body and only directly elected institution in the European Union.

The principal legislative body and only directly elected institution in the EU is the **European Parliament.** It has 732 members, who are elected every five years by European-wide elections. Seats are not apportioned by population, as they are, for example, in the U.S. House of Representatives. A member from small states represents a smaller number of people than one from large states. Representatives do not sit in Parliament in national groups but in seven European-wide political groups, the principal ones being the conservative European People's Party and European Democrats (EPP-ED), the liberal Party of European Socialists (PES), and a smaller centrist group known as the Alliance of Liberals and Democrats for Europe (ALDE). The Parliament has gained wider powers since it was first elected directly in 1979, but its powers still pale in comparison to national parliaments. It cannot initiate legislation, and it approves the budget and other legislation only by co-decision with the Council. It is the weakest institution in the EU, and this fact has given rise to the debate in the EU about the **democratic deficit,** a criticism that points to a gap between Community institutions and the people they represent. The Council and Commission, for example, are not elected by the people but are appointed by national governments. And the Parliament, which is elected by the people, can dismiss the Commission as a whole but not reestablish it. Nor can the Parliament seat or dismiss the European Council. Thus, the most powerful common institutions in Brussels operate once removed from the scrutiny of the people, who elect their own governments but not the principal EU leaders. And the EU Parliament is too weak to fully compensate for this gap.

democratic deficit
the criticism made of the European Union that there is a gap between European Community institutions and the people they represent.

European Court of Justice (ECJ)
the judicial body that has the power to interpret and enforce European Community treaties and law.

The **European Court of Justice (ECJ)** has power to interpret and enforce EC treaties and law. It consists of one judge from each of the twenty-seven member states, but it usually sits in a "grand chamber" of thirteen judges or sometimes in smaller chambers of only three to five judges. It decides on the constitutionality of EU law, offers advisory opinions, and adjudicates disputes not only among EU members and institutions but also between individuals or corporations (NGOs) and the EU. In the latter function, the ECJ goes beyond traditional international courts. Like the European Court of Human Rights under the Council of Europe (see Chapter 15), the ECJ recognizes a right of **individual standing,** which allows individuals to bring cases before the court and thus conveys a sense of European identity or citizenship to the European people independent of national governments. The ECJ superintends the mammoth body of EU law known as the *acquis communitaire,* which new members must accept when they enter the EU. Since 1954, the ECJ has heard over 9,000 cases and rendered 4,000 judgments. When we compare that to the ICJ, which has considered only several hundred cases in recent years, we see why some students of international affairs are more impressed by regional than international organizations. Some of the ECJ's most notable rulings include banning a limit on the number of players from other EU countries that can play on a national soccer team (in other words, all of Germany's national team might, theoretically, come from other EU countries) and declaring parts of the German constitution illegal because they banned women from participating in military combat activities.

individual standing
the right of civilians, as well as states, to bring cases before a court, uncommon in international law until recently.

European Central Bank (ECB)
the banking institution whose Governing Council controls the money supply and sets short-term interest rates for the European Union.

The **European Central Bank (ECB)** is one of the most powerful EU institutions, even though only fifteen of the twenty-seven members currently belong to it. We notice the effect of the ECB immediately when we travel in Europe. There are no more German marks or French francs—these have been replaced by the euro. But you still need pounds in Great Britain because it does not belong to the ECB. The ECB is run by an executive board of the president, vice president, and four other members, all appointed for eight-year nonrenewable terms by agreement among the presidents or prime ministers of the participating member states. The Governing Council, which consists of the executive board and the governors of the fifteen participating central banks, controls the money supply and sets short-term interest rates. The ECB acts independently. It can neither ask for nor accept instructions from any other EU or national body. Yet it controls one of the key levers determining the fate of the European economy.

We can understand why this institution is both so remarkable and controversial. Member states gave up control of their money supply, a critical instrument of national economic sovereignty, when they created the ECB. And they did so without the usual checks and balances of a strong parliament or fully unified political system in Brussels. In the United States, for example, the Federal Reserve acts independently. But it also reports regularly to a very powerful and watchful Congress and consults closely with the Treasury Department on those aspects of economic policy, such as fiscal policy, which the Federal Reserve does not control. The ECB also reports to the European Parliament, but the Parliament, remember, is much weaker than the U.S. Congress. And the ECB consults with finance and economic ministers from the fifteen ECB countries, but the EU has not agreed on a common fiscal policy. The European Council adopted a Stability and Growth Pact that committed member states to keeping fiscal deficits below 3 percent of GDP. In 2005, however, Germany, France, Portugal, Italy, Greece, and the Netherlands—half of the ECB members at the time— were in violation of these limits. If member states fail to control fiscal deficits, that leaves the ECB with two choices. It can loosen money supply to accommodate these deficits, which risks inflation because loose money and loose fiscal policy create more demand than available supply. Or the ECB can ignore the deficits, which risks growth because tight money and loose fiscal policy (government demand for borrowing) raises interest rates and slows growth. The ECB, we could say, is swimming in uncharted waters. Watch the value of the euro. It tells you how the ECB is doing. After declining from 1.10 in dollar terms at its inception in 1999 to about 0.95 in 2002, the euro has risen steadily to above 1.55 in 2008. So far, the world community seems to be gaining confidence in the euro. Stay tuned.

Spotlight on monetary policy

EUROPEAN CONSTITUTION. In 2002, the EU countries convened a convention to draft a **European constitution.** The integrating states of Europe were facing a challenge comparable to that in the United States of America in 1787. This could be seen as another major instance of spillover from economic and monetary to political affairs. With enlargement and monetary union, Europe had become so complex it needed a political and, indeed, constitutional overhaul. The convention, chaired by former French president Valéry Giscard d'Estaing, presented a far-reaching document to an Intergovernmental Conference (IGC) of the European Union. In June 2004, the IGC adopted a somewhat less ambitious yet still substantial document. Among other things, the IGC-approved constitution incorporates a charter of fundamental rights; merges the three pillars of the Community (economic, defense, and justice) into a single European Union, although special procedures still apply in defense, security, and foreign policy; establishes a European Council, distinct

European constitution
a European Union document, not yet ratified, which incorporates a charter of fundamental rights; merges the judicial, economic, and defense aspects of the European Union; establishes the European Council; and raises the numbers of seats in Parliament, among other things.

from the specialized Councils, headed by a president chosen for two and a half years; raises the number of seats in Parliament to 750 and gives the Parliament co-decision rights in roughly 95 percent of all legislation; and creates a new minister of foreign affairs to represent the EU in international affairs. The IGC-approved constitution does not enlarge the Commission; it remains at twenty-seven members until 2014. But the new constitution alters the QMV threshold to require a double majority to pass decisions, 55 percent of the member states representing 65 percent of the population. In addition, a blocking minority must include at least four states to prevent three large countries from gaining a blocking vote through population increases.

However, the IGC-approved constitution was not accepted by the people. As a major political undertaking, it had to be ratified by all member states before it could go into effect. Some states submitted the constitution to popular referenda. In summer 2005, the people of France and the Netherlands rejected the constitution. Although the reasons were many and related to local as well as European politics, the EU confronted a major hurdle. Some wondered if the process of European integration had come to an end. Realist observers saw a revival of nationalism. Liberal proponents stressed the need for more coherent institutions. And identity perspectives blamed the democratic deficit. The debate demonstrated, again, the influence of perspectives in making judgments about institutional movements such as the European Union.

THE LISBON TREATY. After two years of weighing how to proceed in the wake of the constitution's defeat, the European member states decided to move ahead despite popular opposition. They signed the **Lisbon Treaty** in December 2007, which implements many of the provisions of the constitution by intergovernmental agreement. Only parliaments have to ratify an intergovernmental agreement. Nevertheless, Ireland held a public referendum in June 2008 and rejected the treaty. Thus, the situation is once again uncertain. If all twenty-seven states ratify the treaty in time for European Parliament elections in June 2009, the new European Union will have a long-term president elected by the European Council serving for two and a half years; a high representative for foreign affairs acting as the chief diplomat of the EU; a more powerful European Parliament enjoying co-decision rights with the Council on almost all legislation (but still no right to initiate legislation, which only the Commission has and retains); more decisions made using QMV, with a simplified QMV formula taking effect in 2014; and a Charter of Fundamental Rights that makes the rights embodied in the European Convention on Human Rights legally binding on all EU institutions and member states.

With all of its deficiencies, the European Union represents a remarkable instance of institution-building at the regional level, comparable to what the United States undertook in the nineteenth century to bind the states of America to a single federal government. The final outcome in Europe will be different than that in the United States, to be sure, but the comparative exercise suggests the potential for expanding the scope of governance in international affairs that liberal perspectives have often emphasized. The box on page 531 suggests how one analyst evaluates the achievements of the European integration process. While impressed by the liberal features of this process, he judges the identity aspects to be utopian because they ignore the most important realist aspects of international affairs, namely the need for self-defense to survive in a world of continuing anarchy.

Spotlight on
perspectives

Lisbon Treaty

a treaty that implements many of the provisions of the European constitution by intergovernmental agreement.

European Union: Destiny, Dream, or Denial?

In August 2007, Walter A. McDougall, a Pulitzer Prize–winning historian at the University of Pennsylvania, reflected on fifty years of European integration, asking, "Will 'Europe' Survive the 21st Century?" He is doubtful. Let's see why.

McDougall begins by noting the extraordinary process of European integration, almost since the time of Charlemagne in the ninth century:

> The Holy Roman Emperors dreamed of restoring a unity unknown since the fall of ancient Rome. . . . The old dream began to take shape in the late 1940s . . . [when] [t]he French Fourth Republic, inspired by technocrat Jean Monnet and foreign minister Robert Schuman, began the process . . . [and] founded the European Coal and Steel Community. . . . But momentum flagged. . . . Still, the European idea never went into reverse. . . . By the time . . . a revolution would topple the Berlin Wall, . . . Europe not only survived the death of the Cold War, . . . [it] flourished in its absence.

McDougall emphasizes the destiny or spillover effects of integration, important from a liberal perspective, and even cites the "school of political science known as functionalism . . . [that] argued that integration, once begun, must quickly lead to a United States of Europe."

He is impressed, but then he notes a utopian aspect of European integration:

> [M]odern history [the world wars] has been a tale of . . . almost continuous trauma for Europe. . . .

Europeans lost faith in traditional religions, ideologies, and even Enlightenment reason itself. . . . [T]hey relinquished their millenarian or utopian belief in mankind's ability to create heaven on earth and got to work forging a humane, sustainable civilization where no wars of religion, patriotism, or ideology would disturb their personal fulfillment.

Now, he is highlighting the dream or identity aspects of European integration—that Europe may find a future without nation-states and war, perhaps even without the mainstream belief in Enlightenment reason itself. Europe has become postmodern, possibly adopting a critical theory perspective on the future. McDougall is less impressed. Can you guess why?

Let's read further:

> [T]he EU is at best incomplete and at worst a false promise for which its own citizens are unwilling to die. . . . Only . . . a plurality of 42 percent . . . want the EU to take charge of defense. . . . Europeans can trumpet their soft power [of a civilization without wars and patriotism] only because of (a) the absence of any hard power threat in their neighborhood and (b) the willingness of the U.S. to combat terrorists, aggressors, and rogue regimes.

McDougall concludes that Europe is denying the realities of self-defense in a world of continuing threat and danger. Can you see why he ultimately emphasizes the realist perspective in evaluating the significance of the European Union?

Source: Excerpts from Walter A. McDougall, "Will 'Europe' Survive the 21st Century? A Meditation on the 50th Anniversary of the European Community," Pt. I: The Other Age Born in the Year 1957, and Pt. II: The European Union in a Wider World, August 3, 2007, available at www.fpri.org/enotes/200707.mcdougall.willeuropesurvive.html. Published as an FPRI Enote by the Foreign Policy Research Institute (www.fpri.org).

Asian and Other Regional Institutions

Regional developments in Asia and other parts of the world suggest the limits of global governance. While Latin American institutions share many similarities with North American and European political traditions, Asian and African institutions are more distinct. As Professor Peter Katzenstein tells us, "Asian regionalism is shaped by the character of Asian states."[16] And in at least three ways, Asian states are different from western states: they rely less on formal institutions and the separation of powers; they transact business and politics more on a personal and familial basis than through the contracts, law, and courts more familiar in the West; and they place more emphasis on the well-being of the society as a whole than on the freedom or individualism of each citizen. These differences are evident in Asian regional organizations.

ASEAN is the principal Asian IGO. It was founded in 1967 by five countries: Indonesia, Malaysia, the Philippines, Thailand, and Singapore. Brunei joined in 1984, Vietnam in 1995, Laos and Myanmar in 1997, and Cambodia in 1999. It was established primarily to accelerate economic growth and indirectly to shield Asian countries from the Cold War conflicts raging in Indochina. But the approach in ASEAN was never as institutional or centrally directed as in the European Common Market. The originating document contained only five articles, and ASEAN did not start a free-trade area until 1992. While that objective is now more or less in place, ASEAN countries do not have common external tariffs, and free trade is limited to a narrower range of products than in the EU (for example, rice, a principal agricultural product, is excluded). There is no single market with common regulations or currency in ASEAN. And ASEAN avoids legal approaches to dispute settlement, relying on consensus mechanisms rather than court proceedings.

Still, ASEAN has evolved further. In 1994, it initiated along with other Asian countries the ASEAN Regional Forum (ARF). ARF brings together ASEAN and other Asian

Leaders of ten ASEAN nations meet with their counterparts from Japan, South Korea, and China in the ASEAN Plus Three Summit in Singapore in 2007. Pictured from left are Indonesia's president Susilo Bambang Yudhoyono, Laos' prime minister Bouasone Bouphavanh, Malaysia's prime minister Abdullah bin Ahmad Badawi, the Philippines' president Gloria Macapagal-Arroyo, China's premier Wen Jiabao, Japan's prime minister Yasuo Fukuda, Singapore's prime minister Lee Hsien Loong, South Korea's president Roh Moo-hyun, Thailand's prime minister Surayud Chulanont, Myanmar's prime minister Thein Sein, Vietnam's prime minister Nguyen Tan Dung, Brunei's sultan Hassanal Bolkiah, and Cambodia's prime minister Hun Sen.

countries, including China, Russia, Japan, India, and South Korea, to foster constructive dialogue on security and political issues and to contribute to confidence-building measures (such as releasing white papers on defense expenditures) and preventive diplomacy in Asia. The only multilateral security organization in Asia, ARF is based on the strict principle of noninterference in the internal affairs of states. ARF has no secretariat, and its attendees are called participants not members. China resists such institutionalization, preferring to think of international institutions as state-centric actors defending national sovereignty from both other governments and nonstate actors such as NGOs. ASEAN and ARF, for example, do not have any mechanisms to monitor elections or advocate human rights, as the Council of Europe does in the European region.

APEC is another loose institution that is characteristic of the Asian style of international cooperation. Founded in 1989 through an initiative by Australia, APEC is a forum of some twenty-one Pacific-rim countries concerned with economic activities in the region, such as trade and investment. It meets annually, has a small secretariat, and includes Taiwan. For that reason, its annual gatherings are called Leaders' Meetings rather than summits, which usually involve heads of state and government (recall that China does not recognize Taiwan as a state entity). APEC prides itself as the only intergovernmental grouping in the world operating on the basis of nonbinding commitments, open dialogue, and equal respect for the views of all participants.

Critical Theory Perspectives

Critical theory perspectives might point to the very different philosophies toward international institutions reflected in western and Asian approaches as evidence of the limits of global governance in the contemporary world. Western approaches see international institutions largely as problem solvers, finding ways to do things more safely (realist), efficiently (liberal), and democratically (identity). The European Union stands out as the representative model. Eastern approaches see international institutions in more reflective terms, embodying different outlooks and expectations that do not yield a single solution or answer that is applicable to all countries of the world. Critical theory perspectives argue that the solution resides in the process not the outcome—the processes of critically exposing the powerful forces that deny voice and participation to so many groups and of making political and, therefore, contested the underlying assumptions of prevailing approaches. As one critical theorist puts it, multilateralism or global governance must be "schizophrenic—one part . . . being involved in the present predicaments of the state system, another part probing the social and political foundations of a future order." This second part must "respond to the interests and needs of different social groups . . . particularly the needs of the relatively disadvantaged and the imperatives of ecological sustainability."[17] Global governance, in short, is never achieved but is always evolving. Any government, including global government, will mask power, and that facade of institutions must be continuously torn away to expose the face of the interests that it hides.

Summary

The state remains the principal institution in international affairs, but it is facing increasing competition from intergovernmental and regional institutions. IGOs address the increasing requirements of interdependence and globalization. States run IGOs, but IGOs are now so numerous and complex that even advanced states do not have enough time or resources to monitor, let alone control, them all. Regional institutions, in particular, are chipping away at state sovereignty. The EU is a model of functional and neofunctional processes at work, in which states cooperate to address concrete problems and, in the process, reduce the relevance of state authorities and create spillover that eventually transfers state loyalties to wider and deeper supranational institutions.

Realist perspectives accord the least significance to developments of global governance, both because they anticipate that new nonstate, regional, and international institutions will still engage in the struggle for power and because they prefer the checks and balances of decentralized governance and solutions. Liberal perspectives see the greatest prospects for global governance. Technological complexity and environmental concerns compel it, and there seems to be no reason why institutions cannot someday tame violence and the struggle for power at the international level, just as they once did at the national level and are doing already at the regional level. Identity perspectives are both hopeful and skeptical. Some see the pluralization of international institutions as a reflection of growing consensus on democratic norms. If that seems too ambitious, others see opportunities for more limited but essential agreements on basic human rights and for common international procedures to protect them. But still others fear the dilution and potential loss of democratic freedoms in the morass of international actors that are unaccountable and that give, in some cases, tyrannical governments blocking powers on critical political issues. Critical theory perspectives are least willing to offer a solution to the conundrum of global governance. For them, the answer lies in the ongoing struggles to expose the powers that control international institutions and to liberate new voices and participants that can lead the world in new directions.

Which will play the most important role in the future of world governance—the power of states, the common rules of international institutions, the converging and diverging norms and identities of the principal players, or the historical process of contestation and dialectic that eludes rational abstraction?

Key Concepts

collaboration problems 515

coordination problems 515

Council of the European Union 527

democratic deficit 528

epistemic communities 514

European Central Bank (ECB) 528

European Commission 527

European constitution 529

European Council 527

European Court of Justice (ECJ) 528

European Parliament 528

European Union 526

functionalism 514

great power groups 512

IMF quotas 520

individual standing 528

Lisbon Treaty 530

mutual recognition 526

neofunctionalism 515

qualified majority voting (QMV) 527

regional organizations 524

supranational institutions 525

United Nations (UN) 516

Study Questions

1. How do IGOs and TNGOs differ?

2. What are the various challenges to state sovereignty, and how do the three perspectives evaluate the prospects of international institutions transcending state sovereignty?

3. What is the difference between functional and neofunctional studies of international organizations?

4. Discuss the different bases for lawful international intervention in the domestic affairs of sovereign states: peacekeeping, peace enforcement, humanitarian intervention, human rights such as banning genocide, and terrorism.

5. How does the EU differ from the UN? Consider the powers of the Parliament versus the General Assembly, the European Commission versus the UN Secretariat, the Council of the European Union versus the UN Security Council, and the ECJ versus the ICJ.

Conclusion
Applying Perspectives and Levels of Analysis: The Case of the Democratic Peace

Madeleine Albright, then U.S. secretary of state, addresses the Community of Democracies conference in Warsaw, Poland, in 2000, a meeting every two years or so of over one hundred countries that qualify in a minimal sense as democracies.

In an interview with the *Wall Street Journal* in April 2006, George Shultz, secretary of state under Reagan, spoke about the U.S. effort "to spread open political systems and democracy":

> I recall President Reagan's Westminster speech in 1982—that communism would be consigned "to the ash heap of history" and that freedom was the path ahead. And what happened? Between 1980 and 1990, the number of countries that were classified as "free" or "mostly free" increased by about 50 percent. Open political and economic systems have been gaining ground and there's good reason for it. They work better.[1]

In the 1990s, Bill Clinton and Madeleine Albright, ambassador to the United Nations during Clinton's first term in office and secretary of state during his second, went one step further. In his state of the union message in 1994, Clinton tied the spread of democracy directly to national security interests: "The best strategy to ensure our security and to build a durable peace is to support the advance of democracy everywhere. Democracies don't attack each other. They make better trading partners and partners in diplomacy."[2] Albright, who had fled Czechoslovakia as a small girl when German forces invaded in 1939, was also relentless in advocating an expanding community of democracies to end war.

Is this support for what some call the **democratic peace** just American chauvinism and idealism? Critical theory perspectives might think so. Or is there something to Clinton's and Shultz's claims that the spread of democracy is a national security interest because democracies do not fight one another? The mainstream perspectives investigate correlations between democracy and war and test for various causes. The evidence that democracies don't fight one another began to emerge in the late nineteenth century when the United States and Great Britain, then the two dominant powers, did not go to war with one another despite several serious conflicts, such as the boundary dispute in 1895 between Venezuela and what was then British Guiana. Was this an accident? Perhaps. It was only one case. But, as the number of democracies and opportunities for conflict multiplied, gathering evidence tended to support the proposition that democracies rarely if ever go to war with one another. Nevertheless, the evidence remains contentious, subject to debate even among adherents and open to critique from skeptics. We'll look at the evidence for the democratic peace, including some of the statistical problems associated with it, and explore the major explanations researchers have offered.

The democratic peace makes a good topic to wrap up our discussion of international relations because it illustrates nicely the perspectives and levels of analysis we have studied throughout this book. It also illustrates methodological issues and, hence, the potential as well as the limits of social science when we study human subjects that have minds of their own. Last, it reminds us that all knowledge is biased and incomplete in the sense that we select certain facts and cannot know all the facts, so we have to make judgments and trust our values. The democratic peace argument may be self-centered and perhaps even self-righteous for those of us who live in democracies. But do we dismiss the facts because we want to be tolerant of all values, democratic and nondemocratic? Or do we test the facts further because we believe democracy offers a better way to organize human life? Either way, we admit that knowing something is an exercise of both our intellect and our values.

democratic peace

the theory that democratic nations for the most part do not go to war with one another, making the spread of democracy desirable.

Evidence

Statistical findings about democracies over the past thirty years demonstrate a regularity that, as one political scientist concludes, "comes as close as anything we have to an empirical law in international relations."[3] Democracies do not, or at least only rarely, go to war with one another. They are also slightly less inclined than other states to go to war with any state, whether democratic or nondemocratic. To be sure, democracies still fight frequently against nondemocracies, but they are somewhat less inclined to do so than nondemocracies are to fight among themselves. This empirical finding, if it holds up, has revolutionary implications for international affairs, for it suggests that war could be eliminated through the spread of democracy. That conclusion might seem convenient for political scientists and politicians who believe in democracy. But it may also be true. The best explanation to date of this democratic peace points to the internal characteristics of democracies as they interact with one another in the international system. Reviewing democratic peace studies in 2002, Jack Levy, the political scientist quoted earlier, concludes that ideational causes—the joint practice of democracy, that is, a democratic dyad or two democracies interacting at the process level of analysis—appear to trump liberal and realist causes in accounting for the absence of war:

This empirical regularity cannot be explained by the geographic separation of democratic states [a realist factor], by extensive trade among democratic dyads [a liberal factor], by the role of American hegemonic power in suppressing potential conflicts between democracies in the period since the Second World War [a realist factor], or by other economic or geopolitical factors correlated with democracy. . . . There is a growing consensus that the pacifying effects of joint democracy are real.[4]

Despite Levy's confidence, consensus is no more complete in political science than in physical science. (Remember the controversy over global warming?) Debates about the findings of democratic peace researchers continue. The criticisms cluster in two areas: *technical factors* associated with the definitions of democracy and war and the validity of the statistical correlation between them and *theoretical factors* dealing with explanations of this correlation. A correlation, we should note, is not an explanation. It tells us only that two variables appear together with a certain regularity over a large number of cases. War does not appear in relations among democracies, but such a correlation does not tell us *why* war does not occur among democracies. Democracies might not go to war with one another because they share internal democratic norms and practices—identity factors. Or they may not go to war because they trade, participate in lots of international institutions, and negotiate with one another in unique ways—liberal factors. Or they may act peacefully toward one another because they are allies and avoid war among themselves in order to balance power against other alliances—realist factors. In addition, each of these explanations may come from a different level of analysis.

One of the problems confronting democratic peace studies is that relatively few democracies existed before World War II, limiting the total number of cases available for study. The larger the number of cases—the **sample size,** as scientists say—the stronger and more reliable the statistical correlation. Large numbers of cases enable researchers to discover stronger patterns among the variables. If we have only five cases, for example, the chance that no war may occur is greater than if we have fifty cases. With fewer cases, the finding is less reliable. Thus, the result that democracies do not go to war with one another might be a product of chance, a statistical anomaly that would wash out over time in a larger sample.

How do researchers deal with this problem? One way is to define democracy and war more loosely in order to obtain more cases. If the proposition then still holds, the evidence is more persuasive. For instance, let's relax the definition of democracy to include young or weak democracies. Now we find more war among democracies, such as the War of 1812 between Great Britain and the United States. True, the two democracies went to war over disputes in North America, but neither country could be characterized at the time as a particularly robust democracy. In Great Britain, less than 20 percent of white males were eligible to vote, while in the United States all white males could vote, but almost two-thirds of the adult population— slaves and women—could not. Similarly, if we relax the definition of war to include any border incident that involves violence rather than border conflicts that lead to significant numbers of battlefield deaths (say, 1,000, the number used in many democratic peace studies), again we find more wars between democracies, such as the border skirmishes between British Canada and the United States in the late 1830s. Researchers loosen definitions and multiply cases to test the democratic peace proposition more and more rigorously.

As this discussion reminds us, however, the labeling or definition of variables can be very important and may not be completely divorced from biases introduced by the

Spotlight on

correlation

sample size
the number of cases under consideration.

Spotlight on

rationalist methods

Spotlight on

constructivist methods

scholar. This is why constructivist scholars remain skeptical of rationalist methods used in democratic peace studies. They doubt whether we can identify separate dependent and independent variables and say that one variable in a correlation causes the other. Maybe the two variables, instead, constitute or mutually cause one another. Causation is continuous and interactive, not segmented and sequential. Critical theory perspectives go one step further. Not only are the variables inseparable but the historical evolution of capitalism obscures the unrelenting power that spreads democracy by coercion, not consent. As one critical theorist writes, " 'democratic' in this context can only be a code word designating anyone who can be bought or persuaded to work with the penetrating power's foreign policy."[5] The democratic peace is the peace of the democratic hegemon, which in turn is a product of historical circumstances.

Nevertheless, democratic peace researchers are not deterred and have gone on to show that strong democracies not only do not go to war with one another but also do not enter into militarized disputes that threaten war. When studies distinguish along a continuum between strong and weak democracies, they find that new or relatively weak democracies do, in fact, go to war more often with one another.[6] Still, strong democracies do not, and even weak democracies go to war with one another less often than nondemocratic states do. And when democratic peace studies differentiate between wars and militarized disputes—conflicts in which the threat of violence is raised but there is no actual violence—they conclude that "pairs of democracies are much less likely than other pairs of states . . . to threaten each other in militarized disputes less violent than war."[7]

Spotlight on critical theory perspective

At the headquarters building (known as Berlaymont) of the European Union in Brussels, Belgium, a regional grouping of strong democracies pioneers the way to a democratic peace.

Explanations

But, now, what about explanations of the democratic peace? Because a sufficient number of strong democracies have existed only since World War II, the fact that they do not go to war or engage in militarized disputes with one another may be a lingering effect of their Cold War alliance against the Soviet Union. If this realist explanation holds, we may be right back to square one, and the democratic peace would have no significant implications for the future of international relations.

Let's look at different possible mainstream explanations of the democratic peace. By this point (we're almost done with this book!), you should be able to detect the perspective and level of analysis reflected in each explanation. Three major independent variables are involved: democracy, trade and international organizations, and alliances. They correspond with the causes emphasized by our three mainstream perspectives: identity, liberal, and realist. And three major levels of analysis are involved: systemic structure, systemic process, and domestic. (Once you've read the explanations below, see the map on pages 542–543 for a graphical representation of these variables.)

causal ⟶
arrow

Explanation 1: Democracies are more peaceful than all other states.[8]
The statement that democracies are more peaceful than all other states clearly suggests that democracy or identity factors are the cause of the peaceful behavior. Democracies are not only more peaceful toward one another; they are also more peaceful toward non-democratic states. So, the cause does not derive from the interactions between countries (systemic process) because interactions between democracies alone and between democracies and nondemocracies produce the same results. Nor does it derive from how countries are positioned ideologically with respect to one another (relative identity at the systemic structure level) because democracies are more peaceful toward both other democracies and nondemocracies. Relative identities, in other words, cannot be the cause. Instead, the cause comes from inside the democratic country itself and affects that country's behavior in all interactions and all relative ideological configurations—with democracies and nondemocracies. Hence, the level of analysis is domestic.

Spotlight on
identity perspective and domestic level of analysis

Explanation 2: Democracies do not go to war with one another because they share common domestic norms and institutions.[9]
With its emphasis on common norms and institutions, this statement again suggests that identity factors are the cause of the democratic peace, but this result now requires at least two states that are both democratic. It's not enough that just one state is democratic. So, the cause is no longer coming from inside one country alone, or the domestic level of analysis. It is coming from the systemic level. But is it the process or the structural level? The statement tells us how the two countries are positioned with respect to one another—they share common democratic norms and institutions. It does not tell us how those norms and institutions interact, say through greater checks and balances and more openness and trust. Thus, the explanation is from the systemic structural level of analysis, not the systemic process level. It depends on the countries' relative or shared identities as democracies.

Spotlight on
identity perspective and systemic structural level of analysis

Explanation 3: Democracies do not go to war with one another because they trade more with one another and do not want to forfeit the mutual gains from trade.[10]
Now the explanation shifts from an identity to a liberal perspective. The statement says

democracies do not fight, not because they share common values but because they trade more with one another than with other countries. More trade creates a stake in non-zero-sum gains and a reluctance to forfeit those gains through war. Why democracies trade more with one another is another question that may have something to do with their democratic nature. But the statement doesn't explore the explanation any further. The level of analysis is clearly systemic process because the countries have to trade or interact a lot with one another to experience the outcome of peace.

Explanation 4: Democracies do not go to war with one another because they belong to the same international institutions whose laws and practices they follow.[11]
Again the explanation is liberal because the outcome depends on interactions, this time within international institutions rather than through trade. The level of analysis is systemic process if the outcome depends on processes within international institutions or systemic structural if it depends on the roles or specialized functions that states play within these institutions.

Explanation 5: Democracies do not go to war with one another because they have unique contracting or negotiating advantages that allow them to settle disputes without war.[12]
The explanation suggests that negotiations or diplomacy (liberal factors) cause the outcome, although it still doesn't explain why democracies have such unique negotiating advantages. If we argue that democracies have these advantages because they are democracies, identity factors become the independent variable and diplomacy is an intervening variable. But the statement as written implies that negotiating skill is the independent variable. The level of analysis is systemic process because diplomacy involves interactions and democracies achieve peace only through these interactions, not alone or as a result of their relative or shared positions.

Explanation 6: Democracies do not go to war with one another because they belong to the same alliances counterbalancing or fighting other alliances.[13]
Now the explanation shifts to a realist perspective. Alliances and the balance of power explain the outcome, not democracy, trade, or diplomacy. The level of analysis is systemic structural, if we emphasize the relative positioning of opposing alliances within the system, or systemic process, if we emphasize the interactions by which alliances form and change.

Explanation 7: Democracies do not go to war with one another because they successfully use balance-of-power politics to avoid war.[14]
Democracies may not go to war with one another because they are effective at balancing power and avoiding war. This is a realist explanation because peace is a product of balance-of-power politics, not democracy or institutional factors. Of course, the question remains why democratic states are so good at balancing power in that they seem to avoid war more often than nondemocratic states. If the answer is because they are democratic, the explanation becomes identity and policies to balance power become intervening variables. On the other hand, if the peaceful behavior is a product of policies to balance power, the explanation is realist. The level of analysis is systemic process because the outcome is achieved by policy interactions between democracies, not through their relative positions or internal attributes.

Spotlight on
liberal perspective and systemic process level of analysis

Spotlight on
liberal perspective and systemic process or structural level of analysis

Spotlight on
liberal perspective and systemic process level of analysis

Spotlight on
realist perspective and systemic structural or process level of analysis

Spotlight on
realist perspective and systemic process level of analysis

Measures of the Democratic Peace: Democratization, Trade, and Participation in International Organizations (IOs)

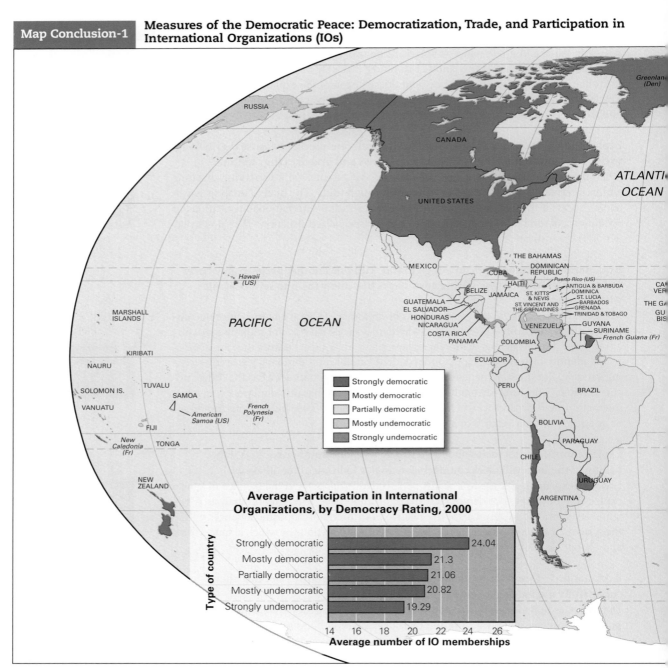

Average Participation in International Organizations, by Democracy Rating, 2000

Legend:
- Strongly democratic
- Mostly democratic
- Partially democratic
- Mostly undemocratic
- Strongly undemocratic

Type of country	Average number of IO memberships
Strongly democratic	24.04
Mostly democratic	21.3
Partially democratic	21.06
Mostly undemocratic	20.82
Strongly undemocratic	19.29

Source: Data on degree of democracy are derived from Freedom House's Freedom in the World 2007 survey. Data on membership in international organizations come from Jon Pevehouse, Timothy Nordstrom, and Kevin Warnke, "Intergovernmental Organizations, 1815–2000: A New Correlates of War Data Set" located at the Correlates of War project, www.correlatesofwar.org. All trade data are derived from Kristian S. Gleditsch's "Expanded Trade and GDP" data set, http://weber.ucsd.Edu/~kgledits/exptradegdp.html. Accessed May 19, 2006.

Note: Data for membership in international organizations for the year 2000 include all three types of membership coded for in the Correlates of War database: full, associate, and observer. Differences would be more pronounced but for the fact that the data weigh IOs and the quality of participation

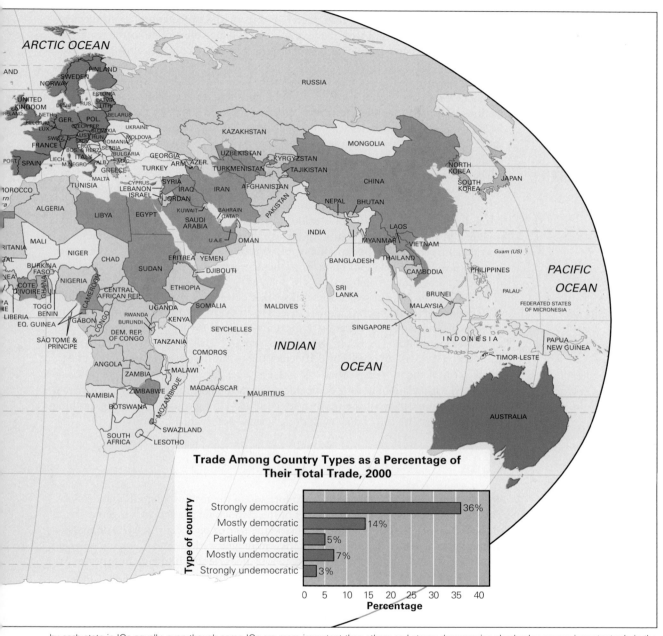

ARCTIC OCEAN

Trade Among Country Types as a Percentage of Their Total Trade, 2000

Type of country	Percentage
Strongly democratic	36%
Mostly democratic	14%
Partially democratic	5%
Mostly undemocratic	7%
Strongly undemocratic	3%

by each state in IOs equally, even though some IOs are more important than others and strong democracies clearly play a more important role in the most important IOs. Trade data given here show the amount of trade that countries in each democracy category do with one another, expressed as a percentage of the total trade those kinds of countries conduct. For instance, strongly democratic countries conduct 36 percent of all their total trade worldwide with other strong democracies, whereas strongly undemocratic countries conduct only 3 percent of their total trade with other strongly undemocratic countries. This result suggests that trade may also be a cause of peace among strongly democratic countries because these countries risk a greater loss of trade, and hence wealth, by going to war with one another.

Summary

As you can tell, sorting through so many variables of and explanations about the democratic peace is difficult, to say the least. Analysts change their mind as the work proceeds. Bruce Russett, a pioneer of democratic peace studies, concludes in an early work that "even when controls for physical distance, alliance, wealth, economic growth, and political stability are incorporated into the analysis, an independent explanatory role for democracy remains."[15] But, in a later study, he finds that trade and international organizations also make democracies more reluctant to go to war.[16] As the map on pages 542–543 shows, democracies tend to trade more with one another and to participate more fully and aggressively in international organizations than nondemocracies. But do trade and international organizations affect the outcome independently, or do they affect peace because democracies are more inclined than other states to trade and join international organizations?[17] Russett, who believed domestic norms and institutions were the best explanation in his early work, now concludes that all three factors—domestic norms and institutions, trade, and international organizations—shape the outcome of the democratic peace. Russett combines identity factors (democracy) and liberal factors (trade and institutions) while rejecting realist explanations of the democratic peace. His explanations come from the domestic and systemic process levels but not from the systemic structural levels of analysis.[18]

In his conclusion, Russett acknowledges that developing overlapping and multiple explanations of the democratic peace can lead to an **overdetermined outcome.** We can't say which factors may be the most important—critical theory perspectives and constructivist methodologies might say, "I told you so." The causes are interactive and cumulative. Peace is not caused by democracy but by the overweening presence of hegemony (critical theory perspective). Or peace is a repetitive and appropriate outcome associated with relations among democracies (constructivist methodology). Notice that this is our old problem of the need to select. If everything causes something, nothing does. Or, at least, we can't know what does. Science has reached its limits.

Coda

Well, we've finished our introductory exploration of the field of international relations. The short excursion through the studies of the democratic peace brings together many of the factors stressed throughout this book: the role of perspectives, levels of analysis, methodological issues, judgment, history (compiling historical cases of relations among democracies), and, ultimately, moral values. Why do we study the democratic peace? Are we being neutral and unbiased, or are we perhaps hoping that the democratic peace is true and that we may work, therefore, toward a world in which democratic values and a democratic way of life prevail? Would we be as enthusiastic if the evidence showed that nondemocracies were more peaceful toward one another than democracies? But, then, maybe we are just taking the facts as we can best assess them. George Shultz says democracies work better, and the most advanced countries, if wealth is one measure of what works, are indeed all democracies. And President Clinton felt strongly that they not only work better but they are also more peaceful.

Take two thoughts away with you as you put this book aside. The ability to know things for sure is very difficult. Science encourages us to think and test our perspectives as systematically and objectively as possible. That's good. But always be modest about

causal arrow

overdetermined outcome

an outcome caused by multiple independent variables, the separate and interactive effects of which are not clear.

what you think you know. Take a course in the philosophy of science, and you'll learn that even natural scientists, who study inanimate objects, can never know the way the natural world really works. They can only know, when their model tests out positively, that the world works in ways consistent with their model. But the world may also work in ways consistent with other, totally different models that have yet to be (and may never be) discovered. So, at a minimum, be prepared to spend the rest of your life learning. Keep an open mind, listen to others, be modest enough not to impugn your neighbor who disagrees with you as being stupid or evil. He or she may be both—ignorance and evil do exist. But we should be aware of our own ignorance and potential for evil as we work to root them out in others.

And that's the second thought. You still have to make judgments, almost always without complete information or knowledge. Don't shy away from making decisions. If you fail to choose—if you always wait for more information—the world may pass you by. Develop trust in your own judgment. Learning and growing, as someone reminded me early in my teaching career, are a full body exercise. You need your head, but you also need your heart and maybe, most of all, your spirit and values. Because we are dealing with one another, not just with physical phenomena, we need a basis that goes beyond physical phenomena even if we ultimately find out that human beings—our mind, spirit, and even our humanity itself—can be understood in purely physical (chemical, biological, and electrical) terms. How will we treat one another if and when we discover that? And if it depends on which electrode we stimulate or which drug we take, who decides what must be done and who administers these remedies? If no one does, if we are all simply products of our physical sensations, what does it mean to be human?

Think, now at the end of this book, about where we began—the situation in Darfur. We can't act responsibly until we know something about Darfur. But we can't read everything about Darfur because that would require too much time and we may never act, especially in a timely way to affect events while they are still fluid. So, we study with diligence and act with modesty using what we know, being aware that we don't know it all, and maintaining a reverence for what we all are—human beings who think and change even as we study and seek to influence one another.

Key Concepts

democratic peace 537
overdetermined
    outcome 544
sample size 538

Study Questions

1. Explain which statement is more reliable: (a) democracies rarely fight one another compared to other states; (b) democracies fight less against all states.

2. How would constructivist methodology critique democratic peace studies?

3. How do researchers generate more cases to test the correlation between democracy and no war?

4. Give an explanation of the democratic peace from each perspective and level of analysis.

5. Why, in your judgment, should the evidence of the democratic peace either play a role or not play a role in American foreign policy?

Notes

Introduction, pages 1–19

1. As one well-known philosopher of science once put it, "philosophers of science have repeatedly demonstrated that more than one theoretical construction can always be placed on a given collection of data." Thomas S. Kuhn, *The Structure of Scientific Revolutions,* 2nd ed. (Chicago: University of Chicago Press, 1970), 76.

2. Ronald Steel, "The Weak at War with the Strong," *New York Times,* September 14, 2001, A27.

3. Caryle Murphy, "A Hatred Rooted in Failings," *Washington Post,* September 16, 2001, B1.

4. Jim Hoagland, "The Mideast's Political Pygmies," *Washington Post,* August 1, 2002, A27.

5. Noam Chomsky, *Failed States: The Abuse of Power and the Assault on Democracy* (New York: Metropolitan/Owl Book, 2006), 14.

6. The labels sometimes differ. Some scholars call rationalist methods naturalist, positivist, or scientific. For a clear introductory discussion, see Jonathan W. Moses and Torbjorn L. Knutsen, *Ways of Knowing: Competing Methodologies in Social and Political Research* (New York: Palgrave Macmillan, 2007).

7. See John Gerard Ruggie, "Continuity and Transformation in the World Polity: Toward a Neorealist Synthesis," in *Neorealism and Its Critics,* ed. Robert O. Keohane (New York: Columbia University Press, 1986), 131–158.

8. He wrote this in a novel about someone losing his mind, suggesting that thinking alternatively is not always consoling. See F. Scott Fitzgerald, *The Crack Up,* ed. Edmund Wilson (New York: New Direction Publishing Corp., 1945).

9. Jim Hoagland, "Little Help Going Forward," *Washington Post,* July 29, 2004, A23.

10. Quoted in James MacGregor Burns, *Roosevelt: The Lion and the Fox* (New York: Harcourt, Brace, 1956), 157.

11. "The Man Who Beat Communism," *The Economist,* June 12, 2004, 13.

12. These three views are labeled variously by international relations scholars, but they represent the same basic points of view. Michael W. Doyle calls the three views revolutionary (universalist), realist (relativist), and rationalist (pragmatist). Joseph S. Nye Jr., calls them cosmopolitan (universalist), state skeptics (relativist), and state moralist (pragmatist). See their books, Doyle, *Ways of War and Peace* (New York:

Norton, 1997), 3; Nye, *Understanding International Conflicts: An Introduction to Theory and History,* 5th ed. (New York: Pearson-Longman, 2005), 23–28.

13. Kofi Annan, "Two Concepts of Sovereignty," *The Economist,* September 18, 1999, 49–50.

14. The story comes from Nye, *Understanding International Conflicts,* 25.

Chapter 1.
How to Think About International Relations, pages 20–71

1. Thomas Risse, "Let's Argue! Communicative Action in World Politics," *International Organization* 54, no. 1 (winter 2000): 3.

2. In the original prisoner's dilemma game, the actors have mixed motives, meaning they have both conflicting (can't go free together) and common (avoid worst outcome of twenty-five years) interests. Changing the goal to frustrating the warden gives the prisoners a dominant interest in common goals and converts the game to a no-conflict situation. Now each actor prefers to cooperate, the upper left box, regardless of what the other actor does. See Arthur A. Stein, *Why Nations Cooperate: Circumstances and Choice in International Relations* (Ithaca: Cornell University Press, 1990), 29.

3. Making the lower right box (DD) least desirable for both prisoners converts the game from prisoner's dilemma to chicken. See Glenn H. Snyder and Paul Diesing, *Conflict Among Nations: Bargaining, Decision Making, and System Structure in International Crises* (Princeton: Princeton University Press, 1977), 43–44.

4. Dates herein use the notation BCE for "before the common era" (rather than BC) and CE for "of the common era" (rather than AD).

5. Kenneth N. Waltz, *Theory of International Politics* (New York: Random House, 1979), 131.

6. Hans J. Morgenthau, *Politics Among Nations: The Struggle for Power and Peace,* 6th ed., ed. Kenneth W. Thompson (New York: Alfred A. Knopf, 1985), 5.

7. Winston S. Churchill, *The Second World War: The Grand Alliance* (Boston: Houghton Mifflin, 1950), 370.

8. Randall L. Schweller, *Deadly Imbalances: Tripolarity and Hitler's Strategy of World Conquest* (New York: Columbia University Press, 1997).

9. Waltz, *Theory of International Politics*; John J. Mearsheimer, *The Tragedy of Great Power Politics* (New York: Norton, 2001).

10. Dale C. Copeland, *The Origins of Major War* (Ithaca: Cornell University Press, 2000).

11. Daniel S. Geller and J. David Singer, *Nations at War: A Scientific Study of International Conflict* (Cambridge, UK: Cambridge University Press, 1998), 117.

12. Morgenthau, *Politics Among Nations*, 12.

13. See Robert Axelrod, *The Evolution of Cooperation* (New York: Basic Books, 1984). As we might anticipate, given the role of perspectives in the study of international affairs, not all scholars agree that reciprocity strengthens cooperation. See Joshua S. Goldstein and Jon C. Pevehouse, "Reciprocity, Bullying, and International Cooperation: Time-Series Analysis of the Bosnian Crisis," *American Political Science Review* 91, no. 3 (1997): 515–529.

14. Ernst B. Haas, *When Knowledge Is Power: Three Models of Change in International Organizations* (Berkeley: University of California Press, 1990).

15. Richard Ned Lebow and Janice Gross Stein, *We All Lost the Cold War* (Princeton: Princeton University Press, 1994).

16. Michael Steiner, "The Legitimacy to Succeed," *Washington Post,* May 18, 2003, B7. (Italics in original.)

17. Joseph S. Nye Jr., *Understanding International Conflicts: An Introduction to Theory and History,* 6th ed. (New York: Pearson-Longman, 2007), 45–50.

18. Robert O. Keohane, *International Institutions and State Power: Essays in International Relations Theory* (Boulder: Westview, 1989), 10.

19. See Edward Hallett Carr, *The Twenty Years' Crisis, 1919–1939* (New York: Harper Torchbooks, 1964), 8, chap. 1.

20. John Gerard Ruggie, *Constructing the World Polity* (London: Routledge, 1998), xi.

21. See Alexander Wendt, *Social Theory of International Politics* (Cambridge, UK: Cambridge University Press, 1999), 1.

22. Risse, "Let's Argue!," 10.

23. Ibid., 23–28.

24. Alexander Wendt, "Anarchy Is What States Make of It: The Social Construction of Power Politics," *International Organization* 41, no. 3 (spring 1992): 391–426.

25. Thomas Risse-Kappen, "Collective Identity in a Democratic Community: The Case of NATO," in *The Culture of National Security: Norms and Identity in World Politics,* ed. Peter J. Katzenstein (New York: Columbia University Press, 1996), 367.

26. For a study that uses ideological distance to explain conflict, see Mark L. Haas, *The Ideological Origins of Great Power Politics, 1789–1989* (Ithaca: Cornell University Press, 2005).

27. Jonathan Mercer, "Anarchy and Identity," *International Organization* 49, no. 2 (1995): 229–253. The realist perspective takes this notion of competitive identity, strips it of any social context, which all constructivists would include, and comes up with the antagonistic identities that populate the world of anarchy and keep states from cooperating and uniting with one another.

28. Social constructivists reduce this individual element of identity to a minimum. See Wendt, *Social Theory of International Politics,* 224–233.

29. See Matthew Evangelista, "The Paradox of State Strength: Transnational Relations, Domestic Structures, and Security Policy in Russia and the Soviet Union," *International Organization* 49, no. 1 (winter 1995): 1–39.

30. Peter J. Katzenstein, "Introduction," in *The Culture of National Security: Norms and Identity in World Politics,* ed. Peter J. Katzenstein (New York: Columbia University Press, 1996), 24.

31. Michael N. Barnett, "Identity and Alliances in the Middle East," in *The Culture of National Security: Norms and Identity in World Politics,* ed. Peter J. Katzenstein (New York: Columbia University Press, 1996), 407.

32. Joseph S. Nye Jr., *Soft Power: The Means to Success in World Politics* (New York: Public Affairs, 2004).

33. See, for example, Judith Goldstein and Robert O. Keohane, eds., *Ideas and Foreign Policy: Beliefs, Institutions, and Political Change* (Ithaca: Cornell University Press, 1993).

34. See Robert Jervis, *Perceptions and Misperceptions in International Politics* (Princeton: Princeton University Press, 1976).

35. For a survey of psychological approaches to international relations, see J. M. Goldgeier and P. E. Tetlock, "Psychology and International Relations Theory," *Annual Review of Political Science* 4 (2001): 67–92.

36. Robert W. Cox, with Timothy J. Sinclair, *Approaches to World Order* (Cambridge, UK: Cambridge University Press, 1996), 90.

37. J. Ann Tickner, *Gender in International Relations: Feminist Perspectives on Achieving Global Security* (New York: Columbia University Press, 1992), 130.

38. Kenneth N. Waltz, *Man, the State and War: A Theoretical Analysis* (New York: Columbia University Press, 1959).

39. Robert D. Putnam, "Diplomacy and Domestic Politics: The Logic of Two-Level Games," *International Organization* 42, no. 3 (summer 1988): 427–461.

40. For details of the Williamsburg Summit, see Robert D. Putnam and Nicholas Baynes, *Hanging Together: Cooperation and Conflict in the Seven-Power Summits* (Cambridge, Mass.: Harvard University Press, 1987), 170–183; Henry R. Nau, *The Myth of America's Decline: Leading the World Economy into the 1990s* (New York: Oxford University Press, 1990), 234–249.

41. Bruce Bueno de Mesquita, *Principles of International Relations: People's Power, Preferences, and Perceptions* (Washington, D.C.: CQ Press, 2003), 7.

Chapter 2.
Perspectives on World History, pages 75–108

1. Renwick McLean, "Growth in Spain Threatens a Jewel of Medieval Islam," *New York Times,* August 16, 2005, A4.

2. Victoria Tin-bor Hui, *War and State Formation in Ancient China and Early Modern Europe* (Cambridge, UK: Cambridge University Press, 2005), chap. 2.

3. Amartya Sen, "The Diverse Ancestry of Democracy," *Financial Times,* June 13, 2005, 13.

4. Sun Tzu, *The Art of War,* trans. Samuel B. Griffith (New York: Oxford University Press, 1963).

5. Thucydides, *History of the Peloponnesian War,* trans. Rex Warner, ed. M. K. Finley (London: Penguin, 1972).

6. John Noble Wilford, "Stone Said to Contain Earliest Writing in Western Hemisphere," *New York Times,* September 15, 2006, A8.

7. Charles Tilly, *Coercion, Capital, and European States AD 990–1992* (Cambridge, Mass.: Blackwell, 1992).

8. I recall a personal experience that registered this fact. On a trip to Europe in the 1960s, my great aunt took me to Beltershausen, a small village in central Germany, where the Nau family lived from the thirteenth century until 1906. Standing on the hills surrounding Beltershausen, my great aunt pointed out the neighboring villages. She specified emphatically which were Protestant and which were Catholic and was clearly very proud that Beltershausen, where she grew up, was Protestant, which was her faith.

9. John Keegan, *A History of Warfare* (New York: Alfred A. Knopf, 1993), 21.

10. Paul Kennedy, *The Rise and Fall of the Great Powers: Economic Change and Military Conflict from 1500 to 2000* (New York: Random House, 1987), 27–28.

11. Quoted in Frederick L. Schuman, *International Politics: Anarchy and Order in the World Society,* 7th ed. (New York: McGraw Hill, 1969), 283.

12. Henry Kissinger, *Diplomacy* (New York: Simon and Schuster, 1994), 130.

13. Quoted in David Fraser, *Frederick the Great King of Prussia* (New York: Fromm International, 2001), 308.

14. Hedley Bull, *The Anarchical Society: A Study of Order in World Politics* (New York: Columbia University Press, 1977).

15. Stuart J. Kaufman, "The Fragmentation and Consolidation of International Systems," *International Organization* 51, no. 2 (spring 1997): 197.

16. Daniel H. Deudney, "The Philadelphia System: Sovereignty, Arms Control, and the Balance of Power in the American States-Union, circa 1787–1861," *International Organization* 49, no. 2 (spring 1995): 191–229.

17. Michael W. Doyle, *Empires* (Ithaca: Cornell University Press, 1986), 52.

18. Robert O. Keohane, *After Hegemony: Cooperation and Discord in the World Political Economy* (Princeton: Princeton University Press, 1984).

19. Robert Axelrod, *The Evolution of Cooperation* (New York: Basic Books, 1984).

20. G. John Ikenberry, *After Victory: Institutions, Strategic Restraint, and Order Building After Major Wars* (Princeton: Princeton University Press, 2001), 59.

21. Kissinger, *Diplomacy,* 19.

22. Paul W. Schroeder, *The Transformation of European Politics 1763–1848* (New York: Oxford University Press, 1994), xiii.

23. Ibid., xii.

24. Paul W. Schroeder, "The Nineteenth-Century International System: Changes in Structure," *World Politics* 39, no. 1 (October 1986): 2.

25. Kalevi J. Holsti, *Peace and War: Armed Conflicts and International Order 1648–1989* (Cambridge, UK: Cambridge University Press, 1991), 167.

26. Robert Jervis, *Perceptions and Misperceptions in International Affairs* (Princeton: Princeton University Press, 1976).

27. For the analysis of French misperceptions, see Thomas J. Christensen, "Perceptions and Alliances in Europe, 1865–1940," *International Organization* 51, no. 1 (winter 1997): 65–99.

28. Stephen M. Walt, *The Origins of Alliances* (Ithaca: Cornell University Press, 1987).

29. Kaufman, "Fragmentation and Consolidation," 193.

30. Rodney Bruce Hall, "Moral Authority as a Power Resource," *International Organization* 51, no. 4 (autumn 1997), quotation from 618.

31. Kissinger, *Diplomacy,* quotations from 63, 65.

32. Paul W. Schroeder, "Historical Reality vs. Neo-realist Theory," *International Security* 19, no. 1 (summer 1994): 135–136.

33. Hans J. Morgenthau, *Politics Among Nations: The Struggle for Power and Peace,* 6th ed., ed. Kenneth W. Thompson (New York: Alfred A. Knopf, 1985), 236.

34. Martha Finnemore, *The Purposes of Intervention: Changing Beliefs About the Use of Force* (Ithaca: Cornell University Press, 2003), 108–124, quotation from 116.

35. John M. Owen IV, "The Foreign Imposition of Domestic Institutions," *International Organization* 56, no. 2 (spring 2002): 375–409; Mark L. Haas, *The Ideological Origins of Great Power Politics, 1789–1989* (Ithaca: Cornell University Press, 2005).

36. Jed Rubenfeld, "The Two World Orders," *The Wilson Quarterly* (autumn 2003): 30.

37. The exchange is recorded in Kissinger, *Diplomacy,* 124–126, quotations from 124, 125, 126.

38. J. Ann Tickner, *Gender in International Relations: Feminist Perspectives on Achieving Global Security* (New York: Columbia University Press, 1992), 42–43.

39. Ibid., 142.

40. Robert W. Cox, "Gramsci, Hegemony, and International Relations: An Essay in Method (1983)," in *Approaches to World Order,* ed. Robert W. Cox with Timothy J. Sinclair (Cambridge, UK: Cambridge University Press, 1996), 126.

41. Immanuel Wallerstein, *The Modern World-System: Capitalist Agriculture and the Origins of the European World-Economy in the Sixteenth Century,* text ed. (New York: Academic Press, 1976), 28–29.

42. Ibid., 239.

Chapter 3.
World War I, pages 109–135

1. For relevant excerpts of the Willy-Nicky telegrams, see Robert K. Massie, *Nicholas and Alexandra* (New York: Dell Publishing, 1967), 269–274.

2. John J. Mearsheimer, *The Tragedy of Great Power Politics* (New York: Norton, 2001), 213.

3. Quoted in Hans W. Koch, *A History of Prussia* (New York: Dorset Press, 1978), 341.

4. Relative wealth is measured in terms of iron/steel production and energy consumption. See Mearsheimer, *Tragedy of Great Power Politics,* 66–71.

5. Ibid., 187.

6. Ibid., 72.

7. Fareed Zakaria, *From Wealth to Power: The Unusual Origins of America's World Role* (Princeton: Princeton University Press, 1998).

8. Stephen R. Rock, *Why Peace Breaks Out: Great Power Rapprochement in Historical Perspective* (Chapel Hill: University of North Carolina Press, 1989).

9. For the relevant paragraph of Crowe's long memorandum, see Joseph S. Nye Jr., *Understanding International Conflicts: An Introduction to Theory and History,* 4th ed. (New York: Longman, 2003), 70.

10. Mearsheimer, *Tragedy of Great Power Politics,* 71.

11. Quoted in Dale C. Copeland, *The Origins of Major Wars* (Ithaca: Cornell University Press, 2000), 63–64.

12. Some German officials, such as von Schlieffen, did advocate preventive war in 1905. See Marc Trachtenberg, *History and Strategy* (Princeton: Princeton University Press, 1991), 60–61.

13. Copeland, *Origins of Major Wars,* 90, 93.

14. This is Copeland's conclusion in ibid., 117.

15. Jack Snyder, *Myths of Empire: Domestic Politics and International Ambition* (Ithaca: Cornell University Press, 1991), 66–67.

16. Ibid., 99.

17. Ibid., 67.

18. For example, Henry Kissinger writes, "Though Bismarck's style of diplomacy was probably doomed by the end of his period in office, it was far from inevitable that it should have been replaced by a mindless armaments race and rigid alliances. . . ." *Diplomacy* (New York: Simon and Schuster, 1994), 165. He admits earlier in this book, however, "the requirements of Realpolitik became too intricate to sustain," 160.

19. Quoted in Otto Pflanze, *Bismarck and the Development of Germany,* Vol. 1 (Princeton: Princeton University Press, 1990), 489.

20. Robert K. Massie, *Dreadnought: Britain, Germany and the Coming of the Great War* (New York: Random House, 1991).

21. Here is another of many examples where scholars interpret the same facts differently. No one disagrees with the fact that Germany issued a blank check. But some analysts believe Germany intended the blank check to encourage an immediate limited action by Austria against Serbia, while others believe the blank check encouraged Austria to delay and provoke a wider war. See Jack S. Levy, "Preferences, Constraints, and Choices in July 1914," *International Security* 15, no. 3 (winter 1990–1991): 171.

22. Massie, *Dreadnought,* 875.

23. Trachtenberg, *History and Strategy,* 59.

24. This history has personal significance for me. My grandfather, then a German citizen, marched into Belgium with the German advance. My father, a four-year-old boy at the time, thinks—because memories usually don't start that early—he remembers his dad's leaving the family in Chemnitz arrayed in battlefield uniform and gear.

25. Trachtenberg, *History and Strategy,* 91–92.

26. See Kier A. Lieber, "The New History of World War I and What It Means for International Relations Theory," *International Security* 32, no. 2 (fall 2007): 155–191, quotations in this paragraph from 157 and 156, respectively.

27. Trachtenberg, *History and Strategy,* 90.

28. Fritz Fischer, *The War of Illusions* (New York: Norton, 1975), viii.

29. Norman Angell, *The Great Illusion* (London: Heinemann, 1912).

30. Quoted in Kissinger, *Diplomacy,* 161.

31. Robert E. Osgood and Robert W. Tucker, *Force, Order and Justice* (Baltimore: Johns Hopkins Press, 1967), quotations from 51, 52.

32. Stephen van Evera, *Causes of War: Power and the Roots of Conflict* (Ithaca: Cornell University Press, 1999).

33. Michael W. Doyle, *Ways of War and Peace* (New York: Norton, 1997), 253.

34. Quoted in Snyder, *Myths of Empire,* 83.

35. Quoted in Walter A. McDougall, *Promised Land, Crusader State* (Boston: Houghton Mifflin Company, 1997), 105.

36. Quoted in Fritz Fischer, *Germany's Aims in the First World War* (New York: Norton, 1967), 33.

37. Quoted in ibid., 33, 59.

38. Quoted in Asa Briggs, *The Age of Improvements, 1783–1867* (London: Longman, 1959), 351. Henry Kissinger, a realist, cites Palmerston's realist quotation from Briggs but not the second, identity-oriented quotation; *Diplomacy,* 96.

39. Mearsheimer, *Tragedy of Great Power Politics,* 214.

40. Levy, "Preferences, Constraints, and Choices," 186.

41. Snyder, *Myths of Empire,* 71.

Chapter 4.
World War II, pages 136–166

1. The Hossbach memorandum raises another problem in the analysis of international affairs—the authenticity of documents. Hossbach drafted it five days after the meeting. Why did he wait so long? Were bureaucratic games being played and memos written to tilt the record? Some German generals, for example, General Werner von Fritisch, objected to Hitler's plans at the meeting. Air Force and Army generals were battling behind the scenes for resources to advance Germany's arms buildup. Hitler never reviewed the Hossbach memorandum, although he was asked to do so twice. So, how official or important was it? Subsequently, the original memo disappeared. It was found in 1943 by a German officer, Count Kirchbach, and copied for the Hossbach German archives. Later, the Americans found it and copied it again for presentation at the Nuremberg trials. Hossbach and Kirchbach subsequently said the Nuremberg copy was shorter than the original and did not include criticisms expressed at the meeting. Did the Americans edit the document to pin blame more emphatically on German leadership for the war? The original document was never found. In this case, there is probably enough other evidence to confirm the general thrust of the meeting. But not everyone agrees. See A. J. P. Taylor, *The Origins of the Second World War* (New York: Atheneum, 1961), xxiii. One side note: my wife and I lived in Bad Godesberg, Germany, in 1969–1970 in the downstairs apartment of the home of Freiherr von Fritsch, a nephew of the general who attended the Hitler meeting. (And you think history doesn't really touch us?) My one regret: I was not yet sufficiently interested to know enough about the Hossbach memorandum to ask the nephew what he or his father (the general's brother) might have known about this controversial document. Don't make my mistake. Get interested now!

2. Quoted in Henry Kissinger, *Diplomacy* (New York: Simon and Schuster, 1994), 127.

3. See Woodrow Wilson's address to Congress, April 2, 1917, available at http://historymatters.gmu.edu/d/4943.

4. Quoted in Kalevi J. Holsti, *Peace and War: Armed Conflicts and International Order 1648–1989* (Cambridge, UK: Cambridge University Press, 1991), 184.

5. Quoted in Inis L. Claude Jr., *Swords into Plowshares: The Problems and Progress of International Organization,* 4th ed. (New York: Random House, 1971), 52.

6. Quoted in Margaret P. Karns and Karen A. Mingst, *International Organizations: The Politics and Processes of Global Governance* (Boulder: Lynne Rienner, 2004), 283.

7. Quoted in Kissinger, *Diplomacy,* 281.

8. Joseph S. Nye Jr., *Understanding International Conflicts: An Introduction to Theory and History,* 5th ed. (New York: Longman, 2005), 93.

9. John J. Mearsheimer, *The Tragedy of Great Power Politics* (New York: Norton, 2001), 71, 305.

10. Ibid., 71.

11. Kissinger is one realist who disagrees: "The destruction of Czechoslovakia made no geopolitical sense whatsoever . . . because Czechoslovakia was bound to slip into the German orbit, and . . . Germany would eventually emerge as the dominant power in Eastern Europe." But that begs the question why Germany had to be dominant in eastern Europe in the first place and why the other powers could not accept this dominance. Maybe structural forces were at work after all. See *Diplomacy,* 316.

12. According to Mearsheimer, Germany was already the wealthiest country in Europe by 1930, but it did not convert this wealth into superior military power until 1939–1940. See *Tragedy of Great Power Politics,* 71, 316–317.

13. Robert Conquest, *The Great Terror* (New York: Macmillan, 1968); *The Great Terror: A Reassessment* (New York: Oxford University Press, 1990).

14. Kissinger, *Diplomacy,* 367–368.

15. Mearsheimer, *Tragedy of Great Power Politics,* 73.

16. Eric Nordlinger, *Isolationism Reconfigured: American Foreign Policy for a New Century* (Princeton: Princeton University Press, 1995).

17. Nye, *Understanding International Conflicts,* 104.

18. Mearsheimer, *Tragedy of Great Power Politics.*

19. Peter Lieberman, *Does Conquest Pay? The Exploitation of Occupied Industrial Societies* (Princeton: Princeton University Press, 1996).

20. Jack Snyder, *Myths of Empire: Domestic Politics and International Ambition* (Ithaca: Cornell University Press, 1991), 105.

21. Ibid., 108.

22. Randall L. Schweller, *Deadly Imbalances: Tripolarity and Hitler's Strategy of World Conquest* (New York: Columbia University Press, 1998).

23. Dale C. Copeland, *The Origins of Major War* (Ithaca: Cornell University Press, 2000), chap. 5.

24. Stephen M. Walt, *The Origins of Alliances* (Ithaca: Cornell University Press, 1987).

25. See, for example, Michael N. Barnett, "Identity and Alliances in the Middle East," in *The Culture of National Security,* ed. Peter J. Katzenstein (New York: Columbia University Press, 1995), esp. 403–413.

26. A. J. P. Taylor, *The Origins of the Second World War* (New York: Atheneum, 1961), quotations in this paragraph from 219 and 216, respectively.

27. Thomas J. Christensen and Jack Snyder, "Chain Gangs and Passed Bucks: Predicting Alliance Patterns in Multipolarity," *International Organization* 44 (1990): 137–168.

28. Copeland, *Origins of Major War,* 238–239.

29. Mark L. Haas, *The Ideological Origins of Great Power Politics, 1789–1989* (Ithaca: Cornell University Press, 2005), chap. 4.

30. Mearsheimer, *Tragedy of Great Power Politics,* 255, 320. A year later, after Roosevelt began a deliberate effort to strengthen America, the U.S. army had grown to 1,460,998.

31. Samuel P. Huntington, *The Third Wave: Democratization in the Late Twentieth Century* (Norman: University of Oklahoma Press, 1991), 17–18.

32. Again as a personal aside to show why history is interesting, my father was a small boy, 8–10 years old, in Berlin at the time and remembers being asked by his mother to forage through garbage cans at the army barracks nearby for potato peelings for the family to eat.

33. Conquest, *The Great Terror; The Great Terror: A Reassessment.*

34. Taylor, *Origins of the Second World War,* 51. Others disagree. Copeland, *Origins of Major War,* 123.

35. Copeland, *Origins of Major War,* 120.

36. Haas, *Ideological Origins,* 113.

37. Charles A. Beard and Mary R. Beard, *The Rise of American Civilization,* Vol. 2 (New York: Macmillan, 1930), 344–345.

38. Charles A. Beard, *President Roosevelt and the Coming of War 1941* (New Haven: Yale University Press, 1948).

39. Quoted in Kissinger, *Diplomacy,* 341–342.

Chapter 5.
The Origins and End of the Cold War, pages 167–204

1. George F. Kennan, *Memoirs: 1925–1950* (Boston: Little, Brown, 1967), 292–293; all quotations in these opening paragraphs are excerpts from the long telegram, 547–559.

2. In later writings, Kennan made explicit that "ideology is a product and not a determinant of social and political behavior." John Lewis Gaddis, *Strategies of Containment: A Critical Appraisal of Postwar American National Security Policy* (New York: Oxford University Press, 1982), 34.

3. [George F. Kennan,] "The Sources of Soviet Conduct," *Foreign Affairs* 26, no. 2 (July 1947): 566–582, quotation from 581. For security reasons, Kennan signed the article "X."

4. Henry Kissinger, *Diplomacy* (New York: Simon and Schuster, 1994), 173, 172, respectively.

5. Quoted in Milovan Djilas, *Conversations with Stalin,* trans. Michael B. Petrovich (San Diego, Calif.: Harcourt Brace Jovanovich, 1962), 114.

6. Quoted in Marc Trachtenberg, *A Constructed Peace: The Making of the European Settlement 1945–1963* (Princeton: Princeton University Press, 1999), 38. Truman made this statement in a letter to Secretary of State James Byrnes in January 1946. The letter was apparently never sent because Byrnes denies receiving it.

7. Ibid., 41.

8. Ibid.

9. Winston Churchill, "The Sinews of Peace" speech, quoted in Robert Rhodes James, ed., *Winston S. Churchill: His Complete Speeches 1897–1963, Vol. 7: 1943–1949* (New York: Chelsea House, 1974), 7285–7293.

10. Ratio drawn from Gordon Wright, *The Ordeal of Total War: 1939–1945* (New York: Harper and Row, 1968), 263–265.

11. Trachtenberg, *Constructed Peace,* 44–46. At Potsdam, Stalin had expressed a preference for a divided Germany: "Germany is what has become of her after the war. No other Germany exists. . . ." Quoted in David McCullough, *Truman* (New York: Simon and Schuster, 1992), 426.

12. Gabriel Kolko and Joyce Kolko, *The Limits of Power: The World and United States Foreign Policy, 1945–1954* (New York: Harper and Row, 1972); William Appleman Williams, *The Tragedy of American Diplomacy* (Cleveland, Ohio: World, 1959).

13. Another personal aside: My parents were close friends with an American soldier, Ray Twork, who was at Torgau when the two armies met. In civilian life, Ray was a graphics designer. So he was given the assignment to design the poster that was used the next day when the official meeting of the two armies was replayed for the military brass and news reporters from all over the world.

14. David P. Calleo, *The German Problem Reconsidered: Germany and the World Order, 1870 to the Present* (New York: Cambridge University Press, 1978).

15. Winston S. Churchill, *Triumph and Tragedy: The Second World War,* Vol. 6 (Boston: Houghton Mifflin, 1953), 227.

16. Quoted in McCullough, *Truman,* 537.

17. Graham Allison and Philip Zelikow, *Essence of Decision: Explaining the Cuban Missile Crisis* (New York: Longman, 1999), 92–93.

18. Richard Ned Lebow and Janice Gross Stein, *We All Lost the Cold War* (Princeton: Princeton University Press, 1994), 25.

19. Nikita Khrushchev, *Khrushchev Remembers,* trans. and ed. Strobe Talbott (Boston: Little, Brown, 1970), 493.

20. Not everyone agrees on the importance of Berlin. Allison and Zelikow conclude that Berlin and closing the missile gap are the most satisfactory explanations of Soviet motives in Cuba; *Essence of Decision,* 107. Lebow and Stein believe the defense of Cuba was more important than Berlin; *We All Lost the Cold War,* 48.

21. Allison and Zelikow, *Essence of Decision,* 104.

22. In an interview on October 29, one day after the Soviets conceded, Kennedy said, "we had decided Saturday night [October 27] to begin this air strike on Tuesday [October 30]. And it may have been one of the reasons why the Russians finally did this [giving in]." Quoted in ibid., 128. We don't know whether this was just postcrisis bravado. Robert McNamara, Kennedy's secretary of defense, insisted that Kennedy did not order an air strike on Saturday night. "If President Kennedy were going to strike on Monday or Tuesday, then he would have told *me* about it so that we could make the necessary preparations. He hadn't told me, so I don't think he *was* going to strike." Quoted in Lebow and Stein, *We All Lost the Cold War,* 128. (Now do you see why it is so hard, in some cases, even to know the facts, let alone interpret them in the same way?)

23. Lebow and Stein, *We All Lost the Cold War,* 294–295.

24. Kennedy Cabinet officials told Congress in January 1963, when speculation arose about secret understandings, that there was no deal or trade. McGeorge Bundy, Kennedy's national security adviser, later said, "we misled our colleagues, our countrymen, our successors, and our allies." Ibid., 123. What is truly mysterious is why the Soviet Union did not leak these secrets. McNamara ordered the Jupiter missiles removed on October 29, confirming that they were part of the deal. They came out six months later when Khrushchev was still in office. Now he had every reason to reveal the secrets because they would have made the outcome of the crisis look much better for him and the Soviet Union. He didn't and was subsequently driven out of office, in part because of Moscow's humiliation in the Cuban Missile Crisis. Now, there is a mystery that could stand further research.

25. David Coleman, "After the Cuban Missile Crisis: Why Short-Range Nuclear Weapons Delivery Systems Stayed in Cuba," *Miller Center Report* 13, no. 4 (fall 2002): 36–39.

26. Allison and Zelikow, *Essence of Decision,* 129.

27. Tony Smith, *America's Mission: The United States and the Worldwide Struggle for Democracy in the Twentieth Century* (Princeton: Princeton University Press, 1994), 226.

28. Paul Kennedy, *The Rise and Fall of the Great Powers* (New York: Random House, 1987).

29. Stephen G. Brooks and William C. Wohlforth, "Power, Globalization, and the End of the Cold War," *International Security* 25, no. 3 (winter 2000–2001): 29.

30. Ibid., 44–49.

31. Quoted in Mark L. Haas, *The Ideological Origins of Great Power Politics, 1789–1989* (Ithaca: Cornell University Press, 2005), 178.

32. Brooks and Wohlforth, "Power, Globalization, and the End," 24. For warhead data, see John J. Mearsheimer, *The Tragedy of Great Power Politics* (New York: Norton, 2001), 229.

33. Quoted in Lou Cannon, *President Reagan: The Role of a Lifetime* (New York: Simon and Schuster, 1991), 286.

34. Robert W. Cox, with Timothy Sinclair, *Approaches to World Order* (Cambridge, UK: Cambridge University Press, 1990), 177–179.

35. Quoted in McCullough, *Truman,* 547.

36. Kissinger, *Diplomacy,* 462.

37. Dean Acheson, "Threats to Democracy and Its Way of Life," address to the American Society of Newspaper Editors, Washington, D.C., April 22, 1950; *Department of State Bulletin* 22, no. 565 (May 1, 1950): 675.

38. Kissinger, *Diplomacy,* 553.

39. Walter Lippmann, *The Cold War: A Study in U.S. Foreign Policy* (New York: Harper, 1947), 60.

40. Thomas Risse-Kappen, "Collective Identity in a Democratic Community: The Case of NATO," in *The Culture of National Security: Norms and Identity in World Politics,* ed. Peter J. Katzenstein (New York: Columbia University Press, 1996), 373.

41. Ibid., 374.

42. See Stalin's Soviet colleague Roy Medvedev, *Let History Judge,* trans. Colleen Taylor (New York: Alfred A. Knopf, 1971), 474–475. Kissinger agrees; see *Diplomacy,* 443.

43. Colin Dueck, *Reluctant Crusaders: Power, Culture, and Change in American Grand Strategy* (Princeton: Princeton University Press, 2006).

44. Quoted in Trachtenberg, *Constructed Peace,* 16.

45. Zbigniew Brzezinski, *Between Two Ages: America's Role in the Technetronic Era* (New York: Viking, 1970), 274, 275.

46. Thomas Risse, " 'Let's Argue!' Communicative Action in World Politics," *International Organization* 54, no. 1 (winter 2000): 1–41.

47. Philip Zelikow and Condoleezza Rice, *Germany United and Europe Transformed: A Study in Statecraft* (Boston: Harvard University Press), 278.

48. Risse, " 'Let's Argue!' " 27.
49. Secretary of State James Baker made this offer to Gorbachev but later backtracked. See Zelikow and Rice, *Germany United and Europe Transformed*, 184.
50. Excerpts are from President Reagan's address before the British Parliament in June 1982. Quoted in Cannon, *President Reagan*, 315.
51. Paul Lettow, *Ronald Reagan and His Quest to Abolish Nuclear Weapons* (New York: Random House Trade Paperbacks, 2005), 63–70. For a summary of NSDD-75, see Jack F. Matlock Jr., *Reagan and Gorbachev: How the Cold War Ended* (New York: Random House, 2005), 53–54.
52. Quoted in Paul Kengor, *The Crusader: Ronald Reagan and the Fall of Communism* (New York: Regan/HarperCollins, 2006), 220.
53. Quoted in Cannon, *President Reagan*, 774.
54. Trachtenberg, *Constructed Peace*, 17.
55. Quoted in Frances Perkins, *The Roosevelt I Knew* (New York: Viking, 1946), 84–85.
56. Quoted in Kissinger, *Diplomacy*, 413.
57. Quoted in McCullough, *Truman*, 376.
58. Ibid., 432.
59. Ibid., 536.
60. See G. John Ikenberry, *After Victory: Institutions, Strategic Restraint, and the Rebuilding of Order After Major Wars* (Princeton: Princeton University Press, 2001).
61. See Trachtenberg, *Constructed Peace*, 119; Ikenberry, *After Victory*, 184.
62. Quoted in Kissinger, *Diplomacy*, 459.
63. See Henry R. Nau, *National Politics and International Technology: Peaceful Uses of Nuclear Power in Western Europe* (Baltimore, Md.: Johns Hopkins University Press, 1974).
64. See Robert E. Osgood, *NATO: The Entangling Alliance* (Chicago: University of Chicago Press, 1962).
65. For a liberal critique of realist versions of the Cuban Missile Crisis, see Lebow and Stein, *We All Lost the Cold War*.
66. See note 22.
67. Lebow and Stein, *We All Lost the Cold War*, 325.
68. Ibid., 323.
69. Thomas Risse-Kappen, "Ideas Do Not Float Freely: Transnational Coalitions, Domestic Structures, and the End of the Cold War," in *International Relations Theory and the End of the Cold War*, ed. Richard Ned Lebow and Thomas Risse-Kappen (New York: Columbia University Press, 1995), 187–223.
70. Quoted in Brooks and Wohlforth, "Power, Globalization, and the End," 38.

Chapter 6.
From 11/9 to 9/11, pages 205–232

1. For excerpts of the "New World Order" speech to Congress on September 11, 1990, see George Bush and Brent Scowcroft, *A World Transformed* (New York: Knopf, 1998), 370. For the UN speech, see President George H. W. Bush, Address Before the 45th Session of the United Nations General Assembly, New York, October 1, 1990; transcript available at http://bushlibrary.tamu. edu/research/papers/1990/90100100.html.
2. Drawn from El-Sayyid Nosair's notebook, quoted in Daniel Benjamin and Steven Simon, *The Age of Sacred Terror:*
Radical Islam's War Against America (New York: Random House, 2003), 6.
3. James A. Baker, *The Politics of Diplomacy: Revolution, War and Peace 1989–1992* (New York: Putnam's, 1995), 605–606. Emphasis in original.
4. U.S. Congress, House Committee on Foreign Affairs, *U.S. Participation in United Nations Peacekeeping Activities*, Hearings Before the Subcommittee on International Security, International Organizations and Human Rights, 103rd Congress, 2nd session, statement by Madeleine K. Albright, June 24, 1994, 3–21.
5. Benjamin and Simon, *Age of Sacred Terror*, 106.
6. William J. Broad and David E. Sanger, "As Nuclear Secrets Emerge, More Are Suspected," *New York Times*, December 26, 2004, 1; David E. Sanger, "Pakistan Leader Confirms Nuclear Exports," *New York Times*, September 13, 2005, A8.
7. James Hoge, "Counting Down to the New Armageddon," *New York Times Book Review*, September 5, 2004, 8.
8. For one such liberal argument, see G. John Ikenberry, *After Victory: Institutions, Strategic Restraint, and the Rebuilding of Order After Major Wars* (Princeton: Princeton University Press, 2001).
9. John J. Mearsheimer, "Back to the Future: Instability After the Cold War," *International Security* 15, no. 1 (summer 1990): 5–56.
10. Bill Clinton, *My Life* (New York: Knopf, 2004), 750.
11. For these phrases, see, respectively, Charles Krauthammer, "The Unipolar Moment," *Foreign Affairs* 70, no. 1 (1990–1991), 23–33; Charles Krauthammer, "Holiday from History," *Washington Post*, February 14, 2003, A31.
12. Henry Kissinger, *Diplomacy* (New York: Simon and Schuster, 1994), 805.
13. Patrick E. Tyler, "U.S. Strategy Plan Calls for Insuring No Rivals Develop," *New York Times*, March 8, 1992, A1.
14. The National Security Strategy, White House, September 2002, Chap. 3, available at www.whitehouse.gov/nsc/nss/2002/nss3.html.
15. William C. Wohlforth, "The Stability of a Unipolar World," *International Security* 24, no. 1 (summer 1999): 13.
16. Henry Kissinger wrote in 1976, for example, that the Soviet challenge "will perhaps never be conclusively 'resolved.' " See his *American Foreign Policy* (New York: Norton, 1977), 304.
17. Quoted in Bush and Scowcroft, *World Transformed*, 515.
18. Quoted in ibid., 541.
19. John J. Mearsheimer, "The Future of the American Pacifier," *Foreign Affairs* 80, no. 5 (September–October 2001): 55.
20. See Henry R. Nau, *The Myth of America's Decline* (New York: Oxford University Press, 1990).
21. Jeffrey E. Garten, *A Cold Peace: America, Japan, Germany and the Struggle for Supremacy* (New York: Times Books, 1992).
22. Kissinger, *Diplomacy*, 23.
23. Mearsheimer, "Back to the Future." In this article, Mearsheimer is thinking like a power balancer, assuming equilibrium in nuclear capabilities equates with stability. In his later book, he thinks like a power transition realist and argues that states will always seek maximum power and disrupt stability based on equilibrium. See *The Tragedy of Great Power Politics* (New York: Norton, 2001).

24. Commission to Assess the Ballistic Missile Threat to the United States, *Executive Summary*, Washington, D.C., July 15, 1998. Available at www.fas.org/irp/threat/bm-threat.htm.

25. Richard K. Betts, "The Soft Underbelly of Primacy: Tactical Advantages of Terror," *Political Science Quarterly* 117, no. 1 (spring 2002): 24.

26. Quoted in Benjamin and Simon, *Age of Sacred Terror*, 106.

27. *The 9/11 Commission Report: Final Report of the National Commission on Terrorist Attacks upon the United States*, authorized edition (New York: Norton, 2004), 59–60.

28. William J. Broad and David E. Sanger, "As Nuclear Secrets Emerge, More Are Suspected," *New York Times*, December 26, 2004, 1; David E. Sanger, "Pakistan Leader Confirms Nuclear Exports," *New York Times*, September 13, 2005, A8; Joby Warrick, "Smugglers Had Design for Advanced Warhead," *Washington Post*, June 15, 2008.

29. Francis Fukuyama, *The End of History and the Last Man* (New York: Avon Books, 1992). Like Huntington, Fukuyama wrote an earlier article that drew wide acclaim, "The End of History," *National Interest*, no. 16 (summer 1989): 3–18.

30. Ikenberry, *After Victory*. See my comment on Ikenberry's book in "Correspondence," *International Security* 27, no. 1 (summer 2002): 178–182.

31. Charles Krauthammer, "In Defense of Democratic Realism," *National Interest*, no. 77 (fall 2004): 15–26.

32. The National Security Strategy, White House, September 2002, Chap. 1, available at: www.whitehouse.gov/nsc/nss/2002/nss3.html.

33. Samuel P. Huntington, "The Clash of Civilizations?" *Foreign Affairs* 72, no. 3 (summer 1993): 22–49, quotation from 25; Samuel P. Huntington, *The Clash of Civilizations and the Remaking of World Order* (New York: Simon and Schuster, 1996).

34. Huntington, "Clash of Civilizations?" 25.

35. Samuel P. Huntington, "The West Unique, Not Universal," *Foreign Affairs* 75, no. 6 (November–December 1996): 28–47.

36. Fareed Zakaria, "The Rise of Illiberal Democracy," *Foreign Affairs* 76, no. 6 (November–December): 42.

37. Andrew J. Bacevich, *American Empire: The Realities and Consequences of U.S. Diplomacy* (Cambridge, Mass.: Harvard University Press, 2002).

38. Ibid., 88.

39. Ibid., 243–244.

Chapter 7.
Terrorism and the World After 9/11, pages 233–271

1. See CNN.com, http://archives.cnn.com/2001/US/11/06/gen.attack.on.terror.

2. See the account by then NATO Supreme Commander Wesley K. Clark, *Waging Modern War: Bosnia, Kosovo, and the Future of Combat* (New York: Public Affairs, 2001).

3. The White House, *The National Security Strategy of the United States of America*, Washington, D.C., September 17, 2002, 6.

4. Robert Kagan, *Of Paradise and Power: America and Europe in the New World Order* (New York: Knopf, 2002).

5. Quoted in Neil King Jr., "Rice's Perplexing Use of History," *Wall Street Journal*, January 19, 2007, p. A4.

6. See "Iran Curveball," *Wall Street Journal*, December 8, 2007, available at www.opinionjournal.com/weekend/hottopic/?id=110010965.

7. *The 9/11 Commission Report: Final Report of the National Commission on Terrorist Attacks upon the United States*, authorized edition (New York: Norton, 2004), 66.

8. "The Inaugural Address," *New York Times*, January 21, 2005, A16–A17.

9. Jim VandeHei, "Bush Calls Democracy Terror's Antidote," *Washington Post*, March 9, 2005, A16.

10. See Francis Fukuyama, "The Neoconservative Moment," *National Interest*, no. 76 (summer 2004): 57–69.

11. Daniel Benjamin and Steven Simon, *The Age of Sacred Terror: Radical Islam's War Against America* (New York: Random House, 2003), 85.

12. Stephen Howarth, *The Knights Templar* (New York: Barnes and Noble Books, 1982).

13. Bernard Lewis, *What Went Wrong? Western Impact and Middle Eastern Response* (Oxford, UK: Oxford University Press, 2002).

14. Abdurrahman Wahid, "Right Islam vs. Wrong Islam," *Wall Street Journal*, December 30, 2005, A16.

15. Benjamin and Simon, *Age of Sacred Terror*, 452.

16. Marc Sageman, *Understanding Terrorist Networks* (Philadelphia: University of Pennsylvania Press, 2004).

17. Oliver Roy, *Globalized Islam: The Search for a New Ummah* (New York: Columbia University Press, 2004).

18. *Global Trends 2015: A Dialogue About the Future with Non-governmental Experts*, National Intelligence Council, Central Intelligence Agency, Washington, D.C., December 2000, 42–45. For update, see www.adherents.com/Religions_By_Adherents.html.

19. A school of psychology known as social identity theory finds that people separate themselves into groups that discriminate against one another for no apparent reason. Thus, "unless the group encompasses all of humanity—and this is improbable at least in part because group cohesiveness decreases as it becomes more abstract—humans will always form groups. And with groups come social comparison and competition." This group dynamic creates anarchy, which other realists see as the root cause of ethnic competition. Jonathan Mercer, "Anarchy and Identity," *International Organization* 49, no. 2 (1995): 250–251.

20. See the discussion in Barbara F. Walter and Jack Snyder, eds., *Civil Wars, Insecurity, and Intervention* (New York: Columbia University Press, 1999), 24–27.

21. Susan L. Woodward, *Balkan Tragedy: Chaos and Dissolution After the Cold War* (Washington, D.C.: Brookings Institution, 1995), 36.

22. Mark Turner, "Under Fire: The United Nations Struggles to Meet the Challenges of a Changed World," *Financial Times*, June 6, 2005, 11.

23. Krishna Guha, "Ethnic Communities Can Be Devout as Well as Good Citizens," *Financial Times*, July 16–17, 2005, 7.

24. Amitai Etzioni, "The Evils of Self-Determination," *Foreign Policy* 89 (winter 1992–1993), 35.

25. Raymond C. Taras and Rajat Ganguly, *Understanding Ethnic Conflict: The International Dimension* (New York: Longman, 2006), 57.

26. David Campbell, *National Deconstruction: Violence, Identity, and Justice in Bosnia* (Minneapolis: University of Minnesota Press, 1998), 242.

27. Ibid., 211.

28. Anthony D. Smith, *National Identity* (Reno: University of Nevada Press, 1991), 40.

29. Kalevi J. Holsti, *Peace and War: Armed Conflicts and International Order 1649–1989* (Cambridge, UK: Cambridge University Press, 1991), 154.

30. Scott D. Sagan and Kenneth N. Waltz, *The Spread of Nuclear Weapons: A Debate* (New York: Norton, 1995).

Chapter 8.
History of Globalization, pages 277–320

1. Thomas L. Friedman, *The World Is Flat: A Brief History of the Twenty-First Century* (New York: Farrar, Straus and Giroux, 2005), quotations from 9–11.

2. Joanne Gowa, *Allies, Adversaries, and International Trade* (Princeton: Princeton University Press, 1994), 7, 9.

3. Professor Hendrik Spruyt has studied this competition between territorial states, city leagues, and city-states in *The Sovereign State and Its Competitors* (Princeton: Princeton University Press, 1994).

4. Charles P. Kindleberger, *The World in Depression 1929–1939* (Berkeley: University of California Press, 1973).

5. Robert O. Keohane, "The Theory of Hegemonic Stability and Changes in International Economic Regimes, 1967–1977," in *Change in the International System*, ed. Ole Holsti et al. (Boulder, Colo.: Westview, 1980), 131–162.

6. Robert Gilpin, *U.S. Power and the Multinational Corporation: The Political Economy of Foreign Direct Investment* (New York: Basic Books, 1975), 86.

7. Kindleberger, *World in Depression 1929–1939*, 28.

8. Here, again, a small bit of our personal entanglement in history. My father's mother came from Chemnitz, Germany. Her father owned a garment factory. After World War I, inflation wiped out the family business. My grandparents, already in America, lent them money throughout the 1920s, ultimately to no avail.

9. Barry Eichengreen, *Globalizing Capital: A History of the International Monetary System* (Princeton: Princeton University Press, 1996), 69.

10. Alfred E. Eckes Jr., *A Search for Solvency: Bretton Woods and the International Monetary System, 1941–1971* (Austin: University of Texas Press, 1975), 19.

11. Kindleberger, *World in Depression 1929–1939*, 219–220.

12. James C. Ingram and Robert M. Dunn Jr., *International Economics*, 3rd ed. (New York: John Wiley, 1993), 181.

13. Angus Maddison, *The World Economy in the 20th Century* (Paris: Development Centre of the Organisation for Economic Co-operation and Development, 1989), 65.

14. Quoted in Daniel Yergin, *The Prize: The Epic Quest for Oil, Money and Power* (New York: Simon and Schuster, 1991), 606.

15. Robert D. Putnam and Nicholas Bayne, *Hanging Together: Cooperation and Conflict in the Seven-Power Summits*, revised ed. (Cambridge, Mass.: Harvard University Press, 1987).

16. Maddison, *World Economy in the 20th Century*, 38–40.

17. Quoted in John Lewis Gaddis, *Strategies of Containment: A Critical Appraisal of American National Security Policy During the Cold War* (Oxford: Oxford University Press, 2005), 356.

18. Quoted in "Business Conditions: How High the Rate?" *New York Times*, July 26, 1981, 18.

19. Henry R. Nau, *The Myth of America's Decline: Leading the World Economy into the 1990s* (New York: Oxford University Press, 1990), 263 (chart).

20. For a recent discussion of this debate, see Kenneth Pomeranz, *The Great Divergence: China, Europe, and the Making of the Modern World Economy* (Princeton: Princeton University Press, 2000). Pomeranz concludes that, while Europe might have had some advantages in technology, China had more developed internal markets than Europe. Thus, Europe's breakout cannot be explained without considering the contribution of colonial exploitation.

21. Maddison, *World Economy in the 20th Century*, 45.

22. Eckes, *Search for Solvency*, 218.

23. Thomas L. Friedman, *The Lexus and the Olive Tree* (New York: Farrar Straus Giroux, 1999), xvi.

24. Joseph S. Nye Jr., *Understanding International Conflicts: An Introduction to Theory and History*, 5th ed. (New York: Pearson-Longman, 2005), 218.

25. Jagdish Bhagwati, "The Capital Myth: The Difference Between Trade in Widgets and Dollars," *Foreign Affairs* 77, no. 3 (May–June 1998): 7–13.

26. David Hale, "The IMF, Now More than Ever," *Foreign Affairs* 77, no. 6 (November–December 1998): 7–14.

27. Max Weber, *The Protestant Ethic and the Spirit of Capitalism*, trans. Talcott Parsons (London: Routledge, 1992), 109. Weber's thesis was first published in articles in 1904–1905 and then as a book in 1930.

28. Ibid., 101.

29. Immanuel Wallerstein, *The Modern World System: Capitalist Agriculture and the Origins of the European World-Economy in the Sixteenth Century* (New York: Academic Press, 1976), 36.

30. For a detailed description of these policies, which are similar in many ways, albeit in a different era, to conservative policies in the 1980s and 1990s, see Maddison, *World Economy in the 20th Century*, 44–45.

31. Karl Polanyi, *The Great Transformation* (Boston: Beacon Press, 1944).

32. Friedrich A. Hayek, *The Road to Serfdom: A Classic Warning Against the Dangers to Freedom Inherent in Social Planning* (Chicago: University of Chicago Press, 1976). The book was first published in 1944; this edition has a new preface by the author.

33. John Gerard Ruggie, "International Regimes, Transactions, and Change: Embedded Liberalism in the Postwar Economic Order," in *International Regimes*, ed. Stephen D. Krasner (Ithaca: Cornell University Press, 1983), 195–233.

34. Herbert Stein, *Presidential Economics: The Making of Economic Policy from Roosevelt to Reagan and Beyond* (New York: Simon and Schuster, 1984), 71–87.

35. Richard N. Cooper, *The Economics of Interdependence: Economic Policy in the Atlantic Community* (New York: McGraw-Hill/Council on Foreign Relations, 1968), 35.

36. Maddison, *World Economy in the 20th Century*, 86–87.

37. Donella H. Meadows et al., *The Limits to Growth: A Report of the Club of Rome's Project on the Predicament of Mankind* (New York: Universe, 1972).

38. Hernando De Soto, *The Other Path: The Invisible Revolution in the Third World* (New York: HarperCollins, 1989).

39. Daniel Yergin and Joseph Stanislaw, *The Commanding Heights: The Battle Between Government and the Marketplace That Is Remaking the Modern World* (New York: Simon and Schuster, 1998), 14–15.

40. See World Bank, *The East Asian Miracle: Economic Growth and Public Policy,* World Bank Policy Research Report (New York: Oxford University Press, 1993).

41. Paul R. Krugman, *Rethinking International Trade* (Cambridge, Mass.: MIT Press, 1990).

42. Paul Krugman, *Peddling Prosperity: Economic Sense and Nonsense in the Age of Diminished Expectations* (New York: Norton, 1994), chap. 9.

43. Joseph E. Stiglitz, *Globalization and Its Discontent* (New York: Norton, 2002).

Chapter 9.
How Globalization Works in Practice, pages 321–344

1. The term *trade account* is sometimes used as shorthand for current account, even by Nobel prize–winning economists, because people know instinctively what trade is but not what a current account is. Nevertheless, dividend and interest income earned on an investment in a foreign stock market is not considered by most people to be trade, even though it is included under the current account. So, we keep the two balances distinct here. See Joseph Stiglitz, "America Has Little to Teach China About a Steady Economy," *Financial Times,* July 27, 2005, 13.

2. Steven Pearlstein, "Tough Choices for World's Finance Leaders," *Washington Post,* April 15, 2005, E1.

3. Robert L. Paarlberg, *Leadership Abroad Begins at Home: U.S. Foreign Economic Policy After the Cold War* (Washington, D.C.: Brookings Institution, 1995), chap. 2. See also Henry R. Nau, "Where Reaganomics Works," *Foreign Policy* no. 57 (winter 1984–1985): 14–38.

4. This period is covered in my book, *The Myth of America's Decline: Leading the World Economy into the 1990s* (New York: Oxford University Press, 1990), chap. 7.

5. Robert D. Putnam and Nicholas Bayne, *Hanging Together: Cooperation and Conflict in the Seven-Power Summits,* rev. ed. (Cambridge, Mass.: Harvard University Press, 1987), 275.

6. I live in Maryland. In 2004, for the first time, I and other power customers could choose from more than one utility to purchase electricity.

7. Barry Eichengreen, *Globalizing Capital: A History of the International Monetary System* (Princeton: Princeton University Press, 1996), quotations from 5–6. Italics in original.

Chapter 10.
Trade, Investment, and Finance, pages 345–377

1. Gary Burtless, Robert Z. Lawrence, Robert E. Litan, and Robert J. Shapiro, *Globaphobia: Confronting Fears About Open Trade* (Washington, D.C.: Brookings Institution, 1998), 69.

2. Adam Smith, *An Inquiry into the Nature and Causes of the Wealth of Nations,* ed. Kathryn Sutherland (Oxford: Oxford University Press, 1993), 13.

3. Ibid., 393–464.

4. This is the conclusion of one of the economists credited with developing the theory. See Paul Krugman, *Peddling Prosperity: Economic Sense and Nonsense in the Age of Diminished Expectations* (New York: Norton, 1994), chaps. 9, 10.

5. Scott Callon, *Divided Sun: MITI and the Breakdown of Japanese High-Tech Industrial Policy 1975–1993* (Stanford: Stanford University Press, 1995).

6. Martin Wolf, *Why Globalization Works* (New Haven: Yale University Press/Notea Sene Book, 2005), 175.

7. Ibid.

8. Burtless et al., *Globaphobia,* 68.

9. Ibid., 46.

10. George P. Shultz and John B. Shoven, *Putting Our House in Order: A Guide to Social Security and Health Care Reform* (New York: W. W. Norton, 2008), 12.

11. Burtless et al., *Globaphobia,* 80.

12. M. P. McQueen and Jane Spencer, "U.S. Orders New China Toy Recall," *Wall Street Journal,* November 8, 2007, A3.

13. Alan Beattie, "Bilateral Trade Agreements 'Betraying' WTO Ideals," *Financial Times,* January 17, 2005; available at http://search.ft.com/ftArticle?dse=true&sortBy=gadatearticle&queryText=Alan+Beattie&y=4&aje=true&x=10&id=050118001201&ct=0&page=87&nclick_check=1.

14. A. K. Cairncross, *Home and Foreign Investment, 1870–1913* (Cambridge, UK: Cambridge University Press, 1953), 3, 23.

15. "A Ravenous Dragon: A Special Report on China's Quest for Resources," *Economist,* March 15, 2008, 1–22.

16. Henry R. Nau, "A Political Interpretation of the Technology Gap Dispute," *Orbis* 15, no. 2 (summer 1971): 507–528. I wasn't making history, but I was commenting on it. This was the first article I published as a young scholar.

17. The CIS is a group founded in 1991, consisting of eleven former Soviet Republics: Armenia, Azerbaijan, Belarus, Georgia, Kazakhstan, Kyrgyzstan, Moldova, Russia, Tajikistan, Ukraine, and Uzbekistan. Turkmenistan discontinued permanent membership as of August 26, 2005, and is now an associate member.

18. Daniel S. Hamilton and Joseph P. Quinlan, *The Transatlantic Economy 2008: Annual Survey of Jobs, Trade, and Investment Between the United States and Europe,* Center for Transatlantic Relations, Johns Hopkins SAIS, 2008, Executive Summary.

19. Raymond Vernon, *Sovereignty at Bay* (New York: Basic Books, 1971).

20. UNCTAD, *World Investment Report 2006: FDI from Developing and Transition Economies: Implications for Development* (New York: United Nations, 2006), 9.

21. Wolf, *Why Globalization Works,* 222.

22. McKinsey Global Institute, *Mapping Global Capital Markets: Fourth Annual Report,* Washington, D.C., January 2008, 13.

23. Wolf, *Why Globalization Works,* 281.

24. For a helpful description of this crisis and the statistics in this discussion, see Serena Ng and Carrick Mollenkamp, "Fresh Credit Worries Grip Markets: Banks' Woes Spur Fear of Reluctance to Lend," *Wall Street Journal,* November 2, 2007, A1.

25. Lee Hudson Teslik, "Sovereign Wealth Funds," Backgrounder, Council on Foreign Relations, January 18, 2008, available at www.cfr.org/publication/15251/sovereign_wealth_funds.html.
26. Ben White, "US Banks Get $21bn Foreign Bail-Out," *Financial Times,* January 16, 2008, 1.

Chapter 11.
Miracle and Missed Opportunity,
pages 378–409

1. Indermit Gill and Homi Kharas, *Overview: An East Asian Renaissance* (Washington, D.C.: World Bank, 2007), 1. Asia here refers to China, Taiwan, South Korea, Singapore, Hong Kong, Indonesia, Thailand, Philippines, Vietnam, Malaysia, and smaller economies, including the Pacific island economies.
2. World Bank, *The East Asian Miracle: Economic Growth and Public Policy,* World Bank Policy Research Report (New York: Oxford University Press, 1993), 1.
3. Charles Wolf, *Markets or Governments: Choosing Between Imperfect Alternatives* (Cambridge, Mass.: MIT Press, 1988), 27.
4. Robert Wade, *Governing the Market: Economic Theory and the Role of the Government in East Asian Industrialization* (Princeton: Princeton University Press, 1990).
5. World Bank, *East Asian Miracle,* 83–84.
6. Alice H. Amsden, *Asia's Next Giant: South Korea and Late Industrialization* (New York: Oxford University Press, 1989), 14.
7. World Bank, *East Asian Miracle,* 84.
8. World Bank, *Economic Growth in the 1990s: Learning from a Decade of Reform* (Washington, D.C.: World Bank, 2005), xiii.
9. World Bank, *East Asia Update: Testing Times Ahead* (Washington, D.C.: World Bank, April 2008), 1.
10. World Bank, *Global Monitoring Report 2005: Millennium Development Goals: From Consensus to Momentum* (Washington, D.C.: World Bank, 2005), 18.
11. Marin Ravalion, "Competing Concepts of Inequality in the Globalization Debate," in *Globalization, Poverty, and Inequality,* ed. Susan M. Collins and Carol Graham (Washington, D.C.: Brookings Institution, 2004), 1–38.
12. World Bank, *Global Monitoring Report 2008: Overview* (Washington, D.C.: World Bank, 2008), 2.
13. Joseph E. Stiglitz, *Globalization and Its Discontents* (New York: W. W. Norton, 2002), 253.
14. Joshua Kurlantzick, "China's Blurred Horizon," *Washington Post,* September 19, 2004, Outlook Section, B2.
15. See "CIA World Factbook," available at www.cia.gov/library/publications/the-world-factbook/index.html.
16. World Bank, *East Asian Miracle,* chap. 1.
17. Ibid., 5.
18. Ibid., chap. 3.
19. Ibid., chap. 4.
20. Ibid., 5–6.
21. Paul Krugman, "The Myth of Asia's Miracle," *Foreign Affairs* 73, no. 6 (November–December 1994): 62–79.
22. Scott Callon, *Divided Sun: MITI and the Breakdown of Japanese High-Tech Industrial Policy 1975–1993* (Stanford: Stanford University Press, 1995), 170.
23. See Henry R. Nau, *At Home Abroad: Identity and Power in American Foreign Policy* (Ithaca: Cornell University Press, 2002), 181 (table).
24. "Foreign Investment in China," The US-China Business Council, February 2007, available at www.uschina.org/info/forecast/2007/foreign-investment.html.
25. Martin Wolf, "On the Move: Asia's Giants Take Different Routes in Pursuit of Economic Greatness," *Financial Times,* February 23, 2005, 13.
26. Edwin O. Reischauer, *The Japanese Today: Change and Continuity* (Cambridge, Mass.: Belknap Press, 1988), 33.
27. Quoted, respectively, in Fareed Zakaria, "A Conversation with Lee Kwan Yew," *Foreign Affairs* 73, no. 2 (March–April 1994): 111; John Bresnan, *From Dominoes to Dynamos: The Transformation of Southeast Asia* (New York: Council on Foreign Relations, 1994), 55.
28. Quoted in Kazuo Ogura, "A Call for a New Concept of Asia," *Japan Echo* 20, no. 2 (2002): 40.
29. Data in the preceding two paragraphs are from Angus Maddison, *The World Economy in the 20th Century* (Paris: Development Centre of the Organisation for Economic Co-operation and Development, 1989), 35, 69–72, 90–97.
30. World Bank, *Economic Growth in the 1990s,* 36.
31. Ibid., 36–37.
32. See World Bank, "America Latina and the Caribbean Regional Brief," April 2008, available at http://web.worldbank.org/WBSITE/EXTERNAL/COUNTRIES/LACEXT/0,,contentMDK:20340156~menuPK:815394~pagePK:146736~piPK:226340~theSitePK:258554,00.html.
33. World Bank, *Economic Growth in the 1990s,* 50.
34. Ibid., 53.
35. Edward L. Gibson, "Conservative Party Politics in Latin America: Patterns of Electoral Mobilization in the 1980s and 1990s," in *Constructing Democratic Governance: Latin America and the Caribbean in the 1990s,* ed. Jorge I. Dominguez and Abraham F. Lowenthal (Baltimore: Johns Hopkins University Press, 1996), 26–42.
36. Leslie Bethell, "From the Second World War to the Cold War: 1944–1954," in *Exporting Democracy: The United States and Latin America,* ed. Abraham F. Lowenthal (Baltimore: Johns Hopkins University Press, 1991), 41–71.
37. Tom Farer, "Collectively Defending Democracy in the Western Hemisphere," in *Beyond Sovereignty: Collectively Defending Democracy in the Americas,* ed. Tom Farer (Baltimore: Johns Hopkins University Press, 1996), 2.
38. Maddison, *World Economy in the 20th Century,* 92.
39. Ibid., 94.
40. World Bank, *Economic Growth in the 1990s,* 147.
41. Geraldo Samor, "Brazil Is Driven to Bad Roads," *Wall Street Journal,* May 25, 2005, A10.
42. Data in this paragraph are from World Bank, *World Development Report 2005: A Better Investment Climate for Everyone* (Washington, D.C.: World Bank, 2005), Overview, 1–20; Matt Moffett and Geraldo Samor, "In Brazil, Thicket of Red Tape Spoils Recipe for Growth," *Wall Street Journal,* May 24, 2005, A1.
43. World Bank, *Informality: Exit and Exclusion* (Washington, D.C.: World Bank, 2007), 4.
44. World Bank, *World Development Report 2005,* Overview, 1–20.

45. World Bank, *Economic Growth in the 1990s,* 68.

46. World Bank, "America Latina and the Caribbean Regional Brief."

47. Tony Smith, "The Alliance for Progress: The 1960s," in *Exporting Democracy,* 71–90.

48. Harvey F. Kline, "Colombia: Building Democracy in the Midst of Violence and Drugs," in *Constructing Democratic Governance: Latin America and the Caribbean in the 1990s,* ed. Jorge I. Dominguez and Abraham F. Lowenthal (Baltimore: Johns Hopkins University Press, 1996), 20–42; Anita Issacs, "Ecuador: Democracy Standing the Test of Time," in *Constructing Democratic Governance: Latin America and the Caribbean in the 1990s,* ed. Jorge I. Dominguez and Abraham F. Lowenthal (Baltimore: Johns Hopkins University Press, 1996), 42–58.

49. Deborah J. Yashar, "Indigenous Protest and Democracy in Latin America," in *Constructing Democratic Governance: Latin America and the Caribbean in the 1990s,* ed. Jorge I. Dominguez and Abraham F. Lowenthal (Baltimore: Johns Hopkins University Press, 1996), 87–105.

Chapter 12.
Foreign Aid and Domestic Governance, pages 410–435

1. See Stephen C. Smith, *Ending Global Poverty: A Guide to What Works* (New York: Palgrave McMillan, 2005); he argues for a "holistic understanding of poverty" (24).

2. Jeffrey D. Sachs, *The End of Poverty: Economic Possibilities for Our Time* (New York: Penguin Books, 2005).

3. *Arab Human Development Report 2004: Towards Freedom in the Arab World,* report by the United Nations Development Programme, Arab Fund for Economic and Social Development, and Arab Gulf Programme for United Nations Development Organizations (New York: United Nations Development Programme, Regional Bureau for Arab States, 2005), 8–9.

4. Quoted in Daphne Eviatar, "Spend $150 Billion per Year to Cure World Poverty," *New York Times Magazine,* November 7, 2004, 48.

5. World Bank, *Global Monitoring Report 2008: Overview* (Washington, D.C.: World Bank, 2008), 2.

6. For these and other data, see World Bank, *World Development Indicators* (Washington, D.C.: World Bank, 2008), available at http://devdata.worldbank.org/wdi2006/contents/Section1.htm.

7. World Bank, *Can Africa Claim the 21st Century?* (Washington, D.C.: World Bank, 2000), 9.

8. Amy Chua, *World on Fire* (New York: Anchor Books, 2004), 147–148.

9. Richard Joseph, "Progress and Retreat in Africa: Challenges of a 'Frontier' Region," *Journal of Democracy* 19, no. 2 (April 2008): 96.

10. Larry Diamond, *The Spirit of Democracy: The Struggle to Build Free Societies Throughout the World* (New York: Times Books, 2008); quoted in ibid., 100.

11. "Zimbabwe Law Gives Business Control to Blacks," *Wall Street Journal,* March 10, 2008, A4.

12. Michael Wines, "Zimbabwe, Long Destitute, Teeters Toward Ruin," *New York Times,* May 21, 2005, A1.

13. World Bank, *Global Monitoring Report 2008,* 2.

14. World Bank, *Global Monitoring Report 2005: Millennium Development Goals: From Consensus to Momentum* (Washington, D.C.: World Bank, 2005), 25–26.

15. Ibid., 44.

16. Ibid., chap. 4.

17. Donald G. McNeil Jr. "U.N. Agency Denies Inflating Cases of H.I.V. Deliberately," *New York Times,* November 21, 2007, A11.

18. Data are from UNAIDS/WHO, available at http://data.unaids.org/pub/EPISlides/2007/2007_epiupdate_en.pdf.

19. Jim Kling, "The Vaccine That Almost Wasn't," *MIT Technology Review,* June 2005, 36–38.

20. World Bank, *Global Monitoring Report 2008,* 3.

21. World Bank, "Better Governance for Development in the Middle East and Africa: Enhancing Inclusiveness and Accountability," MENA Development Report (Washington, D.C.: World Bank, 2003), 8.

22. International Monetary Fund, *World Economic Outlook* (Washington, D.C.: IMF, April 2008), 98.

23. Mustapa K. Nabli, "Middle East and North Africa: 2007 Economic Development and Prospects," World Bank, Cairo, Egypt, May 31, 2007.

24. World Bank, "Better Governance," 6.

25. Ibid., 64.

26. Ibid., 98.

27. World Bank, "Trade, Investment and Development in the Middle East and North Africa: Engaging with the World," MENA Development Report (Washington, D.C.: World Bank, 2003), 110.

28. Ibid., 93.

29. Faiza Saleh Ambah, "Saudi Women See a Brighter Road on Rights," *Washington Post,* January 31, 2008, A15.

30. World Bank, *Gender and Development in the Middle East and North Africa: Women in the Public Sphere,* MENA Development Report (Washington, D.C.: World Bank, 2004), 2–6.

31. Ibid., 4.

Chapter 13.
Global Inequality, Imperialism, and Injustice, pages 436–455

1. Max Weber, *The Protestant Ethic and the Spirit of Capitalism,* trans. Talcott Parsons (London: Routledge, 1992).

2. Jared Diamond, *Guns, Germs and Steel: The Fates of Human Societies* (New York: Norton, 1999).

3. Paul Kennedy, *The Rise and Fall of the Great Powers* (New York: Random House, 1987), 28.

4. Immanuel Wallerstein, *The Modern World-System: Capitalist Agriculture and the Origins of the European World-Economy in the Sixteenth Century* (New York: Academic Press, 1976).

5. Douglass C. North, *Institutions, Institutional Change and Economic Performance* (Cambridge, UK: Cambridge University Press, 1990), 122. On the development of property rights, see also John Gerard Ruggie, "Continuity and Transformation in the World Polity: Toward a Neorealist Synthesis," *World Politics* 35, no. 2 (January 1983): 261–285.

6. John Micklethwait and Adrian Wooldridge, "The Hidden Promise: Liberty Renewed," in *The Globalization Reader,*

3d ed., ed. Frank J. Lechner and John Boli (Malden, Mass.: Blackwell, 2008), 11.

7. Robert W. Cox, with Timothy J. Sinclair, *Approaches to World Order* (Cambridge, UK: Cambridge University Press, 1996), 7.

8. Quoted in Robin Broad, "Part II: The Historical Context," in *Global Backlash: Citizen Initiatives for a Just World Economy,* ed. Robin Broad (Lanham, Md.: Roman and Littlefield, 2002), 66.

9. Frances Moore Lappé and Joseph Collins, "Why Can't People Feed Themselves?" in *Food First: Beyond the Myth of Food Scarcity* (Boston: Houghton Mifflin, 1977), 75.

10. Georg Lukacs, "The Marxism of Rosa Luxemburg," in *History and Class Consciousness* (London: Merlin Press, 1967), 27.

11. Raymond Vernon, *Sovereignty at Bay: The Multinational Spread of U.S. Enterprises* (New York: Basic Books, 1971).

12. Robin Broad, "Part IV: Challenging Corporate Conduct," in *Global Backlash: Citizens Initiatives for a Just World Economy,* ed. Robin Broad (Lanham, Md.: Rowman and Littlefield, 2002), 177.

13. Thomas L. Friedman, *The Lexus and the Olive Tree* (New York: Farrar, Strauss and Giroux, 1999), quotations in this paragraph from 27–29.

14. Subcommandante Marcos, communiqué entitled "The Southeast in Two Winds, A Storm and A Prophecy." Marcos's writings are collected in *Our Word Is Our Weapon: Selected Writings of Subcomandante Insurgente Marcos* (New York: Seven Story Press, 2002). Subcommandante Marcos is a pseudonym adopted by this Zapatista leader.

15. Manisha Desai, "Transnational Solidarity: Women's Agency, Structural Adjustment, and Globalization (2002)," in *The Globalization and Development Reader: Perspectives on Development and Change,* ed. J. Timmons Roberts and Amy Bellone Hite (Malden, Mass.: Blackwell, 2007), 410.

16. Joseph E. Stiglitz, *Globalization and Its Discontents* (New York: Norton, 2002), 5–6.

17. Dani Rodrik, *Has Globalization Gone Too Far?* (Washington, D.C.: Institute for International Economics, 1997), 2.

18. Martin Wolf, *Why Globalization Works* (New Haven: Yale University Press, 2004), 142–143.

19. Ibid., 158.

20. Ibid., 150–151.

21. Robert Wade, "Winners and Losers" and "Of Rich and Poor," *Economist,* April 28, 2001, 72–74, 80.

22. Wolf, *Why Globalization Works,* 149.

23. Jeffrey A. Frieden, *Global Capitalism: Its Fall and Rise in the Twentieth Century* (New York: W. W. Norton, 2006), 2.

Chapter 14.
World Environment, pages 460–482

1. Norman J. Vig, "Introduction: Governing the International Environment," in *The Global Environment: Institutions, Law, and Policy,* ed. Regina S. Axelrod, David Leonard Downie, and Norman J. Vig (Washington, D.C.: CQ Press, 2005), 5.

2. John McCormick, "The Role of Environmental NGOs in International Regimes," in *The Global Environment: Institutions, Law, and Policy,* ed. Regina S. Axelrod, David Leonard Downie, and Norman J. Vig (Washington, D.C.: CQ Press, 2005), 85.

3. Ibid., 84.

4. William B. Karesh and Robert A. Cook, "The Human-Animal Link," *Foreign Affairs* 84, no. 4 (July–August 2005): 50.

5. *Global Trends 2015: A Dialogue About the Future with Non-governmental Experts,* National Intelligence Council, Central Intelligence Agency, December 2000, 19.

6. *State of the World 1999: A WorldWatch Institute Report* (New York: W. W. Norton, 1999).

7. Richard P. Cincotta, Robert Engelman, and Daniele Anastasion, *The Security Demographic: Population and Civil Conflict After the Cold War* (Washington, D.C.: Population Action International, 2003).

8. Robert Kagan, *Of Paradise and Power: America and Europe in the New World Order* (New York: Vintage Books, 2004), 88–89.

9. Robert J. Samuelson, "Geopolitics at $100 a Barrel," *Washington Post,* November 14, 2007, A19.

10. Fiona Harvey, "A Costly Thirst: Proper Pricing of Water Could Ease Shortages," *Financial Times,* April 4, 2008, 7.

11. The irony is that after more than ten years of no logging on some 24 million acres in Washington, Oregon, and California, the spotted owl population continues to decline by 7 percent per year. Biologists think it may be due to another owl that kills or mates with the spotted owl. Kimberly A. Strassel, "Owls of Protest," *Wall Street Journal,* October 19, 2005, A12.

12. Karen A. Mingst, *Essentials of International Relations,* 3d ed. (New York: Norton, 2004), 295.

13. Donella H. Meadows, et al., *The Limits to Growth: A Report for the Club of Rome's Project on the Predicament of Mankind* (New York: Universe, 1972).

14. J. Ann Tickner, *Gender in International Relations* (New York: Columbia University Press, 1992).

15. Horace Freeland Judson, "The Great Chinese Experiment," *Technology Review* 108, no. 6 (December 2005–January 2006): 52.

16. Edward Cody, "Toxic Slick Contaminates Water Supply of Chinese City," *Washington Post,* November 25, 2005, A1.

17. For IPCC reports, see www.ipcc.ch.

18. Lisa Randall, "Dangling Particles," *New York Times,* September 18, 2005, WK 13.

19. John R. Christy, "My Nobel Moment," *Wall Street Journal,* November 1, 2007, A19. Christy was a member of the IPCC, which received the Nobel Prize in 2007.

20. David G. Victor, *Climate Change: Debating America's Policy Options* (Washington, D.C.: Council on Foreign Relations, 2004), 12–16.

21. Daniel B. Botkin, "Global Warming Delusions," *Wall Street Journal,* October 17, 2007, A19.

22. Thomas Catan, "Oil Chiefs Disagree on Global Warming Strategy," *Financial Times,* July 7, 2005, 3.

23. See *Copenhagen Consensus 2004,* available at www.copenhagenconsensus.com. See also Bjorn Lomborg, "How to Think About the World's Problems," *Wall Street Journal,* May 22, 2008, A15.

24. Fiona Harvey and John Aglionby, "Who Bears the Load? Bali Leaves Big Concessions Needed on Climate Change," *Financial Times,* December 18, 2007, 7.

25. Michael T. Osterholm, "Preparing for the Next Pandemic," *Foreign Affairs* 84, no. 4 (July–August 2005): 26.

26. Laurie Garrett, "The Next Pandemic?" *Foreign Affairs* 84, no. 4 (July–August 2005): 14.

27. Michael T. Osterholm, "Unprepared for a Pandemic," *Foreign Affairs* 86, no. 2 (March–April 2007): 48.

28. Justin Gillis, "Cure for Neglected Diseases: Funding," *Washington Post,* April 25, 2006, D1.

29. Garrett, "Next Pandemic?" 17.

30. James Gustave Speth, *The Bridge at the Edge of the World: Capitalism, the Environment, and Crossing from Crisis to Sustainability* (New Haven: Yale University Press, 2008); quotations from a review of this book by Ross Gelbspan, *Washington Post Book World,* April 27, 2008, 4.

Chapter 15.
Global Civil Society, pages 483–509

1. Francis Fukuyama, *America at the Crossroads: Democracy, Power, and the Neoconservative Legacy* (Princeton, N.J.: Princeton University Press, 2006), quotations from 162–163.

2. Anne-Marie Slaughter, *A New World Order* (Princeton, N.J.: Princeton University Press, 2004), 6–7.

3. Peter J. Katzenstein, *A World of Regions: Asia and Europe in the American Imperium* (Ithaca: Cornell University Press, 2005).

4. Stephen D. Krasner, *Sovereignty: Organized Hypocrisy* (Princeton, N.J.: Princeton University Press, 1999).

5. Union of International Associations, *Yearbook of International Organizations 2005/2006* (Munich: Thomson Verlag, 2005).

6. Salman Masood, "Pakistanis Back Off Vow to Control Madrassas," *New York Times,* January 2, 2006, A6.

7. See Margaret P. Karns and Karen A. Mingst, *International Organizations: The Politics and Processes of Global Governance* (Boulder: Lynne Rienner, 2004), 245–246.

8. United Nations Conference on Trade and Development, *World Investment Report 2007: FDI from Developing and Transition Economies* (New York: United Nations, 2007), xvi.

9. "Sudan: Talisman Energy Must Do More to Protect Human Rights," Amnesty International Index AFR 54/010/2001— News Service Nr. 78, 1 May 2001, available at www.amnesty.org/en/library/asset/AFR54/010/2001/en/dom-AFR540102001en.html.

10. Stephanie Strom, "Poor Nations Complain That Not All Charity Reaches Victims," *New York Times,* January 26, 2006, 12.

11. For details, see the World Wildlife Fund at www.worldwildlife.org/what/howwedoit/conservationfinance/item7065.html.

12. Karns and Mingst, *International Organizations,* 420.

13. See Amnesty International Financial Reports, available at www.amnesty.org/en/who-we-are/accountability/financial-reports.

14. Ann Marie Clark, *Diplomacy of Conscience: Amnesty International and Changing Human Rights Norms* (Princeton, N.J.: Princeton University Press, 2001).

15. Kofi Annan, *Annual Report of the Secretary-General to the General Assembly,* SG/SM/7136 GA/9596, September 20, 1999.

16. International Commission on Intervention and State Sovereignty, *The Responsibility to Protect: Report of the International Commission on Intervention and State Sovereignty* (Ottawa: International Development Research Centre of ICISS, 2001), 32.

17. Hans Peter Schmitz and Kathryn Sikkink, "International Human Rights," in *Handbook of International Relations,* ed. Walter Carlsnaes, Thomas Risse, and Beth Simmons (London: Sage, 2002), 517–536.

18. David P. Forsythe, *Human Rights in International Relations* (Cambridge, UK: Cambridge University Press, 2006), 60.

19. Karns and Mingst, *International Organizations,* 233.

20. See Judith Sunderland (Human Rights Watch), "Will the UNHRC Fulfill Its Promise?" available at http://ourkingdom.opendemocracy.net/2008/04/10/will-the-unhrc-fulfill-its-promise.

21. For text of the convention, see www.un.org/womenwatch/daw/cedaw/cedaw.htm.

22. For more details on these and other cases, see www.echr.coe.int/ECHR/EN/Header/Pending+Cases/Pending+cases/Cases+pending+before+the+Grand+Chamber.

23. Forsythe, *Human Rights in International Relations,* 127.

24. Ibid., 144.

25. See Roy W. Brown, "Vote on Freedom of Expression Marks the End of Universal Human Rights," International Humanist and Ethical Union, available at www.iheu.org/node/3123.

26. Martha Finnemore, *The Purposes of Intervention: Changing Beliefs About the Use of Force* (Ithaca: Cornell University Press, 2003), 79.

Chapter 16.
Global Governance, pages 510–535

1. J. Martin Rochester, *Between Peril and Promise: The Politics of International Law* (Washington, D.C.: CQ Press, 2006), 42.

2. John J. Mearsheimer, "The False Promise of International Institutions," *International Security* 19, no. 3 (winter 1994–1995): 5–50.

3. Robert O. Keohane and Lisa L. Martin, "The Promise of Institutionalist Theory," *International Security* 20, no. 1 (summer 1995): 39–52.

4. John O. McGinnis, "Individualism and World Order," *National Interest* 78 (winter 2004–2005): 41–52.

5. David Mitrany, *A Working Peace System,* 4th ed. (London: National Peace Council, 1946).

6. On epistemic communities and scientific problem solving, see Peter M. Haas, "Introduction: Epistemic Communities and International Policy Coordination," *International Organization* 46, no. 1 (winter 1992): 1–35; Ernst B. Haas, *When Knowledge Is Power: Three Models of Change in International Organizations* (Berkeley: University of California Press, 1990). Peter is Ernst's son.

7. Robert O. Keohane, *International Institutions and State Power* (Boulder, Colo.: Westview Press, 1989).

8. Robert Axelrod, *The Evolution of Cooperation* (New York: Basic Books, 1984).

9. Colum Lynch, "U.N. Finds Fraud, Mismanagement in Peacekeeping," *Washington Post,* December 18, 2007, A6.

10. *A More Secure World: Our Shared Responsibility,* report of the Secretary General's High-Level Panel on Threats, Challenges and Change (New York: United Nations, December 2005).

11. Mark Turner, "Wrongdoing Costs UN up to $298m," *Financial Times,* January 24, 2006, 3.

12. Peter J. Katzenstein, *A World of Regions: Asia and Europe in the American Imperium* (Ithaca: Cornell University Press, 2005).

13. The father of neofunctionalism is Ernst B. Haas. See, among others sources, his *The Uniting of Europe: Political, Social, and Economic Forces, 1950–1957* (Palo Alto, Calif.: Stanford University Press, 1958); *Beyond the Nation-State: Functionalism and International Organization* (Palo Alto, Calif.: Stanford University Press, 1964).

14. See my review essay examining this shift from integration to interdependence studies. Henry R. Nau, "From Integration to Interdependence: Gains, Losses and Continuing Gaps," *International Organization* 33, no. 1 (winter 1979): 119–147.

15. For a thorough and lucid treatment of the EU, see Roy H. Ginsberg, *Demystifying the European Union: The Enduring Logic of European Integration* (Lanham, Md.: Rowman and Littlefield, 2007); *The European Union in International Politics: Baptism by Fire* (New York: Rowman and Littlefield, 2001).

16. Katzenstein, *World of Regions,* 223.

17. Robert W. Cox, with Timothy J. Sinclair, *Approaches to World Order* (Cambridge, UK: Cambridge University Press, 1996), 534–535.

Conclusion, pages 536–545

1. Quoted in Daniel Henninger, "Father of the Bush Doctrine," *Wall Street Journal,* April 29–30, 2006, A8.

2. Quoted in Bruce Russett and John R. Oneal, *Triangulating Peace: Democracy, Interdependence, and International Organizations* (New York: W. W. Norton, 2001), 218.

3. Jack S. Levy, "Domestic Politics and War," *Journal of Interdisciplinary History* 18 (spring 1988): 662.

4. Jack S. Levy, "War and Peace," in *Handbook of International Relations,* ed. Walter Carlsnaes, Thomas Risse, and Beth A. Simmons (London: Sage, 2002), 358–359.

5. Robert W. Cox, with Timothy J. Sinclair, *Approaches to World Order* (Cambridge, UK: Cambridge University Press, 1996), 490.

6. On the relationship between new democracies and war, see Edward D. Mansfield and Jack Snyder, "Democratization and the Danger of War," *International Security* 20 (summer 1995): 5–38. Russett and Oneal dispute this conclusion; see *Triangulating Peace,* 51, 120.

7. Russett and Oneal, *Triangulating Peace,* 46.

8. R. J. Rummel, "Democracies ARE Less Warlike than Other Regimes," *European Journal of International Relations* 1 (December 1995): 457–479.

9. Bruce Russett, *Grasping the Democratic Peace: Principles for a Post-Cold War World* (Princeton, N.J.: Princeton University Press, 1993).

10. Russett and Oneal, *Triangulating Peace,* chap. 4.

11. Ibid., chap. 5.

12. Charles Lipson, *Reliable Partners: How Democracies Have Made a Separate Peace* (Princeton, N.J.: Princeton University Press, 2003).

13. Joanne Gowa, *Ballots and Bullets: The Elusive Democratic Peace* (Princeton, N.J.: Princeton University Press, 1999).

14. Christopher Layne, "Kant or Cant: The Myth of the Democratic Peace," *International Security* 19 (fall 1994): 5–49.

15. Russett, *Grasping the Democratic Peace,* 30.

16. Russett and Oneal, *Triangulating Peace,* chap. 2.

17. John Ikenberry argues, for example, that democracies are better able than nondemocracies to bind themselves in international institutions. See G. John Ikenberry, *After Victory: Institutions, Strategic Restraint, and the Rebuilding of Order After Major Wars* (Princeton, N.J.: Princeton University Press, 2001). See also my comment on Ikenberry's book in "Correspondence," *International Security* 27, no. 1 (summer 2002): 178–182.

18. Russett, *Grasping the Democratic Peace,* 400.

Glossary of Key Concepts

A

absolute advantage: when a country can produce most or all products more efficiently than another country.

absolute gains: the increase each side gains over what it had before.

acid rain: condensation-borne pollutants that may be transported through the upper atmosphere over long distances.

agent-oriented constructivism: an identity perspective that allows for greater influence on the part of independent actors in shaping identities.

aggressive Keynesians: economists who favor more extensive government intervention to achieve full, not just high, employment and are less averse to inflation, price controls, or other forms of government intervention in the domestic economy.

alliances: a formal defense arrangement wherein states align against a greater power to prevent dominance.

American Declaration on the Rights and Duties of Man: the world's first international human rights instrument of a general nature, adopted by the nations of the Americas in April 1948.

anarchy: the decentralized distribution of power in the international system; no leader or center of authority exists that monopolizes power and has the legitimacy to use it.

Anti-Ballistic Missile (ABM) Treaty: a treaty signed by the United States and Soviet Union in 1972 limiting anti-ballistic missiles except for two installations on each side.

appeasement: a policy of making concessions to a stronger foe because a nation is less willing to consider the use of force.

arms race: the competitive buildup of weapons systems.

Asian values: the Confucian ideas that motivated economic success in Asia; based on cultural/ethical principles such as the privileging of authority—family or community—over the individual.

asymmetric threat and warfare: the exploitation of technology and psychology to target the peripheral vulnerabilities of a larger foe.

authoritarian states: states that typically restrict civil rights in key sectors of society such as political parties and the media but allow some independent activities in commerce and other areas.

B

balance of payments: a country's current and capital account balances plus reserves and statistical errors.

balance of power: the process by which states counterbalance to ensure that no single state dominates the system, or an outcome that establishes a rough equilibrium among states.

balance of terror: a situation in which two countries fear that, if either side attacks, the other side might use nuclear weapons, resulting in both countries being forced to prepare for the full range of possible conflicts to avoid all-out nuclear war.

bandwagoning: the aligning of states with a greater power to share the spoils of dominance.

Baruch Plan: a proposal made by the United States in 1946 to create an international agency under the United Nations to control and manage nuclear weapons cooperatively.

beggar-thy-neighbor policies: competitive economic policies to reduce imports by raising tariffs and to increase exports by lowering the value of currencies, with the net result that global markets shrink.

behind-the-border policies: domestic economic policies that affect all domestic goods, services, capital, and labor, whether traded or not.

beliefs: ideas about how the world works as emphasized by identity perspectives.

belief systems: ideas about how the world works that influence the behavior of policymakers.

Berlin Blockade: the first physical confrontation of the Cold War, taking place from 1948–1949, in which Stalin blocked the land routes into Berlin.

biodiversity: the multiple species of plant and animal life found in nature.

Biological Weapons Convention (BWC): an agreement made in 1972 to ban the production and use of biological weapons.

bipolar: when two states dominate a distribution of power.

bonded labor: a form of unfree or indentured labor, typically a means of paying off loans with direct labor instead of currency or goods.

border policies: foreign economic policies that affect goods, services, capital, and people only as they cross national boundaries.

buckpassing: a free-riding strategy wherein one country allows others to fight conflicts while it stays on the sidelines.

C

capital accounts: the net flows of capital, both portfolio and foreign direct investment, into and out of a country.

capital account deficit: the net amount that a country lends out to other countries when it exports more than it imports.

capital account surplus: the net amount that a country has to borrow from abroad when it imports more than it exports.

capital flight: moving money out of the local currency and country because of inflation and economic or political instability.

capitalism: a system that concentrates economic and social power in the hands of bankers and corporations (bourgeoisie), exploiting the labor of workers and farmers (proletariat).

causation: one fact or event causing another.

chain-ganging: the creation of a rigid defensive alliance.

Chemical Weapons Convention: agreement made in 1993 to ban the production and use of chemical weapons.

Chicago School of economics: an economic model that allows for fiscal and monetary policies to manage domestic demand, but sharply limits government spending and taxation and seeks to reduce tariffs and maintain relatively stable exchange rates to ensure more competitive and, hence, efficient domestic and international markets.

chlorofluorocarbons (CFCs): chemicals that break down the ozone layer.

city leagues: collections of city-states united for protection or trade.

city-states: cities that are controlled by sovereign governments.

civic identity: identity constructed when people are willing to submit to the laws of a common government rather than those of separate ethnic or religious groups.

civil rights: rights for participants in civil society, regarded in democratic societies as existing before government and as inalienable by governments.

civil society: the nongovernmental sector.

clash of civilizations: a thesis advanced by Samuel Huntington that past and future global conflicts can be traced along the fault lines between nine major world civilizations.

classical economic liberalism: an economic orientation that holds that parties have a right to own property and exchange goods in a relatively free and competitive marketplace without violence and coercion.

Colbertism: an economic policy based on high tariffs; named after seventeenth-century Frenchman Jean Baptiste Colbert.

Cold War: the putatively bloodless conflict, starting after World War II and lasting forty-five years, between the United States and the Soviet Union, which nonetheless resulted in massive arms buildups, international conflicts, and proxy wars worldwide.

collaboration problems: problems that can be resolved only when parties cooperate, usually through institutional means.

collective goods: goals, such as clean air, which are indivisible, meaning they exist for everyone or not for any one particular person or group, and which cannot be appropriated, meaning that they do not diminish as one party consumes them.

collective security: the establishment of common institutions and rules among states to settle disputes peacefully and to enforce agreements by a preponderance, not a balance, of power.

colonization: the establishment of outposts or colonies within a foreign population with the intention of dominating resources and indigenous peoples.

common market: a transnational market system that reduces internal tariffs to zero and establishes a common external tariff.

comparative advantage: a relationship in which two countries can produce more goods from the same resources if they specialize and trade products rather than produce them separately.

competition policies: policies that deal with monopolies by authorizing, deregulating, or privatizing them.

competitive advantage: a trade advantage created by government intervention to exploit monopoly rents in strategic industries.

complex interdependence: a dense network of interconnections emphasizing horizontal rather than vertical relationships that benefits more and more countries but also exposes them to more and more risks.

Comprehensive Test Ban Treaty (CTBT): a 1996 agreement to stop the testing of nuclear weapons both above and below ground.

compromise: swapping the achievement of an interest in one issue area for the achievement of another interest in a second issue area.

Concert of Europe: a system of conferences and consultations, in the early nineteenth century, among the great powers to manage the balance of power.

concessional loans: loans made to developing nations at subsidized interest rates.

conditionality: a requirement by the IMF that, in exchange for balance of payment assistance, a country alter its policies to correct its balance of payment deficit.

Congress of Vienna: a major international conference (1814–1815) that shaped Europe by setting up the Concert of Europe.

constitutional governments: governments that reserve a large space for civil society to act independently.

constitutional orders: international orders based on constitutional rules and institutions such as those that exist in the case of constitutional domestic governments.

constitutional solutions: resolutions to ethnic and religious conflicts that implement a constitution and promulgate norms of equality and human rights.

construction of identities: a process of discourse by which actors define who they are and how they behave toward one another.

constructivism: a perspective that emphasizes ideas, such as word content and social discourse, over institutions or power.

constructivist methods: methods that pay more attention to the way that meaning is formed discursively, through language, and that see events as mutually causing or constituting one another rather than causing one another sequentially.

containment: the policy of the United States during the Cold War that checked aggressive Soviet actions by military alliances.

coordination problems: problems that can be resolved by informal means rather than institutional cooperation.

core states: large and leading countries that produce most of the leading or quasi-monopoly products.

correlation: one fact or event occurring with another fact or event.

corruption: violations of the rule of law on the part of government officials that divert public resources to private gain and create an unpredictable investment climate.

Council of Europe (CE): the oldest (founded in 1949) and broadest (forty-seven member countries) organization working for European integration, focusing on legal standards and the protection of human rights, democratic development, and the rule of law in Europe.

Council of the European Union: the assembly bringing together the member states of the European Union.

counterfactual reasoning: a method of testing claims for causality by inverting the causal claim. The counterfactual of the claim "event A caused event B" is to ask, "if event A had not happened, would event B have happened?"

counterforce weapons: nuclear missiles aimed at other missiles rather than at population or industrial centers.

countervalue weapons: nuclear missiles aimed at population and industrial centers rather than at other missiles.

critical theory perspective: a perspective that questions whether events can be explained apart from historical circumstances and focuses instead on social and political change that unfolds within history; it offers broad critiques of international relations and generally advocates radical solutions such as revolution.

crony capitalism: noncompetitive lending and investment relationships between financial institutions and industry, such as between government banks and private manufacturing companies.

cult of the offensive: a belief in offensive military power.

currency markets: the market that involves transactions that swap one currency for another.

current accounts: the net border flows of goods and services, along with government transfers and net income on capital investments.

customs fees and duties: charges added to the import price of goods.

D

debt relief: the rescheduling of loans to developing nations to stretch the loans over longer periods of time or the forgiving of the loans altogether.

decolonization: the process by which a colony gains its independence from a colonial power.

deconstructivists: theorists who seek to deconstruct social reality wherever they find it and show that all politics conceals the exercise of power through words and discourse.

democratic deficit: the criticism made of the European Union that there is a gap between European Community institutions and the people they represent.

democratic peace: the theory that democratic nations for the most part do not go to war with one another, making the spread of democracy desirable.

demographic transitions: periods of accelerating population growth as living standards increase because death rates decline faster than birth rates.

dependency theory: theory developed by Latin American economists that explains the lack of growth in terms of external or colonial exploitation and oppression.

derivatives market: the market that exchanges existing loans and financial assets and hedges them as derivatives against future prices, earnings, or interest.

détente: a phase of the Cold War beginning in the 1960s when France and Germany initiated diplomatic overtures to Moscow and western countries subsequently concluded agreements with the Soviet Union.

deterrence: preventing an attack by threatening retaliation against the potential attacker.

development: the process of material, institutional, and human progress in a particular country or region.

diplomacy: discussions and negotiations among states as emphasized by the liberal perspective.

disarmament: the process of mutual reduction of military arms by international agreements or convention.

distribution of identities: the relative relationship of identities among actors in the international system in terms of their similarities and differences.

division of labor: division of world markets into core, peripheral, and semi-peripheral states.

Doha Round: the ninth and most current round of trade talks, which has as its goal to aid developing countries with respect to agricultural subsidies, more favorable systems for the manufacture and distribution of medical drugs, and the improvement of infrastructure, while still lowering barriers for advanced countries on industrial, service, and investment flows.

dollar standard: the fixed exchange rate system established by Bretton Woods, that pegged the U.S. dollar to gold and other currencies to the dollar.

domestic governance: the domestic institutions and policies that govern the local economy.

domestic level of analysis: a level that focuses on domestic features of a country as a whole, such as its capitalist economic system or nationalist ideology, from which the causes of a realist, liberal, or identity perspective come.

domino theory: fear of the superpowers that if one country in a developing region went over to the other side, other countries would fall like dominoes.

E

East Asian Miracle: a period of unprecedented economic growth and development in East Asia between 1965 and 2005.

economic autarky: a closed domestic economic system based on protectionism and state-owned industries.

economic nationalism: the approach of assisting domestic industries to catch up with and compete with more advanced foreign industries through protectionism, high tariffs, and subsidies.

economies of scale: the larger the amount of a good that is produced, the lower the cost of production.

ejido **system:** Mexican land reform project that redistributed some land to peasants; however, the plots were owned collectively, not individually, and depended on government development banks for financing.

elite manipulation: leaders' exploitation of people's fears to advance their own personal and group interests; the principal cause, according to liberal perspectives, of ethnic conflicts.

embargoes: trade policies that effectively reduce imports or exports to zero.

embedded liberalism: an interpretation of the Bretton Woods system that held that governments accepted the discipline of free trade and relatively stable exchange rates in the international economy in return for "embedding" these liberal commitments in domestic government policies to intervene extensively to achieve full employment, control prices, and prevent disruptive capital flows.

empire: a configuration of government where a hegemon consolidates power primarily through conquest.

end of history: an idea advanced by Francis Fukuyama that with the spread of democracy and the achievement of universal and equal recognition of all human beings and states the struggle for recognition, and hence violent conflict, will end.

Entente Cordiale: an agreement signed in 1904 between Britain and France that settled colonial disputes between them and ended a century of British isolation from conflicts on the continent.

epistemic communities: groups of experts who share and are motivated by the same set of scientific ideas and training.

equilibrium: a distribution of political or economic power in which the different parts of the world interact on a more or less decentralized basis.

escalation dominance: a strategy of deterrence designed to resolve conflicts without the use of unacceptable force whereby a state incrementally matches the arms capabilities of another state at all levels of potential conflict, ultimately discouraging the other state from escalating the conflict to higher levels where it could not prevail and forcing it to choose compromise.

ethics: standards of good conduct for human behavior.

ethnic cleansing: the systematic persecution, torture, and killing or removal of a religious or ethnic group with the intent to take over the territory of that group.

ethnic groups: social organizations in which the group is primarily defined by families and blood relatives or by the idea of some kind of kinship.

ethno-national communities: groups of people in which ethnic and national identities overlap substantially.

European Central Bank (ECB): the banking institution whose Governing Council controls the money supply and sets short-term interest rates for the European Union.

European Commission: the organ of the European Union that has the exclusive authority to initiate legislation and pursue the goals of an ever-closer union.

European constitution: a European Union document, not yet ratified, which incorporates a charter of fundamental rights; merges the judicial, economic, and defense aspects of the European Union; establishes the European Council; and raises the numbers of seats in Parliament, among other things.

European Convention on Human Rights and Fundamental Freedoms: the convention adopted by the Council of Europe in 1950 that establishes basic protections that block governments from violating citizens' rights to due process (legal rights, trial by jury, and so on) and political participation.

European Council: summit meetings of the Council of the European Union, involving heads of state and government, to deal with issues that cut across jurisdictions and resolve issues that are blocked at lower levels of the organization.

European Court of Human Rights: the court, established under the European Convention on Human Rights and Fundamental Freedoms of 1950, that enforces compliance with the convention's stipulations.

European Court of Justice (ECJ): the judicial body that has the power to interpret and enforce European Community treaties and law.

European Parliament: the principal legislative body and only directly elected institution in the European Union.

European Payments Union: a predecessor to European integration in the 1950s that allowed European countries to settle their import and export accounts first with one another and then with the United States, thus discriminating against U.S. imports and exports.

European Union: an intergovernmental and supranational organization that superseded in 1993 the various institutions of the European Communities to which most European democracies belong.

exceptionalism: the view that a particular state, and especially the United States, is distinct due to its specific history and unique institutions.

exchange market intervention: the buying or selling by a government's central bank of its own currency in large quantities hoping to affect the currency's market price.

exchange rate policies: policies affecting the price of one country's currency in relation to another country's currency.

exogenous variables: autonomous factors that come from outside a particular model or system and that are not explained by the system.

exploitation: extracting profits from the use of resources or workers in an unjust way.

export subsidies: reductions on the price of exported products.

export taxes: taxes levied on exported goods, perhaps in order to keep at home products that are in short supply.

extended deterrence: a strategy of deterrence in which a country agrees to strike back at missile attacks against its allies from its own territory.

external identity: the international dimension of identity of a country; it is determined by its historical and external relationships with other states.

F

failed states: states whose domestic institutions have collapsed.

federalism: a method of decentralizing power to accommodate tribal and regional differences.

feminism: a theory that critiques international relations as a male-centered and -dominated discipline.

financial economy: portfolio, financial, and currency transactions involving money exchanges.

financial repression: a system in which states extract savings from one sector, usually agriculture, by not paying market prices for the goods produced by that sector.

Finlandization: a solution to conflict whereby the Soviet Union agrees to tolerate different domestic systems within its alliance as long as its allies cooperate on foreign policy; contrasts with Stalinization in which the Soviet Union imposes its domestic system on its allies.

first-strike capability: the capacity to use nuclear missiles preemptively to destroy most or all of the missiles of the other side.

fiscal policies: policies affecting a government's budget; when revenues exceed expenditures, the budget surplus restrains the domestic economy; when expenditures exceed revenues, the budget deficit stimulates the domestic economy.

fixed exchange rate system: a system in which governments fix exchange rates to gold, another currency, or a basket of currencies.

flexible response: the strategy of retaliating selectively to fight wars at conventional levels without immediately risking nuclear war or, if the nuclear threshold is crossed, engaging in limited nuclear wars.

foreign direct investment (FDI): capital flows involving the acquisition or construction of manufacturing plants and other facilities to a foreign country.

foreign policy level of analysis: a level of analysis between the systemic process and domestic levels where foreign policy officials actually make decisions.

fossil fuels: coal, oil, and natural gas.

free riders: states that allow another to pay the costs of a particular transaction while at the same time receiving the benefits of that state's actions.

free-trade area: a market that reduces internal tariffs to zero, but whose members retain different external tariffs.

free-trade export-processing zones: separate industrial areas established within developing countries that give foreign firms profitable concessions as long as these companies produce goods primarily for export.

functionalism: an approach that argues that states will decline in significance as expert intergovernmental organizations solve practical problems.

G

General Agreement on Tariffs and Trade (GATT): the Bretton Woods economic institution that supervised multilateral trade negotiations to reduce trade barriers.

Generalized System of Preferences (GSP): a proposal to grant developing countries tariff preferences in violation of MFN rules.

genocide: the systematic persecution and extermination of a group of people on the basis of their national, ethnic, racial, or religious identity.

geoeconomics: the regional or global struggle for relative power and geopolitics through economic competition.

geopolitics: a focus on a country's location and geography as the basis of its national interests.

global civil society: the international network of nongovernmental organizations that seeks to influence governments and intergovernmental organizations in numerous issue areas such as development and the environment.

global governance: the various international institutions and great powers groups that help govern the global economy.

global warming: the heating up of the Earth's atmosphere due to greenhouse gases.

global war on terror: a military campaign to defeat nonstate terrorist groups such as Al Qaeda and rogue state actors that assist terrorists by supplying training facilities, as the Taliban government did, or potentially WMDs, as it was thought that Iraq or a radical government in Pakistan might do.

globalization 1.0: one of three periods of globalization; it lasted from 1492 to 1800 and was characterized by mercantilism and colonialism.

globalization 2.0: one of three periods of globalization; it lasted from 1800 to 1950 and was characterized by the emergence of multinational corporations and institutions.

globalization 3.0: one of three periods of globalization; it started in the second half of the twentieth century and continues into the twenty-first and is characterized by the flattening of the global playing field and reliance on the knowledge economy more than on military power or big institutions.

gold standard: a pre–World War I system of international payments based on gold, which was fixed in price with respect to local currencies.

graying population: the demographic pattern in which a substantial percentage of a country's population is growing progressively older than sixty-five.

great power groups: assorted informal groupings of the major economic and financial powers that supplement formal international institutions in managing global economic affairs; examples are the G-7, G-8, and G-20.

greenhouse gases: emissions from fossil fuels and other sources that can cause climate change.

green revolution: international research that led to new and more efficient varieties of crop seeds, fertilizers, and pesticides.

gross domestic product (GDP): the quantification of a country's production of goods and services at home.

Group of 7 (G-7): starting in 1975, an annual process of economic summits among the heads of state and governments of the United States, Great Britain, France, Germany, Japan, and, after 1976, Canada and Italy.

Group of 77 (G-77): originally a collection of seventy-seven developing countries, organized to champion cartels and the regulation of other world resource markets.

H

Hecksher-Ohlin theory: the theory that over time trade will not only equalize the prices for products from different countries but also the prices for labor and other inputs or factors of production.

hegemon: the dominant power in the international system.

hegemonic stability: stability provided by a hegemon rather than through equilibrium or a balance of power.

hegemonic stability theory: the theory that a hegemonic power is necessary to support a highly integrated world economy.

hegemony: a situation in which one country is more powerful than all the others.

Helsinki Accords: a series of agreements between East and West concerning arms control, trade, and human rights signed by thirty-five nations in 1975, which encouraged exchanges and interdependence.

Hickenlooper Amendment: post–World War II legislation that called for the United States to cut off all foreign aid to a country if U.S. company property was seized without adequate compensation.

Holy Alliance: an alliance established in 1815 that proclaimed the adherence of all rulers to the principles of Christianity, with God as the actual sovereign of the world.

human rights: the most basic protections against human physical abuse and suffering.

human security: a focus on violence and security within states and at the village and local levels, particularly against women and minorities.

hypernationalism: a form of nationalism in the early twentieth century, most prominent in Germany, that stirred together race and culture to heighten national cohesion.

I

ideal types: perspectives or simplified characterizations of theories that identify the most important aspects, not all of the intricacies and variations.

identity: the ideas that shape an entity's sense of self either through a shared or collective relationship with others or through relative similarities and differences with other groups.

identity perspective: a perspective that emphasizes the importance of ideas that define the identities of actors and that motivate the use of power and negotiations by these actors.

IMF quotas: the maximum amounts of money that countries provide to the International Monetary Fund for lending to correct balance of payment problems. A country's vote in the IMF is based on its share of total quota contributions.

immigration: the movement of peoples across national boundaries.

imperialism: the forceful extension of a nation's political authority by territorial conquest establishing economic and political domination of other nations.

imperial overstretch: the squandering of resources by superpowers in proxy conflicts.

import substitution policies: policies developed in Latin America that substitute domestic industries for imports.

individual level of analysis: a level at which individuals or small groups of individuals make decisions and cause events using power, institutions, or ideas.

individual standing: the right of civilians, as well as states, to bring cases before a court, uncommon in international law until recently.

infant industries: developing industries that require protection to get started.

informal sector: business activities that take place outside the legal system of a country and that involve no legal titles or tax payments.

information revolution: the latest stage of the technological revolution that transforms the world economy through communications, digitization, and software management of data and voice transactions.

infrastructure: a country's ports, roads, electric power, and other basic facilities that provide the framework for its economy.

Inter-American Convention on Human Rights: an international human rights instrument adopted by the nations of the Americas in 1969; its purpose is to report, investigate, and conduct diplomacy to protect and promote human rights in Latin America.

Inter-American Court of Human Rights: the court charged with implementing the Inter-American Convention on Human Rights.

interdependence: the mutual dependence of states and nonstate actors in the international system through conferences, trade, tourism, and the like.

intergovernmental organizations (IGOs): formal international organizations established by governments.

interindustry trade: trade between separate industries, such as manufactured goods for agricultural materials.

internal identity: the domestic dimension of identity of a country; it derives from individual self-reflection and national memory.

International Court of Justice (ICJ): the UN's main judicial institution, made up of fifteen judges elected by a majority of the UN Security Council and General Assembly and designed to arbitrate disputes among nations.

International Criminal Court (ICC): a permanent tribunal started in 2002 to prosecute war crimes.

international institutions: formal international organizations and informal regimes that establish common rules to regularize contacts and communications.

international law: the customary rules and codified treaties under which international organizations operate; it covers political, economic, and social rights.

International Monetary Fund (IMF): the international economic institution that supervises the exchange rate system, provides external loans to countries undergoing balance of payment adjustments, and reviews domestic policies in member countries.

international regimes: a network of international institutions.

intifada: Arabic term for uprising; often refers to Palestinian campaigns to end Israeli military occupation and oppose U.S. policies supporting Israel.

intra-industry trade: trade of component parts within the same industry.

invisible hand: the economic theory that says that, if each nation or individual acts in its own best economic interests, the common good will be served.

inward-first approach: an approach to international economic cooperation in which countries act first to fix their problems at home and then, if successful, push other countries toward compatible policies abroad.

iron curtain: a metaphor for the political, ideological, and physical (no-man's land) separation of the Soviet Union and western countries during the Cold War.

irredentism: the annexation of or claim to territory in one state by another on historical or purported grounds of common race, ethnicity, or culture.

J

jihad: for Muslim fundamentalists, a "holy war" or the physical struggle against western civilization in the name of Islam.

judgment: the broader assessment of what makes sense after accumulating as many facts and testing as many perspectives as possible.

K

Kennedy Round: the sixth round of trade talks under which across-the-board trade negotiations took place, reducing tariffs by an average of 35 percent; this was the first round of talks in which EC countries negotiated as a group.

Keynesian economics: an economic model that calls for more activist government intervention to stimulate domestic growth, protect imports, and adjust exchange rates more frequently.

Korean War: A war that started in June 1950 by a Soviet-blessed North Korean invasion of South Korea and ended in July 1953 by an armistice agreement (but no peace treaty) that divided the country along the thirty-eighth parallel, roughly where the war had begun.

Kyoto Protocol: an agreement reached in 1997 that set deadlines of 2008–2012 for industrial countries to cut their greenhouse gas emissions.

L

labor laws: microeconomic policies that set minimum wages and working conditions for factory and other workers.

laissez-faire or free trade: the economic model based on the idea of comparative advantage, calling for a country to reduce tariffs and specialize in products that it produces most efficiently while importing products that other countries produce more efficiently.

land reform: domestic policies to redistribute land for the purposes of equity and development.

League of Nations: an institution founded after the Paris Peace Conference in 1919; it was the first international institution to embody the collective security approach to the use of military power.

Lebensraum: the Hitlerian expansionist ideology that proposed a larger living space for the German racial community.

legitimacy: the right to use power in international affairs.

level of analysis: the direction, or "level," from which different causes of international change emerge. Four types are identified in this book: the systemic, domestic, foreign policy, and individual.

liberal nationalism: a form of nationalism emerging in the nineteenth century focusing on political ideologies and calling for wider participation and the rule of law in both domestic and international politics.

liberal perspective: a perspective that emphasizes relationships and negotiations among actors in international affairs, as well as how groups interact, communicate, and transact exchanges with one another, such as trade; liberal perspectives tend to focus on the role of institutions in solving international conflicts.

limits to growth: limits on industrialization proposed in the 1970s to slow consumption, conserve resources, and preserve natural habitats and wildlife.

Lisbon Treaty: a treaty that implements many of the provisions of the European constitution by intergovernmental agreement.

long telegram: George Kennan's diplomatic telegram of 1946 outlining the U.S.-Soviet conflict and arguing for the policy of containment.

long-term investments: investments of more than a year, typically less volatile than short-term investments.

lost decade: economic stagnation in Latin America brought on by domestic policies, the oil crises, and high debt, lasting from the early 1970s to the late 1980s.

M

macroeconomic policies: fiscal and monetary policies that affect the domestic economy as a whole.

madrassas: Muslim religious schools, some of which teach hatred and holy war toward the West.

major suppliers: countries that produce a great deal more of a product than other countries; a criterion for negotiations during trade rounds that called for countries that were major suppliers of a particular product to offer to lower tariffs, primarily to the benefit of those same countries.

managed or dirty float: exchange rates that are not fixed but are kept within certain ranges or go up and down gradually by governments intervening (sometimes secretly) in exchange markets.

marginalization: the social process of making unimportant or powerless certain groups within a society especially indigenous peoples and women.

Marshall Plan: the U.S. post–World War II economic plan that provided loans for the reconstruction of war-torn economies in Europe.

Marxism: a theory that emphasizes the dialectical or conflictual relationship between capitalist and communist states in the international system leading to the triumph of communism, not democracy.

massive retaliation: the strategy of threatening to unleash a general nuclear war against the Soviet Union if it attacked western Europe.

mercantilism: an economic philosophy that holds that the central objective of a state's policy is to increase the state's wealth relative to that of other states and to pursue that economic development independently, in a zero-sum struggle for material advantage.

methods: the formal rules of reason (rationalist) or appropriateness (constructivist) for testing perspectives against facts.

metropole: the metropolitan (political, commercial, and military) centers of imperial powers.

microeconomic policies: government policies usually taking the form of regulations, subsidies, price controls, competition or antitrust policies, and labor laws that apply to a specific sector, industry, or firm in the domestic economy, not to the economy as a whole as in the case of macroeconomic policies.

microlending: small loans made to individual farmers and merchants who would not otherwise have access to credit.

militant nationalism: a form of nationalism emerging in the nineteenth century focusing on cultural and racial differences and advocating an aggressive, heroic approach to international relations.

minimum deterrence: a strategy of deterrence that calls for a relatively few nuclear weapons that can survive an enemy strike and threaten unacceptable damage in retaliation on civilian and industrial centers.

moderate Keynesians: economists who favor accepting some government intervention in the domestic economy to achieve high, but not necessarily full, employment while still favoring the classical market policies of low inflation and sound money, deregulated or flexible labor and capital markets, and open international trade.

modernization: the transformation of human society from self-contained autarchic centers of agrarian society to highly specialized and interdependent units of modern society.

monetary policies: government policies that seek to control the money supply and affect the economy as a whole.

monopoly rents: a firm's dominating a market and setting prices above what the market would ordinarily permit because of lack of market competition.

Montreal Protocol: an agreement reached in 1987 that set the specific goal of reducing chlorofluorocarbons by 50 percent by 1998.

morality: standards of good conduct for human behavior.

most-favored-nation (MFN) principle: the principle in trade agreements by which nations that negotiate tariff reductions offer the same low tariff to all nations that they offer to the most-favored nation, meaning the nation that pays the lowest tariffs.

Multi-fiber Agreement (MFA): an agreement imposing direct quotas on the imports of textiles and apparel.

multilateral trade liberalization: a Pax Americana trade system in which nations negotiate reciprocal tariff reductions rather than one nation reducing tariffs unilaterally.

multilateral trade rounds: trade negotiations in which multiple countries participate and reduce trade barriers simultaneously.

multipolar: when three or more states are involved in a balance of power.

Mutual Assured Defense: the strategy, proposed by Reagan with his Strategic Defense Initiative, that defensive systems could be built up and offensive weapons built down to ensure deterrence, with the United States sharing defense technology with the Soviet Union to preclude a first strike advantage.

Mutual Assured Destruction (MAD): the deterrence strategy that called for the dominance of offensive over defensive weapons at each level of potential conflict or escalation, including the targeting of missile sites to avoid immediately attacking civilian and industrial centers; if each side could retaliate and assure a certain amount of destruction to the other side at each level of escalation, neither side would risk escalation.

mutual gains: the increase each side gains over what it had before.

mutual recognition: a way of reconciling different regulatory standards across nations by requiring that all participants recognize the right of companies to operate within their borders as long as the companies apply the standards accepted in their home country.

N

national industry champions: industries that are protected and subsidized by the state so as to dominate home markets and gain an edge in world markets.

national security export controls: limitations on the trade of military and dual-use (having both commercial and military applications) products and technology.

national treatment: the treatment of foreign firms on the same terms as local firms.

national wars of liberation: Soviet term for revolutions in developing countries against western colonialism and for proxy wars during the Cold War.

nationalism: a sentiment, emerging in the 1800s, that sees nations as the core unit of identity.

nation-building: process by which ethnic groups evolve toward nationhood.

nationhood: a status acquired by states strong enough to protect their borders and command the loyalty of their citizens.

nation-states: states defined by fusion of the masses and the state, which occurred in the aftermath of the French Revolution.

neoclassical liberalism: an interpretation of the Bretton Woods system that held that an international system of relatively free trade and fixed exchange rates effectively limited the ability of governments to intervene in the domestic economy because such intervention would ultimately contravene commitments to keep markets open, inflation down, and exchange rates stable.

neocolonialism: the post-colonial domination of the developing world by multinational corporations.

neofunctionalism: an approach that argues that intergovernmental organizations, such as the institutions of the European Community/Union, transform state loyalties and identities directly.

New International Economic Order (NIEO): A set of economic proposals put forward in the 1970s by the Group of 77 developing nations that challenged the Bretton Woods system.

newly exporting countries (NECs): another term for the Asian tigers (Japan, South Korea, Taiwan, Singapore, Malaysia, and later Thailand, the Philippines, Indonesia, and Chile, among others); the term focuses on their use of exports to develop.

newly industrializing countries (NICs): another term for the Asian tigers (Japan, South Korea, Taiwan, Singapore, Malaysia, and later Thailand, the Philippines, Indonesia, and Chile, among others); the term focuses on their use of manufacturing to develop.

nonaligned movement: a coalition led by India, Yugoslavia, and Egypt that stressed neutrality in the Cold War, nonintervention in the domestic affairs of newly independent nations, and international aid for third-world development.

nongovernmental organizations (NGOs): nonstate actors such as student, tourist, and professional associations that are not subject to direct government control.

nontariff barriers (NTBs): policy instruments other than price, such as quotas and qualitative restrictions, designed to limit or regulate imports and exports.

non-zero sum: situations and goals in which all parties can gain.

norms: ideas that govern the procedural or substantive terms of state behavior, such as reciprocity or human rights.

nuclear triad: the combination of nuclear land-, sea-, and air-based retaliatory weapons.

O

official development assistance (ODA): aid from advanced governments to developing nations.

offshore investment: the production of the components of a product overseas, followed eventually by the assembly of the components abroad as well.

opportunity costs: the relative costs associated with using the same resources to produce one product compared to another.

Organization of Petroleum Exporting Countries (OPEC): a cartel of the oil-producing states formed in the 1960s; led by the major Middle East oil-reserve countries.

Oslo Accords: a series of agreements reached in 1993 between the Palestine Liberation Organization and Israel calling for Israel to withdraw troops from Gaza and areas of the West Bank and for Israel and the PLO to recognize one another.

out-of-area missions: NATO missions outside the central European area as defined by the Cold War threat.

outsourcing: sending in-house payroll, software, and data processing tasks to other, often foreign, firms for execution via the Internet, requiring no transfer of physical production facilities.

outward-first approach: an approach to international economic cooperation in which countries agree first on common international policies and then change their separate national policies to conform to international agreements.

overdetermined outcome: an outcome caused by multiple independent variables, the separate and interactive effects of which are not clear.

ozone layer: the outer layer of the Earth's atmosphere that protects the planet from solar radiation.

P

pandemics: diseases such as AIDS, the avian flu, and SARS, which spread or threaten to spread worldwide.

partition: the separation of hostile ethnic or religious groups into different territories or states.

paternalism: institutions such as the church or state providing for the needs of individuals or groups but without granting them real rights or responsibilities, thus stifling individual initiative and entrepreneurship.

path dependence: a process emphasized by liberal perspectives that results in outcomes from a long sequential historical chain of cause and effect; for example, the kind of institutions a state develops depends on earlier developments because, once a country starts on a certain path, it accumulates advantages or disadvantages along that path.

patient capital: money invested by the government or government-directed banks over the long term to develop dominant industries for the future; common in Japan and other Asian economies.

Pax Americana: American hegemony after World War II during the third period of globalization.

Pax Britannica: British hegemony before World War I during the second period of globalization.

peace-enforcement activities: UN actions compelling countries by force or threat of force to follow the terms of UN resolutions.

peacekeeping activities: the UN monitoring of cease-fires and separating combatants.

peace research studies: scholarly inquiry dedicated to the study of the potential for international peace, emphasizing collective and common humanity approaches rather than balance of power.

perimeter deterrence: Cold War strategy of confronting disputes early in peripheral and former colonial areas and preventing them from escalating to the central states in Europe.

peripheral states: smaller and less-developed countries that produce most of the competitive or lagging products after their monopoly qualities have been lost.

perspectives: hypotheses or explanations that emphasize one of three causes (power, institutions, or ideas) of world events over the others.

petrodollar recycling: the recycling by private banks in Europe and the United States of dollars deposited by oil exporters through loans to oil-importing countries.

polarity: the number of states holding significant power in the international system.

pollution rights: a country's credits toward meeting the overall cap on pollution emissions; when an individual country exceeds the cap on pollution emissions, it may trade for credits with another country that has not exceeded its cap.

portfolio investments: transfers of money to buy stocks, bonds, and so on.

post-conflict reconstruction: activities to resettle and rebuild areas ravaged by ethnic conflict.

postmodernists: theorists who seek to expose the hidden or masked meanings of language and discourse in international relations in order to gain space to imagine alternatives.

Potsdam Conference: the meeting among wartime allies in July 1945 in which they were unable to reach an agreement on the unification of Germany, and other issues.

power: material capabilities of a country such as size of population and territory, resource endowment, economic capability, and military strength.

power balancing: a school of realism that sees hegemony as destabilizing and war as most likely when a dominant power emerges to threaten the equilibrium of power among other states.

power conversion: the administrative capacity of a country to convert wealth to military power.

power transition: a school of realism that sees hegemony as stabilizing and war as most likely when a rising power challenges a declining one and the balance of power approaches equilibrium.

pragmatism: the idea that morality is proportionate to what is possible and that one should do what one can to uphold proper standards under present and potential future circumstances but that one should not be dogmatic.

predictable domestic politics: the prerequisite for a stable domestic economy that a government not be run by weak or unstable coalitions or experience frequent changes in leadership and policies.

preemption: a policy of using force to attack challengers when they prepare to attack you; blurs with preventive war when the preparation of challengers such as terrorists is not readily visible.

preemptive war: an attack against a country that is preparing to attack you.

preponderance of power: an aggregation of the power of all states (rather than a balance of power) to deter or punish aggressors in a collective security arrangement.

preventive war: a war against a country that is not preparing to attack you but is growing in power and may attack you in the future.

price controls: microeconomic policies designed to keep prices down.

price supports: microeconomic policies designed to keep prices up.

prisoner's dilemma: a game illustrating the realist perspective in which two prisoners rationally choose not to cooperate in order to avoid even worse outcomes.

procedural norms: norms that govern how states interact; emphasized by liberal perspectives.

process tracing: a method of examining events in detail to identify cause and effect.

product life cycle: a theory that argues that high-tech product development goes through various stages, explaining why foreign direct investment most often goes to advanced, not developing, countries.

Protestant ethic: the Reformation idea, formulated by sociologist Max Weber, that each individual lives out God's will in a specific vocation and demonstrates his or her faith by the works of his or her vocation, an idea that ultimately justifies the rational pursuit of wealth.

proxy wars: conflicts sponsored by superpowers elsewhere—in third-party states or through terrorists—as a substitute for direct conflict.

psychological studies: studies that emphasize ideas that define actor personalities, although the ideas may not be conscious but subconscious and sometimes irrational.

puppet governments: governments that are installed, controlled, and/or supported by foreign states or other external parties and that act in the interests of those states or parties.

purchasing power parity exchange rates: exchange rates that adjust for the local purchasing power of currencies recognizing that prices are generally lower in a developing than developed country.

Q

Quadruple Alliance: an alliance established in 1814 by Britain, Russia, Prussia, and Austria to prevent another revolution in France.

qualified majority voting (QMV): the principle that decisions are made by majority vote, not consensus or great power veto; this is how some decisions are made today in the European Union.

qualitative regulations: restrictions on traded products to protect safety, health, labor standards, and the environment.

Quintuple Alliance: an alliance established in 1818 when France joined the four nations of the Quadruple Alliance in which members assumed special rights and responsibilities to settle international disputes peacefully and, if necessary, enforce them.

quotas: quantitative limits on imports or exports regardless of price.

R

raison d'état: the principle of national interest or what the state requires.

rationalist methods: methods that assume that causal factors can be disaggregated and described objectively, explaining one event by a second event occurring in sequence.

real economy: the trade and investment markets involving production activities.

realist perspective: a perspective that sees the world largely in terms of a struggle for power in which strong actors, especially states, seek to dominate weak ones and weak actors resist strong ones to preserve their interests and independence.

reciprocity: states behaving toward one another based largely on mutual exchanges that entail interdependent benefits or disadvantages.

regionalism: a norm of global governance that tolerates different substantive ideologies based on regions rather than on states or universality.

regional organizations: organizations whose members come from and are limited to a specific geographic region of the world.

regulations: standards that are established for health, safety, labor, and the environment that apply to all domestic, including traded, products through various qualitative restrictions.

relative gains: the increase one side gains over the other.

relative identities: identities that position actors' self-images with respect to one another as similar or dissimilar.

relativism: a position that holds that truth and morality are relative to each individual or culture and that one should "live and let live."

religious sects: social organizations in which the group is defined by participation in a particular religion or subgroup (or denomination) of a religion.

rent-seekers: firms that lobby to limit competition, extracting monopoly rents by producing at low costs while selling at high prices.

reparations: large fines in the form of payments levied against an aggressor (in the case of World War I, Germany) to help rebuild nations affected by war (for example, Britain and France).

resource curse: a phenomenon that occurs when an abundance of natural resources prevents development by encouraging overvalued exchange rates, corruption, and lack of diversification into industry.

revisionist interpretation: an interpretation of the origins of the Cold War that emphasizes American ideological or economic aggression against the Soviet Union and its allies.

river and ocean pollution: waterway contaminants from industrial and agricultural run-off, garbage, and human sewage.

rogue states: states that seek systematically to acquire nuclear weapons with the possible intent of passing them on to nonstate terrorists.

rollback: John Foster Dulles's policy in the 1950s of liberating the eastern European countries from Moscow's control.

S

sample size: the number of cases under consideration.

savings and investment policies: domestic economic policies that influence savings and investments.

Schlieffen Plan: Germany's plan (named after General Alfred von Schlieffen, who first developed the plan in 1892; it did not become official strategy until 1913) that called for an attack on France first, by way of Belgium, followed by an attack on Russia.

second-strike capability: protecting nuclear missiles so that enough will survive a first-strike attack to be used to retaliate and ensure a level of unacceptable damage, thereby deterring the first strike.

security: the prerequisite for a stable domestic economy that a government not be engulfed in civil or guerrilla war.

security dilemma: the situation that states face when they arm to defend themselves and in the process threaten other states.

self-determination: the right of autonomy for nations; that is, nations may adopt whatever substantive identities they wish, democratic or nondemocratic.

self-help: the principle of self-defense that arises from the situation of anarchy in which states have no one else to rely on to defend their security except themselves.

semi-peripheral states: states that produce a nearly even mix of monopoly and competitive products.

sensitivity interdependence: situation in which a country is affected economically or politically by what happens in other parts of the world, whether it is directly involved or not.

seven sisters: the seven major western oil companies of the twentieth century that controlled most of the production and distribution of Middle East oil.

shared identities: identities that overlap and fuse based on norms and images that cannot be traced back to specific identities or their interrelationships.

Shiites: members of the minority sect of Islam that identifies with a renegade group in the seventh century that advocated divine rather than elective succession.

short-term investments: investments of less than a year, typically volatile.

side payments: offers made by a hegemon (in effect, bribes) to get smaller nations to cooperate.

smog: air pollution, especially as a result of industry.

social constructivism: an identity perspective in which states and other actors acquire their identities from collective discourses in which they know who they are only by reference to others.

Social Darwinism: a worldview that emerged in the nineteenth century that claimed that, as in the natural world described by the scientific writings of Charles Darwin, there exists a struggle among nations for a survival of the fittest.

socialism: big government policies that call for strong labor unions to match big corporations as well as state regulations and ownership to control substantial sectors of the economy.

socialist nationalism: a form of nationalism emerging in the nineteenth century that sought greater economic equality and social justice, especially in class and colonial relationships.

soft power: the attractiveness of the values or ideas of a country as distinct from its military and economic power or its negotiating behavior.

sovereignty: a condition under which a state yields to no other authority in matters of religion or power.

sovereign wealth funds (SWFs): state-controlled investment companies that manage large chunks of central bank foreign exchange reserves in such countries as United Arab Emirates, China, Singapore, Kuwait, Norway, Canada, and Russia.

spheres of influence: areas of contested territory divided up and dominated by the great powers; the great powers then agree not to interfere in one another's territory in order to preserve the relative balance of power.

spillover: the idea that, once interdependence starts down a certain path in one sector such as trade, it creates issues that can be resolved only by extending interdependence to other sectors such as finance.

stagflation: slow growth accompanied by high inflation.

states: the largest actors in the contemporary international system that can legitimately use military force.

sterilization: central bank action to offset the increase or decrease of local currency in circulation caused by interventions to affect exchange rates.

Strategic Arms Reduction Talks (START): meetings that produced agreements (including START I in 1991 and START II in 1993) that lowered by two-thirds the number of offensive ballistic missiles and warheads maintained by Russia and the United States.

Strategic Defense Initiative (SDI): the space-based anti-missile systems that formed the core of Reagan's program to enhance missile defense.

strategic trade: trade policies that rely on competitive advantage through government targeting of technology and capital, rather than comparative advantage derived from fixed land, labor, or raw material resources, and that emphasize getting into markets first and eventually dominating them when the economies of scale are so large that only one firm or country can make a profit.

strongpoint deterrence: Cold War strategy of concentrating on the central points of a conflict and on not spreading the conflict to other, perimeter regions.

subsidies: grants and loans at below-market interest rates.

substantive norms: norms that involve the values states share or do not share; emphasized by identity perspectives.

Sunnis: members of the majority branch of Islam that identifies with the caliphs, the elected successors of Muhammad dating back to the seventh century.

supranational institutions: institutions above the level of the state that are motivated by common, rather than state-specific, goals; for example, the European Commission in the EU.

sustainable development: an economic approach that calls for smaller-scale development that works in harmony with resource, population, land, and environmental constraints.

systematic inequality: deep-seated disparity in the distribution of wealth and/or power generated by colonialism and dependency.

systemic level of analysis: a level that identifies causes that come from the positioning and interaction of states in the international system.

systemic process level of analysis: the interaction of states; this involves which countries are aligned with which other countries and which countries negotiate with which other countries.

systemic structural level of analysis: the position of states; this involves the relative distribution of power, such as which country is a great, middle, or small power, and geopolitics.

T

tariffs: taxes on goods and services crossing borders.

tax cut and deregulation movement: A set of policies advocated by Margaret Thatcher and Ronald Reagan that drove up interest rates to kill inflation, reduced taxes and deregulated markets to restructure investment incentives, and liberalized trade and capital markets to spur efficiency.

technological change: the application of science and engineering to increase wealth and alter human society.

technology gap: the feared dominance of high-tech U.S. companies in Europe in the 1960s, limiting critical European research and development resources and preempting independent European technological and industrial development.

territorial states: highly centralized administrations emerging in the late tenth century CE that consolidated feudal authorities and asserted independence from the holy Roman emperor.

terrorism: the use of violence against innocent civilians to advance political aims.

Tokyo Round: the seventh round of trade talks, which moved trade liberalization forward by reducing tariffs further across the board and, among other means, granting developing countries tariff preferences.

totalitarian governments: governments that try to control all or most of civil society.

toxic and hazardous wastes: pollutants from the disposal of petrochemicals, nuclear waste, and other dangerous materials.

trade policies: policies that affect the prices of goods and services when they cross borders by either taxing or subsidizing the price or restricting the quantity of those goods.

trade-related intellectual property issues (TRIPs): the policies of a country that require foreign companies, before they can invest in the country, to share their technology to help local suppliers reach international standards.

trade-related investment measures (TRIMs): the policies of a country that require foreign companies, before they can invest in the country, to export a large share of their production or source many of their inputs from local suppliers.

transaction costs: the expenses incurred in long-distance exchanges or large markets in which people do not know one another personally, namely the costs of finding appropriate buyers and sellers, establishing appropriate prices, and enforcing contracts.

transnational nongovernmental organizations (TNGOs): international not-for-profit advocacy organizations typically independent of and not founded by governments.

transnational relations: relations among nongovernmental as opposed to governmental authorities.

Treaty of Utrecht: a multistate European treaty established in 1713 that helped end the War of Spanish Succession and eventually signaled the rise of Great Britain.

Treaty of Westphalia: a multiparty European treaty signed in 1648 establishing the modern international system of state sovereignty.

Treaty on Conventional Forces in Europe (CFE): treaty reducing and establishing a roughly equal balance of major conventional weapons systems (tanks, artillery, aircraft, and so on) and personnel strength among some thirty countries in Europe.

Treaty on the Non-Proliferation of Nuclear Weapons (NPT): a 1968 treaty that seeks to prevent the spread of nuclear weapons and materials while fostering the civilian development of nuclear power.

Triple Alliance: an alliance first between Germany and Austria-Hungary in 1879, which then added Italy in 1882, that accounted for 50 percent of all European wealth in the early twentieth century.

Triple Entente: an agreement signed in 1907 in which Great Britain and France expanded the Entente Cordiale to include Russia, accounting for 50 percent of European wealth at the time.

tripolar: when three states dominate a distribution of power.

U

UN Convention on the Elimination of All Forms of Discrimination Against Women (CEDAW): a 1979 UN convention broadly prohibiting all discrimination against women to which 185 members are parties and 8 (including the United States) have yet to ratify.

UN Convention on the Rights of the Child (CRC): a UN convention adopted in 1989 to protect the rights of children, defined as anyone under eighteen years of age unless adult status has been attained earlier under national law, to life, to freedom from abuse, and to food, shelter, education, conscience (including religion), and participation in the community.

UN Economic and Social Council (ECOSOC): a major organ of the UN General Assembly; among other things, until 2006 it elected the members of the UN Human Rights Commission based on geographic representation.

UN Human Rights Commission: the commission that drafted and implements the Universal Declaration of Human Rights, passed by the UN as a nonbinding resolution in 1948.

UN Human Rights Council: the 2006 successor of the UN Human Rights Commission.

unanimity: a principle in Article 5 in the Covenant of the League of Nations that established that all nations, no matter what size, must agree on what constitutes a threat to international peace and security.

unfair trade: trade by a firm or government that violates an international trade agreement or trade practices by a firm or government not covered by agreements and that are unjustifiable, unreasonable, and discriminatory.

unilateral trade liberalization: one county's lowering or elimination of tariffs without asking other countries to reciprocate.

United Nations (UN): the principal general-purpose intergovernmental organization that deals with collective security, economic and social development, and international law and human rights.

Universal Declaration of Human Rights: a UN declaration approved in 1948 prescribing the obligations of states to individuals rather than of individuals to states.

universalism: a position that holds that truth and morality are universal; one cannot adjust moral behavior to circumstances without sliding down the slippery slope to relativism.

Uruguay Round: the eighth round of trade talks and the first to bear the name of a developing country; it extended the principle of free trade to services, investment, agriculture, and intellectual property.

V

values: ideas that express deep moral convictions.

voluntary export restraints (VERs): agreements in which exporting countries "voluntarily" (actually under pressure) agreed to limit exports of specific products.

vulnerability interdependence: situation in which a country is put at risk if interdependence is cut and it can no longer get resources or capital from external sources.

W

Wahhabism: a rigid and puritanical form of Islam originating in the eighteenth century with the Arabian spiritual leader, Muhammad ibn Abd al-Wahhab.

Washington Consensus: the policy movement in the 1990s advocating market-oriented ideas for developing nations.

water tables: the aquifers below the Earth's surface that supply freshwater.

weapons of mass destruction (WMDs): weapons that can kill large numbers of humans and/or cause great damage to fabricated and natural structures and to the biosphere in general; they include nuclear, biological, chemical, and, increasingly, radiological weapons.

World Bank: the international economic institution set up to provide long-term financing for infrastructure development and basic human needs such as health and education; originally called the International Bank for Reconstruction and Development.

world systems: theories (updating Marxism) that explain how colonialism reinforced capitalism and enabled capitalism to survive by exploiting the peripheral countries of the world.

Y

Yalta Conference: a wartime conference held in February 1945 where the United States, Soviet Union, and Great Britain agreed on the unconditional surrender of Nazi Germany and postwar occupation of Europe and where the United States conceded Soviet influence over Poland; considered a sell-out, especially in eastern Europe, of small powers by the great powers.

youth bulge: the demographic pattern in which a substantial percentage of the population in a given country is young, typically below the age of fifteen.

Z

zero sum: situations in international affairs in which what one actor gains, the other loses.

Zollverein: a customs union created by Prussia involving other German states that lowered barriers to trade and ignited rapid industrial development beginning in the 1830s.

Photo Credits

Front cover (left to right): iStock; © Andy Rain/epa/Corbis; iStock
About the Author (page viii): Elise Frasier, CQ Press

Introduction

Chapter 1: How to Think About International Relations

Chapter 2: Perspectives on World History

Chapter 3: World War I

Chapter 4: World War II

Chapter 5: The Origins and End of the Cold War

Chapter 6: From 11/9 to 9/11
Page 205: AP Photo/Sadayuki Mikami
Page 212: *Israel Sun*/Landov
Page 224: Reuters
Page 228: Getty Images/Photo by Scott Peterson

Chapter 7: Terrorism and the World After 9/11
Page 233: AP Photo/Portland Police Department
Page 237: Ray Stubblebine/Reuters/Landov
Page 240: AP Photo/Jerome Delay
Page 250: AP Photo/Emilio Morenatti

Chapter 8: History of Globalization
Page 277: AP Photo/Greg Baker
Page 281: The Granger Collection, New York
Page 302: AP Photo/J. Scott Applewhite
Page 316: AP Photo

Chapter 9: How Globalization Works in Practice
Page 321: AP Photo
Page 330: Reuters/Enny Nuraheni
Page 335: AP Photo/Winfried Rothermel
Page 339: Reuters/Francois Lenoir FLR
Page 340: AP Photo/Oleg Romanov

Chapter 10: Trade, Investment, and Finance
Page 345: AP Photo/Richard Vogel
Page 353: Reuters/Yuriko Nakao
Page 362: Rabih Moghrabi/AFP/Getty Images
Page 366: AP Photo

Chapter 11: Miracle and Missed Opportunity
Page 378: Mario Guzman/EPA/Landov
Page 389: AP Photo/Ahn Young-joon
Page 393: Reuters/Luis Enrique Ascui
Page 403: Reuters/Landov
Page 407: AP Photo/Dado Galdieri

Chapter 12: Foreign Aid and Domestic Governance
Page 410: Reuters/Jason Reed
Page 422: AP Photo/Tsvangirayi Mukwazhi
Page 433: Reuters/Ahmed Jadallah

Chapter 13: Global Inequality, Imperialism, and Injustice
Page 436: AP Photo/Eduardo Verdugo
Page 445: AP Photo/Gunnar Ask
Page 450: AP Photo/Shib Shankar Chatterjee

Chapter 14: World Environment
Page 460: Reuters/Gregg Newton
Page 471: AP Photo/Siddharth Darshan Kumar

Page 473: Reuters/Shamil Zhumatov
Page 478: Reuters/Grant Neuenberg

Chapter 15: Global Civil Society
Page 483: The Granger Collection, New York
Page 493: AP Photo/Greg Baker, File
Page 498: Reuters/Chaiwat Subprasom
Page 504: Reuters/Vincent Kessler

Chapter 16: Global Governance
Page 510: Daniel Acker/Bloomberg News/Landov
Page 513: Denis Sinyakov/Reuters/Landov
Page 522: Stringer/AFP/Getty Images
Page 532: AP Photo/Pool photo by Kyodo News

Conclusion
Page 536: AP Photo/Czarek Sokolowaki
Page 539: AP Photo/Yves Logghe

Index

Note: page numbers followed by *b, t, f, m,* or *p* indicate boxes, tables, figures, maps, and photos, respectively.